American Democracy in World Perspective

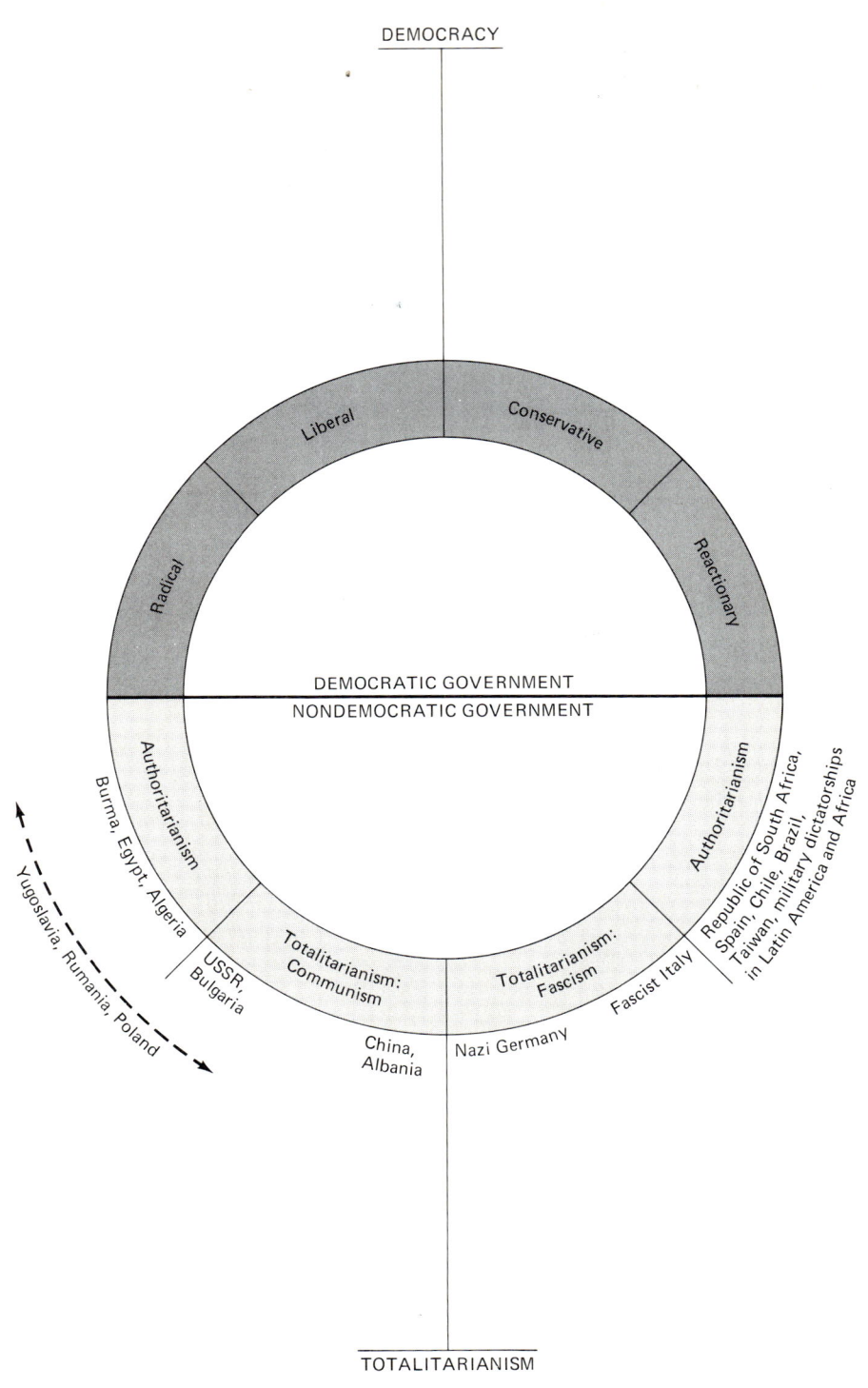

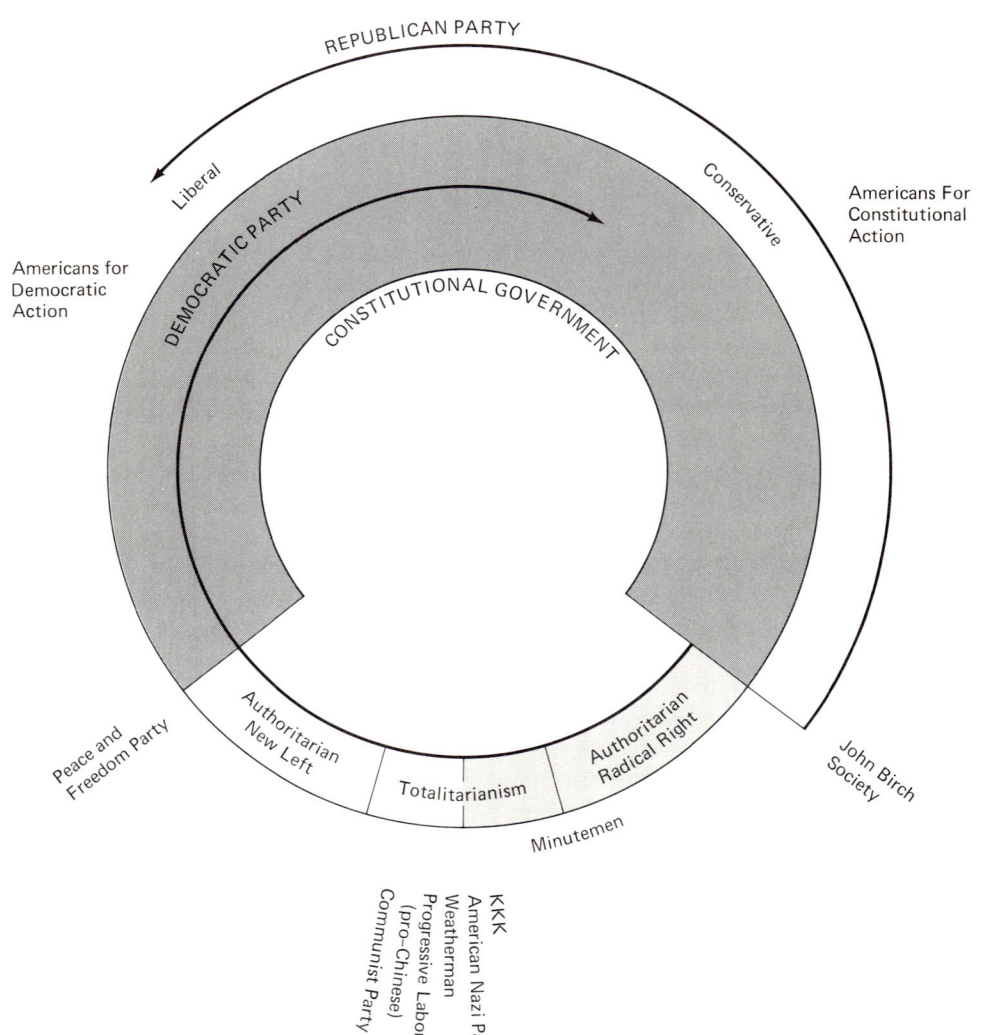

American Democracy in World Perspective

William Ebenstein
C. Herman Pritchett
Henry A. Turner
Dean Mann

UNIVERSITY OF CALIFORNIA,
SANTA BARBARA

HARPER & ROW, PUBLISHERS
New York   Hagerstown   San Francisco   London

Sponsoring Editor: Dale Tharp
Project Editor: Ralph Cato
Designer: Rita Naughton
Production Supervisor: Will C. Jomarrón
Compositor: V & M Typographical, Inc.
Printer and Binder: The Murray Printing Company
Art Studio: Vantage Art Inc.

AMERICAN DEMOCRACY IN WORLD PERSPECTIVE, Fourth Edition

Copyright © 1970, 1973, 1976 by William Ebenstein, C. Herman Pritchett, Henry A. Turner, and Dean Mann. Copyright © 1967 by Harper & Row, Publishers, Inc.

All rights reserved. Printed in the United States of America. No part of this book may be used or reproduced in any manner whatsoever without written permission except in the case of brief quotations embodied in critical articles and reviews. For information address Harper & Row, Publishers, Inc., 10 East 53rd Street, New York, N.Y. 10022.

Library of Congress Cataloging in Publication Data

Main entry under title:

American democracy in world perspective.

    Bibliography: p.
    Includes index.
    1. United States—Politics and government—Handbooks, manuals, etc. 2. Comparative government. I. Ebenstein, William, Date-
JK261.A66   1976   320.4'73   75-33916
ISBN 0-06-041866-4

PHOTOGRAPHY CREDITS

1 Wide World/ 2 Wide World/ 3 Tass from Sovfoto; American Airlines; Wide World / 4 Wide World/ 5 Wide World/ 6 Wide World/ 7 National Archives/ 8 Wide World/ 9 G. Arvid Peterson, Photo Researchers/ 10 Wide World/ 11 Beckwith Studios/ 12 Wide World/ 13 Wide World/ 14 Wide World/ 15 Wide World/ 16 Wide World/ 17 Wide World/ 18 Wide World

The chapters . . .

      1 Concepts of Democracy   1
      2 Conflict Resolution in the Political Process   31
      3 Constitutional Government   53
      4 Federalism   77
      5 The Courts and Judicial Review   96
      6 Criminal Punishment and the Constitution   122
      7 Liberty   143
      8 Equality   172
      9 Public Opinion and Political Participation   188
     10 The Party System   219
     11 The Electoral Process   250
     12 Political-Interest Groups   276
     13 Congress   296
     14 The Presidency   330
     15 Running the National Government   365
     16 The American Political Economy   385
     17 The Welfare State   413
     18 American Foreign Policy   434
Appendix 1 The Declaration of Independence   457
Appendix 2 The Constitution of the United States   461
Appendix 3 Articles of Impeachment Against Richard M. Nixon   486
           Bibliography   492
           Index   503

Contents

PREFACE xxv

1 CONCEPTS OF DEMOCRACY 1

CONFLICT, POLITICAL POWER, AND GOVERNMENT 2
Man—a political animal 2
Collective needs 2
Cooperation and conflict 3
Power 3
    The pluralist conception of power 3
    The elitist conception of power 4
Pluralism and elitism: theoretical analyses or political ideologies? 6
    Political power 6

GOVERNMENT AS INSTITUTIONALIZED POLITICAL POWER 7

CONCEPTS OF DEMOCRACY 7
Democracy as a system of power 7
    Anarchism and communes 8
    Voluntary associations 9
Historical overview 9
    Greek city-states 9
    Roman rule of law 10
    Feudalism 10
The modern Western concept of democracy 10
Key principles of the American political commitment 12
    Limited government 12
    Equality 13
Gaps between commitment and performance 14
The operational concept of democracy 16
The democratic political order: limits and potentialities 20
    Moral integrity and free government 22

AUTHORITARIAN AND TOTALITARIAN GOVERNMENTS 23

THE MARXIST-COMMUNIST CONCEPT OF DEMOCRACY 26

DEMOCRACY IN DEVELOPING COUNTRIES   **27**

    Capitalism and developing countries   28
    Single-party dominance   28

2   CONFLICT RESOLUTION IN THE POLITICAL PROCESS   31

PROCESSES OF CONFLICT RESOLUTION   31

The crucial role of leadership   31
    The transfer of power   32
Majority and minority   33
Government and opposition   35

GOVERNMENT BY DISCUSSION AND CONSENT   36

Free flow of information and communication   36
    The Freedom of Information Act   37
    The Pentagon Papers   37
Frustration and aggression   39
Freedom of expression as a safety valve   40
    Taboo issues   40
Functional limits of free speech as a safety valve   41
    Common agreement on fundamentals   42

AMERICAN DEMOCRACY UNDER PRESSURE   43

The new era of political frustration   43
Rising expectations of government   44
The impact of the postindustrial society on political democracy   46
    The dossier society   47
Violence   47
    Violence in the 1960s   48
    The revolutionary experience   48
    Racial violence   49
    Labor-management violence   49
    Crime and the social order   50
    Political crime   51
    Governmental lawlessness   52

3   CONSTITUTIONAL GOVERNMENT   53

THREE CONSTITUTIONS COMPARED   55

The English constitution   55
The case for an unwritten constitution   56
Protection under an unwritten constitution   57

The Soviet constitution   58
The American Constitution   59

KEY PRINCIPLES OF THE AMERICAN CONSTITUTION   60
Popular sovereignty   61
Federalism   63
Separation of powers   65
Limited government   67

CONSTITUTIONAL AMENDMENT   68
Amendments to the Constitution   68
The amending process   69
Amendment by the convention method   70
Appraisal of the amending process   70

CONSTITUTIONAL INTERPRETATION   71
Interpretation by Congress and the President   72
Judicial interpretation   72

WORLD SIGNIFICANCE OF THE AMERICAN CONSTITUTION   74

4 FEDERALISM   77

THE CASE FOR FEDERALISM   79

Establishing the viability of the American federal system   80
   Interposition   81
   Nullification   82
   Secession   82

THE CONSTITUTION AND FEDERAL-STATE RELATIONS   82
Republican form of government   83
Domestic violence   83
Admission of new states   83
Interstate relations   85
   Interstate compacts   85
The states and commerce   85
Interstate privileges and immunities   86
   The right to interstate travel   86
   Full faith and credit   86
   Extradition   87

WEAKNESSES OF THE STATES   88
   Revival of state government   89
Federal grants-in-aid   89
   Effects of federal grants   90
   Objections to federal grants   91

Revenue sharing   92

FEDERAL CENTRALIZATION   93

THE FUTURE OF THE STATES   95

5 THE COURTS AND JUDICIAL REVIEW   96

THE FEDERAL COURT SYSTEM   98
Federal courts   98
    The Supreme Court   99
Jurisdiction   100

STATE COURTS   101

RELATIONS BETWEEN FEDERAL AND STATE COURTS   102

SELECTION OF JUDGES   103
The federal judiciary   104
    Appointment of judges for lower courts   104
    Appointment of Supreme Court justices   104
The state judiciary   107

TENURE OF JUDGES   108

THE SUPREME COURT   109
How the Court operates   109
Concurring and dissenting opinions   110
The role of the Chief Justice   111

THE POWER OF JUDICIAL REVIEW   111
Review of congressional and presidential acts   112
    Marbury v. Madison   112
Review of the constitutionality of state legislation   114
Interpretation of congressional statutes   116
Controversy over judicial review   116
    The Court and the New Deal   117
Is judicial review compatible with democracy?   119
Judicial review in other countries   120

6 CRIMINAL PUNISHMENT AND THE CONSTITUTION   122

THE FEDERALISM PROBLEM   125

RIGHTS OF THE CRIMINAL SUSPECT   126

Unreasonable searches and seizures 126
Wiretapping and electronic eavesdropping 128
Self-incrimination and coerced confessions 129

RIGHTS OF THE ACCUSED 132
Indictment by grand jury 132
Admission to bail 132
Trial by jury 133
The right to counsel 133
Double jeopardy 134

PUNISHMENT AND REVIEW OF CONVICTIONS 135
Cruel and unusual punishment 137
Habeas corpus 139

JUSTICE FOR JUVENILES 139

MILITARY JUSTICE 139

CRISIS IN THE AMERICAN COURT SYSTEM 140

ENGLISH CRIMINAL JUSTICE 141

7 LIBERTY 143

CONSTITUTIONAL BACKGROUND 145

FREEDOM OF EXPRESSION 146
Methods of restraint on freedom of expression 147

FREEDOM OF THE PRESS 148
Censorship of the press 148
   The Pentagon Papers 148
   The Post Office 148
   Free press and fair trials 149
Libel 150
Obscenity 152

FREEDOM OF SPEECH 155
Speech and breach of the peace 155
Conspiracy prosecutions for speech 157

FREEDOM TO DEMONSTRATE 157
Constitutional status of demonstrations 158
Demonstrations and breach of the peace 159
Symbolic speech 161

DIRECT ACTION AND CIVIL DISOBEDIENCE 161

FREEDOM OF ASSOCIATION 162
NAACP activities   162

INDIVIDUAL FREEDOM AND NATIONAL SECURITY   163
The status of the Communist party   164
Legislative investigations   165
The English policy on totalitarian parties and political violence   166

RELIGIOUS LIBERTY   166
Freedom of religion   166
Religion and the establishment clause   168
   Aid to parochial schools   169

THE RIGHT TO PRIVACY   170
   Abortion laws   171

8 EQUALITY   172

EQUALITY OF OPPORTUNITY   173

EQUAL VOTING RIGHTS   176

EQUAL ACCESS TO PUBLIC ACCOMMODATIONS   177

EDUCATIONAL EQUALITY   178
Segregation in education   178
Steps toward desegregation   180
Equality in financial support for schools   182

EQUAL ACCESS TO HOUSING   183

RACIAL DISCRIMINATION IN BRITAIN   184

THE EQUAL-PROTECTION EXPLOSION   184

9 PUBLIC OPINION AND POLITICAL PARTICIPATION   188

PUBLIC OPINION   189
What is public opinion?   190
   General and special publics   190
   The role of opinion leaders   191
The function of public opinion   192
   Supportive function   192
   Directive function   193

Permissive function   *193*
Assessing public opinion   *193*
    The mass media as a means of assessing public opinion   *194*
    Political-interest groups   *194*
    Communications with private citizens   *194*
    Elections   *195*
    Public-opinion surveys   *195*
The impact of the mass media on public opinion   *197*
    Patterns of government control   *198*
    The performance of the mass media   *198*

POLITICAL PARTICIPATION   202

Political socialization and electoral behavior   *204*
    The family   *205*
    Socioeconomic class   *206*
    Occupation   *207*
    Income and education   *208*
    Regional and residential influences   *209*
    Religion and race   *210*
    Influence of age   *211*
Influence of parties, candidates, and issues   *212*
    Party affiliation   *212*
    The impact of candidates and issues   *213*
Trends in political participation   *214*
    Increase in voting and office-holding by blacks   *214*
    Women elected officials   *215*
    Nonvoting   *215*

10 THE PARTY SYSTEM   219

THE DEVELOPMENT OF AMERICAN PARTIES   219

The first American parties   *221*
Eras of one-party dominance   *222*
    First period: the election of Jefferson, 1800   *222*
    Second period: the election of Lincoln, 1860   *224*
    Third period: the election of Franklin D. Roosevelt, 1932   *225*
Reasons for periods of one-party dominance   *226*
The Republicans and Democrats today   *227*

PARTY ORGANIZATION   230

National party organization   *231*
    The national convention   *231*
    The national committee   *231*

The national chairman 232
Campaign committees 232
State and local party organizations 232
State party organization 233
Local party organization 234

CHANGING ATTITUDES TOWARD POLITICAL PARTIES 235
Increase in independents, ticket-splitting, and switch-voting 235
Ticket-splitting 236
Switch-voting 237
A better informed and activist electorate 237

FUNCTIONS OF AMERICAN PARTIES 237
Providing personnel for government 237
Organizing and conducting the government 238
Serving as a countercheck to the party in power 238
Representing group interest 239
Educating and informing the electorate 239
Socialization of conflict 240
Unifying the nation 241

CHARACTERISTICS OF THE AMERICAN PARTY SYSTEM 241
A two-party system 241
American parties are multigroup organizations 242
American parties are pragmatic, nonideological organizations 242
American parties are decentralized 242
Why the two-party system in the United States? 243
Minor parties 245
Long-range doctrinal parties 245
Splinter or secessionist parties 246
Independent short-term parties 246
The two-party versus the multiparty system 247

ONE-PARTY GOVERNMENTS: COMPATIBLE WITH DEMOCRACY? 248

11 THE ELECTORAL PROCESS 250

THE ELECTORATE 251
Voting requirements 252

NOMINATIONS 252
The direct primary 254
Recruitment and nomination of candidates 255

NOMINATING AND ELECTING THE PRESIDENT 255
The national convention 255

    Selecting the delegates   *256*
    Presidential primaries   *256*
    Allocation of delegates   *257*
    Convention procedure   *257*
    Vice-presidential nominations   *258*
Presidential campaigns and elections   *258*
    Winning the nomination   *258*
    Campaign strategy   *259*
    Campaign organizations   *260*
    Professional campaign management and opinion surveys   *260*
    Electoral college   *261*
    Presidential elections classified   *262*

CONGRESSIONAL CAMPAIGNS AND ELECTIONS   *263*

POLITICAL FINANCE   *264*
What campaigns cost   *264*
Regulation of campaign finance   *266*
    1972 presidential campaign finance   *266*
    Campaign finance abuses   *268*
The Federal Campaign Election Act of 1974   *270*
    Limitations on contributions and expenditures   *270*
    Publicity of income and expenditures   *271*
    Public financing of presidential elections   *272*
    Federal Election Commission   *272*
    How the money is spent   *273*
Sources of campaign funds   *273*
Additional political finance reforms   *274*

12 POLITICAL-INTEREST GROUPS   276

FUNCTIONS OF POLITICAL-INTEREST GROUPS   *278*

GROUP TACTICS AND TECHNIQUES   *278*
Influencing the membership and other groups   *279*
Interest groups and the public   *280*
Interest groups and political parties   *281*
Pressures on legislators   *282*
Influencing the executive branch   *283*
Interest groups and the courts   *284*

THE VARIETY OF INTEREST GROUPS   *285*
Business groups   *285*
Agricultural groups   *287*
Labor organizations   *287*
The professions   *288*

The educational lobby   *289*
　The medical lobby   *289*
　The legal lobby   *289*
Other interest groups   *290*
The radical right and the radical left   *291*

PRESSURE GROUPS AND DEMOCRACY: THE DILEMMA OF REGULATION   *293*

13 CONGRESS   *296*

LEGISLATURES IN THE POLITICAL PROCESS   *297*
Legislative-executive struggle in the United States   *297*
The office of the member of Congress   *298*
The perquisites of office   *300*

HOW REPRESENTATIVE IS CONGRESS?   *300*
Method of representation   *300*
The politics of districting   *301*
Impact of apportionment on the system of representation   *302*
The recruitment process and membership in Congress   *302*

THE LAWMAKING FUNCTION   *304*
Consensus-building and legitimation   *305*
Providing funds   *305*

THE REPRESENTATIVE FUNCTION   *306*
Relationships to the electorate   *306*
Determinants of congressional voting   *307*
How congressmen promote constituent interests   *308*

THE OVERSIGHT FUNCTION   *309*
The informing function   *310*
Congressional studies and investigations   *310*
Advise and consent   *311*
　Treaties   *312*
　Appointments   *312*
Judicial functions   *313*

CONGRESSIONAL ORGANIZATION: FORMAL AND INFORMAL   *314*
Differential access to congressional power   *315*
The role of party   *315*

THE AGENTS OF LEADERSHIP   *317*
The elected leaders   *317*

The committee system of Congress   318
    Committee staff   320
    Chairmanships and the seniority rule   320

THE LEGISLATIVE PROCESS   322
The rules of Congress   322
Committee deliberations   324
The House Rules Committee   324
Consideration on the floor of the House of Representatives   325

THE SENATE   326
The filibuster   326
    The cloture rule   327
The conference committee   328
The President decides   328

14 THE PRESIDENCY   330

ASPECTS OF THE PRESIDENCY   331
Qualifications and perquisites   331
Presidential succession   332
Growth of the presidency   333

THE ROLES OF THE PRESIDENT   334
The President as chief of state   335
    Ceremonial head of the nation   335
    Chief magistrate   335
The President as national leader   336
    Presidential leadership in economic policy   336
    Leading public opinion   337
The President as party leader   338
The President as chief legislator   339
    Constitutional powers   341
    Extraconstitutional powers   342
The President as chief administrator   343
    Means of administrative control   344
The President as chief diplomat   347
    Conducting foreign relations   347
    Treaties and executive agreements   349
The President as commander-in-chief   349
    Wartime powers   350

THE PRESIDENT'S ASSISTANTS   351
The Executive Office of the President   351

The White House office   352
The Office of Management and Budget   353
The Council of Economic Advisers   354
The National Security Council   354
The Domestic Council   354
Other Units of the Executive Office   355
The Cabinet   356
Selection of cabinet members   356
The role of the cabinet   357
The Vice-President as presidential assistant   358

THE IMPLICATIONS OF WATERGATE   360
The abuse of executive power   360
Explanations for Watergate   362
A post-Watergate presidency   363

15 RUNNING THE NATIONAL GOVERNMENT   365

DIMENSIONS OF THE BUREAUCRACY: SIZE AND VARIETY OF ITS ACTIVITIES   366

THE RISE OF THE ADMINISTRATIVE STATE   367

THE SPIRIT OF THE BUREAUCRACY   368

BUREAUCRACY AND POLICY-MAKING   369
Policy promotion   369
Policy implementation   370

POLITICAL LEADERSHIP AND CONTROL   370

ORGANIZATION OF THE EXECUTIVE BRANCH   371
Departments   373
Independent agencies   373
Independent regulatory commissions   374
Corporations   374
Internal organization and processes   375
Equal treatment and decentralization   376
Planning and budgeting   376

ADMINISTRATIVE MEASURES AND PROCEDURES   377
Regulatory and enforcement measures   377
Providing government services   378

THE PUBLIC SERVICE   379
Political executives   380

The Civil Service: recruitment, selection, and classification *381*
The problems of neutrality, loyalty, and ethnic employment *382*
    Restrictions on political activities *382*
    Loyalty *383*
    Employment of minorities *383*

A RESPONSIBLE BUREAUCRACY IN THE DEMOCRATIC SYSTEM *384*

16 THE AMERICAN POLITICAL ECONOMY *385*

AMERICAN ATTITUDES TOWARD GOVERNMENT INTERVENTION IN THE ECONOMY *386*
The dominance of empiricism? *386*

THE CONSTITUTION AND ECONOMIC POLICIES *386*
Flexibility of constitutional language *386*
Private property and eminent domain *387*
"Business affected with a public interest" *387*
No specific economic theory enshrined in the Constitution *388*

CURBING CONCENTRATION OF ECONOMIC POWER *389*
The rise of trusts *389*
The Sherman Antitrust Act *389*
    Breakup of monopolies *390*
    Criminal prosecutions under the Sherman Act *390*
A new approach in the fight against monopoly: the factor of size *390*
Expanding governmental protection of the free market: the Clayton Act *391*
    The Federal Trade Commission *391*
Curbing the urge to merge *392*

GOVERNMENT AND LABOR *392*
Areas exempt from antimonopoly policies *392*
The rationale behind the encouragement of labor unions *393*
The National Labor Relations Act: the Magna Carta of labor *394*
The Taft-Hartley Act *394*
The Landrum-Griffin Act *395*

PUBLIC POLICIES FOR ECONOMIC GROWTH AND STABILITY *396*
The Employment Act of 1946 *396*
    The Joint Economic Committee and the Council of Economic Advisers *396*
The problem of inflation *396*
The use of fiscal and monetary policies *397*
    The use of fiscal policies *398*
    The use of monetary policies *398*

Limits of monetary policies 399
Federal insurance of deposits and credits 399

BUILT-IN STABILIZERS OF THE ECONOMY 400
Government spending 400
"Transfer payments" 401

EXECUTIVE POWER IN DEFENSE OF PRICE AND WAGE STABILITY 401
Holding the line in basic industries 401
Economic controls in the late 1970s 402

FEDERAL SUBSIDIES 403
Subsidies to transportation 403
   Amtrak 403
   Urban mass transportation 404
   Air carriers 404
   Shipping 404
Subsidies through postal services 404

GOVERNMENT AND THE ENERGY CRISIS 405
Project independence 406
   Conservation of energy 406
   Expansion of energy production 406
   Energy Research and Development Administration 407

GOVERNMENT AND AGRICULTURE 408
The growth of farm productivity 408
Reasons behind government aid to farming 409
"Parity" prices 410
Price-support programs 410

THE MIXED ECONOMY 411

17 THE WELFARE STATE 413

REASONS FOR THE GROWTH OF THE WELFARE STATE 414
Changing structure of the population 414
The political factor: the welfare state as a response to popular demands 415
The welfare state and the voter 416
Welfare policies as insurance premiums 416

SOCIAL SECURITY AND WELFARE 417
Old-age, Survivors, and Disability Insurance 418
Private pensions 420
   Employee Benefit Security Act 420

Unemployment insurance   *420*
Public assistance   *421*
    Supplementary security income   *421*
Food stamps   *423*
Aid to families with dependent children (AFDC)   *423*

HEALTH AND MEDICARE   425
Government involvement in health services   *425*
    Medicare: toward a national health insurance program?   *427*
    State medical programs   *427*

THE EXPANDING FEDERAL EFFORT IN EDUCATION   428
The role of education in American development   *428*
The magnitude of the educational effort   *428*
Federal aid to education   *429*
The Elementary and Secondary Education Act of 1965   *429*
The Higher Education Act of 1965   *430*

HOUSING AND URBAN RENEWAL   431
    Slum clearance and public housing   *432*
    Urban renewal and community development   *433*

18 AMERICAN FOREIGN POLICY   434

FROM COLONY TO WORLD POWER   435
Domestic and foreign affairs   *436*

DEMOCRACY AND FOREIGN POLICY   438
Inherent tensions between democracy and foreign policy   *438*
Weakness of the rule of law and of a sense of community   *440*
Collective defense agreements as a substitute for the rule of law   *440*
    The Korean conflict   *441*
    Vietnam   *441*
Changing attitudes toward America's role in the world   *442*

THE EMPHASIS ON POWER AND NATIONAL INTEREST   444
Difficulty of defining the national interest   *445*
    Civilian supremacy over the military   *445*
    The national interest and foreign policy   *446*

DEMOCRATIC CONTROL OF FOREIGN POLICY   448
Low level of interest and information in foreign affairs   *448*
The growing role of science and technology   *449*
The changing role of Congress   *450*
    The National Commitments Resolution   *450*

      The War Powers Act   *451*
      The role of Congress in the decision-making process   *451*
Veto-limits of public opinion   *451*
Bipartisanship in foreign policy   *452*

THE LONG-RANGE CHALLENGES TO AMERICAN FOREIGN POLICY   453
The widening gap between rich and poor countries   *453*
      The oil crisis   *455*
The paradox of power and influence   *456*

APPENDIX 1   THE DECLARATION OF INDEPENDENCE, 1776   457

APPENDIX 2   THE CONSTITUTION OF THE UNITED STATES   461

APPENDIX 3   ARTICLES OF IMPEACHMENT AGAINST RICHARD M. NIXON, PRESIDENT OF THE UNITED STATES   486

BIBLIOGRAPHY   492

INDEX   503

Preface

The continuously friendly and generous reception accorded to the previous three editions of this book by both students and teachers of American government and politics has encouraged publication of a Fourth Edition, completely revised and reset. It appears at a time when American government is experiencing profound stresses in its domestic policies, ideas, and institutions, as well as in its relations with the rest of the world. Vice-President Spiro T. Agnew's resignation and conviction on a felony charge in 1973 was without parallel in American political history. Even more shattering was President Richard M. Nixon's resignation in 1974, when such action became the only alternative to certain impeachment and conviction by Congress. After the resignation of Nixon—the first president to resign from office—American government and politics will never be the same again, and the long-term effects of Watergate and Nixon's involvement in its cover-up will be felt for generations to come. As a result of the Nixon-Agnew upheavals, fundamental principles as well as basic political and social institutions have been reexamined, nothing is taken for granted any longer, and no principle of American government and politics can henceforth rely on unquestioning acceptance rooted in conventional wisdom. Similarly, the defeat of American political and military objectives in Southeast Asia, particularly in Vietnam and Cambodia, has led to a thorough reexamination of the role of the United States in the world in years to come.

Because the world is of concern to the United States, and the United States to the world, we have tried to make appropriate comparisons of American political ideas and practices with those of other prominent democratic and nondemocratic systems. There is no area of American political experience which cannot be illuminated by drawing on similar or contrasting experiences of other nations. The traditional method of comparing American government and politics solely with their own historical antecedents is no longer sufficient. While we have sought to provide the essential historical experience where it is indispensable to the understanding of contemporary trends, we feel that the student gains even more by looking at American political aspirations, achievements, and failures in contemporary world perspective.

In trying to present a fair and balanced picture of political behavior and the political process, we have paid special attention to critical and controversial issues. The United States owes its existence to controversy and conflict, and during its history, as today, there has never been a dearth of highly controversial political questions. Throughout the book we therefore focus on such issues as the role of violence in the political process, civil rights, racial tensions, equality for women, political participation, new party alignments, the role of money in election campaigns, the welfare crisis, and problems of the developing nations.

The present edition stresses brevity more than have the preceding editions, so that the student can make use of more supplementary readings on any specific topic. The streamlining of this edition has enabled us to add new topics and to expand the analysis of others, including such issues as: integrity in government; governmental lawlessness; obscenity; abortion; capital punishment; the record of the Burger Court; new voter attitudes and the phenomenal numerical growth of independents, ticket-splitters, and vote-switchers; the presidency in the post-Watergate political climate; domestic and international implications of the energy crisis; and the problems of galloping inflation and high unemployment.

We have not hesitated to express our own views in many places, in order to stimulate thought and discussion rather than to lay down final certainties. We hope that this new edition, combining succinctness of treatment with a wider range of coverage, will prove even more useful to the beginning student of American government and politics.

W. E.
C. H. P.
H. A. T.
D. M.

1 Concepts of Democracy

CONFLICT, POLITICAL POWER, AND GOVERNMENT

Man—a political animal

Aristotle wrote in his *Politics* over two thousand years ago that only a beast or a god can live outside a political community, without the protective shelter of government, for "man is by nature a political animal."

Government emerges from the mists of the early historical experience of man as one of his oldest institutions. We do not know precisely the conditions in which government was conceived and born; but we dimly see in even the most rudimentary forms of social organization elements of political authority and control—of government. Throughout the ages, men have tolerated inefficient, corrupt, and repressive governments, but at all times even the worst government has seemed preferable to anarchy, or the absence of government.

Collective needs

Government is a persistent part of human experience because it reflects and fulfills basic human needs that the individual cannot satisfy independently. No single person can secure through his personal effort alone the advantages that are provided to him by his government—the ability to walk safely on the streets, the power to repel foreign invaders, the security of being able to provide for himself and his family when he is unemployed or when he is disabled, or the confidence that the air he breathes will be fit for human consumption.

These are all *collective* needs and must therefore be met by collective effort and organization; some of these collective needs—as in health and education, for example—may be satisfied, to some extent, by private organizations; however, when private organizations cannot meet the public's needs, this responsibility belongs to a public organization or government. In some areas—such as national defense, domestic security, environmental control, economic policy—only government has the resources and authority to fill the gap between individual capacity and society's demands for survival and well-being.

Cooperation and conflict

Human needs and relations are anchored in two deep-seated psychological forces: the cooperative impulse that leads to integration and association, and the aggressive impulse that results in hostility and conflict. The perennial ambiguity of human relations lies in the fact that these two contradictory forces operate simultaneously. Individuals within a group, or groups within society, express the cooperative impulse in the very existence of the group, but at the same time they pursue objectives that are mutually incompatible.

One of the main sources of conflict in society is that individuals and groups want more than is available. Not only are material goods and services in short supply, but so also are nonmaterial or intangible goods and values, such as respect, security, status, and power. This scarcity inevitably results in conflict.

Power

If the integrative and associational bonds of society are not to be constantly threatened by the disruptive forces of anarchy and disintegration, there must be a cut-off point at which individual or group conflicts can be authoritatively settled by decisions that are accepted as binding. This requires that some members of society have power over others. Power is a relation between persons or groups in which one person or group controls the actions of others by means of effective sanctions. Such sanctions may be rewards or punishments. Power may have its base or source in corporate wealth, labor unions, military expertise, technological skill, religion, or political organization.

Power in any society or political system may be centralized—that is, it may be held by a small *elite*—or it may be shared by a *plurality* of groups. With respect to the analysis of power in the United States, two main approaches or interpretations have been advanced: the pluralist and the elitist.

The pluralist conception of power. The multiplicity of the sources of power in developed countries is reflected in the pluralist concept. According to that concept, in every sector of social life there is a twofold power structure, a functional one and a territorial one. Functionally—in the economy, the political order, the military establishment, and major interest groups—power is structured in terms of role differentials: Within each power structure, a relatively small group of the most active and committed persons—the leaders, the elite—holds the largest amount of power, sharing it to some extent with the rank and file. Territorially, power structures are differentiated according to the local, state, regional, national, or international units in which they operate. The power of a boss of a local party machine, for example, is circumscribed by the machine's narrow territorial dimensions, whereas a multinational corporation, such as Exxon, exercises its power and influence in several dozen countries throughout the world.

In the pluralist interpretation of power, the various power structures in such liberal capitalistic societies as the United States or Canada do not merge into one unified, monolithic power elite, but rather cooperate or compete with each other. Regardless of whether these power structures cooperate or compete, their relations do not lead to the permanent dominance of one power structure over the others. In general, each elite exercises its strongest power and influence within its own sphere. Politicians are most powerful in the governmental sphere, and business leaders are most powerful in the economic sphere.

The pluralist concept of power also emphasizes the varied subsystems of power within each power structure. The economic sector of society is not capped by a single unified power elite, because in that sector there are competing leadership groups—labor unions and corporate business, for example. By the same token, neither labor nor business is led by a single elite, but rather by various competing leadership groups. Similarly, while there is cooperation between the different political elites, there is also conflict and competition between them, espcially between the two major political parties, neither of which is dominated by a single unified power elite.[1]

The elitist conception of power. By contrast with this pluralist interpretation, the "elitist" interpretation views the various leadership groups or elites not as being coordinate, but rather as being hierarchically related.[2] In this pyramidal view of society, the apex is occupied by the economic power structure, which is regarded as a unified elite of wealthy businessmen. Only two other power elites are credited with substantial importance: the political leadership and the high military, but in the last analysis the business elite is regarded as dominant. To the extent that the elitist interpretation stresses the pivotal role of the corporate rich, it uses basic Marxist concepts of social power.[3] Many adherents of the elitist interpretation of power stress the imperialist character of Western societies; in their view the military acquires a high degree of importance, since military power is considered to be the indispensable means of imperial expansion.

[1] The best exposition of the pluralist conception of power from a broad social perspective is Arnold M. Rose, *The Power Structure: Political Process in America Society,* New York: Oxford University Press, 1967. Rose calls his interpretation a "multi-influence hypothesis," thus emphasizing that in the multiplicity of power structures no single one has predominance over all others.

[2] The most influential presentation of the elitist interpretation of power is in C. Wright Mills, *The Power Elite,* New York: Oxford University Press, 1956. Mills was both an outstanding American sociologist and a leading Marxist.

[3] The elitist emphasis on the military and the political derives from Lenin rather than from Marx. Lenin stressed, as Marx did not, the importance of the political element in history, and he also saw in imperialism a major force of capitalist states.

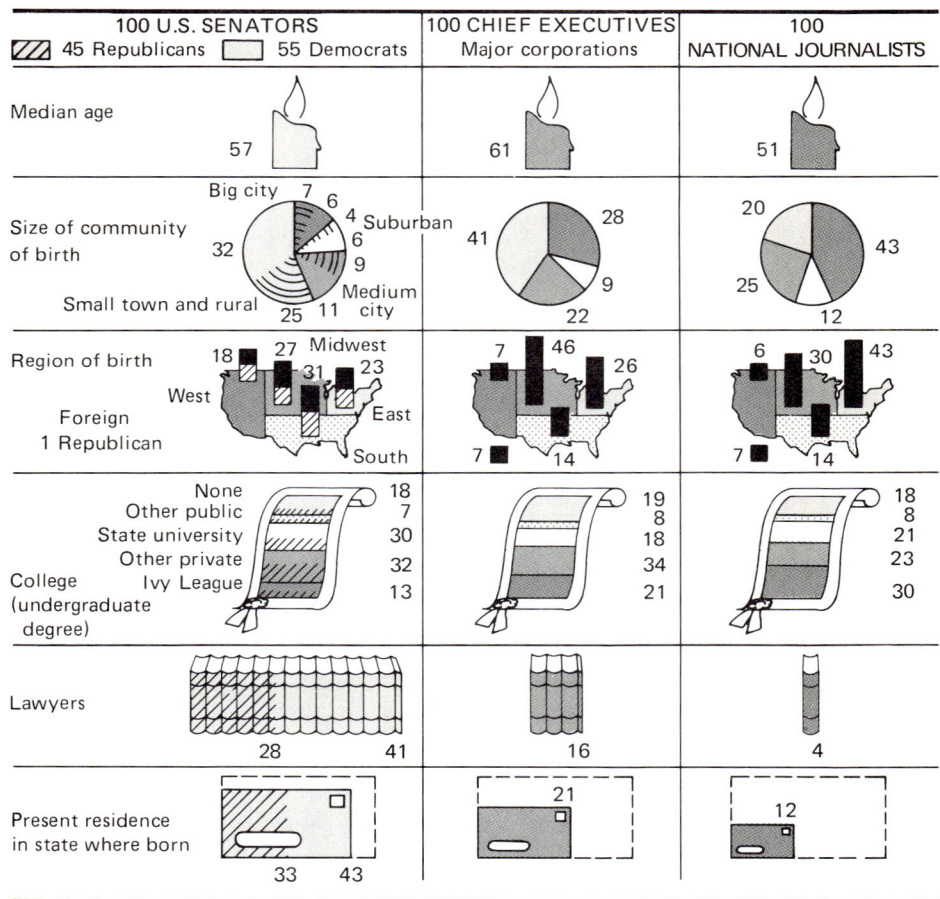

Three Kinds of Leaders: A Group Portrait
Tom Cardamore for *Fortune,* September, 1971, p. 91.

The unified character of the power elite is seen by the elitist analysts not only in terms of its control over men, ideas, and resources, but also in terms of its psychological and social integration. The "big three" elites (economic, political, and military) are said to be composed of men of similar social background and education, whose similar life styles facilitate social intermingling and intermarriage. They can easily move from one elite group to another, always with the understanding that the commanding heights of decision-making and financial rewards are to be found in the economic elite of the corporate rich.

Pluralism and elitism: theoretical analyses or political ideologies?

Neither the elitist nor the pluralist interpretations of power can be proved to be factual in the sense that a mathematical or chemical formula can be proved to be true or false. Both analyses of power seek to interpret facts—but both either draw different conclusions from the same facts or rely on different sets of facts. In general, the elitist interpretation of power appeals most to those who tend toward the extreme right or left of the political spectrum. The rightist holds that under any system the majority of the people are incapable of rational thought or responsible action and must therefore be led by a cohesive elite. The leftist believes that under capitalism the masses of the people are manipulated by a small economic oligarchy that controls all media, so that capitalism will have to be overthrown before power—social, economic, and political—can be broadly shared by a plurality of groups.

From the pluralist's viewpoint, the principle of countervailing powers—of restraints and limits—is not only operative in the political order of the United States, but is also, to a considerable extent, an active influence in the United States' social and economic domains. The validity of the pluralist or elitist interpretation of power in a society like the one existing in the United States thus relates to the broader issue of whether such a society is judged to be essentially liberal—a society limiting the power of all organized groups and interests—or whether it has already become, or is in the process of becoming, a totalitarian political order that protects the economic interests of a small class of the rich.

Political power. Political power is distinct from other forms of power in two basic criteria. First, political power relates to society as a whole, rather than to a particular social group. Every social group or association manifests phenomena of power, both internally and externally. By contrast, political power potentially relates to every segment of society. If one seeks to effect major changes in society, one cannot bypass the political process. College students, for example, may be able to produce changes in colleges and universities through campus activities, but they cannot change society to any significant extent by such means. The lowering of the minimum voting age to 18 years now provides the college-age generation with direct access to the political decision-making process. As a result, the student is likely to have a more profound and lasting effect on society as a whole than when his actions were, for the most part, limited to the college campus.

The second principal difference between political and other types of power is that the sanctions at the disposal of power holders in specific social groups are limited: An employer may fire a recalcitrant employee, or a medical association may exclude a physician from access to some hospitals. But such sanctions are limited by comparison to the sanctions available to the holders of political power. They—and they alone—possess the authority to inflict on the individual all kinds of deprivation and punishment, including physical coercion, imprisonment, and even death. Government, of course, may also impose limitations on itself as to the type of sanctions that it may use—for example, the Eighth Amendment prohibits "cruel and unusual punishments." Nevertheless, the potential "omni-concern" of political power holders with respect to the whole society's tensions and conflicts is reflected in the vast scope of sanctions that are forbidden to private power holders.

Although political power includes the potential use of force and coercion, it must not be confused with them. Most people, for example, obey the law not because they are afraid of the sanctions threatened, but because they believe that the law is fair or just; or because they accept the legitimacy of the democratic process, under which both wise and unwise laws are passed; or because they feel indifferent toward a specific law and obey it out of a generalized habit of obedience, abandoning the stance of unreflecting obedience only when a vital issue of conscience or interest is involved.

GOVERNMENT AS INSTITUTIONALIZED POLITICAL POWER

In the early stages of social evolution, small, nonliterate societies may get along without specialized political institutions. The head of a tribal clan may act as its familial chief, its religious leader, and also as the authority that settles disputes among members of the clan. But in later stages of social evolution, specific social functions are carried on by specific social institutions, and the political function, too, becomes specialized by the establishment of political norms and institutions—laws, representative councils, and executive and judicial institutions.

These governmental institutions may be set up and developed in many different ways: Power may be held and exercised in a relatively more or less diffused or monopolistic manner. From the earliest beginnings in ancient Greece, political writers have been aware of these differences, and the typologies of government have generally centered on the issue of whether a single person possesses political power (autocracy), whether a few privileged persons rule (oligarchy), or whether political power is held by leaders elected by the majority of voters in free and periodic elections (democracy).

CONCEPTS OF DEMOCRACY

Democracy as a system of power

If all politics is concerned with attaining, distributing, and exercising power, democratic politics and government must *also* be a system of power. To some people, this inevitable relationship between democratic politics and power is unappealing or even repugnant, but they confuse power with physical compulsion and violence and fail to see that power encompasses a wide range of means from physical compulsion to persuasion and the peaceful force of habit.

The second reason why people sometimes feel uncomfortable with the relationship between democracy and power is the idea of consent. From a normative viewpoint, democratic politics ought to be based entirely on consent, in which case no interpersonal or intergroup conflicts would arise that could not be settled without resorting to the superior force of society, that is, the government. This normative ideal of democracy must not be confused, however, with the empirical facts of social life. These facts indicate that no society based entirely on persuasion and consent has ever existed or is likely to exist, if one assumes that the things and values wanted by individuals and groups are always in short supply.

Anarchism and communes. Anarchism is the only political doctrine that affirms the desirability and possibility of a society without binding norms and the political power and institutions of enforcing them. Anarchists believe that man is innately benevolent and cooperative, and that he is prevented from being his good spontaneous self by the corrupt institutions and practices of government, religion, education, and the economy. There have been—and there are today—anarchist thinkers, movements, and parties, but there has never been an anarchist state or society, because the very concepts of state and society imply norms, laws, and authoritative agencies and institutions enforcing binding rules. As the Romans put it: *Ubi societas, ibi ius* (Where there is society, there is law).

Whenever even small groups of people with shared goals and ideals get together to set up "unstructured" communities without power and government, as has happened in hundreds of American communes in the last decade, they inevitably discover that even small communes cannot do without some forms of government and power. A founder-member of a successful commune in Virginia writes, after five years of experience:

> *A group that chooses to have no government is not thereby going to go without one. It is merely going to deliver government into the hands of the head of the dominance hierarchy—to those people who just naturally rise to the top. There, without guidelines or rules of any kind, the natural leader will exercise his power for good or bad, and recognize or not recognize his responsibility to the other people, depending on his ideas and conditioning.*[4]

[4]Kathleen Kinkade, *A Walden Two Experiment: The First Five Years of Twin Oaks Community*, New York: Morrow, 1973, p. 23.

Of course, the very existence of communes, whether in the United States or in other countries, is possible only because the larger society supplies protection against theft, robbery, and physical violence to which even members of anarchically inspired communes are exposed.

All of us rebel to some extent against power and authority, and many have dreamed of a society in which political power and compulsion would be kept to a minimum. But even the most committed Jeffersonian recognizes that there can be no society without political power and authority, and that the realistic objective should be, first, to devise a political system in which power is widely diffused, and, second, to set up procedures through which the exercise of political power can be kept within legitimate bounds.

Voluntary associations. Finally, the statement that democratic government is *also* a system of power clearly implies that it is *not only* a system of power. Democratic political systems at their best encourage and utilize *voluntary* activities and associations of citizens and citizen groups, because democracy can best be practiced in small groups. In fact, it can be argued that the degree to which a political system can be called democratic is proportionate to the extent to which voluntary activities and associations arise. Before a voter can choose between two or more candidates for public office, it is necessary for citizens to band together voluntarily to form political parties, and those who run for public office know that at the end of the road there may be, not victory and glory, but defeat and frustration. The First Amendment guarantees "the right of the people peaceably to assemble," but such constitutional provision is based on the optimistic expectation that the people actually will assemble, that they will care, and that they won't lazily and apathetically withdraw into their little private worlds. This presupposition of voluntary effort and participation applies also to nongovernmental organizations. In democratic political systems, labor unions, professional associations of lawyers, boy scout organizations, and baseball clubs are not created and run by government, but owe their existence and operation to voluntary citizen effort.

Historical overview

Greek city-states. To the ancient Greeks the world owes the first experience and conceptual formulation of democracy. Democracy developed in a few small Greek city-states, where the voting citizens—free male adults—numbered only several thousand. They met in popular assemblies and approved or disapproved the measures proposed by the officials, most of whom were elected by lot. Representation was largely unknown, and the rapid turnover of officials enabled many citizens to hold public positions at one time or another.

Roman rule of law. After the brief Greek experience with democratic government, it took nearly 2,000 years to revive the practice of democratic government in the West. The government of Republican Rome included democratic elements, but its mixed constitution generally favored the aristocratic element. After Rome became an empire with heavy military commitments, its mixed constitution was replaced by more or less autocratic forms of monarchical government. The Roman concept and practice of the rule of law (or the supremacy of law over arbitrary power and the equal treatment of all before the law) is often cited as a Roman contribution to democracy. However, the rule of law—certainly indispensable to liberal, constitutional democracy—may also be found to a varying extent in authoritarian governments.

Feudalism. During the Middle Ages some important contributions were made to democratic theory and practice. The medieval invention of representation of interests (nobility, clergy, towns) in a king's council or parliament paved the way for later democratic forms of representation. The medieval system of feudal relations between lord and vassal rested on a mutuality of rights and duties. The lord had claims of loyalty, obedience, and service against the vassal, but he also had duties and obligations to protect and care for the vassal, and this mutuality of rights and duties between governors and governed later contributed to the social-contract doctrine of government based on consent, as expressed in the Declaration of Independence. Finally, the medieval concept of law as limited by social custom and divine reason contributed to the classical democratic and liberal idea that there are areas outside of political power and decision, and that government must be limited with respect to means and ends if it is to be democratic.

The modern Western concept of democracy

Democracy in the seventeenth and eighteenth centuries can best be defined by what it opposed rather than by what it advocated and practiced. First, it opposed royal absolute authority. The beheading of Charles I of England in 1649 and the execution of Louis XVI and Marie Antoinette of France in 1793 reflected the original egalitarian impulse in the growth of democratic attitudes and institutions.

Second, democracy opposed, and the French Revolution abolished, aristocratic titles; the American Constitution provides that "no title of nobility shall be granted in the United States." Third, it opposed the principle of hereditary nobility. In Britain, the influence of the House of Lords, based on this principle, was continually curbed after the Glorious Revolution of 1688–1689 until the supremacy of the House of Commons was permanently established in 1911. It is possible that before long, the House of Lords may be abolished altogether, or, if retained, its members will very likely be selected on the basis of public service rather than of birth.

Finally, democracy opposed arbitrary government. In the predemocratic age and in the early phases of democratic government, hostility to arbitrary government demanded basic procedures of the rule of law, such as judicial independence, freedom from arbitrary arrest, no taxation without representation, and basic freedoms of speech and association.

The word *democracy* was in ill repute in the eighteenth century. So-called men of substance and their ideological apologists considered democracy to be synonymous with mob rule, unrestrained popular majorities, unreasoning imprudence, internecine factionalism, chaotic turbulence, and tyranny of the ill-bred and uneducated over the well-bred and the educated. The plus-word in the eighteenth century for opponents of royal absolutism and arbitrary government was *republic*. It meant responsible government by a leadership of carefully chosen representatives, who were intelligent and moderate, considerate of minorities, dedicated to the achievement of a rational balance between conflicting interests, and filled with patriotic devotion to the public good.

This eighteenth-century distrust of democracy was reflected in the American Constitution. Only the House of Representatives was to be elected directly by the people, whereas the President and the Senate were to be elected by the more indirect means of the Electoral College and state legislatures. It was assumed that these methods would protect the republic against the rash and impulsive actions resulting from the people voting directly. Direct election of senators was not introduced until the Seventeenth Amendment was passed in 1913; women were not guaranteed the suffrage until the Nineteenth Amendment was passed in 1920; and many black people were not guaranteed the right to vote until 1965, when the Voting Rights Act enabled the federal government to register black voters directly in areas of discrimination.

In colonial times, American hostility to the word *democracy* and what it represented faithfully reflected the dominant European prejudice.[5] John Winthrop, governor of Massachusetts through most of the 1630s and 1640s, called democracy "the meanest and worst of all the forms of government." Even Jefferson, who symbolized the democratic ideal more than any other statesman in the American political experience, shied away from the word *democracy,* although he frequently expressed faith in the "people," "freedom," and "self-government." In the last years of his life Jefferson became less cautious in his language and used the word *democracy* more often. In 1816, for example, he described the American people as being "constitutionally and conscientiously democrats."

[5]For a presentation of the evolving uses of the word *democracy* in America, see Saul K. Padover, *The Meaning of Democracy: An Appraisal of the American Experience,* New York: Praeger, 1963, pp. 12–29.

When Jefferson organized his own party in the 1790s, it was called the Republican party; later it became the Democratic–Republican party; and since the days of Andrew Jackson's administration it has been known as the Democratic party. The era of Jackson marks the turning point for the words "democracy" and "democratic." Since that time they have become plus-words—regardless of what social and political reality hides behind them.

From respectability to apotheosis was only a short step, and the generation after Jackson established Walt Whitman, the author of *Democratic Vistas* (1871), as the national poet of democracy. The power of the word *democracy* became manifest in World War I, when President Wilson assured the American people that the purpose of American intervention in the conflict was "to make the world safe for democracy."

Key principles of the American political commitment

In England, the Magna Carta and the Glorious Revolution decisively influenced English political development, but neither created England as a nation. If the French Revolution had failed, there would still be a French nation today. By contrast, the United States as a nation is the creation of a few political acts and documents. The Declaration of Independence laid down a few principles containing the commitment to a goal that the United States was to follow in its quest for nationhood. In drawing up the Constitution, the framers found that the job was more difficult than stating the general principles of the Declaration of Independence, and subsequent experience has shown that living up to the Constitution has been much more complex than drafting it. Yet the principles of the Declaration are all the American people have as official tenets of political belief. Documents such as the Declaration and the Constitution are the American equivalents of the nonpolitical attachments and articles of faith possessed by older nations.

The Declaration of Independence contains the basic principles of the American political commitment to democracy.

> *We hold these truths to be self-evident; that all men are created equal, that they are endowed by their Creator with certain unalienable rights, that among these are life, liberty, and the pursuit of happiness. That to secure these rights, governments are instituted among men, deriving their just powers from the consent of the governed; that whenever any form of government becomes destructive of these ends, it is the right of the people to alter or to abolish it, and to institute new government, laying its foundation on such principles, and organizing in such form, as to them shall seem most likely to effect their safety and happiness.*

Limited government. The first important principle of the American political commitment to democracy, expressed here in eighteenth-century language, is the assertion that man-made laws and government action have limits, set by the "self-evident truths" of the laws of God and nature. In twentieth-century parlance, our courts have ruled that governmental actions are invalid if they are "arbitrary" or "unreasonable"; however, the significance of these terms in relation to governmental practice has never been clearly defined. The important point is that our courts assume, as did the Declaration, that there are certain principles behind governmental actions that need not be proved and that serve as criteria for judging whether governmental actions are right or wrong. This concept of *limited government* is necessarily implied in any doctrine of democracy, because opposition to unlimited government has always been one of the driving forces behind the democratic impulse. The concept of what the specific limits are varies from time to time, and the Declaration wisely refrained from laying down any specific limits.

Equality. The phrase "all men are created equal" is the hardest phrase in the Declaration to define in concrete terms. In his original draft of the Declaration, Jefferson had included a long passage condemning the British monarch for capturing slaves and carrying them from Africa to America. But Jefferson was induced to remove that passage. In his *Autobiography* (1821), Jefferson explains why the antislavery statement had to be deleted. Southern states wanted to continue slavery, and "our northern brethren," he wrote, "though their people had very few slaves themselves, yet they had been pretty considerable carriers of them to others."[6]

The authors of the Declaration were fully aware that human beings are not equal in background, upbringing, physical and intellectual endowment, or motivation. They also knew that they could not abolish differences between individuals and groups by fiat. In the Declaration, they tried to steer a middle course between two concepts of equality that seemed to them unsatisfactory. First was the Stoic-Augustinian concept that the only equality that mattered was the equality of the human soul before God, and that, therefore, to a true Christian differences of social status and power were basically unimportant. The authors of the Declaration, divided as they may have been in their religious outlook, were too this-worldly to accept life here and now as a trifle.

Second, equality in the Declaration does not mean uniformity through the steamroller of social pressure, integration of all into one pattern, but rather the right not to be punished for being different. In the eighteenth century, people *were* penalized for being different: Women suffered for not being men, Jews for not being Christians, Catholics for not being Protestants, atheists for not being believers, blacks for not being white, the poor for not

---

[6]Dumas Malone (ed.), *The Autobiography of Thomas Jefferson*, New York: Capricorn, 1959, p. 35.

"If you hold those truths to be so self-evident, how come you keep harping on them?"
Drawing by Weber; © 1968 The New Yorker Magazine, Inc.

being affluent, the uneducated for not having attained prescribed educational credentials. Psychologically, difference easily arouses hostility, and because this tendency in man's feeling and behavior is only too natural, the Declaration sought to lessen it through an explicit commitment to equality.

Socrates summarized his philosophy of the good life in two words: "Know thyself." The democratic ideal of equality seeks to embrace the whole personality of every human being, even those who never will know themselves, and the democratic ideal could be summarized also in two words: "Be yourself." The right to be oneself, to be happy, did not originate with the authors of the Declaration, but in the Declaration we have the first case of a whole political community officially committing itself to that philosophy.

Gaps between commitment and performance

The key principles of the American political commitment obviously do not describe the actual American political performance. In fact, the very ambitiousness of the American commitment magnifies the tension between ideal and reality, because living up to the high ideals of the Declaration has always proved difficult and has often been impossible. Such failures create feelings of guilt in the United States and charges of hypocrisy abroad. The higher a nation sets its sights, the more it may achieve—but the more it may also fail as measured by its own professed standards.

All social and political systems reveal serious discrepancies between promise and performance, idea and reality. Democracy, by encouraging criticism and protest, is particularly sensitive to such discrepancies, and protracted failure to deal with them carries the seeds of violence, if peaceful criticism and protest persistently cannot bring about the needed changes. Such dissatisfaction is particularly dangerous when it affects a major identifiable group. If the ranks of the dissatisfied are made up of individuals or comparatively small groups scattered throughout the population, such dissatisfaction should not pose a serious threat to the stability and peace of a democratic polity. But when a major group feels that it is not being treated fairly, when such feeling of deprivation and alienation is protracted, and when a group begins to feel that it is permanently outside the system, it is inevitable that trouble will develop.

In the 1930s, for example, organized labor reached the conclusion that it could not peacefully get what it felt it should get in political power and economic benefits. A wave of sit-down strikes, or the occupation of factories, ensued. The National Labor Relations Act of 1935 and its later administration by the National Labor Relations Board finally convinced organized labor that its fundamental demands for recognition of status and fair shares in the economy had been substantially met, and since then organized labor has been rightly considered by the still powerless groups as part of the "establishment."

In the 1960s, black people showed their accumulated resentment against their status as "outs" both in the political process of decision-making and in the economic process of creating and distributing wealth. Seven out of ten poor families are white; but this fact does not generate political dynamite, since in proportional terms only one in ten white families is poor, whereas the incidence of poverty is three out of ten nonwhite families. Moreover, among the nonwhite poor there is further concentration geographically. In central-city areas, 42 percent of all poor families are black—considerably higher than the incidence of black poverty throughout the country. Central-city areas have also been the places in which riots have occurred.

Democracy can stand the strain of temporary ins and outs. In fact, after every election there are ins and outs. But *the game of ins and outs works only as long as the outs believe that there is a chance for them next time, and only as long as the ins are willing to acknowledge that chance.* When the outs feel that they will never be ins, democracy loses its meaning for them, and society faces the danger of becoming split permanently into those for whom the system works and those for whom it does not. Paradoxically, as the number of the contented increases and becomes a permanent majority, the danger of disregarding still dissatisfied minority groups assumes major dimensions. Of the issues unresolved by the Western affluent democracies, *The Economist* argues:

> ... the most explosive is what you do when a relatively well-to-do and contented majority sits on its plump bottom and ignores the sort of people who are condemned, by the colour of their skin or by being born hard-luck cases, to the status of a permanent minority. That is a new problem because a contented majority is a brand-new phenomenon.[7]

The operational concept of democracy

The ambiguities and failures of the democratic experience are partly related to the high expectations entertained by early democratic thinkers and statesmen with respect to popular self-government. In the eighteenth century—before democratic government was a reality—there was the cheering hope that government by the people would put an end to the ills that had always afflicted the human condition. Yet, in a literal sense, the classical formulation of the concept of democracy as government by the people can operate only in a community that is small enough to let the individual be heard in public assembly and to vote there on specific policies and laws. Operationally, such *direct democracy* has functioned, where it has existed at all, in the small city-states of ancient Greece and in the small towns of Switzerland and New England.

In large communities—nations, states, provinces, and cities—the definition of democracy as government by the people runs into serious difficulties, so serious that some observers believe democracy in the large community is an impossibility and can be retained only as a "hurrah word," a manipulative term with which to bamboozle the people at home into docile submission, and which can also be used in foreign policy as an ideological weapon against communism. Other students of democratic government have been impressed, and distressed, that in modern large-scale societies, political democracy is a system of power, and since in the mind of such observers power and democracy are *ipso facto* incompatible, they view democracy as a "mythical conception" until the day comes when democracy will be not a system of power but a "system of participation."[8]

Ordinary observation and common sense tell us that a definition of political democracy as a system in which people govern themselves has little reference to reality, if "self-governing" is taken to mean what it means to,

---

[7]October 24, 1970 (London), p. 13.

[8]For a fuller treatment of democracy as a system of participation versus democracy as a system of power, see Robert J. Pranger, *The Eclipse of Citizenship: Power and Participation in Contemporary Politics,* New York: Holt, Rinehart & Winston, 1968.

say, the small businessman, who is self-governing in the sense that he expresses his will each day in a host of decisions that he believes serve his interest. Obviously, a nation of over 200 million people cannot be self-governing in this sense, since such vast numbers of people—by the sheer fact of size—would produce only chaos if each individual were trying to make the policy decisions or perform the administrative actions of the national or local political communities to which he belongs. No political system can be devised in which the individual wills or interests of over 200 million people could be realized, if one assumes the practical impossibility of perfect harmony among so many individual wills and interests.

Therefore in the large society—the society beyond the dimensions of a small Swiss commune or a small Quaker meeting—there has to be a division of labor. Some persons have to make the important political decisions for the whole society, and some specialists in administration have to perform the tasks of management and administration for society as a whole. Because of the inevitable impact of size and dimension on the political process, the method of selecting political decision-makers and administrators is highly significant. Are they to come from royal families by divine grace? Are they to come from self-appointed rulers who acquired their position by the gun and perpetuate their power by the threat of the gun? Or are there other methods?

Democracy is another method. Operationally, modern democracy may be defined as a *political order in which adult citizens freely choose representatives in regularly scheduled competitive elections.* Whereas citizens in the direct democracy of small communities decide specific policies through their votes in popular assemblies, in the *indirect democracy of representative government* citizens express their preferences for a cluster of political views by voting for representatives who favor, in general, the same policies that they do. In the large-scale democracy of the nation, state, province, or city, voters participate in the political process in many ways other than through voting (involvement in party activities, campaign contributions, influencing others through the spoken or written word), but voting is the central act of influencing policy formation.

Elections of representatives, of the political leadership, are indispensable to a democratic political order, but not every political system is democratic just because it holds elections. In making his choices, the citizen must be free—free from governmental coercion to vote in a particular way, and free to obtain all the available information about the various candidates and parties. Freedom of choice therefore implies freedom of speech, assembly, and the press, including radio and television. A free choice can also be made only if the election is free from fraud and deception, such as occurred in the presidential election of 1972 in the Watergate scandal: burglarizing and bugging the opposition party's headquarters; "dirty tricks," libel, and slander; exacting illegal campaign contributions from corporate managers;

and abusing federal agencies (Internal Revenue Service, Federal Bureau of Investigation, Central Intelligence Agency) for partisan political purposes.

The classical definition of democracy as government by the people implied that each citizen be well informed and that he take a strong and active interest in public affairs. There is ample empirical evidence, however, that a considerable minority of citizens in modern democracies are very poorly informed about public policies and political leaders, and that only a very small minority take an active part in public affairs. Thus the temptation is great to conclude that democracy *is* a myth and will remain so until all the people are Platonic "philosopher-kings," wise, well informed, and able and willing to play a part in the political process. However, if one abandons the classical definition of democracy as unsuited for modern times, the operational definition given above provides an approximately correct approach, since it allows for the fact that most people find politics less interesting than some political observers and civic boosters can bring themselves to admit.

In the "psychic budget" of most people, government and politics are of less interest than such personal matters as improving one's standard of living, good health, and a happy family life. In a series of surveys made in the 1950s, 1960s, and 1970s, respondents were asked to describe, in their own words, what they wanted from life, what meant most to them in the light of their own perceptions and hopes. In tabulating the responses, the directors of the surveys included only those items that appeared in at least 5 percent of the answers. As Table 1–1 shows, nearly all the items mentioned by at least 5 percent of the respondents reflect nonpolitical, personal concerns for better living standards, good health, and happy family life. Interestingly, the single political item—the desire for peace—is broad and noncontroversial, affecting everybody in a direct, personal way. If democratic politics implies a principle of competition, of alternative policy choices, the desire for peace is so generally shared by all citizens that it cannot be called political in terms of controversial "democratic politics."

About one-third of the American public is largely unaware and uninformed about political issues. About 40–60 percent vote, but otherwise confine their political interest and activity to spectator roles, such as watching political television broadcasts, reading political news in the papers, and discussing politics with their friends. About 10-12 percent contribute money to their favorite political causes, but only 3–5 percent engage in active party work.[9]

---

[9]See Lester W. Milbrath, *Political Participation,* Chicago: Rand McNally, 1965; Angus Campbell et al., *The American Voter,* New York: Wiley, 1960, pp. 90 ff.; V. O. Key, Jr., *Public Opinion and American Democracy,* New York: Knopf, 1961, pp. 494 ff.; and Robert Lane, *Political Life,* New York: Free Press, 1959, chaps. 6, 22. For a five-country comparison with respect to levels of political knowledge and involvement, see Gabriel A. Almond and Sidney Verba, *The Civic Culture: Political Attitudes and Democracy in Five Nations,* Princeton, N.J.: Princeton University Press, 1963, chaps. 3, 6–9.

Table 1–1 *Personal hopes, in percentages (specified by 5 percent or more of sample[a])*

	1959	1964	1971	1972
Peace in the world; no wars	9	17	19	32
Better standard of living	38	40	27	29
Good health for self	40	29	29	27
Aspirations for children (opportunities, especially education; success; happiness)	29	35	17	23
Happy family life	18	18	14	18
Own house or live in better one	24	12	11	12
Good health for family	16	25	13	12
Good job; congenial work	7	9	6	10
Wealth	—	5	7	8
Leisure time; recreation; travel	11	5	6	8
Peace of mind; emotional stability and maturity	5	9	8	7
Economic stability in general; no inflation	—	—	6	7
Safety from crime	—	—	—	7
Employment	5	8	6	6
Social justice (greater equality, elimination of discrimination)	—	—	—	6
Happy old age	10	8	6	6
Self-improvement or development	—	—	—	5
Christian revival	—	—	—	5

[a] A dash (—) indicates mention by less than 5 percent of the sample. A shift of 4 percentage points between studies is considered statistically significant.
Source: William Watts and Lloyd A. Free (eds.), *State of the Nation,* New York: Basic Books, 1973, p. 259.

How then are the voters equipped to select or remove a government? The situation here is not so different from many others encountered in daily life. We constantly enlist the authority and skills of people whose qualifications we cannot judge professionally, such as physicians, lawyers, tax accountants, and auto mechanics. We judge them on the basis of what we think they will do for us and what they have done for our friends and acquaintances whose judgment we trust. This does not mean that such judgments are entirely based on provable fact—there will always be a nonrational element of like or dislike, sympathy or hostility, or plain ignorance. But flunking a questionnaire on simple political facts and issues no more disqualifies a person from exercising his judgment of whom to vote for than the total ignorance of the way an automobile engine works disqualifies someone from making an intelligent purchase of the car most suited to his needs.

Without attempting to settle the question of the capacity and rationality of the American voter in a permanently valid and philosophical way, V. O. Key, Jr., one of the foremost American political scientists, studied the presidential election campaigns between 1936 and 1960. His main finding was that

> *voters are not fools. To be sure, many individual voters act in odd ways indeed; yet in the large the electorate behaves about as rationally and responsibly as we should expect, given the clarity of the alternatives presented to it and the character of the information available to it.*[10]

In selecting (or rejecting) a group of political leaders who will compose the government, the voter is greatly helped by the fact that the more important the office sought, the higher is his familiarity with the candidate—at least in a general way. Presidential candidates are nearly always well known before the race starts. In Congress, too, the voter generally does not have to evaluate novices. In the last three decades, the House of Representatives has averaged 65 freshman members (out of 435) in each Congress, and the Senate 13 freshmen (out of 100). Moreover, freshmen members of the House and the Senate do not emerge from a political no-man's land, but generally have had substantial experience in government and politics before being elected to Congress. Candidates for important state and local offices are also usually political professionals or semiprofessionals.

The democratic political order: limits and potentialities

The operational definition of democracy as a political order in which the citizens freely choose their government in competitive elections states only *how* public policies are arrived at, but says nothing about their *content*. In a democratic political order, the majority of the voters may favor—through the election of representatives broadly reflecting their views—all kinds of public policies that are mutually contradictory. Democracies may pursue economic policies inspired by the philosophies of laissez-faire, state intervention, social welfare, or public ownership of the means of production. In the field of education, democracies may provide a college education for the majority of high school graduates or for only a small minority. In the field of health, democracies may establish national health plans in which the patient makes no payment for the specific health service received, or they may accept a market relation in which the recipient of a health service pays for each service received, or democracies may enact a mixture of private and public elements in medical and hospital services. In religion, democracies may follow policies of strict separation of state and church, of support for all religions, or may even favor one church. In foreign policy, democracies may withdraw into isolation, vigorously cooperate in

---

[10] V. O. Key, Jr., *The Responsible Electorate: Rationality in Presidential Voting, 1936–1960*, Cambridge: Harvard University Press, 1966, p. 7.

internationalist efforts, or pursue imperialist policies. In regulating family relations and sexual morality, political democracies may enact restrictive or lenient policies on divorce, abortion, and pornography.

Not only do differences and contradictions between specific policies exist between democratic systems of different nations, but the same democratic political order may enact specific policies today that totally repudiate the policies of yesterday. Therefore, the question of whether such policies are democratic cannot be answered with reference to their content but only to the method by which they are made. Some people find this limitation of democracy to method and procedure unsatisfactory and seek to incorporate into the meaning of democracy such broad terms as "the good society," "liberty," "equality," "justice," and the like. However, such broad moral terms do not lend themselves to empirical verification.

There are as many conceptions of the good society as there are persons holding them. What seems to be a good society to one person may appear to be barely tolerable or outright repugnant to another person. By contrast, the meaning of democracy in procedural terms can be easily verified: A political system that has only one party, little or no freedom of speech and the press, that holds no elections or only infrequent elections, that coerces citizens to vote in a particular way, or that punishes political opposition as a crime, is not a democratic order, regardless of the content of its policies.[11]

Even when functioning at its best—that is, when faithfully reflecting the policy preferences of the majority of voters—a democracy will never be able to solve all of society's problems to everybody's satisfaction. Much of the criticism of American democracy, for example, has stressed the excessive power of special-interest groups at the expense of the majority of the people. Recently, radical criticism has been directed against contemporary American government because it *does* reflect the attitudes and preferences of the majority, rather than because it does not. The democratic political process provides means for changing other people's attitudes, but there is no guarantee that such efforts will always be successful. The democratic political process does not ensure that majorities of voters or legislators will be sufficiently intelligent, sensitive to necessary changes, and mindful of the feelings and interests of minorities.

Those who prefer democracy cannot base their preference on the illusionary ground that democracy is perfection, utopia here and now, or that it will ever approach utopia. Given the undeniable shortcomings of democracy at any time in any place, the limits of democracy can be accepted on the

---

[11] See Dorothy Pickles, *Democracy,* New York: Basic Books, 1970, pp. 9–93; Deane E. Neubauer, "Some Conditions of Democracy," *The American Political Science Review,* 61 (December, 1967), pp. 1002–1009; and Felix E. Oppenheim, "Democracy—Characteristics Included and Excluded," *The Monist,* 55 (January, 1971), pp. 29–50.

pragmatic ground that the shortcomings of an undemocratic system—one in which the preferences of a minority prevail over those of the majority—are even more serious.

Yet the very criterion that is democracy's most serious limitation—the fact that democracy is a set of methods and procedures of *how* public policies are to be arrived at rather than *what policies* are to be effected—is also democracy's greatest potential strength. Precisely because the rules of the democratic political game relate to no one specific social or economic issue, they potentially affect all. In general, experience has shown that if the political procedures of democracy are practiced over any length of time, they will eventually be applied to social, economic, educational, religious, and racial issues. So far, there is less evidence of the reverse. For example, in eighteenth-century Prussia religious toleration did not lead to political democracy. By contrast, in nineteenth-century Britain and the United States, the growth of political democracy eventually led to freedom and equality of status for religious minorities and nonbelievers.

The focus of democracy on specific procedures rather than on specific policies enables it to adapt to many kinds of political and economic institutions. Despite the American bias in favor of the republican form of government, some of the most effective and stable democracies—such as Britain, Holland, and the Scandinavian countries—function under monarchical forms of government. Similarly, the common American belief that democracy works best in a two-party system is no more than a prejudice, since most democratic systems—such as those in Belgium, France, Canada, Finland, Holland, Israel, and Japan—take a multiparty system for granted. Lastly, the typically American coupling, or even identification, of democracy with capitalism is not borne out by the facts. Spain, Taiwan, Brazil, and the numerous military dictatorships in Africa and Latin America are capitalistic economies combined with nondemocratic, authoritarian political regimes. Conversely, some democratic nations (Britain, Sweden, Norway, Australia) have moved in the direction of socialism without loss of democratic vitality.

Moral integrity and free government. The limits and potentialities of the democratic political order are not wholly determined by its procedural, operational elements: they are a necessary but not sufficient condition for the functioning of democracy. While democracy requires a particular kind of political machinery, it is more than a piece of machinery. The Founding Fathers clearly saw that, as George Washington put it in his Farewell Address (1796), "virtue or morality is a necessary spring of popular government." Jefferson and Madison were also deeply convinced that "the new science of government" had to be more than a set of mechanical devices or governmental institutions, that "republican government" had to be nourished by "republican morality" and "civic virtue" if the experiment in self-government was to endure. Above all, the founders held that the moral qualities of moderation, self-discipline, the ability to put the common good above private gain and interest, and faithful adherence to the Constitution were indispensable to the survival and flourishing of free government. The unbreakable link between moral integrity and free government was perhaps most pungently expressed by the great eighteenth-century British statesman Edmund Burke:

> *Men are qualified for civil liberty in exact proportion to their disposition to put moral chains upon their own appetites; in proportion as their love to justice is above their rapacity; in proportion as their soundness and sobriety of understanding is above their vanity and presumption; in proportion as they are more disposed to listen to the counsels of the wise and good, in preference to the flattery of knaves.*[12]

In the era of Watergate, Burke's words sound uncannily contemporary.

AUTHORITARIAN AND TOTALITARIAN GOVERNMENTS

Of the 140 states in the world today, about three-quarters have nondemocratic political orders. Such regimes vary from country to country according to political traditions, levels of social and economic development, and the cultural contexts within which they operate. These nondemocratic governments may be divided into two broadly defined groups: *authoritarian* and *totalitarian* systems. (See Figure 1–1.)

Both types of government deny their citizens the basic democratic political rights of freely selecting their political leaders in competitive elections, and therefore also forbid the complementary political freedoms of speech, assembly, association, and the media (press, radio, and television). Generally, both types of government tolerate only one party—the party of the government. All political power is concentrated in the executive, and the legislative and judicial branches play only minor roles, subordinated as they are to the executive. Elections may be held periodically, but no opposition party is allowed to participate, and the announced election results generally give the government party a comfortable margin of 90 percent or more of the total vote. The media are under strict government control—at least as far as political issues are concerned. Finally, both authoritarian and totalitarian governments typically employ a secret political police to watch over actual or potential dissidents, to track down oppositional groups or activities, and to ferret out unreliable elements in the government itself.

---

[12]Edmund Burke, *Reflections on the Revolution in France: And Other Writings*, New York: Oxford University Press (World's Classics), 1950, p. 319. See also Irving Kristol, *On the Democratic Idea in America*, New York: Harper & Row (Harper Torchbooks), 1973.

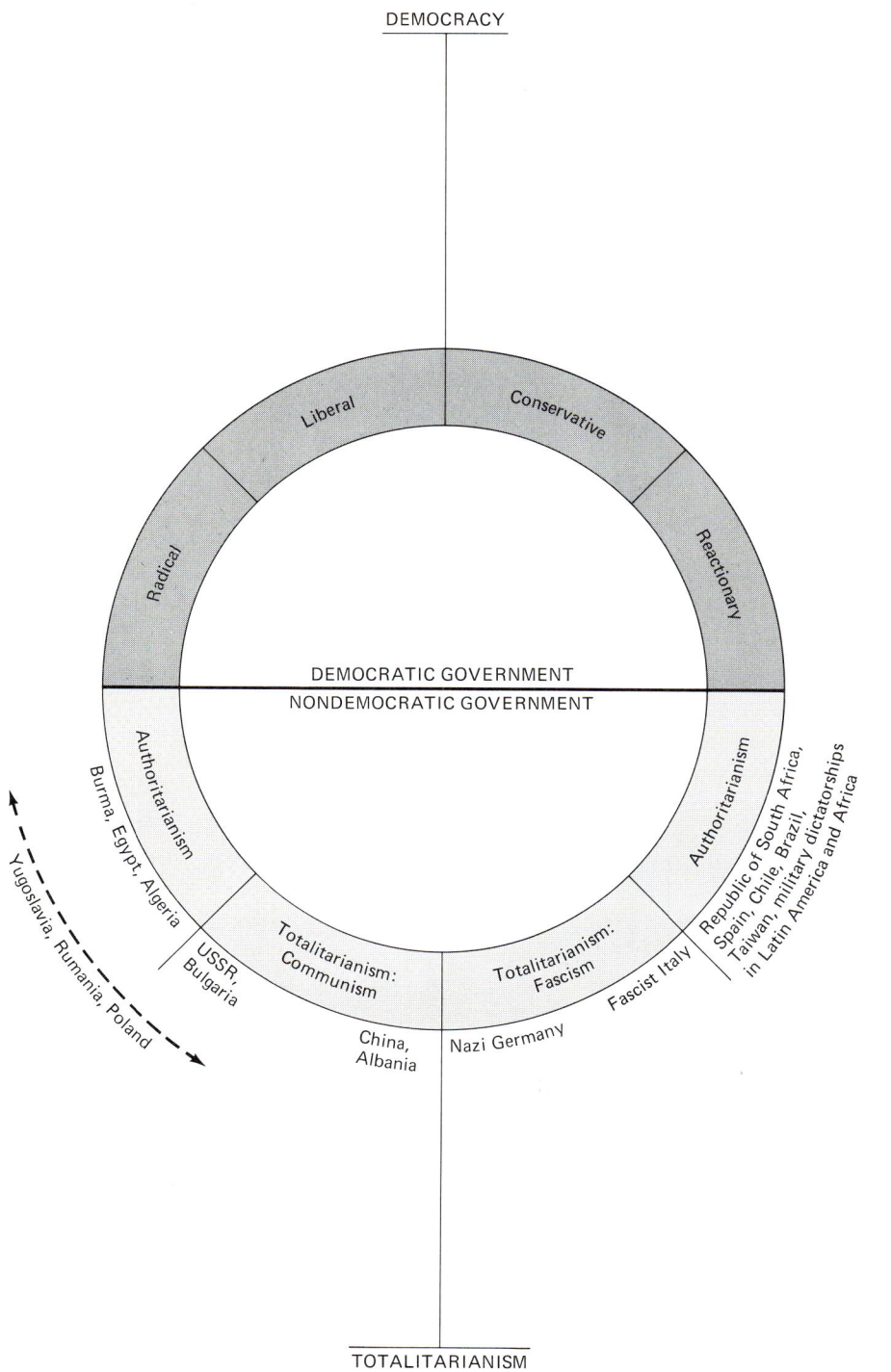

Figure 1-1 *The world political spectrum*

Similar as authoritarian and totalitarian governments are in their rejection of basic democratic political processes, they also differ in important ways with respect to both goals and means. As to goals, authoritarian governments seek to control primarily the political aspects of the individual's behavior and activities, leaving him substantial freedom of choice in his religious, family, cultural, and economic activities. Even with respect to politics, authoritarian regimes often leave the citizens some channels of expression, called the "freedom of the coffeehouse." A person may express his critical ideas freely while conversing with his friends, but he does not have the liberty to address a group without permission of the police, or to publish ideas that are hostile to the government. One political liberty that authoritarian regimes usually grant to their citizens is access to foreign newspapers and magazines: Although the press in authoritarian countries, such as Yugoslavia and Spain, always expresses the official line, foreign publications are freely sold in major cities.

In contrast with authoritarian regimes, totalitarian governments aim at a much wider range of controls over the individual and society. As a general principle, the totalitarian state recognizes no human sphere that is exempt from governmental control. Nazi Germany attempted to eradicate Christianity and replace it with pre-Christian pagan cults, and the Soviet Union has turned most churches and temples into warehouses, movies, and similar facilities. Worship in the remaining churches is still tolerated, but religious instruction is forbidden. In the field of cultural activity, totalitarian governments prescribe what types of music or painting or literature are to prevail: In Nazi Germany, artists had to promote the ideal of the pure Nordic Aryan; and in the Soviet Union, the government frequently forbids the publication or display of works of art that do not conform to "socialist realism." In the economy, the totalitarian state seeks to maintain complete control, either through minute regulation (as in the case of Nazi Germany) or through a combination of public ownership and control (as in the case of the Soviet Union and China), whereas in authoritarian Communist states, such as Yugoslavia and Poland, about 90 percent of the farms are privately owned and small businesses are tolerated.

Finally, one important freedom that the totalitarian state generally denies its citizens is the right of emigration. In China and the Soviet Union, illegal attempts to emigrate are crimes punished by years of prison or labor camp. This again is in sharp contrast with authoritarian states, such as Spain, Yugoslavia, and Brazil, which allow their citizens to work abroad temporarily or to emigrate permanently. A correlative of the right to emigrate is another basic human right—the right *not* to emigrate, the right of a citizen to live in his native land. This right is recognized by democratic and authoritarian governments, but not by totalitarian regimes: After resisting governmental pressures to leave the Soviet Union "voluntarily," author

Aleksandr Solzhenitsyn was forcibly expelled from the Soviet Union in 1974.

As to means, authoritarian governments use physical sanctions against political opponents, but such penalties generally do not go beyond imprisonment or exile; by contrast, totalitarian governments have not hesitated to "liquidate" "undesirable" individuals or groups. One of the semantic contributions of totalitarianism is the term "genocide," meaning the destruction of entire national groups.

While the concepts of political authoritarianism and totalitarianism are useful as rough guides, it should be borne in mind that no state or society is static. For example, under Stalin the Soviet Union experienced a perfected form of totalitarianism, with respect to both goals and means. After Stalin, the Soviet Union moved, under Khrushchev's leadership, toward "liberalization," which in practice meant the substitution of authoritarian for totalitarian policies. Under Brezhnev, the Soviet Union underwent a slow process of "re-Stalinization," without, however, moving back to full-fledged Stalinism. Nigeria, Africa's most populous state, was at first governed by democratic methods after becoming independent in 1960. Yet within six years democratic government disintegrated, and since 1966 Nigeria has been ruled by a succession of military strongmen—the form of authoritarianism most common in Africa, Asia, and Latin America. Democracies, too, are not static, and have had their periodic flirtations with anarchist tendencies on the one extreme and authoritarian pressures on the other.

THE MARXIST-COMMUNIST CONCEPT OF DEMOCRACY

In typically nineteenth-century fashion, Karl Marx's thinking centered on economics rather than politics. The root of all power, in his view, was economic, and political power was merely part of the "superstructure" erected on the foundation of economic power. Those who hold economic power by owning the means of production also control, directly or indirectly, the levers of political power and government. The control is exercised, Marx held, by the economic ruling class for the purpose of suppressing the exploited working classes. In the economic stage of capitalism, government—whether monarchy or republic, democracy or dictatorship—is but the "executive arm of the bourgeoisie," the instrument for oppressing the workers. Marx believed that only after the class rule of capitalism had been replaced by the classless society of communism would repressive political force no longer be necessary. In the classless society, therefore, the state would wither away, since the need for repression would have disappeared. True democracy would then come into being, a society in which there would be not the domination of man over man, but the "administration of things," as stated by Friedrich Engels, Marx's collaborator.

Marx thus combined in his thinking about political power and democracy an unusual mixture of realism and utopianism. Looking at society as it had hitherto existed, he realistically saw the importance of political power and the many obstacles to achieving democracy. Looking into the future classless society, Marx adopted the utopian view that political power would vanish and that democracy would automatically and spontaneously come into being in a society without any power, political or otherwise.

In typical twentieth-century fashion, Lenin gave politics priority over economics. Long before the Russian Revolution of 1917, Lenin argued that the working class was incapable of wresting power from the capitalist ruling class, and that a vanguard of trained professional revolutionaries had to be created to destroy capitalism and its institutions of political power. But even after the destruction of capitalism, the working class, corrupted, as Lenin viewed it, by the ideological superstructure of capitalism, would not have the capacity of self-government and would therefore have to be directed by the Communist party, a minority of the proletariat.

Claiming democracy as their objective, Communists argue that government is democratic if, and only if, it rules *in the interests* of the people, regardless of the political forms in which this is done. The Western concept of democracy stresses method and procedure; Marxists and Communists argue that the crucial point is not the means of obtaining power but the source and objective of power. From their viewpoint, as long as political power is held by the Communist party, as long as the working class is directed by the Communist party, and as long as governmental policies aim at the benefit of the people, a political system is by definition democratic.

In the Communist perspective, Britain is a capitalist dictatorship, although the Communist party is able to get only 0.1 percent of the popular vote in completely free elections, with no prohibitions or repressions of its press, propaganda, or political activities. In spite of the tiny electoral support of the Communist party, Britain could become a democracy only, in the Marxist-Communist view, if the party were to take power in Britain, since only Communist parties rule in the interest of the people. By contrast, Communists regard East Germany as a democracy because capitalism has been abolished there, although the Communist regime requires the use of political prisons and correctional labor camps, not to speak of frontiers of barbed wire and concrete walls designed to prevent the escape of East Germans into West Germany.

DEMOCRACY IN DEVELOPING COUNTRIES

Since the 1950s, both the newly independent countries and the older developing nations have increasingly made their weight felt in the world's balance of power. The political experience and the social setting of governments in the developing countries are different from those in the economically and politically advanced Western nations as well as from those in the Communist states.

Capitalism and developing countries. The ideas and practices of democracy in developing countries lack the individualistic streak of Western societies, since that individualism was largely the result of the capitalist market society and its stress on competition. The preindustrial peasant economies of the developing countries lack this tradition and ideal of individual competition as the driving force in politics or economics. Family and tribal cooperation rather than individual enterprise and self-enrichment have been the dominant elements of the cultures of the developing countries. The fact that capitalist competition was largely introduced into the Third World by foreign imperialist powers did not add to the prestige of competition and individualism. Community rather than individual choice is still the watchword in these largely preindustrial societies.

Yet in rejecting the extremes of economic and political individualism of Western democracies, the developing countries have also found the Communist approach to democracy wanting. The Marxist emphasis on class makes little sense in the developing countries for two reasons. First, the main political struggles of developing countries have not been, and are not, class struggles against an internal enemy, but are national struggles against foreign imperialism. An intense national consciousness rather than class consciousness has been, and is, the driving political force in the developing countries. Second, the Marxist emphasis on class makes sense only in societies that have undergone considerable industrialization, and even in pre-1917 Russia there was an important industrial working class in the big cities. In the developing countries, the majority of the people, or at least of the political leaders and intellectuals who speak for them, reject capitalism, but they do not necessarily advocate economic collectivism of the Soviet or Chinese type. The main root of anticapitalism in developing countries is opposition to *imperialist* capitalism, the form of capitalism the developing countries have known in the past. What developing countries are searching for is a communitarian economy in which there is a mixture of private and public ownership, but whose main characteristic is—or is to be—a sense of social responsibility pervading the economic life.

Single-party dominance. Rejecting, in general, both the political free-for-all of competing parties of Western democracies and the rigid political monopoly of Communist party regimes, developing countries have produced the interesting phenomenon of *single-party dominance*. During the struggle for independence, the need for successful action required one broad political mass movement that could unite the politically active elements of the people for the achievement of the supreme goal: national independence. After independence is achieved, there is a new task for which national unity must be mobilized: *modernization*. Like winning the political or military struggle for independence, the struggle for social and economic modernization seems above party, and a single party can well maintain its predominance even where interparty competition is legally and politically feasible.

These political patterns are not rigid, and there are many varieties. In India, democratic government was based on the dominant Congress party in the 1950s and 1960s, but it was replaced by authoritarian rule in 1975. Mexico has followed a different path. The single-party dominance of its government party (Institutional Revolutionary party) has been successfully maintained since the 1930's, although other parties enjoy considerable freedom—particularly between elections. Some developing countries practice competitive party systems, with no single party being dominant (as in Colombia and Venezuela), but such patterns of effective political competition are the exception rather than the rule. The typical government in the developing nations is authoritarian, often headed by military leaders, with no party or with a single, official government party.

2
Conflict Resolution in the Political Process

2

PROCESSES OF CONFLICT RESOLUTION

All political systems are caught in the tension between conflict and consensus. All types of systems, even the most authoritarian, prefer consensus based on shared values and loyalties to compliance based on feared or actual repression, but all, even the most permissive of democratic political orders, must recognize the reality of conflict and abandon any utopian dream of a society of universal agreement. The key issue is: How do different political systems go about securing maximum consensus and preventing or resolving conflicts?

Conflicts arise between individuals or groups over (1) the distribution of scarce goods and values (such as status, power, income, or preferred ecological space) and (2) the means by which mutually incompatible goals are to be reconciled. Consensus involves either agreement over goals, or if agreement is lacking and conflict emerges, agreement over the means by which the conflict should be resolved. The term *consensus* also implies the normative element of common attachment to moral and legal rules and institutions as well as the emotional or psychological element of a sense of identity among members of a group.

The crucial role of leadership

The scope and intensity of conflict and consensus are strongly influenced by those in the group who lead, that is, by those who make the decisions, and who give a sense of direction and orientation to the group. For a long time, students of democracy neglected the problem of leadership in the political process, since the conventional definition of democracy as "government by the people" seemed to focus on the voter rather than on the elected leadership. With the rise of a more realistic and empirical study of politics and government, the crucial role of leaders has gradually been recognized, since the essence of political democracy is now seen to lie in the choosing of political leaders in competitive elections. A renowned student of democracy even argues that the "effectiveness of democracy depends first and foremost on the efficiency and skill of its leadership."[1]

---

[1] Giovanni Sartori, "Democracy," *International Encyclopedia of the Social Sciences,* vol. 4, New York: Macmillan and Free Press, 1968, p. 119.

This "modern" recognition of the importance of leadership in democracy is perhaps no more than a rediscovery of older verities. Thomas Jefferson, the apostle of the ideal of equality among the Founding Fathers, rejected leadership by an "artificial aristocracy" based on wealth and birth, but believed in the indispensable role of a "natural aristocracy" founded on "virtue and talent." Talent—or ability—was not enough for Jefferson. Leaders also had to be persons of "virtue," or character and moral integrity. For Jefferson, that form of government was the best which elected members of the natural aristocracy to public offices, and he was confident that, in a system of popular government, the citizens would be able to separate "the wheat from the chaff." Jefferson foresaw that, on occasion, wealth and birth would blind and corrupt the judgment of the people, "but not in sufficient degree to endanger the society."[2]

The transfer of power. In choosing between competing leadership groups, the voters must have confidence that all will abide by the rules of the democratic game, that the ins will leave peacefully and make room for the outs if the latter win an election. Generally, contestants in democratic elections have been willing to accept the possibility of defeat and to bow out gracefully if defeated. On occasion, fanaticism weakens that ability to play by the rules. One of the main roots of the political pathology of Watergate in 1972 was the determination of some high-level persons in the Nixon camp to prevent a Democratic victory in the presidential election by any means, whether unethical, illegal, or criminal.

If the transfer of power in a democracy is to be peaceful, the choice of alternative leaders and policies must not be tied to issues that large segments of the voting public consider "nonnegotiable." In separating church and state—a radical innovation at the time—the founders wisely sensed that the issue was too divisive and emotional to be subject to political bargaining and manipulation. A century ago, the issue of slavery was too deeply felt by the South to be amenable to solution by the ballot. In the presidential election of 1964, Barry Goldwater made the fatal mistake of proposing, or seeming to propose, radical changes in the social-security system—a nonnegotiable issue for too many voters.

If irreconcilable differences of outlook among competing leadership groups are inimical to the effective functioning of democratic politics, there exists also the opposite danger: The differences between rival leaders may be perceived by the public to be so minimal as to make a choice between the ins and outs seem unimportant, subjecting democracy to the strain of apathy and atrophy. For example, the low turnout in 1968 was attributed by many to the belief that the Nixon-Humphrey race did not offer a genuine choice between alternative leaders and policies.

[2]John Dewey (ed.), *The Living Thoughts of Thomas Jefferson,* London: Cassell, 1946, pp. 62–63.

Majority and minority

Democracy is often described as a combination of majority rule and minority rights. On the surface this formula seems to offer the best of all possible worlds, yet when it is looked at more closely, the concept of democracy as a happy mix of majority rule and minority rights raises many perplexing issues. The majority-rule principle, carried to its logical conclusion, could make life for the minority intolerable or could dispose completely of the minority as a political entity. Conversely, the minority-protection principle, if carried to its conclusion, could make democratic government—or any government—impossible by sabotaging the majority at every conceivable stage.

Fortunately for most working democracies, neither the majority-rule principle nor the minority-protection principle has been carried to its ultimate potential, although the balance between the two principles is always tenuous at best. In every democracy, there are those who claim the majority principle will best advance the welfare of the whole community, or at least of the largest number of its members, and those who claim that society as a whole benefits most from the expansion of individual self-fulfillment and that the cumulative effect of protecting individual prerogatives safeguards the minorities from suppression by the majority, even a democratic majority.

The rationale of the majority principle can hardly be satisfactorily based on arithmetic, for if the majority principle is justified solely on the ground that it expresses more individual wills than the minority, then "more wills" can be easily interpreted as meaning "more force." However, if superior force of the majority is the determining criterion, then the minority would ostensibly have the right to overthrow the majority by force, if it had the capacity to do so. In the last analysis, the majority principle is based on the belief that the citizen's life experience is more important than his knowledge. The average person does not need to be a professional economist to know whether a major tax or welfare policy affects him favorably or unfavorably, nor does he have to be an expert in educational administration to judge whether the school in his district does a good job in teaching his children.

Nondemocrats claim to pursue perfect or absolute justice, but democrats merely claim that the majority principle produces less injustice than rule by the minority. Although majority rule does not promise perfect justice for everybody, it at least ensures that fewer persons will be frustrated than under the rule of a minority. In other words, democrats believe that although justice under majority rule is imperfect, it is still "more just" than it can be under minority rule.

This theoretical rationale of the majority principle will not work if a society is divided politically into a permanent majority and a permanent minority, because minorities are willing to acknowledge the majority principle only under two conditions.

The first condition is that the majority will not take undue advantage of its numerical force and violate the basic rights and deep feelings of the minorities. In situations requiring major policy decisions, the ruling majority does generally seek the views and consensus of the minority before it acts. After World War II, for example, the United States made a historic turnabout in its foreign policy by committing itself to NATO and thus to the military defense of many nations. This policy decision was possible only because the Republican minority, formerly isolationist, decided to support the Democratic majority. And in the 1960s the Democratic majority in Congress could hardly have enacted the civil-rights legislation without the cooperation of the Republicans.

The second condition that is necessary for the acceptance of the majority principle by minorities is that the minority or a coalition of minorities has a reasonable chance of becoming the governing majority. No one is willing to play a game in which he knows in advance he can only lose. When India became independent in 1947, it had to be divided in two because the Muslim minority had little or no confidence that, as a permanent minority, it would get a fair deal from the Hindu majority.

In working democracies, the dilemma of majority versus minority is substantially reduced by the fact that the electorate does not consist of *a* majority opposed by *a* minority. In a multiparty system, this can be easily seen, since the government generally consists of a coalition of several parties, each of which is a minority. But even in a two-party system, such as exists in Britain and the United States, there is no *permanent* political majority, because each of the two parties consists of a coalition of various social, economic, and sectional interests. Under the circumstances, the so-called electoral majority is no more than an aggregate of minorities. Such aggregates never hold together in any permanent fashion. The most successful coalition of various sectional, social, economic, and ethnic minorities resulted in the Democratic dominance from the 1930s to the 1960s, which was interrupted only briefly by the two Eisenhower victories in the 1950s. In 1936 and 1964, the Republican party was declared by some to have virtually no prospect of a comeback as the majority party. Yet the 1968 and 1972 presidential elections not only saw the Republicans winning, but also suggested that the Democratic coalition had begun to dissolve, most conspicuously in the "solid South."

The complexity of majority rule is further increased whenever more than two candidates compete. In about one-third of all presidential elections, the winning candidate polled under 50 percent of the vote, and in several cases the winner polled only slightly over 40 percent. In the six presidential elections from 1948 to 1968, Truman, Kennedy, and Nixon won without receiving 50 percent of the popular vote. In such cases, the weaker plurality principle rather than the majority principle rules, and this lack of majority support is a further deterrent to arrogant conduct and policies on the part of the winning party. Thus while each party in its propaganda tries to convince the voters that it is completely right and the other party completely wrong, the voters have generally been fairly evenly divided between parties and the margins of victory have often been amazingly narrow.

Finally, the growing practice of split-ticket voting has substantially blurred the lines of demarcation between majority and minority. In 1952, 66 percent of the voters voted a straight party ticket in a national election; in 1972, only 42 percent of the voters did so. In the elections of 1974, voters in 11 of the 25 states electing senators and governors chose a U.S. senator of one party and a governor of the other party. Thus there are millions of individuals who, at one and the same time, when voting for one party belong to the majority, and when voting for another party belong to the minority.

The public rhetoric of politicians and much of the literature dealing with the majority-minority relationship centers on the threat of majority tyranny. In Britain and the United States, however, the danger has not been the threat of tyrannical majorities but the impotence of government. In recent years, for example, government in the United States has been unable to cope effectively with the problems of energy and inflation. Governmental impotence has been even more dramatically demonstrated on the issue of illegal aliens in the United States. According to a statement by the Commissioner of the Immigration and Naturalization Service in 1974, about five to seven million illegal aliens were estimated to be in the United States in that year, fed by an annual increase of two to three million in recent years.[3] Although this problem has assumed crisis proportions, the Immigration Service has not had the administrative capacity or manpower to deal with it.

Government and opposition

In every democracy there is a government and an opposition. But these two terms are generally used with special reference to two-party systems, such as Great Britain and the United States, since in multiparty systems both government and opposition are temporary coalitions of several parties, none of which commands a majority in the legislative body. By contrast, in two-party systems, the majority party forms the government and the minority party the opposition.

The relations between government and opposition reflect the complexities of the majority-minority phenomenon in the daily decision-making processes in representative legislative bodies. The government knows it

[3]*U.S. News & World Report,* July 22, 1974, p. 27.

cannot ride roughshod over the opposition, and the opposition knows it cannot indefinitely oppose, block, and sabotage policies solely for the sake of opposition. It is an unwritten law of American politics that the President consults in advance with the leaders of the opposition on important policy proposals, domestic and foreign.

The language of politics reveals an important difference between democratic and undemocratic politics. In a democratic political system, the minority party is called "the opposition" and is conceived as a group of persons loyal to the nation and its system but opposed to specific policies of the government of the day. Britain has gone further than other democracies in recognizing the opposition as an integral part of the system by salarying the leader of the opposition, by officially referring to the party as "Her Majesty's Loyal Opposition," and by regarding it as an equal partner with "Her Majesty's Government."

In undemocratic systems, oppositionists are branded as "enemies of the state" or "enemies of the people." During the Vietnam war, both Presidents Johnson and Nixon charged some critics of their war policies with disloyalty and "aid to the enemy." More seriously still, the Senate hearings on Watergate revealed that the totalitarian concept of "enemy" had burrowed deeply into the highest echelons of President Nixon's staff in the White House. From 1971 on, lists of administration "enemies" were periodically compiled by White House staff members. On August 16, 1971, John W. Dean, counsel to President Nixon, wrote a confidential memorandum to H. R. Haldeman, White House Chief of Staff, and John Ehrlichman, the President's chief assistant for domestic affairs. The memorandum was entitled "Dealing with Our Political Enemies," and the opening paragraph reads as follows:

> *This memorandum addresses the matter of how we can maximize the fact of our incumbency in dealing with persons known to be active in their opposition to our Administration. Stated a bit more bluntly—how can we use the available federal machinery to screw our political enemies.*[4]

GOVERNMENT BY DISCUSSION AND CONSENT

Free flow of information and communication

The democratic process in which majorities make up the government and minorities form the opposition requires free speech, free discussion, and a free flow of communication. Freedom of speech in the political process

[4]*Presidential Campaign Activities* of 1972. Hearings Before the Select Committee on Presidential Campaign Activities of the U.S. Senate: Watergate and Related Activities, Book 4, Washington, D.C.: U.S. Government Printing Office, 1973, p. 1689.

sometimes leads to results that many find disturbing, and at times even intolerable. Although freedom of expression stimulates some great masterpieces, it also gives rise to mediocre, and even spurious, criticisms, calumnies, falsehoods, and insults. Not everybody is willing to be subjected to such criticisms, and for this reason many persons are reluctant to engage actively in politics. However, as President Truman was fond of saying, "If you can't stand the heat, get out of the kitchen."

The free flow of communication requires that politicians be willing to hear opinions expressed by the different segments of the public. Even so, some opinions never reach the politicians, usually because they are not expressed in any organized manner. Thus the opinions of the 25 million United States poor are hardly ever listened to because they are not presented in a collective, coherent fashion. The poor—subsistence farmers, migratory workers, unskilled service workers, the aged—do not form a cohesive group with authoritative spokesmen. As Michael Harrington has put it:

> *The poor are politically invisible. It is one of the cruelest ironies of social life in advanced countries that the dispossessed at the bottom of society are unable to speak for themselves. The people of the other America do not, by far and large, belong to unions, to fraternal organizations, or to political parties. They are without lobbies of their own; they put forward no legislative program. As a group, they are atomized. They have no face; they have no voice.*"[5]

The Freedom of Information Act. The free flow of communication requires not only the freedom to express information or opinion but also the freedom to have access to information. The Freedom of Information Act of 1966 spells out the duty of executive officials to disclose information, but translating this principle into practice has not been easy, especially since the tendency of bureaucrats under any political system is "When in doubt, don't give it out." Because the act did not live up to expectations, and partly as a result of the post-Watergate atmosphere, Congress amended the Freedom of Information Act in 1974, limiting bureaucratic delay in giving out information and also strengthening the role of the courts in the designation of information as classified (such as in cases of national security or diplomacy, or of confidential economic or financial data).

The Pentagon Papers. The tendency of the executive to suppress embarrassing information and the right of the public to have access to it came to a dramatic clash in one of the great test cases in American political history

---

[5]Michael Harrington, *The Other America: Poverty in the United States,* Baltimore: Penguin, 1963, p. 14.

""Well, we certainly botched this job. What'll we stamp it—'Secret' or 'Top Secret'?"
From *Herblock's Special for Today,* New York, Simon & Schuster, 1958.

in 1971. In that year, the *New York Times* and several other newspapers came into possession of a secret Department of Defense study of American policy in Vietnam in the period 1945–1967. When the newspapers began to publish excerpts from the collection of 7,000 pages of narrative and documents, the government sought to stop publication of these classified materials on the grounds that their release would jeopardize national security. The Supreme Court upheld the right of the newspapers to publish the excerpts from the Pentagon Papers. Justice Black most poignantly expressed the relation of the government and the press in the light of both democratic principles and the First Amendment as follows: "The Government's power to censor the press was abolished so that the press would remain forever free to censure the Government" (*New York Times Company* v. *United States* [1971]).

In the United States, the attempt of the government to prevent the publication of "classified" documents produced a public reaction of surprise, shock, and indignation. But in other democratic nations, such as Britain and France, it seemed even more astounding that such secret government documents as the Pentagon Papers could be published at all. In Britain, for example, the Official Secrets Act makes it a crime to publish anything from official documents of any government department, unless the release of such material has been authorized. A former British attorney general was quoted as saying that a British paper could violate the law if it reported "the number of cups of tea consumed per week in a Government department."[6] In the case of unauthorized publication of sensitive materials, British law is even more drastic and severe; there was "no doubt" among British newspaper editors that "they would have been promptly jailed if they had published anything resembling the Pentagon papers."[7]

Frustration and aggression

Social psychologists have long held that aggression is closely linked to frustration. From earliest infancy, the human being learns to accept some frustration as the indispensable condition of living with others in the family, group, or society. Such minor frustration usually does not lead to aggressive behavior. Major frustration, however, such as the despair that occurs when an individual's or group's life goals are interfered with, does often lead to major aggression.

Aggression is most clearly manifested in physical violence. It may take other forms, however; an outburst of anger, malicious rumors, hostile sarcasm, or facial expression may also reflect aggressive attitudes. Even pacifists, who intellectually condemn all forms of war and aggression, may be so militant in their behavior as to betray deep-seated aggressive tendencies. When the person or group inflicting deprivation is too powerful or is not readily available for retaliation, aggression resulting from this frustration may be "displaced" from the original source to substitute targets or even to oneself. Unpopular minorities often serve as "scapegoats," that is, as safe targets for accumulated hostility resulting from acts or conditions unrelated to the minorities. The person suffering frustration may also direct the ensuing hostility against himself in a physical manner, as in suicide, or he may develop hatred against himself or the group he belongs to. Self-hatred as a form of displaced aggression may be seen among some members of religious or racial minorities that are subject to unjust discrimination, and it may also be observed among members of the majority who are at the bottom of society. Thus self-hatred helps to perpetuate the unequal relations between those who inflict deprivations and those who experience them.

The democratic society seeks, not always successfully, to lessen frustration by attacking its causes and by providing socially useful outlets for aggressive and competitive impulses. The American philosopher William James brilliantly expressed this problem by stating that, if civilization is to survive, we must discover the "moral equivalent of war." He wisely real-

[6]*New York Times,* September 30, 1972
[7]*New York Times,* December 26, 1972, in a report from its correspondent in London.

ized that man's aggressive impulses cannot be abolished; rather, useful outlets are needed for them, such as fighting disease, want, and hunger, or trying to solve the riddles of nature.

Freedom of expression as a safety valve

The most important safety valve for aggressive impulses is free speech and criticism. Freedom of expression fulfills a person's intellectual need to make his opinion known to his fellows, to have his mind appreciated by others, and to count as a thinker. But a person also has an emotional need to get off his chest the feelings that lie behind his ideas. This emotional need is satisfied when he is allowed to express his ideas—even if nothing much happens as a result.

As long as communication between people flows freely, conciliation is always possible. When people are unable to talk to each other because of political sanctions or because there is too much hate between them, then human relations face disaster. This is as true in a personal relationship such as marriage as in a collective process such as politics.

In democratic government, politicians frequently "knock off" their opponents in fiery speeches, but these acts of verbal violence are socially more acceptable than silencing an opponent with a bullet or a prison term. Freedom of expression in democratic societies does not abolish hostility and resentment; it allows them to be expressed in tolerable doses, thus contributing to the mental hygiene of the individual and to the social peace of the whole community.

Loss of the ability to communicate can have profoundly disturbing effects on both individual and society. Although we do not know yet exactly how or why they work, all the different methods of psychiatric therapy have one trait in common: They encourage the patient to talk, and by discussing his troubles the patient is to some degree relieved of them. A whole society that has lost the ability to communicate cannot go to a psychiatrist for help, so social mechanisms must be set up to provide the society with new channels of communication.

Taboo issues. Maximum communication in a free society implies that there be no taboo issues, no set of final truths that must not be questioned. The primary taboo issue in Communist states is Marxism-Leninism, a set of final social, economic, and political truths that must be accepted—or else. In addition, other subjects may be tabooed by the top party leaders. For example, a Soviet citizen who publicly criticizes the military occupation of Czechoslovakia may find himself in jail for having slandered the Soviet Union and its government.

If democracy is true to its principles, it recognizes no taboo issues, not even the validity of democracy itself. In practice, democracies at times

Through History With J. Wesley Smith
"It's called dialog, and it's much more flexible than monolog. The way it works out is—you ask me a come-on question, and I give you a smart answer."
Saturday Review, August 10, 1974, p. 22.

violate their own principles and restrict—in fact, if not in law—the discussion and challenge of those political, economic, or moral principles that are accepted by most members of the community as so true as to be "beyond discussion."

Since the mid-1960s, the United States has gone through a period of unparalleled freedom of expression on all subjects, political and nonpolitical, ranging from pornography in papers, books, movies, and theaters to the most inflammatory revolutionary rhetoric, including the incitement to the murder of public officials. Far from ignoring and suppressing the lifestyle and revolutionary politics of the leaders of the counterculture, the media, especially television, turned them into celebrities. Whether the counterculture and revolutionary politics have been effective in changing the mores and priorities of Americans is a matter of controversy. That they have provided some with handsome monetary benefits is a matter of record.

Functional limits of free speech as a safety valve

The function of free speech and criticism as a safety valve should be kept in proper perspective. The functional utility of freely expressing conflict depends on whether such expression is merely a safety valve, providing release from psychological tension, or whether it leads to a modification of the social relations that have resulted in conflict. Even totalitarian systems allow the expression of mild antiregime hostility on the stage or in cartoons and jokes, because they know that this type of criticism serves to release tension and anxiety without necessitating any remedial action on the part of the government. Long ago the autocratic Roman emperors understood that giving the people outlets for tension, *panem et circenses* (bread and circuses), could divert them from the more serious business of political interference.

Modern democratic political systems can tolerate large amounts of dissent and criticism in particular areas of social conflict, yet may fail to remedy the causes of this conflict. What is true of the democratic political process as a whole—that its practitioners cherish it primarily for its nonpolitical effects—is also true of free communication. If it degenerates in specific policy areas into a mere ceremonial testifying to the existence of democratic procedures, if it results in no remedial action, then the value of *all* free communication is proportionately undermined. Once a significantly large group of people loses faith in the function of political dialogue to resolve social conflicts, once the suspicion grows that the safety valve of free criticism is only a device for maintaining the status quo, direct action and violence not infrequently replace the more rational processes of the dialogue.

Common agreement on fundamentals. Disagreement is the lifeblood of the democratic society, but disagreement is negative and sterile unless the society first agrees to commit itself to the *right* to disagree. The only indispensable agreement to the functioning of political democracy is the agreement of the citizenry to remain faithful to the democratic process, and this means agreeing to adhere to *nonviolent procedures of resolving social and political conflicts.*

Every government, whether democratic or not, has a monopoly on the use of force and physical compulsion. In denying individuals and groups the right to use physical force against either public officials or other citizens, the democratic political system acts like any political system that seeks to survive by preventing anarchy. However, where the political system acts as a democratic system is in tolerating substitutes for force—free speech, protest meetings, demonstrations, strikes—in the process of resolving social conflicts. It does not tolerate the use of Molotov cocktails, arson, firebombs, or physical violence against those who disagree with dissenting demonstrators or strikers. Thus abstention from violence in the political process is the only commitment that must be commonly accepted and practiced in a political democracy.

The great paradox of democratic political systems is that they make violence less necessary, but also more appealing. The antiauthoritarian bias in a political democracy undermines the respect for authority, including the authority of democratic government itself; yet the penalty for violence in the democratic system is generally much milder than in authoritarian or totalitarian systems. Thus the tolerant atmosphere of a democratic political system, which greatly stimulates all kinds of peaceful expressions of dissent and protest, simultaneously encourages civil disobedience and confrontation politics.

Although there is no written constitution in Britain, there are few, if any, other nations in which dissenters and nonconformists are so fully protected by law and public opinion. At the same time, Britain strictly controls private ownership of guns, forbids political uniforms and paramilitary political organizations, and severely and swiftly punishes political violence or the threat of violence. What is true of Britain is also true of other democratic nations (Switzerland, the Scandinavian countries, Australia) that tolerate high levels of peacefully expressed dissent and nonconformity but react vigorously to violence or the threat of violence.

The great political problem of modern France is not so much its multiparty system as the lack of agreement on the kind of government that is to prevail. Some French parties (such as the Communists and extreme rightists) want dictatorship; others want parliamentary supremacy over a weak executive; and the Gaullists believe in strong presidential leadership over an impotent legislature. Events will show whether Gaullism without De Gaulle can effectively continue in France.

AMERICAN DEMOCRACY UNDER PRESSURE

The new era of political frustration

Since the mid-1960s the American political process has shown persistent symptoms of crisis and malfunctioning. There have been riots and civil disorders in big cities, violent confrontations between revolutionary groups and the police, and thousands of bombings of government buildings, banks, and corporate offices. Beneath these symptoms of turbulence and violence, the traditional American optimism has been substantially undermined by feelings of pessimism, doubt, unease, and frustration. Such erosion of confidence was greatly intensified by the Watergate scandal. In a survey conducted by the University of Michigan's Institute for Social Research late in 1973, 66 percent of the interviewees said that they could trust the government only "some of the time," and 53 percent of the interviewees believed that "quite a few" of the people running the government are crooked.[8] These percentages were higher than any figures in similar surveys conducted since the early 1960s by the University of Michigan pollsters.

The feelings of unease and frustration among the middle classes, particularly the white-collar and new professional middle classes in the suburbs, do not derive from specific causes, such as poverty or racial dis-

[8] *Los Angeles Times*, January 13, 1974.

crimination, since the suburban middle classes are typically white and relatively well-off. Their "rebellion without cause" stems from a generalized and diffused feeling of powerlessness, of an inability to control one's own personal life and environment. Unsafe streets, polluted air, polluted water, traffic snarls, and urban decay are just a few of the symptoms of environmental deterioration of which even the affluent middle classes are painfully aware. The Vietnam war and racial conflict at home intensified attitudes of pessimism, alienation, and anger, but they did not create them, since other advanced Western societies have shown similar symptoms. Even rigidly controlled states, Communist and non-Communist, have not escaped the spread of disillusionment with the existing establishments.

Rising expectations of government

Part of this new atmosphere of doubt and unease is due to the people's rising expectations of government. The demands made on government in eighteenth-century America were comparatively simple: Government was expected to provide for public order; supply highways and a postal system for commerce and communication; and protect the individual against the arbitrary actions of the government itself. In the nineteenth century and the first half of the twentieth century, particularly after the rise and dominance of the industrial economy, government could still do what was expected of it: It could curb economic monopolies; regulate public carriers, radio and television, and labor-management relations; fix minimum wages; and provide old-age pensions. In all these cases, government was expected to deal with specific situations that could be resolved by more public expenditures, an enlarged public administration, or both. Today government is increasinly expected to deal with, and solve, the broadest range of conceivable problems: It must rebuild cities; provide clean air and water; keep a full-employment economy humming without inflation or deflation; supply guaranteed annual incomes; eliminate racial tension; and ensure a general quality of life that is economically efficient, socially just, and esthetically pleasing.

The phenomenon of rising expectations of government is built into the American political system, as it is into every democracy. As Tocqueville noted over a century ago in *Democracy in America*, Americans do not believe in intervention by government as a general principle,

> but, by an exception to that rule, each of them craves for its assistance in the particular concern on which he is engaged, and seeks to draw upon the influence of the government for his own benefit, though he would restrict it on all other occasions.[9]

---

[9] Alexis de Tocqueville, *Democracy in America*, vol. 2, New York: Knopf, 1945, p. 294.

Rising expectations of government result also from the dynamics of the democratic process. People gradually learn that their votes and other pressures that they apply to decision-makers are the most potent weapons they have in asserting their claims, and the appetite grows with eating, as the French proverb has it. Making demands on government is a never ending process, and each satisfaction before long produces more demands. Politicians often try to anticipate popular demands by making a political issue of them. They may sincerely believe in the justness and fairness of these expanding demands, and they rarely feel guilty about having made political capital out of them.

Governments have not always increased their capacity to meet demands at the same rate that demands on governments have increased. As demands become more complex, the job of satisfying them by governmental action becomes proportionately more difficult. Since the 1930s, for example, the federal government and local governments have run joint slum-clearance programs. At first this seemed to be a comparatively simple operation, consisting essentially of tearing down old, deteriorated dwellings and replacing them with better housing accommodations. But this simple approach quickly proved unsatisfactory. Because a community is more than a collection of individual dwellings, the people in slum-clearance projects increasingly expect the government to provide them with the physical facilities that go with a real community: hospitals, educational complexes, recreation centers, parks, and sources of employment.

Even if government had the know-how and means to provide the physical ingredients of a total community, what about the human variable involved? How does the government ensure the right racial and soioeconomic balance? And what *is* the right balance? Finally, can government provide a "sense of neighborhood," the most important ingredient that goes into the making of a community?

A sense of neighborhood or community in an urban environment may, but need not, mean a sense of belonging to and identifying with a particuar group. It also implies a concern for proper and considerate behavior on the part of the residents of the community in the places in which they live, shop, and walk. In a survey of Boston, James Q. Wilson, a leading American urbanist, found that the interviewees (both white and black) regarded as the single most important issue facing the city not housing, pollution, transportation, or employment, but the quality of life in the city.[10] The police can arrest a person who commits a crime, but they cannot deal with complaints

---

[10]James Q. Wilson, "The Urban Unease: Community vs. City," *The Public Interest*, no. 12 (Summer, 1968), pp. 34–35. Surveys in Harlem, the black section of New York City, in 1974 largely confirm the earlier Boston study. The interviewees, mostly black, considered the following problems, in this order, as the most serious ones: crime in the streets, drug addiction, burglarizing of apartments, youth unemployment, dirty streets and pollution, and poor housing conditions (*New York Times*, November 21, 1974).

that a neighbor's lawn is a jungle of weeds, that his children are wild and undisciplined, or that gangs of teenagers make a sport of taunting passersby. Yet today the American people increasingly expect their government to deal with those matters that contribute to the quality of life in general.

The impact of the postindustrial society on political democracy

Political democracy is now facing the impact of technology on the postindustrial society. In an industrial society, the manufacturing of goods is the central economic activity. But in a postindustrial society, of which the United States is the most prominent example, more people are producing services than are producing goods. In the mid-1970s, some 62 percent of the civilian labor force in the United States was employed in the service sector —49 percent as white-collar workers (professionals, technicians, managers, officials, office personnel, salespeople) and 13 percent as service workers (repairmen, waiters, domestics). In 1950, blue-collar workers still outnumbered white-collar workers, but currently the latter outnumber the former by four to three.

The fastest growing group among the white-collar workers is that of professionals and technicians, constituting in 1950 only about 20 percent of white-collar workers, but rising to 30 percent by the mid-1970s. The growing role of professionals and technicians points to the increasing importance of knowledge and research in the postindustrial society. The expanding role of professionals permeates all spheres of social organization, including government. Don K. Price, a leading American student of the relations between science and government, holds that the development of public policy and administrative methods owes less "in the long run to the processes of conflict among political parties and social or economic pressure groups than to the more objective processes of research and discussion among professional groups."[11]

The increasing importance of persons of knowledge and research will not necessarily give them the power to make formal decisions of a political character, but it will greatly enhance their role in the decision-making process, since their advice has strong persuasive force. In the political process, the growing importance of the professional expert may still further strengthen presidential power, for the President is the final destination of all information and intelligence that impinges on major policy issues.

The advanced technology of the postindustrial society is not only producing more rapid social and technological changes and innovations, but producing them at a faster rate. Will the pressures of the new technological skills put a growing strain on democratic institutions and procedures?

---

[11]Don K. Price, *Government and Science: Their Dynamic Relation in American Democracy*, New York: Oxford University Press Galaxy Books, 1962, p. v.

Before long, computerized retrieval of information may revolutionize, and partly replace, the traditional methods of libraries and book publishers and make possible a federal retrieval center that will provide the government with a complete dossier on every citizen in the United States. Such a national data center might be the realization of a dream for a national chief of police, but it could also be a nightmare for the citizen who values his privacy.

The dossier society. The danger of the United States becoming a "dossier society" was brought to the attention of the public by the Senate Subcommittee on Constitutional Rights. Probing into alleged abuses of government snooping and surveillance, the subcommittee found that a vast mass of computerized data has been made available to the federal government, without safeguarding affected individuals from having false or adverse information entered against their names. The Federal Bureau of Investigation has fingerprints of 86 million persons, only 19 million of whom have been arrested on criminal charges. The Internal Revenue Service has information, to which some federal and state officials have access, on 75 million taxpayers. The Department of Defense retains data on 15 million persons, military and civilian, who have been subjected over the years to security, loyalty, criminal, and related types of investigation. The total number of items in federal data banks amounted to 1.25 billion in 1974, according to the Senate Subcommittee on Constitutional Rights. In addition to federal data banks, there are also data banks maintained by state and local governments as well as by private commercial enterprises. After Watergate, Congress enacted legislation in 1974 aimed at regulation of federal data banks and increased protection of individuals.

Violence

Until the 1960s, American history and politics were viewed by scholars largely from the perspective of consensus, the basic assumption being that American political behavior was comparatively free from ideological dogma, and that the issues that occasionally divided the nation had always been, and would continue to be, resolved peacefully. Analyses of American politics since the 1960's, however, have found the consensus perspective to be too narrow, and have given greater recognition to the role of conflict and violence.

Neither the consensus nor the conflict approach is without flaw. The consensus approach tended to minimize the numerous conflicts and violent clashes that periodically racked the nation, but the conflict perspective fails to explain how the basic institutions of our political system have continued to exist, and how the nation itself managed to survive a bloody civil war.

If, in recent years, there has been a tendency to emphasize the role of conflict and violence in the American political process, this may be due to the fact that political scientists and historians have been made so keenly aware of that violence by recent political assassinations, urban riots, and campus disturbances.

The assassinations of President John F. Kennedy in 1963, of Dr. Martin Luther King, Jr., and Senator Robert F. Kennedy in 1968, and the assassination attempt on Governor George Wallace in 1972 convinced Americans that violence was a persistent phenomenon of American public life. The role of political violence in the United States has no counterpart in other major democratic nations. Between 1865 and 1963, four presidents (Lincoln, Garfield, McKinley, and Kennedy) were assassinated, and attempts were made to kill four others. The chief executives of most European democracies and of Canada travel throughout their countries with little protection, but the U.S. President is always heavily guarded when appearing in public, and public appearances are being increasingly replaced by the safer atmosphere of the television studio.

In 1969 the National Commission on the Causes and Prevention of Violence issued a report comparing civil strife in 114 nations and colonies from mid-1963 to mid-1968. The report found that the United States ranked first among 18 Western democracies and 24th among the 114 nations and colonies of the world in magnitude of civil strife. Eleven out of every 1,000 Americans participated in civil strife, as compared with a participation ratio of 7 out of 1,000 in the other 17 democracies.

Violence in the 1960s. Those who argue that the upsurge of violence in the 1960s was due to America's racial conflicts and her involvement in Vietnam forget that violence also exploded in other democracies in the late 1960s—notably in Italy and Japan—which were not involved in wars and had no racial conflicts. The American experience of the frontier is often cited as a major source of the infatuation of Americans with violence, but Australia, Canada, and Brazil had a frontier experience too, and there is no persistent addiction to violence in those countries. Nor can the large-scale violence in recent years be interpreted mainly as a protest of alienated and frustrated persons against the bureaucratization of public and economic institutions, since bureaucratization does not seem to produce the same violent reactions in other highly industrialized nations, such as West Germany, Great Britain, and Sweden. Finally, the sociological interpretation of crime as an effect of poverty has been substantially controverted by experience: The more affluent a society is, the higher the rate of crime. This does not suggest that affluence produces more violence, but it does undermine the cause-effect explanation of poverty and criminal violence.

The revolutionary experience. The American historical experience has much in common with that of other Western societies, but there are some factors that are specifically American and that may supply a clue to the violent strain in American society. The United States as a political community owes its very existence to the acts of rebellion and violence that culminated in the American Revolution. Other Western nations have had their revolutions, too: the English in the 1640s and the French in 1789. But the revolutionary experience of these nations was only one stage in their development, whereas in the United States the existence of the nation derived directly from the act of revolution. Politically, this has made it difficult in the United States to develop the "sense of state" that in other democracies survives from their prerevolutionary periods. Antiauthoritarian as French republicanism and British democracy may be in ideological outlook, both political systems still benefit from the respect for political authority that is older, and deeper, than their revolutionary experiences.

Racial Violence. The revolutionary act of violence from which the United States emerged as a political entity was followed, during the settling of the vast continent, by two other major types of violence that are deeply embedded in the American experience and consciousness: the killing of Indians and the use of slaves transported from Africa. In the years 1882–1938, 4,687 lynchings occurred, involving 3,398 blacks and 1,289 whites. Many additional lynchings were attempted but were frustrated by the interference of police officers.[12] Race riots also produced a heavy casualty list. In 1917 in East St. Louis, 47 were killed; in 1919 in Chicago, 36; and in 1943 in Detroit, 29. These riots—and many others—were true interracial conflicts, whites pitted against blacks. In the urban riots of 1964–1968, which were largely confined to the black ghettos, 191 persons were killed, most of whom were black.

Labor-management violence. Throughout the period of urban growth and industrialization in the United States, violence in labor-management disputes was greater than in any other country undergoing a similar experience under representative government. For a long time, labor had to contend with the pro-management attitudes and policies of legislative, executive, and judicial bodies as well as various forms of intimidation and physical terror employed by management itself. Large corporations employed their own spies and strikebreakers or those supplied by "detective agencies," and some large corporations also maintained huge arsenals of assorted weapons and called upon the National Guard and the police whenever necessary. In the railroad strikes of 1877, some 150 persons were killed; 30 were killed in the Pullman strike of 1894, after federal troops were brought into the conflict. In the Rocky Mountain mining strikes around the

---

[12]V. O. Key, Jr., *Politics, Parties, and Pressure Groups*, 2nd ed., New York: Crowell, 1948, p. 635.

turn of the century, 198 persons were killed. Bloody conflict continued well into the twentieth century, with the last major outbreak of violence occurring in 1937 in Chicago and claiming the lives of 10. Since then, violence in labor disputes has dramatically declined, largely perhaps because public policy and administrative regulation (the National Labor Relations Act of 1935 and the National Labor Relations Board) have provided workable channels for the resolution of labor conflicts.

Crime and the social order. Most people regard "ordinary crime" as being free from political connotations. This may be true from the perspective of the individual lawbreaker or law-enforcement officer, but in a larger perspective the amount of crime in a nation is one indicator of the fragility of the social order that the political system is designed to protect. During 1960–1970, violent crime (murder, robbery, aggravated assault, forcible rape) rose by 156 percent. Murder increased by 76 percent, robbery by 224 percent, aggravated assault by 117 percent, and forcible rape by 121 percent. During the same period, the population of the United States increased by only 13 percent, indicating that the rate of increase for violent crime was 12 times greater than the growth rate for the population. Crimes against property (burglary, larceny, auto theft) increased by 180 percent during 1960–1970, or by an even faster rate than violent crimes. The combined total of violent and property crimes rose from slightly over 2 million in 1960 to almost 5.6 million in 1970, an increase of 176 percent. (See Figure 2–1.)

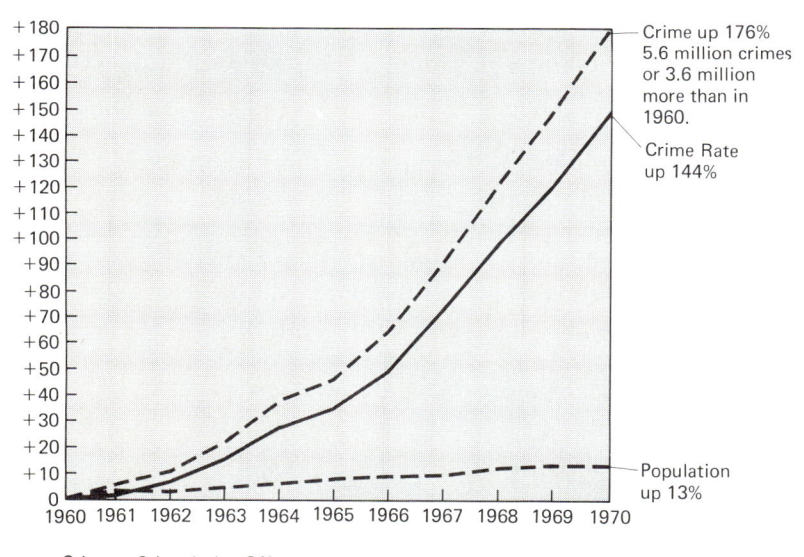

Crime = Crime Index Offenses
Crime Rate = Number of Offenses per 100,000 Population

Figure 2–1 *National crime increase. Percent change in 1970 over 1960*
SOURCE: *U. S. Department of Justice.*

"Don't consider this a stickup. Consider it a manifestation of the socio-economic malaise which has gripped our modern urban environment."
Saturday Review, May 4, 1974, p. 5.

The high and growing rate of crime in recent years points to serious symptoms of social disorganization, deeply reflected also in Congress. Despite the public outcry for stricter gun-control laws after the assassinations of Martin Luther King, Jr., and Robert F. Kennedy in 1968 (over 70 percent of those queried in a Harris poll favored strict antigun laws), Congress, largely influenced by the powerful National Rifle Association lobby, passed only a weak and ineffective law. States with strong gun laws show lower rates of crimes of violence than weak gun-law states, and foreign countries with strong gun-control laws show a much lower rate of crimes of violence than does the United States. Murder by firearms is, in proportion to population, about 40 times higher in the United States than in England, and over 100 times higher than in Japan. Among developed countries, there is no nation whose murder rate comes even close to that of the United States.

Political crime. The problem of lawlessness and violence in the United States is complicated by two factors. First, in recent years there has emerged a growing advocacy of violence for political ends. This new ideology, a mixture of revolutionary, terroristic, and anarchist elements, is more than innocuous rhetoric, as is evidenced by the many thousands of bombings in recent years as well as by the rapidly rising numbers of killings of police officers. In 1963, 55 state, county, and local law-enforcement officers were killed; in 1973 the number was 127—of which number almost half were slain in ambush situations.

Governmental lawlessness. Second, the rule of law is gravely endangered whenever the government itself—sworn to uphold the law—commits illegal or criminal acts. Shortly after the first portions of the Pentagon Papers appeared in the *New York Times* on June 13, 1971, a special investigative unit (called the "Plumbers," because they were supposed to stop "leaks") was set up in the White House. The most notorious of the activities of the Plumbers was the covert break-in, on September 3, 1971, of the office of Dr. Lewis Fielding, the psychiatrist of Daniel Ellsberg, who had been identified as the source of the disclosure of the secret Pentagon materials. When testifying before the Senate Watergate Committee in 1973, John Ehrlichman, who was deeply involved in the organization of the Plumbers and the burglary of Dr. Fielding's office, stated that neither he nor President Nixon had authorized the burglary, but even if they had, such an action was "well within both the constitutional duty and obligation of the President." Senator Herman Talmadge of Georgia, a member of the Senate Watergate Committee, reminded Ehrlichman of the ancient rule in Anglo-Saxon law that "no matter how humble a man's cottage is, even the King of England cannot enter without his consent." Whereupon Ehrlichman retorted: "I am afraid that has been considerably eroded over the years." Finally, the following exchange between Senator Talmadge and John Ehrlichman took place:

Senator Talmadge: *Now, if the President could authorize a covert break-in, and you do not know exactly [by] what that power would be limited, you do not think it could include murder or other crimes beyond covert break-ins, do you?*
Mr. Ehrlichman: *I do not know where the line is, Senator.*[13]

---

[13]*Presidential Campaign Activities of 1972. Hearings Before the Select Committee on Presidential Campaign Activities of the U.S. Senate: Watergate and Related Activities,* Book 6, Washington, D..C.: U.S. Government Printing Office, 1973, pp. 2600–2601.

3
Constitutional Government

3

Government is power. Constitutional government is power limited by law. It stands in contrast to government by fiat, government with unlimited power, government at the whim of power holders, government with rules subject to change without notice, government that does not recognize or assure any substantial body of liberties or rights for its citizens.

A constitution, it follows, is the general system of limitations—laws, customs, institutional patterns, rules—pertaining to the government of a country. It grants powers but also specifies how they are to be used. A constitution is both the instrument for achieving limited government and the product of a regime that recognizes that it is limited by law.

The distinction between a constitution and a government is fundamental. If the distinction is not observed, there is in fact no constitution, because the will of the government is unrestrained. A constitution is antecedent to a government, either in bringing the government into being or in the sense that it is superior to the government in character and authority. Since a constitution imposes limits on a government, any exercise of authority by government beyond these limits is *unconstitutional*.

The individual citizen in a constitutional system has rights that the government is obligated to observe, and the constitution provides methods for asserting and enforcing these rights. But citizens are also restrained by the constitution. The rule of law applies to both governors and governed. Individuals in a constitutional system are bound *by* the constitution, which they can change only by procedures specified *in* the constitution. Some Americans may wish the income-tax amendment were not in the Constitution, but it is there, and they are obliged to pay income taxes. There are always many Americans who oppose the incumbent President, but they are forced to recognize his authority until his constitutional term expires or until he is removed by the constitutional process of impeachment or by resignation.

One of the great merits of constitutional government is that it provides for the most dangerous incident in the life of a governmental system: the transfer of power from one individual or group to another. It foresees the inevitability that power holders will die or lose their bases of power, and so it arranges a peaceful and orderly system of succession to avoid murders, intrigues, or *coups d'état*.

Constitutional government is not necessarily republican or democratic government. There can be constitutional monarchies or constitutional aristocracies. But in the twentieth century, constitutionalism is inseparable from democracy and both systems reinforce each other. Under a constitutional system, individuals have freedom to read and to talk, to form groups, to become informed about public affairs. They will not for long accept restraints on their right to vote or limits on their areas of public concern, as is evident in the history of the American constitutional system. Payment of property taxes as a prerequisite for voting has long been abolished, and suffrage, originally limited to males, was extended to women in 1920. The President, originally named by a process of indirect election, soon came to be chosen by procedures that in effect amounted to popular vote, and the United States Senate, originally elected by the state legislatures, is now elected by the people of the states. The poll tax as a prerequisite for voting in federal elections was abolished by the Twenty-Fourth Amendment and declared unconstitutional for state elections by the Supreme Court in *Harper v. Virginia State Board of Elections* (1966). And in 1971, the Twenty-Sixth Amendment granted 18-year-olds the right to vote in all elections, federal, state, and local.

THREE CONSTITUTIONS COMPARED

The heart of a constitutional system is typically a written document drafted by a constitutional convention or assembly and made effective by legislative ratification or popular referendum. Constitutional provisions have a status superior to that of ordinary legislation, and the constitution can be revised or amended only by a difficult procedure. However, England, which has one of the most successful constitutional systems in history, does not follow this pattern and is the principal example of a nation with an "unwritten" constitution.

The English constitution

The English constitution is a combination of statutes and judicial decisions, plus unwritten customs and conventions. The English have never attempted to list and define their principles of government in a single written document. There is an English constitution, but one cannot go into a library and ask for a copy of it. England's constitutional convention has been a thousand years of history. Whenever Parliament enacts an important statute granting authority, establishing an institution, or limiting the powers of an office, it is creating part of the constitution. The Magna Carta (1215), the Petition of Right (1628), and the Bill of Rights (1689) are constitutional landmarks in bringing the power of the Crown under parliamentary control. The Act of Settlement (1701) regulated succession to the throne and established the irremovability of judges. The Parliament Acts of 1911 and 1949 reduced the power of the House of Lords and limited the duration of Parliaments to five years. The Representation of the People Act (1949) was the latest in a series of statutes dealing with voting and elections.

The decisions of the superior courts have supplied another important section of the English constitution. Principles of the common law, deduced from the decisions in countless individual cases, control many relations between the ndividual and the state. However, when Parliament speaks on a subject, it supersedes any conflicting judicial rules.

Custom and convention have great weight in supplying principles for the English constitution. Custom controls much of the procedure in Parliament, such as the status of the impartial Speaker of the House of Commons, questions by members to ministers, the protection of the rights of the legislative minority, and the allocation of time for parliamentary business. Conventions establish many of the basic operating conditions of the parliamentary system—for example, that a government outvoted in the House of Commons may dissolve the House and appeal to the electorate; that if the electorate returns a majority against the government, it must resign; that the Prime Minister, on his resignation, advises the Crown as to who should be his successor; that the Cabinet is collectively responsible for general policy; and that there must be at least one session of Parliament each year.

The case for an unwritten constitution

Why have the English never gathered these scattered statutes, judicial principles, customs, and conventions into a single constitutional document? The answer is that they have never found it imperative or even desirable to do so. Unlike the United States, England never had to overthrow a foreign ruler and establish a new system of self-government. For the past three hundred years, they have had a Parliament with both the power and the ability to meet the nation's crises with appropriate legislation.

Instead of one concise written constitutional document, the English now have hundreds of statutes and declarations in Parliament of basic constitutional character, and thousands of decisions in cases before the courts that have bearing on fundamental liberties and powers. These are all written. Even the various usages and conventions are recorded in documents of the Cabinet and the Crown or in constitutional treatises. Thus, in a sense, it is not really true to say that the English constitution is unwritten; it is just, as Giovanni Sartori has said, that it is "written differently."

The English would not want to try to condense all these constitutional principles into a single document. Writing a constitution is not easy, as the founders of the American Constitution discovered in Philadelphia. It is much more feasible to approach one constitutional issue at a time, rather than to expose to controversy the entire governmental framework. Moreover, as soon as a constitution is written, it must be adapted to new and changing conditions. So written constitutions must provide for the possibility of amendment. But amendment is typically more complicated than the enactment of ordinary legislation, and desirable amendments are often delayed or defeated by these complications. The English can respond to any need for constitutional change by ordinary legislative procedures.

Protection under an unwritten constitution

How much protection is there in a constitution that is subject to change by any parliamentary majority? Most Americans would feel uneasy if the only limits on Congress were its own good sense. Englishmen, however, appear to have greater trust in government than Americans do. The United States was born in rebellion against an unpopular government, and although that was long ago, an element of suspicion of *all government* has always been part of the American outlook. In this respect, American political feeling resembles more that of the French than of the British.

The aristocratic origins of English government are perhaps another factor in the success of the unwritten constitution. Among gentlemen, written pledges are unnecessary and almost an affront to the parties to an agreement. Under Oliver Cromwell, when the aristocracy was temporarily out of power, a constitution was written. Since Cromwell, there has never been a revolutionary break with the past, and therefore there has been no need for a comprehensive constitutional document.

Generally speaking, in England the freedom to make constitutional changes has not been used rashly or irresponsibly. Constitutional reforms have usually occurred only after thorough discussion and the securing of a mandate from the electorate. For example, the reform of the House of Lords in 1911, which largely stripped that body of its powers, was preceded by two general elections in 1910 in which the status of the Lords was the paramount issue. On such major issues as extending the franchise, all changes since 1918 have been preceded by an all-party conference under the chairmanship of the nonpartisan Speaker of the House of Commons. It has also been the custom for important legislative proposals to be investigated by royal commissions of inquiry, which include distinguished private citizens and experts as well as members of Parliament.

The English constitution does in fact exercise a definite restraining influence on government power. In theory, Parliament is omnipotent; it was once said that "Parliament can do everything but make a woman a man, and a man a woman." But in fact Parliament is limited. The limits are not the American limits of a written constitution enforced by the Supreme Court. They are the limits of usages, of conventions, of understandings, and of attitudes of mind. Moreover, Parliament is not a monolith; it is an amalgam of Crown, Cabinet, Commons, and Lords. The Crown will not let the Cabinet abuse its powers of resignation and dissolution. The Cabinet is limited to policies that it can get the Commons to accept. The House of Lords, even with its reduced powers, can still force the Cabinet and the Commons to take a second look at a proposed constitutional change.

Nevertheless, because there are no enforceable constitutional limits on the power of Parliament and no comprehensive bill of rights, there is thus no bar to the adoption of repressive legislation when popular pressure is sufficient to override traditional standards. Following the deadly bombing of two Birmingham pubs by the Irish Republican Army in 1974, the English government adopted emergency legislation outlawing the IRA, authorizing the arrest of suspected terrorists without warrant and detention without charges, and giving immigration officers the power to arrest, detain, and search suspects at airports and docks. These measures, unprecedented in peacetime, could not be challenged as unconstitutional. While comparable legislation has sometimes been adopted in the United States, it is always subject to challenge, often successful, in the courts.[1]

The Soviet constitution

The power of the constitutional idea is demonstrated by the fact that even political despotisms have used the symbolism or semantics of constitutionalism. The Soviet Union promulgated written constitutions in 1918, 1924, and 1936. The 1936 constitution was particularly noteworthy for the impressive list of civil rights it purported to guarantee; among the rights promised to Soviet citizens were freedom of speech, freedom of the press, freedom of assembly and of holding mass meetings, freedom of street processions and demonstrations, the inviolability of persons and of the homes of citizens, and secrecy of correspondence. Yet the 1936 constitution was promulgated during perhaps the most intense period of terror and repression in the history of the USSR. In fact, at the time the leading Soviet jurist argued that the very concept of law was a product of the capitalist market enconomy and would wither away in the planned communist society.

A new party line was presented in 1938 by Andrei Vishinsky in his book *The Law of the Soviet State;* under this doctrine, law was restored to its role in the protection of personal, property, family, testamentary, and other rights and interests. But political dissent has remained outside the protection of the law and the constitution. "Counterrevolutionaries" and "enemies of the people" have generally been tried in secret proceedings before administrative or military courts.[2] Another method of handling dis-

[1] Enforcement of the 1954 act outlawing the U.S. Communist party was never attempted because of administrative doubts as to its constitutionality. The 1940 Smith Act, making it a crime to advocate the overthrow of the government by force, was rendered unusable by Supreme Court interpretation in *Yates v. United States* (1957).

[2] See Aleksandr I. Solzhenitsyn, *The Gulag Archipelago,* New York: Harper & Row, 1973.

senters is to confine them to mental institutions or, as in the case of Aleksandr Solzhenitsyn, expel them from the country.

While Russians generally recognize that their constitution is a facade and place no reliance on it, there have been a few scattered efforts to invoke its protection. The author Andrei Amalrik, who was sentenced in 1970 to three years in a labor camp for "slandering" the USSR in his book *Will the Soviet Union Survive Until 1984?*, invoked the constitution unsuccessfully at his trial. So did Vladimir Bukovsky, who told how dissidents were placed in mental hospitals and treated with drugs in a clandestine interview with the Columbia Broadcasting System in 1970. The nuclear physicist Andrei Sakharov proposed in 1972 a bill of rights for the Soviet Union.

The American constitution

The American written constitution, unlike the Russian, is effective because the limitations that it imposes on governmental powers are founded in American political theory, are recognized as binding by government officials, are enforceable in the courts, and have general public support.

The American Constitution is now by far the oldest written constitution in modern history. In the period since 1789, states and nations have drafted scores of constitutions, which have subsequently been outgrown or abandoned or destroyed by violent change. France, for example, has had 14 constitutions since 1789.

Why has the American Constitution proved to be so effective and so enduring? How has a nation of over 200 million people, of continental proportions and worldwide responsibilities, with a government that spends over $350 billion annually, been accommodated within the confines of a document drafted almost 200 years ago for a handful of people in 13 isolated states along the Atlantic seaboard?

One reason for the success of the Constitution is that its framers were wise enough to avoid being too specific in drafting key provisions of the document. The entire original Constitution is only 6,000 words long. By contrast, many American state constitutions are massive compendiums regulating state and local governmental procedures and powers down to the pettiest details. These constitutions require constant amendment to keep up with current changes and to remain applicable.

The general intent of the framers in 1787 was to limit themselves to the fundamentals and leave implementation to subsequent legislative decisions. For example, Congress was permitted to decide such matters as the departmental organization of the executive branch, presidential succession beyond the Vice-President, and whether a system of lower federal courts would be established.

As a result of this approach, there are gaps in the Constitution sufficiently wide to allow entire political institutions to grow within these gaps and be almost free of constitutional restrictions. No provision is made for the Cabinet as an institution, nor are political parties, such an essential feature of American government, mentioned in the Constitution. Political parties were regarded as dangerous when the Constitution was drafted, and the framers deliberately tried to prevent the rise of a party system. Even today, after 180 years of party government, there are no direct references to parties or nominating procedures in the Constitution.

Consequently it may be argued that in addition to the written Constitution, the United States also has an unwritten constitution that is similar to the English model. The written, enforceable Constitution is supplemented by a multitude of usages and conventions that are generally accepted as rules for the operation of the political system but which have no binding force other than tradition. One such example is the requirement that representatives in Congress must be residents of the district they represent (which incidentally is contrary to the English practice). Another example was based on the decision of both Washington and Jefferson to retire after their second terms as President. Their action established a two-term limitation which was treated as binding by all subsequent presidents until 1940, when Franklin Roosevelt was reelected to a third term. After Roosevelt had breached the tradition still further by going on to a fourth term, Congress adopted the Twenty-Second Amendment, which makes the two-term limit a part of the written Constitution.

If the American Constitution resembles the English model in that it is partly unwritten, it also bears a slight resemblance to the Soviet Constitution in that it states some noble goals or broad principles which have not always been realized. For example, the Fifteenth Amendment guarantees the right to vote regardless of race or color. But this amendment was virtually ignored in some parts of the country until the Voting Rights Act of 1965 was passed. The Fourteenth Amendment requires that states that deny the right to vote be penalized by having their representation in Congress reduced. However, this provision has never been enforced. Most important, the "equal protection of the laws" guaranteed by the Fourteenth Amendment has all too often been denied to racial minorities, the poor, and other disadvantaged members of the American community.

KEY PRINCIPLES OF THE AMERICAN CONSTITUTION

The Constitution of the United States was written between May 14 and September 17, 1787, by 55 men meeting in the city of Philadelphia. The Continental Congress, which had directed the American colonies through the war against British rule, had been succeeded in 1781 by the Articles of Confederation. Both concentrated all governmental power in a one-house legislature. Under the Articles, each state had one vote, just as in the United

Nations Assembly today, and two-thirds of the states had to vote in favor of an important measure in order for it to be adopted. Amendments could be added to the Articles only if they were passed with the unanimous consent of the states. The Confederation lacked most of the powers essential to an effective central government: Congress could not levy taxes or regulate commerce among the states, for instance, and there was no executive and only a very limited system of courts.

The impossibility of governing with such a weak instrument soon became apparent to the leading figures in the new nation, and early in 1787 Congress authorized a convention to meet for the "sole and express purpose" of revising the Articles of Confederation. When the notable group of delegates met, they quickly decided to override their instructions, and abandon the confederation principle in favor of a strong central government.

Moreover, the Constitutional Convention bypassed both Congress and the state legislatures and submitted the new constitution to state conventions that had been elected for the specific purpose of considering ratification. The Constitution was to become effective once it had been ratified by nine state conventions. The ratification campaign left as a legacy the most famous commentary on American government, *The Federalist,* a collection of newspaper articles written by James Madison, Alexander Hamilton, and John Jay. These articles were intended to influence the vote in the undecided state of New York. The essays have been accepted as authoritative guides to constitutional interpretation.

The absence of a bill of rights was the feature most widely criticized in the ratifying conventions, and in several states the promise that a bill of rights would be added was instrumental in securing the votes needed for ratification of the new Constitution. In pursuance of this understanding, ten amendments, commonly referred to as the Bill of Rights, were adopted by the First Congress in 1789 and ratified in 1791; these amendments are generally regarded as a part of the original Constitution.

The ideas embodied in the Constitution were not wholly new. They were drawn from the European political heritage of the new nation. The genius of the Convention was in its practicality and willingness to compromise dogmatic principles in order to achieve a workable basis for union. The key principles of the document are (1) popular sovereignty, (2) federalism, (3) separation of powers, and (4) limited government.

Popular sovereignty

The Declaration of Independence, the cornerstone of American ideas about government, is the most representative and influential statement of American political theory. Its basic conception came from the English philosopher John Locke, but the doctrines were sharpened by the experience of resistance to British rule. These principles were so much a part of American thinking that the Declaration referred to them as "self-evident." The state constitutions that were adopted between 1776 and 1780 also abound in statments of then-current political assumptions.

The basic political premise of the day was that people are by nature endowed with certain inalienable rights. This concept assumed that a state of nature had existed prior to the establishment of civil government. In this primeval condition, all people were free, in the sense that they were subject to no one and equal in the right to rule themselves. As persons, they possessed a body of natural rights, including the right to "life, liberty, and the pursuit of happiness." These rights not only antedate the existence of government but are superior to it in authority.

The exercise of coercive power by governments over persons born free and equal can be justified, then, only by the consent of the governed. The process as expressed by the Massachusetts Bill of Rights was that "the body politic is formed by a voluntary association of individuals; it is a social compact by which the whole people covenants with each citizen, and each citizen with the whole people, that all shall be governed by certain laws for the common good."

The exact nature of this contract on which government was based, or the circumstances under which it was agreed upon, were not much discussed. But the concept was given a sense of reality by the numerous written compacts that had contributed to American development, especially the Mayflower Compact of 1620 and the colonial charters. The slogan "No taxation without representation" was a particular application of the consent theory, with roots deep in English constitutional history.

Government is created by contract to serve the welfare of the people. Quoting again from the Massachusetts document, the aim of government is "to secure the existence of the body politic, to protect it, and to furnish the individuals who compose it with the power of enjoying in safety and tranquillity their natural rights, and the blessings of life." A government that has failed to serve the ends for which it was established has breached the contract that brought it into existence and has forfeited the loyalty of its citizens. On this basis, the right of revolution, obviously fundamental to legitimizing the American nation, was established. The Declaration of Independence justified revolutionary action as follows:

> *Whenever any form of government becomes destructive of these ends, it is the right of the people to alter or to abolish it, and to institute new government, laying its foundation on such principles and organizing its powers in such forms, as to them shall seem most likely to effect their safety and happiness.*

When faced with the problem of constructing a governmental system in which these basic principles would be realized, the framers of the Constitution proved to be somewhat divided as to what extent the government would be subjected to popular control. Direct election was provided for the House of Representatives, but the Senate was to be chosen by the state legislatures. Judges were not to be elected, and only a few of the delegates favored direct popular election of the President.

The Constitution clearly bases the government on the representative, or republican, principle, but the only time the term *republican* appears in the Constitution is in Article IV, which provides that the United States shall guarantee "a republican form of government" to every state in the Union. Some have argued that since the United States was created as a republic, it is a serious mistake to speak of it as a "democracy." This is the usual position of conservatives who treasure the aristocratic manifestations in the initial constitutional provisions, and who disapprove of modern trends toward egalitarianism, direct democracy, and mass society in general. Unquestionably, the original republic has evolved into a representative democracy, but this development has taken place within the framework of constitutional principles. The transformation of presidential choice, for example, from indirect to direct election occurred without any relevant change in the language of the Constitution.

Federalism

The most novel feature of the Constitution was the federal structure of the government it created. American federalism is a form of political organization in which authority is divided between two levels of government, each possessing its powers as a matter of right, and each acting directly on the citizens. Midway between a confederation, or league of states, and a completely centralized, unitary government, the American federal pattern was a unique invention combining the principles of unity and diversity.

The powers of the new central government were taken from the existing state governments and "delegated" to the United States.[3] The most significant listing of powers delegated to Congress is found in Article I, Section 8. These powers range from punishing counterfeiters to declaring war. These authorizations were typically stated rather broadly—for example, the power to regulate commerce or to levy taxes. Backing up these broad grants of specific powers, moreover, was the general authorization to Congress in the last clause of Article I, Section 8, "to make all laws which shall be necessary and proper for carrying into execution the foregoing powers. . . ."

In the Constitution as originally drafted, no effort was made to state

[3]Except for the power to conduct foreign relations. The Supreme Court held in *United States v. Curtiss-Wright Export Corp.* (1936) that the individual states had never possessed any competence in foreign relations, and that at the time of the Revolution this power passed directly from Britain to the Continental Congress and then to the Confederation.

any general formula reserving to the states the powers not delegated to Congress. That these undelegated powers remained with the states was regarded as so obvious that it did not need to be spelled out. However, specific reassurances were demanded during the ratification debates, and were met by the Tenth Amendment: "The powers not delegated to the United States by the Constitution, nor prohibited by it to the States, are reserved to the States, respectively, or to the people."

The Constitution thus established ground rules for the federal system by allocating authority between two levels of government. But this was not sufficient. Conflicts between the states and the nation over the division of functions were inevitable. The federal system could work only if there were rules for deciding such contests, and if an umpire was appointed to apply those rules. The principal rule supplied by the Constitution is the "supremacy clause" of Article VI:

> *This Constitution, and the laws of the United States which shall be made in pursuance thereof, and all treaties made, or which shall be made, under the authority of the United States, shall be the supreme law of the land; and the judges in every state shall be bound thereby, any thing in the Constitution or laws of any State to the contrary notwithstanding.*

This meant that no state was to have any power to retard, impede, or burden the operations of any constitutional powers exercised by Congress. When Congress entered a field in which it was authorized by the Constitution to act, its legislation would void all incompatible state regulations. Enforcement of the supremacy clause was entrusted in the first instance to the "judges in every state," but in the Judiciary Act of 1789, the First Congress provided for review of state court decisions by the Supreme Court, which has ever since functioned as the umpire of the federal system.

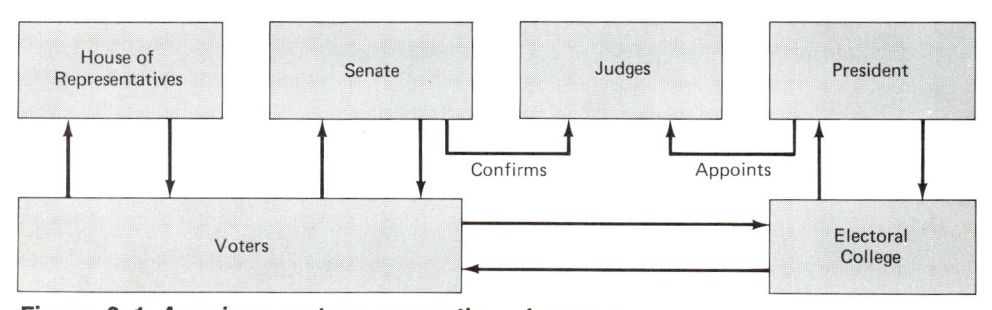

Figure 3–1 *American system: separation of powers*
Presidential System.

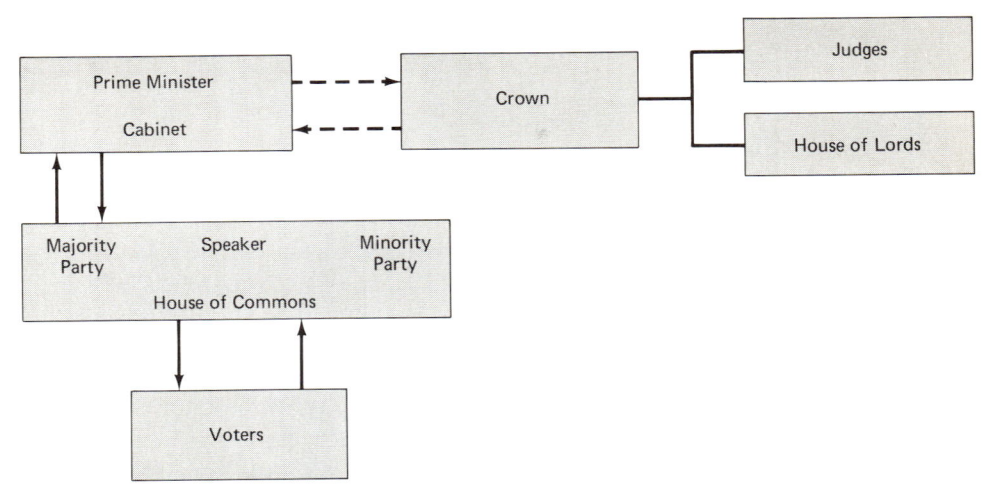

Figure 3-2 *British system: concentration of powers*
Parliamentary System.

Separation of powers

The Constitution established American governmental institutions on the separation-of-powers principle, with legislative, executive, and judicial functions entrusted to three separate branches of government (see Figure 3-1). The executive and the legislative are independent of each other in that each is elected by separate electoral processes for assured terms of office. The President cannot dissolve Congress or shorten its term or remove any of its members. The Congress, even though it may have a majority that does not support the President, cannot remove him from office except by the difficult process of impeachment.[4] The federal judiciary, although appointed by the President and confirmed by the Senate, is independent in the sense that the judges have tenure for life; judicial authority to enforce constitutional requirements on both the President and Congress is universally acknowledged.

By way of contrast, the English constitution concentrates authority in the legislature (see Figure 3-2). The English executive is a cabinet or council of ministers, headed by the prime minister, which is in effect a committee of the majority party in the House of Commons. The Cabinet remains in power only so long as it retains the confidence of the House. The English

---

[4]President Andrew Johnson was impeached but not convicted in 1868. In 1974 impeachment proceedings were begun against President Richard Nixon and three articles of impeachment were voted by the House Judiciary Committee, but the proceedings were dropped after his resignation.

judiciary has great prestige and security, but it cannot challenge the legitimacy of parliamentary action. Thus the English system is based on legislative supremacy.

Although the phrase "separation of powers" has a measure of accuracy in describing American constitutional arrangements, it is in many respects a most misleading description. It is more accurate to say that the American Constitution, through a system of "checks and balances," provides for a government of separated institutions sharing powers. The great task of American government is to get these separate institutions to work together with some measure of effectiveness.

The Constitution vests the executive power in the President, but many of his most important executive functions involve congressional participation. The Senate must confirm all important appointments. The organization of and allocation of powers to executive departments depends on congressional legislation. The President has great independent power in the field of military and foreign affairs, but he must secure the approval of two-thirds of the Senate for the ratification of treaties, and all presidential programs, both foreign and domestic, depend on congressional appropriations of the necessary funds.

Congress, for its part, is granted "all legislative powers," but the President is authorized to "recommend to their consideration such measures as he shall judge necessary and expedient." In fact, the initiation of legislative programs has become almost entirely the President's responsibility. After passage by Congress, all legislation must be submitted to the President for his signature before it becomes effective, and a presidential veto can be overridden only by a two-thirds majority of each house of Congress. The President has thus become the major architect of congressional legislative programs.

Federal judges are completely independent once they are on the bench, but they must be appointed by the President and their appointments must be confirmed by the Senate. They are subject to impeachment; in fact, impeachment proceedings have been brought against ten federal judges, four of whom were convicted. Congress can change the number of justices on the Supreme Court and can exercise some measure of control over the Court's power to hear cases. In their turn, the federal courts can invalidate any presidential actions and congressional statutes that they find to be contrary to the Constitution. No specific authority for such judicial review is stated in the Constitution, but this power has been exercised by the federal courts since 1803.

Thus it is clear that there is no rigid separation of powers in American government. The President is chief executive, chief legislator, and through the power of judicial appointment, a major force in determining the constitutional positions taken by the judicial branch. Congress, through its powers of appropriation, investigation, and confirmation, goes far beyond a mere legislative role to intervene in the administrative side of government. The courts through their authority to interpret the Constitution and federal statutes can exercise a major role in the formulation of policy. This may appear to be a blueprint for confusion, and in fact the separation of powers has been responsible for much deadlock, frustration, and lack of direction in American government, but occasional confusion is better than disaster, which would certainly have been the result if the goal of separation of powers had been sought by attempting to divide the executive, legislature, and judiciary into separate watertight compartments.

Limited government

Basic to the entire idea of constitutionalism is the concept of limited government. Under a constitution, governmental power is both authorized and limited by undertakings arrived at in advance, consented to by those affected, and given continuing validity by appropriate enforcement processes. The rule of law and of representative institutions with defined authority stands under the American Constitution as a guarantee of individual liberty against the exercise of arbitrary power.

In part, the idea of limited government is implemented by constitutional provisions that specifically deny certain powers to the government. Thus the Constitution prohibits the suspension of the writ of *habeas corpus* or the passing of laws impairing the obligation of contracts. More important are the prohibitions added to the Constitution by the Bill of Rights, particularly the First Amendment, which guarantees that speech, press, assembly, and religion will be free from congressional restraint. The Fourteenth Amendment, added to the Constitution after the Civil War, forbids the states to deprive any person of life, liberty, or property without due process of law, or to deny equal protection of the laws.

In part, also, the goal of limiting government power is achieved through the system of checks and balances that has just been discussed. The executive and the legislative are the major power centers; Hamilton symbolized their roles as those of the sword and the purse. It is largely to offset and restrain their power that the Supreme Court has been permitted to develop its unusual role of judicial review. The fact that judicial determinations can occasionally override executive and legislative action has led some commentators to refer to the American system as one of judicial supremacy. Admittedly, the courts do play a significant role in making a reality out of the limitations of a written constitution, but even courts would be helpless without the support of a tradition that makes freedom a value of the highest order, and unless there are the resources, the opportunities, and the will to protect the principles of an open society from attack or frustration. As

Judge Learned Hand said, "In a society which evades its responsibility by thrusting upon the courts the nurture of [the spirit of moderation], that spirit in the end will perish."[5]

There may be some risk that in stressing the limitations on governmental power, one may forget that the purpose of those limits is not to produce a weak government. A government unable to deal effectively with the cataclysmic challenges of the modern world is as dangerous for its citizens as one that bears too heavily on them. The American Constitution, it has been well said, is both an instrument of power and a symbol of restraint. The lesson of the Articles of Confederation—that governmental weakness and incompetence will not safeguard liberty or foster the good life—had been well learned by 1787. The founders at Philadelphia sought to establish a government strong enough to protect against foreign enemies, preserve domestic peace, and foster commercial development and the general welfare. At the same time, they wanted a national governmnt limited so as not to obliterate the states or threaten individual rights of liberty and property.

CONSTITUTIONAL AMENDMENT

If a constitution can be changed by simple act of the legislature (as is the case in some countries), then its status is no higher than statute law. But the process for amending the American Constitution is difficult and imposes a real barrier to direct constitutional change. As a result only 16 amendments have been adopted since 1791.

Amendments to the constitution

Apart from the Bill of Rights (1791), the most important group of amendments—the Thirteenth (1865), the Fourteenth (1868), and the Fifteenth (1870)—were adopted after the Civil War to abolish slavery and protect the rights of the newly freed blacks.

The remaining amendments have had a variety of purposes. In three cases, they were adopted to reverse decisions of the Supreme Court. The Eleventh Amendment (1795) overrode a 1793 court decision allowing states to be sued in federal courts by citizens of other states. The Sixteenth Amendment (1913) authorized the federal government to levy an income tax, which the Court had held unconstitutional in 1895. The Twenty-Sixth Amendment (1971) forbade the states to deny the vote to citizens 18 years of age or older on account of age, an action which the Court had ruled Congress could not take by statute so far as state elections were concerned.

---

[5] Irving Dilliard (ed.), *The Spirit of Liberty: Papers and Addresses of Learned Hand*, New York: Knopf, 1959, p. 125.

Four amendments have dealt with presidential elections and terms of office. When the original language on presidential election proved to be faulty, the Twelfth Amendment (1804) made some necessary corrections. The Twentieth (1933) changed the beginning of presidential terms from March 4 to January 20, and the Twenty-Second (1951) limited the President to two terms. The Twenty-Fifth Amendment (1967) provided improved arrangements for presidential disability and succession.

The Nineteenth Amendment (1920) gave women the vote, and the prospective Twenty-Seventh (which had been ratified by 34 of the required 38 state legislatures by 1975) guaranteed women equality of rights under the law. The Twenty-Third (1961) allowed residents of the District of Columbia to vote in presidential elections, and the Twenty-Fourth (1964) forbade the poll tax as a prerequisite for voting in federal elections. Finally, there was the ill-starred Eighteenth Amendment (1919), authorizing the federal government to prohibit intoxicating liquor, which was repealed in 1933 by the Twenty-First Amendment.

The amending process

Article V provides two methods for proposing amendments: (a) by a two-thirds majority of each house of Congress, or (b) by a convention summoned by Congress at the request of the legislatures of two-thirds of the states. Only the first of these methods has so far been employed. There are likewise two ways by which amendments may be ratified: (a) by three-fourths of the state legislatures, or (b) by ratifying conventions in three-fourths of the states. (See Figure 3–3.) In only one of the amendments thus far adopted, the Twenty-First, did Congress specify the use of conventions. The reason for this exception was the fear in Congress that overrepresentation in the state legislatures of rural areas, which tended to be "dry," might imperil adoption of the amendment repealing prohibition, whereas conventions would more equitably represent the views of the urban areas.

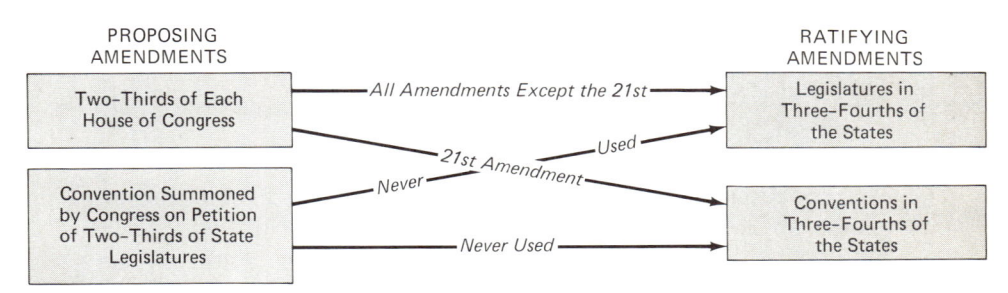

Figure 3–3 *Four methods of amending constitution*

Amendment by the convention method

On numerous occasions, state legislatures have unsuccessfully petitioned Congress to call a constitutional convention under Article V. In the early part of this century, some 31 states, meeting the two-thirds requirement at that time, submitted petitions for an amendment to provide for direct election of senators. Congress failed to call a convention, but eventually proposed the amendment itself. After the Supreme Court ruled in 1964 that members of both houses in all state legislatures must be elected from districts of equal population, a national campaign was mounted to persuade the state legislatures to call for a convention to nullify this ruling, and 33 of the required 34 legislatures took such action.

This near-miss concentrated attention on the many uncertainties surrounding the convention method. For example, if two-thirds of the legislatures submit petitions, must they be in identical language, and must they be received within a limited time period? May Congress decline to act on the petitions? If a convention is called, how are the delegates to be chosen, and what are the voting rules in the convention? How can a convention be prevented from going beyond the subject for which it was convened, as the Constitutional Convention did in 1787?

These uncertainties are so serious that it would be wise for Congress to adopt general implementing legislation before it is faced with a valid call for a convention. However, it would be preferable if the convention method of amendment were not used at all. Its principal recent support has come from interests sponsoring proposals that could not gain congressional approval. It is an alternative attractive to those who find it more congenial to work in the recesses of 50 state legislatures than in the pitiless publicity of the congressional forum. The national interest in the amending process is best protected by leaving the responsibility for proposing amendments in the hands of Congress, where the necessity of securing a two-thirds vote in each house lessens the possibility of hasty or ill-considered action.

Appraisal of the amending process

Perhaps the most striking fact about the amending procedure is the relative infrequency with which it has been used. For more than 40 years following the Civil War the Constitution appeared unamendable. This was an era of agrarian discontent, industrial unrest, and growing pressure for political and economic reforms. The conservatism of the Supreme Court, symbolized by its invalidation of the income tax in 1895, made constitutional amendment seem to be a necessary step toward achieving liberal legislative goals, but the necessary two-thirds majorities in Congress could not be secured.

In 1913, however, the long liberal campaigns for the income tax and direct election of senators succeeded, and the women's suffrage amendment followd shortly thereafter. With six amendments added to the Constitution between 1913 and 1933, the amending process no longer seemed to be so formidable. In fact, adoption of the Enghteenth Amendment showed that even a small but dedicated pressure group could sucessfully manipulate the amending machinery.

The liberalization of the Supreme Court's views as a result of President Roosevelt's appointments substantially diminished liberal interest in further amendments. In a dramatic turnaround, pressure for amendments shifted almost entirely from the liberals to conservative sources. The increase in executive power and congressional expenditures, the acceptance of new welfare functions internally and new responsibilities internationally by the federal government, and the reduced role of the states all stimulated the resistance of various conservative groups. Lacking the power to block these developments through the regular political processes, conservatives relied instead on the strategy of constitutional amendment. During the 1950s, conservative measures that failed to be adopted were the Bricker Amendment to limit the federal government's power to enter into international agreements, various proposals for revising the presidential election process so as to reduce the importance of the large industrial states, and a proposal to place a ceiling on federal income taxation. In the 1960s, proposed amendments to nullify the Supreme Court's decisions on school prayer and legislative apportionment were defeated.

The only amendment secured by this drive from the right was the Twenty-Second Amendment, adopted in 1951. The limitation of the President to two terms was initially proposed by the Republican party after it had suffered four defeats at the hands of Franklin Roosevelt, but the measure was subsequently supported by conservatives of both parties who feared strong executive leadership. Ironically, the first President affected by the amendment was a Republican, Dwight Eisenhower.

The adoption of the Twenty-Sixth Amendment demonstrates how fast the amending machinery can work when the political climate is right. The Supreme Court invalidated the 18-year-old vote in state elections on December 21, 1970. The amendment lowering the voting age to 18 for all elections cleared Congress on March 23, 1971, and the 38th state ratified the amendment on June 30, 1971, bringing it into effect.

CONSTITUTIONAL INTERPRETATION

Almost as important as the amending process in adapting the Constitution to changing conditions is the device of constitutional interpretation. In fact, the possibility of modifying constitutional meanings gradually over the years to meet new times and new necessities has accounted for the relative infrequency of formal amendment.

Interpretation by Congress and the President

In a sense, Congress interprets its power under the Constitution every time it passes a law or holds a hearing. There are always a substantial number of members in Congress who pride themselves on their knowledge of the Constitution, and whenever a new legislative program is being considered, much of the congressional debate will be concerned with the constitutional justification for it.[6]

In the same way, the President interprets the Constitution whenever he makes a decision, issues an executive order, or signs a bill into law. The Constitution is manifested in the historic crises that Presidents have met—Lincoln facing the disintegration of the Union, Roosevelt facing the collapse of the national economy. Their actions were based on explicit or implicit interpretations of executive power. When the President has any doubt about the sufficiency of his constitutional authority, or when he wishes to provide the firmest possible basis for his action, he will ask the Attorney General for a legal opinion covering his proposed action.

Judicial interpretation

The most highly rationalized type of constitutional interpretation, however, is that engaged in by judges, and particularly those on the Supreme Court. No matter how great the prestige of the President or Congress, there is a general assumption that until the Supreme Court has spoken, the Constitution has not been officially interpreted. And almost invariably the President and Congress, even when they hold opposite views, yield to the Court's position. Thus judicial interpretation is the final arbiter in most areas of constitutional meaning.

The Constitution contains many broad phrases such as "due process of law" and "freedom of speech." How does the Supreme Court decide what these words mean? One test that is often suggested is the *intention of the framers*. It does seem logical that where the language of the Constitution is vague or subject to diverse interpretations, the Court should try to resolve the uncertainties by seeking guidance from the understandings of the men who wrote the document.

However, there are more difficulties than one might imagine in determining the intent of the framers of Constitution. Fifty-five delegates were present at one or more sessions of the Convention, but some took little or no part in the proceedings. Some propositions on which they voted were carried by narrow majorities. What was said, and the reasons given for votes cast, are known almost entirely through James Madison's incomplete notes. On no issues did all members speak; on few did a majority

---

[6]See Donald G. Morgan, *Congress and the Constitution*, Cambridge: Belknap Press of Harvard University Press, 1966.

speak. Many decisions must have been compromises that fully pleased no one.

If the intention of the 55 men at Philadelphia cannot be discovered with assurance, what chance is there of determining the intention of the delegates to the state ratifying conventions whose votes put the Constitution into operation? The ultimate in uncertainty is reached if we seek to discover the intention of the people who elected the delegates to the state conventions.

In spite of these complications, there are some areas where the purpose of the drafters may seem reasonably clear and where legitimate use can be made of historical data in discovering these purposes. Thus in *Barron v. Baltimore* (1833) the Supreme Court had to decide whether the first ten amendments were limitations on the states as well as on the national government. Chief Justice John Marshall held that they were not, and based his decision primarily on the historical fact that the Bill of Rights had been drafted to meet the objections of those who were afraid of the power of the new central government.

All too often, however, persons who seek to settle constitutional arguments by appealing to the intention of the framers are simply reading their own policy preferences into the language of the Constitution. When the Supreme Court was trying to decide in *School District v. Schempp* (1963) whether the First Amendment makes it unconstitutional to read the Bible in public schools, Justice Brennan expressed his opinion that it would be "futile and misdirected" to ask what the Founding Fathers had intended on this point.

First, Brennan said, "the historical record is at best ambiguous, and statements can readily be found to support either side of the proposition. . . . Second, the structure of American education has greatly changed since the First Amendment was adopted." Justice Brennan thought it would be a more fruitful inquiry for the Court to ask "whether the practices here challenged threaten those consequences which the Framers deeply feared; whether, in short, they tend to promote that type of interdependence between religion and state which the First Amendment was designed to prevent."

Another major issue for the Court is what degree of responsibility it can assume in modifying previous constitutional interpretations to meet new situations and new needs. Once the meaning of a particular constitutional provision is authoritatively determined, is the Court bound to that interpretation for all time? Some members of the Court have thought so. Chief Justice Roger B. Taney said, in the famous *Dred Scott* case in 1857:

> *[The Constitution] speaks not only in the same words, but with the same meaning and intent with which it spoke when it came from the hands of its framers, and was voted on and adopted by the people of*

> the United States. Any other rule of construction would abrogate the judicial character of this court, and make it the mere reflex of the popular opinion or passion of the day.

More recently, Justice Frankfurter took this same position in *Ullmann* v. *United States* (1955): "Nothing new can be put into the Constitution except through the amendatory process. Nothing old can be taken out without the same process."

The Supreme Court has generally rejected this rigid view, which would make the nation a prisoner of its past and deny the legitimacy of amendment by consensus and usage. It was such narrow textualism that Chief Justice Marshall was warning against in *McCulloch* v. *Maryland* (1819) when he said: "We must never forget, that it is a constitution we are expounding ... a constitution intended to endure for ages to come, and, consequently, to be adapted to the various crises of human affairs."

WORLD SIGNIFICANCE OF THE AMERICAN CONSTITUTION

The era of the written constitution was ushered in by the American and French revolutions in the late eighteenth century. Up to that time, the dominant conception of a constitution was the English evolutionary idea stated by the English statesman Lord Bolingbroke in 1793:

> By constitution we mean, whenever we speak with propriety and exactness, that assemblage of laws, institutions and customs, derived from certain fixed principles of reason, directed to certain fixed objects of public good, that compose the general system, according to which the community hath agreed to be governed.

But the American and French constitution framers were dealing with a revolutionary rather than an evolutionary situation. They meant to break with the past, to make a new start, and so they sat down and thought out a government. They put down in writing a framework of administration and an allocation of powers and a system of restraints on power. Their invention of the written constitution has been subsequently adopted by every nation that faces the problem of starting a new government and operating under the rule of law.

The fact that the French have had 14 constitutions since 1789 suggests that there are some problems in thinking out a government. A constitution in and of itself does not bring stability to a country split by religious, racial, or class conflicts, a country threatened by powerful foreign neighbors, or a nation enduring a tradition of violence in its public life. It is necessary that there be some correspondence between constitutional goals and political realities.

The survival of the American Constitution of 1789 is certainly due in part to the favorable circumstances of its national setting. It was framed in a new country which was still malleable, protected by two oceans from foreign conquest, without sharp class distinctions, with great natural resources and vast areas of unsettled land to absorb the discontented and disadvantaged, and with considerable experience in self-government. But recognition of these features should not prevent us from crediting the founders for the wisdom of their basic decisions.

The American Constitution has had tremendous impact on world opinion and unusual value for the framers of other constitutional systems, particularly during the nineteenth century, when the struggling American nation was a symbol of freedom to much of the world. The French and American Constitutions started what has been called a "constitutional cult." Even Tsar Alexander of Russia corresponded with Thomas Jefferson to learn how the American Constitution functioned, and the abortive Russian Constitution of 1820 was the first constitutional attempt by a European ruler to combine the federal and monarchical principles.

The revolutionary movements of the mid-nineteenth century in Europe got much of their inspiration from America. This was especially true in Germany, where the revolutionists of 1848–1849 constantly referred to the American example and wanted to create a Germany that was free "like America." The Frankfurt Constitution of 1849 borrowed from the American Constitution both in broad matters of principle and in matters of drafting and detail. Key articles were drawn almost textually from the American document, which had been translated into German and widely circulated.

For the Latin American countries that gained their independence in the nineteenth century, it was the federal character of the American Constitution and the strong independent executive that were most attractive. The highly centralized bureaucratic organization that Napoleon had developed in France was similar to that in Latin America and might have seemed better adapted to the conditions prevailing there. But centralism was associated with conservatism, whereas federalism had a liberal image and was favored regardless of whether it was appropriate for local political or geographic conditions. When the Brazilian monarchy was overthrown in 1889, a federal republic, with a constitution modeled after that of the United States, took its place.

The American federal pattern was more successfully followed by the Swiss constitution of 1848, and by two countries in the British Commonwealth, Canada (1867) and Australia (1900). Decisions by the United States Supreme Court regulating relations between the federal government and the states are cited and often followed by the courts of Canada, Australia, and other federal countries.

In the twentieth century, when the United States became rich, powerful, and conservative, its example was less attractive to developing nations, which found it hard to identify with the American colossus. To some extent, the American Constitution has remained a model for other nations; this is largely due to the influence of two of its liberal features—the Bill of Rights and judicial protection for the individual. The institution of a strong Supreme Court, with power to enforce constitutional restrictions on the executive and the legislature, was adopted in several of the post–World War II constitutions, notably those of West Germany, Italy, and India. The American Bill of Rights has symbolized in many lands the goal of individual freedom and the right to resist governmental oppression. Carl J. Friedrich states, "Wherever men have gathered to draft a constitution, they have drawn upon American constitutional theory and practice."[7]

---

[7] Carl J. Friedrich, *The Impact of American Constitutionalism Abroad,* Boston: Boston University Press, 1967, p. 11.

4 federalism

4

One of the serious reservations that the framers had in setting up a new constitution was whether a large country under a powerful central government would be a threat to the freedom of its citizens. The delegates who opposed a strong central government had a picture in their minds of the "small republic" as the ideal form of government, a picture drawn in part from their knowledge of the Greek city-states. Roger Sherman of Connecticut put it this way: "The people are more happy in small than large States."

The problem was that small republics were too weak, standing alone, to protect their independence and their economies, and so they had to associate in some common organization for mutual protection. But some members of the Constitutional Convention, generally from the smaller states, believed that a confederation limited to the functions of keeping the peace among the states and defending them against foreign enemies was all that was needed.

It was James Madison's role to answer the small-republic argument. He contended that from antiquity small republics had been beset by conflicts between classes that were fatal to liberty. A large republic would be preferable, for there, he argued, liberty would be protected by "the great variety of interests, parties, and sects which it embraces." An "extended republic of the United States" would be divided into many groups, no single one amounting to a majority. Only as smaller groups associated together could majorities be formed, a process that would force each group to moderate its position and protect the liberties of all.

The Convention was persuaded by Madison's argument and by the realization that security, peace, and economic development could be achieved only through a strong central government. But this created a coexistence problem. How could this new power center be accommodated within the same governmental structure with the existing and powerful state establishments? The framers found a solution. They invented the federal system.

We now think of the threefold distinction between a *confederation*, a *federal* system, and a *unitary* government as routine and obvious. (See Figure 4–1). But in 1787 only the confederation and the unitary government were recognized. As the Virginia delegation to the Convention said at the opening of its proceedings, the two possible forms of governmental organization were a "merely federal" union or a "national government." By

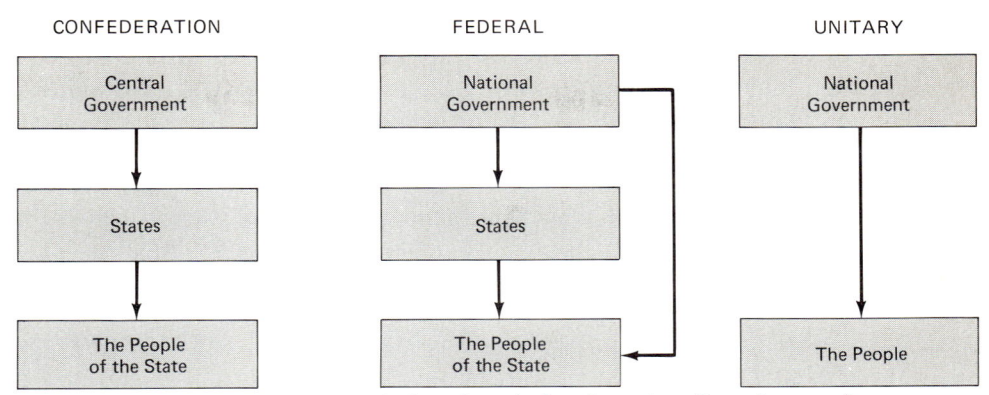

Figure 4-1 Comparison of confederation, federal, and unitary types of government

"merely federal" they meant a confederation such as was then in existence. Because this "merely federal" plan had failed, Virginia supported the "national" alternative. But what actually emerged from the Convention was a compromise between these two forms, a blueprint for a large republic whose goals of liberty and security were to be achieved by a division of responsibilities and functions between the central government and the states. This American invention has come to be considered the true form of federalism.

THE CASE FOR FEDERALISM

Since 1787 the federal system has been adopted in many countries, including Canada, Australia, Switzerland, India, Germany, Russia, and Mexico. By contrast, well-established democracies such as England, France, and Italy operate on the unitary system, with all governmental power vested in the central government; local districts are only administrative areas for carrying out national programs under central direction.

Federal systems have the following advantages over unitary systems:

1. Federalism tends to offer a more effective plan of government for big countries. Switzerland is an exception to the rule that large size and federalism go together. The difficulty of governing from one capital a country as large in area and population as the United States or India is obvious. Under federalism many functions are performed at the state or provincial level and need never concern the central authorities.

2. Federalism is well adapted to a country with strong regional differences. Diversities of race, language, tribe, and religion, are accommodated by federal systems in Switzerland, India, and Canada. Even in a country as relatively homogeneous as Great Britain, there is a separate parliament for Northern Ireland and a strong movement toward one in Scotland, and

even in Wales. One of the foremost accomplishments of the Tito regime in multinational and multilingual Yugoslavia has been the organization of the government and economy along the lines of federal balance and equity.

There is always the possibility that loyalty to a region may be so strong as to conflict with loyalty to the federal union, as is illustrated by the separatist movement in Quebec and the bitter language conflicts in India. American federalism has been successful partly because its federal units are based not on differences of race, national origin, religion, or language, but merely on geography.

3. The states or provinces in a federal system bring government closer to the people. Important centers of influence and decision are widely enough distributed to encourage popular participation in elections and other political activities. While it is often true that citizens are better informed about what happens in Washington than in their state capital, the possibility of interaction with their neighbors on local issues is greater.

4. The state level is an important training ground for national politics. Woodrow Wilson, Franklin Roosevelt, and Nelson Rockefeller are among those who got their first significant political experience as governors of important states. State legislators and state judges often move up into corresponding positions in the national government.

5. The states are political laboratories where new ideas can be tested without committing the whole country. Wisconsin first experimented with unemployment compensation. Georgia was the first state to reduce the voting age to 18. Prohibition on a national scale in the United States was a disaster, but if individual states wish to try to make it work they are free to do so. New Hampshire revived the state lottery as a revenue device; Massachusetts pioneered no-fault auto insurance. Many other states then followed their lead.

6. A federal system permits more effective forms of administrative decentralization. In a unitary system, the central government uses the local districts as administrative areas; in a federal system, the states can be treated as partners and share the responsibility for initiating and directing important programs. Thus the United States pays 90 percent of the cost of the interstate highway program, but the planning and construction of the system is delegated to the states.

Establishing the viability of the American federal system

On the other hand, the greater complexity of the federal system creates special problems for this form of government. It is inevitable that there will be disputes between the states and the central government over the allocation of functions and resources, as well as competition and conflict among the states themselves. The loyalty of citizens may be divided between state and nation. "States' rights" has been a perennial political issue in the

American federal union, and it finally took a bloody civil war to establish the viability of the federal system.

Interposition. The first state challenge to federal power came within a decade of the founding of the United States. As the Federalists began to lose ground to Jefferson's new Republican party, they reacted by passing in 1798 the Alien Enemies Act (aimed at Jefferson's French supporters) and the Sedition Act (aimed at critics of the national government). The Jeffersonians, outraged by what they regarded as an unconstitutional abuse of congressional power, protested by drafting the famous Kentucky and Virginia Resolutions (so called because of their adoption by the legislatures of those two states). These resolutions argued that under the Constitution the states, which were "integral parties" to the compact, had the right to judge when the federal government exercised powers that had not been granted by the compact, and could "interpose" state authority "for arresting the progress of the evil, and for maintaining within their respective limits, the authorities, rights, and liberties" guaranteed by the Constitution.

The resolutions did not specify how interposition was to be carried out. One suggestion was to call for the submission to the states of a constitutional amendment authorizing the allegedly improper assertion of federal power. If such an amendment failed to be ratified by three-fourths of the states, the federal action would be nullified as an act of usurpation not warrranted by the Constitution.

Jefferson's victory over the Federalists in the elections of 1800, due in no small part to popular resentment over the Alien and Sedition Acts, terminated this episode. But the concept of interposition has periodically been rediscovered. During the War of 1812 the New England states, suffering because of the disruption of their trade with England, joined in the Hartford Convention of 1814–1815 to recommend to the state legislatures that they pass measures to protect their citizens from the operation of unconstitutional national acts. But before the resolutions were even delivered, the war was over, the complaints forgotten, and the Federalist party annihilated.

In 1956 the long-slumbering doctrine of interposition was revived by southern opponents of the Supreme Court's decision banning racial segregation in the public schools. Almost 100 congressmen from 11 southern states issued a manifesto charging the Court with a clear abuse of judicial power encroaching on the reserved rights of the states and the people, and commending those states "which have declared the intention to resist forced integration by any lawful means." Legislatures of most of the southern states proceeded to draft declarations of interposition purporting to relieve their states from the necessity of enforcing the Court decision. When the governor and legislature of Arkansas argued in the 1958 Little Rock case, *Cooper v. Aaron,* that they were not bound by the segregation decision, the Supreme Court sharply and decisively restated the principles of federal supremacy that make the claims for interposition incompatible with the American federal system.

Nullification. Nullification was originally a part of the interposition doctrine, but it also had a history of its own, particularly as developed by John C. Calhoun in the pre–Civil War period. The theory of nullification originated with Jefferson's statement in the Kentucky Resolutions of 1798 that "where powers are assumed which have not been delegated, a nullification of the act is the rightful remedy."

This idea was later developed as a rationalization for southern opposition to the increase in tariff rates between 1816 and 1828. Calhoun, alarmed at the open talk of secession in the South, offered the doctrine of nullification as a substitute, contending that it was a logical extension of the Virginia and Kentucky Resolutions.

A South Carolina convention then declared the federal tariff acts null and void and forbade federal agents to collect them in the state. President Jackson immediately challenged this action, saying that the power of nullification was "incompatible with the existence of the Union," and sent gunboats into Charleston Harbor to enforce the tariff. The nullification statute was eventually repealed by the state after Congress had worked out a compromise measure on the tariff rates.

Secession. As the slavery issue increased in intensity, southern statesmen shifted their ground from nullification to secession as the means to preserve their economic life and social institutions. For Calhoun, secession was justified as a final remedy for preserving a state's rights. If the character of the Constitution was radically changed (as by the abolition of slavery), even through the amending process, Calhoun contended that any state, "acting in the same capacity in which it ratified the constitution," would have the right to depart from the Union.

Lincoln's decision to use force to keep the southern states in the Union and the victory of the North in the Civil War closed the debate over the legality of secession. In *Texas v. White* (1869) the Supreme Court summed up the principle that had taken a civil war to establish: "The Constitution, in all its provisions, looks to an indestructible Union, composed of indestructible States."

THE CONSTITUTION AND FEDERAL–STATE RELATIONS

The Constitution imposes several important obligations on the national government with respect to the states. For example, no state may be denied equal representation in the Senate without its consent, and Congress must respect the territorial integrity of existing states in forming new states. Other guarantees deserve fuller consideration.

Republican form of government

The Constitution provides that "the United States shall guarantee to every State in this Union a republican form of government. . . ." No definition is given of a republican form of government, but presumably the requirement contemplates a form of representative government in which basic democratic procedures, such as regular elections and civil and political rights, are protected.

The Supreme Court has on several occasions declined to attempt to interpret the republican form of government guarantee. In *Pacific States Telephone & Telegraph Co. v. Oregon* (1912), it was alleged that the insertion in the Oregon constitution of a provision for direct legislation by way of the initiative and referendum deprived the state of a republican form of government and made it a pure democracy. The Court's reply was that in the absence of any determination on this point by the executive and legislative branches of the government, it would refuse to consider such charges. Similarly, in 1964, the Court refused to rely on the republican-form-of-government provision to justify its decision in favor of "one man, one vote" in legislative elections, although some critics argued that it would have offered stronger support for the ruling than the equal-protection clause that the Court did invoke.

Domestic violence

The federal government must intervene in a state to protect it against "domestic violence," if requested by the state legislature or executive. On at least 16 occasions, states have sought federal assistance in dealing with violent outbreaks. It was under this provision that federal troops were sent into Detroit during the summer of 1967 to quell the disastrous rioting in that city.

A request for aid from the state legislature or governor is not necessary if domestic violence threatens the enforcement of national laws. Under the Constitution, Congress can summon the militia to execute the laws of the Union, suppress insurrections, and repel invasions. President Eisenhower had to use federal troops in 1957 to control violence in Little Rock, Arkansas, and to enforce the order of a federal court desegregating the local high school. Again, in 1962, federal troops were called in by President Kennedy to deal with violence at the University of Mississippi caused by an integration order.

Admission of new states

Thirty-five new states were admitted to the Union between 1791 and 1912. (See Figure 4–2). Five were carved out of the territory of older states—

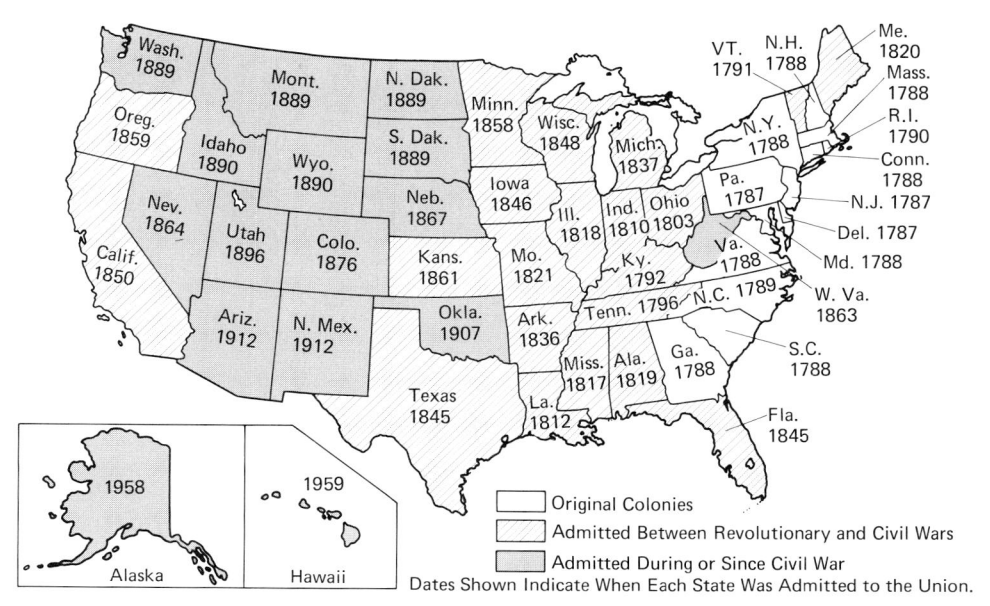

Figure 4–2 *Admission of states to the Union*
Adapted from Statistical Abstract of the United States, 1974.

Vermont, Kentucky, Tennessee, Maine, and West Virginia. In the first four cases, the legislature of the older state gave its consent. But West Virginia was formed from the western counties of Virginia during the Civil War when Virginia was in military opposition to the Union. However, after the war, Virginia formally consented to the dismemberment.

Of the remaining 30 states, all but two went through a probationary status as organized territories before they were admitted as states. The exceptions were Texas, which, upon its admission in 1845, was an independent republic, and California, which was formed out of a region ceded by Mexico in 1848.

Hawaii and Alaska were strong candidates for admission from at least 1944, when the platforms of both political parties recommended statehood, but various political considerations delayed action by Congress. Alaska finally won admission in 1958, and Hawaii in 1959; these were the first states to join the Union since 1912. There is some "statehood" sentiment in Puerto Rico.

Although there is no such provision in the Constitution, the Supreme Court has held that each state is admitted to the Union on an "equal footing" with the other states.[1] However, an exception to the "equal footing"

[1] *Coyle* v. *Smith* (1911).

doctrine arose under the Submerged Lands Act of 1953, which ceded to the states ownership of land and resources under adjoining seas to a distance of three miles from shore or to the state's "historic boundaries." The Supreme Court interpreted this statute to grant Florida and Texas jurisdiction ten miles into the Gulf of Mexico, since their "historic boundaries" were three marine leagues, whereas all other states have only three miles.

Interstate relations

Fifty quasi-sovereign states cannot operate within the same union and govern their respective territories without conflict and consensus. The Constitution makes provision for both situations. When controversies between states prove to be irresolvable, they can be submitted to a federal court for decision. In fact, any case in which a state is a party can go to the Supreme Court in its original jurisdiction.

Interstate compacts. As for cooperation between states, the Constitution makes available the device of the interstate compact. The consent of Congress is required for such compacts, but a great number have been authorized, covering such diverse problems as conservation of natural resources, sharing of water in interstate streams, flood and pollution control, provision of educational and health facilities, and supervision of parolees.

New York and New Jersey entered into one of the most famous compacts when they established the Port of New York Authority to develop and operate harbor and transportation facilities in the bistate area. In 1953 the same states signed another compact regulating labor practices in the New York port. Because of evidence of crime and racketeering on the waterfront, the states agreed to set up a bistate waterfront commission to regulate employment on the docks.

The states and commerce

The Constitution gives Congress sole power to regulate commerce among the states. The states can, of course, levy taxes for services that they supply to interstate commerce, such as highways for interstate trucks, and they can make border inspections to prevent anyone from bringing into a state fruit or plants that might introduce insects or disease. But the Supreme Court is particularly alert to strike down regulations adopted solely to favor local commerce at the expense of the national free-market system.

The commerce clause may also be utilized by Congress to achieve noneconomic goals in the states. For example, the Civil Rights Act of 1964 banned racial discrimination in hotels, motels, restaurants, and other facilities serving travelers in interstate commerce.

Interstate privileges and immunities

The various states have different systems of criminal, family, business, and tax laws, and with a highly mobile population these differences can cause problems. But certain basic rights are protected by the Constitution, which provides that "the citizens of each state shall be entitled to all privileges and immunities of citizens in the several states." Such privileges and immunities include the right to pass through or reside in another state, to institute or maintain court actions in any state, and to be exempt from having to pay higher taxes than are paid by the state's own citizens.

But there are some acceptable reasons for a state treating an out-of-state citizen differently from of a citizen of its own. State universities may charge a higher tuition for out-of-state students than for their own residents. Persons licensed by one state to practice law, medicine, or other professions involving the public interest must prove their competence and secure licenses in any other state in which they propose to practice. Higher fees for hunting or fishing may be charged to outsiders, on the ground that local citizens pay taxes that are used in part for the upkeep of the public domain. However, if the fees are exorbitantly discriminatory, they will be held invalid. Finally, a state can impose a reasonable residence requirement that must be satisfied before a new resident is allowed to vote in state elections. In 1972 the Supreme Court held that a one-year residence requirement was unreasonably long, and suggested that 30 days appeared to be ample time to register new arrivals to vote, but in 1973 it accepted a 50-day period.

The right to interstate travel. The right to travel from one state to another and to the seat of the national government has long been recognized as a basic privilege derived from the nature of the federal system. In *Shapiro* v. *Thompson* (1969) the Supreme Court ruled that it was unnecessary to ascribe the right to interstate travel to any particular constitutional provision, mentioning the commerce clause, the privileges and immunities clauses of Article IV and the Fourteenth Amendment, and the due process clause of the Fifth Amendment as possible constitutional supports for the right to travel. In the *Shapiro* case the Court invalidated state and District of Columbia statutes that denied welfare assistance to persons who had not been resident in the state for one year.[2]

Full faith and credit. Another unifying influence in the federal system is the provision in the Constitution that each state must accord full faith and credit to three types of official acts of sister states: public records, statutes, and court decisions. Public records create no problem, but the effect of

[2]In 1975 a federal appeals court ruled that an effort by Petaluma, California, to limit its growth was not an unconstitutional violation of the right to travel.

state statutes and court decisions in other states requires some explanation.

No state is obliged to enforce the criminal laws of another state. For other types of statutes, the general principle is that the full faith and credit clause does not necessarily require a state to subordinate its own policy to that of another state in case of conflict. The matter must be settled by appraising the respective interests of each state.

So far as judicial proceedings are concerned, the full faith and credit clause requires judgments conclusive in one state to be recognized as final in all states. This conclusiveness is not automatic. A litigant who has secured a court order in one state and wants to have it enforced against a person who has since gone to another state must bring a new legal action in the latter state. The court there will accept the original decree and examine it. If the court finds the order to be properly authenticated, it will issue an enforcement order of its own. The defendant may appear in court and contest the order, but he may not reargue the merits of the case.

Because of the lenient divorce laws in some states, major problems have arisen as to whether other states are required to give full faith and credit to "quickie" divorces. In the cases of *Williams* v. *North Carolina* (1942, 1945), two residents of North Carolina, which had relatively rigid divorce laws, went to Nevada, lived in a motel for six weeks, shed their respective spouses, married each other, and then returned to North Carolina. That state refused to recognize the validity of the Nevada decrees and brought bigamy charges against the couple, contending that six weeks' residence in Nevada was not enough to establish domicile there or give that state claim to jurisdiction over North Carolina residents. The Supreme Court in its 1945 decision upheld the right of North Carolina courts to decide for themselves, before giving full faith and credit to out-of-state decrees, whether or not residents of the state had established a bona fide domicile outside the state.

The *Williams* decision has not been overruled, but the chaos that this doctrine might cause if widely followed is so obvious that it is now generally agreed that "quickie" divorces do terminate the marriage in all states. However, some states have refused to accept such divorces as altering rights to property, alimony, or the custody of the children of their residents. The recent relaxation of divorce laws in most states has eased the situation, since fewer persons feel obliged to resort to out-of-state divorces.[3]

Extradition. Although the full faith and credit clause, as just noted, does not require a state to enforce the criminal laws of another state, there is a provision in the Constitution that a person charged with a crime who flees

---

[3]In 1975 the Supreme Court upheld a state law requiring residence of one year in the state to qualify for a divorce, rejecting the contention that this requirement was an unconstitutional interference with the right to travel *(Sosna v. Iowa)*.

to another state "shall on demand of the executive authority of the state from which he fled, be delivered up. . . ." Congress in 1793 passed a statute implementing this provision. But in *Kentucky* v. *Dennison* (1861), the Supreme Court held that Congress had not provided any means to compel the execution of this duty, and that the federal government could not constitutionally force a state official to take such action. Thus governors can, and occasionally do, refuse to honor a request for extradition. However, most of the states have adopted a uniform criminal extradition act. Also, Congress has helped out by adopting a law making it a federal offense for a person to go from one state to another with the intent of avoiding prosecution or imprisonment.

WEAKNESSES OF THE STATES

The states perform many of the functions that touch the lives of citizens most directly. By far the greater responsibility for the administration of the American system of justice resides with the state courts. The states plan, construct, and maintain the highway system. They have major responsibility for education, welfare, health, police, and safety functions. They register births, examine and license various professions and occupations, control the laws of marriage and divorce, and administer estates.

Yet state government was for many years the "dark continent" of American politics. State constitutions were ridiculously detailed—Louisiana's had 253,830 words, California's 82,570—so that adjustments to meet changed conditions could not be effected without amending the constitution.[4] The executive leadership of the governor was usually weak because of restrictions on his powers and tenure and the sharing of executive responsibilities with other elective officers. Patronage controlled appointment to many posts in state government. Special interests influenced the action of many legislators, and in some states major industries dominated the legislative channels—copper in Montana, oil in Louisiana, Texas, and California, Du Pont in Delaware, insurance in Connecticut. Most state legislatures were grossly unrepresentative and malapportioned, resulting in rural domination and lack of concern for the problems of the cities. State revenues were drawn primarily from the general property tax and the sales tax, both regressive in their impact.

The imbalance between the federal and state governments became acutely evident in the 1930s, during the New Deal period, when Washington came alive with a multitude of ambitious and novel programs and developed a well-trained bureaucracy to manage them. That was the period when the cities, struggling with depression problems, learned to look to Washing-

---

[4]In 1975 Louisiana replaced its constitution, which had been amended 537 times, by one only 35,000 words long.

ton for aid, rather than to the state capitals, still mired in the nineteenth century.

Revival of state government. All this has changed, or is changing. Under the mandate of the Supreme Court's "one person, one vote" decision, state legislatures have been more equitably reapportioned. The increased urbanization of the country has doomed the earlier rural domination. By the mid-1970s only 11 states (seven of them in the South) were less than 50 percent urban, and they contain only about 10 percent of the nation's population.

Staffing of executive offices has improved both in the cities and in the states. Mayors and governors are increasingly using planning staffs as resources for controlling and coordinating the activities of their governments. State and local administrators in the various social and technical services tend to approach the level of competence of their federal counterparts, since all are drawn from the same professional backgrounds and have the same professional goals.

State functions have grown and diversified. States are no longer mere road-builders and operators of prisons and mental institutions. A 1974 survey showed that the states were spending 40 percent of their revenues to support education, while another 25 percent went for welfare. In fact, state services were expanding much more rapidly than those of the federal government. From 1950 to 1970 the number of federal employees increased from 2.1 million to 2.9 million, but state employment went from 1.2 million to 3.0 million. Between 1960 and 1970 federal expenditures rose 69 percent (including the costs of the Vietnam war), but state and local expenditures rose 76 percent.

Again, state fiscal systems have become more equitable. By 1974 only five states had no income tax, and the states were drawing 23 percent of their revenues from personal income taxes, compared with only 9 percent some 15 years earlier. There was still heavy local reliance on the regressive general property tax, but many states were providing some relief for low-income taxpayers.

Federal grants-in-aid

State and local government functions have historically been financed in part from federal funds. In 1837 the federal government distributed surplus revenues to the states, and many public school systems, public institutions, and even highways of today trace their origins to that federal largesse. In 1862 the Morrill Act authorized massive grants of public lands to the states for the establishment of agricultural colleges. In 1887 Congress provided cash grants for the maintenance of agricultural stations, followed by grants for forestry in 1911, highways in 1916, vocational education in 1917, health

Table 4–1 *Federal aid to state and local governments, selected years (in millions of dollars)*

	1970	1972	1974
Health and medical care	3,831	5,974	7,542
General revenue sharing	—	6,636	6,147
Income maintenance, welfare	4,194	6,652	5,347
Highways	4,333	4,696	4,602
Housing and community development	2,432	3,427	3,878
Food stamps and child nutrition	938	2,571	3,837
Education	2,824	3,270	3,414
Environment and pollution control	606	907	2,732
Social services and vocational rehabilitation	963	2,442	2,650
Manpower and employment security	830	2,237	2,343
Agriculture and rural development	661	880	1,445
Law-enforcement assistance	41	321	708
Urban transportation	104	179	405
Total (includes other programs)	24,015	35,940	48,293

Source: Statistical Abstract of the United States, 1974.

in 1918, the social-security system in 1935, public housing in 1937, airports and hospitals in 1946, libraries in 1956, elementary and secondary education in 1965, urban development in 1966, and law enforcement in 1968. By the 1970s roughly one-fourth of all state and local revenues came from federal sources. Highway construction historically received the largest amount of federal grants, but in 1967 public assistance payments, primarily for welfare, took first place, and by 1974 health and medical care programs were receiving the most support. (See Table 4–1.)

Effects of federal grants. The purpose of federal grants is to promote activities that Congress regards as beneficial to the public welfare but which the states might not undertake without federal stimulus or be able to afford without federal financial support. To a certain extent, federal grants, which are distributed among the states according to formulas specified by Congress in each grant statute, can perform an equalizing function and enable the poorer states to bring their services up to an acceptable national minimum. For example, New Mexico received federal grants of $252 per capita in 1972, while Indiana got only $92. For every federal grant, the state is required to contribute some prescribed amount, but the proportion of this amount will vary from program to program. For the interstate highway program, the federal contribution is a high 90 percent, while the states contribute only 10 percent.

Another effect of the grant-in-aid system has been to revitalize some areas of state activity and enable the states to retain certain activities that might otherwise have become federal responsibility by default.

Federal grants are accompanied by regulations and requirements intended to ensure that state administration of the programs will meet acceptable standards; the threat of withdrawal of federal funds is a potential sanction against the states, although one that is seldom employed. Federal supervision over state highway building performance has been characterized as being limited to two concerns—"pour concrete and don't steal."

Two of the newer grant programs demonstrate how profound an influence federal money can have on local situations and institutions. Until recently, federal grants to education had been limited to specialized fields such as vocational training, but the Russian success with Sputnik in 1957 aroused concern about American scientific capabilities and led to the passage of the National Defense Education Act of 1958. Further aid to higher education and to the construction of higher education facilities followed, and, finally, elementary and secondary education was included on a massive scale by the act of 1965. These grants give Congress and federal officials the opportunity to influence local educational policies on such matters, for example, as rate of racial desegregation or the use of busing to achieve racial balance in the schools.

Even more unsettling to traditional practices was the Economic Opportunity Act of 1964, authorizing a number of antipoverty programs and giving the Office of Economic Opportunity great flexibility in dealing with state, local, or private organizations. The act's most distinctive creation was the "community-action agency" (CAA), a public or private nonprofit agency designed to coordinate a locality's existing institutional resources and utilize them in a community-action program (CAP) to alleviate poverty. The CAA was required to be broadly representative of community opinion in social welfare matters, and the CAP was to be developed and administered with "maximum feasible participation" of residents in the area and the groups served. Grants were made directly to the CAAs. A state governor could veto a contract, but his veto could be overridden by the OEO director in Washington. One of the most significant and controversial activities of OEO was the funding of a number of private nonprofit legal aid or "poverty law" offices throughout the country, which brought legal services for the first time to many poor people. This legal aid program was transferred to a new Legal Services Corporation when OEO was dismantled in 1974.

Objections to federal grants. A general objection to the grant system is that it limits state discretion in the spending of funds, and it forces the states to give priority to those activities that will bring in federal money. Another contention is that grants from Washington merely return to the states the tax receipts taken from their citizens, and that this is an unnecessary and costly process. The wealthy states, in particular, object that the federal grants that they receive represent a smaller proportion of the taxes paid by their citizens to the federal government than is the case with the poorer states.

In recent years, criticism has centered particularly on the "categorical" character of most grants, which specify in detail what local governments can spend for particular projects and encumber local officials in a maze of federal regulations. A count taken in 1969 revealed the existence of nearly 1,100 grant-in-aid programs, each with its separate set of specifications and requirements. As a corrective measure, it was proposed that federal funds be made available by "block grants," that is, in lump sums which the states or localities would be free to allot toward specified aid programs. Block grants were initially provided to cities in the Model Cities program, and to states for improvement of law enforcement under the Crime Control Act of 1968. In 1974 eight federal programs, including model cities and urban renewal, were consolidated into one block grant of $11.2 billion for housing and community development, designed to give local governments more control over the way federal aid money was spent.

Revenue sharing

An alternative to categorical or block grants is revenue sharing, under which the federal government simply returns to the states a designated amount of federal funds without any stipulations as to the purposes for which the

"I'm instituting a revenue-sharing program. I want you to share your revenues with me."
Drawing by Farris; © 1971 Saturday Review, Inc.

money must be spent. It was first proposed by the Council of Economic Advisers in the Johnson administration, and President Nixon made it a major plank in his domestic program. His initial proposal in 1969 generated considerable public support, but it was not until 1972 that a revenue-sharing act was passed by Congress, making available the sum of $30.2 billion over a five-year period. One-third of each state's share would go to the state government and two-thirds to local governments in the state. Allocation formulas took into account population, tax effort, and relative income. For New York the combined state and local grant totaled $591 million annually, for California $555 million.

Revenue sharing has proved understandably popular with state and local officials, and appears certain to be a permanent feature of federal-state relations. It will not, however, displace completely the categorical grant programs. Moreover, revenue sharing is not without its problems. It has the defects of its virtues, in that it permits federal funds to be spent without national purpose or direction, and without any requirement of specific performance from recipients. While Nixon said that revenue sharing would return power to the people, the act makes no stipulation about community participation in deciding on the disposition of funds. Some jurisdictions, however, have involved the local citizenry in these decisions. One of the few requirements in the act is observance of federal antidiscrimination statutes, but by 1974 there were only two civil-rights compliance field officers to check on annual grants amounting to $6 billion.[5]

Early experience with revenue-sharing decisions showed that the states tended to use their money to pay bills, lower or hold down taxes, balance budgets, or avoid borrowing money. Cities were more likely to spend their money on new programs involving environmental protection, transportation, recreational facilities, and public safety. Relatively small amounts were allocated to the poor and the elderly. A questionable aspect of revenue sharing is the distribution of funds to 38,745 units of local government, along with 178 Indian tribes and Alaskan villages, some of which have neither demonstrated a need nor provided a use for them. Moreover, the allocation formula fails to assure that jurisdictions with the greatest need get the greatest assistance.

FEDERAL CENTRALIZATION

Nearly everyone agrees in theory that too many domestic functions are concentrated in the federal government, and that the flow of power to Washington should be reversed. However, in actual practice, it is almost impos-

---

[5] The first enforcement effort occurred in late 1974 when a federal judge ordered a halt in revenue-sharing payments to the city of Chicago until the city ended discrimination in its police department. Revenue-sharing funds constituted 12 percent of the Chicago city budget for 1975.

sible to decentralize the functions of the federal government. Any effect that revenue sharing may have is likely to be offset by countervailing pressures on Washington for the assumption of additional functions.

The welfare system is probably the best example. The Social Security Act of 1935 established three "welfare" programs—aid to families with dependent children (AFDC), old-age assistance, and aid to the blind. Aid to the disabled was added in 1950. All programs were operated by the states, which made monthly cash payments to eligible indigents, with the federal government reimbursing the states for part of their costs.

By the 1960s there was universal agreement that this experiment in federalism had failed. The welfare outlays had risen so sharply that they placed a crushing burden on the taxpayers of the big cities and industrial states, where the indigents were concentrated. Standards of support vary enormously from state to state. In 1973 the average monthly AFDC payment for a family ranged from $52 in Mississippi to $269 in New York. Welfare families were consequently tempted to move to the higher level states, which in turn sought to reduce the inflow by imposing residence requirements for eligibility.

Appalled by what he called the "welfare mess," President Nixon, in spite of his principles against big government, proposed to replace welfare by a federally guaranteed family income plan. This idea proved to be too radical for many conservatives, and too conservative for many liberals. Consequently it failed in Congress, but no solution for the welfare problem can be visualized which does not involve increased federal participation.

It is axiomatic that national problems lead to pressure for national action. The crisis in medical and hospital costs makes national health insurance inevitable. Pollution of the nation's air and water and destruction of the environment by heedless exploitation of irreplaceable natural resources were too urgent perils to wait for individual state action. Since the 1930s no one questions the responsibility of the federal government to deal with the human consequences of a faltering economy. In the recession of 1974–75 the question was not whether but only how the federal government should respond to unemployment.

State racial discrimination in voting led to adoption of the Voting Rights Act of 1965, which denied states their traditional authority over voter qualifications. State failure to act against destructive strip mining has resulted in agreement that federal standards must be set. State regulation of the gigantic life and casualty insurance industry has been so ineffective in many states that federal regulation may be imminent.

Experiences such as these demonstrate that shifts of powers and functions from the states to the federal government are not the result of ideologies or conspiracies or Supreme Court decisions, but are the consequences of wars, depressions, increased population, new means of communication, urbanization, technology, and all the other factors that have shrunk the size of our world, endangered the environment, and created problems so large and so urgent that of necessity they require the attention of the national government. Slogans like "new federalism" will not reverse this process.

THE FUTURE OF THE STATES

Does this mean that the states have no future, or that they will wither away? It seems very unlikely. Obsequies have been pronounced over the states on many occasions, but for all their troubles the states continue to be active, essential, and in many respects successful partners in American federalism.

There are important administrative tasks for the states, not only in dealing with their traditional functions, but also in helping to meet the physical and social problems stemming from urbanization and suburbanization. The New Deal formula for handling each new need was to establish a new federal agency, but the recent political temper has been more favorable to local participation. There is no doubting the developing distaste for "big government." For that reason, it is particularly important to realize that an increase in federal responsibiilties does not mean that the federal government must do everything. In fact, many of the functions of the federal system have historically been performed jointly by two or all three levels of government. In the public health field, for example, federal, state, and local programs are so intertwined that it may be difficult for an official to know in what capacity he is operating at a particular time.[6]

The states have a strong bastion of support in the American party system. The national parties are merely federations of state and local parties, which join every four years, more or less loosely, to elect a President, and then go their separate ways for another four years. No movement for centralizing control over either major party has had the slightest success. So long as the power bases of the state parties remain untouched, so long as the states have equal representation in the Senate, so long as members of the House must live in the districts they represent and rely on local support to get elected, the political foundation of the states will be impregnable.

---

[6]For this reason it has been suggested that the proper analogy for the federal administrative system is not a three-layer cake, but rather a marble cake of merging and cooperative activities. Morton Grodzins, *The American System*, Chicago: Rand McNally, 1966, part II.

5
The Courts and Judicial Review

5

In Europe, courts were created by royal authority and evolved under royal direction. Judges were appointed and dismissed at the pleasure of the monarch. England was the first country to adopt the principle of judicial independence. Under the Settlement Act of 1701, judges were given security of office "during good behavior," and other European constitutional governments later followed the English example.

By contrast, in the United States there are no historical memories of a judiciary created by, or subservient to, the other two branches of government. The judicial branch was created directly by Article III of the Constitution at the same time and with the same status as the other two branches; it was neither inferior nor superior to them. At the time of the adoption of the Constitution, the judiciary might well have been regarded as a very junior partner in the governmental enterprise on the basis of its power potentialities. Alexander Hamilton made such an estimate in No. 78 of *The Federalist*:

> *The Executive not only dispenses the honors, but holds the sword of the community. The legislature not only commands the purse, but prescribes the rules by which the duties and rights of every citizen are to be regulated. The judiciary, on the contrary, has no influence over either the sword or the purse; no direction either of the strength or of the wealth of the society; and can take no active resolution whatever. It may truly be said to have neither FORCE nor WILL, but merely judgment. . . ."*

However, equipped only with the power of judgment, the Supreme Court has so utilized its moral and intellectual resources as to earn respect and authority equal to, if not in some degree greater than, that of the executive and Congress. It has come to occupy the position of official constitutional interpreter, philosopher, and umpire of the federal system. In its application of the Bill of Rights, it has functioned as the nation's principal forum for considering the operating conditions of a free society. Sometimes it has appeared to be a brake on progress, and sometimes it has been thought to be too progressive. Its decisions have often been unpopular. But even its strongest critics generally agree that it performs an essential function.

THE FEDERAL COURT SYSTEM

The Constitutional Convention created the Supreme Court, but left to Congress the decision whether there should be a system of lower federal courts. In the first Congress, the Anti-Federalists argued that one federal court (that is, the Supreme Court) was enough, and that the responsibility of enforcing federal law should be mainly entrusted to the existing state courts. But this view was defeated, and the Judiciary Act of 1789 provided for a complete set of federal trial and appellate courts. This was a decision of tremendous consequences for the strength of the central government. If state courts alone had been charged with the responsibility of trying cases involving federal law, they could hardly have been expected to be generous in their interpretations of federal power, and the Supreme Court as the sole federal court would have faced a hopeless task in trying to correct the errors of 50 state supreme courts.

Federal courts

The federal courts are organized in a three-level hierarchy. (See Figure 5–1.) The district courts, one or more of which is located in every state and in the District of Columbia, are the trial courts of the federal system. There are 93 district courts, with 400 district judges in 1975. Trials are held in the

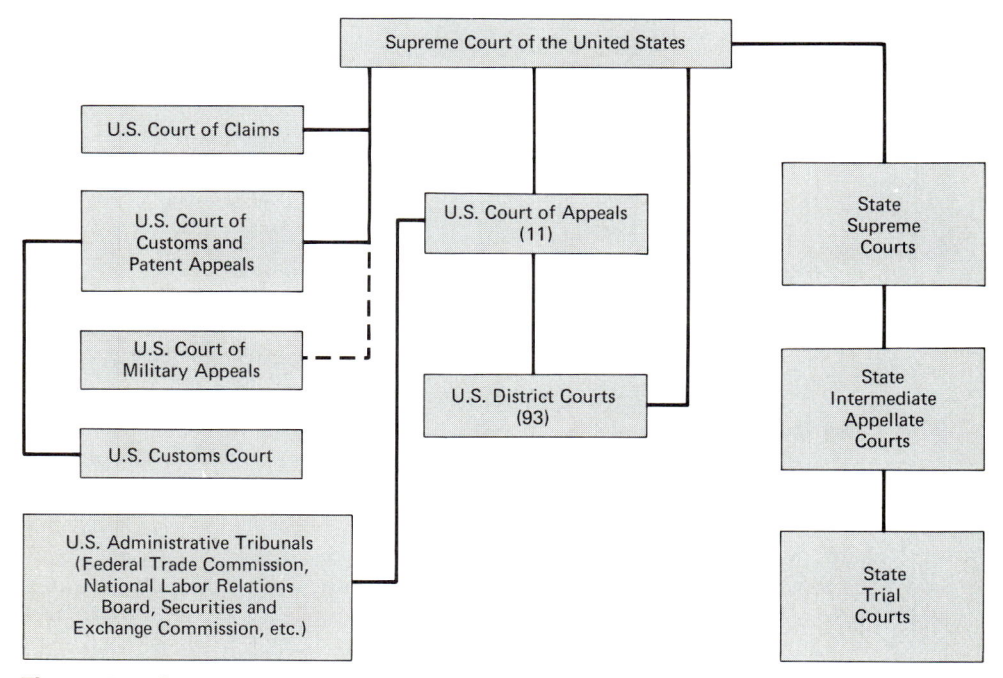

Figure 5–1 *Organization of the judicial system of the United States*

district courts before a single judge, except that when the constitutionality of a federal statute is questioned, and in certain other situations, three judges must sit in the trial of a case. Juries are frequently employed in both civil and criminal cases.

Appeals from the district courts go to the federal courts of appeals. The 50 states are divided into 10 judicial circuits, with an appeals court for each circuit, plus an additional appeals court for the District of Columbia. There are 97 judges for these courts, and appeals are usually heard by a panel of three judges. The courts of appeals also review orders of certain administrative agencies, such as the Federal Trade Commission and the National Labor Relations Board.

The Supreme Court. At the apex of the federal judicial hierarchy stands the U.S. Supreme Court. It is primarily an appellate court, but the Constitution does define two categories of cases that can be heard in the Court's *original jurisdiction,* that is, without prior consideration by any other court. These are cases in which a state is a party, and those affecting ambassadors and other diplomatic personnel. However, the Court generally does not accept a suit invoking its original jurisdiction unless it feels that there is a compelling reason of public policy for doing so.

All the remaining business of the Supreme Court comes to it in its *appellate jurisdiction,* which it exercises, as the Constitution says, "with such exceptions, and under such regulations as the Congress shall make." The number of cases filed with the Supreme Court every year (4,187 in the 1973–1974 term) is so great that of necessity it can consider and decide only a small proportion. It is true that Congress has provided for an *appeal* as a matter of right to the Supreme Court in certain classes of cases—for example, where a state court has upheld a state law against a claim that it violates the federal Constitution. In theory, the Supreme Court is obligated to accept all such appeals, but in fact it dismisses many of them on the ground that they do not present a substantial federal question.

In all other cases, review is sought from the Supreme Court by filing with the Court a petition for writ of *certiorari* (Latin for "to be certified"), which, if granted, directs the lower courts to send up the record in the case for review. Granting of the writ is completely at the discretion of the Court. The petitions are examined by the law clerks of the justices and then reviewed by all members of the Court. Petitions are granted if four justices vote in the affirmative. Usually no reason is given when petitions are denied, but, in general, the Court accepts only cases that present substantial issues of law or policy.

Petitioners who are unable to pay court costs of an appeal ask leave to proceed *in forma pauperis* (in the manner of a pauper). This relieves them of the docketing fee of $100, and of the necessity of having their court papers printed. Such petitions are often filed by prisoners seeking review of

Table 5–1 *Review granted in paid and* **in forma pauperis** *cases, U.S. Supreme Court, 1973–1974 term*

	PAID CASES		IN FORMA PAUPERIS CASES	
	No.	%	No.	%
Cases granted review	229	11.8	30	1.5
Cases summarily decided	147	7.5	41	2.0
Cases denied, dismissed, or withdrawn	1,572	80.7	1,942	96.5
Total	1,948	100.0	2,013	100.0

their convictions. It was a handwritten petition on yellow lined paper from a prisoner in Florida that inaugurated the famous case of *Gideon* v. *Wainwright* (1963).[1] While *in forma pauperis* petitions are given the same consideration as those submitted regularly, they are less likely to present substantial issues, and a smaller percentage are granted. (See Table 5–1.)

Jurisdiction

The jurisdiction of the federal courts is defined by Article III on two different bases: (a) subject matter, and (b) nature of the parties involved. The subject-matter classifications are:

1. All cases in law and equity arising under the Constitution
2. All cases in law and equity arising under the laws of the United States
3. All cases in law and equity arising under treaties made under the authority of the United States
4. All cases of admiralty and maritime jurisdiction[2]

Any case falling in these four fields can be brought in the federal courts, regardless of who the parties to the controversy may be.

Issues arising under the first three of these headings are referred to generally as "federal questions." A plaintiff seeking to bring a case in the federal courts on one of these grounds must set forth in his complaint a substantial claim as to the federal question involved, showing that an interpretation or application of the Constitution or a federal statute or treaty is essential to judicial decision of his case.

---

[1] In this case the Supreme Court established the principle that in every criminal case the defendant must have the assistance of counsel. See the fascinating account of the case in Anthony Lewis, *Gideon's Trumpet,* New York: Random House, 1964.

[2] This provision was included in the Constitution to promote uniform regulation of commerce.

The second basis for federal court jurisdiction is the nature of the parties involved. Article III extends federal jurisdiction to:

1. Controversies to which the United States is a party
2. Controversies between two or more states
3. Controversies between a state and citizens of another state
4. Controversies between citizens of different states
5. Controversies between a state, or the citizens thereof, and foreign states, citizens, or subjects
6. All cases affecting ambassadors, other public ministers, and consuls

Cases involving these classes of parties can be brought in the federal courts, regardless of the subject matter of the controversy.

Of these six classes, the first and the fourth generate the greatest amount of litigation. Suits in the fourth category, between citizens of different states, are commonly referred to as *diversity of citizenship* cases. The original purpose of opening the federal courts to these cases was to provide a neutral forum for the determination of such disputes, because the state courts might be biased in favor of their own citizens and against "foreigners" from other states. Today there is less likelihood of such bias, and many persons have urged the abolition or limitation of this class of federal jurisdiction, which imposes a very great burden on the federal courts.

The fact that a legal dispute meets the test of federal jurisdiction does not mean that it must be filed in a federal court. It is true that Congress has given the federal courts exclusive jurisdiction in some areas, notably in federal criminal, admiralty, patent, and bankruptcy cases. But in all other areas the state and federal courts enjoy *concurrent* jurisdiction over Article III cases, and the plaintiff can choose whether he wishes to file his suit in a state or federal court. Where such a suit is filed in a state court, however, the defendant can, if he prefers, by appropriate and timely action have the case transferred to a federal court for trial.

Where state courts do try cases involving the application of federal law, they are bound by the *supremacy clause* of the Constitution. Article VI, after making the Constitution, laws, and treaties of the United States "the supreme law of the land," continues: "And the judges in every state shall be bound thereby, any thing in the Constitution or laws of any state to the contrary notwithstanding."

STATE COURTS

The pattern of state judicial organization has been strongly localistic. When the country was sparsely settled and methods of communication and transportation were primitive, courts needed to be close to be convenient. The result was the widespread adoption of the justice-of-the-peace system to provide courts on a neighborhood basis. At the next higher level, courts tended to be established with reference to the distance a man could travel in a day on horseback. These local courts and judicial districts, once set up, proved very difficult to modify.

State courts are organized in hierarchies, often with overlapping jurisdiction. Justices of the peace or other part-time magistrates, where they still exist, constitute the lowest level of trial court. They typically are authorized to grant small money judgments, and as criminal courts to try minor offenses. They are not courts of record (that is, their proceedings are not recorded), and if their decisions are appealed, a new trial must be held in the next highest court.

Municipal or county courts are the courts of first instance for most civil, criminal, and probate (wills and estates) proceedings. Circuit or district courts are also trial courts, typically covering several counties and handling the more important civil and criminal cases.

Above the trial courts are generally two levels of appellate courts that review lower-court decisions; there are several intermediate appellate courts and one state supreme court. The easy availability of appellate consideration and the tremendous volume of appeals carried to the higher courts are characteristics in which the American legal system differs markedly from English and continental systems of justice. The technicalities and formalities of appellate consideration make the process very costly and time-consuming. Multiple appeals are possible and may keep a case pending in the courts for years.

The American state judicial system has traditionally been a very decentralized operation. There has been no central authority with responsibility for the conduct of judicial business, or with power to reassign judges where needed to deal with congested calendars. Judges have usually had to answer to no one for the efficiency of their courts or the volume of work they perform. Judicial independence, it has been assumed, requires judicial autonomy. However, under pressure of heavier case loads and public criticism, state court systems are increasingly supervising or monitoring the performance of judges through such devices as administrative judges in multijudge districts, state judicial councils, or offices of judicial administration operating under the chief justice of the state supreme court.

RELATIONS BETWEEN FEDERAL AND STATE COURTS

The U.S. Supreme Court is the final appellate tribunal for both the federal and the state courts. Any decision of a state supreme court that involves a substantial federal question (that is, application of the Constitution or the validity of federal laws or treaties) is subject to review by the Supreme Court. This power was not established without some resistance, however. Initially, many states could not reconcile themselves to the idea that their supreme courts could be checked by any higher authority, and there were some historic confrontations on this issue.[3]

Challenges to the power of the Supreme Court over state courts have been repeated occasionally during crisis periods, most recently after the Supreme Court's decision in *Brown v. Board of Education* (1954), holding racial segregation in the public schools unconstitutional. Several southern states adopted statutes of interposition or nullification, purporting to release the courts of their states from obedience to the *Brown* decision. In *Cooper v. Aaron* (1958), the Supreme Court was faced with the claim by the governor and legislature of Arkansas that they were not bound by the *Brown* holding. In rejecting this claim, the Supreme Court pointed out that "the principle that the federal judiciary is supreme in the exposition of the law of the Constitution" had been established as early as 1803 in the vital case of *Marbury v. Madison,* and that this principle "has ever since been respected by this Court and the Country as a permanent and indispensable feature of our constitutional system."

Even when the authority of the Supreme Court is fully recognized, there are numerous opportunities for conflict between the two systems of courts. In general, neither state nor federal courts may interfere with each other's proceedings or judgments by issuing writs of injunction; this is referred to as the doctrine of "equitable abstention." However, federal courts can enjoin state officials from enforcing unconstitutional statutes, and they can also enjoin state prosecutions in unusual cases which threaten great, immediate, and irreparable injury to a defendant's civil rights.[4] Also, under an 1866 act, defendants in state courts who are being prosecuted under laws denying their equal civil rights may have their cases removed to federal courts for trial.[5]

SELECTION OF JUDGES

Judges are selected by two principal methods. One is the pattern that prevails on the European continent and generally in the countries with the Roman civil-law tradition. There the judiciary is a professional career distinctly separate from the practice of law. Students intending to become judges take a special set of examinations after completing their law training. The successful candidates become career civil servants in the ministry of justice. They are assigned first to minor positions, and then by the process of promotion they may rise to the more important posts in the judicial hierarchy.

This system guarantees that its judges will be able and well trained. On

---

[3]The principal Supreme Court decision was *Martin v. Hunter's Lessee* (1816).
[4]*Dombrowski v. Pfister* (1965); *Younger v. Harris* (1971).
[5]*Georgia v. Rachel* (1966); *City of Greenwood v. Peacock* (1966).

the other hand, it leads to bureaucratization of the judiciary and some limitation on judicial independence, since advancement depends on pleasing one's superiors in the ministry.

By contrast, the Anglo-American pattern is to select judges from the practicing bar. There is no special training or internship for judges in England or America. In both countries, it is assumed that individuals who have achieved distinction or recognition in the practice of law will have the qualities needed to be a good judge. All English judges are appointed, as are all federal judges in the United States and some state judges. In many states, however, judges are elected.

The federal judiciary

The appointment of federal judges is frankly and entirely a political process. During the present century over 90 percent of all judicial appointments have gone to members of the President's party. For example, of the 176 judges named to the federal bench in the first Nixon term, 165 were Republicans. Appointees have typically been active in state or national party affairs, usually officeholders or perhaps unsuccessful candidates for office.

Appointment of judges for lower courts. In the nomination of judges for the lower federal courts, senators of the President's party from the state and state party officials play the dominant role, though the Department of Justice also conducts an active search for promising candidates. If there is a conflict of views between the senator and the Justice Department, the senator can threaten to block a nomination to which he is opposed at the confirmation stage, and so a compromise is usually arranged. Since the courts of appeals cover more than one state, vacancies must be allocated to the various states on some basis satisfactory to the party organizations. When the list of candidates has been narrowed, the FBI runs a full loyalty-security check, and the Justice Department seeks the approval of the American Bar Association Committee on the Federal Judiciary. This committee conducts its own inquiry, securing the views of the legal profession in the area concerned.

Appointment of Supreme Court justices. Vacancies on the Supreme Court present major policy problems for the President. He receives suggestions from many sources, particularly from his Attorney General, but he makes his own decisions. Often he has his own ideas on the subject, either as to specific candidates or as to the qualifications he wants. Presidents are usually interested in the political viewpoint of a possible nominee, and the line he is likely to take in deciding cases. Of course, predicting the future decisions of a man to be placed in a lifetime position on the bench is risky business. Theodore Roosevelt was unusually careful in picking men who could be expected to vote "right" on the big issues, and he was very angry when Justice Oliver Wendell Holmes, soon after his appointment to the Court, disappointed his expectations in an important antitrust case. President Taft felt that the most significant thing he had done during his administration was to appoint six justices who shared his conservative views. "And I have said to them," Taft chuckled to newspapermen when his term was expiring, "damn you, if any of you die, I'll disown you." President Nixon announced on taking office that he would appoint only "strict constructionists" to the Court.

The Senate must confirm all judicial appointees, and can thus impose effective restraints on executive choice. Washington saw one of his Supreme Court nominees rejected by the Senate, and in the nineteenth century over 25 percent of the nominations failed to negotiate the Senate hurdle. By contrast, during the first two-thirds of the twentieth century only one nominee was rejected by the Senate: John J. Parker was defeated in 1930, partly because of the opposition of labor and black organizations. There had been strong conservative opposition to Louis D. Brandeis in 1916, while liberals sought to defeat Charles Evans Hughes in 1931, but both were confirmed by substantial majorities. It was therefore a stunning reversal of precedent when within the space of two years, 1968 to 1970, both Johnson and Nixon saw two of their nominees fail to secure confirmation.

In June, 1968, Chief Justice Earl Warren notified Lyndon Johnson of his desire to retire, effective on confirmation of his successor. The President then nominated as Chief Justice his long-time friend and former legal counsel, Abe Fortas, whom he had appointed to the Court in 1965. Opposition developed to Fortas as a result of partisan politics, objections to the liberal decisions in which he had participated, and the revelation that he continued to act as a presidential adviser while he was on the bench. When a filibuster prevented the Senate from voting on the nomination, it was withdrawn at Fortas' request.[6] The following year, evidence that Fortas had agreed to accept an annual fee from a private foundation for research and advisory services while on the bench made it clear that he had failed to conform to accepted standards of judicial propriety, and he resigned, the first justice to leave the Court under such circumstances.

President Nixon's nomination of Warren Burger for the chief justiceship in 1969 was confirmed almost without opposition, in spite of his strongly conservative record. But the Senate, alerted to the issues of judicial ethics by the Fortas affair, carefully examined Nixon's nominee for the Fortas vacancy, federal appellate court judge Clement F. Haynsworth, Jr., of South Carolina. Certain indications of ethical insensitivity in his judicial record

[6]As a result, Chief Justice Warren remained in office for an additional year, and President Nixon was given the opportunity to name the new Chief Justice. On the Fortas case, see Robert Shogan, *A Question of Judgment: The Fortas Case and the Struggle for the Supreme Court,* Indianapolis: Bobbs-Merrill, 1972.

"I think I'll retire while I'm still young enough to enjoy the ruckus over the selection of my successor."
Drawing by Sabo; © 1971 Saturday Review, Inc.

were discovered which led to his rejection by the Senate by a vote of 55 to 45 in November, 1969.

The President then nominated another "strict constructionist," federal appellate court judge G. Harrold Carswell of Florida. His lack of intellectual qualifications for the position became obvious under Senate scrutiny, and he was rejected 51 to 45 in April, 1970.[7] Not since 1894 had two successive Supreme Court nominations been rejected by the Senate. Angrily charging that the Senate would not confirm a southerner, President Nixon then named another federal appellate court judge, Harry A. Blackmun of Minnesota, who was confirmed 94 to 0.

Both Justices Black and Harlan retired in the summer of 1971 for reasons of health, and both died shortly thereafter. Although these two men were among the most distinguished in the history of the Court, President Nixon's insistence on finding "strict constructionists" led him to propose to the American Bar Association committee for review a slate of six persons, all

---

[7]The story of the Carswell rejection is told in Richard Harris, *Decision,* New York: Dutton, 1971.

of whom were unknown nationally or obviously lacking in qualifications for the high court. The two candidates he preferred—one was the first woman seriously considered for the Court—were in fact rated as unqualified by the ABA committee. In a quick switch, the President avoided another bruising battle with the Senate by naming two much more able conservatives, a noted Richmond lawyer and former ABA president, Lewis F. Powell, Jr., and Assistant Attorney General William H. Rehnquist. Powell was quickly confirmed by a vote of 89 to 1, but Rehnquist encountered more opposition and the vote was 68 to 26, the largest vote against confirming a Supreme Court justice since Charles Evans Hughes was confirmed as Chief Justice in 1930.

It is sometimes argued that only persons with previous judicial experience should be given federal judicial appointments. Four of Eisenhower's five nominees were judges, as were Nixon's first four nominees. However, it would be unfortunate for presidential freedom of selection to be limited by a judicial-experience requirement, particularly at the Supreme Court level. The major questions confronting the Supreme Court require political judgment more than technical proficiency in private law. If judicial experience had been a prerequisite in the past, most of the greatest Supreme Court justices would have been ineligible for appointment, including Marshall, Story, Taney, Miller, Bradley, Hughes, Brandeis, Stone, Black, Frankfurter, and Warren.

The state judiciary

In the states, judges are both appointed and elected. The practice of electing judges was one of the bequests of Jacksonian democracy to the American system of government. Prior to 1832, only one state elected all its judges, but every state admitted to the Union from 1846 to 1959 provided for election of most or all of its judiciary. In spite of great current dissatisfaction with elective judges, two-thirds of the states still use election as a principal means of choosing their judges.

One problem with electing judges is that voters generally have no basis for deciding on the relative merits of candidates. Usually all they can do is to vote blindly for the candidates nominated by their party. This means that the judges are not really elected at all, but are in effect appointed by the party leaders who make up the ticket. The local bar associations usually poll their members on the relative merits of the candidates, and although even these results are not necessarily reliable, they are about all the independent voter has to go on in making his decisions.

Another objection is that judges who have to win elections are necessarily obligated to their political sponsors and supporters. Where judges run on a party ticket, they are expected to make a substantial contribution to the party campaign fund. Where judges are elected for a long term, the assessment may be one year's salary or more. Many lawyers who would make excellent judges refuse to submit themselves to the pressures, costs, and obligations of a political campaign.

Appointment of state and local judges by responsible political executives—governors or mayors—has generally come to be regarded as preferable to election. Although there is no guarantee that appointment will eliminate undesirable political influence, the responsibility for bad selections will be focused directly on the official who made the appointment.

The bar associations have urged that they be given greater responsibility for the selection of judges, on the grounds that this would take the process "out of politics." They propose that commissions of lawyers and other responsible citizens be established to name candidates who would be suitable for judicial positions, and that the appointments then be made from among these nominees. This idea was incorporated into a combined system of appointment and election adopted by Missouri in 1940. Under this plan, commissions are established to nominate judges at the various court levels. For the higher courts, the commission consists of seven members: the chief justice of the state supreme court, three lawyers elected by the state bar association, and three persons appointed by the governor, none of whom can hold public office or be a party official. This commission nominates three persons for each judicial vacancy, and the governor must appoint one of the three.

The elective feature of the Missouri Plan is that at the next election the new judge's name is placed on the ballot and the voters are asked whether the judge shall be retained in office. If the vote is favorable, the judge then serves out a specified term of years and is eligible for reelection. Some 11 states have now adopted the Missouri Plan or a variation of it.

TENURE OF JUDGES

Judicial independence and guaranteed tenure are among the most important criteria in determining how democratic a political system is. The independence of judges was established in England by 1701, long before broadly based political democracy had developed, and this was an important feature of the American heritage.

Recent experience in the Republic of South Africa has shown how the disintegration of a democratic system is signaled by attacks on the independence of the judges. Conversely, the courage and stature achieved by judges in West Germany and Italy after World War II constituted hopeful signs of the political maturity of those countries.

In the United States, most state judges serve for specified terms of years, but federal judges hold office during "good behavior," which in practice means life tenure. They can be removed only by impeachment; only four federal judges have ever been convicted on impeachment. Because some federal judges have insisted on remaining in office after their mental powers failed, Congress has encouraged the withdrawal of older judges by setting up attractive retirement arrangements. Life tenure, plus the constitutional provision that a judge's compensation may not be reduced while in office, constitute a strong guarantee of independence for the federal judiciary.

THE SUPREME COURT

The Supreme Court is composed of the Chief Justice and eight associate justices. Initially the Court had six members, but Congress later increased its size five times and reduced it twice. Since 1869 the membership of the Court has been stabilized at nine. In 1937 President Roosevelt's "Court-packing" plan would have authorized appointment of one new justice for each sitting justice who remained on the Court after reaching the age of 70, up to a maximum of 15. The plan failed to win general support and was defeated in Congress.

How the Court operates

The Supreme Court meets annually in October and remains in session, although with periodic recesses, until the following June. The Court formerly sat in the old Senate chamber in the basement of the Capitol, but it now occupies a palace of white marble so elegant that when it was completed in 1935, one justice suggested that the members of the Court ought to ride in on elephants.

The Court sits for four hours daily, Monday through Wednesday, in an impressive high-ceilinged courtroom, with enormous pillars and red velvet hangings. The justices meet in the robing room behind the drapes shortly before ten o'clock. By tradition, each justice shakes hands with every one of his colleagues. Promptly at ten the court crier raps his gavel, spectators rise, the velvet curtains part, and the justices come through to take their places behind the long bench as the crier chants:

> *The Honorable, the Chief Justice and Associate Justices of the Supreme Court of the United States! Oyez, Oyez, Oyez! All persons having business before the Honorable the Supreme Court of the United States are admonished to draw near and give their attention, for the Court is now sitting. God save the United States and this Honorable Court.*

During its public sessions the Court hears oral arguments in scheduled cases and announces its decisions. For every case on the docket, the record of the proceedings in the lower courts and briefs stating the arguments for each side are filed with the Court. The justices study these materials before the case comes up for hearing. The time for oral argument is strictly limited; except in the most important cases, counsel for each side will have one hour or less to address the Court. When time is up, a red light goes on at the lectern where the counsel stands facing the Court, and he must stop immediately. Legend has it that Chief Justice Hughes once called time on a lawyer in the middle of the word *if*.

Counsel seldom have an opportunity to make their arguments without interruption. The justices frequently break in with questions, comments, or requests for clarification. From the questions asked, it is often possible to predict how the individual justices are likely to vote in deciding the case. Probably their minds are not often changed by the oral argument, but it does give counsel a chance to emphasize what they feel are the main points for their side.

On Friday of each week when the Court has been sitting, the justices meet in conference to decide the cases heard that week. The proceedings are absolutely secret. Only the justices are present. The Chief Justice presents each case that is ready for decision, making such comments and offering such opinions as he chooses. Discussion then goes down the table, each associate justice speaking in order of seniority. When all have given their views on the case, voting begins. Now the order is reversed, the most junior justice voting first and the Chief Justice last. This proceedure maximizes the role of the Chief Justice, because he has the chance to formulate the issues initially and to break the tie if the associate justices are evenly divided.

Following the vote, the Chief Justice assigns the writing of the opinion of the Court to himself or one of his colleagues. However, if there is a divided vote and the Chief Justice is in the minority, the senior associate justice who voted in the majority controls the assigning of the Court's opinion. Drafts of opinions are circulated among the justices, and the author may revise the final opinion on the basis of comments by his colleagues. Justice Holmes once commented that this process amounted to taking out all the raisins and leaving the dough.

Concurring and dissenting opinions

In the early years of the Court, it was customary for all justices to give their opinions seriatim in a case, and there was no single opinion "of the Court." However, when Marshall became Chief Justice, he wrote the opinion for the Court in almost all important cases. Justices were still free to write *concurring* or *dissenting* opinions, but there was a tendency for them to go along with the Court unless they sharply disagreed. The fame of Justices Holmes and Brandeis as dissenters was based on the quality rather than the quantity of their dissents. Beginning about 1935, however, dissenting opinions became more frequent, and for the past several decades, non-unanimous opinions have far outnumbered unanimous ones.

In civil-law countries (continental Europe and Latin America), when the judges disagree, only the opinion of the majority is announced. There it is thought that a court must speak with one voice, disagreements being concealed behind the veil of official unanimity.

The Anglo-American common-law tradition has given more freedom to the judge, however. The possibility of registering dissents from the bench encourages and protects the independence of the judiciary and permits the development or maturing of alternative legal theories, which, although held by a minority today, may in time prove their greater vitality and become the accepted view. Chief Justice Hughes made this point.

A dissent in a court of last resort is an appeal to the brooding spirit of the law, to the intelligence of a future day, when a later decision may possibly correct the error into which the dissenting judge believes the court to have been betrayed.[8]

The role of the Chief Justice

The Chief Justice is extremely important, because he can develop a substantial position of leadership on the Court. His formal authority stems primarily from his role as presiding officer at Court sessions and in the conference, and from his power to assign the writing of opinions. But he is also the symbolic head of the Court, and if he has the skill and tact and prestige of a Hughes or a Warren, he can use his position to guide the decision-making process toward consensus and to keep discussion from bogging down in quibbling and personalities.

The most famous Chief Justice in Supreme Court history was John Marshall, the third Chief Justice (1801-1835), who used his influence so effectively that he must rate as one of the founders of the republic. For 35 years he dominated the Court, and he was second only to Washington in determining the initial character of the federal constitutional system.

THE POWER OF JUDICIAL REVIEW

The Supreme Court's power of judicial review can be separated into two categories. First is the power to declare acts of Congress unconstitutional, which Marshall claimed for his Court in *Marbury v. Madison* in 1803, and which also came to include the power to review the constitutionality of presidential actions. Second, the Supreme Court has the power of judicial review over the constitutionality of state legislation. (See Figure 5-2.)

---

[8] *The Supreme Court of the United States,* New York: Columbia University Press, 1928, p. 68.

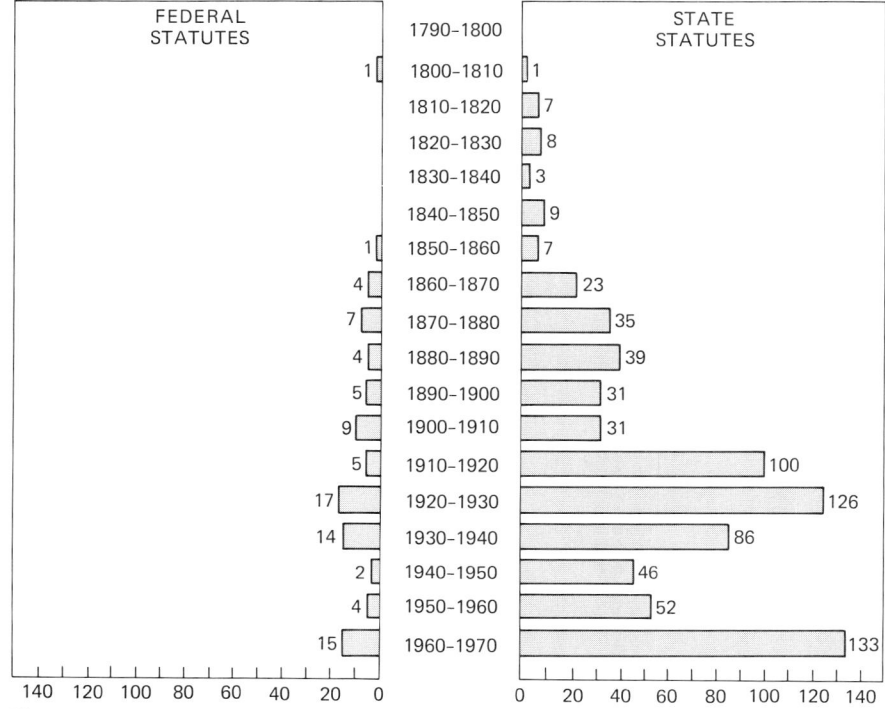

Federal Statutes	Decade	State Statutes
	1790–1800	
1	1800–1810	1
	1810–1820	7
	1820–1830	8
	1830–1840	3
	1840–1850	9
1	1850–1860	7
4	1860–1870	23
7	1870–1880	35
4	1880–1890	39
5	1890–1900	31
9	1900–1910	31
5	1910–1920	100
17	1920–1930	126
14	1930–1940	86
2	1940–1950	46
4	1950–1960	52
15	1960–1970	133

Figure 5–2 *Supreme Court decisions holding federal and state statutes unconstitutional, 1790–1970, by decades*
Based on data from The Constitution of the United States of America: Analysis and Interpretation, Senate Doc. No. 39, 88th Cong., 1964, pp. 1387–1522, supplemented by the authors for period 1964–1970.

Review of congressional and presidential acts

It is primarily the authority of the Supreme Court to judge the constitutionality of congressional and presidential acts that has made it the world's most powerful judicial institution. Surprisingly enough, this power was not specifically authorized by the Constitution, and this has led to endless and fruitless arguments as to whether the framers intended the Supreme Court to have such authority.

Marbury v. Madison. The case of *Marbury v. Madison* (1803) arose in the following way: Marbury had been appointed a justice of the peace for the District of Columbia by President Adams before he went out of office in 1801. The commission was signed and sealed, but the Federalist Secretary of State, none other than John Marshall, failed to deliver it on March 3. When President Jefferson took office on March 4, he instructed Madison, the new Secretary of State, not to deliver the commission. Marbury then filed a petition for mandamus to compel Madison to deliver the commission.

He filed it directly in the Supreme Court, thus invoking the Court's original jurisdiction under the Judiciary Act of 1789.

As Chief Justice,[9] Marshall seemed to have two alternatives: The Court could grant Marbury's petition, or it could deny it. Whichever Marshall did, it seemed that he was bound to lose the contest for power and prestige to his great antagonist, Jefferson. If the writ was issued, Madison, with Jefferson's support, would refuse to obey it, and the Court would have no practicable means of compelling him to do so. If the Court refused relief to Marbury, it would be admitting officially that it was powerless to control the executive. In either event, the judiciary and the Federalists would be humiliated, and the triumph of Jefferson and the Democrats would be complete and obvious.

In this situation, Marshall's decision was a masterful stroke. He ruled that the Judiciary Act of 1789, in authorizing the Supreme Court to grant writs of mandamus in its original jurisdiction, had unconstitutionally extended the Court's original jurisdiction beyond that provided for in the Constitution. The Court consequently declined to issue the writ, leaving Madison and Jefferson with nothing to deny or resist. The writ was refused not because the Court lacked power to give relief against executive officers, but because the Court asserted and exercised the much greater power of finding an act of Congress unconstitutional.

There were three steps in Marshall's argument as to why the Court should not enforce a statute that was contrary to the Constitution. First, the written Constitution is the fundamental law, superior to common and statute law, and subject to change only by the amending process. Second, the powers of the various branches of government are limited by the terms of the Constitution, and their actions are valid only when in conformity with those limits. Third, the judges had sworn to enforce the provisions of the Constitution as the superior law, and were therefore obligated to refuse to enforce any legislative act or executive order that was in conflict with the Constitution.

This is a powerful argument, but it is not without its flaws. The President also takes an oath to support the Constitution. Does this give him the right to refuse to enforce a duly adopted act of Congress that he regards as unconstitutional? Marshall's argument rested on a basic, but unstated, assumption that the Supreme Court is better qualified to interpret and to apply the Constitution than the other two branches. This is not necessarily true, but it has now been accepted as true for over a century and a half, and it constitutes a fundamental premise of judicial review.

It was proposed as an alternative to Marshall's position that each of

---

[9]Marshall had been appointed Chief Justice by President Adams on January 20, 1801, and had been confirmed by the Senate on January 27, so he was Chief Justice and Secretary of State at the same time for more than a month.

the three branches should be the final interpreter of its own powers under the Constitution. Actually, this principle would have been adequate to sustain the *Marbury* decision, because the Court was there passing on the issue of its own original jurisdiction. But recognition of three final interpreters of the Constitution would have led to great confusion in the many constitutional areas where there is no strict separation of functions.

The importance of the Court's role as sole authoritative interpreter of the Constitution was not simply that it justified the Court in declaring acts of Congress unconstitutional. It enabled the Court to exert a continuing influence on the development of the nation, and to operate as a major participant in American political life. The Court could check not only Congress but also the President, as was demonstrated when it undertook to declare President Roosevelt's New Deal unconstitutional by declaring its most important legislative enactments invalid in 1935 and 1936. It could also serve as umpire in disputes between the President and Congress, such as occurred in 1952 when President Truman seized the steel mills to prevent a strike that might have cut off needed munitions for American troops in Korea. The Court appreciated the President's motives, but concluded that Congress had made clear its intention that the President should not possess the seizure power, and so ordered the mills returned to their owners. The Court's decision in *United States* v. *Nixon* (1974) ordering President Nixon to turn over White House tapes essential to the Watergate cover-up trial of five Nixon aides exposed his participation in the cover-up and forced his resignation.

Review of the constitutionality of state legislation

The second aspect of judicial review is the Supreme Court's authority to pass on the constitutionality of state legislation. As already explained, any decision of a state supreme court involving a "federal question," that is, one arising under the Constitution, laws, or treaties of the United States, can be appealed to the Supreme Court. Only in this way can constitutional provisions be given uniform interpretation and effective application throughout the United States.

By this power over state legislation, the Supreme Court is also enabled to serve as umpire in disputes between the nation and the states. Every federal system requires an allocation of authority between the two levels of government, and conflicts over the division of functions are bound to occur. To make the federal system work, there must be rules for deciding such contests and an umpire to apply these rules. In all the successful federal systems—Canada, Australia, Switzerland, West Germany, as well as the United States—the highest court performs this function.

As umpire of the American federal system, the Supreme Court must necessarily have power to declare invalid any state legislation or other state action that infringes on the constitutional authority of the central government or the other states in the federal union. By 1970 the Court had held unconstitutional provisions of state constitutions or statutes in 737 decisions, as well as invalidating some 90 municipal ordinances. Justice Holmes thought it was more important for the Supreme Court to have the power to review state legislation than acts of Congress. He said:

> *I do not think the United States would come to an end if we lost our power to declare an act of Congress void. I do think the Union would be imperilled if we could not make that declaration as to the laws of the several States. For one in my place sees how often a local policy prevails with those who are not trained to national views. . . .*[10]

In its role as umpire of the federal system, the Supreme Court enforces three kinds of restrictions on the states.

First, it measures state legislation by constitutional standards. The original Constitution contained certain provisions aimed directly at the states. But by far the most important constitutional limitations on the states are those imposed by the Fourteenth Amendment, which forbids them to deprive any person of life, liberty, or property without due process of law, or to deny to any person within their jurisdiction the equal protection of the laws. The due process clause is important not only in itself, but also because the Supreme Court has interpreted it as making the First Amendment and most of the other provisions of the Bill of Rights effective against the states. The next three chapters are largely concerned with discussing the Supreme Court's application of the due process and equal protection standards to the states.

Second, as umpire of the federal system, the Court must determine whether state legislation conflicts with congressional legislation. While state statutes may infringe on acts of Congress in many areas, the most persistent problems arise in connection with the regulation of commerce. The first case the Supreme Court ever decided involving the commerce clause, *Gibbons v. Ogden* (1824), concerned New York's effort to establish a monopoly on steamboat transportation in its waters. The states do possess considerable power to regulate commerce, but they must yield if Congress has "preempted" the field by adopting regulations of its own. Since Congress often does not make clear in passing a regulatory statute whether it intends to exclude state regulation, the Supreme Court may have to use its own judgment as to whether enforcement of the state law would be harmful to national interests. In this field, the Supreme Court has performed one of its most important functions by protecting the national economy from discriminatory local regulation and taxation.

Third, the Supreme Court acts as arbiter of the federal system by set-

---

[10] "Law and the Court," *Speeches*, Boston: Little, Brown, 1934, p. 102.

tling disputes among the states. Litigation between states is handled by the Court in its original jurisdiction. Typical subjects of controversy are boundaries, water rights, and monetary obligations. In 1963 the Supreme Court finally settled in favor of Arizona a 40-year-old contest between that state and California over water rights in the Colorado River and its tributaries (*Arizona v. California* [1963]).

Interpretation of congressional statutes

The Supreme Court has another function which, although less dramatic than reviewing the constitutionality of acts of Congress or serving as umpire of the federal system, is very important in its total impact. This is interpreting Congressional legislation as it is applied in lawsuits decided by the Court. The Court held only 21 acts of Congress unconstitutional between 1940 and 1970, but during that period it determined the meaning of federal statutes in hundreds of cases whose results were often more significant than those occasioned by a ruling of unconstitutionality. For example, in 1957 the Court practically knocked out the Smith Act as a weapon for jailing Communists by the interpretation it gave to the word "organize" in that statute (*Yates v. United States* [1957]). Again, in 1958, the Court held that the State Department could not refuse to grant passports to Communists, because the statute on which it was relying did not grant that authority (*Kent v. Dulles* [1958]).

It is always possible for anyone who dislikes the Supreme Court's interpretation of a statute to appeal to Congress and ask that the offending interpretation be reversed by new language. In 1958, after the passport decision, the State Department and President Eisenhower made an urgent appeal to Congress for statutory authorization to deny passports to Communists, but Congress, taking a less serious view of the problem, failed to act and hence let the Supreme Court interpretation stand. On many occasions, business interests have gone to Congress seeking reversal of unfavorable Supreme Court statutory interpretations, and often these efforts are successful. One example concerned the Supreme Court ruling that the Du Pont Company must dispose of its vast holdings of General Motors stock. Congress passed a law confirming that the stock must be disposed of, but under more favorable conditions than the Court had imposed.

Controversy over judicial review

The Supreme Court, because of the great powers it wields, has been the perennial center of controversy. In the nineteenth century, according to Charles Evans Hughes, the Court made three major errors, which he characterized in a famous phrase as "self-inflicted wounds." The first was the Dred Scott decision in 1857, which held that Negroes could not be citizens of the United States and helped to bring on the Civil War. The second was the post–Civil War Legal Tender Cases, where the Court first ruled by a vote of 4 to 3 that the paper money issued to finance the war was unconstitutional, and then after President Grant had filled the two vacancies on the Court promptly reversed itself and upheld paper money by a 5-to-4 vote. Third was the ruling in 1895 that the federal income tax was unconstitutional, a holding subsequently reversed by the Sixteenth Amendment.

The Court and the New Deal. The conservative Court was finally defeated by the Depression of the 1930s and President Roosevelt's legislative program for restoring prosperity. Ignoring the changed temper and economic conditions in the country, the Court in 1935 and 1936 declared unconstitutional a whole series of New Deal recovery statutes, usually by votes of 5 to 4 or 6 to 3. Although Roosevelt's effort to change the Court's thinking by "packing" it failed, in several key cases in the spring of 1937 the Court upheld New Deal legislation by a vote of 5 to 4, and the crisis was over. This was "the switch in time that saved nine." Soon afterward there were vacancies to be filled and within a few years the Court was composed almost entirely of Roosevelt appointees.

The Roosevelt revolution precipitated a remarkable change in the relation of the Court to American politics and in the character of its public support. For the first time in history, the Court began to move ahead of public opinion instead of lagging behind, particularly in controversial areas involving civil liberties and political rights. But the Court itself was split on these issues. In a classic confrontation, Justices Hugo Black and Felix Frankfurter, representing the contrasting positions of judicial activism and judicial restraint, disagreed on the extent to which the Court should intervene to support libertarian values.

Justice Black believed that the First Amendment freedoms occupied a *preferred position* among American liberties, because a free and democratic society could not exist without freedom of speech, press, and assembly. He tended to be an absolutist in the enforcement of these freedoms. When the First Amendment says, "Congress shall make no law," he insisted that it meant what it said, and the Court should not hesitate to strike down legislation that violated this command. Justice Frankfurter, on the other hand, was reluctant to declare legislation unconstitutional, because he regarded legislatures as the most democratic branch of government and thought judges should defer to their decisions except in highly unusual cases. He insisted that the values of rights and liberties were not absolute; they must be balanced against the claims of authority and order.

In 1954, however, both sides united in the Court's portentous ruling that racial segregation in the public schools was unconstitutional (*Brown* v. *Board of Education of Topeka*). The *Brown* decision inaugurated a period of almost continuous controversy for the Warren Court. Opposition to the ruling was in part reasoned, but also in part vituperative in the extreme, calling into question not only the ability but also the motives and the patriotism of the justices.

In 1957 the Court raised up additional enemies when it handed down decisions limiting the investigation of Communists by congressional committees and their criminal prosecution under the Smith Act (*Watkins* v. *United States; Yates* v. *United States*). In some quarters these decisions were regarded as a threat to national security, and in the 1958 session of Congress these forces joined with opponents of the *Brown* decision to support a number of measures to "curb" the Court. With one minor exception, all of these bills were defeated, some by very narrow margins. Court-curbing was no more acceptable in 1958 than court-packing had been in 1937.

In the 1960s the Warren Court's difficulties were compounded by controversial decisions in three areas. First, two decisions held that it was an unconstitutional establishment of religion for a state to require prayer or Bible-reading in the public schools (*Engel* v. *Vitale; School District* v. *Schempp*). Second was the line of "one man, one vote" decisions, initiated by the Court's ruling in *Baker* v. *Carr* in 1962, in which the Court held that in the national House of Representatives and in both houses of state legislatures the districts from which legislators were elected must be approximately equal in population. Finally, there was an entire series of cases, beginning with *Mapp* v. *Ohio* (1961), and including the famous decisions in *Escobedo* v. *Illinois* (1964) and *Miranda* v. *Arizona* (1966), in which the Court imposed stricter standards on state criminal investigations and prosecutions.

Concerted efforts were made in Congress to overturn the first two groups of decisions by constitutional amendment. The amendment authorizing prayer in the public schools failed initially, but was still a live issue in Congress in 1975. An amendment to exempt one house in each bicameral state legislature from the equal-population district requirement, sponsored by Senator Everett Dirksen, failed to obtain the necessary two-thirds vote in the Senate in 1965 and 1966. His subsequent campaign to induce two-thirds of the state legislatures to call for a constitutional convention to achieve the same end fell barely short of its goal, securing approval by 33 of the required 34 states.

Perhaps the greatest opposition was reserved for the Court's criminal procedure decisions (to be discussed in more detail in Chapter 6). Attacks on the Warren Court for "coddling criminals" and weakening the "peace forces" of the country were responsible for inclusion of some anti-Court provisions in the Crime Control and Safe Streets Act of 1968, and reached a climax in Richard Nixon's campaign for the presidency in 1968 on a "law and order" platform. Nixon's four appointments gave the Court a substantially more conservative orientation, particularly in the criminal punishment field, where important Warren Court decisions were modified or reversed. However, the Court still remained a center of controversy. Over the opposition of the four Nixon appointees, capital punishment was held to be unconstitutional in 1972 (*Furman* v. *Georgia*), and by a 7 to 2 vote in 1973 the Court invalidated state criminal abortion laws, a subject of enormous sensitivity which previous courts had never dared touch.

Is judicial review compatible with democracy?

Throughout its history, opponents of the Supreme Court, from Jefferson to the John Birch Society, have complained that it was exercising political power and that the justices were misusing their judicial authority to make policy decisions which, in a democratic system, belong to the elected branches of the government. *Brown* v. *Board of Education of Topeka* in 1954 and *Baker* v. *Carr* in 1962 demonstrated how in fact the judges can seize the leadership in dealing with problems vital to the public welfare. The issue is whether American democracy is stronger or weaker because of the possibility of judicial participation in national policy-making.

The case against a strongly activist Court has been soberly stated by members of the Court itself. During the 1920s and 1930s, when the conservative majority on the Court was declaring liberal legislation unconstitutional, Justice Holmes was constantly telling his colleagues that they must not prevent the enforcement of laws that reasonable men could regard as helpful in solving society's problems. When the Court's interference with the legislative will reached its climax in 1936, Justice Stone warned the Court that "the only check upon our own exercise of power is our own sense of self-restraint," and he added: "For the removal of unwise laws from the statute books appeal lies not to the courts but to the ballot and to the processes of democratic government" (*United States* v. *Butler*).

As the Court of the 1950s and 1960s actively intervened to promote civil and political rights, it heard similar warnings about the dangers of political involvements. Justice Frankfurter questioned the credentials of the Court for making policy judgments: "Courts are not representative bodies. They are not designed to be a good reflex of a democratic society" (*Dennis* v. *United States* [1951]). Justice Harlan, objecting to the Court's getting involved in the "political thicket" of legislative apportionment, protested the "current mistaken view . . . that this Court should 'take the lead' when other branches of the government fail to act." The Supreme Court, he said, is "a judicial body," not "a general haven for reform movements" (*Reynolds* v. *Sims* [1964]).

The opposing view, that an activist Court is not incompatible with democracy, stresses two main considerations. First, the Court, although not elected, is dependent in many ways on the elected branches of the government, and so is not free from popular control. For example, the Court may need help from the executive or legislature to get its decrees enforced. President Jackson is reported to have said, concerning one of the Supreme Court's rulings: "John Marshall has made his decision. Now let him enforce it." In 1954 the Supreme Court handed down its ruling that racial segregation in the public schools was unconstitutional, but it was not until Presidents Kennedy and Johnson took an interest in the problem and Congress applied the pressure in the Civil Rights Act of 1964 and the Education Act of 1965 that compliance with the ruling began to be achieved in the more recalcitrant states.

Of course, the President's greatest impact on the Court is through the power of appointment. Given a normal rate of turnover on the Court, a President can make its membership representative of current political ideas. If he is unhappy with the trends of decisions on the Court, he can let the Court know about it, as President Roosevelt did.

As for Congress, the senatorial power of confirmation, as demonstrated by the Fortas filibuster, can be the occasion for flashing warnings of legislative displeasure to the Court. Judicial decisions based on statutory interpretation can be appealed to Congress by a request for new legislation. If it ever became sufficiently aroused, the Congress could completely abolish the Court's appellate jurisdiction. In fact, Congress can pass any legislation it likes concerning the Court, short of reducing the salaries of sitting justices, taking away its original jurisdiction, or abolishing the Court entirely.

Second, it can be argued that when the Supreme Court's activism takes the form of protecting individual rights against infringement by federal or state governments, it is performing a most valuable democratic function. Perhaps more important than any other feature of the judicial process for democratic theory is its accessibility to individuals and minorities. Executives and legislatures are responsible to mass constituencies. Only large interests and effective pressure groups have the chips to get into the game of politics today.

The courts, however, are open to anyone with a valid case or controversy. America's largest racial minority, even after it had begun to organize through such groups as the NAACP, lacked the political power to secure an effective hearing from a series of Presidents and Congresses. It was only in the courts that its constitutional claims to equal protection could be registered. Even a penniless convict in a state penitentiary who claims he has been denied due process of law can have his case considered by the Supreme Court by mailing it a handwritten petition.

Judicial review in other countries

The American system of judicial review has few parallels elsewhere in the world. In most democratic countries, the tendency is to regard constitutional provisions more as guidelines for legislative acts or statements of fundamental principles of government, rather than as strict rules of law to be authoritatively interpreted and enforced by the judiciary. In Britain, the defense of individual rights and liberties has been centered in Parliament rather than in the courts. Parliament concerns itself not only with general principles of individual liberty through legislative measures but also with issues affecting individual violations of civil liberties. Thus the government is under constant pressure to observe and enforce accepted standards of civil liberty.

It is noteworthy, however, that following World War II several countries—including the three defeated Axis powers, Germany, Italy, and Japan—did follow the American example by establishing strong supreme courts with responsibilities for constitutional interpretation. The West German Federal Constitutional Court of 16 judges deals with constitutional disputes between state and federal governments, between states, and between high federal departments, controversies involving the validity of state or federal legislation; and constitutional complaints by private citizens alleging violation of their basic rights. The Court also has important authority over political parties, with power to declare a party unconstitutional if its purpose is to impair the democratic order or jeopardize the existence of the Federal Republic. In 1975 this court struck down a liberalized abortion law as in violation of the constitutionally protected "right to life." Within the same week the Italian Constitutional Court of 15 members upheld abortion as legal if pregnancy threatened a woman's health.

The Supreme Court of Japan was created as part of the legal reforms imposed by the Allied Occupation under General Douglas MacArthur after World War II. Composed of 15 members appointed by the Cabinet, it has not achieved a high level of visibility, nor have its decisions often touched on major public issues. The principal exception was a 1959 decision upholding the treaty providing for the stationing of U.S. troops in Japan.

The Indian Supreme Court of 11 members is appointed from the regional high courts by the prime minister and the Cabinet. It has original jurisdiction over disputes among states and claims of infringement of constitutionally protected fundamental rights, as well as a broad appellate jurisdiction. Fundamental rights include rights to property, freedom of speech and expression, freedom of religion, equality before the law, and the right of minorities to conserve their culture and language.

In 1974 France amended its constitution to permit a limited form of judicial review by a nine-member Constitutional Council. On petition by 60 members of either house of the legislature, the Council will determine whether a law passed by the legislature violates civil liberties.

6
Criminal Punishment and the Constitution

6

The principal protections provided to the individual suspected of a criminal act are found in the Bill of Rights (specifically, the Fourth through the Eighth Amendments). The Fourth guarantees protection from unreasonable searches and seizures. The Fifth contains not only the due process clause, but also the assurance of trial by jury and freedom from double jeopardy and self-incrimination. The Sixth specifies the essential features of a fair trial, including notice to the defendant of the accusation against him, confrontation with witnesses, and impartiality of the jury. The Eighth forbids excessive bail, excessive fines, and cruel and unusual punishment. (See Figure 6–1.)

In addition to these provisions, there are other fundamental tenets of Anglo-Saxon criminal law that were such a basic part of the American heritage that they were not specifically mentioned in the Constitution. Among these principles were that an accused person is innocent until proved guilty; that the burden of proof rests on the prosecution; that guilt must be established beyond a reasonable doubt; that guilt is personal; and that no one can be punished because of acts of others for which he had no responsibility.

These provisions and principles are not self-enforcing, however, and their implementation will depend upon the conception held by the courts and the public concerning the nature and purposes of criminal punishment. In an influential book Herbert Packer hypothesized two opposing models of the criminal process.[1] One, which he called the due process model, begins with the presumption of legal innocence, which may be overturned only through the full operation of adversary trial proceedings. The model relies on formal procedures as a guard against the abuse of discretionary power by the police, prosecutors, and judges. It recognizes that strict enforcement of formal procedures may result in the factually guilty going free. It stresses the primacy of the individual in confrontation with the awesome power of the law-enforcement machine.

The crime control model, on the other hand, assumes that the repression of criminal conduct is the most important function to be performed

---

[1] Herbert L. Packer, *The Limits of the Criminal Sanction,* Stanford, Stanford University Press, 1968.

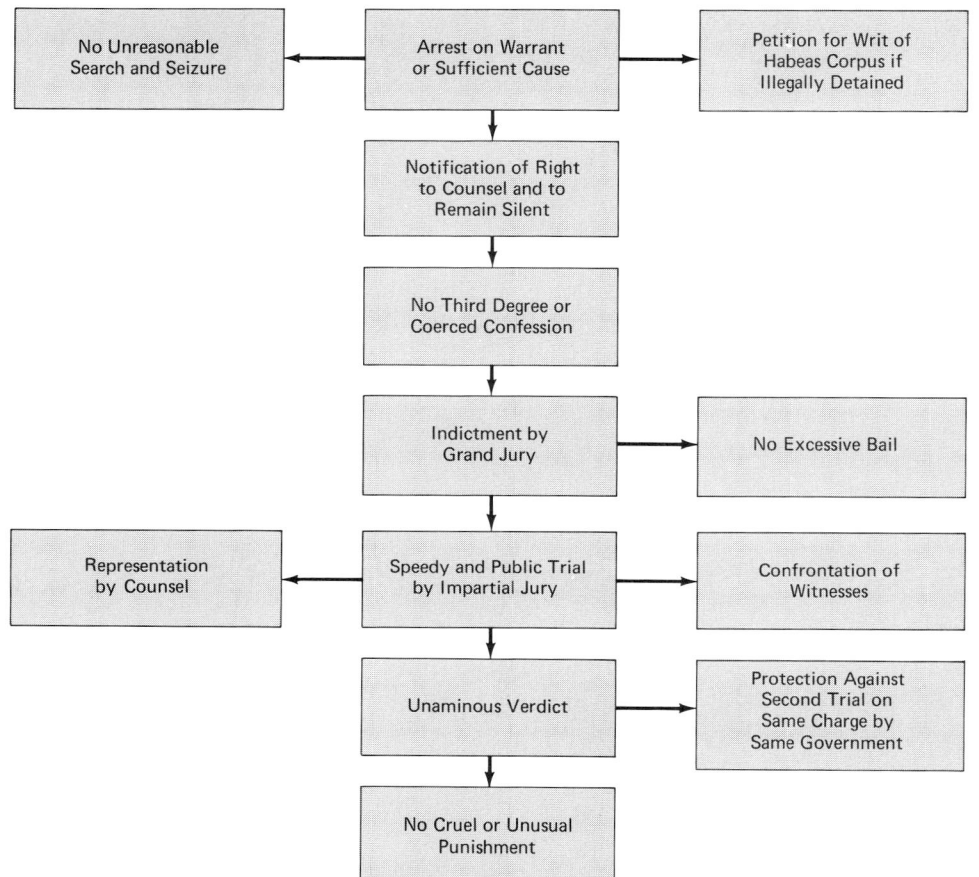

Figure 6-1 *Constitutional protection for persons accused of crime in federal courts*

by the criminal process, and that maximum efficiency in catching and convicting criminals is its goal. Efficiency requires informal procedures and the elimination of obstacles to the fact-finding process. Once a *prima facie* case has been established by preliminary fact-finding, there is a presumption of guilt which reduces the significance of the adversary trial.

Packer sums up: The crime control model resembles an assembly line, while the due process model looks very much like an obstacle course. In the discussion that follows, it may appear that the Warren Court exemplified the due process model, while the Burger Court sought to reestablish the earlier dominance of the crime control model.

THE FEDERALISM PROBLEM

Before looking at American practices of criminal prosecution, we must clarify an important preliminary issue related to the American dual court system. In *Barron* v. *Baltimore* (1833), the Supreme Court ruled that the Bill of Rights was a limitation only on the federal government and not on the states. Consequently, state criminal prosecutions were not controlled by national standards. Not until the Fourteenth Amendment was adopted in 1868 was there any constitutional basis for federal concern about the standards and processes of state criminal justice. And even then, state courts were controlled only by the general standard of due process of law.

An interesting problem was thus created for the federal system and for the Supreme Court, which was ultimately responsible for determining the constitutional standards for both federal and state courts. For a long time the Supreme Court held that the *state* courts, bound only by the need to give due process, were free to adopt practices that would be unconstitutional in the *federal* courts because they were forbidden by specific provisions in the Bill of Rights. "Due process" was a comparatively loose requirement, the Court thought. It left the states free to experiment and to adopt diverse approaches toward their practices of criminal justice. As Justice Cardozo said in *Palko* v. *Connecticut* (1937), the states were free to adopt any standards so long as they were not in conflict with "the concept of ordered liberty" and did not violate principles of justice "so rooted in the tradition and conscience of our people as to be ranked as fundamental."

Although this rule gave interesting recognition to the diversities of American federalism, it did create two major difficulties. One was the problem for the Court itself of deciding which procedures were necessary to ordered liberty and which might be ignored without denying equal justice under law. The members of the Court often disagreed on what was essential and what was nonessential; Justice Black charged that the "ordered liberty" test permitted the Court to substitute "its own concepts of decency and fundamental justice for the language of the Bill of Rights."

The second difficulty involved explaining to ordinary citizens, untrained in the intricacies of constitutional law, how it was that the American Constitution did not equally protect defendants in state and federal courts. How could one explain why a federal court had to appoint counsel for a defendant too poor to hire one, whereas a state court did not? How could it be justified that a defendant could be convicted in a state court on evidence that could not have been legally presented in a federal court?

The pressure of such anomalies led the Warren Court very largely to abandon the effort to apply differing constitutional tests to state and federal courts, but after 1969 the Burger Court began to return to the states some of their earlier exemptions from federal constitutional standards.

RIGHTS OF THE CRIMINAL SUSPECT

Unreasonable searches and seizures

Evidence of lawbreaking must be secured by law-enforcement officers to support a criminal prosecution. The Fourth Amendment imposes a substantial handicap on the police by protecting individuals "in their persons, houses, papers and effects, against unreasonable searches and seizures." As the test of reasonableness, the amendment relies primarily on requirement of a search warrant, issued "upon probable cause, supported by oath or affirmation, and particularly describing the place to be searched, and the persons or things to be seized." Warrants must be obtained from judicial officers, who are expected to prevent overzealous or unjustified police action.

Searches and seizures may be made without search warrants in connection with lawful arrests, and the test for a lawful arrest is "probable cause." Search of the person arrested can be undertaken to find concealed weapons or evidence of crime. Even when there is no probable cause for arrest, police may stop, question, and search the outer clothing of suspicious persons, the Court ruled in *Terry* v. *Ohio* (1968). When making a lawful but warrantless arrest in a house or office, the police can seize evidence of crime which is in plain sight, but cannot search the entire premises, the Court held in *Chimel* v. *California* (1969), overruling several decisions to the contrary.

So far as automobiles are concerned, the constitutional rule is that they may be stopped and searched, provided again that there is probable cause to do so. The police, however, tend to interpret "probable cause" very loosely, and the stopping and searching of autos is a common tactic, which the Supreme Court has generally been reluctant to control.[2] In two 1974 cases the Court approved warrantless searches of the persons of drivers who had been stopped and arrested for minor traffic violations.[3] Searches of persons boarding airplanes present some constitutional questions, but have been generally accepted as necessary to prevent hijackings.

Evidence of crime that is seized without warrant and without justification cannot be used in a judicial prosecution. This is the "exclusionary rule," adopted by the Supreme Court for federal prosecutions in *Weeks* v. *United States* (1914).

The Supreme Court had no occasion to decide whether the state courts were bound by the unreasonable-search-and-seizure rule until 1949. The

---

[2]See, for example, *Cady* v. *Dombrowski* (1973), *Schneckloth* v. *Bustamonte* (1973), and *Cardwell* v. *Lewis* (1974). However, in *Almeida-Sanchez* v. *United States* (1973) the Court declared unconstitutional the practice of the U.S. Border Patrol of seeking to discover illegal immigrants by warrantless stopping and searching of autos in California twenty miles north of the Mexican border.

[3]*United States* v. *Robinson* (1974), *Gustafson* v. *Florida* (1974).

case of *Wolf* v. *Colorado* involved an abortionist who had been convicted on the basis of records seized by the police in an unauthorized search of his office. The Supreme Court held that the "security of one's privacy against arbitrary intrusion by the police" was an essential element in the concept of "ordered liberty," and so entitled the criminal suspect to Fourteenth Amendment protection against state action. But the Court majority then illogically went on to hold that the exclusionary rule did not apply in state courts, and that consequently illegally secured evidence could still be used to send a man to jail.

During the next decade, the Supreme Court was confronted with some shocking cases of local police methods; in one instance, the police secured evidence to convict a man for possessing drugs by having his stomach pumped to bring up morphine tablets he had swallowed (*Rochin* v. *California* [1952]). After a few experiences like this, the Court concluded in the 1961 case of *Mapp* v. *Ohio* that the exclusionary rule should also be applied to the states.

On the Burger Court, however, the exclusionary rule came under increasing attack. There has always been respectable opposition to the rule. For instance, Justice Benjamin Cardozo thought it unacceptable that "the criminal should go free because the constable has blundered." There was uncertainty as to whether the rationale of the rule was as a sanction against police misconduct, a protection of the purity of judicial proceedings, or a constitutional right of the accused. In a 1971 case Chief Justice Burger expressed the view that the rule was "conceptually sterile and practically ineffective."[4] In *United States* v. *Calandra* (1974) a Court majority partially infringed the rule by holding that a witness before a grand jury may not refuse to answer questions based on evidence resulting from an unlawful search.

The Crime Control Act of 1968 contained a "no-knock" provision authorizing federal agents to invade dwellings without notice, on the theory that surprise entry would prevent the destruction of drugs. This tactic backfired when in several widely publicized cases agents invaded the wrong house and terrorized and manhandled innocent occupants. The reaction was so severe that Congress abolished the "no-knock" law in 1974.

Welfare recipients cannot resist home visits by social service caseworkers; the Court ruled in *Wyman* v. *James* (1971) that requiring access as a condition of continued benefits did not constitute an unconstitutional search. However, administrative searches by municipal health and safety inspectors of dwellings or businesses do require a warrant and probable cause.[5]

---

[4]*Bivens* v. *Six Unknown Named Agents* (1971).
[5]*Camara* v. *Municipal Court* (1967).

Wiretapping and electronic eavesdropping

An English maxim states that a man's house is his castle, across whose threshold not even the king is entitled to pass. The Fourth Amendment attempted to make this ideal a reality in the United States. But modern technology has permitted the police to invade personal privacy without using such crude measures as the breaking down of doors and the rifling of desks. Wiretapping, electronic eavesdropping (bugging), and even more sophisticated methods of surreptitious surveillance are now commonplace and widely employed.

The Supreme Court originally excluded wiretapping from the restrictions imposed by the search-and-seizure rule; this was because nothing tangible was seized and the wiretapping was usually done outside the constitutionally protected living quarters of the victim. This reasoning was expounded in the famous case of *Olmstead* v. *United States* (1928). However, Congress in 1934 reacted to the ruling by forbidding the use in court of evidence secured by wiretapping.

Where telephone wires were not involved, of course, the federal statute did not apply. Consequently, evidence secured by electronic "bugs" placed where they could pick up conversations could be used in court, provided there had been no trespassing on the victim's living space when the bug was placed. However, in *Katz* v. *United States* (1967), the Supreme Court reconsidered its position and abandoned the *Olmstead* reasoning, ruling that the Fourth Amendment did cover the "search and seizure" of words, and that it protected people, not places. In this case, federal agents had secured evidence against a gambler by putting a bug on top of a public telephone booth that they had observed him using to place bets. The Court ruled that even though Katz was in a public, glass-enclosed booth, he was constitutionally entitled to make a private telephone call that would not be relayed to government agents. The new rule was: "What a person knowingly exposes to the public, even in his own home or office, is not a subject of Fourth Amendment protection. But what he seeks to preserve as private, even in an area accessible to the public, may be constitutionally protected."

The Court went on, however, to explain that the requirements of the Fourth Amendment could be satisfied if law-enforcement agents secured advance judicial approval for the placing of an eavesdropping device. The *Katz* opinion stated that if agents presented reliable evidence that a law was being violated, a judge could authorize eavesdropping under strictly limited conditions. Congress promptly wrote such an authorization into the Crime Control Act of 1968. In the next five years some 3,500 wiretaps and bugs were authorized, and some 160,000 persons were overheard by federal and state agents. Judges almost never declined to issue the authorizations requested, which were used primarily in gambling and drug investigations. In addition, much unauthorized tapping and bugging was carried on by the

F.B.I. on "national security" grounds. In 1972 the Supreme Court unanimously ruled that the government could not use this justification to eavesdrop on domestic organizations, but in 1974 the Court refused to decide whether the President could legally order wiretaps to detect and counter foreign espionage, without securing judicial approval.

Self-incrimination and coerced confessions

One of the important provisions of the Fifth Amendment is that no one "shall be compelled in any criminal case to be a witness against himself." This protection has been interpreted to cover witnesses before congressional committees and grand juries as well as defendants in criminal cases. There has been sharp difference of opinion about the desirability of the self-incrimination rule, but it embodies a basic principle of Anglo-Saxon jurisprudence: No individual is obliged to help the government prove that he committed a crime. Thus it is the prosecutor's responsibility to prove his case by adducing evidence against the defendant; for this reason the American system of criminal procedure is referred to as "accusatorial" in comparison with the "inquisitorial" system of the civil-law countries.

The Fifth Amendment's protection against self-incrimination allows the criminal suspect to refrain from making any statements in response to police interrogation. However, if the law enforcers feel that a person's testimony is essential to the incrimination of others, they can, under several federal statutes, request a federal judge to grant the witness immunity from prosecution for any criminal action he may reveal (*Ullmann* v. *United States* [1956]). If he continues his refusal after immunity is granted, he can then be jailed for contempt.

A grant of immunity generally protects the individual from prosecution for any criminal act revealed—so-called transactional immunity. But a 1970 statute authorized a more limited "use immunity," under which the government, while forbidden to use any evidence revealed by the witness, is still free to prosecute him if evidence of crime is independently secured. Use immunity was upheld by the Supreme Court in *Kastigar* v. *United States* (1972).

The Supreme Court initially held that the privilege against self-incrimination was not applicable at the state level (*Twining* v. *New Jersey* [1908]; *Adamson* v. *California* [1947]). However, here again the Court has reversed itself. In *Malloy* v. *Hogan* (1964), a majority ruled that protection against self-incrimination was an "essential mainstay" of the American accusatorial system, and that it would be "incongruous to have different standards determine the validity of a claim of privilege . . . depending on whether the claim was asserted in a state or federal court."

Confessions extorted by force or violence (the "third degree") are forbidden in the federal courts by the Fifth Amendment, because in such cases the defendant would obviously have been under compulsion to testify against himself. The same rule was adopted for state courts under the due process clause in 1936 (*Brown v. Mississippi*). Subsequently, the Court extended the ban to confessions secured by nonviolent means where there is mental or psychological pressure of an "inherently coercive" character. Convictions founded in whole or in part on involuntary confessions are a denial of due process of law, without regard for the truth or falsity of the confession, even though there is evidence aside from the confession to support the conviction.[6]

More recently, the Supreme Court has sought to bar even voluntary confessions if they are secured in violation of constitutional rights. The Court first moved in this direction in the famous case of *Escobedo v. Illinois* (1964), where a suspect was refused the right to see his lawyer while he was being held and questioned in a police station as a murder suspect. The Court ruled that whenever a police investigation ceased to be general and focused on a specific suspect, he was entitled to the assistance of counsel, and a subsequent conviction would be invalid if he was denied access to counsel.

Two years later, in *Miranda v. Arizona* (1966), the Court went further and in a 5-to-4 decision laid down a stiff code of conduct for police interrogation, including the following requirements:

1. *If a person is held in custody for interrogation, he must first be informed in clear and unequivocal terms that he has the right to remain silent.*
2. *He must be warned that anything he says can and will be used against him in court.*
3. *He must be given the right to consult with counsel prior to questioning, and to have counsel present during questioning if he desires.*
4. *Failure to request counsel does not constitute a waiver of the right to have counsel.*
5. *If the accused is unable to secure a lawyer, one must be appointed for him.*

The Court recognized that a lawyer would probably advise the suspect not to talk to police until he had investigated the case, and said this would be merely good professional judgment on the attorney's part. The Court warned that if interrogation proceeded without the presence of counsel and a confession was secured, a heavy burden would rest on the state to demonstrate that the defendant knowingly and intelligently waived his privilege against self-incrimination and his right to retained or appointed counsel.

---

[6]The Supreme Court has held (*Schmerber v. California* [1966]) that a state-compelled blood test for drunken drivers does not involve either self-incrimination or unreasonable search and seizure.

"According to U.S. v. Miranda, you're violating my civil rights."
Saturday Review, July 27, 1974, p. 54.

The dissenters in *Miranda* argued that the Court was really expressing a distrust of all confessions and saying that it was inherently wrong to secure evidence from the accused himself. They thought that society's interest in the detection and prevention of crime was being downgraded in preference to the rights of criminal suspects.

The *Miranda* decision precipitated a nationwide debate. On behalf of the Court, it was argued that the police, who have tended to concentrate on getting confessions because that is easier than looking for evidence, would be forced by *Miranda* to do a more creative job. Also, several studies purported to show that the number of confessions was not being substantially reduced under the new rules. On the other hand, many law-enforcement officers contended that it would no longer be possible to solve crimes by securing confessions. The Burger Court in several decisions indicated an intention to retreat somewhat from the *Escobedo* and *Miranda* rules.[7]

[7]See *Harris v. New York* (1971), and *Michigan v. Tucker* (1974).

RIGHTS OF THE ACCUSED

Indictment by grand jury

The Fifth Amendment provides: "No person shall be held to answer for a capital, or otherwise infamous crime, unless on a presentment or indictment of a grand jury...." The purpose of the grand jury provision is to require prosecuting officers to prove to a body of laymen that there is a *prima facie* case of criminal violation, so that citizens will not be subjected to the expense and indignity of a criminal trial without reasonable cause. If the grand jury finds the evidence sufficiently strong, it votes an indictment or a "true bill."

A grand jury generally consists of from 12 to 23 members; these jurors are selected by lot from the voting rolls, or are chosen by judges or by other local officials. The district attorney meets with the grand jury, whose sessions are secret. The grand jury has the power to inquire into any alleged offense called to its attention by the judge in his charge to the jury, or any offense within the personal knowledge of any of its members, but the usual practice is for the group to confine its attention to issues presented by the district attorney, and that official is, in fact, often charged with dominating the grand jury.

This is one of the few areas where the states are not required to follow federal constitutional standards. In about half of the states, a prosecuting officer may bring a person to trial by filing an "information" against him. The Supreme Court upheld this practice in *Hurtado* v. *California* (1884) and has never reversed this decision.

Admission to bail

The Eighth Amendment provides that "excessive bail shall not be required." Bail is the pledge of money or property by an accused person or his sureties for the purpose of guaranteeing his appearance for trial. Bail bondsmen customarily operate around courthouses, providing bail for the usual fee of 10 percent of the amount of the bond.

A large proportion of the occupants of the nation's jails are persons who cannot pay the costs of bail and may thus be incarcerated for months awaiting trial. Public reaction against this practice has led many jurisdictions to provide for release on personal recognizance in cases where investigation indicates that the individual is unlikely to flee. The federal Bail Reform Act of 1966 requires release on recognizance or unsecured bond of persons charged with noncapital offenses unless a judicial officer finds that release would not reasonably assure appearance.

Trial by jury

The Sixth Amendment (and also Article III of the Constitution) provides for jury trials in criminal cases. In federal criminal trials the jury must be the common-law jury of 12 persons, with a unanimous verdict required. An accused can waive jury trial, and Congress has provided for the trial of petty crimes without a jury. In federal civil cases tried by jury the 12-member rule is not mandatory; a number of federal district courts have experimented with six-member juries.[8]

The states must provide for jury trial in all criminal prosecutions except those for petty crimes, which are defined as offenses punishable by confinement for less than six months (*Duncan* v. *Louisiana* [1968]; *Baldwin* v. *New York* [1970]). However, the states can use a six-member jury in criminal cases (*Williams* v. *Florida* [1970]), and two 1972 decisions held that unanimous verdicts are not required for conviction in state criminal cases (*Johnson* v. *Louisiana, Apodaca* v. *Oregon*).

Both the due process and equal protection clauses forbid racial discrimination in jury selection at the state level. In fact, intentional exclusion of any group in the population from jury lists, or any system of weighting or preference that will render any group in the community more or less likely to be represented on juries, will create constitutional questions.

The right to counsel

The Sixth Amendment specifies certain rights essential to an adequate defense in criminal cases, including the right of the defendant "to be informed of the nature and cause of the accusations; to be confronted with witnesses against him; to have compulsory process for obtaining witnesses in his favor . . . and to have the assistance of counsel for his defense." This last right is the only one that has given rise to controversy.

The principal problem that arises is in situations where the defendant is too poor to hire a lawyer to defend him. In 1938 the Supreme Court ruled that defendants must be represented by counsel in all federal criminal proceedings (*Johnson* v. *Zerbst*). Consequently, the trial court must assign counsel for any defendants who come to court without legal representation. At the state level, the Court first dealt with this problem in the famous First Scottsboro Case, *Powell* v. *Alabama* (1932), involving seven black youths, ignorant and illiterate, who were charged with the rape of two white girls on a freight train passing through Alabama. They were brought to trial under conditions of extreme public hostility, with only the most nominal kind of representation by counsel, and they were quickly sentenced

---

[8]In *Colgrove* v. *Battin* (1973) the Supreme Court ruled that a six-member jury in federal civil cases does not violate the Seventh Amendment.

to death. The Supreme Court reversed the convictions on the ground that

> in a capital case, where the defendant is unable to employ counsel, and is incapable adequately of making his own defense because of ignorance, feeble-mindedness, illiteracy, or the like, it is the duty of the court . . . to assign counsel for him as a necessary requisite of due process of law.

It was not clear from this decision whether in a noncapital case, where the defendant did not suffer from the disabilities of the Scottsboro youths, the requirement of counsel would also apply. The Supreme Court had such a case 10 years later. In *Betts* v. *Brady* (1942), the defendant, who was white, of ordinary intelligence, and charged with robbery, requested the court to appoint counsel for him, because he was financially unable to secure a lawyer. The trial court refused on the ground that in that Maryland county it was the practice to appoint counsel only in murder and rape prosecutions. The Supreme Court upheld this practice, holding that historical research showed "appointment of counsel is not a fundamental right, essential to a fair trial." Counsel had been necessary in the Scottsboro case only because of the "special circumstances" of those defendants.

For the next 20 years, the Court struggled with the task of deciding when the circumstances were "special" enough to require counsel. Finally, in the celebrated case of *Gideon* v. *Wainwright* (1963), the Court overruled *Betts* v. *Brady* and held that representation by counsel was a constitutional necessity in criminal cases. The decision was generally well received in the legal profession, and programs for supplying counsel to indigent defendants were promptly inaugurated or improved throughout most of the states. In 1972 the Court extended the requirement of counsel to misdemeanor trials for offenses involving any possibility of imprisonment (*Argersinger* v. *Hamlin*).

Double jeopardy

The Fifth Amendment forbids the government to place any person "in jeopardy of life or limb" twice for the same offense. The underlying idea, as Justice Black said in *Green* v. *United States* (1957),

> is that the State with all its resources and power should not be allowed to make repeated attempts to convict an individual for an alleged offense, thereby subjecting him to embarrassment, expense and ordeal and compelling him to live in a continuing state of anxiety and insecurity, as well as enhancing the possibility that even though innocent he may be found guilty.

The double-jeopardy provision means that after an accused has been acquitted in a federal court, the government cannot appeal the decision or try him again for the same offense. If a jury fails to agree on a verdict and is discharged, however, a second trial *is* permissible. An accused waives his immunity against double jeopardy when he requests a new trial or appeals from a verdict of guilty. If a conviction is set aside on appeal, the defendant may be tried a second time for the same offense, but according to *Green v. United States* (1957), he cannot be subjected to the risk of being convicted on a more serious charge than in the first trial. He does assume the risk of a heavier penalty than was given in the first trial, but only if justified by some "identifiable conduct" occurring after the original sentencing (*North Carolina v. Pearce* [1969]).

The double-jeopardy rule also applies to the states, according to *Benton v. Maryland* (1969), which overruled the famous decision to the contrary in *Palko v. Connecticut* (1937). A macabre situation arose while the *Palko* rule was in effect when the state of Louisiana proposed to take a condemned man to the electric chair for the second time, after mechanical failure had prevented electrocution from being effective on the first trip. The Supreme Court held that this was not double jeopardy in the constitutional sense (*Louisiana ex rel. Francis v. Resweber* [1947]), and the man was electrocuted.

Under the federal system, the same action may be made a crime by both federal and state law—for example, robbing a national bank. The Supreme Court has ruled that both federal and state prosecution in such cases is not double jeopardy (*Abbate v. United States* [1959]; *Bartkus v. Illinois* [1959]). But it is double jeopardy for both a state and a city in that state to prosecute a person for the same act (*Waller v. Florida* [1970]).

PUNISHMENT AND REVIEW OF CONVICTIONS

The American prison population is declining at a time when the crime rate is rising. Part of the explanation for this paradox is that judges across the nation are so aware of the brutalizing conditions in American prisons that they tend not to commit persons convicted of relatively minor crimes. Prisons are almost complete failures at rehabilitation. Once a man has served a prison term, the chances are 60 to 70 percent that he will return. Recently, resentment against prison conditions has tended to become a racial issue because such a substantial proportion of the prison population are blacks—for example, in New York State 70 percent of the prison inmates are black. In 1973 the National Advisory Commission on Criminal Justice Standards found that the prison system

> *is obsolete, cannot be reformed, should not be perpetuated through the false hope of forced "treatment," and should be repudiated as useless for any purpose other than locking away persons who are too dangerous to be allowed at large in free society.*

"Five years! I thought the courts were coddling punks like me!"
Drawing by Lorenz; © 1968 The New Yorker Magazine, Inc.

Supervised probation has been increasingly used as an alternative to imprisonment, and some judges have experimented with sentences to some form of community service. A number of states have work-release programs whereby convicts can leave the prison to work at civilian jobs during the day and then return to the prison at night. There have been some attempts to deal with the problem of homosexuality by allowing prisoners to have visits from their spouses. By going to court, convicts have established that they must be granted certain civil rights. For example, *Procunier* v. *Martinez* (1974) limited censorship of prisoners' mail. The federal government operates several minimum security facilities that depart so far from the traditional prison pattern that they have been dubbed "country clubs." But in general, society locks up its prisoners and forgets about them until it is shocked into awareness of this national scandal by prison riots or takeovers such as the one in Attica, New York, in 1971, which was repressed at the cost of 42 lives.

The sentencing practices of judges have increasingly come under attack. It is well known that "street crimes" generally draw heavier sentences than white-collar crimes. But there are wide disparities among sentences for comparable offenses, determined solely by judicial discretion. It has been suggested that legislatures should spell out sentencing criteria in more detail, and that appellate court review of sentences should be increased.

Cruel and unusual punishment

The only constitutional provision specifically limiting criminal penalties is the Eighth Amendment's ban on "cruel and unusual punishment." Until 1972, this language had not been officially interpreted to forbid or limit capital punishment. However, sentiment against the death penalty had been gradually increasing, 11 states had abandoned it, and no convict had been legally executed in the entire nation since 1967, though over 600 were being held in death rows. The principal reason for this moratorium was the fact that cases were pending before the Supreme Court attacking the constitutionality of the death penalty.

The Court proved to be reluctant to tackle this issue. In *Witherspoon* v. *Illinois* (1968) it did declare unconstitutional the general practice of excluding from juries in capital cases all persons conscientiously opposed to capital punishment. A jury drawn only from that minority that has no doubts about imposing the death penalty would not be impartial, the Court thought; indeed, it would be a "hanging jury." But it was not until 1972 that the Court met the issue directly. Then in a 5-to-4 decision in *Furman* v. *Georgia* the justices ruled that, as imposed in three cases before them, the death penalty was cruel and unusual. However, only two justices would have totally abolished capital punishment. The other three in the majority stressed the denial of equal protection in a system where, out of all the perpetrators of serious crimes, only a "random few" are given the death penalty, and they are "capriciously selected."

On the theory that the decision would not apply to legislation leaving no discretion in imposition of the death penalty, a number of states promptly passed new laws making the death penalty mandatory for specific crimes.[9] Under these laws, death rows in state prisons, which had been emptied by the *Furman* decision, began filling up again. In North Carolina, 65 death sentences had been meted out by the end of 1974, and one of these cases, *Fowler* v. *North Carolina*, testing the revised death penalty laws, was to be decided by the Supreme Court in its 1975–1976 term.

The cruel and unusual punishment test was also invoked in *Robinson* v. *California* (1962) to strike down a state law making narcotics addiction a crime to be punished rather than an illness to be treated. However, in

---

[9]But, as Charles L. Black, Jr., has pointed out, no amount of specificity in statutes imposing capital punishment can ever eliminate "the possibility of *mistake* in the infliction of the penalty and the presence of standardless *arbitrariness* in its infliction." *Capital Punishment: The Inevitability of Caprice and Mistake* (New York: W. W. Norton & Co., 1974).

Powell v. *Texas* (1968) the Court denied that criminal conviction of chronic alcoholics constituted cruel and unusual punishment.

Habeas corpus

The purpose of the writ of *habeas corpus* (Latin for "have the body [in court]") is to provide a judicial remedy for arbitrary arrest or unlawful punishment. The writ, when issued by a court on petition of a person who is imprisoned or being held by police, requires the officers involved to bring the prisoner before the court and show that there is just cause for depriving him of his liberty. If the court is not satisfied, it can order the prisoner's immediate release. *Habeas corpus* is the most powerful weapon for enforcing the protections in the Bill of Rights. As Zechariah Chafee, Jr., has said: "This one human right is the safeguard of most other human rights."[10]

Initially *habeas corpus* was not available to prisoners who had been duly convicted and sentenced by a court. But in 1867 Congress passed a law authorizing the federal courts to issue writs of *habeas corpus* to prisoners in custody "in violation of the Constitution or of any treaty or law of the United States." Under this provision, persons convicted of crime in state courts who claim that their constitutional rights were denied in the trial can, after failing to get redress in the state courts, have their charges reviewed by a federal court through writ of *habeas corpus,* and this is very often done.

Article I, Section 9, of the Constitution provides that the writ of *habeas corpus* "shall not be suspended, unless when in cases of rebellion or invasion the public safety may require it." The Constitution does not say who is to suspend the writ, but since this provision is in the legislative article of the Constitution, it was generally assumed that the power belonged to Congress. However, early in the Civil War, President Lincoln ordered the writ suspended in various parts of the country. Chief Justice Taney vigorously criticized this action, but Congress subsequently passed a statute authorizing the President to suspend the writ when in his judgment such action was necessary.

After the Civil War, the Supreme Court in *Ex parte Milligan* (1866) held that the President had no power to suspend the writ in areas outside an actual theater of war. Again, after World War II, the Court in *Duncan* v. *Kahanomoku* (1946) ruled that the declaration of martial law in Hawaii and the suspension of *habeas corpus* until 1944, long after the threat of invasion was over, was unjustified.

---

[10]*How Human Rights Got into the Constitution,* Boston: Boston University Press, 1952, p. 53.

JUSTICE FOR JUVENILES

The theory of special courts for juveniles has been that the state can act through them in a protective capacity and not as an adversary, and that the proceedings are civil and not criminal. Consequently, it has been the usual practice that the child is not entitled to the constitutional rights of adult offenders in criminal cases, such as bail, indictment, public or jury trial, immunity against self-incrimination, or counsel. However, in *Kent* v. *United States* (1966) and *In re Gault* (1967) the Court expressed serious misgivings about the denial of basic procedural rights to juveniles.

In the *Gault* case, a 15-year-old boy was judged to be a delinquent for making an obscene telephone call and was sentenced to a state industrial school, with the possibility of remaining there until he was 21. The maximum penalty for an adult on this charge would have been a fine of $50 and two months' imprisonment. The Court in *Gault* held that certain rights must be provided in juvenile proceedings—specifically, notice of charges, counsel, confrontation of witnesses, and adequate warning of the privilege against self-incrimination. *Breed* v. *Jones* (1975) added double jeopardy to this list. But *McKeiver* v. *Pennsylvania* (1971) held that there is no right to jury trial in juvenile courts.

MILITARY JUSTICE

The armed forces maintain a system of courts-martial for punishment of offenses by their members, under regulations prescribed by Congress. The right to indictment by grand jury is specifically made inapplicable by the Fifth Amendment to "cases arising in the land and naval forces." Because courts-martial provide less procedural protection than civil courts, the Supreme Court held in *O'Callahan* v. *Parker* (1969) that military courts can try only service-connected offenses.

In general, courts-martial constitute a system of justice completely separate from the civilian courts. The decision of a court-martial must be affirmed by the appropriate command officers, and a final appeal may be taken on matters of law to the Court of Military Appeals, a bench of three civilian judges established by Congress in 1950. Appeal from this court to the Supreme Court is specifically prohibited by the 1950 law.

However, the writ of *habeas corpus* supplies a method whereby detention resulting from a court-martial decision can be reviewed by the civil courts. Such review is strictly limited, but it does permit the conformity of court-martial procedures to constitutional standards to be examined.

The principal objection to court-martial procedure is "command influence." The commanding officer appoints the pretrial investigation officers, authorizes searches and arrests, convenes the court-martial, decides whether the accused shall remain in pretrial confinement, selects the prosecutor and often the defense counsel, chooses the members of the court (the equivalent of jurors), decides whether a sentence to confinement will be deferred pending appeal, and makes the initial review of the case. Proposals have been made in Congress to eliminate command influence by establishing in the armed forces a separate and independent court-martial command, which would be modeled after the civilian courts.

Criticism of military justice was heightened by the record in the My Lai atrocity cases. Out of a total of 25 enlisted men and officers charged in connection with the 1968 mass murders in Vietnam, only six were brought to trial, and only one—Lieutenant William Calley—was convicted. His conviction was set aside in 1974 by a federal judge on the ground that massive publicity about his case had denied him a fair trial.

Article 133 of the Uniform Code of Military Justice provides for the punishment of a commissioned officer for "conduct unbecoming an officer and a gentleman." This provision, which dates back to the Revolutionary War, has often been challenged as irrelevant to today's armed forces, but it was held not to be unconstitutionally vague in *Parker* v. *Levy* (1974).

CRISIS IN THE AMERICAN COURT SYSTEM

The American court system is widely regarded as being in a state of crisis. The public considers courts to be expensive, time-consuming, and inefficient arms of justice to be avoided if at all possible. The log jam of court cases makes the "speedy trial" promised by the Sixth Amendment a hollow mockery.[11] The bulk of the jail population in every state is composed of defendants who, unable to make bail, must remain in jail, perhaps for months, awaiting trial. In this situation, even the innocent are under great pressure to plead guilty to some crime in order to bring their cases to a speedier final disposition. "Plea bargaining" is the process by which the defendant's attorney agrees to plead his client guilty in return for a reduction in the charge. The court system would break down completely from overload if many trials were not avoided by this device.[12]

In civil jury suits in metropolitan courts there is usually an interval of three years or more from the date of filing to the time of trial. This causes all parties to suffer. Physically or economically injured plaintiffs must wait

[11] In 1974 Congress adopted a law to implement the "speedy trial" provision. It requires automatic dismissal of federal charges if a defendant is not indicted within 30 days of arrest, not arraigned within 10 days of indictment, or not tried within 60 days of arraignment.

[12] In 1964, guilty pleas accounted for 90.2 percent of all criminal convictions in federal district courts. In *Santobello* v. *New York* (1971) the Supreme Court held that if a guilty plea is induced by promises made by the prosecutor, such promises must be fulfilled, or the defendant must be given the opportunity to withdraw his plea of guilty.

years for compensation, and often settle out of court for a fraction of their losses. Defendants may suffer injury to their credit or reputation while suits against them pend. In metropolitan criminal courts, delays of up to two years are not uncommon. As time passes, witnesses disappear and memories fade. In jury trial cases, jury selection may take weeks as the two sides seek to exclude from the panel anyone who might be hostile to their cause.

Standards of courtroom behavior have deteriorated, particularly under the stress of "political trials." Defendants have been unruly in court, lawyers have been cited for contempt, and some judges have engaged in sarcastic and undignified repartee with counsel. In *Illinois* v. *Allen* (1970), the Supreme Court held that as a last resort a disruptive defendant could be bound and gagged in court, as was done to Bobby Seale in the Chicago conspiracy trial in 1969; however, the Court suggested that it would be preferable simply to exclude the defendant from the courtroom.

Appellate practices permit cases to drag on for years before a final decision is reached. The process of appeal is expensive, since trial transcripts and elaborate briefs must be prepared and printed. Multiple appeals are possible, proceeding through all the levels of the court system. Convicts under sentence of death have spent many years in death-row cells while their appeals were being heard.

ENGLISH CRIMINAL JUSTICE

American criminal justice is often compared unfavorably with English procedures. Under the English system, justice is swift and most cases come to trial within one month; the average serious criminal case takes only one or two days to try. The longest murder trial in English history lasted less than two months. It takes only a few minutes to seat a jury. Unlike the *voir dire* examination in America, in England counsel cannot question members of the jury panel to determine their fitness to serve. All that counsel know about a prospective juror is his name and occupation, so challenges for cause are almost never made. Recent acceptance of less than unanimous verdicts means that there are fewer hung juries. Moreover, the great majority of criminal cases are heard by justices of the peace in magistrates' courts without a jury, and juries are seldom used in civil cases.

The English judge exercises absolute discipline in the courtroom. Only a highly select group of barristers (2,600 in all of England) may appear in court, and they behave with exquisite decorum. Neither prosecution nor defense counsel can approach the jury, the witnesses, or the accused. Presentations are sober, without histrionics. Moreover, there is in England no official like the American district attorney, whose reputation and political advancement depend upon the number of convictions he secures. There is a national director of public prosecutions who acts in the more important cases and who has coordinating responsibilities for the entire system. But most prosecutions are handled directly by the police or by barristers who are employed to prosecute particular cases. Thus a barrister may handle a case for the government one day and for a defendant the next day.

English convictions are relatively final, and cannot be overturned after they have been reviewed once on appeal. Frivolous appeals are screened out; a single appellate judge can reject an appeal without hearing if he finds no grounds for it. The English style of appeal relies largely on oral arguments and an oral ruling from the bench, in contrast with the expensive and time-consuming written records and briefs required in American appeals.

In several respects, criminal suspects have fewer rights in England than in the United States. The English police have greater power to detain and arrest suspects. A warrant is required to enter private premises, but the police can use any evidence they may discover, whether the evidence is covered by the warrant or not. Evidence obtained illegally is still admissible in court; the English system does not employ the American exclusionary rule. "Preventive detention" of suspects while they await trial, a very controversial subject in the United States, is widely practiced in England. While suspects are informed of their right to remain silent, there is no right to pretrial assistance of counsel, as required by *Escobedo* and *Miranda*. English police are trusted with such authority in part because they are considered to be better trained and more professional than most American police, and because with few exceptions they are unarmed. The latter is made possible by an absence of a tradition of violence in England. English judges, all appointed rather than elected, are universally respected by the English public, not only for their high professional competence but also for their unquestioned integrity.

The English model of criminal justice could not and should not be transferred to the United States, but reforms consistent with American conditions and the requirements of the Bill of Rights are possible. Since his appointment, Chief Justice Burger has devoted considerable effort toward stimulating more effective judicial administration and reforms in the penal system. But, as he himself has recognized, "efficient administration is the tool, not the goal of justice."[13] Moreover, it is important to remember, as Justice Frankfurter once said, that the constitutional protections of the criminal law are provided "not out of tenderness for the accused but because we have reached a certain stage of civilization"—a civilization which, Justice Douglas added, "by respecting the dignity even of the least worthy citizen, raises the stature of all of us."

[13] 57 *American Bar Association Journal* 425, 430 (1971).

7
Liberty

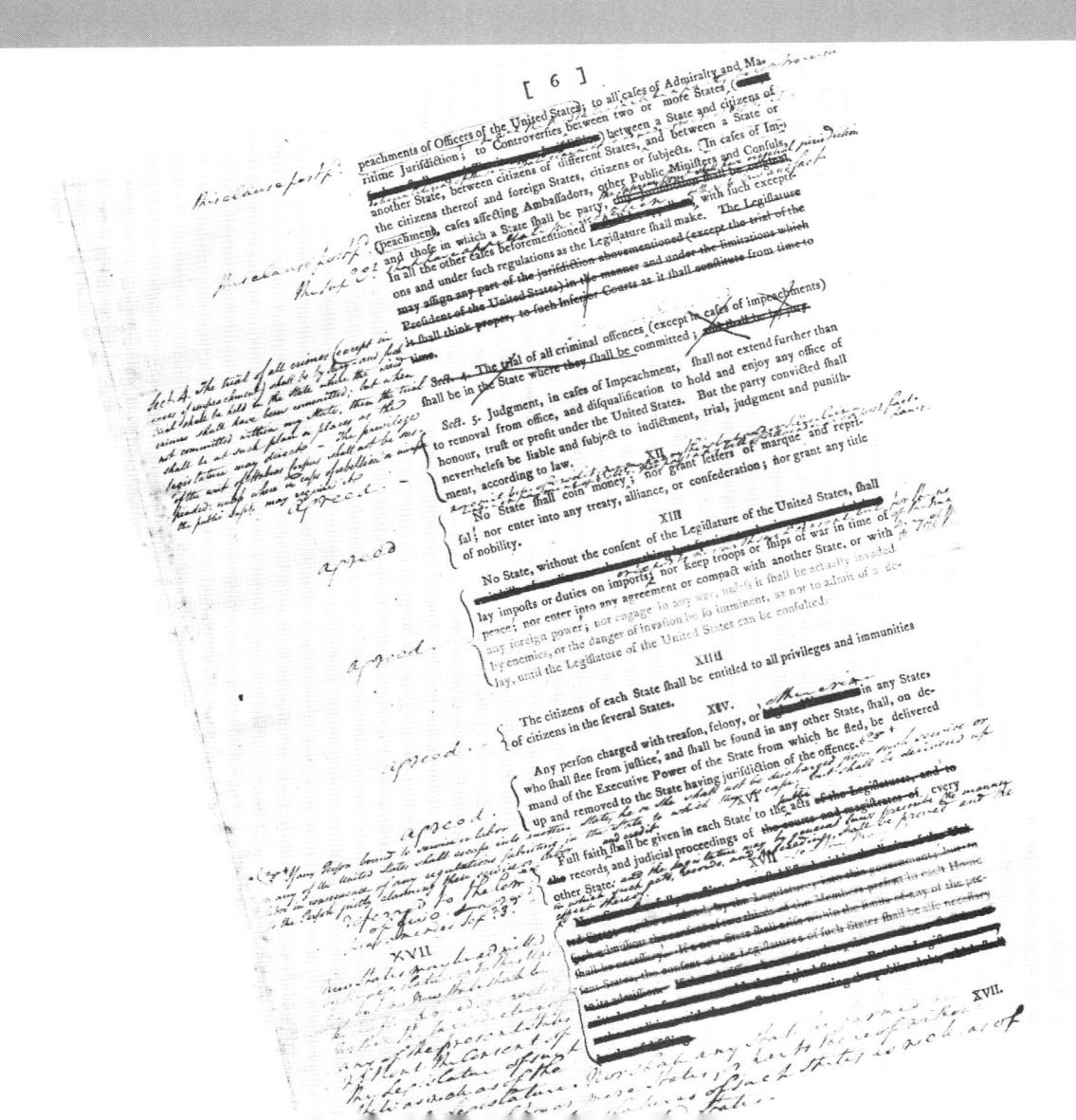

7

Liberty has meant widely different things at different times to different people. In the Declaration of Independence, the liberty at issue was freedom from English rule for the American colonies, the liberty that comes with self-government. In 1863, when Lincoln issued the Emancipation Proclamation liberating the slaves in rebellious territory, liberty meant the termination of a legal status of involuntary servitude. In 1936, to the conservative organizers of the Liberty League, liberty meant repeal of the New Deal laws regulating the stock exchanges and promoting the growth of labor unions. To the American Civil Liberties Union (ACLU), liberty means the right to form organizations, to picket, to speak freely, to hold unpopular views.

In every sense in which it is used, however, liberty has a basic connotation of *freedom from control*—whether control by a foreign power, control by a human master, or control by laws or government agencies that are conceived to be unduly restrictive of individual expression or initiative. Liberty is in constant rebellion against authority. Yet it is the great paradox of liberty that it cannot exist except within a framework of authority. A system of unlimited liberty, where anyone is free to do anything he likes at any time, would constitute a condition of anarchy. It would be that "war of each against all" that Hobbes described, a state of nature in which life would be "solitary, poor, nasty, brutish, and short." As the Declaration of Independence goes on to say in the next sentence after its praise of liberty, "governments are instituted among men" precisely with the intent "to secure these rights."

And so the American colonies that rebelled against English authority set up a new government with more authority to tax and to regulate commerce than the English king had exercised. The blacks who emerged from the Civil War as freedmen needed, but for a long time did not get, the vigorous support of governmental authority to help them emerge from the shadow of bondage. The Liberty Leaguers who objected to the National Labor Relations Act and the National Recovery Act of the New Deal saw nothing wrong with the Old Deal, under which federal authority was used to levy protective tariffs and enjoin labor unions from striking or picketing. The ACLU does not want cities to censor motion pictures, but it expects the police to protect the street demonstrations of unpopular groups.

The tension between liberty and authority, then, is absolutely necessary for the existence of people in communities, and the larger the community, the greater the tension. The question is never one or the other, but how much of each.

CONSTITUTIONAL BACKGROUND

Considering the great concern of the Founders for liberty, it is surprising that the original Constitution contained so few indications of this interest. The theory of the Constitutional Convention was that traditional American liberties did not need much in the way of specific constitutional protection. The basic concept of limited national government was to be achieved by a division of functions, separation of powers, and checks and balances calculated to frustrate any abuse of power. The drafters of the Constitution relied on the open spaces of the American continent to guarantee escape from confining situations. They saw the boundless resources of the country as insurance of economic opportunity. They conceived that the broad expanse of the republic would encompass such a variety of interests that combination into a domineering majority would be difficult. Thus individual liberty did not need to be planned. It would come automatically as the by-product of a system of economic opportunity, social mobility, and political responsibility.

But when the proposed Constitution went to the states for ratification, it quickly became apparent that not many people agreed with the framers that civil liberties required no special protection. In several of the important states, ratification was secured only on the understanding that amendments protecting individual rights would be immediately added. James Madison took the lead in bringing together the various suggestions for amendments in the First Congress. Twelve were presented to the states and 10 were ratified by 1791, constituting what soon came to be known as the Bill of Rights.

Only six of these amendments are of direct importance in our present discussion. The First, justly the most famous, covers freedom of speech, press, assembly, and religion. The Fourth through the Eighth deal primarily with procedural protections in criminal trials, but certain other matters are also covered, such as the prohibition on taking private property for public use without just compensation.

For the most part, the restraints imposed by these amendments are stated in general language. The only two that by their terms apply to the federal government are the First, which specifically mentions "Congress," and the Seventh, which refers in one clause to "any court of the United States." However, the general understanding was that the amendments were being drafted to impose limitations on the new government set up by the Constitution, and the Supreme Court confirmed this understanding when in *Barron v. Baltimore* (1833) it held that the due process clause of the Fifth Amendment did not apply to the states.

This meant that the states were left free, so far as the federal Constitution was concerned, to deny freedoms protected by the Bill of Rights. But the post–Civil War amendments, particularly the due process and equal protection clauses of the Fourteenth, finally brought the states within federal constitutional controls. As for the freedoms of the First Amendment, with which this chapter is particularly concerned, the Supreme Court held in *Gitlow* v. *New York* (1925) that the freedoms of speech and press guaranteed against congressional infringement by the First Amendment were also among the fundamental personal rights and "liberties" protected by the Fourteenth against impairment by the states. In 1940, the Court similarly brought the religion clauses of the First Amendment into effect against the states. Thus the libertarian principles of the First Amendment apply at all levels of American government.

FREEDOM OF EXPRESSION

Apart from voting, there are three principal ways by which citizens in a free community express themselves on public issues.

First, they can talk—talk to their friends, their relatives, their neighbors, even to total strangers. They can talk at meetings, and if they are not invited to be on the platform, they can ask questions from the floor or heckle the speakers. They can be interviewed on radio or television.

Second, they can get their views into print. Most people, of course, do not own newspapers, but they can write letters to the editor. They can print up a handbill or leaflet and distribute it on street corners or send it out by mail. A few can even write books and can sell them.

Third, they can organize or assemble with other like-minded persons and make their views known by carrying signs in a parade, by marching in a picket line around city hall, by signing petitions addressed to the government, or by volunteer work in the office of a propaganda organization or political party.

All three of these types of expression are protected by the First Amendment, which provides that "Congress shall make no law . . . abridging the freedom of speech, or of the press; or the right of the people peaceably to assemble, and to petition the Government for a redress of grievances." (See Figure 7–1.) But, in fact, the degree to which one is free to express his views is largely dependent on the manner of the expression. This is so because, in spite of the flat statement in the First Amendment, there is no absolute right to freedom of expression at all times and in all places.

For example, we are all familiar with situations where speech is abridged or restrained with common consent. One may not talk freely in a library reading room, or during a church service, or while a court is in session. There are rules of order governing legislative assemblies or public meetings, which restrain people from talking at the same time, or which

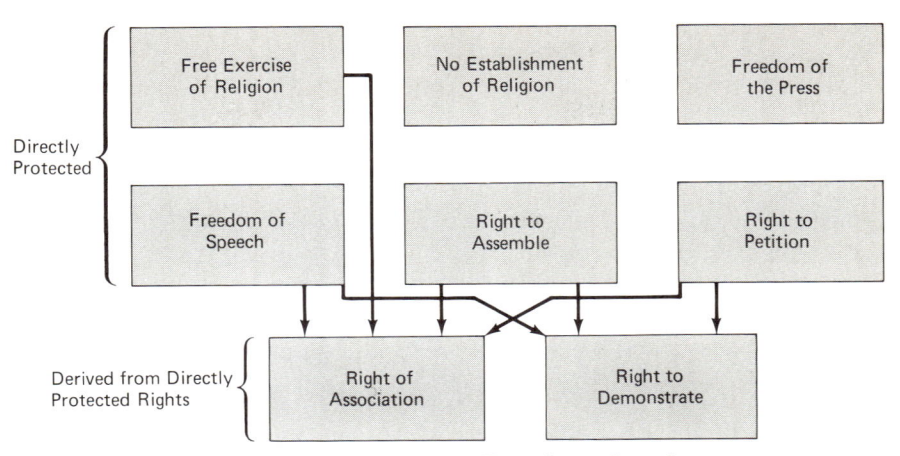

Figure 7-1 *Rights protected under the First Amendment*

prevent speech irrelevant to the issue under discussion. Clearly, the extent of one's right to self-expression depends on what other rights may be competing for consideration. There is a right to speak, but there is also a right to privacy. There is a right to parade in the streets, but there is also a right to use the streets for transportation.

Methods of restraint on freedom of expression

Governmental limitations on freedom of expression may take two different forms. Sometimes public officials act to prohibit or restrain speaking or publishing or assembling. This is *censorship* or *prior restraint*. Sometimes public officials act to prosecute persons for speech or publication or assembly that has already occurred. This is *subsequent punishment*.

Prior restraint is generally regarded as more dangerous to freedom of expression than subsequent punishment, because it throttles the expression of opinion and prevents communications from ever reaching the marketplace of ideas. Prior restraint is aimed at what *may* be said or done if a meeting is held; it is justified by probabilities; it anticipates that abuses are going to occur. Moreover, prior restraint is dangerous because it is relatively easy to impose. It requires only a decision by the police or other public officials, which can often be taken behind a screen of informality and partial concealment.

In contrast, a system of subsequent punishment does not operate until after the communication has occurred. For whatever it may be worth, the people involved have been able to present their message to the public. If their communication has resulted in a violation of the law, they can be punished only after the illegality of their actions has been established by a criminal prosecution in which they will have all the safeguards of due process. The court will be dealing not with hypothetical possibilities but with what actually happened.

FREEDOM OF THE PRESS

Among the three forms of expression described above, print has the greatest claim to freedom because its social setting makes it the least likely to be in conflict with other rights. Communication by way of the printed page is essentially a solitary process. The reader makes no noise; he creates no disturbance; he causes no problems. Consequently, the right to print and to publish is least likely to be limited by the claims of competing rights.

Censorship of the press

It has been so well understood that the First Amendment forbids prior restraint of the press that few such efforts have been made. The principal anticensorship decision is *Near v. Minnesota* (1931). Here a newspaper had been enjoined from publication under a state statute providing that "malicious, scandalous, and defamatory" newspapers could be treated as a public nuisance. The Supreme Court declared the law unconstitutional by a vote of 5 to 4.

The Pentagon Papers. This position was challenged in 1971 when the government sought an injunction against *the New York Times* and the *Washington Post* to prevent them from continuing their publication of the so-called Pentagon Papers. These papers came from a many-volumed study, made at the direction of the Defense Department, of how the United States became involved in the war in Vietnam. The study was classified as secret, but Daniel Ellsberg, who had access to the papers through his employment by a private research agency, in violation of government security rules furnished copies to the press. By a vote of 6 to 3, the Supreme Court in *New York Times v. United States* (1971) dissolved a lower court injunction that had interrupted publication of the papers. However, this was not an impressive free press victory. There was no majority opinion, only a short *per curiam* statement that the government had not met the heavy burden of showing justification for the restraint on publication. Each of the nine justices filed an individual opinion, from which it appeared that a majority of the Court would have been willing to enjoin publication if the government had made a stronger case that publication would endanger national interests.

The Post Office. Obviously, it does little good to print one's ideas if the printed matter cannot be circulated. There are several ways in which that prime medium of circulation, the Post Office, has attempted to use its position to limit the freedom to print. One relates to the granting of second-class mailing privileges, which amount to a subsidy, since the rates are much below the cost of service. During both World Wars I and II, various radical or antiwar publications were denied second-class privileges, but when the Postmaster General attempted to withdraw second-class privileges from *Esquire* magazine on the ground that it was not published "for the public welfare and the public good," the Supreme Court unanimously reversed him in *Hannegan v. Esquire* (1946). A 1962 statute authorizing the Postmaster General to detain "communist political propaganda" and to deliver it only upon the addressee's request was held unconstitutional in *Lamont v. Postmaster General* (1965).

Free press and fair trials. An aspect of press freedom under considerable pressure is the right of the press to print information about pending criminal prosecutions or trials in progress. In England, restraints on press comments about criminal trials are very strict; only the barest facts of the case can be published. But the United States has been much more permissive toward outside comment on judicial proceedings, and the Supreme Court has generally protected this freedom *(Bridges v. California* [1941]).

Currently, however, there is widespread concern that when police and prosecutors make public, and the communications media circulate, evidence against suspects before their trials are held, they jeopardize the suspect's rights to a fair trial and make the task of securing an unbiased jury very difficult. In *Sheppard v. Maxwell* (1966), the Supreme Court reversed the second-degree murder conviction of Dr. Samuel H. Sheppard on the ground that "massive" and "virulent" publicity generated by a Cleveland newspaper had denied him a fair trial. The Court held that the trial judge had permitted a "carnival atmosphere" and even "bedlam" resulting from activity of newsmen in the courtroom, and had failed to isolate the jury from the publicity that attended this notorious prosecution.

Since the *Sheppard* ruling, trial judges have generally been much more disposed to grant changes of venue (transfer to a different court and locality) when the defense alleges that publicity concerning the crime has made it impossible to secure an unbiased jury in the area. Also it has become fairly common for judges in sensational cases to issue "gag orders" prohibiting law-enforcement officers, prosecutors, and counsel from discussing the pending case. The press has objected strenuously to these orders, but no significant constitutional tests have occurred. The press did lose an important test case in 1972, when in *Branzburg v. Hayes* the Supreme Court ruled 5 to 4 that newsmen have no First Amendment right to refuse to answer questions of grand juries. The press had contended that such compulsion would dry up newsmen's sources of information and in effect make them investigative arms of the government. But the Court did rule in 1974 against a Florida statute requiring newspapers that commented unfavorably on a political candidate to afford free space to the candidate to reply, holding that this was an unconstitutional intrusion into the editorial function *(Miami Herald Publishing Co. v. Tornillo).*

Libel

Libel is the defamation of character by print or other visual presentation such as television. It has long been understood that false and malicious statements about an individual damage him in his legal rights and make the publisher subject to prosecution for libel.

Some states have laws for punishing libel aimed not at private individuals but at groups. Group libel laws are directed at those who make false, abusive, hatemongering attacks on racial, religious, or other groups in our society. Proponents of group libel laws argue that they are needed because the ordinary law of libel will not reach defamers of a group, and that individual members of the group may suffer severely because of defamatory comments about their group. It is noteworthy that England, which had never known racial problems until recent years, in 1965 adopted a Race Relations Act making racial defamation and incitement to race hatred a crime.

In 1952 the Supreme Court upheld by a vote of 5 to 4 the constitutionality of a group libel law *(Beauharnais v. Illinois).* Beauharnais, who headed an antiblack organization, stood on a Chicago street corner and handed out petitions to the city council, asking the use of the police to protect white citizens from the "rapes, robberies, knives, guns and marijuana" of the Negro. The Supreme Court upheld his conviction for violation of the group libel statute, Justice Frankfurter holding that libelous utterances, affecting either private individuals or groups, are not within the scope of "constitutionally protected speech." But Justice Black, dissenting, thought that "no legislature is charged with the duty or vested with the power to decide what public issues Americans can discuss." If the question were brought before the Court again, it seems almost certain that the *Beauharnais* decision would be regarded as a mistake and that group libel laws would be declared unconstitutional, because they punish statements pertaining to social and political issues of public importance.

The Supreme Court's more recent and more considered position on libel prosecutions was announced in the 1964 case of *New York Times v. Sullivan.* Here the problem was not libel of private individuals or groups, but alleged libel of a public official by a newspaper. The *New York Times* had printed as a paid advertisement a criticism of the treatment of blacks in Montgomery, Alabama. The ad was submitted by reputable persons, but it was later discovered that it contained some factual errors.

The police commissioner of Montgomery, although not mentioned in the ad either by name or by specific reference to his office, contended that criticism of the Montgomery "police" constituted libel of him, and an

Alabama jury awarded him damages of $500,000. Another commissioner who sued on the basis of the same ad also got a $500,000 judgment. Eleven additional libel suits were filed against the *Times* seeking a total of $5,600,000, and five suits asking $1,700,000 were brought at the same time against the Columbia Broadcasting System on the basis of its coverage of Alabama civil-rights controversies.

Clearly, libel judgments of this magnitude, secured with such ease, could effectively silence all comment or reporting by the communications media in controversial situations. Such a result, the Supreme Court held, would be in conflict with "the principle that debate on public issues should be uninhibited, robust, and wide-open. . . ." At times, public discussion "may well include vehement, caustic, and sometimes unpleasantly sharp attacks on government and public officials." Sometimes, the Court granted, there may even be false statements, damaging to official reputations. That is inevitable in free debate, the Court said. But "erroneous statements honestly made" cannot be punished as libel.

So the Court's conclusion in the *New York Times* case was that a public official cannot recover damages for a defamatory falsehood relating to his official conduct unless he proves that the statement was made with "actual malice"—that is, "with knowledge that it was false or with reckless disregard of whether it was false or not."

In 1967 the Court extended the *New York Times* rule from public officials to public figures; that is, private citizens who had engaged in or become objects of public controversy. By this standard the Associated Press was held not to have libeled a right-wing retired general in its account of his activities during the University of Mississippi rioting in 1962 *(Associated Press v. Walker)*. Similarly in *Rosenbloom v. Metromedia* (1971) a distributor of nudist magazines arrested for obscenity, but subsequently cleared, lost his libel suit against a radio station that referred to him as a "smut distributor." But in *Gertz v. Robert Welch* (1974) the Court ruled that a Chicago lawyer, who had been falsely charged by a John Birch Society magazine with being a "communist-fronter" and having a criminal record, was not a "public figure," and that consequently the publication was not protected by the *New York Times* rule.

The First Amendment has generally protected the press against complaints that articles about newsworthy persons have invaded their privacy. In *Cox Broadcasting v. Cohn* (1975) the Court refused to apply a state law forbidding news media to disclose the names of rape victims, when the information had been secured from official court records.[1] By contrast, a 1974 ruling held that the *Cleveland Plain Dealer* had invaded the privacy of a

---

[1] There was a similar ruling in *Time Inc. v. Hill* (1967), where *Life* magazine was held not to have invaded the privacy of a family by printing, three years after the event, a distorted account of their experience when their home was taken over by a trio of escaped prisoners.

family by an article containing gross and knowing inaccuracies and untruths (*Cantrell* v. *Forest City Publishing Co.*).

Obscenity

Obscenity, like libel, has long been punishable under state laws, and there is also a federal obscenity statute applying to the mails. It was not until 1957 that the Supreme Court gave serious attention to the obscenity problem. Then, in *Roth* v. *United States,* it upheld laws punishing obscenity on the ground that obscenity was completely outside the area of "constitutionally protected speech." The First Amendment, the Court recognized, extends to "all ideas having even the slightest redeeming social importance —unorthodox ideas, controversial ideas, even ideas hateful to the prevailing climate of opinion." But obscenity, the Court went on, is "utterly without redeeming social importance," and so it does not share in the protection of the First Amendment.

This holding, however, still left the Court with the task of deciding what *was* obscene. In the *Roth* case, the Court's test for obscenity was whether "to the average person, applying contemporary community standards, the dominant theme of the material taken as a whole appeals to prurient interest." Later, in *Manual Enterprises* v. *Day* (1962), Justice Harlan added a second test: The material must be "patently offensive," its indecency "self-demonstrating." Then, in *Jacobellis* v. *Ohio* (1964), the Court made its *Roth* rationalization that obscenity was utterly without redeeming social importance into a third test: Anything *with* redeeming social importance could not be obscene.

In the 1966 *Fanny Hill* case (*A Book* v. *Attorney General of Massachusetts*), the Court held that a book must fail all three tests before it could be regarded legally as obscene. Since the trial court admitted that *Fanny Hill* had "a modicum of social value," it could not be branded obscene. In fact, almost the only class of material likely to be regarded as obscene under these tests is "hard-core pornography." Even that is difficult to define, as Justice Stewart said in the *Jacobellis* case. But, he added, "I know it when I see it, and the motion picture involved in this case is not that."

The Supreme Court, however, departed from its liberal policy on obscenity in *Ginzburg* v. *United States* (1966), where it upheld a criminal conviction and five-year sentence for violation of the federal obscenity law. The Court conceded that the materials published by Ginzburg, standing alone, might not have been obscene under the three original tests, but they now held that the "context" and "setting" in which the publications were presented could be considered as relevant to a determination of obscenity. The Court found that Ginzburg had been engaged in "commercial exploitation of erotica solely for the sake of their prurient appeal" and in the "sordid business of pandering"; consequently, these transactions were "sales of illicit merchandise, not sales of constitutionally protected matter."

In addition to a finding of pandering, the Supreme Court indicated that it would uphold two other types of obscenity convictions. The first is under laws aimed to safeguard the welfare of juveniles by punishing the sale of obscene materials to them *(Ginzburg v. New York* [1968]). The second is where individual privacy is invaded by circulation of objectionable material in such an obtrusive manner that unwilling individuals cannot avoid exposure to it. In 1967 Congress passed a law providing that a person receiving in the mail what he regarded as obscene material could demand the removal of his name from the firm's mailing list, after which a second mailing would be a basis for prosecution. This law was upheld in *Rowan v. Post Office Department* (1970).

In *Stanley v. Georgia* (1969), the Supreme Court ruled that a man could not be punished for having obscenity in his home. But under subsequent decisions he might have trouble getting it there, because the federal statute against sending obscene materials through the mail was upheld in *United States v. Reidel* (1971), and the right of customs agents to seize obscene pictures being imported was approved in *United States v. Thirty-Seven Photographs* (1971).

A substantial change in the Court's definition of obscenity occurred in 1973. In *Miller v. California* and several companion cases the Burger Court substituted for the permissive holdings of the Warren Court a new rule permitting findings of obscenity where the material lacked serious literary, artistic, political, or scientific value. The "patent offensiveness" test was maintained, but offensiveness was to be judged by local, not national, community standards.

The threat thus posed to national distribution of books or motion pictures was demonstrated when a Georgia jury held a widely acclaimed film obscene. The Court in *Jenkins v. Georgia* (1974) felt compelled to reverse the conviction, cautioning that *Miller* did not mean to give local juries unbridled discretion. However, the Court reasserted that juries could base their determinations of offensiveness on the prevailing moral standards of their communities, thus seeming to guarantee continuing confusion in legal prosecutions for obscenity.

American limits on obscenity, which formerly were much stricter than in France or England, now tend to be more lenient than in those countries. Under the earlier standards, books that could not be published in the United States, such as James Joyce's *Ulysses,* were published in France. Now the situation has been reversed. England has an Obscene Publications Act under which, if one item in an article is obscene, the whole article is considered obscene, a position long abandoned by American courts.

England's censorship of stage plays by the Lord Chamberlain, dating back to 1737, was abolished in 1967, but the English film industry maintains its own board of censors. Movie censorship by American states and cities has been held constitutional by the Supreme Court, but it has insisted on such strict procedural protections for film distributors that most censor-

"It's too obscene for Georgia and not obscene enough for New York."
The New Yorker, August 20, 1973, p. 29.

ship systems have now been abandoned. Instead, attention has shifted to the possibility of a labeling system, such as is used in England, where some films are given a universal license, and others are limited to adults. The American film industry in 1968 adopted its own voluntary labeling system.

The American attitude toward obscenity is approaching that prevailing in Denmark and Sweden, the two most permissive countries in this area. Denmark has legalized the sale of pornography, removed obscenity as a ground for any action under the criminal code, and abolished the already lax censorship of motion pictures. Scandinavians have always found the horror and violence in American films more objectionable than the sex in theirs.

FREEDOM OF SPEECH

Speech by its nature is more likely than print to result in a conflict of rights, because speech involves the interaction of at least two persons. However, censorship of speech is just as objectionable in principle as censorship of the press, and it is only in unusual situations, where the social setting of the speech is such as to threaten danger to the public order, that controls over speech may be constitutionally imposed. The use of public streets, sidewalks, or parks for speech purposes may create traffic problems or potential disturbances. Consequently, municipalities usually require advance notification of meetings in public places and issue permits to the speakers.

Such permit systems have been held constitutional by the Supreme Court, provided they are administered under standards that prevent discrimination. If permits are issued to some groups and not to others, this is not only interference with freedom of assembly but also a denial of equal protection of the laws. Thus in *Niemotko v. Maryland* (1951), the Court invalidated as arbitrary and discriminatory the refusal of a city council to allow Jehovah's Witnesses to hold a meeting in a public park because the councilmen did not like the sect's views on saluting the flag.

The Supreme Court's insistence on strict standards for permit systems is illustrated by *Kunz v. New York* (1951). Here the Court reversed the action of New York City in removing a bigoted preacher from the public streets by revoking his permit for street preaching. The Court's objection to the permit ordinance was that it gave to an administrative official "discretionary power to control in advance the right of citizens to speak on religious matters on the streets of New York," with "no appropriate standards to guide his action." In *Walker v. Birmingham* (1967), the Court held the Birmingham parade permit ordinance unconstitutional on its face, but because Martin Luther King, Jr., had ignored a court injunction against parading without a permit, his jail sentence was upheld.

Amplification of sound creates a different problem, and may make speech liable to control as a public nuisance and an invasion of privacy (*Kovacs v. Cooper* [1949]). Local ordinances may also protect privacy by forbidding commercial canvassers or salesmen to sell from door to door (*Breard v. Alexandria* [1951]), but such limitations cannot be imposed on persons going from door to door on public policy or religious errands (*Martin v. Struthers* [1943]).

Speech and breach of the peace

The freedom to speak, then, is generally protected from advance restrictions, but if speech results in unlawful action of some kind, the speaker may be liable to punishment. One of the most common problems is that speech may inflame tempers and lead to violence. Preservation of order is a prime responsibility of every community, and in all states there are statutes punishing breach of the peace, disorderly conduct, inciting to riot, and like offenses. Where speech is an element in these offenses, serious questions arise in balancing the right to speak against the necessity of maintaining public order. The Supreme Court has worked out three tests to be applied in passing on the constitutionality of punishment for speech.

First, is the speech of a type that is entitled to constitutional protection? In *Chaplinsky* v. *New Hampshire* (1942), a member of Jehovah's Witnesses had cursed a city marshal, calling him a "damned racketeer" and "a damned Fascist," and he was convicted for calling the marshal "offensive and derisive" names in public. The Supreme Court upheld the conviction on the ground that such language is not constitutionally protected. Insults and "fighting words" are "no essential part of any exposition of ideas, and are of such slight social value as a step to truth that any benefit that may be derived from them is clearly outweighed by the social interest in order and morality."

Subsequently the Court has been less certain about the right to punish "fighting words." In *Gooding* v. *Wilson* (1972) the Court reversed the conviction of a black who used threatening language to a white police officer, holding that the Georgia statute making unlawful the use of "opprobrious words or abusive language" was too vague and overly broad.

The recent Court has also tended to extend protection to the public use of language regarded as offensive because of its vulgarity. *Cohen* v. *California* (1971) voided the conviction of a young man who had been charged with breach of the peace because he wore a jacket bearing a four-letter word expressing his opposition to the draft. Justice Harlan noted that words have an "emotive" as well as a "cognitive" function, and suggested that the emotive role "may often be the more important element of the over-all message sought to be communicated." Most of the other currently popular vulgarisms have also been cleared by the Court of charges of offensiveness or obscenity.[2]

The second test is: Does the ordinance or statute for violation of which the speaker is being punished validly recognize the constitutional necessity for protection of speech? In *Terminiello* v. *Chicago* (1949) the Court invalidated a breach-of-the-peace conviction under an ordinance that made it unlawful to "stir the public to anger" or "incite dispute." The evils had to be greater than that to justify a speech conviction, the Court said. *Street* v. *New York* (1969) involved a state law punishing expression of contempt for the flag "by words or act," and the Court reversed Street's conviction because no law can constitutionally make it a crime merely to speak "defiant or contemptuous words."

The third consideration in determining whether a speaker should be punished is whether a clear and present danger of actual breach of the peace resulted from the speech. In answering this question, a reviewing

---

[2]See *Papish* v. *University of Missouri* (1973); *Eaton* v. *City of Tulsa* (1974).

court of necessity has the difficult task of evaluating the correctness of the judgment of the police officers or others on the scene as to the potentialities for violence. In *Feiner v. New York* (1951) the Supreme Court was unwilling to question the judgment of the police and the trial court. But later, in such decisions as *Edwards v. South Carolina* (1963) and *Cox v. Louisiana* (1965), it did substitute its judgment for theirs and reversed the convictions of black demonstrators.

Conspiracy prosecutions for speech

Two prosecutions for alleged speech offenses achieved great notoriety during the violent 1960s, those of Dr. Benjamin Spock and the Chicago Seven.[3] Both involved charges of conspiracy, which are more difficult to defend against than charges of individual wrongdoing, since a conspiracy to commit an illegal act is a crime even if the act itself never occurs.

Dr. Spock and three other opponents of the war in Vietnam were convicted of conspiring to encourage resistance to the draft, but the convictions were reversed on appeal in 1969 because of errors in the trial. The Chicago Seven were participants in the disorders at the 1968 Democratic Convention in Chicago and were charged with violation of the federal Anti-Riot Act, which defines as a criminal act the crossing of state lines to incite or participate in a riot. Five of the defendants were convicted after a very turbulent trial before Judge Julius Hoffman, but two were held innocent by the jury, and all seven were freed of the conspiracy charge. The court of appeals subsequently reversed the convictions for errors in the trial, but by a 2-to-1 vote upheld the constitutionality of the Anti-Riot Act.

FREEDOM TO DEMONSTRATE

The organized demonstration is a form of communication that almost necessarily involves serious impact on other community interests. Demonstrations nearly always take place in public areas—the streets, the sidewalks,

---

[3]See Jessica Mitford, *The Trial of Dr. Spock,* New York: Knopf, 1969; and Jason Epstein, *The Great Conspiracy Trial,* New York: Random House, 1970. A third major conspiracy trial was that of the Reverend Philip Berrigan and six others at Harrisburg, Pennsylvania, in 1972 for allegedly conspiring to kidnap presidential adviser Henry A. Kissinger and blow up underground heating tunnels in Washington. The case ended in a mistrial when the jury was unable to reach a verdict. See John C. Raines (ed.), *Conspiracy: The Implications of the Harrisburg Trial for the Democratic Tradition,* New York: Harper & Row, 1974; Jack Nelson and Ronald J. Ostrow, *The FBI and the Berrigans: The Making of a Conspiracy,* New York: Coward, McCann & Geoghegan, 1973.

the parks. Demonstrators use public places because they want to make contact with the public. They want to bring their views to the attention of people who do not know about them, who have not asked to be informed concerning them, and who may very well object to them. An organized demonstration on public streets or sidewalks is bound to interfere to some degree with the normal use of these public facilities. A parade or a picket line, with songs and slogans and signs, is "speech," but it is also action. As the Supreme Court has put it, it is "speech *plus*."

Because of these facts, it is clear that the community is justified in requiring advance notification and permits for demonstrations. The Supreme Court so held in Cox v. *New Hampshire* (1941), where a group of Jehovah's Witnesses had marched single file along city streets carrying placards to advertise a meeting, without securing the license required by state law for "parades or processions" in public streets. The Court upheld this statute as a reasonable police regulation, administered under proper safeguards.

Picketing initially came to the Court's attention in connection with labor disputes. In the nineteenth century, labor picketing was unlawful, but in the 1940 case of *Thornhill* v. *Alabama*, the Supreme Court finally brought picketing within the protection of the free-speech clause, saying: "In the circumstances of our times the dissemination of information concerning the facts of a labor dispute must be regarded as within that area of free discussion that is guaranteed by the Constitution." However, the Court quickly made clear that it realized labor picketing was more than discussion. It was also economic coercion, which could lead to violence or be exercised for unlawful ends. So in an important series of cases from 1941 to 1957, the Court uniformly upheld various legislative and judicial restrictions on picketing.

Constitutional status of demonstrations

The constitutional aspects of demonstrations and picketing in connection with the civil-rights and peace movements of the 1960s presented difficult problems for the courts. The starting point, of course, is that a demonstration is conduct as well as speech, and as conduct it is subject to regulation. As Justice Goldberg said in *Cox* v. *Louisiana* (1965):

> *We emphatically reject the notion . . . that the First and Fourteenth Amendments afford the same kind of freedom to those who would communicate ideas by conduct such as patroling, marching, and picketing on streets and highways, as these amendments afford to those who communicate ideas by pure speech.*

Although demonstrations are not the same as "pure speech," they are important instruments for expression of opinion, and consequently they are entitled to some measure of constitutional protection. A city could not ban all demonstrations on its streets, except for limited emergency periods or in specific locations. There is, of course, no right to hold "a street meeting in the middle of Times Square at the rush hour" (*Cox* v. *Louisiana* [1965]). In *Cameron* v. *Johnson* (1968), the Court upheld a Mississippi antipicketing law forbidding mass demonstrations that interfered with free access to any public building. The mayor of Philadelphia banned all public gatherings of more than 12 persons during the emergency period following the assassination of Martin Luther King, Jr., and in *Stotland* v. *Pennsylvania* (1970), the Supreme Court failed to invalidate this action. Federal and state statutes forbid picketing around courthouses with the intention of influencing pending trials, and the Supreme Court upheld such a law in *Cox* v. *Louisiana* (1965).

These are exceptional situations, however. The basic principle, as stated in *Hague* v. *C.I.O.* (1939), is that the use of the streets and public places "for purposes of assembly, communicating thoughts between citizens, and discussing public questions [is] a part of the privileges, immunities, rights, and liberties of citizens." The right to picket the White House has been protected by courts in the District of Columbia. Although there is normally no right to stage demonstrations on private property without permission, in 1968 the Court upheld picketing in the parking lot of a shopping center, which was technically private property but to which the public had free access. In 1972 the Burger Court held that this decision did not open shopping centers to general propaganda efforts, but only authorized union picketing directed specifically at businesses operating in the shopping center (*Lloyd* v. *Tanner*).

Demonstrations and breach of the peace

If the police undertake to arrest demonstrators for breach of the peace or other unlawful acts, they must be prepared to justify the arrests. Of course, if demonstrators obstruct traffic by lying down in the streets, or if they physically attack the arresting officers, their conduct is clearly illegal. But more difficult problems arise when picketers simply disobey police orders to discontinue their demonstration. In *Brown* v. *Louisiana* (1966), five blacks walked into a segregated library, asked for a book, and remained after the librarian had told them the book was not available and requested them to leave. No one else was in the library, and they stood quietly until the sheriff arrived and arrested them for breach of the peace. The Supreme Court by a vote of 5 to 4 held that their action did not amount to a violation of the breach-of-the-peace law.

A few months later, however, the Court reached an opposite conclusion, also by a vote of 5 to 4, in *Adderly* v. *Florida*. A sizable group of black students had gathered on jailhouse property to protest segregation in the jail. The sheriff ordered them off as trespassers, and the Supreme Court agreed that they had no right to demonstrate on property that was not open to the public and where security was essential.

When a hostile crowd has formed around the demonstrators and violence seems likely, the police have a very difficult problem. Should they seek to preserve order by ending the demonstration and, if necessary, arresting the demonstrators? Or should they let the demonstration continue and seek to control the crowd, arresting the principal troublemakers if necessary?

Obviously, the police have to base their decision on their judgment of the facts in each specific situation. As we have seen, in the *Feiner* case the police arrested the speaker, and the Supreme Court approved. But in *Edwards* v. *South Carolina* (1963), involving a demonstration by some 200 black students on the grounds of the state capitol that seemed much more likely to lead to violence than the Feiner situation, the Court reversed the convictions of the demonstrators who had defied police orders to disband. The Court said: "The Fourteenth Amendment does not permit a State to make criminal the peaceful expression of unpopular views."

In the late 1960s, unrest on the nation's campuses and protests against the war in Vietnam led to massive demonstrations and violent disorders. Police and National Guard troops were called onto a number of campuses. Violence by both demonstrators and police at the 1968 Democratic Convention in Chicago amounted to a national scandal. The importance of rational foresight and planning by the authorities is demonstrated by comparing the Chicago disaster with the march on the Pentagon by the anti-Vietnam National Mobilization Committee in October, 1967. In Washington, the government granted permits for the demonstration, in spite of the threats of participants to close down the Pentagon, and was able to control a crowd of some 30,000 with only a minimum of force. In Chicago, on the other hand, city officials denied permits for the demonstration and the use of public parks, and with no legitimate arena, the protest escalated into a bloody confrontation between demonstrators and police.[4]

Massive antiwar demonstrations were held in Washington, D.C., in May, 1971. When a complete traffic tieup was threatened in downtown Washington, the capital police abandoned normal field arrest procedures, which require photographing each suspect and filling out a brief form, and made mass arrests of over 10,000 persons who were crowded into jails and detention centers where they were held for several days incommunicado and without adequate food or facilities. Practically all of these cases were subsequently dismissed because there were no arrest records and the police could not identify individuals alleged to have broken the law. During the same period the police also arrested some 1,200 demonstrators peaceably

---

[4]See Norman Mailer, *The Armies of the Night*, New York: New American Library, 1968; and *Rights in Conflict: The Walker Report to the National Committee on the Causes and Prevention of Violence*, New York: Bantam Books, 1968.

assembled on the Capitol steps to hear speeches by sympathetic members of Congress. In 1975 a Washington jury held that these demonstrators had been denied their civil rights and awarded them $12 million in damages.

Symbolic speech

Freedom of speech may also be invoked to justify forms of expression in which speech is not used, but where ideas or protests are communicated by conduct, as by burning a draft card or pouring blood over draft files to express opposition to the war in Vietnam. Such action serves as a surrogate for speech, and conveys an ideational message perhaps more effectively than speech would do. But is this type of "symbolic speech" entitled to the constitutional protection of normal speech? In *Tinker* v. *Des Moines School District* (1969), school officials had forbidden pupils to wear black armbands as a protest against the war on the ground that this gesture might cause controversy in the school. The Court, however, upheld the students, saying that "apprehension of disturbance is not enough to overcome the right to freedom of expression." But draft-card burning did not win the Court's approval. Chief Justice Warren wrote in *United States* v. *O'Brien* (1968): "We cannot accept the view that an apparently limitless variety of conduct can be labeled 'speech' whenever the person engaging in the conduct intends thereby to express an idea."

Disrespect for the American flag has sometimes been used as a method of expressing opposition to government policy. In *Street* v. *New York* (1969) the Court appeared to assume that burning the flag could be punished. But in *Smith* v. *Goguen* (1974) conviction of a youth for wearing an American flag on the seat of his pants was reversed on the ground that the statute against treating the flag "contemptuously" was too vague.

DIRECT ACTION AND CIVIL DISOBEDIENCE

Direct action is a very broad term covering a wide range of challenges to established laws or practices. Direct action may be nonviolent or violent. It may operate within legal limits, or it may deliberately and intentionally violate the law. The purpose of direct action is to dramatize issues, to force grievances on the attention of the community, to create trouble and expense for the community involved, and to compel the "establishment" and the "power structure" to enter into negotiations for correcting the conditions protested. As the late Martin Luther King, Jr., the acknowledged philosopher of the direct-action movement, put it: "Nonviolent direct action seeks to create such a crisis and establish such creative tension that a community that has constantly refused to negotiate is forced to confront the issue."[5]

[5]"A Letter from Birmingham Jail," July, 1963.

The direct-action program that Dr. King led was nonviolent and operated in large part through legal methods such as parades and demonstrations. His program, however, did include the violation of laws he regarded as unjust. He said: "I would agree with Saint Augustine that 'an unjust law is no law at all.' "

Civil disobedience is an extreme form of direct action. It involves deliberate violation of the law, but the violation is not necessarily limited to laws the protesters regard as unjust. Rather, practitioners of civil disobedience will violate admittedly valid laws, such as traffic regulations, in order to dramatize their grievances by creating maximum confusion, trouble, and danger for the community. Thoreau and Gandhi agreed that persons who engaged in civil disobedience should expect to go to jail, but some recent practitioners of civil disobedience have demanded amnesty from prosecution for law violations.

FREEDOM OF ASSOCIATION

Freedom of association is not mentioned in the Constitution, but it is an important civil liberty derived from the right of assembly and the freedoms of speech, press, and religion. One of the most effective methods of expression is to associate oneself with other like-minded persons for the achievement of common goals. Americans are inveterate "joiners," and the right to belong to groups is so universally assumed that it is seldom challenged. However, groups that are unpopular or are regarded as dangerous—the Communist party, the Ku Klux Klan, the National Association for the Advancement of Colored People (NAACP), the John Birch Society—may find their associational freedom subject to attack. The Communist party is a special problem to be considered later. Among other organizations, the experience of the NAACP has been the most important in stimulating judicial statements on freedom of association.

NAACP activities

After the *Brown* decision in 1954, the activities of the NAACP in seeking to promote school desegregation aroused bitter hostility in most of the southern states. Its members were subjected to economic coercion and often to physical abuse. There were also efforts through legislation and court action to hamper or terminate the work of the organization.

In Alabama, the attorney general sought to enjoin the NAACP from operating in the state on the pretext that as an out-of-state corporation it had not filed the necessary papers to qualify it to carry on activities in Alabama. As a part of this action, the attorney general demanded a list of all the NAACP members in the state, but the organization refused on the ground that making the list public would subject members to harassment and unconstitutionally restrain their freedom of association. The Supreme Court upheld this refusal in *NAACP* v. *Alabama* (1958).

The NAACP concentrated much of its efforts on court suits to compel desegregation, and here also it was subjected to pressure. A Virginia law, typical of those in many other states, forbade the stirring up of litigation or the improper solicitation of legal business. This legislation was aimed at "ambulance-chasing" and other unethical legal practices, but because the NAACP admittedly seeks out test cases on which it can go to court, it was accused of violating the statute in Virginia.

In *NAACP* v. *Button* (1963), the Supreme Court upheld the association's litigation procedures, and in the decision recognized litigation as a "form of political expression." The Court said that "in the context of NAACP objectives, litigation is not a technique of resolving private differences; it is a means for achieving the lawful objectives of equality of treatment by all government, federal, state, and local, for the members of the Negro community in this country." Indeed, "for such a group, association for litigation may be the most effective form of political association."

INDIVIDUAL FREEDOM AND NATIONAL SECURITY

The severest test of constitutional freedom occurs in periods of war and civil emergency, when danger or disorder threatens, passions become inflamed, and there is no longer toleration of the unorthodox and the extremists who are accepted in less tense times. The favorable geographical position of the United States, protected by two oceans, for a long period minimized any threat of foreign involvement. To be sure, this was not true during the early period of the nation, and in the bitter conflict between the partisans of England and France, the Federalist majority in Congress sought reprisals against the Jeffersonians by passing the Alien and Sedition Acts. At the time there was no constitutional test of the Sedition Act, but in 1964 the law was declared unconstitutional retrospectively by the Supreme Court.

After more than a century of freedom from serious foreign involvements, the United States was not psychologically prepared for the strains of World War I. The country reacted hysterically, first to the German threat and then, after the Bolshevik revolution in Russia, to the specter of communism. Congress adopted the Espionage Act in 1917 and the Sedition Act in 1918, under which many persons were jailed for criticizing the war effort.

Justice Holmes was the spokesman for the Court in its first encounters with these World War I cases, and he developed, in *Schenck* v. *United States* (1919), the famous "clear and present danger" test to measure the extent of the government's power to punish the spoken or written word because of its connection with illegal action:

> *The question in every case is whether the words used are used in such circumstances and are of such a nature as to create a clear and present danger that they will bring about the substantive evils that Congress has a right to prevent. It is a question of proximity and degree.*

However, the clear-and-present-danger test proved to have little protective effect. In *Abrams* v. *United States* (1919) the Court upheld the conviction of Communists who printed leaflets urging munitions workers to strike to demonstrate their disapproval of American armed action against the Russian revolution. *Gitlow* v. *New York* (1925) and *Whitney* v. *California* (1927) upheld convictions of Communists under state criminal anarchy or syndicalism laws.

The status of the Communist party

After World War II, the American Communist party came under intensive pressure. Prosecution of its national leaders was begun in 1948 under the Smith Act, which makes it unlawful knowingly to advocate the overthrow of any government in the United States by force or violence, or to organize or knowingly become a member of any group that so advocates. The Supreme Court upheld the conviction of the party leaders in *Dennis* v. *United States* (1951). Although they were not charged with having taken any action for the immediate purpose of initiating a revolution, the Court majority, applying the clear-and-present-danger test, decided that the Communist party constituted an evil of sufficient gravity to justify punishing its leaders for their advocacy of revolutionary principles. Later, in *Scales* v. *United States* (1961), the Court upheld the provision of the Smith Act making active and knowing membership in the Communist party a crime.

The Internal Security Act of 1950 requiring all Communist-action organizations to register with the government was upheld in 1961, but the government was unable to force the Communist party to register because such action would constitute self-incrimination. The principal sanctions in the same law, forbidding Communists to apply for passports or work in defense plants, were declared unconstitutional on the ground that mere membership in the party could not be treated as criminal.[6] *Brandenburg* v. *Ohio* (1969) completed the reversal of the Cold War decisions by striking down the Ohio criminal syndicalism law, thereby overruling the *Whitney* decision.

The Supreme Court thus restored freedom of association for the Communist party and accepted as constitutional the right to advocate overthrow of the government as an abstract doctrine. The party, which during the Cold War had been forced off the ballot in all states, reappeared, and in

---

[6]*Aptheker* v. *Secretary of State* (1964); *United States* v. *Robel* (1967).

1974 the Court invalidated an Indiana law that required the party to file a loyalty oath as a condition of gaining a place on the ballot. Similarly, loyalty-oath requirements for public employees, which had been widely prescribed during the Cold War, were gradually restricted by court decisions until they amounted to little more than affirmations of support for the federal and state constitutions.[7]

Legislative investigations

Congress has broad power to investigate as an aid to its legislative function, and to punish for contempt persons who refuse to testify before its committees. Although this authority is used to secure information on every aspect of congressional activity, the most publicized investigations since World War II have involved suspected subversive activities and organizations.

The investigations conducted by the House Committee on Un-American Activities and Senator Joseph McCarthy were particularly controversial.[8] Many persons contended that these committees were interested not in securing information for legislative purposes but in exposing individual Communists and forcing witnesses to invoke the Fifth Amendment to avoid self-incrimination. The Supreme Court warned in *Watkins* v. *United States* (1957) that there is no power to expose for the sake of exposure. But since the Court accepted the position that the Communist party was not a legitimate political party, it upheld legislative inquiries into Communist activity as fulfilling a proper legislative purpose, and ruled that individuals, unless they took the Fifth Amendment, could be required to reveal whether they were members of the Communist party. However, the Court has insisted that congressional committees give witnesses procedural protections and not ask questions outside their authorized area of investigation. Since 1961, the Court has reversed a substantial number of contempt convictions on these grounds.

The 1973 investigation by the Senate Select Committee on Watergate, under the chairmanship of Senator Sam Ervin, and the 1974 public hearings of the House Judiciary Committee, under the chairmanship of Peter Rodino, on the impeachment of President Nixon were both conducted with careful concern for the rights of all involved, and demonstrated before nation-wide television audiences the essential value of the investigative function.

[7]*Elfbrandt* v. *Russell* (1966); *Cole* v. *Richardson* (1972).

[8]In 1969 the House Committee on Un-American Activities, in an effort to dispel its unfavorable image, changed its name to the Committee on Internal Security. In 1975 the committee was abolished, its functions being transferred to the House Judiciary Committee.

The English policy on totalitarian parties and political violence

The English policy of dealing with the Communist party and fascist groups has been quite different from the American. While the government does concern itself with any underground or conspiratorial activities of such parties, no effort has been made in England to deprive these parties of their freedom to organize in the open and to conduct propaganda activities. The British concept, in which all the democratic parties—Conservative, Labour, and Liberal—concur, is that if the totalitarian parties are given enough rope they will hang themselves. Although the Communist party of Britain has contested a number of seats in Parliament without any harassment or governmental curbs, since 1950 it has not been able to elect a single member to Parliament. In contrast to the organizational freedom allowed to extremist groups in England, the English courts have been quick to punish political violence and riotous demonstrators.

RELIGIOUS LIBERTY

The First Amendment guarantees freedom of religion and forbids the "establishment" of religion. Of these two principles, religious freedom or toleration was the older and more firmly grounded when the First Amendment was adopted in 1791. The tragic results of religious discrimination and persecution, of punishment because of belief or conscience, had long been demonstrated in England and in Europe by the time the American nation was founded, and the theoretical and practical case for toleration was well developed in English writing.

The establishment provision, on the other hand, was in flat contradiction to the English practice of an official established church, and some variety of establishment prevailed in several of the American states at the time the Constitution was adopted. Thus the principle of separation of church and state was an American invention whose application remained to be worked out in practice.

Freedom of religion

The government cannot force or influence a person to go to or remain away from church. It cannot require anyone to profess a belief or disbelief in any religion, or punish anyone for entertaining or professing religious beliefs or disbeliefs. Parents cannot be forced by state law to send their children to public schools if they prefer that they receive a religious education in parochial schools meeting state standards (*Pierce v. Society of Sisters* [1925]). A state cannot require persons to secure permission from a public official before soliciting for religious causes, because this would amount to state censorship of religion (*Cantwell v. Connecticut* [1940]).

However, it often happens that general regulations adopted in good faith to promote the general welfare—compulsory education, public health, limitation of child labor or hours of work, licensing of occupations, social security—conflict with the practices or beliefs of some religious groups. The courts generally deal with such conflicts by the so-called secular-regulation rule, which states that there is no constitutional right to exemption on religious grounds from the compulsion of a general regulation dealing with nonreligious matters.

The Supreme Court first applied this rule in holding that a congressional statute making polygamy criminal did not deny free exercise of religion to Mormons, for whom plural marriage was a religious tenet (*Reynolds v. United States* [1878]). In the *Sunday Closing* cases of 1961, the Court held that Sunday closing laws do not infringe the religious freedom of Jewish merchants, whose religion requires them to close their stores on Saturday, because Sunday observance, while originally religiously motivated, had become a secular device for providing a uniform day of rest. Other applications of the secular-regulation rule have upheld compulsory vaccination and laws prohibiting snake-handling in religious services.

The secular-regulation rule, however, may on some occasions seem to be unduly harsh in refusing to make any allowance for deviant religious practices that are based on sincere beliefs and do not threaten any vital public interests. If a legislature wishes, it may grant exemptions to religious groups from general secular laws. Thus, in 1965, Congress gave exemption from the social-security laws to the Amish, a small religious sect that believes that any form of insurance shows a lack of faith in God. Similarly, in *Sherbert v. Verner* (1963) the Court made an important concession to a religious claim, holding that a state unemployment-compensation law could not be applied to force a Seventh-Day Adventist to violate the religious teachings of that church by working on a Saturday. The *Sherbert* holding was subsequently cited by state courts in overturning the conviction of Navajo members of the Native American Church for using the drug peyote in their religious ceremonies, and in freeing from a contempt sentence a woman who had refused on religious grounds to serve on a jury. The refusal of Amish parents for religious reasons to send their children to school beyond the eighth grade was upheld by the Supreme Court in *Wisconsin v. Yoder* (1972).

All American draft laws have granted exemption from military service to religious objectors to war. The 1948 statute granted exemption to persons whose opposition to war was based on "religious training and belief," which was defined as "an individual's belief in a relation to a Supreme Being involving duties superior to those arising from any human relation, but [not including] essentially political, sociological, or philosophical views or a merely personal moral code." In *United States v. Seeger* (1965), the Supreme Court interpreted this language broadly enough to cover quite unorthodox religious beliefs. The Court then went further in *Welsh v. United States* (1970) and upheld conscientious objection on purely moral and ethical grounds.

The statute provides that objectors must be "conscientiously opposed to participation in war in any form." Attitudes toward the Vietnam war caused some young men, who did not reject all wars, to profess "selective conscientious objection," that is, the right to object to service in particular wars of which they disapproved. The Supreme Court rejected this contention in *Gillette v. United States* (1971), saying it was in direct contradiction to the statute.

Religion and the establishment clause

There are two general views as to the meaning of the establishment clause. The first holds that it outlaws only the kind of establishment that existed in Europe in 1791, namely, one official tax-supported church. This view contends that what the framers wanted to prevent was *preference* for one religion over others. State contacts with religion or state support of religion would be proper unless discrimination between religions is involved.

The second view contends that the establishment rule outlaws *any* government support of, or connection with, religion. Complete separation of church and state is demanded, and no public financial support to religious institutions is permissible, even if made available on a nonpreferential basis. The Supreme Court has consistently supported this second position.

Establishment issues have been raised on many occasions in American history—the official designation of Thanksgiving Day, the provision of chaplains for Congress and in the armed services, compulsory chapel services at U.S. military academies. The Supreme Court's first important consideration of the issue came in the 1947 New Jersey bus case, *Everson v. Board of Education.* Justice Black summarized the Court's understanding of the establishment clause as follows:

> *Neither a state nor the Federal Government can set up a church. Neither can pass laws which aid one religion, aid all religions, or prefer one religion over another. . . . No tax in any amount, large or small, can be levied to support any religious activities or institutions, whatever they may be called, or whatever form they may adopt to teach or practice religion. . . . In the words of Jefferson, the clause against establishment of religion by law was intended to erect "a wall of separation between church and State."*

In the *Everson* case, public funds were being used to pay the bus fare of children to parochial as well as public schools, but the majority of the Court held that these payments were for the benefit of the child and so did not constitute financial assistance to religious schools.

"Released-time" programs of religious education, where children are excused from regular public-school classes to take religious instruction from teachers supplied by local religious groups, are constitutional, provided the classes are held off the school premises. This was the Court's holding in *Zorach* v. *Clauson* (1952), although three members of the Court charged that the use of the public-school machinery to provide students for these classes made the program an unconstitutional joinder of church and state.

Religious observances in the public schools—the saying of prayers and the reading of the Bible—were held unconstitutional by the Supreme Court in 1962 and 1963 (*Engel* v. *Vitale; School District* v. *Schempp*). These decisions created a great public furor, and an effort to amend the Constitution to permit prayers in the public schools was begun. However, many religious leaders supported the decisions as wise steps toward keeping the divisive influence of religion out of the public schools. The charge by the Court's opponents that it would logically have to proceed to root out all religious manifestations in public life, such as the offering of prayers at the opening of legislative sessions or the words "In God We Trust" on coins, was refuted by the Court itself in 1964 when it refused to review a New York state court ruling upholding the use of the words "under God" in the pledge of allegiance by public-school pupils.

Aid to parochial schools. A serious new establishment problem was raised by the passage of the Elementary and Secondary Education Act of 1965. Previous efforts to give federal financial aid to education had always foundered on the issue of inclusion of the parochial schools. President Johnson successfully bypassed this problem by proposing assistance primarily to schools serving children of low-income families, and the act as passed made funds available in various ways for improving the education of students in both religious and public schools.

Most of the funds go to public-school districts in "poverty-impacted" areas, to be used to meet the special educational needs of educationally deprived children, but through "shared-time" or "dual-enrollment" programs, eligible children attending nonpublic schools also participate in these benefits. The act also provides funds for the purchase of textbooks and library materials. The title to these books remains in the public-school district, but in fact they are used by the pupils of both public and nonpublic schools. Finally, the act provides for supplemental education centers where remedial instruction, laboratories, specialized teachers, and counselors are available for students of both public and nonpublic schools.

It was recognized in Congress that the act raised establishment issues, and there was some fear that the Supreme Court would not be able to pass on them because of a 1923 decision denying taxpayers the right to bring suits against federal spending. However, the Court in *Flast* v. *Cohen* (1968) did grant standing to taxpayers where First Amendment rights were at stake. The Court had not by 1975 ruled directly on the constitutionality of the Education Act. It had, however, generally rejected all state efforts to provide financial help for hard-pressed parochial schools. In *Board of Education v. Allen* (1968) the Court did uphold a New York law under which textbooks were provided for parochial as well as public-school students. But a group of 1973 decisions, headed by *Committee for Public Education v. Nyquist,* rejected an assortment of state aid plans, including state reimbursement or tax credits to parents for tuition in parochial schools. *Meek v. Pittinger* (1975) upheld state loans of textbooks to children in nonpublic schools, but struck down all the other provisions of a Pennsylvania parochial aid package.

Likewise *Lemon v. Kurtzman* (1971) ruled unconstitutional state grants to supplement the salaries of teachers of secular subjects in parochial schools, Chief Justice Burger saying that this relationship would result in excessive "entanglement" of government and religion. However, federal and state building grants for construction of nonsectarian facilities at church-related colleges was upheld as meeting the "no entanglement" test (*Tilton v. Richardson* [1971], *Hunt v. McNair* [1974]).

THE RIGHT TO PRIVACY

There is no general language in the Constitution protecting the right to privacy, and yet such a right is one of the underlying conditions of a free society. Justice Brandeis once referred to the "right to be let alone" as the "most comprehensive of rights and the right most valued by civilized men." The Constitution comes closest to spelling out this right in the Fourth Amendment provision against "unreasonable searches and seizures," which protects the privacy of one's home from invasion by the police unless they have sufficient evidence of commission of a crime to secure a search warrant from a court.

The more interesting and difficult problems of privacy have occurred in recent decades with the development of means of surveillance that can invade privacy without any physical incursion into a home. Tapping of telephone lines was one of the first of these methods. Scientific advances have now made possible even more effective forms of surveillance, so that government agents or anyone else can penetrate easily and effectively the privacy of houses, offices, and vehicles, or monitor the basic channels of communication. In the area of psychological surveillance, techniques such as the polygraph (lie-detector test) and personality testing that probe interior thought processes of their subjects have become widely used since World War II. Use of "truth drugs" and brain-wave analysis can carry these incursions even further. Computers have made possible the collection and instant availability of masses of information, so that "data surveillance" of individuals, businesses, and groups has become possible on a scale hitherto unknown.[9]

What will remain of the right to privacy under this technological assault is not clear. However, it is interesting that the Supreme Court has discovered the existence of a general right to privacy under the Constitution. The occasion was *Griswold* v. *Connecticut* (1965), where the Court held unconstitutional a state statute forbidding the use of birth-control devices. In this case, a doctor who had given birth-control information to married couples had been convicted of violating the law. Justice Douglas for the Court recognized "zones of privacy" contained in the "penumbra" of various provisions in the Constitution, including the First, Third, Fourth, Fifth, and Ninth Amendments. In the marriage relationship, he concluded, "We deal with a right of privacy older than the Bill of Rights. . . ."

Abortion laws. In two sensational 1973 decisions, *Roe* v. *Wade* and *Doe* v. *Bolton,* the Court invoked the right of privacy in holding unconstitutional the criminal abortion laws of two states, and announced guidelines limiting the power of states to regulate abortion. By a vote of 7 to 2 the Court ruled that during the first three months of pregnancy, the decision to have an abortion must be left entirely to the woman and her physician. During the second trimester the state can set standards for the conditions under which abortions are performed, in the interest of preserving the health of the mother or the potential life of the unborn infant. In the third trimester the state, to safeguard the unborn infant, can ban all abortions except those performed to save the mother's life. The Court declined to find that the word "person" in the equal protection clause includes unborn children. These rulings were highly controversial, and several "right to life" constitutional amendments were immediately introduced in Congress, generally intended to forbid abortion except in medical emergencies when the life of the mother was threatened.

---

[9]*California Bankers Association* v. *Shultz* (1974) upheld the Bank Secrecy Act, which requires all banks to maintain records and make reports of their customers' transactions which will be useful in criminal, tax, or regulatory proceedings.

8 Equality

8

The Declaration of Independence affirmed that "all men are created equal," yet there was no language in the Constitution reflecting this concern. There were, to be sure, provisions protecting various civil rights, particularly the guarantees of uniform standards of criminal justice in the Fourth through the Eighth Amendments, but there was nothing specifically affirming the equality of all persons under law. On the contrary, there were several provisions accepting and guaranteeing the institution of human slavery.

All this was changed by the Civil War and the passion for equality that it unloosed. Slavery was abolished by the Thirteenth Amendment, and the Fourteenth undertook to guarantee that the freedmen would enter fully into the privileges of their new status. However, the equal protection of the laws promised to blacks by the Fourteenth Amendment remained a promise only. Neither the country, the Congress, nor the Court was prepared to translate these fine words into deeds. Ironically enough, the original beneficiaries of the equal-protection clause were not blacks but business corporations, which in case after case were able to get tax or regulatory statutes declared unconstitutional on the ground that their impact was not equal on all corporations. The constitutional standing of the equal-protection clause fell so low that in 1927 Justice Holmes deprecated it as the "usual last resort of constitutional arguments" (*Buck* v. *Bell*). But a change was finally at hand. Within a few years the equal-protection clause became the foundation of a massive midcentury drive for civil rights and equality of opportunity.

EQUALITY OF OPPORTUNITY

Equality of opportunity has been one of the great boasts of American democracy. Our folklore is full of success stories of people who, like Horatio Alger's storybook heroes, rose from poverty to wealth and power by means of their hard work and winning personalities. Being born in a log cabin was a positive advantage in running for the presidency during the nineteenth century. Yet at the same time, no one could help recognizing the grievous inequalities of opportunity in American life. One reaction to this conflict of dream and reality is the cynicism of George Orwell: "All men are created equal, but some are more equal than others." Abraham

Lincoln thought there was a better way to regard the idealism of the Declaration of Independence:

> [It] meant to set up a standard maxim for free society which could be familiar to all, and revered by all; constantly looked to, constantly labored for, and even though never perfectly attained, constantly approximated, and thereby constantly spreading and deepening its influence, and augmenting the happiness and value of life to all people of all colors everywhere.

In fact, the process that Lincoln described has been enormously successful. American society has been remarkably open and has offered tremendous opportunity for recognition of individual merit while imposing comparatively few arbitrary barriers to personal fulfillment. There have been many reasons for this favorable situation. In the beginning, the American settlers were relatively homogeneous in social status, language, and religion. The rich natural resources of the new country offered great opportunity to anyone with industry and initiative. The frontier was always just over the horizon for those who felt hemmed in by the more settled communities. Of course, classes developed, based, as in Europe, on birth and wealth, but class lines were not as rigid or taken as seriously as in England, and upward mobility was constantly possible. It was not utopia, but opportunity was real.

The inequalities that have marred American society in the past century have their basis in social, economic, or legal disadvantage or some combination of these factors. The immigrants who came to America in a swelling tide from 1850 to the 1920s often encountered social and economic discrimination. The Irish, for example, were initially despised and given only the most menial jobs, but they quickly made their way into political life and used their political skills to improve their economic and social position.

The poor, whether native or foreign-born, have never shared fully in American opportunities. Although not subject to actual legal disabilities, they have generally lacked the motivation or the resources to secure an adequate education, and so have been deprived of the most important requisite for individual advancement. Until fairly recently, only the children of middle- and upper-class parents went to college.

Women as a class have had to struggle against many kinds of discrimination. They are less likely to go to college, they were and are still discouraged from entering many professions and many types of employment, their pay scales have generally been lower than those for men, and their legal situation subordinates them in various respects to their husbands.

Some inequalities stem from geographic location. Americans living in regions that lack natural resources or industrial development tend to suffer from malnutrition, ill health, and lack of education and opportunities for employment because of the poverty of their surroundings. The coal industry until recently yielded a poor living for residents of Kentucky and West Virginia. The cut-over forest land of Wisconsin and Michigan, the exhausted iron-ore quarries of Minnesota, the overcropped dust bowls of the Great Plains all created economic and social inequalities.

In the programs of the New Deal, the federal government made the first concerted attack on inequality of opportunity. President Franklin Roosevelt inaugurated a series of emergency programs to relieve unemployment, to restore confidence in private enterprise, and to start up the machinery of a stalled economy. Unemployment compensation and the social-security system met some of the basic social and human needs, and a fascinating experiment in reducing regional inequalities was conducted by the Tennessee Valley Authority. The major lesson of the New Deal was that never again could the government permit a nationwide depression to occur without taking vigorous steps to combat it.

World War II brought full employment and job opportunities for all previously disadvantaged groups, including women. At the close of the war, fear of a postwar depression led the government to assume further responsibilities for the health of the economy by adopting the Full Employment Act of 1946. In spite of the Republican philosophy of reducing the sphere of the federal government that had been widened during 20 years of Democratic administration, President Eisenhower did not find it desirable to dismantle any of the machinery intended to create the economic base for greater equality of opportunity.

The innovative spirit of the New Deal was revived under Presidents Kennedy and Johnson. The most ambitious and comprehensive program ever undertaken in the United States for remedying inequalities included such features as area-redevelopment programs for the Appalachian region; a federal equal-pay act for women; improvement of educational opportunities for the children of poor families by an extensive program of federal financial grants to elementary and secondary schools; and a wide-ranging "poverty program" aimed at training dropouts, illiterates, and the unemployables for useful jobs and reentry into society.

The most important target of these new efforts was the Negro. From the time of emancipation, the plight of the black American had been by all odds the most glaring and persistent contradiction of the American claim of equality of opportunity. For a few years after the Civil War, the federal government devoted some attention to improving the lot of the newly freed slaves, but these efforts were soon abandoned. Concentrated largely in the southern states, deprived of the vote, offered a racially segregated education of the most primitive kind, limited in employment opportunities to manual and domestic labor, kept in their "place" by a rigid code enforced by sanctions ranging from insult and economic pressure to lynching, blacks lived as a lower caste almost completely excluded from sharing in the American heritage.

Only after the twentieth century was half over did the situation of the blacks begin to improve. Although many factors were at work, by far the most important was the Supreme Court's electrifying decision on May 17, 1954, in *Brown* v. *Board of Education of Topeka,* that racial segregation in the public schools was unconstitutional. While the civil-rights revolution can be dated from this event, it is desirable first to review some of the background for this ruling.

EQUAL VOTING RIGHTS

One of the major factors in black inequality was denial of the right to vote. The states determine who is eligible to vote in state and local elections, and the Constitution also permits the states to determine the federal electorate. However, racial discrimination is forbidden by the Constitution, both by the equal-protection clause of the Fourteenth Amendment and by the Fifteenth Amendment, which specifically guarantees that the right to vote shall not be abridged on account of race, color, or previous condition of servitude. Unfortunately, these provisions are not self-enforcing, and aside from certain civil-rights statutes after the Civil War, the federal government for almost a century gave no attention to the problem of black voting.

Denial of the franchise to blacks was accomplished in large part by intimidation and violence, but the southern states also sought to discover "legal" methods for accomplishing their purpose. The most successful devices were tests for literacy and "understanding the Constitution," which could be manipulated with great effectiveness to disfranchise blacks. A Mississippi law requiring voters to be able to read, understand, or interpret any section of the Constitution was upheld in *Williams* v. *Mississippi* (1898) because on its face it was not discriminatory. Another type of restriction, the so-called grandfather clause, was declared unconstitutional. An Oklahoma law imposed a literacy test for voting, but exempted persons whose ancestors had been entitled to vote in 1866. The Supreme Court in *Guinn* v. *United States* (1915) held this provision to be an obvious attempt to evade the Fifteenth Amendment.

Another device for achieving discrimination was to bar blacks from primary elections. The Supreme Court abetted this tactic when in *Newberry* v. *United States* (1921) it ruled that party primaries were not part of the election process, and consequently constitutional protections on voting did not apply to them. When the Texas Democratic party confined membership and participation in its primaries to white citizens, the Supreme Court upheld this action in *Grovey* v. *Townsend* (1935).

The propositions that primaries are not elections and that political parties are private clubs that can choose their own members were both so absurd that the Supreme Court could not long maintain them. Primaries were declared to be part of the election process in *United States* v. *Classic* (1941), and *Smith* v. *Allwright* (1944) reversed the private-club rule. But this was about as far as the Supreme Court could go. Intimidation, coercion, and inertia still prevented most blacks from voting in the South, and this situation could be changed only by intervention on the part of the federal government to enforce constitutional rights.

Effective voting rights for blacks became a reality in 1965, when Congress decided to make it a responsibility of the federal government to register voters in areas where racial discrimination was evident. The Voting Rights Act of 1965 suspended the use of literacy tests or similar voter-qualification devices in states and voting districts that had less than 50 percent of voting-age residents registered in 1964 or actually voting in the 1964 presidential election, and authorized the appointment of federal voting examiners who would go into these areas to register blacks. When the Voting Rights Act expired in 1970, it was renewed for five years with an amendment suspending literacy tests in all states. In 1975 the act was extended for ten years, its coverage expanded to include Spanish-speaking Americans, and the nationwide ban on the use of literacy tests made permanent.

The poll tax, which was an additional bar to black voting, was abolished as a voting requirement in federal elections when the Twenty-Fourth Amendment was adopted in 1964, but it remained as a requisite for state and local elections in five states. In *Harper* v. *Virginia State Board of Elections* (1966), the Supreme Court held that the requirement to pay a fee as a condition of obtaining a ballot was an invidious discrimination contrary to the equal-protection clause. Thus all the remaining poll-tax systems were rendered unconstitutional.

EQUAL ACCESS TO PUBLIC ACCOMMODATIONS

One of the abortive efforts that Congress made after the Civil War to protect the civil rights of blacks was passage of the Civil Rights Act of 1875, which forbade racial separation or discrimination in public conveyances, hotels, and theaters. The Supreme Court declared this law unconstitutional in the *Civil Rights Cases* (1883), on the ground that the Fourteenth Amendment forbade only *state* action, not discrimination by private individuals or corporations. This decision stripped Congress of any power to prevent racial discrimination by railroads, bus lines, restaurants, hotels, and other privately owned facilities of public accommodation. And so Jim Crow flourished for three-quarters of a century.

It was not until 1946 that the Supreme Court took the first step toward breaking this impasse by finding segregation of the races on interstate buses to be an unconstitutional burden on commerce (*Morgan v. Virginia*). The Interstate Commerce Commission followed with a 1955 order banning racial segregation on all interstate facilities. In 1956 the Court struck down Jim Crow rules for local transportation as a denial of equal protection (*Gayle v. Browder*).

Discrimination continued to be the rule, however, in many hotels and eating places. Beginning in 1960, the "sit-in" was widely employed against segregated restaurants. Blacks would take seats at "white-only" lunch counters and, after being refused service, continue to sit there until arrested or ousted by force. They were customarily charged with breach of the peace or criminal trespass (that is, remaining on private property after being requested to leave).

While the Supreme Court decided a number of sit-in cases between 1961 and 1964, it never found a case that would require it to pass squarely on the constitutional situation of trespassers. However, the legal situation was changed when Congress passed the Civil Rights Act of 1964, making unlawful racial discrimination in public accommodations such as restaurants, hotels, and motels. Under the 1964 Act, it is the owner of the restaurant who refuses service for racial reasons who is guilty of unlawful conduct, not the person who enters the restaurant demanding service. The statute, which is based on the power of Congress to regulate interstate commerce and facilities used by travelers in interstate commerce, was upheld by the Supreme Court in *Heart of Atlanta Motel v. United States* (1964).

EDUCATIONAL EQUALITY

Segregation in education

The practice of racial segregation in the public schools was so firmly established in the South, as well as in certain northern states and cities, that it was not even challenged in the courts until the 1930s. Constitutional support for segregated schools was supplied by the famous Supreme Court decision in *Plessy v. Ferguson* (1896), which announced the doctrine of "separate but equal"—that is, it was not unconstitutional to provide separate public-transportation facilities for the two races if the facilities were equal. Justice Brown wrote in that decision:

> *The object of the [Fourteenth] amendment was undoubtedly to enforce the absolute equality of the two races before the law, but in the nature of things it could not have been intended to abolish distinctions based upon color, or to enforce social, as distinguished from political equality, or a commingling of the two races upon terms unsatisfactory to either.*

Actually, of course, facilities in the segregated black schools were never "equal," but the Supreme Court for years avoided recognizing that fact. It was not until a 1938 decision (*Missouri ex rel. Gaines* v. *Canada*) that the Court finally began to enforce the equality requirement for separate educational facilities. This and subsequent decisions stimulated many school districts to start programs for raising the level of their segregated schools.

But it was too late for half measures. The time of "separate but equal" was running out. The Supreme Court was moving swiftly toward its epoch-making decision of May 17, 1954. In *Brown* v. *Board of Education of Topeka* and four other cases, the Court held that "segregation of children in public schools solely on the basis of race, even though the physical facilities and other 'tangible' factors may be equal, deprive[s] the children of the minority group of equal educational opportunities. . . ." Separating children in grade and high schools "from others of similar age and qualifications solely because of their race generates a feeling of inferiority as to their status in the community that may affect their hearts and minds in a way unlikely ever to be undone."

This was the reply of the 1954 Supreme Court to the 1896 Court, which had denied in *Plessy* v. *Ferguson* that separation of the races stamped blacks with a "badge of inferiority," and had asserted that "if this be so, it is not by reason of anything found in the act, but solely because the colored race choose to put that construction upon it."

By its decision in the *Brown* case, the Supreme Court assumed the most stupendous task in its entire history—to enforce and supervise the changing of social habits and customs amounting to a way of life in many sections of the country. Obviously, no judicial fiat could change men's minds overnight or wipe out the consequences of decades of inequality, poverty, and neglect.

The Supreme Court fully appreciated the enormity of the task it had undertaken. Its plan of action was to remand the cases to the courts where they had originated, which were to work out decrees of enforcement on equitable principles, with regard for "varied local school problems." The local courts would consider whether the actions or proposals of the various school authorities constituted good-faith progress toward full compliance with the *Brown* ruling "with all deliberate speed."

At first it seemed that the prestige of the Supreme Court might substantially temper the expected resistance to the decree. The Court may have expected that it would receive some support from Congress and the President in winning acceptance for its ruling, but no such aid was forthcoming. On the contrary, 96 southern congressmen signed a manifesto in 1956 challenging the legality of the Court's decision, and President Eisenhower, while declaring that he would enforce the law, persistently declined to attempt to organize popular support for the desegregation ruling. Thus the responsibility for effecting this tremendous social revolution was left primarily to some 58 federal judges in the southern states, many of whom were personally opposed to the principle of the *Brown* decision.

Steps toward desegregation

Under these circumstances it was not surprising that progress toward the goal of desegregation of the schools was slow and uneven. In the border states, a considerable measure of integration was soon achieved, but in the "Old South" the ruling was almost completely frustrated by a variety of methods. The most publicized resistance was the violence associated with integrating the Little Rock, Arkansas, high school in 1957. President Eisenhower was forced to send federal troops to control the riotous situation there and to enforce federal court orders aimed at accomplishing gradual desegregation of the high school.

The role of the different actors in this enormously difficult and complex movement toward racial equality in the schools can be summarized briefly.

First, local pressure groups would raise the issue of segregation in local school systems and file suits to bring the matter into court. Often the National Association for the Advancement of Colored People (NAACP) performed this function, although other civil-rights groups of a more activist temper were also involved. In some sections of the South, reprisals against those active in civil-rights organizations were so severe and effective that initially few dared to protest segregated schools.

Second, local school boards and officials, acting on their own initiative or under the compulsion of a district court order, would prepare a desegregation plan. School officials, even when they were willing to act, usually preferred to wait for the pressure of a court order to justify themselves to the segregationists of the community.

Third, the state legislatures' initial contribution in the southern states was to pass, usually under their governors' leadership, a bewildering mass of laws aimed at preventing or punishing steps toward integration. They adopted legislation purporting to nullify the Supreme Court's *Brown* decision and to "interpose" state authority to protect state rights. Most of the laws passed were generally recognized even by their sponsors to be unconstitutional, but the process of litigation took time and delayed the progress of desegregation programs.

Fourth, the federal district court judges occupied a central strategic position in achieving integration "with all deliberate speed." They could order school boards to act, or they could sabotage the Supreme Court order by employing all the delays that the technicalities of the law afford. Of equal importance were the judges of the federal courts of appeals, principally of the Fifth Circuit (Alabama, Florida, Georgia, Louisiana, Mississippi, and Texas), who reviewed the decisions of the district courts in those states. Generally, the appellate court justices, somewhat further removed from the pressures of local situations than the district judges, took a conscientious view of their obligation to enforce the Supreme Court's ruling.

Fifth, there was the Supreme Court itself. After handing down the enforcement plan in 1955, the Supreme Court for a time deliberately sought to stay above the battle and let the lower courts work out the problems. But in 1958, when a federal district judge ordered a 30-month delay in the modest Little Rock integration program, the Supreme Court met in an unusual special summer session and upheld the court of appeals reversal of this order in *Cooper v. Aaron*. The Court flatly charged that the governor and legislature of Arkansas had caused the violent resistance in that state and reaffirmed the constitutional obligations of the states to obey the Court's mandate.

Another noteworthy enforcement decision was *Griffin v. School Board of Prince Edward County* (1964), declaring unconstitutional the action of a Virginia county that had closed its public schools rather than integrate them. In *Green v. School Board of New Kent County* (1968) the Court held that a freedom-of-choice plan, which was supposed to permit pupils to choose the school they would attend, did not meet the school board's obligation to take positive action to desegregate.

Finally, there was the major role of the President and Congress, who belatedly assumed their responsibilities for carrying on the revolution the Supreme Court had begun. In the fall of 1962, President Kennedy had to send federal marshals and troops to enforce a court order to admit a Negro student to the University of Mississippi. After police dogs, cattle prods, and fire hoses had been used against demonstrating blacks in Birmingham in 1963, President Kennedy proposed new federal civil-rights legislation. Following the assassination of President Kennedy, President Johnson made adoption of the Kennedy civil-rights bill one of his primary purposes, and with his persuasive leadership a bipartisan majority in Congress passed the Civil Rights Act of 1964. As far as education is concerned, this statute authorized the Attorney General to bring school desegregation suits in the name of the United States, a power Congress had refused to provide in the Civil Rights Act of 1957.

The 1964 act also included a general provision prohibiting racial discrimination in any local program receiving federal financial assistance. This sanction became of very great importance in 1965, when Congress adopted President Johnson's plan for federal financial assistance to elementary and secondary schools. To become eligible for these grants in the fall of 1965, all public schools had to certify that they were integrated or had to file acceptable plans for achieving complete integration.

The Nixon administration, with its "southern strategy," brought some relaxation in federal pressure toward achievement of desegregation, but initial efforts by the Justice Department to have the Supreme Court modify its position failed. In *Alexander* v. *Holmes County Board of Education* (1969), the Court, in fact, abandoned its policy of "deliberate speed" and warned that every school district must "terminate dual school systems at once and . . . operate now and hereafter only unitary schools." Again, in 1971, the Court rejected the advice of the Justice Department to move more slowly toward integration, and in *Swann* v. *Charlotte–Mecklenburg Board of Education* it upheld judicially designed desegregation plans, including school busing and the assignment of teachers to achieve faculty desegregation.

By 1972 court-ordered busing of children out of their neighborhoods to achieve racial balance was developing into a major political issue. A new factor was that northern cities, in many of which schools were more segregated than in the South, were being affected. Segregation in the North, while sometimes intentional, was usually *de facto,* the result not of law or school policies but of ghetto housing barriers that created all-black neighborhood schools.

In 1972 Congress refused to accede to Nixon's request for legislation to halt, delay, or minimize court-ordered busing. But the Supreme Court, with four Nixon appointees, did respond to increased concern about busing. In 1973 the Court's unbroken record of unanimity on *Brown*-related issues was ended by a 4-to-4 split on a city-county integration plan for the schools of the Richmond, Virginia, area. Then in *Milliken* v. *Bradley* (1974) the Court by a 5-to-4 vote held that the white suburban school districts outside Detroit could not be forced to integrate with the city's predominantly black schools by court-ordered busing across city-county boundaries. This decision took the pressure off Congress, where the House and Senate had been at odds over antibusing provisions in the $25 billion Education Act of 1974. As passed, the act banned court-ordered busing past a student's second nearest school, but courts could ignore this ban if they found it violated the constitutional rights of minority children.

Equality in financial support for schools

Another kind of educational equality suddenly emerged as a national issue in 1971 as a result of court decisions challenging the school financing systems in several states. In every state except Hawaii, public schools have traditionally been financed primarily by local property taxes, resulting in wide variations in financial support between rich and poor districts. State equalization grants failed by a wide margin to correct these inequities. In California, for example, wealthy Beverly Hills spent $1,638 per pupil in 1971, while depressed Baldwin Park, with a tax rate twice as high, could scrape up only $690 per pupil. The California supreme court and federal courts in Minnesota and Texas all held that a system where educational expenditure is a function of local wealth discriminates against children in poorer communities and is a violation of the equal-protection clause. However, in *San Antonio School District* v. *Rodriguez* (1973) the Supreme Court rejected the claim that education is a fundamental right, and ruled that existing systems of school finance, heavily relying on the general property tax, are not constitutionally objectionable.

EQUAL ACCESS TO HOUSING

Equal access of black families to housing remains a goal for the future. The Supreme Court has done what it can to invalidate discrimination in housing. In 1917, a Louisville segregation ordinance that prevented blacks from buying property in certain sections of the city was declared unconstitutional by the Court (*Buchanan* v. *Warley*). Then the "restrictive covenant" was adopted, under which property owners bound themselves not to sell or lease their property to blacks or certain other groups. But in 1948, the Court held that such covenants were not judicially enforceable (*Shelley* v. *Kraemer*).

These rulings did little to break the housing barriers, however. Positive legislation at the city and state levels was needed to require property owners and real estate agents to offer housing for rent or sale without racial restrictions. Many such "open-occupancy" laws have been passed, usually after bitter political resistance by organized property owners and real estate interests.

In California, a state open-occupancy law was repealed in 1964 when by referendum vote a constitutional amendment was adopted guaranteeing the right of any property holder to sell, lease, or rent his property to anyone he chose. However, in 1966, the state supreme court declared the amendment unconstitutional as discriminatory state action in violation of the equal-protection clause, thus bringing the open-occupancy law back into effect. The state ruling was upheld by the U.S. Supreme Court by a 5-to-4 vote in *Reitman* v. *Mulkey* (1967), the reasoning being that the constitutional amendment, while appearing only to guarantee the freedom of property owners to sell, actually made the right to discriminate one of the basic policies of the state. "Those practicing racial discriminations need no longer rely on their personal choice. They could now evoke express constitutional authority."

In 1968, following the assassination of Martin Luther King, Jr., Congress for the first time passed a civil-rights act containing comprehensive open-housing provisions applicable to a broad range of discriminatory practices. A few weeks later the Supreme Court, in *Jones* v. *Alfred H. Mayer Co.* (1968), ruled that a provision of the Civil Rights Act of 1866, although never previously interpreted so broadly, had actually made illegal every racially motivated refusal by property owners to rent or sell. Thus a national policy forbidding private racial discrimination in access to housing finally came into effect.

Zoning restrictions remain, however, as effective housing barriers, walling off the affluent suburbs from the central-city areas. As industries flee the congested inner cities, workers are often unable to follow the jobs into the suburbs because of the difficulty of securing suitable housing. While exclusionary zoning seems a clear challenge to equal protection, feasible distinctions between legitimate and discriminatory zoning standards have been difficult to develop. In *Belle Terre* v. *Boraas* (1974) the Supreme Court upheld use of the zoning power by towns and villages to restrict land use to one-family dwellings.

RACIAL DISCRIMINATION IN BRITAIN

The English formerly tended to be rather condescending in their attitude toward American racial problems. However, after World War II, an increasing number of nonwhite citizens of Commonwealth countries left their native lands to reside in England. This stirred up severe friction and made it clear that English law was unprepared to counter racial discrimination. In fact, the common law's rigid theory of freedom of contract guaranteed employers, banks, insurance companies, and renters of rooms complete discretion in making their services available. Consequently, courts in England could not take the initiative, as the Supreme Court did in the United States, against restrictive covenants in housing and segregated education.

Action to provide equal opportunities regardless of race had to come through legislation, and Parliament was slow to move. In fact, its first response was a 1962 statute limiting immigration from Commonwealth countries, a move that escalated racial antagonisms, although nonwhites comprise only 2 percent of the British population. When a Race Relations Act was adopted in 1965, it was a comparatively weak measure that established machinery of investigation and conciliation for handling complaints of racial discrimination. Admittedly, racial problems in England are less serious and far more recent than in the United States, and there has been no discrimination in voting; however, the public action in England against racial inequality has fallen far short of that in the United States.

THE EQUAL-PROTECTION EXPLOSION

The American drive toward equality has not been limited to the attempts to eliminate racial discrimination. By the 1970s, the women's liberation movement, which had its origins in the nineteenth century, had become much more than the target of jokes by male chauvinists. Congress passed the Equal Pay Act in 1963, requiring equal pay for equal work regardless of

"I'll tell you what I want. I want self-actualization as a woman in a societal modality in which a viable life-style is divorced from preconceived ideas of sexual role-conditioning, and I want it now!"
Saturday Review, March 22, 1975, p. 22.

sex, and the Civil Rights Act of 1964 banned discrimination in employment on the basis of sex as well as race, color, religion, or national origin.[1]

A constitutional amendment removing all legal disabilities based on sex and guaranteeing women equal rights with men, a goal long sought by women activists, was passed by the House in 1971 and the Senate in 1972. During congressional consideration of the amendment, objections were raised that its adoption would subject women to the draft and would invalidate all labor legislation designed to protect women in industry. However, proponents of the amendment insisted that they wanted complete elimination of all legal inequalities, and as adopted the amendment guarantees full "equality of rights under the law." If ratified by 38 states (34 had done so by mid-1975) it would become the Twenty-Seventh Amendment.

It appears that the Supreme Court never considered until recently that the equal-protection clause might refer to women. In 1872 the Court upheld an Illinois law denying women the right to practice law, and in 1875 it ruled that women had no constitutional right to vote. It took a century for the Court to reverse its position on women's rights. In *Reed* v. *Reed* (1971), the Court unanimously declared unconstitutional as a denial of equal protection

---

[1] For representative decisions, see *Phillips* v. *Martin Marietta Co.* (1971), *Cleveland Board of Education* v. *LaFleur* (1974), and *Corning Glass Works* v. *Brennan* (1974).

an Idaho statute requiring that men be given preference over equally qualified women in the court appointment of administrators of estates. *Frontiero v. Richardson* (1973) ruled that spouses of female members of the armed forces must receive equal treatment with spouses of male members in terms of allowances and benefits. However, the Burger Court majority has declined to consider all classifications based on sex as "suspect," like those based on race. For example, in *Kahn v. Shevin* (1974) the Court approved a Florida law giving widows, but not widowers, a $500 property tax exemption.[2]

The equal-protection explosion has also benefited the poor. Many legal rights that in theory are equally available to all persons have, in fact, been foreclosed to the poor because of their poverty. This situation is now changing, largely as a result of the Supreme Court's new emphasis on equal protection. The *Gideon* decision requiring that counsel be supplied to all defendants in criminal cases who are unable to employ counsel has already been noted, but there are several other decisions of similar import. In *Griffin v. Illinois* (1956), the Court held that defendants could not be denied the opportunity to appeal their convictions because they could not pay for the necessary trial transcripts.[3] In *Boddie v. Connecticut* (1971), it ruled that a state cannot deny a person the right to file for a divorce because he cannot pay court costs. In *Williams v. Illinois* (1970), the Court held that indigent convicts who cannot afford to pay fines and court costs cannot be held in jail beyond the maximum term specified for their crimes. Legal-aid programs for the poor have begun to bring legal services to sectors of the population never before able to seek legal protection for their rights.

The implications of the equal-protection explosion have not yet been fully realized. Its impact on the legal, economic, and social position of women has only begun to be felt. The National Advisory Commission on Civil Disorders charged in 1968 that the nation was "moving toward two societies, one black, one white—separate and unequal," but subsequent opinion polls show that in some respects racial prejudice has diminished sharply.

The drive for equality is challenging many long-established institutions. Some aspects of the present system of local government are simply incompatible with the guarantee of equal protection of the laws. The neighborhood-school system is under pressure, and probably can be maintained only if segregation in housing can be reduced or eliminated. To accomplish this

---

[2]But in *Weinberger v. Wiesenfeld* (1975) the Court held invalid a provision of the Social Security Act providing less in the way of survivor's benefits for widowers than for widows.

[3]But in *Ross v. Moffitt* (1974) the Court ruled that states need not furnish free attorneys to indigent defendants wishing to appeal their convictions to the highest state court and to the Supreme Court.

goal, the right of the suburbs to wall themselves off from the social and fiscal problems of the inner cities will have to be attacked by judicial or legislative means. Equal education clearly demands a new pattern of financing public schools. Building a new system of taxation and fund distribution for schools will necessarily change patterns of land, housing, and industrial development. Equal protection may require state legislatures to redefine the lines drawn around the areas of local government.

Economic inequalities, which fall outside the constitutional guarantee of equal protection of the laws, have so far scarcely been touched by the drive toward legal equality. However, proposals for a guaranteed annual income or a national income floor now have responsible sponsors. But optimism concerning trends toward equality must be tempered by recognition that much remains to be done to fulfill the obligation of equal protection of the laws and the boast of equality of opportunity.

9
Public Opinion and Political Participation

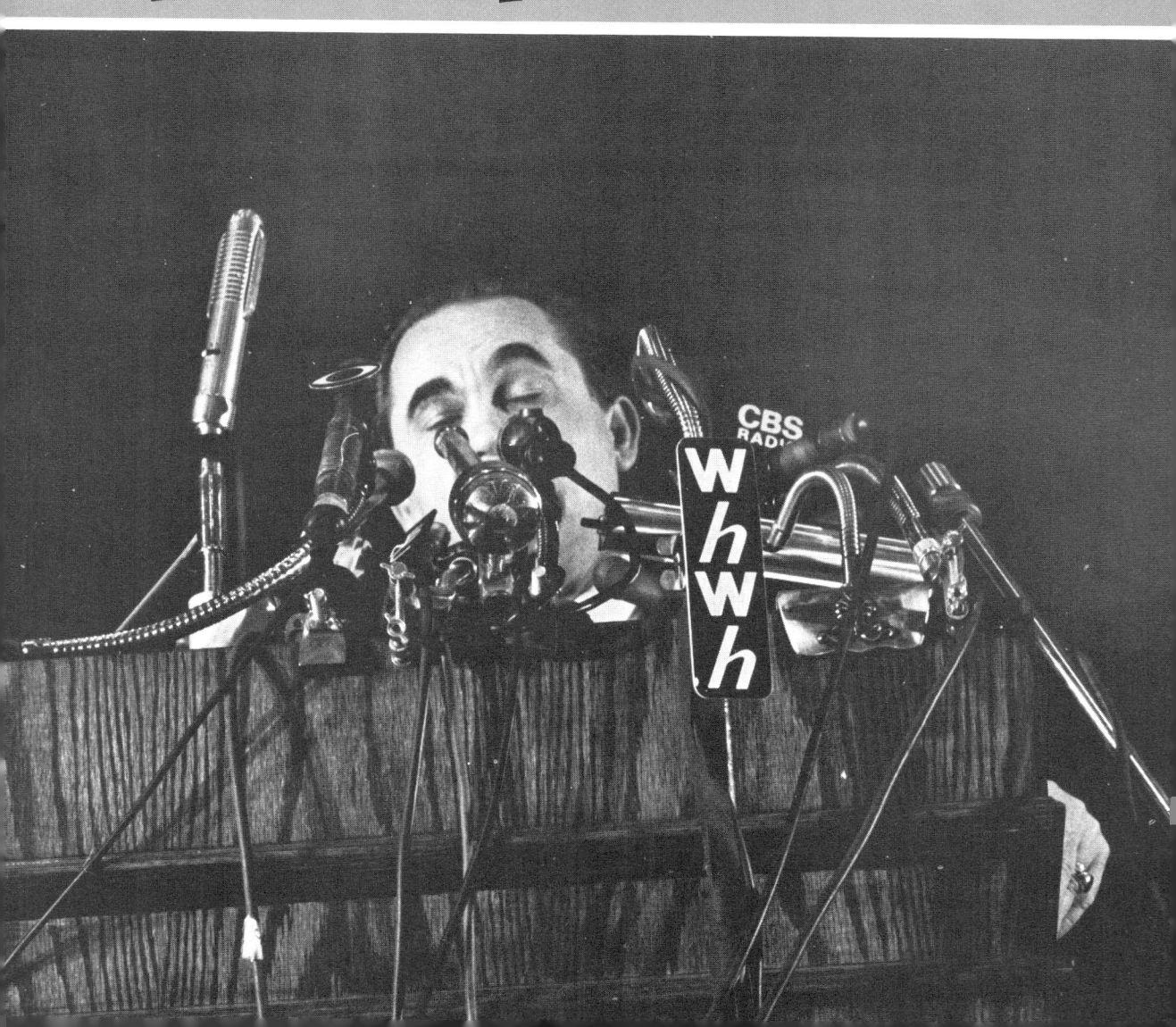

9

Politics is most commonly defined in terms of a *struggle for power* or of an *allocation of values*. "Politics," wrote Max Weber, "means striving to share power or striving to influence the distribution of power, either among states or among groups within a state." David Easton, writing in a similar vein, described politics as an "authoritative allocation of values for a society."[1] While these definitions apply equally to politics in the United States and in other countries, the manner in which the struggle for power or the allocation of values take place and the people who participate differ greatly from one country to another. For instance, in a country ruled by a military junta the participants may be limited primarily to the officers of the armed forces. In a Communist country, the struggle is principally among the leaders of the Communist party. In the United States, it is possible for all people to take part in the political process, and the means by which persons may participate are varied—including running for office or seeking appointment to an administrative position, becoming leaders in a political party or political interest groups, attempting to influence public opinion, and, of course, voting. In actual practice, the barriers to political participation are far greater for some people than for others, and the extent to which individuals participate in American politics and influence political decisions varies widely.

PUBLIC OPINION

The concept of *government based on public opinion* is relatively new in history. It developed simultaneously with the evolution of democratic government and the extension of the suffrage, and even today it is not accepted by the rulers of authoritarian regimes. Thus the attitude toward public opinion as a political force differs greatly in countries such as the United States and Great Britain on the one hand, and the Soviet Union and Libya on the other.

---

[1] H. H. Gerth and C. Wright Mills (eds.), *From Max Weber: Essays in Sociology*, New York: Oxford University Press, 1946, p. 78; David Easton, *The Political System: An Inquiry into the State of Political Science*, New York: Knopf, 1953, p. 135.

What is public opinion?

When men first began to reflect on the influence of public opinion on the governmental process, political regimes were less complex than most present-day democracies. Prior to the advent of the airplane, radio, and television, when the literacy rate was much lower and the suffrage was more limited, public opinion was considered to be primarily the opinions held by the upper and upper-middle classes on political issues, which were generally less complicated and more slow to change than today's issues. Early scholars often regarded public opinion as a type of organic entity or mystical force. For instance, James Bryce, a brilliant British scholar, writing at the beginning of this century, described public opinion as "a real force, impalpable as the wind, yet a force which all are trying to discover and nearly all to obey."

In recent decades, political scientists, social psychologists, and sociologists have learned much about public opinion, but no universally acceptable definition of it has yet been devised. V. O. Key, Jr., suggested what is perhaps the most useful definition of public opinion: "those opinions held by private persons which governments find it prudent to heed."[2] Many other scholars insist that for the term to have any meaning it must apply to a particular public and to opinions regarding some specific issue or issues.

General and special publics. Although on some broad topics there is sufficient interest on the part of the entire citizenry to have a general public opinion, surveys have shown that only a small proportion of the population has sufficient information and interest to form an opinion on many political issues. When one is considering most political questions, therefore, it is useful to think of those with opinions as special or "attentive" publics, and those with no opinions as "inattentive" publics. For instance, the attentive public on the question of the nation's entry into a war would be virtually the entire populace or the general public. If the question were the acquisition of property for a city park, the attentive public would be the interested local citizens. It is thus apparent that the issue determines the "public."

As the political issues change, the relationship of the attentive and inattentive publics may shift, with an attentive public becoming inattentive and vice versa. In actuality, often one issue will elicit the attention of one group or groups, a different problem may interest a second element of the citizenry, and a third might attract the attention of still another public. Thus the publics group and regroup depending on the particular issue or controversies.

The inattentive public should not be considered unimportant. They may make little effort to be informed, and what knowledge they have is usually

---

[2]V. O. Key, Jr., *Public Opinion and American Democracy*, New York: Knopf, 1961, p. 14.

superficial, but from the standpoint of policy formation, they are important because if they are activated, they become part of the attentive public and may assist in establishing the limits within which the government must act.

On some political questions there may be no sharp distinction between the attentive public and the inattentive; instead, the population could figuratively be placed on a spectrum, with the highly attentive public at one end, the inattentive at the other end, and the remainder of the population spaced along the spectrum according to their interest and opinions on the specific question.

The role of opinion leaders. From the standpoint of the process by which opinions are formed, it is also useful to conceive of the attentive publics as being composed of two groups—the formal and informal opinion leaders, and those who are informed but take a more passive role. Of these, the opinion leaders, and in particular the formal opinion leaders, are the most important. The primary relevance of public opinion in the governmental process must be considered from the standpoint of the existence of this elite of political activists. These are the individuals who are most active in originating new policies, in suggesting changes in existing policies, and in activating and converting other individuals to their views. As Gabriel Almond has remarked, "Who mobilizes elites, mobilizes the public."

It is difficult to say precisely who should be included in the group of opinion leaders, for the membership is indefinite and changeable. Undoubtedly, the foremost formal opinion leader is the President, whose pronouncements and activities are daily reported on television, on radio, and in the press. Also included among the formal opinion leaders are many other elected public officials; leaders of economic, religious, ethnic, and other interest groups; syndicated columnists, journalists, and news commentators; political party leaders; and numerous other political activists who function in a variety of middle-level and top-level capacities. These political elites are tremendously important in the opinion-formation process. Whereas most of the formal opinion leaders are from the upper and upper-middle strata of the population, informal opinion leaders are found at all levels in society. The latter include persons who hold no official positions in the government or political parties, but who are well informed politically and discuss political issues with numerous friends, acquaintances, and even casual contacts.

Some political observers believe that to a large extent the character and quality of the nation's political opinions and policies are dependent on the nature and behavior of these opinion leaders. In the words of Professor Key:

> *The longer one frets with the puzzle of how democratic regimes manage to function, the more plausible it appears that a substantial part of the explanation is to be found in the . . . leadership echelon. . . . Focus of*

attention on this sector of the opinion system . . . does not deny the importance of mass attitudes. It rather emphasizes that the pieces of the puzzle are different in form and function and that for the existence of a democratic opinion-oriented system each piece must possess the characteristics necessary for it to fit together with the others in a working whole.[3]

In addition to opinion leaders, the attentive publics include those who are aware of the political issues of the day—or at least those issues that relate directly to them—but who are comparatively passive. While not originators of opinions, these individuals often discuss public affairs, make some attempt to keep informed, and help to modify and mold political attitudes. For many of these individuals, opinion formation is a two-step or multistep process, with much of their information being received directly or indirectly from opinion leaders. Aware of the significance of political decisions, the persons in this second category may be stimulated to take actions that shape public policies. They therefore play an important role in the development of public opinion and in bringing it to bear on public policy.

The function of public opinion

Observers of democratic government have long pondered the relationship of public opinion to governmental actions. Obviously, the impact of public opinion on public policy will vary according to different circumstances and political problems. Depending on the particular issue and set of conditions, public opinion may be considered to perform any one of at least three different functions—supportive, directive, or permissive.[4]

Supportive function. For most continuing programs, public opinion performs a supportive function. From the adoption of the Constitution—which was originally opposed by a large segment of the population—to the present, most programs, after being established, have been supported by the public. In fact, public support for existing programs is commonly taken for granted, and its significance is usually overlooked until proposals are made for changing such programs. For example, President Nixon in 1972, after finding that public-opinion surveys showed widespread opposition by both whites and blacks to the busing of schoolchildren to achieve racial balance in neighborhood schools, indicated his support for the existing policy of desegregation without forced busing. On the other hand, the *lack* of public

---

[3]*Ibid.,* p. 537.
[4]This concept of the role of public opinion is based on the discussion by V. O. Key, Jr., *ibid.,* pp. 29–37.

support for prohibition made it extremely difficult to enforce prohibition laws and led to the repeal of the Eighteenth Amendment.

Directive function. Under some circumstances, the public may be so united in its opinions about an issue that public opinion may be said to be directive. For example, the growing discontent with the Vietnam war persuaded President Johnson to declare in the spring of 1968 that he would not run for reelection—a rare decision for an incumbent President. Another example occurred in 1975 when the public reaction to President Ford's proposal for tax increases to combat the dual problem of inflation and recession led him to reverse his position and propose instead a reduction in taxes.

Permissive function. In the formation and enactment of governmental policy, public opinion commonly performs a permissive function. On most public problems, the political attitudes of the general populace do not require the adoption of a specific policy, but allow the elected officials wide latitude in working out solutions. Often, because of the low intensity of opinion of many individuals and the lack of information or apathy of others, public opinion permits the policy-makers to select any one of a number of alternatives, including doing nothing, without having to fear reprisals at the polls. Indeed, on some questions, actions favored by a majority who do not hold strong views may be defeated or delayed by an organized and active minority. For example, shortly after President Truman presented his government health-insurance proposal in 1949, congressmen's correspondence indicated general public approval. Yet owing to the efforts of the American Medical Association, the proposal was defeated, and it was not until 1965 that a modification of it, Medicare, was enacted.

We know that public officials and government agencies make extraordinary efforts to assess public attitudes, yet we find instances in which opinion surveys show a majority favoring a particular proposal, but in which no action on the proposal is taken. On the other hand, we sometimes find Congress acting in the interests of a small special public by adopting a measure in which the majority of the people have no interest. The relationship between governmental policy and public sentiment thus may appear ambiguous at times. Nevertheless, astute public officials seldom question the importance of the permissive role of public opinion.

Assessing public opinion

Government officials have the responsibility of informing the people regarding political questions and heeding their opinions in formulating public policies. They inform the public in a variety of ways, including public addresses, press conferences and press releases, meetings with private citizens and organized groups, and appearances on television programs.

But how do public officials learn the views of the general and specialized publics so that they may reflect those opinions in their decisions? In considering this question, it is well to remember the distinction between general public opinion and specialized opinions held by attentive publics. On broad issues of public policy, it is essential that the government have the support of the general public, but it is not necessary to seek their concurrence on the detailed application of those policies. As the majority of the people probably will have no opinions on more specialized issues, the views officials will seek are usually those of political interest groups and other attentive publics.

The mass media as a means of assessing public opinion. Most public officials attempt to keep abreast of public events through the mass media of communication. Aware that opinions are shaped by interpretations of events as well as by events themselves, many top officials read several daily newspapers and one or more weekly news magazines. For years, it has been customary for certain members of the White House staff and also staff members of other government offices to devote full time to analyzing sources of expressed opinion. For example, under President Ford each day a staff of four White House employees, often assisted by others, prepares for the President and his assistants a folder entitled "The President's Daily News Briefings," which presents summaries of news accounts gained from reading more than 50 newspapers and 40 major periodicals, and monitoring news tickers and television newscasts.

Political-interest groups. On many issues, the opinions held by the public are largely shaped by political-interest groups, which tend to equate their interests with the public welfare and to exaggerate the extent to which the general public shares their opinions. Hence, while such groups provide one means of assessing public attitudes, experienced political officials usually check the statements of interest-group leaders and lobbyists with other sources to determine the degree to which the general public concurs with the goals of a specific group.

Communications with private citizens. Officials learn much regarding mass opinions from direct communications with private citizens. Letters, telegrams, telephone calls, and personal conversations provide a means for assessing opinions. Public officials soon learn to distinguish between such communications that are initiated by personal interest and those that are stimulated by pressure groups. In order to be cognizant of their constituents' views, most congressmen visit their districts to consult individual opinion leaders and to talk to rank-and-file voters.

Elections. In democracies, elections not only perform the function of determining who will hold public office but also reflect public opinion. Presidential elections have been the primary means by which the American citizenry has voiced a collective opinion. In actuality, the extent to which an election measures public opinion varies from one election to another. Because Americans reach their individual voting decisions for a variety of reasons, it is often difficult to determine what mandate was received by the winning candidate. But most presidential elections provide a crude measurement of the direction in which the electorate wishes the government to move, and in some presidential elections—such as 1932 and 1964—the voters spoke with a clear and forceful voice, at least on general social policies if not on administrative and legislative details.

In a number of states, in addition to selecting public officials, the electorate may vote to *recall* officials and may participate directly in the legislative process through the *initiative* and *referendum*.[5] Through the recall, a public official may be removed from office prior to the expiration of his term. The initiative permits a specified number of voters to propose a statute or constitutional amendment by petition and have it submitted for approval or rejection by the electorate. Through the referendum, a bill or a constitutional amendment that has been adopted by the legislature is submitted to the voters for their approval. Opinion is divided concerning the relative merits of the recall, initiative, and referendum. However, proponents argue that these three governmental devices provide an additional means by which mass opinions may influence public policy.

Public-opinion surveys. Public-opinion polls or surveys provide the most effective means for assessing the opinions of large numbers of individuals on a variety of topics. By combining a knowledge of social psychology with mathematical probability, the polling organizations are able to ascertain with a high degree of accuracy the opinions of the entire American public through interviews with a carefully selected sample of 1,500 to 6,000 persons. Although efforts at sampling opinion and predicting election results have been made for more than a century, modern public-opinion polling may be said to date to the 1930s when Dr. George Gallup organized the American Institute of Public Opinion (AIPO) and Elmo Roper established his Roper Survey. Today more than a thousand organizations are engaged in opinion surveys; however, most are engaged in marketing research and do not conduct polls on political issues or attempt to predict election results. In addition to the Roper and Gallup polls, other well-known organizations that conduct surveys of political opinions include the Center for

---

[5]Twenty-one states make provision for the initiative or referendum, 12 states authorize the recall of state officials, and approximately three-fourths of the states provide for the recall in some or all cities.

"Make that upper-middle class."
Drawing by Porges; © 1968 Harper's Magazine, Inc.

Political Studies of the University of Michigan, which has been publishing survey results since 1948, and the Harris Survey, which was established by Louis Harris in 1954. In recent years, more than 30 additional organizations have published polls on state or local elections, and a number of other firms have conducted private polls for candidates and political parties.

Although opinion polling is now a well-established occupation, it is still the subject of criticism. Some critics believe that most commercial pollsters have not emphasized sufficiently that within the total process of drafting a questionnaire, selecting the sample, conducting the interviews, and tabulating and analyzing the results, decisions must be made that make errors possible in the final results. Other critics maintain that the surveys in general have neglected the impact of opinion leaders on political attitudes. Most opinion surveys have ignored the fact that while one person's vote counts the same as another's, one person's opinion may be more important than another's in the determination of mass attitudes.

Predicting election results is the activity that attracts both the most interest in opinion polls and the most criticism. Some people allege that newspaper polls on political races tend to distort and undermine the electoral process. In brief, the principal criticisms are that polls may have a significant impact on the campaigns and the outcome of some elections. In particular, polls that show a candidate running considerably behind his opponent can have an adverse effect on fund raising, coverage of the candidate by the media, staff morale, and even voter turnout. Various changes have been suggested, including publishing no polls more than three or four months before an election or within the final days of the campaign. Others suggest that polls concentrate more on voters' general attitudes toward the candidates and the major issues and not on the "horse race question" of who is ahead and by how many points.

Opinion surveys may help illuminate the significance of election returns; from such surveys one may learn what specific political forces and issues contributed to the victory of the winning candidates. Surveys have shown not only the proportions of the population favoring a given proposal but also the areas of apathy, ignorance, and misinformation. Efforts have been made to probe such properties of mass opinion as the intensity of the strength with which views are held and the stability of opinions or the likelihood that opinions will change.

Sample surveys provide a valuable supplement to the other means of assessing political opinions. Opinion polls may indicate the extent to which the views expressed by the press, the personal communications to public officials, and the opinions of interest-group leaders are shared by the general public. In the words of one political observer, "The polls permit the voice of the majority to be heard against that of the clamorous minority." Most agree that the polls, although an imprecise measure, are more accurate than any other measure available.

The impact of the mass media on public opinion

Viewed broadly, the mass media include all of the ways by which vast audiences may be informed. From the standpoint of providing information to the public, "the press"—now generally considered to include television and radio as well as newspapers and news magazines—is, of course, by far the most important. One student of American politics has written:

> The power of the press in America is a primordial one. It sets the agenda of public discussion. . . . It determines what people will talk and think about. . . . No major act of the American Congress, no foreign adventure, no act of diplomacy, no great social reform can succeed in the United States unless the press prepares the public mind.[6]

---

[6]Theodore H. White, *The Making of the President, 1972,* New York: Atheneum, 1973, p. 245.

Patterns of government control. The extent to which the communications media are controlled or regulated by governments ranges from the complete control that characterizes totalitarian regimes to virtually no control and a minimum of regulation, as in the United States and other democracies. The practices followed by governments fall into four general categories.

First, in totalitarian states, all of the mass media are customarily strictly controlled by the government. Virtually all newspapers, periodicals, and other publications are published by the government or under government supervision, the radio and television are state-operated, and the motion pictures are government-produced. Even the novelists, poets, and artists have been instructed by the government regarding permissible themes and content.

Second, in authoritarian states such as Spain and Egypt, the government operates the radio and television stations and often publishes one or more newspapers, but it permits privately owned newspapers and periodicals to be published under rigid censorship regulations. Any privately owned press that criticizes the government or prints any prohibited information or ideas may expect to lose the right to publish.

A third pattern prevails in a number of democracies, including Great Britain, West Germany, and the Scandinavian countries. In these countries, the press is free from government control and censorship, but governmental agencies operate all or most of the radio and television stations. However, such "public corporations" in radio and television are free from government control with respect to the contents of the programs.

In the United States, there is a fourth pattern of relationship between the government and the mass media. All elements of the mass media are privately owned, and any type of censorship over the opinions or information disseminated by the communications media is prohibited by the Constitution. The Federal Communications Commission (FCC) grants licenses to radio and television stations in accordance with the "public interest, convenience, and necessity"—terms never adequately defined by Congress or the FCC. The commission exercises a degree of control over the operations of the licensees but not the content of the programs.

The performance of the mass media. The communications media rival the family, the school, and religious institutions in molding general attitudes and values, and are no doubt most important in shaping opinions on current political issues. Because of their importance, considerable attention has been directed to the manner in which the newspapers, radio, and television perform their function of providing the people an intelligible account of political events and issues. With eight out of 10 Americans having access to daily newspapers and with nine out of 10 being exposed to television, one might assume that the people are amply informed regarding political issues. Yet a number of professional journalists and other students of the mass media have called attention to disturbing shortcomings in the functioning of the mass media.

Despite the daily torrents of words, it is asserted, the people are not provided an account of significant political events and issues in a context that explains their meaning. Much of the reporting in the press and on television and radio is either of trivial events or "spot" news, with very little, if any, interpretive material. Often, superficial reports are given of major political issues with little background information, whereas detailed accounts will be presented of crimes, scandals, athletic events, and the private lives of celebrities.

Television has been criticized even more strongly than the newspapers for failing to inform and educate the people. The charge has been made that television is neither an educational nor an entertainment medium, but that it is primarily an advertising medium operated largely for the benefit of the network and station owners and advertisers. Although this criticism may appear to some to be too harsh, many will agree that the violence, sentimentality, and banality of many television programs help to document the statement of a former chairman of the FCC that television has become a "vast wasteland." On the other hand, television does provide many informative daily newscasts, often with insightful interpretations; and on-the-spot and in-depth coverage of special events has given the public unique opportunities to become informed.

The trend toward increased concentration of ownership of newspapers, periodicals, and radio and television stations has been a source of concern to many persons. Fear has been expressed that such concentration will create inordinate power in the hands of a relatively few individuals and will reduce the free flow of ideas and opinions. Newspaper chains now control 60 percent of the total daily circulation. In addition, approximately one-third of the television stations are affiliated with newspapers and thus are under the same overall management.

The trend toward monopoly conditions is further illustrated by the decline in the number of cities with competing daily newspapers. The proportion of cities with competing newspapers declined from 60 percent in 1919 to 15 percent in 1950 and to less than 4 percent in the early 1970s, and the sole newspaper in many of these cities is owned by a chain.[7] In New York City, for example, the number of general daily newspapers shrank from 12 in the 1930s to 3 in 1975.

Formerly, the extent to which the communications industry had been permeated with a conservative business bias disturbed many who believed that most owners considered their newspapers or broadcasting stations not as social institutions with public responsibilities, but as business enterprises

---

[7]Robert L. Bishop, "The Rush to Chain Ownership," *Columbia Journalism Review*, 11 (November–December, 1972).

to be managed as the owner desired. The charge was commonly heard that as businessmen they often shared a conservative political outlook which was sometimes reflected in the news columns of papers as well as on the editorial pages. As is true of other business groups, most newspaper publishers usually support Republican candidates. Only once in this century, in 1964, has a majority of the nation's newspapers supported the Democratic candidate for President. For instance, in 1968, a total of 483 daily American newspapers supported Nixon, 93 backed Humphrey, and 10 supported Wallace. Four years later, 735 endorsed Nixon while only 56 supported McGovern. In spite of this widespread endorsement by newspapers, Nixon and various members of his administration, in particular Vice-President Agnew, often complained that the more liberal metropolitan press, such as the *New York Times* and the *Washington Post,* did not report some news stories accurately. Most presidents have complained about their treatment by the press, but undoubtedly the Nixon administration more than any other sought to stifle press criticism. Methods employed ranged from verbal attacks by Agnew and others on certain newspapers and television networks to having the F.B.I. and the Internal Revenue Service conduct investigations of some newspaper and television reporters. Some of the reaction by Nixon administration officials undoubtedly stemmed from what Supreme Court Justice Potter Stewart calls "the twin phenomena" of "investigative reporting and an adversary press." These phenomena have come about because some reporters have taken the view that, under the Constitution, their proper role is to investigate and expose questionable practices on the part of public officials.

In recent years, the government has frequently been charged with managing the news. While most misgivings regarding the mass media relate to the operation of the press, the criticism of "managed news" has been made by journalists who assert that government officials—by emphasizing certain information and withholding other items—have attempted to control the news. The question of what information the government may withhold from the public attracted nationwide attention in 1971 when the *New York Times* published the so-called Pentagon Papers, which were position papers written earlier by public officials concerning American involvement in Vietnam.

For many years, political observers have pointed out that it is more difficult to develop a national opinion in the United States than in Great Britain. In addition to the vastly larger territory and the less homogeneous population, there are no national newspapers comparable with those in Britain. For instance, *The Times* (London) is read by opinion leaders throughout Great Britain, but the *New York Times,* which is the most influential newspaper in the United States, is read by relatively few individuals in the South, Midwest, or West. Although there are no national newspapers in the United States, developments in mass communication have made it more possible for Americans throughout the nation to receive via the various

"Aren't you glad you're a nobody and not a big shot with the media picking on you all the time?"
Saturday Review, July 27, 1974, p. 48.

syndicated news services the same radio and, in particular, television accounts of international and national events. The daily news programs broadcast by the three national television networks and the time allotted to special news events—such as the President's State of the Union address, the hearings of the Senate committee investigating the Watergate scandals, and the House committee hearings on the impeachment of Richard Nixon—have contributed significantly toward both informing the people regarding important political issues and creating a national opinion.

Although the current performance of the American press could be improved, it compares favorably with that of any earlier period in the United States and with the mass media of most other countries today. Reporting in the American press is undoubtedly less biased and more objective and responsible than in previous eras; this is probably partly because Americans are better educated today than ever before.

POLITICAL PARTICIPATION

The right of all citizens to attempt to influence public opinion and participate in the political process in other ways is protected by several sections of the Constitution, including provisions relating to freedom of speech, press, and association, and the right to assemble, to petition Congress, and to vote. Most political activists, realizing that they can exert relatively little influence alone, join political parties and interest groups, organizations whose right to exist is implicitly guaranteed by constitutional provisions.

Although democracies provide opportunities for political participation denied by authoritarian governments, only a small proportion of the population are active participants. These political activists

> *talk up their beliefs, criticize or praise the government, and push their ideas through their membership in this group and that. They may discuss the campaign with their friends and acquaintances. . . . They write to their Congressmen. They serve the party's cause by working at the polls, ringing doorbells, addressing envelopes, and doing other chores. . . . In a sense they vote many times.*[8]

For the political system to function satisfactorily, it is not, of course, necessary that the whole population be actively involved. Indeed, if everyone were a political activist, the system might be destroyed by fanaticism or extremism.

Lester Milbrath has suggested that the various forms of political participation might be conceived as a hierarchy of political involvement.[9] The list of political acts in Figure 9–1 is based on the proportion of Americans who engage in various types of political activity, with the acts at the bottom of the hierarchy performed more generally and those at the top less commonly. For instance, in an election, 40 to 70 percent of the electorate obtain political information and vote. However, only about 24 percent of adult Americans belong to political interest groups, only 17 to 20 percent contact public or political leaders, only 10 to 12 percent make campaign contributions, and fewer than 1 percent are candidates for public office or are party or public officials.[10] Milbrath notes that political participation tends to be

---

[8]V. O. Key, Jr., *Politics, Parties, and Pressure Groups,* New York: Crowell, 1964, p. 592.

[9]Lester W. Milbrath, *Political Participation,* Chicago: Rand McNally, 1965, pp. 16–19.

[10]The percentages are taken from Gabriel A. Almond and Sidney Verba, *The Civic Culture,* Princeton, N.J.: Princeton University Press, 1963, p. 306; Sidney Verba and Norman Nie, *Participation in America: Political and Social Equality,* New York: Harper & Row, 1972, p. 31; and the studies cited by Milbrath, *op. cit.,* p. 19.

Holding
office
Running
for office
Soliciting
political funds
Attending a caucus
or a strategy meeting
Becoming an active
member in a political party
Contributing time
in a political campaign
Attending a political meeting or rally
Making a monetary
contribution to a party or a candidate
Contacting a public official or a political leader
Wearing a button or putting a sticker on a car
Joining a political-interest group
Attempting to talk another into voting a certain way
Initiating a political discussion
Voting
Obtaining political information

Figure 9–1 ***Hierarchy of political involvement***
Adapted from Lester Milbrath, *Political Participation,* Chicago, Rand McNally, 1965, p. 18.

"cumulative" in that those who perform acts at the top of the hierarchy of involvement usually engage in most of the lower-ranked activities as well. Hence, party officials and public officeholders are typically active in a political party, attend political meetings, contact other public figures, discuss politics, vote, and attempt to be informed politically.

The degree of citizen involvement in public affairs is related to the general political culture. A study of the United States, Great Britain, Germany, Italy, and Mexico revealed different national attitudes regarding political participation. Table 9–1 summarizes the views of the respondents concerning the obligation of citizens to be politically involved. In each of the five countries, a surprisingly small proportion of the population—approximately one out of five in the United States and Great Britain, one out of eight in Germany, one out of 10 in Mexico, and one out of 20 in Italy—indicated they believed the ordinary person should take an active part in his local governments. When all types of political involvement are considered, of the nationalities polled, more Americans (78 percent) and fewer Italians (32

Table 9-1 *Attitudes toward political participation, in percentages*

	United States	United Kingdom	Germany	Italy	Mexico
Attitudes toward active participation in local community:					
Activities of local government	21	22	13	5	11
Activities of political parties	6	4	4	1	5
Nongovernmental activity and organizations interested in local affairs	32	17	9	5	10
Attitudes toward more passive community activities:					
Being interested and trying to keep informed	24	24	30	21	33
Voting	40	18	15	2	1
Total percentage of respondents who mention some political activity	78	70	60	32	59

Source: Adapted from Gabriel A. Almond and Sidney Verba, *The Civic Culture*, Princeton, N.J.: Princeton University Press, 1963, pp. 170, 171.

percent) stated that the average person should participate in some form of political activity.

Political socialization and electoral behavior

The term *political socialization* refers to the process by which individuals gain the attitudes, values, interest, and information that influence their political decisions and actions and lead them to perceive political events in a particular manner. The extent to which a person participates in public affairs is significantly influenced by his experiences and his political environment, which includes the governmental system and the social, psychological, and physical factors and forces that have an impact on political attitudes and behavior.

How a person's political loyalties, values, and beliefs are developed is a question that has intrigued political scientists as well as psychologists and sociologists. Research studies regarding political socialization indicate that the manner in which adult political attitudes are formed is highly complicated. It is now generally accepted that political socialization is a continuous process beginning in early childhood in nonpolitical as well as political experiences and continuing throughout adolescence and adulthood. In brief, "political learning continues throughout life and follows a roughly sequential development."[11]

Of the various forms of political participation, voting is the most im-

---
[11] Richard E. Dawson and Kenneth Prewitt, *Political Socialization*, Boston: Little, Brown, 1969, p. 43.

portant act engaged in by the great majority of Americans. The factors related to voting and party affiliation have been studied more intensively than other forms of political behavior. The following discussion focuses primarily on those factors and will also elucidate other aspects of political behavior and participation.

The family. The family is the most important force in an individual's social and physical environment. The family serves as the principal early determinant of information and ideas regarding political parties, government, social problems, religion, and ethnic groups. David Wallace has noted that by the time a child enters kindergarten "this new semisocial being has already acquired the equivalent of 350 college courses, enough for an A.B. degree more than eight times over, in learning the values, customs, and attitudes that are sanctioned by his own unique family."[12] The ideas and concepts gained directly from parents are usually reinforced by newspapers, periodicals, and books in the home, by friends and occupational associates of the parents, and by the community or neighborhood.

The impact of the family on the development of early attitudes is difficult to overstate. In the early formative years, individuals develop various political attitudes, some of which are retained for much if not all of their lives. As Fred Greenstein has observed: "Early impressions tend to coalesce into a natural view of the world. All later experiences then tend to receive their meaning from this original set."[13] These attitudes often lead to specific types of overt political behavior. They also condition a person's political outlook, so that later in life he may be inclined either to accept or "screen out" certain kinds of information, depending on whether it conforms or conflicts with his preestablished political orientation.

Voting is essentially a group phenomenon, and the family is the most important and influential group to which a person ever belongs. Professor Lazarsfeld found in his Erie County, Ohio, survey that disagreement regarding presidential candidates occurred between husband and wife in only one couple out of 22. Other studies have shown that among voters whose parents had the same party affiliation, approximately eight out of 10 stated that their first vote was for that party.

Since parental influences are so strong, how does one account for those individuals whose party affiliations are dissimilar from their parents'? To a considerable degree, the answer is mobility—occupational, economic, and geographic mobility. In the United States, young people frequently do not follow the vocations of their parents, and many enter occupations that place

---

[12]David Wallace, *First Tuesday, A Study of Rationality in Voting*, Garden City, N.Y.: Doubleday, 1964, p. 231.

[13]Fred I. Greenstein, *Children and Politics*, New Haven: Yale University Press, 1965, p. 81.

them in different strata of society and different geographic regions. In their new situations and associations, they may encounter new political perspectives and information that may erode parental influences. In recent years, a considerably larger proportion of young people than formerly have adopted political attitudes and party affiliations different from those of their parents.

Socioeconomic class. The American egalitarian heritage and relatively high degree of social and economic mobility has resulted in less class consciousness than in western Europe and in many other countries. Nevertheless, in the United States, too, socioeconomic class has a bearing on political behavior. Class status is determined by a combination of factors, including occupation, education, economic resources and income, place of residence, and social standing. Objectively, a person's class standing would be ascertained by an analysis of such factors. For many individuals, however, class identification may be largely subjective, and it is not uncommon for a person to believe that he is in a class different from that indicated by his socioeconomic characteristics. From the standpoint of political behavior, a person's own analysis of his class status may be more important than his actual class level. Although the relationship between class status and affiliation with a particular party apparently has diminished, data obtained from several studies show that the higher a person's class status, the greater his tendency to vote Republican.

Investigations of political participation in five countries—United States, Britain, West Germany, Italy, and Mexico—indicate a close relationship between class status, membership in organizations, and political participation. The investigators found that, in each country, the higher a person's social status and involvement in organizations, the greater the tendency to be politically active. Table 9–2 shows the proportion of persons politically active in the five countries for each of four groupings—persons with high and low organizational involvement and high and low social status.

Table 9–2 *Political participation among status and involvement groups*

Organizational Involvement Level	Social Status Level	PERCENTAGE OF ACTIVE PARTICIPANTS				
		U.S.	G.B.	Germany	Italy	Mexico
High	High	75	77	62	66	61
High	Low	67	67	65	53	71
Low	High	32	38	21	10	16
Low	Low	10	21	14	11	8

Source: Adapted from Norman H. Nie, G. Bingham Powell, Jr., and Kenneth Prewitt, "Social Structure and Political Participation: Developmental Relationships, Part I," *American Political Science Review,* 63 (1969), p. 371. This table shows actual political participation of various groups as contrasted with attitudes toward political participation illustrated in Table 9–1.

Occupation. Of the various attributes of class, the factors that especially influence political attitudes and behavior are occupation, income, and education. Considering the proportion of a person's time devoted to his occupation (possibly in close contact with fellow workers) and its influence on his socioeconomic status, where he lives, his choice of friends, and the use of his leisure time, it is not surprising that the way one earns his livelihood is an important determinant of political behavior. Table 9-3 shows the percentage of different occupational groups voting for Democratic presidential candidates from 1948 through 1972. As would be expected, the strongest support for Republican candidates came from the professional and managerial class. Union members are among the most consistent Democratic supporters. As the percentages indicate, farmers have the most unstable voting pattern. One explanation for this is that, living and working more in isolation than most other people, the farmer is less likely to be swayed by membership in organized groups, by co-workers, or by party activists, and is more likely to vote for the party that offers the most attractive farm program.

Although these data are useful, much of their significance is lost because they apply to broad analytical categories. The gross percentages presented in this table fail to illustrate fully the cleavages within these categories and the importance of group influences on electoral behavior. For example, within the "professional and managerial" classification are corporation executives, small shopkeepers, attorneys, doctors, college professors, and several other subgroupings. The aggregate figures indicate that historically the group as a whole supports the Republicans, and some within the group have voted overwhelmingly for Republican candidates, but others have supported Democrats by equally large margins. For example, the proportion of top-level business executives and northern doctors voting the Republican ticket during the 1950s and 1960s was undoubtedly higher than these figures indicate, because large proportions of other groups in this broad category supported Democratic candidates.

Studies of subgroups within the academic profession indicate both the

Table 9-3 *Percentage of occupational groups voting for Democratic candidate for President, 1948–1972*

	1948	1952	1956	1960	1964	1968	1972
Professional and managerial	19	31	31	44	57	35	31
Clerical and sales	47	35	39	48	63	41	32
Skilled and semiskilled	72	51	44	57	76	45	35
Unskilled	67	67	47	59	80	56	55
Union members	76	55	51	62	83	49	41
Farm	59	37	46	33	63	37	31

Source: *Center for Political Studies*, University of Michigan.

fallacy of using broad categories in classifying individuals and the correlation between a person's job category and his partisan attachments. Two surveys, made a decade apart, of more than 4,000 professors teaching in 12 different subject-matter areas in American colleges revealed that the proportion of Democrats, Republicans, and independents depends on the area of specialization. While a majority of social scientists classified themselves as Democrats, less than 30 percent of the mathematicians and engineers so categorized themselves. This research suggests that for these individuals the information gained in their professions and contacts with colleagues may be more important than parental influences in determining their political preferences.

Income and education. In virtually every demographic grouping, the more income a person has, the greater the likelihood that he will be a Republican voter. This is true of occupational categories, individuals living in different regions and in urban and rural communities, all educational and age groups, and all racial and religious groups. This does not mean, of course, that there are not many wealthy Democrats.

Opinion surveys have indicated a correlation between education and voting. Various studies have shown that college graduates vote Republican

"I bet you thought you'd never find a conservative this far down the economic scale."
Wall Street Journal, June 21, 1971. By permission of artist and Wall Street Journal.

in higher proportions than high-school graduates, who in turn cast their ballots for Republicans in larger percentages than those with only a grade-school education. Undoubtedly, the tendency of those with higher educations to vote Republican may be attributed in part to their economic status and occupations. Among university professors, the field of specialization apparently has an influence on partisan preference, with a large proportion of those in the social sciences supporting the Democratic party.

Regional and residential influences. Owing in part to historical reasons, the people in certain regions of the nation have been predominantly Republicans, while in other regions most of the voters were Democrats. After the Civil War, the states below the Mason-Dixon line so consistently supported the Democratic party that this area became known as the "solid South." Regardless of religion or ancestry, most southerners—whether lawyers, merchants, doctors, bankers, factory workers, or tenant farmers—have been Democrats. The strongest and most consistent support for the Republicans has been found in Maine and Vermont in the Northeast, and in North Dakota, Nebraska, and Kansas in the Midwest. All of these states were in the Republican column in every presidential election starting with 1940 until 1964, all except Maine went Republican in 1968, and all supported Nixon in the Republican landslide of 1972. Regional influences on party identification have thus contributed to the multigroup character of each party; if it were not for regional influences, party preferences throughout the nation would be more distinctly a matter of class and economics. In recent years throughout the nation regional influences on party politics have declined, with the Republican party gaining strength in the South and the Democrats in the previously Republican-dominated northern states. In the 1974 Democratic electoral victory, Republicans in the South suffered sizable setbacks, but the long-run trend appears to be an increase in the proportion of southerners identifying as Republicans and the further growth of a two-party system in the South.

Political attitudes may also be shown to vary with the size of the communities—that is, different voting patterns can be seen in large cities, suburbs, small cities, and rural areas. Election statistics show that in every presidential election from 1928 to 1972, a majority of the voters in the 12 largest northern cities have voted Democratic, whereas in the nearby suburbs a majority have voted Republican in every presidential election except for 1936 and 1964. This does not mean that all suburbs are Republican strongholds. There are all types of suburbs, and in many the majority of voters are Democrats.

Generally, in small cities outside the South the voters tend to support the Republican party in larger proportions than they do in large cities. As William H. Flanigan has observed, "The Republican Party . . . is disproportionately a small-town and medium-size city party."[14] In cities of 10,000 to 50,000 population, the business community—functioning through the local Chamber of Commerce, service clubs, and other organizations—often exerts a more pervasive influence on the entire community than in larger cities, where labor unions and other groups are more likely to operate as competing political forces. Thus in small cities, laborers, government employees, and others are more likely to vote the Republican ticket than in major cities.

Religion and race. In a number of countries—such as Italy, France, Germany, Ireland—religion has served as the basis for organizing some parties. In the United States, Protestants, Catholics, and Jews are found in both parties, but not in the same proportions. Northern Protestants tend to support the Republican party, Catholics tend to be Democrats, and since the 1930s the great majority of Jews have voted the Democratic ticket. Historical factors account in part for this alignment of voters. Protestant groups generally came to the United States first, became established, and often prospered. Most Catholics and Jews came later, often were considered by the earlier arrivals to be minority groups, and customarily settled in cities where Democratic party organizations aided them to become citizens and voters. Franklin Roosevelt and subsequent Democratic presidents, with their emphasis on social reforms, helped to cement the ties of most minority groups to the Democratic party.

As in the case of other variables, the candidates and the issues may alter the voting patterns of each group. Note the variations in the percentage of each group voting for Democratic candidates in the presidential elections of 1948 through 1972, as shown in Table 9–4. The candidacy in 1960 of John F. Kennedy, the first Catholic to be elected President, illustrates the salience of religion to electoral behavior. As the table indicates, numerous Catholic Democrats who had voted for Truman in 1948 supported Eisenhower in 1952 and 1956, but returned to the Democratic fold in 1960. Of

Table 9–4 *Religious groups voting for Democratic candidates, in percentages*

	1948	1952	1956	1960	1964	1968	1972
Protestant	43	36	35	36	61	35	30
Catholic	62	51	45	82	79	56	37
Jewish	(a)	71	77	89	89	85	66

[a]Too few cases to compute.
Source: *Center for Political Studies*, University of Michigan.

[14]William H. Flanigan, *Political Behavior of the American Electorate*, Boston: Allyn & Bacon, 1968, p. 46.

the Catholics who voted for Eisenhower in 1956, nearly six out of 10 supported Kennedy in 1960.

The importance of ethnic or racial background as a determinant of voting behavior no doubt declines with each generation. Yet in certain areas —in particular, a number of cities east of the Mississippi and north of the Ohio River—ethnic voting is a fact of political life, and it is likely to continue for decades to come. In New York City, for example, each party appeals for the votes of the major ethnic and racial groups in the city by nominating persons from each of these groups. The voting behavior of blacks, who constitute the single most important racial minority in the United States, will be discussed in a later section in this chapter.

Influence of age. Election studies have correlated age with party preference and voting. During recent decades, the proportion of older voters who have voted Republican has exceeded the percentage of the national vote received by the Republican party. The Democrats have experienced similar success with the younger voters (see Table 9–5). The reasons for this phenomenon are not fully known, but it has been suggested that as people grow older they receive higher incomes, acquire more property, become more conservative, and are more disposed to support the Republican party. Public opinion surveys have indicated that young people are somewhat more liberal than their elders and have different partisan orientations. For instance, a Gallup

Table 9–5 *Percentage of vote by groups in Presidential elections, 1956–1972*

	1956 Dem.	1956 Rep.	1960 D	1960 R	1964 D	1964 R	1968 D	1968 R	1968 Wallace	1972 D	1972 R
National	42.2	57.8	50.1	49.9	61.3	38.7	43.0	43.4	13.6	38	62
Men	45	55	52	48	60	40	41	43	16	37	63
Women	39	61	49	51	62	38	45	43	12	38	62
White	41	59	49	51	59	41	38	47	15	32	68
Nonwhite	61	39	68	32	94	6	85	12	3	87	13
College	31	69	39	61	52	48	37	54	9	37	63
High school	42	58	52	48	62	38	42	43	15	34	66
Grade school	50	50	55	45	66	34	52	33	15	49	51
Under 30 years	43	57	54	46	64	36	47	38	15	48	52
30–49 years	45	55	54	46	63	37	44	41	15	33	67
50 years and older	39	61	46	54	59	41	41	47	12	36	64
Republicans	4	96	5	95	20	80	9	86	5	5	95
Democrats	85	15	84	16	87	13	74	12	14	67	33
Independents	30	70	43	57	56	44	31	44	25	31	69

Source: *Gallup Opinion Index*, Princeton, N.J.

poll[15] conducted in mid-1974 showed that of the 18-to-24 age group 15 percent said they were Republicans, 37 percent Democrats, and 48 percent independents. In comparison, of the voters 50 and over, 29 percent preferred the Republican party, 49 percent the Democratic party, and 22 percent said they were independents. Other surveys have shown that young people in college are more liberal and more likely to favor the Democratic party or to be independents than those not in college.

It is no doubt true that classifying voters according to social characteristics may explain little about the factors influencing voting, unless those factors are related in some fashion to political decisions made by public officials. Being a businessman, doctor, Negro, or Catholic may influence a person's electoral decision only if he believes that the victory of a party is relevant to him as a businessman, doctor, Negro, or Catholic. Thus when a large proportion of a given category of voters supports a party, it is not due merely to the impulse of social forces, but to what appears to be a rational decision based on the best available information.

Influence of parties, candidates, and issues

An analysis of the economic and demographic bases of partisan preferences implies a static quality of political behavior and may lead one to the erroneous conclusion that the act of voting is simply an unthinking response to social forces. The sociological factors related to voting are, of course, not static; indeed, major changes have occurred in the past decade. Yet in order to understand the dynamism that characterizes the American electoral process and the extent to which voters make rational, purposive decisions, one must examine the voters' perceptions of the political parties, candidates, and issues. As has been indicated, a person's perception of these will be influenced by the information he receives through the mass media, his friends, occupational associates, family, and other social forces.

Party affiliation. The influence of political parties on voting behavior has diminished significantly in recent years, and some writers believe the impact of the parties will continue to decline.[16] However, for many individuals, the party is an important "reference group," that is, a group with which the individual significantly identifies and from which he derives some basic values and goals. The influence of party attachments tends to be in proportion to the strength of those attachments, with persons classifying

---

[15]*New York Times*, July 18, 1974, p. 24.

[16]For instance, see David Broder, *The Party's Over: The Failure of Politics in America*, New York: Harper & Row, 1971; and Walter Dean Burnham, *Critical Elections and the Mainsprings of American Politics*, New York: Norton, 1970.

themselves as "strong" Republicans or Democrats more likely than the "weak" Republicans or Democrats to vote for candidates of their party.

Political party affiliation provides a stabilizing force in American politics. Many Americans choose their party early in life and do not change. Regardless of the candidates or the issues, millions of voters can be counted on by each party. The Survey Research Center found that 56 percent of voters interviewed stated that they had never voted for a presidential candidate of the opposite party. There is a continuous movement of voters from one party to the other, and many voters will cast ballots for candidates of the opposite party, but major shifts in party affiliation have occurred only as a result of some national crisis such as the Civil War or the Great Depression. Individuals who change their party affiliations at other times usually do so because of some marked change in their own lives, such as marriage, moving, a new job, or a change in economic status.

From the standpoint of the stabilizing role of parties, it is significant that more than half of the electorate have always voted for their party's presidential candidate; from the standpoint of political dynamism, it is equally noteworthy that more than four out of 10 persons have voted or are willing to vote for presidential candidates of the other party.[17] Thus, while partisan psychological attachments are not changed lightly, many voters will cross party lines in elections.

The voter's perceptions of candidates and issues and the looseness of partisan attachments help to account for the dynamic character of American elections. This characteristic is dramatically illustrated by recent election returns. For instance, the Republican percentage of the vote varied from 57.4 to 49.5 to 38.5 to 43.5 to 60.8 in 1956, 1960, 1964, 1968, and 1972 respectively. Although the change in the Republican vote is important, equally significant is the fact that the change occurred in virtually every socioeconomic category of voters.

The impact of candidates and issues. Although social forces and partisan affiliation influence electoral decisions, the candidates and the issues may be the most important factors in determining the success of a party in a particular election. Indeed, since the mid-1960s there has been a definite increase in those who have cast their ballots because of preference for particular candidates and issues, and a decline in partisan voting.

The term *candidate orientation* refers to interest in candidates separate from their party affiliations and the political issues. From this standpoint, candidates are viewed on the basis of both their presumed effectiveness in office and their personality characteristics. Each candidate is judged on the basis of his past record and his personal appearance and style. As partisan

---

[17] Angus Campbell, Warren E. Miller, Philip E. Converse, and Donald S. Stokes, *The American Voter*, New York: Wiley, 1960, p. 148.

affiliations continue to weaken, some voters who are apparently confused by the issues—or possibly indifferent to them—vote for the man they "can trust." For example, in 1952 and 1972, millions of Democrats crossed party lines and voted for Eisenhower and Nixon respectively.

For issue-oriented individuals, public policies provide the strongest norm according to which they make their electoral decisions. While most candidates conduct their campaigns largely on promises of future action, voters tend to judge the parties retrospectively; they respond more to events they have experienced and to policies enacted by a party than to new proposals. Parties are rewarded for enacting policies considered beneficial, and many voters react emphatically if they believe favored policies might be jeopardized by the election of a particular candidate.

Trends in political participation

During the 1960s and 1970s several changes and trends have occurred regarding the political behavior of Americans. Of major importance is the increase in numbers of blacks voting and holding public office, the number of women elected to office, and a decline in the percentage of the electorate who vote.

Increase in voting and officeholding by blacks. Although the Fifteenth Amendment, ratified in 1870, granted black Americans the right to vote, they have until recently constituted the largest group of disfranchised citizens in the United States. Means that have been used in the past to prevent blacks from participating in politics are discussed in Chapter 8. In southern states, constitutional provisions, statutes, administrative regulations, and threats of violence have prevented blacks from voting or running for public office. Under the federal system, voting, elections, and the enforcement of criminal law are considered to be primarily the responsibility of the states. However, the federal government, in order to correct the inequitable treatment of blacks, undertook to guarantee the Negro his political rights by enacting the civil-rights acts of the 1950s and 1960s. The most important of the provisions authorized federal examiners to oversee the registration or directly to register blacks in several southern states and to prevent the intimidation of voters by making it a federal offense to injure or threaten any person for voting or campaigning for public office.

Largely as a result of these statutes, black political participation has greatly increased during recent years. For example, in the 11 southern states that formed the Confederacy, the proportion of registered voting-age blacks increased from 43 percent in 1964 to 70 percent in 1972. Black voting in national elections increased from 6 million in 1964 to over 7 million in 1972. The number of blacks elected to public office also increased sharply. In 1967 only an estimated 475 blacks held public office, but in 1974 the number had increased to 2,991.[18] Black mayors have been elected in such major cities as Gary, Indiana; Detroit, Michigan; Cincinnati and Cleveland, Ohio; Los Angeles, California; Washington, D.C.; Atlanta, Georgia; and approximately fifty smaller cities. In California, blacks have been selected for two state-wide elective offices, lieutenant governor and superintendent of public instruction. In addition, considerably more blacks have been recruited for high administrative positions than had been chosen for these positions at any previous time in history. The number of blacks in the House of Representatives has been increasing, and in 1974 sixteen were elected to Congress. Considering that blacks constitute approximately 11 percent of the American population, the number of offices they hold is still disproportionately small, but important gains were made during the 1960s and 1970s.[19]

Women elected officials. In addition to the election of more blacks and other minority members to public office, an increased number of women have been elected to public office in recent years. For example, in Connecticut in 1974 Ella Grasso became the first woman to be elected governor of a state without succeeding her husband to the office. Minnesota and California elected women as their secretaries of state, the third highest ranking state officer; and North Carolina was the first state to elect a woman as chief justice of the state supreme court. Almost yearly larger numbers of women have been elected to other state offices, and by 1974 nearly 600 were members of state legislators. In 1975, 19 women were members of the House of Representatives, but with the defeat in 1972 of veteran United States Senator Margaret Chase Smith of Maine, there were no women in the Senate.

Nonvoting. Much has been written regarding the large proportion of nonvoters in the United States in comparison with other democracies. For example, in recent elections in Austria and Italy 90 percent or more of the qualified voters have participated, in West Germany from 78 to 88 percent, and approximately 80 percent in Canada. By comparison, in presidential elections in the United States the percentage of voting-age persons going to the polls has been as low as 51.6 percent in 1948, and no higher than 63.8 percent in 1960. Two questions are raised by these data: Why are the figures cited on voter participation lower in the United States than in sev-

[18] U.S. Bureau of the Census, *Statistical Abstract of the United States: 1974*, Washington, D.C.: U.S. Government Printing Office, pp. 436, 437. In two southern states, Arkansas and Texas, a larger percentage of blacks than whites registered to vote in 1971.

[19] Besides the increased political participation by black citizens, there has been an increase of other minorities, especially Mexican-Americans and Asian-Americans, elected to office.

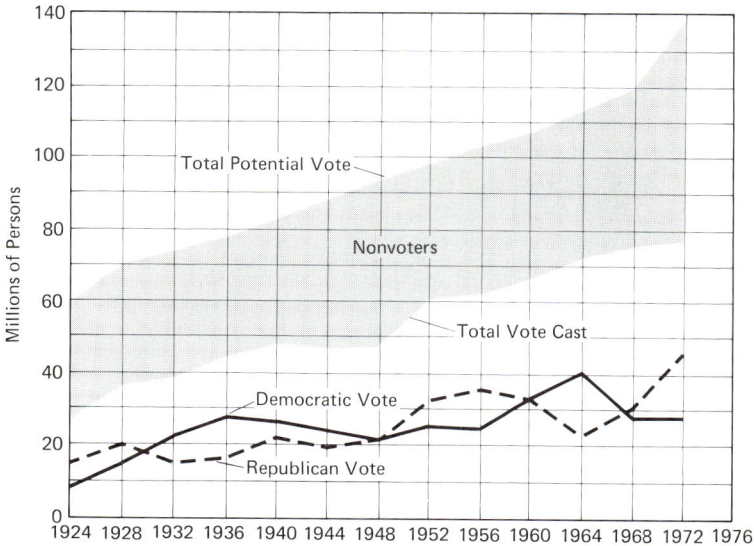

Figure 9-2 *Votes cast in presidential elections, 1924-1972*

eral other democracies? What factors are related to nonvoting in the United States?

The lower proportion of persons cited as voting in the United States may be explained in part by the manner in which the statistics are presented and in part by legal and administrative obstacles to registering and voting. According to the statistics commonly quoted, of the approximately 140 million persons of voting age in 1972, slightly more than 77 million cast ballots for a presidential candidate. (See Figure 9-2.) However, these figures are misleading if they are interpreted to mean that only slightly more than 55 percent of the qualified voters cast ballots in 1972. First, 5 to 10 percent more people usually vote in a presidential election year than the published figures on presidential voting indicate—some people vote in the primary elections but not in the general election, some vote in the general election but not for a presidential candidate, and some ballots are invalidated owing to technical errors by the voter. Second, because of legal and administrative requirements for voting, the number of qualified voters is considerably lower than the number of persons of voting age. According to estimates at the time of the 1972 election there were slightly more than 95 million registered voters. Thus, of the legally qualified voters, 80 to 85 percent actually voted.

According to a Gallup poll, 28 percent of the nonvoters in the 1972 election said they were not interested in politics, and 38 percent stated they had not met the residency requirements or had failed to register. This latter group could have voted if the United States employed automatic

"I'm not voting this year. They're not going to get me as an accessory to anything."
Los Angeles Times, Sunday, October 27, 1974 (Part VIII, p. 18).

registration, as is done in most European countries and Canada. Among others who did not vote, several million were disqualified because they were not American citizens, were confined to a mental institution, or had been convicted for criminal acts.

Psychological factors are important in determining the level of voting as well as other forms of political participation. As the preceding data indicate, many fail to vote because of indifference, noninvolvement, or alienation. Others, questioning the efficacy of their vote, may simply not make the effort. Political observers believe that the growing feeling of cynicism and disaffection toward government during the late 1960s and early 1970s was largely responsible for the decline in voting. For instance, there was a decrease in the proportion of the electorate who voted, from 63 percent in 1960 to less than 56 percent in 1972—the smallest percentage since 1948.

Another reason for the relatively low level of electoral participation in the United States may be the similarity of the two parties. A study of voters in the United States and four other countries—Great Britain, West Germany, Italy, and Mexico—revealed that a smaller proportion of the people in the United States than in the other countries were fearful of the possible victory of an opposition party.[20]

---

[20]Robert E. Lane, "The Politics of Consensus in an Age of Affluence," *American Political Science Review*, 59 (December, 1965), p. 890.

10
The Party System

10

From a historical standpoint, party government is a fairly recent development. Political parties originated in England in the late seventeenth century as a necessary element in the evolution of representative government; as government became more representative, the influence of parties increased proportionately. Competitive political parties developed in the United States near the end of the eighteenth century, were not established in other countries until the nineteenth or twentieth centuries, and in many countries are yet to be established.

Prior to the development of parties, authority was held by individuals because of particular circumstances—royal birth, military leadership, religious position, wealth, or specialized knowledge or training. In these earlier regimes, short-lived oligarchies or factions occasionally arose which resembled certain political parties of today. These groupings were basically different from present-day parties, however, because they were extraconstitutional or even anticonstitutional. Political parties today, through either legal provisions or custom and practice, have acquired a constitutional status. (See Figure 10–1 showing the United States political spectrum.) In brief, in most modern countries the only legitimate means by which persons now acquire political authority is through political parties. As a consequence, parties have become semigovernmental organizations and are as essential to the functioning of democratic governments as are legislative bodies or judicial agencies.

A political party may be defined as an organization that has as its basic purpose controlling the choice of governmental personnel and policies. Although parties differ greatly from country to country and even within countries, this definition applies to all true political parties. Unorganized cliques and other types of organizations, such as political–interest groups, may be found that attempt to influence the choice of public officials and policies, but only a political party has as its *raison d'être* the selection of governmental personnel and policies.

THE DEVELOPMENT OF AMERICAN PARTIES

Political parties in the United States are almost as old as the country itself. The Democratic party traces its origin to Thomas Jefferson, who was elected President in 1800, and the Republican party was first formed in 1854. Be-

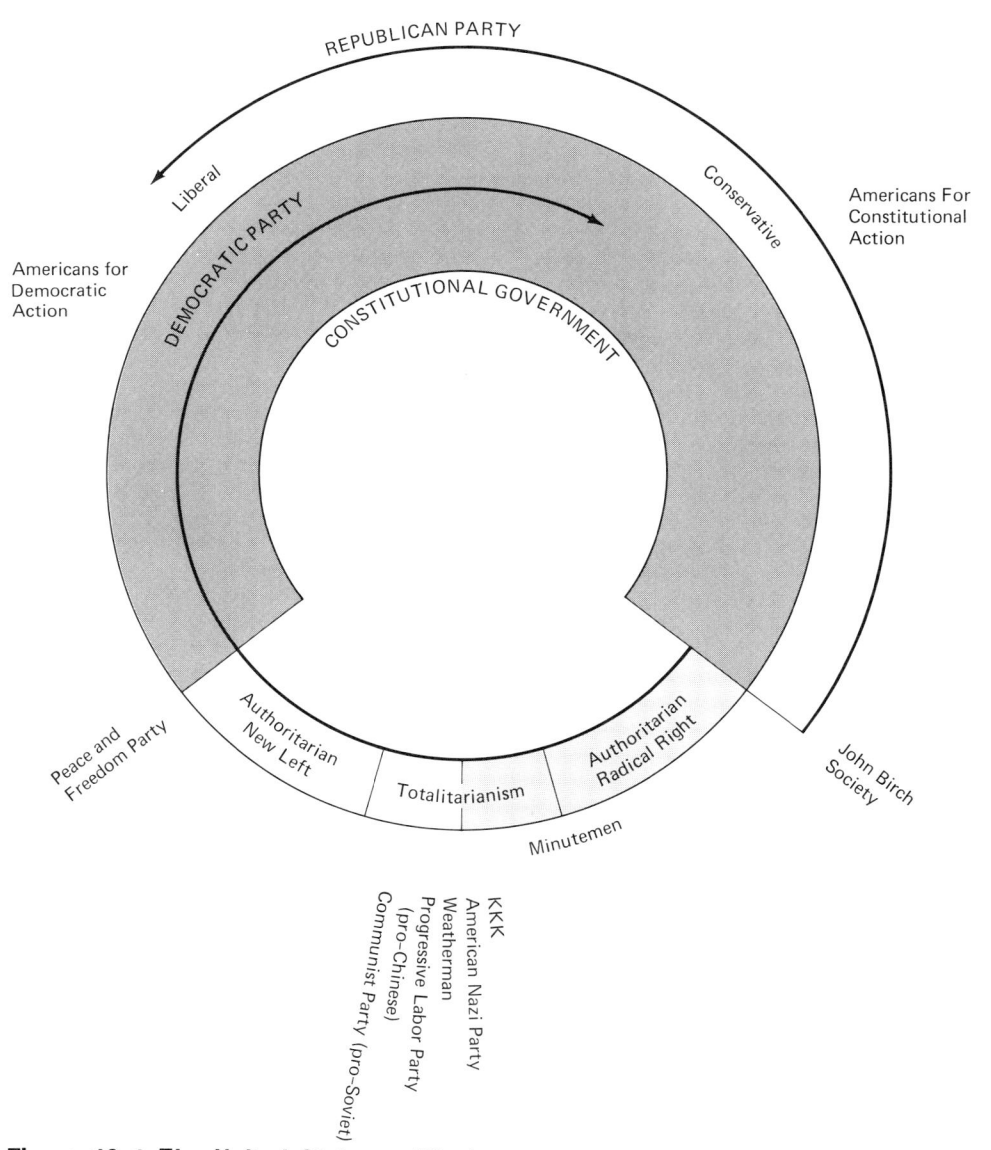

Figure 10–1 *The United States political spectrum*

cause American parties have developed in a pragmatic fashion and are shaped by past customs and practices as well as by influential party leaders, one cannot fully appreciate and understand politics today without some knowledge of the past.

No provision was made in the Constitution for political parties. To provide for the selection of the President and Vice-President, the Founding Fathers devised the Electoral College system, which fulfilled the function of both nominating and electing these officials. Nominations for other offices were by self-announcement or by caucuses of local leaders. The Founding Fathers, like the leaders of many recently created nations, hoped to see the country move ahead as one united citizenry rather than divide into opposing factions or parties. President George Washington reflected the opinion of many of his contemporaries when, in his Farewell Address, he warned of "the baneful effects of the spirit of party."

The first American parties

Washington, who was unanimously elected President by the electors, sought to direct the government in a nonpartisan fashion, but political parties developed during his administration. The formation of the first two parties may be attributed to Alexander Hamilton, the first Secretary of the Treasury, and Thomas Jefferson, the first Secretary of State. Hamilton, who lived in New York City, was the founder and acknowledged leader of the Federalist party. An exponent of the principle that "the rich, the well-born, and the good" should rule, Hamilton advocated a government based on strong executive leadership, centralized power, and policies beneficial to the business and commercial community. Although Washington attempted to be nonpartisan, he came to accept the policies of his Secretary of the Treasury.

Jefferson, a Virginia plantation owner, led the opposition to Hamilton. Basically equalitarian, he favored a limited and decentralized government, a strong legislature, and policies that would benefit the small shopkeepers, workers, farmers, and planters. Shortly after Washington's second inauguration, Jefferson left the Cabinet to organize and lead his party, which was first known as the Anti-Federalist, then as the Jeffersonian–Republican, and later as the Democratic party. The first electoral contest between the two parties occurred in 1796 when John Adams, the Federalist candidate for President, defeated Jefferson. Four years later, Jefferson was elected President, and Federalist control of the national government was ended.

Eras of one-party dominance

Most students of American politics now accept the view that our history has been characterized by relatively long periods during which one of the major parties has dominated the political scene.[1] Although scholars have varied analyses of the eras of party dominance, there is general agreement that each era reflects a major phase of American social and economic development and the dominant party tended to establish the "agenda" for the nation. Considered from the standpoint of the presidency, political party history since 1800 may be divided into three periods starting respectively with the elections of 1800, 1860, and 1932.

First period: the election of Jefferson, 1800. In the 60 years between the election of Jefferson in 1800 and the Civil War, the party founded by Jefferson and reorganized by Jackson lost only two presidential elections. Initially the competition was between the Jeffersonian Republicans and the Federalists, with both parties consisting primarily of elected officials and making little effort to organize the electorate. Following Jefferson's victory in 1800, the Federalist party gradually declined. For several years after 1817 the only national party was that of the Jeffersonian Republicans, and the principal competition for national office was between opposing candidates of that party.

The 1828 election ushered in Jacksonian democracy. Previously, the political leaders had come largely from the eastern states and from the gentry. As new states were admitted to the Union and as suffrage restrictions were gradually removed, there was a shifting of political power from the seaboard states to the western and southern states, and from the upper to the middle and lower classes. The election of Jackson, the first "man of the people" to occupy the White House, illustrates this shift in political power and initiated modern mass parties.

In the three decades prior to the Civil War, the parties underwent a number of changes, and experienced several developments that had a lasting impact on American politics. With the expansion of the suffrage there occurred a notable increase in popular participation in the government, more elaborate political organizations developed, the party boss appeared in many cities, and the patronage system became the order of the day. Certain present-day practices of the parties date from these years, including the drafting of party platforms. The first national committee was established in 1848, and it became standard practice for all the electoral votes in a given state to be cast for the one candidate receiving the plurality of the popular votes. From the standpoint of American politics, possibly the most

---

[1] For somewhat differing analyses of this phenomenon see Henry A. Turner, "National Politics: Eras of One-Party Control," *Social Science*, 28, no. 3 (June, 1953), pp. 137–143; Walter Dean Burnham, *Critical Elections: The Mainsprings of American Politics*, New York: Norton, 1970; Everett Carll Ladd, Jr., *American Political Parties: Social Change and Political Response*, New York: Norton, 1970; and James L. Sundquist, *Dynamics of the Party System*, Washington, D.C.: Brookings Institution, 1973.

important contribution of these decades was the firm entrenchment of the two-party system. A single party has been able to win most presidential elections for long periods, but in every election since 1824, two parties have competed seriously and vigorously and usually on fairly even terms.

Table 10–1 *Political eras*

	FIRST DEMOCRATIC ERA	
	Federalist, Whig	Jeffersonian-Republican, Democrat
1801		Jefferson
1805		Jefferson
1809		Madison
1813		Madison
1817		Monroe
1821		Monroe
1825		J. Q. Adams
1829		Jackson
1833		Jackson
1837		Van Buren
1841	Harrison-Tyler	
1845		Polk
1849	Taylor-Fillmore	
1853		Pierce
1857		Buchanan

	REPUBLICAN ERA	
	Republican	Democrat
1861	Lincoln	
1865	Lincoln-Johnson	
1869	Grant	
1873	Grant	
1877	Hayes	
1881	Garfield-Arthur	
1885		Cleveland
1889	Harrison	
1893		Cleveland
1897	McKinley	
1901	McKinely-T. Roosevelt	
1905	T. Roosevelt	
1909	Taft	
1913		Wilson
1917		Wilson
1921	Harding-Coolidge	
1925	Coolidge	
1929	Hoover	

Table 10–1 *Political eras (continued)*

	SECOND DEMOCRATIC ERA	
	Republican	Democrat
1933		F. Roosevelt
1937		F. Roosevelt
1941		F. Roosevelt
1945		F. Roosevelt-Truman
1949		Truman
1953	Eisenhower	
1957	Eisenhower	
1961		Kennedy-Johnson
1965		Johnson
1969	Nixon	
1973	Nixon-Ford	

Second period: the election of Lincoln, 1860. The Civil War, a major landmark in American politics, introduced a new political era. In 1860 the Democratic party split into northern and southern wings, each nominating its own presidential candidate. With the Democrats divided, the Republican party elected Abraham Lincoln, although he received less than 40 percent of the popular vote. This first Republican victory was followed by the secession of the South and the Civil War.

The Civil War and Reconstruction periods profoundly affected party history in the United States. One result was the "Solid South"—a one-party region in which the Democratic party was supreme. Another result, largely attributable to the war and its aftermath, was the virtual monopolization of the presidency by the Republicans for nearly three-quarters of a century. It would be incorrect, however, to assume that the Democrats were completely submerged. Actually, until 1896 the electoral strength of the two parties was very similar.[2] Moreover, on several occasions the Democrats controlled one or both houses of Congress, and Democratic presidential candidates outpolled their Republican opponents on six occasions. But between 1860 and 1932 only two Democrats, Cleveland and Wilson, occupied the White House.

---

[2] The election of 1896 has been considered a "critical election," because in that year the Republicans gained new voters from most socioeconomic classes, creating a new alignment that enabled them to dominate national politics for the next three decades. Theodore Roosevelt, one of the most skilled political leaders in American history, contributed significantly to the maintenance of the North-West sectional alliance. V. O. Key, Jr., "A Theory of Critical Elections," *Journal of Politics,* 17 (February, 1955), pp. 3–18.

In 1912, when Taft was nominated for a second term, Theodore Roosevelt, who desired the nomination, led his supporters out of the Republican national convention and organized his Progressive party. With the Republican voters divided between Taft and Roosevelt, the Democratic nominee, Woodrow Wilson, was elected President. Four years later, while Europe was at war, Wilson was reelected by a very narrow margin.

During his administration, Wilson, through his legislative program and the precedents he established for strong presidential leadership, brought about a reversal of the positions of the two parties regarding states' rights versus federal power. The Democrats from the days of Jefferson had traditionally stood for states' rights and limited government, whereas the Republicans had favored a strong central government and the use of federal power to promote national interests. Wilson led the Democratic party away from its states' rights, laissez-faire position, and helped forge it into the party that advocates a strong national government and the utilization of that government to solve social and economic problems. The Republicans, in turn, have become known as the party favoring more power for the states and limited action by the national government.

Third period: the election of Franklin D. Roosevelt, 1932. The period of Republican domination of national politics was terminated with the election of Franklin D. Roosevelt in 1932, which, like the election of 1860, is one of the landmark elections in American history. Following his victories in 1932 and 1936, Roosevelt ended the no-third-term tradition in 1940, and in 1944 was elected to a fourth term. After Roosevelt's first election as President, the Democrats dominated national politics in a fashion reminiscent of the earlier period of Democratic rule and the subsequent interval of Republican hegemony. Although there is evidence that a realignment of the parties had started with the 1928 election, the Great Depression was the fundamental reason for the abrupt transfer of electoral power from the Republicans to the Democrats.

Since 1932 the Republicans have won only four presidential elections and have had majorities in either house of Congress for only four years— 1947–1949 and 1953–1955. In 1952 and 1956 the Republicans marched to victory under the banner of World War II hero General Dwight D. Eisenhower. In 1960 John F. Kennedy became the first Roman Catholic to occupy the White House when he won a narrow victory over Eisenhower's Vice-President, Richard M. Nixon. In 1964, in a second precedent-breaking election, Lyndon B. Johnson, who had been elevated to the presidency upon the assassination of President Kennedy, became the first southerner to be elected since the Civil War. In 1968 Nixon made a dramatic comeback and defeated Lyndon Johnson's Vice-President, Hubert H. Humphrey, by a margin only slightly larger than that by which he had lost eight years before. In 1972 Nixon defeated Senator George McGovern in a landslide victory, but

"If President Roosevelt has been dead for 30 years, why are you still mad at him?"
Saturday Review, January 11, 1975, p. 27.

the Democrats retained control of both houses of Congress. (See Figure 10–2.) What effect the resignation of Vice-President Agnew, the Watergate scandals, the appointment of Gerald Ford as Vice-President, the resignation of Nixon, the subsequent elevation of Ford to the presidency, and the appointment of Nelson Rockefeller as Vice President will have on the fortunes of the two parties remains to be seen.

Reasons for periods of one-party dominance

A number of reasons may be given to explain why for as long as seven decades one party has been able consistently to win national elections. First, of course, is the obvious reason that the party in power simply espoused policies that appealed to more voters than did the opposition party. In brief, it was able to organize a coalition representing the leading socioeconomic interests of that era. In the past, the party in control of the government has often been alert to changing conditions and has adjusted its policies to meet the new problems. Moreover, the party in power is in the position of recommending programs, so it has first choice among available policies, and its opponents then have the unfortunate alternatives of supporting the same policies, opposing them, or proposing other policies that they hope will be appealing to the voters but which, in fact, may be less popular.

The old adage that success breeds success applies in politics, and the very fact of its position of leadership brings other advantages to the party in power. It has, for instance, certain prerequisites—honors, favors, and preferments; it can award appointive offices, grant contracts, select locations for governmental facilities; it can provide its younger men with the experience and publicity essential for aspirants seeking higher elective office, and this may encourage able party members to enter politics and induce ambitious persons in the opposition to change party affiliation. Controlling the presidency tends to reduce substantially the problem of raising campaign funds. Furthermore, Americans tend to vote for incumbents, so the party with the largest number of officeholders may expect to benefit at the polls in subsequent elections. After a party has been in office a number of years, it continually attracts more and more loyal supporters until it becomes firmly entrenched as the majority party.

In the past, major changes in political orientation have taken place at times of national crisis. At the beginning of each of the three periods cited in Table 10-1 (page 223), the party that was ousted from power had to operate at a disadvantage for years. After 1800, the Federalist party was discredited by the Hartford Convention and the Alien and Sedition Acts; after the Civil War, the Democrats were stigmatized as the party of rebellion; and for at least two decades after 1929, the Republicans were criticized as being responsible for the Depression. Regardless of the relevance of the accusations, the party in power in each instance missed few opportunities to exploit them to their advantage.

The Republicans and Democrats today

Although the two major American parties are more similar than are the parties of Great Britain or of any other major power, an analysis of the Republican and Democratic parties today reveals differences regarding both their concepts of the proper function of government and their chief sources of electoral support. Any comparison of the Republicans and Democrats, however, should be prefaced with the observation that there are greater divergences of viewpoints within each party than between the two parties.

Although there is danger of overgeneralization, it may be said that history and circumstances have placed the present-day Democratic party in the role of exponent of positive governmental programs, whereas the Republican party occupies the position of advocate for less governmental action and more individual responsibility. The Democratic party has gained a reputation for being more willing than the Republicans to utilize government to

228 10 / THE PARTY SYSTEM

1968   Electoral Vote   Popular Vote

Millions

31.8   31.3

10.1

Democratic: 191
Republican: 301
American Independent: 46

1972

46

29

Democratic: 17
Republican: 521

0.013

☐ Republican   ▨ Democratic   ▥ Other

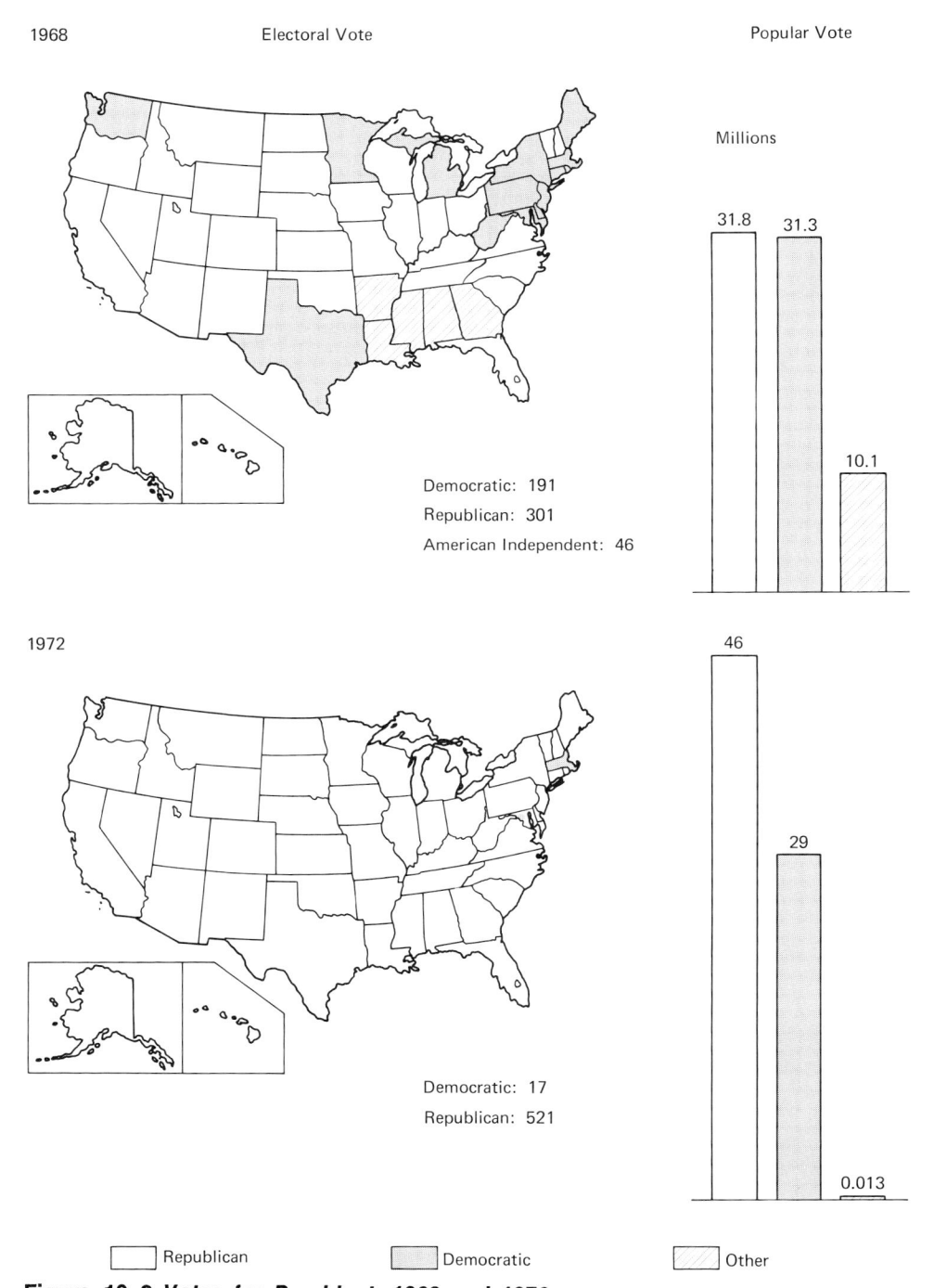

Figure 10–2 *Votes for President, 1968 and 1972*
SOURCE: *Pocket Data Book, USA.* Washington, D.C.: Bureau of the Census.

"Republican?"
The New Yorker, June 17, 1972, p. 35.

attack social and economic programs. Today the Democratic party is credited —or blamed—for initiating such legislative measures as old-age pensions, unemployment insurance, medical-care programs, labor and farm programs, federal aid to education, antipoverty programs, civil-rights legislation, tariff reforms, and foreign-aid programs. In some states—particularly the industrial states in the East and on the West Coast—Republican governors and legislators have initiated similar measures, but the Republican party nationally has the image of reluctantly accepting such programs while urging a reduction in government expenditures, lower taxes, less government regulation, and more responsibility on the part of the individual citizen for handling social and economic problems. For example, in the mid-1970s the Republicans were more fearful of rampant inflation than of rising unemployment, and thus favored restrained federal expenditures; the Democrats feared unemployment more than inflation, and favored increased federal expenditures and bigger tax cuts, even if more inflation were to result from such policies.

One reason for the differing reputations of the two parties regarding the proper function of the federal government is that the membership of the two parties is dissimilar. The most solid block of support for each of the two parties differs, as shown in Chapter 9. From the election of Lincoln, the "center of gravity of wealth" has been in the Republican party. The GOP dominated national politics during the period of spectacular business growth, and since that time business generally has been associated with the Republican party. Public-opinion surveys have shown that a majority of those in the upper-income groups have consistently voted the Republican ticket. Many business executives, independent entrepreneurs, and members of certain professional groups—including physicians, dentists, attorneys, engineers, and others—have durable psychological attachments to the Republican party. Although there are numerous wealthy individuals in the Democratic party as well as many intellectuals, the party finds that most of its support is in the ranks of the middle and lower classes, labor, and minority groups.

There is considerable evidence that the political parties have been in a state of flux or "partisan fluidity" during the 1960s and 1970s. The Republicans have obtained additional voters from the ranks of labor and from the South, while the Democrats have gained support from persons in the expanding middle class of professional and managerial workers. Moreover, as will be explained, the percentage of independents among the electorate has increased substantially during the past decade.

PARTY ORGANIZATION

Political parties in the United States have two general types of formal organization, each of which is directly related to a major function of political parties—winning elections and conducting the government. The term *party organization,* as commonly used, refers to the party machinery for nominating and electing candidates for public office, and will be described in this chapter. The other kind of party organization, the "party in the government," which is concerned with running the government, will be discussed in the chapter on the Congress. Political parties in the United States may be considered as three interacting elements—these two types of party organizations and the party voters, the "party in the electorate."

National party organization

The national convention. At the national level, political parties are organized primarily for the purpose of electing the President and Vice-President and members of Congress. The national convention, composed of delegates from the 50 states and the territories, convenes quadrennially to nominate candidates for the Presidency and Vice-Presidency and to adopt a platform. The convention has no other major functions. Unlike the conventions of European parties, the national conventions in the United States exercise no control over candidates for legislative offices.

Responding to criticisms of their 1968 convention, the Democrats changed the rules for selection of delegates in 1972 to provide for the selection of more delegates among racial minorities, women, and the younger voters. As a result, fewer of the delegates in 1972 were established party leaders and representatives of organized labor. Another change adopted by the Democrats provided for conventions, popularly referred to as "miniconventions," to be held halfway between presidential elections, to be devoted primarily to discussing party rules and current political issues. At the first midterm convention in 1974 the Democrats abandoned the much criticized quota system of the 1972 convention, while at the same time affirming the necessity of more delegates from hitherto underrepresented groups.

The national committee. During the four-year interval between meetings of the national convention, the national committee and the national chairman, in theory, direct and guide the party. The national committees of both parties formerly consisted of one man and one woman from each state and territory. In 1964 the Republicans added as an *ex officio* member the state chairman of the party in the states carried by the Republicans in the preceding election, and in 1972 the Democrats enlarged their national committee by granting additional members to the more populous states. In most states the committee members are selected by the delegates to the national convention, but in some states they are chosen by state conventions or committees or in direct primaries.

The national committee does not direct the party affairs in the sense that similar party committees do in Great Britain, Germany, and other countries. The reason for this lies in the decentralized character of American parties. Instead of being considered as a governing body, the national committee should be viewed as a gathering of representatives from autonomous or semiautonomous organizations. One of the powers of the national committee is to fill vacancies on the national ticket should the candidate for President or Vice-President die or resign between the time of the national convention and the election. In 1972 the Democratic National Committee, upon the request of the party's presidential nominee, George McGovern, formally selected R. Sargent Shriver as the Democratic vice-presidential nominee, after the unprecedented withdrawal of Senator Thomas Eagleton, who had been chosen previously by the Democratic National Convention as the vice-presidential nominee.

The national chairman. According to custom, the national chairman is appointed by the presidential nominee chosen by the convention and then is formally elected by the national committee.[3] Usually his initial task is to direct the presidential campaign. If his party's nominee is elected President, the national chairman will probably continue in that capacity, but only as long as the President desires his services. Although he holds the highest position in his party, he remains the agent of the President. Concerned with strengthening the party throughout the nation, he delivers addresses, keeps in touch with state and local party organizations, and assists in various fund-raising activities. He shares with the House and Senate campaign committees the responsibility of assisting in the off-year congressional campaigns. Prior to President Lyndon Johnson's administration, the national chairman normally had considerable influence. However, both Johnson and Nixon downgraded the position of the national chairman and the national committee. As will be explained in the next chapter, Nixon set up a separate committee for his reelection, with the top positions held by a former Cabinet member and White House aides.

Campaign committees. Each party has separate Senate and House campaign committees to assist candidates seeking election to Congress. These committees, responsible to the legislators and not to the national committee or chairman, illustrate the influence of the separation of powers. In brief, realizing that the national committee and chairman are primarily concerned with the election of the President, the national legislators have formed their own committees, which are in no respect subordinate to the national chairman or the national committee.

State and local party organizations

Unlike the national party organization, which is not established or regulated by Congress, the state party organizations have been prescribed by each of the state legislatures, which often have set forth in considerable detail how the parties are to be organized and what functions they are to perform. Although all states provide for similar party organizations, the detailed party structures vary widely from state to state. Specifically, all

---

[3]In 1972 the Democratic presidential nominee, George McGovern, selected as national chairperson Jean Westwood, the first woman to hold that position in either the Democratic or Republican party. Two years later President Ford selected Mary Louise Smith to head the Republican National Committee.

states provide for two levels of organizations—state and county or local. Commonly, the most important organization units are the state central committee and the county central committees. In addition, there is usually a state convention, as well as district committees created to assist candidates whose constituencies are not statewide but cover more than one county. Often there are also city, ward, and precinct organizations. (See Figure 10–3.)

State party organization. State statutes typically give the state central committees the responsibility for directing and coordinating party activities throughout the state, assisting in statewide campaigns, supervising fund-raising activities, and calling the state conventions. The extent to which the state central committees actually carry out such activities differs considerably among the states. During the decades following World War II there has been a gradual decline in the influence of state and local party organizations, in particular in eastern and midwestern states that formerly had strong party organizations.

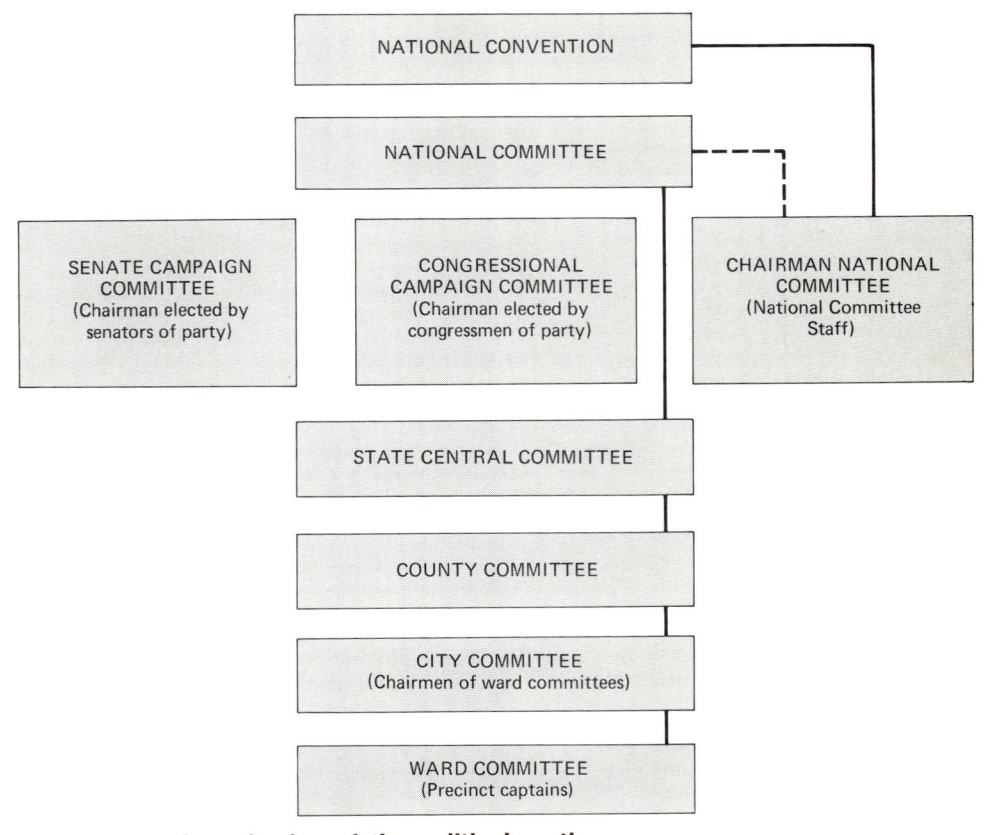

Figure 10–3 *Organization of the political parties*

Methods of selecting committee members vary from state to state and include indirect election by county or congressional district committees, appointment by officeholders and nominees, and election in direct primaries. State committees range in size from only a few in some states to more than 900 in California. The larger committees commonly select an executive committee, which, in conjunction with the chairman, will perform most of the committee's duties.

Local party organization. The county central committee is usually the basic organizational unit below the state level. County committees have such responsibilities as coordinating the work of other local party units, helping organize campaigns, securing candidates for local offices, raising funds, and making recommendations on patronage appointments. County committee members in some states are elected in party primaries, but more commonly they are party leaders of county subdivisions—usually precincts or townships.

Some urban communities often have party committees for each city ward. The ward leaders together may form a city committee that will conduct and coordinate citywide party activities. The individual ward committeemen may supervise the work of the precinct committeemen or captains. The precincts usually range in size from 100 to 600 voters. The precinct committeeman is the party's representative in his district and has the responsibility to see that the voters are registered and go to the polls on election day. In many cities, the parties have active precinct captains only during campaigns, if at all. But in the more highly organized cities, one or both parties still attempt to have a captain or committeeman active in most precincts throughout the year.

Although a chart outlining the structure of a party would indicate that it is organized in a hierarchical pattern similar to a business corporation or a military unit, there is little similarity in the way that they actually function. In a political party, there is no top authority comparable to a corporation president or an army general. Whatever power the parties possess tends to be at the state and local levels rather than at the top of the party structure. Moreover, each level of party organization is primarily concerned with its own problems and usually functions independently of the other levels. One scholar has used the term *stratarchy* to describe this distribution of power within the typical state party organization. He has explained, "Although authority to speak for the organization may remain in the hands of the top elite nucleus, there is great autonomy at the lower 'strata' or echelons of the hierarchy, and . . . control from the top is minimal and formal."[4]

---

[4]Samuel J. Eldersveld, *Political Parties: A Behavioral Analysis,* Chicago: Rand McNally, 1964, pp. 99–100.

CHANGING ATTITUDES TOWARD POLITICAL PARTIES

During the past few years an increasing number of Americans have developed feelings of cynicism and alienation toward political parties and public officials. This attitude has been manifested in various ways. Whereas earlier studies indicated that a person's party identification was the most reliable predictor of his vote, in a 1974 study in Wisconsin two-thirds of the voters agreed that "it would be better if in all elections we put no party labels on the ballot," and five out of six voters thought that the parties "had done no good" for people like themselves.[5] As noted previously, the decline in the proportion of the electorate who have voted can be traced largely to apathy and alienation. Moreover, in 1958 over 88 percent of the people believed they could "trust the government" to do what was right all or most of the time; but by 1972 that figure had declined to 55 percent. With the revelation of the involvement of Richard Nixon and his top assistants in the Watergate scandals, trust in other elected officials and institutions of government plummeted to record lows.[6]

Increase in independents, ticket-splitting, and switch-voting

The declining influence of the political parties may be illustrated by the increase in the number of people who consider themselves to be independents and the decrease in partisan identifiers. According to Gallup Poll surveys, the proportion of the electorate who classified themselves as independents rose from 23 percent in 1960 to 33 percent in 1975. At that time the independents outnumbered the Republicans by 10 percent, and the remaining 44 percent classified themselves as Democrats. Undoubtedly, part of the Republican loss may be traced to Watergate.[7] Another indication of the decline of party loyalty was the election in 1974 of James B. Langley as governor of Maine, the first independent elected to a governor's office in nearly half a century.

Survey research findings indicate that in the past two decades there has been a change in the kinds of people who identify themselves as independents. Public-opinion polls prior to 1960 led to the conclusion that in-

---

[5]Jack Dennis, "Trends in Public Support for the American Political Party System" (mimeographed). Paper presented at the 1974 annual meeting of the American Political Science Association.

[6]Arthur H. Miller, "Political Issues and Trust in Government: 1964–1970," *American Political Science Review*, 68 (September, 1974), pp. 951–972; and William Watts and Lloyd A. Free, *State of the Nation 1974*, Washington, D.C.: Potomac Associates, 1974, pp. 70–74.

[7]*New York Times*, July 18, 1974. A poll conducted in January, 1975, for the Republican National Committee found that only 18 percent identified themselves as Republicans, 42 percent said they were Democrats, and 40 percent considered themselves independents. *Los Angeles Times*, January 26, 1975.

"I'm not cynical about politicians. I believe everything the Democrats say about the Republicans, and everything the Republicans say about the Democrats!"
Santa Barbara News–Press, March 11, 1975.

dependents generally were less attentive, informed, and interested than partisan identifiers.[8] The "new" independents of the 1960s and 1970s are a different breed. They tend to be similar to partisan identifiers in most respects except that they are more likely to be younger, and to have higher than average education, income, and occupational status. For example, a Gallup poll in 1974 showed that among persons under 30 years of age who were college graduates and whose occupations were classified as business or professional, there were more independents than either Democrats or Republicans.[9] Other research indicates that these new independents often have psychological attachments with one of the major parties, and some consistently vote for candidates of that party; but for several reasons, including political events and personalities of the past two decades, they do not wish to identify with either party.

Ticket-splitting. Other evidence of the reduced role of political parties is the increased proportion of ticket-splitters—those individuals who in a single election vote for candidates of both parties. This trend may be illustrated by the number of congressional districts won by presidential and congressional nominees of different parties. The number of such districts rose from about 20 percent in 1948 to approximately 45 percent in 1972.[10]

---

[8]Angus Campbell et al., The American Voter, New York: Wiley, 1960, p. 143.
[9]New York Times, July 18, 1974.
[10]Walter De Vries and W. Lance Tarrance, The Ticket-Splitter: A New Force in American Politics, Grand Rapids, Mich.: W. E. Eerdmans, 1972, p. 185.

In 11 of the 25 states electing both a governor and a senator in 1974, a majority of the electorate split their tickets to place in office members of different parties for the two offices.

Switch-voting. The willingness of sizable numbers of Americans to switch-vote in presidential elections also reflects a decline in party loyalty. In any presidential election, the voters might be considered to be composed of three groups: the standpatters, the new voters, and the switchers. The standpatters are those who vote for the same party as in the previous election. The new voters are the ones who did not vote in the previous election because they were too young or for some other reason. The switchers are those persons who vote for a different party than in the preceding election. While the standpatters are most numerous, research indicates that there are more switchers than previously thought. For example, one survey of over 1,100 college professors voting in the four consecutive elections of 1956 through 1968 showed that approximately one-third switch-voted one or more times in that series of four elections. Research on switchers indicates that they are not dissimilar in interest, involvement, or education to the standpatters. Self-identified independents are more likely to switch-vote than partisan identifiers, but most of the switch-voters consider themselves affiliated with one of the parties, but have voted for the opposite party in order to support a particular candidate.

A better informed and activist electorate

Simultaneously with the increase in independents, ticket-splitting, and switch-voting, more people than previously have contributed funds and volunteered time in support of candidates whose stands on issues correspond with their own. Such presidential candidates as Barry Goldwater, Eugene McCarthy, George Wallace, and George McGovern, as well as numerous persons seeking lesser offices, have been assisted by financial contributions and volunteer labor from thousands of persons, many of modest means, who previously had not been active in politics. Thus while many Americans have become apathetic and alienated from partisan politics, others have become more ideological and activist, and have taken the more positive approach of actively supporting candidates and issues that they favored.

FUNCTIONS OF AMERICAN PARTIES

Providing personnel for government

The primary function of political parties is to provide personnel for government. In the United States and in other democratic countries, this function is accomplished principally by the recruitment, nomination, and election of public officials. This electoral function is the one activity that distinguishes American parties most effectively from other organizations. Only political parties have as their basic purpose mobilizing voters in support of candidates for public office.

In addition to presenting a choice of candidates for public office, political parties in a democracy provide a peaceful means for succession to office, a major concern in any political regime. Often, in authoritarian regimes, the only method for removing public officials is through the use of force. American parties concentrate more on the electoral function and place less emphasis on other activities than do parties in most other countries.

Organizing and conducting the government

A second purpose of political parties is to organize and conduct the government. If one party controls the presidency and Congress, it organizes both branches and attempts to secure the enactment and execution of its program. The party thus serves to bridge the gap between the two branches created by the separation of powers. Because of the nature of American politics, members of the President's party in Congress will not necessarily support him on every issue, but the common desire to establish a record that will attract votes in future elections provides an incentive for cooperation between the President and Congress. Even if the opposition party controls the legislature, responsibility for administering the government is still centered in the Chief Executive and the party he represents. When one party controls the presidency and the other Congress, the party system may, of course, create obstacles to the smooth operation of the government.

Serving as a countercheck to the party in power

Third, the opposition party serves a useful function in American politics. In a two-party system, the opposition party, by checking on and criticizing the party in power, helps to ensure that the government will be responsible. In the United States, the concept of the "loyal opposition" has not been institutionalized to the extent that it has in Great Britain; nonetheless, it is considered the role of the defeated party to scrutinize and point out defects in governmental policies and present alternative proposals. Although the criticism is often not entirely constructive and at times appears to be intended merely to harass the party in power, the opposition role of checking and criticizing is an important party function and helps to prevent the adoption of unwise policies and to lessen inefficiency and malfeasance in government.

Representing group interest

A fourth function of the parties in America is the important representative one. Political parties and legislative bodies together serve as the two principal representative agencies of popular power. The parties thus serve as the linkage between the people and the public officials. In the process of developing and promoting party programs, political parties perform the function of articulating and aggregating the interests and demands of many interest groups, which often find they must obtain party support in order to achieve their goals. From the myriad interests asserted by groups, political parties reject some issues and select others that they articulate, explain, debate, and promote. The parties thus serve as "political brokers," modifying and compromising the proposals of various groups as they develop party programs.

Educating and informing the electorate

A fifth function of political parties is to participate in the process of educating and informing the electorate regarding political issues. It is true that parties in the United States place less emphasis on their educational role than do their European counterparts. This is because the United States has no "ideological parties" based on well-defined general philosophies. Even in Britain there are Labour party organizations of physicians, lawyers, students, and others. Although such party organizations do not exist in the United States, American parties do help to educate and inform the voters in a variety of ways. In articulating group interests, parties are, of course, helping to inform the people, but the educational function encompasses more than merely explaining and advocating specific policies. Through public addresses, campaign communications, legislative debates, news conferences, and press releases, political leaders inform the citizenry on a variety of issues of concern to the majority of the population.

The educational role of parties also includes participating in the political socialization of the electorate. As was explained in Chapter 9, "political socialization" is the term used to describe the process by which citizens acquire the attitudes, values, and information that influence their political decisions and actions. Political parties share with the family, other groups, and the media of communications in the socialization of the populace. Research on attitude formation reveals that for many dedicated partisans the party to which they belong serves as an important reference group and is one of the most influential determinants of attitudes on political issues and candidates. By accepting the position of party spokesmen, these individuals are able to simplify and clarify the confusing array of domestic and foreign problems that confront them. Thus, depending on a person's point of reference—his party—a proposed policy may be "right" or "wrong" and a particular official a public-spirited statesman or a venal politician.

Socialization of conflict

A sixth function of political parties in democratic political systems is to socialize conflict. To socialize conflict means to transfer it from a private context to a public context. To the extent that parties operate within an open society, they frequently magnify conflicts, particularly if political capital can be made out of such intensification and exaggeration. A mink coat given to the wife of a presidential aide, improprieties of a labor-union leader, cries for "law and order"—no conflict is so small that political parties will not pick it up and turn it into a national issue. The more a society and its political system are responsive to complaints and conflicts, the more will political parties exploit such conflicts for their benefit and their opponents' detriment.

In both the United States and Great Britain, where two major parties dominate the field, many individuals and groups with segmented and specific conflicts are associated for practical and specific reasons. Instead of possessing one fundamental base of conflict—such as religion—which colors and dominates all others and which makes compromise difficult, pragmatic parties are coalitions of a variety of interests and conflicts. It is a general principle of conflict resolution that *"multiplicity of conflicts stands in inverse relation to their intensity."*[11] Since in a pluralistic society individuals participate in a multiplicity of association, opponents on one issue may be allies on another; this overlapping of group memberships and group conflicts has the effect of mitigating specific conflicts.

Political parties provide the individual not only with an important source of personal identification and loyalty, but also with a legitimate outlet for hostility. Extreme partisans may express this hostility in extreme ways, such as denigrating adherents of the opposite political persuasion—particularly during election campaigns, when deep feeling is more likely to weaken discretion. But even the ordinary man who identifies with a political party expresses some criticism and hostility, if not toward individual followers of the opposing party, at least toward that party and what it stands for, as he perceives it. The edge of such hostility is generally blunted by the fact that the political partisan expresses his hostile feelings toward the party as an impersonal abstraction, while still observing the ordinary proprieties of behavior toward individual members of the opposing party. Finally, even when one's preferred party is defeated in an election or on a

---

[11] Lewis A. Coser, *The Functions of Social Conflict*, New York: Free Press Paperbacks, 1964, p. 153 (italics added).

specific issue, party identification allows the individual to become involved in a conflict without having to suffer personal defeat; that is, parties allow the depersonalization of conflict.

Unifying the nation

Finally, the major political parties in the United States have helped to integrate the country. Because they usually adopt moderate, middle-of-the-road policies, the parties unify rather than divide the people. Today, regardless of where one lives, the majority of Americans consider themselves to be Republicans or Democrats. Common membership in the two parties throughout the 50 states has assisted in drawing together the most heterogeneous population of any country of the world.

An activity of parties in an earlier age which aided in this unification process was their assistance in the "Americanization" of immigrants. This function was not performed by parties in any other country. Aside from the school, the party was perhaps the most important influence in the Americanization of the 45 million immigrants who have come to the United States since 1820.

CHARACTERISTICS OF THE AMERICAN PARTY SYSTEM

Political party systems are generally classified according to the number of parties competing effectively for control of the government: one-party, two-party, and multiparty systems. In some countries only a single party is allowed; in other countries there are no constitutional restrictions on the number of parties, but one party has been able to exercise dominant control over the government, and the lesser parties wield little influence. If two parties customarily have a chance to win control of the government, the country is commonly considered to have a two-party system, although one or more minor parties may also nominate candidates. If more than two parties share governmental power, the country is considered to have a multiparty system.

A two-party system

The most apparent and basic characteristic of the American party system is that it is a two-party system. Although more than two parties have nominated candidates in virtually every national election, with rare exceptions the real contest for control of the national government has been between two major parties. Other features of American parties result from the basic fact that the United States has a two-party system.

American parties are multigroup organizations

Because the electorate in the United States is a heterogeneous mixture of many social, economic, ethnic, and religious groups spread through 50 states, any party that obtains a majority of the vote must of necessity be composed of different groups. In an effort to achieve a majority coalition, both parties make some appeal to every major segment of the population—business, labor, farmers, the professions, and others. A party program is thus determined both by the desire to attract new voters and by the need to retain the support of groups within the party. As a result, party programs tend to be compromises negotiated by party leaders between the often conflicting policies advocated by different groups.

American parties are pragmatic, nonideological organizations

The British statesman Edmund Burke once defined a political party as "a body of men united for promoting . . . the national interest upon some particular principle in which they are all agreed." Major parties in the United States do not conform to this definition. Because of their histories, traditions, leaders, and membership, each of the two parties takes fairly consistent stands on certain issues. But within each party, disagreement may be found on virtually any question. Neither of the two parties is fully united on any principle, and both are largely uninterested in doctrine or ideology. As each party is composed of groups with varying opinions, party programs are often expressed in broad, general terms. Such programs are usually adopted in order to win votes and to maintain coalitions, and both parties attempt to avoid issues that will repel voters and divide their party.

Many individuals (including some political scientists) have criticized American parties for not providing the voters with clear choices on public policies. They argue that the parties should draft party platforms that contain specific policies which differ from the policies of the opposition. According to this view, parties should be programmatic organizations, and party members should be united in support of a general philosophy of government. They argue that, once a party espouses a policy, all elected officials should be obligated to support it. Although many European parties conform to this pattern, American parties have not done so and undoubtedly will not in the foreseeable future.

American parties are decentralized

Because of the federal form of government, political parties in the United States are decentralized. The national parties, in addition to being coalitions of a variety of socioeconomic groups, are confederations, or alliances, of state and local party organizations. As the state and local party organizations are largely autonomous units, the national leaders seldom have sanctions that may be employed to discipline them. Although the two-party system is firmly entrenched in national politics, it is not in all states. If the party systems in the states were plotted on a political spectrum, they would range from two nearly equal parties through modified one-party systems to a few states with virtually one-party systems. In only half of the states do the two parties compete on fairly even terms.

A comparison with the British system is instructive. Great Britain has a unitary form of government, and British parties are highly centralized. Once a British party adopts a policy, all party members in Parliament may be required to vote for that policy. In Great Britain, the national party leaders may determine who may "stand" for Parliament in an electoral district. In the United States, anyone with the necessary legal requirements may "run" for Congress, regardless of his philosophy of government or the wishes of the national party leaders. A candidate once elected may consistently oppose the policies of his party and still be returned to office as long as a majority of his constituents vote for him. Moreover, a Democratic congressman from California and one from Mississippi may regularly take opposing positions on important partisan issues, and the same may apply to Republican senators from New York and Arizona.

Why the two-party system in the United States?

Of the approximately 20 governments that might be classified as "Western democracies," no more than six have two-party systems.[12] Because most countries do not operate under a two-party system, the question naturally arises: Why does the United States, with the most diverse population of any country in the world, have a two-party system?

Of the factors contributing to the two-party system, undoubtedly the most significant is the method used to elect members of Congress and the President. Members of Congress are elected under the single-member, simple plurality system: The one candidate in each geographic district with the largest number of votes is elected. This "winner take all" system works to the disadvantage of all except the two leading parties.[13] A third party cannot anticipate victory unless it either joins a major party or draws support from one. Faced with these prospects, most third-party adherents, or groups that might otherwise form minor parties, join a major party. If a system of

---

[12] Leon Epstein, *Political Parties in Western Democracies*, New York: Praeger, 1967, p. 59.

[13] This point may be illustrated by noting that in Great Britain, where a similar single-member electoral system is used, in the 1974 election the Liberal party polled 18 percent of the popular vote, but elected only 13 (approximately 2 percent) of the 635 members of the House of Commons.

proportional representation with multiple-member districts were used, each party would gain seats in the legislature proportionate to the number of popular votes it received.

The separate election of the President, which in effect takes place in a "single-member district" consisting of the 50 states, also helps to create and to maintain the two-party system. Under the prevailing arrangement, one nominee customarily receives the entire electoral vote of a state, and the candidate who receives the highest number of electoral votes becomes President. Political leaders and party organizations in the various states know that in order to participate in this, the ultimate victory, they must join one of the two leading parties. If the United States had a parliamentary form of government, it is possible that there would be two parties in each state, but not the same two parties throughout the nation, as is the case in Canada. In a few instances, third parties—such as the Farmer-Labor party of Minnesota and the Progressive party of Wisconsin—have elected governors, other state officers, and national legislators, but they subsequently merged with a major party or disappeared.

Other factors—historical, legal, and psychological—have been influential in the establishment or maintenance of the biparty system. The United States inherited many political institutions and practices from the British, and the early American leaders, although reluctant to form political parties, were influenced by the British bipartisan practices.[14] Once the two-party system was firmly entrenched, legal provisions and practices militated against third parties. Congress is organized along bipartisan lines; hence members of minor parties cannot expect to be appointed to important committees or to become committee chairmen. Statutes provide for bipartisan appointments to a variety of committees, commissions, and boards. Legal impediments in a number of states make it difficult for persons wishing to organize a new party to obtain a place on the ballot. The loyalty of voters to the party of their choice strengthens the present two-party alignment. Many people accept the party affiliation as well as the religion of their parents, and are only slightly less inclined to change their religion than their partisan allegiance.

In explaining the reasons for the two-party system in the United States, it has been suggested that certain problems dividing other countries into three or more parties have been avoided, and that most troublesome American problems have been of a bimodal character. Regarding the first point,

---

[14]It has been suggested that the British aristocrats who originated the two-party system were influenced by their interest in sports or games that were played by two competing individuals or teams. The early ideal of political behavior in English party politics was "fair play," such as is found in a game played by gentlemen. Even today, only in English-speaking countries does one hear references to the "rules of the game" in talking about politics.

it is correct that the United States—with its comparative lack of class consciousness and the separation of church and state—has avoided some problems that have encouraged the development of a multiplicity of parties in other countries.

The inherent dualism of American political issues is another matter. Those who assert this position call attention to such dichotomous issues as the early question of the "strict" versus the "loose" interpretation of the Constitution, the issue of property rights versus the rights of people, the division of the nation along sectional lines, and the separation of the citizenry into conservative and liberal camps. In brief, it has been argued that these issues have divided the American electorate naturally into two parties, whereas the political questions confronting the French or Italian voters have been responsible for their multiparty systems. One may ask, however, whether the dualism of political issues has been a *cause* or a *result* of the party system. One characteristic of the biparty system is that it forces individuals to compromise their demands and unite with others in order to share political power. Hence, if the United States had a multiparty system, political issues might appear in a different form.

Minor parties

The monopolization of the electoral process by the Republicans and Democrats during the past century tends to obscure the fact that in virtually every national election a number of minor or third parties nominate candidates. The variety of these parties makes it difficult to classify them. For instance, some parties have limited their activity to one state, some to one geographic area, and others have sought votes throughout the nation. Most minor parties have short histories, but a few have existed for several decades. Some minor parties promote a single issue or doctrine, but others have broader, more practical programs.

Although no means of classifying these myriad parties is entirely satisfactory, an examination reveals that minor parties with long histories have characteristics different from those of transient third parties. Minor parties that have existed for several decades tend to be doctrinal or ideologically oriented, whereas short-lived third parties often are protest movements of voters who have disassociated themselves from the major parties.

Long-range doctrinal parties. The long-range doctrinal parties do not exist to elect candidates, but to propagate a particular ideology or to advocate a specific cause. Examples of such parties are the Prohibition, the Socialist, and the Socialist-Labor parties, each of which originated prior to the turn of the century. These parties, not expecting or hoping to win elections, are essentially different from the major parties. In a sense, they operate outside the two-party system, because they have little or no influence on the outcome of elections or on the programs of the major parties. Although they call themselves parties and often nominate candidates, they consider the ballot primarily as an inexpensive means of propagandizing their program. From the standpoint of their basic purpose, these organizations might correctly be considered pressure groups and not parties.

Splinter or secessionist parties. Of the transient parties, two general types may be identified. First there have been several splinter or secessionist parties, each consisting of a specific segment of a major party that has temporarily broken away from the older organization. Examples of splinter parties include the Progressive party of 1912, which was formed when Theodore Roosevelt failed to receive the Republican presidential nomination, and the States' Rights or Dixiecrat movement of 1948, which consisted of disaffected southern Democrats who broke away because of disagreement over the party's stand on civil rights. In 1912, Roosevelt, the candidate of the Progressives, actually polled more votes than the Republican nominee, but the party dissolved after the election. In the 1948 election the Dixiecrats carried several southern states, but realizing that they could not hope to elect a President and that as Dixiecrats their members in Congress would lose their committee chairmanships, most of them rejoined the Democratic party shortly after the election.

Independent short-term parties. In addition to the splinter parties, there have been a number of short-term parties that developed because of dissatisfaction with the programs of the major parties. Until recent years, most of these parties have been of a reformist nature, advocating social and economic reforms that were ignored by the major parties. Of these, the most successful was the Populist party, which in 1892 polled over a million votes for its presidential nominee and elected several members of Congress. Four years later, the Democrats adopted most of the planks of the Populist platforms, with the result that the Populists lost most of their appeal. In recent years, several small conservative parties have appeared that have favored such policies as repealing the income tax and the withdrawal of the United States from the United Nations. These groups, taking such names as the Constitution party and the National States' Rights party, usually appear on the ballots of very few states—often only one or two—and receive minuscule electoral support.

In 1968 George Wallace, then former governor of Alabama, formed the American Independent party, which became the first third party to gain a place on the ballots of all 50 states; this party received a larger proportion (over 13 percent) of the popular vote than any third party since Robert La Follette's Progressive party in 1924. In 1972 George Wallace entered several Democratic presidential primaries, but his candidacy was ended when he was shot while campaigning in the Maryland primary. With Wallace out of the race, the American Independent party, renamed the American party, nominated for the presidency John G. Schmitz, a former congressman from California and a member of the John Birch Society. Eight other minor parties nominated candidates and obtained places on the ballots of some states. Schmitz polled slightly more than one million votes. Dr. Benjamin Spock, baby-care author and antiwar activist, as the nominee of the People's party obtained approximately 75,000, and all other candidates received only limited support.

The two-party versus the multiparty system

A comparison of the two-party system with the multiparty system provides an additional perspective for viewing American political parties. Multiparty systems exist in a number of countries, including most western European countries, India, Israel, and Japan. Because of the differences between the party systems in the various multiparty states, it is difficult not to overgeneralize. For instance, the Scandinavian countries, where a Labor party generally predominates, have usually only four or five parties seriously competing for votes, whereas in Italy and France as many as 10 or 12 parties have contested elections. As Giovanni Sartori has noted, "It is wrong to deal with multipartism as a single category."[15]

The principal argument offered in favor of the multiparty system is that it reflects more accurately differing political viewpoints. In some countries, the several parties represent virtually every shade of the political spectrum, ranging from the extreme left to the extreme right. In France, for example, in the past the voters have been able to choose between candidates advocating communism, socialism, a moderate democratic system, extreme authoritarianism, or even the reestablishment of a monarchical regime. We have observed that various viewpoints are represented in each major party in the United States, but such a variety of choice obviously is not available to the electorate. Proponents of multiparty systems argue that in the United States not only are the voters limited to candidates of two parties, but also these choices are relatively meaningless because both parties have similar programs.

Advocates of the two-party system assert that a comparison should be made on the basis of how the government actually operates under each type of party system and not on the theoretical grounds of the variety of choice offered the voters. In the two-party system, majorities in the legislature are produced automatically by elections. When the votes are counted, one party has won and has received a mandate for organizing and conducting the government. The other party stands in opposition and has the responsibility for criticizing those in power and offering an alternative program. More-

---

[15]Giovanni Sartori, "European Political Parties: The Case of Polarized Pluralism," in Joseph LaPalombara and Myron Weiner (eds.), *Political Parties and Political Development*, Princeton, N.J.: Princeton University Press, 1966, p. 137.

over, the victorious party will be in power until the next regularly scheduled election, which means that it is assured time to implement its program. If the voters become dissatisfied, they may at the next election vote into office the opposition party. Thus, while the voters have a limited choice from the standpoint of who is to represent them, they have an "either-or" choice from the standpoint of selecting the party that will have responsibility for conducting the government.

By comparison, governments in multiparty systems are composed of combinations or coalitions of parties, so there is seldom a clear division between the government and the opposition. Moreover, there is no alternative party to whom the voters may turn if they become displeased with those in power. If one coalition is replaced by another, the new governing combination may contain some of the parties in the previous government. However, proponents of multiparty competition assert that such coalition governments provide a desired continuity not found where the party in power may be replaced by the opposition party.

Multiparty states differ considerably from the standpoint of continuity and stability of their governments. Some multiparty countries—such as the Netherlands, Switzerland, the Scandinavian countries—have had stable and effective multiparty governments for many decades. In the Netherlands, which has five or more active parties, only five cabinets over an 80-year period have lost power prior to the general election, and the average life of a cabinet has been four years. In other countries—such as France under the Third and Fourth Republics and Italy—electoral support has been so fragmented and unstable that the governments have found it difficult to handle critical social or economic problems without being voted out of office. In France from 1951 to 1956, under the Fourth Republic, cabinets lasted an average of only seven months, and in Italy between 1947 and 1975 there were 34 cabinets.

No objective appraisal of the comparative merits of a two-party system versus a multiparty system is possible. First, the systems are not the products of deliberate choice but rather a reflection of different historical contexts and political experiences. Second, each of the two systems has a major advantage which cannot be compared or measured in quantitative terms. The great appeal of the multiparty system is its faithful reflection of all shades of political opinion in a nation. To some, this is the essence of democracy. The great appeal of the two-party system is the opportunity it provides for effective government.

ONE-PARTY GOVERNMENTS: COMPATIBLE WITH DEMOCRACY?

Americans have a tendency to equate one-party systems with totalitarian regimes, although in fact the one-party systems found in various nation-states may be grouped into several categories. The question of whether one-party states are compatible with democratic government must be answered separately for each category.

First, there are the Communist and fascist totalitarian states, in which all parties are prohibited except the single official state party. Obviously, these party systems are not compatible with democratic government.

The second category includes those one-party states in Asia and Africa —such as Burma, Egypt, and Zaire—which are not totalitarian, but which allow only one political party. In such cases, the official party is not ideological, as are Communist or fascist parties, but is generally tailor-made for the needs of the current ruler. Such single-party states tend to be authoritarian rather than totalitarian, and therefore less extreme than Communist or fascist systems with respect to either aims or methods. For instance, the typical penalty for the political dissenter in such a regime is imprisonment or exile rather than death. Given educational and economic advances, such one-party systems may develop in the direction of multiparty or two-party states.

Mexico exemplifies a different situation. Numerous parties freely exist, from Communists to near-fascists. All parties are permitted freedom of expression, the press, assembly, and association, but only the official government party, the *Partido Revolucionario Institucional,* is allowed to win national elections. In congressional elections, the government party decides how many seats are to be allocated to opposition parties, and in presidential elections its candidate is always elected.

The most important point in appraising one-party, or nearly one-party, states is the direction in which the country is moving. There is no doubt, for example, that Mexico has steadily moved toward a more mature democracy in the last 30 years under the guidance of a dominant party that is committed to democracy.

11
The Electoral Process

11

A persistent problem of governments is the establishment of orderly, legitimizing procedures for the transfer of authority. In most ancient governmental systems, rulers customarily inherited their positions. Even today in countries such as Saudi Arabia and Iran, virtually unlimited political powers are exercised by monarchs who presumably will be succeeded by royal princes. In other countries, for example Syria and Argentina, a military junta often exercises political power until forcibly removed by another junta. In modern democracies, the question of who shall succeed to political authority and through what process has been answered by political parties and the electoral process.

THE ELECTORATE

Obviously, an important factor affecting the outcome of elections is who may vote. Universal suffrage is today so commonplace among Western democracies that one often forgets that it is a recent phenomenon. In Great Britain, where modern democratic government first developed, no more than two-thirds of the adult males had the vote at the turn of this century. Women were not given the suffrage in the United States until 1920, in Britain until 1928, in France and Italy until 1946, in Switzerland in 1971; and in some countries women are still disfranchised.

In the United States, owing largely to the inability of the Founding Fathers to agree on specific requirements, the Constitution left to the states the establishment of voting qualifications. When George Washington was elected President, probably not more than one man out of 15 could vote. The first struggle over the expansion of the electorate occurred during the early part of the nineteenth century when the states one by one removed the taxpaying and property-owning requirements for voting, and universal white manhood suffrage was achieved. The second effort to extend voting rights followed the Civil War with the adoption of the Fifteenth Amendment, which was intended to grant the vote to male Negroes. The third extension of the right to vote came at the close of World War I with the adoption of the Nineteenth Amendment, which established women's suffrage. The fourth major move toward a full realization of universal suffrage occurred in the post–World War II period when federal legislation was adopted aimed at guaranteeing to blacks the right to register and vote in all states. The most recent enlargement of the electorate occurred in 1971 with the adoption of the Twenty-Sixth Amendment, which reduced the voting age to 18.

Voting requirements. In every state a voter, in addition to being 18 years old, must be a citizen of the United States and meet residential requirements. Congress has established 30 days as the maximum residency requirement for voting in a presidential election, and in 1972 the Supreme Court in effect ruled that 50 days was the maximum period of residency which may be required for voting in state and local elections. Formerly, residential requirements for voting in state and local elections ranged from two years in Mississippi to three months in New York, New Jersey, and Pennsylvania, and approximately two-fifths of the states had some form of literacy test for voting. Most states specifically disqualify from voting those who are classified as mentally incompetent and those who have been convicted of a felony.

In the United States, registration is generally a prerequisite for voting. In some places, such as North Dakota and in rural areas of several states, registration is not required, but elsewhere prospective voters must register personally in advance in order to vote. Registration is required so that the election officials in each precinct will have a list of the qualified voters. In most European countries, the local government officials compile the register of voters; hence, each voter's name appears on the list without any effort on his part, and no one is disqualified by failing to register.

Two types of registration systems—periodic and permanent—are employed by the various states. In 14 states, a voter must register periodically, usually every two or four years. The other states employ permanent registration. In these states, once a person is registered he need not reregister unless he moves, changes his name, wishes to change his party affiliation (in states with closed primaries), or has failed to vote. A study of registration and voting in American cities confirmed what many had long assumed: Differences in voter turnout are related to "rates of registration, and these in turn reflect to a considerable degree local differences in the rules governing, and arrangements for handling, the registering of voters."[1]

NOMINATIONS

One of the basic purposes of political parties is to nominate candidates for public office. The method by which this is done varies considerably from one political system to another. In the United States, the nominating pro-

[1] Stanley Kelley, Jr., Richard E. Ayers, and William G. Bowen, "Registration and Voting: Putting First Things First," *American Political Science Review*, 61 (1967), pp. 373–374.

cess differs in two respects from that of most other countries. First, the rank-and-file American voters may participate more directly in the nomination of candidates than voters elsewhere. In authoritarian regimes, the leaders of the government party make the nominations by preparing a list of candidates, who will be unopposed in the election. In most democracies other than the United States, candidates are commonly selected by a caucus or committee of dues-paying members in accordance with rules drawn up and enforced by the party. In no country other than the United States do persons who are not party dues-payers or otherwise enrolled as party members participate directly in nominating candidates. Second, there are more legal regulations governing the nominating process in the United States than in other countries, where nominations are subject to few if any governmental regulations. In the United States, however, almost every phase of the nominating process, with the exception of the national nominating convention, is regulated by legislation to provide for maximum participation by voters. These two features of the American party system help to explain why our parties are different from political parties in other countries.

In each electoral district in the United States, the local party members have complete control over the choice of candidates. Although a President may encourage an individual to run for office, neither he nor any other national party official can actually designate the party's candidate. In Great Britain, by comparison, both Conservative and Labour party executives have authority to approve candidates for public office. Although the power is not often used, the British national party organizations may veto any local choice for nomination and deny the unauthorized candidate the use of the party name. Moreover, as there are no local residence requirements for holding office in Great Britain, the national party organization may have a person nominated (with the approval of the local party) in a "safe" district even though he lives elsewhere.

During early American history, nominations were usually made in caucuses of party leaders. By the 1830s, the convention system began to replace the party caucuses and soon became the most widely used method for making nominations. During the second half of the nineteenth century, conventions fell into disrepute owing to the commonly held belief that they were controlled by party bosses and pressure groups. In an effort to make the nominating process more democratic, reformers began advocating the direct primary, which would permit the voters to make the final decision regarding the party nominees. Wisconsin, in 1903, became the first state to adopt a mandatory direct–primary law.

Although all states have now adopted the direct primary, the caucus and the convention still have limited use in the making of nominations. In some New England and midwestern states, caucuses open to all party members are held in certain areas for making nominations for local offices, and a few states hold conventions for nominating candidates for important, statewide positions. The great majority of candidates today, however, are nominated in direct primaries.

The direct primary

From the standpoint of procedure, the direct primary resembles the general election. In both cases, the state prepares the ballots, provides for them to be counted, and certifies the results. From the standpoint of purpose, the direct primary and the general election are different: Direct primaries are held *to nominate candidates;* general elections are held *to elect public officials.*

Two types of primaries are used—the closed and the open. Approximately 40 states have closed primaries, which means that only those voters who have registered with a party or who make known their party identification at the polling place may participate in the selection of that party's nominees. In states using open primaries, a voter need not declare his party affiliation, but may participate in the nomination of candidates of either party. The state of Washington has a variation of the open primary called the "blanket type," in which a voter is permitted to split his ticket and vote for candidates of both parties in the primary, just as a voter may do in any state in a general election.

In many electoral districts, winning the nomination of the majority party virtually assures victory in the general election. This is the case generally in several southern states, in other states in regions in which one party predominates, and in some electoral districts that have been gerrymandered so that the nominee of the larger party in the district will consistently be elected. In 1974, for example, three senators and 60 candidates for the House of Representatives had no major party or significant minor party opposition in the general election. Because winning the nomination is tantamount to being elected in so many electoral districts, the nominating process assumes greater importance than it would if two-party competition existed in elections throughout the nation.

Some southern states, recognizing that winning the Democratic nomination virtually assures victory in the general election, have provided that if no candidate receives a majority of the vote in the first primary election, a runoff primary will be held between the two candidates who received the most votes in the first primary.

Nonpartisan primaries are used to nominate state legislators in Minnesota and Nebraska and are employed in several states for the nomination of judicial and local officials. In nonpartisan primaries, no party labels appear on the ballots, and the individuals receiving the highest and second highest number of votes become the candidates. Frequently, if one candidate receives a majority he is declared elected.

Recruitment and nomination of candidates

While nominating candidates is a basic function of political parties, in the United States the activity is not monopolized by the parties. Many candidates are self-recruited; they secure a place on the ballot by circulating their own petitions, and they conduct their own campaigns without support from party organizations. Also, political-interest groups sometimes recruit candidates and assist in their nomination campaigns. Undoubtedly, however, most candidates for public office are recruited, assisted, or at least encouraged by party officials.

Although the direct primary was adopted to further democratize the nominating process, the extent to which the voters participate in the actual designation of candidates varies considerably from one electoral district to another. In some constituencies, the primaries are usually hotly contested, and the party members may choose between two or more prospective nominees for most offices. At the other extreme are localities in which the party leaders still prepare a slate that will seldom be opposed in the primary. Incumbents seeking reelection often have no opposition in the party primary, or if they are opposed, they win the nomination anyway. For instance, in 1974, of 391 congressmen seeking renomination by their parties, only eight were unsuccessful. This is a striking illustration of the advantage of being an incumbent.

NOMINATING AND ELECTING THE PRESIDENT

The national nominating convention is a peculiarly American institution. The chief executive of no other major power is nominated by a comparable procedure. In most modern democracies, the person who becomes the nation's chief executive must first be selected the leader of his party, a position usually achieved only after years of legislative and party experience. Then, if his party gains a majority in the legislature, he becomes the chief executive.

In the United States, a person generally becomes the acknowledged leader of his party only after being nominated for the presidency. The national convention makes it possible for an individual to follow a variety of routes for advancement to this, the highest elective office. In most cases, presidential nominees have had experience either in Congress or as state governors. On occasion, persons with no political background or experience have been nominated for the presidency, as happened in the nominations of Wendell Willkie in 1940 and General Eisenhower in 1952.

The national convention

The national convention illustrates how political institutions in a free society evolve to meet the needs and temperament of the people. The Constitution provided for the President and Vice-President to be chosen by the electors, who would be selected in a manner to be determined by the individual state legislatures. However, the entire process of nominating and electing the President and Vice-President was soon assumed by the parties, and the Electoral College has not functioned as anticipated by the Founding Fathers. Through custom and practice, the parties have amended the Constitution and have changed the process by which the President is elected. In 1832 the Democrats became the first major party to hold a national convention, and since that time, presidential candidates of major parties have been nominated by national conventions.

Selecting the delegates. The only governmental regulation of the national conventions are the state laws that prescribe how the delegates are to be chosen. The parties themselves establish the rules for allocating delegates among the states and for all other matters relating to the convention. The state legislatures have provided for delegates to be selected by presidential primaries or state and local conventions. Although the states may decide how the delegates are to be chosen, the Supreme Court ruled in 1975 (*Cousins* v. *Wigoda*) that each national political party has the right to determine the eligibility of its convention delegates.

Presidential primaries. Wisconsin, in 1903, was the first state to adopt a presidential primary. Currently more than half of the states and the District of Columbia hold presidential primaries, and about two-thirds of the convention delegates are selected in these primaries.

Various criticisms have been voiced regarding the presidential preferential primaries. As presidential hopefuls commonly enter only those primaries they believe they can win, in only a few states are the voters able to indicate a choice among the leading contenders in either party. For instance, in 1968, Nixon formally entered six primaries, all of which he won, but he had no opposition in one state and only token opposition in others. In 1972, George McGovern contested 17 primaries, 10 of which he won.

Among other criticisms of the preferential primaries are the following: Voter participation in some states may be very low; primaries are expensive and give an advantage to individuals with large sources of funds; they physically exhaust prospective candidates; they may be decided on local and not on national issues; and a defeat in an early primary may eliminate a potential presidential nominee.

On the positive side it should be noted that presidential primaries provide the opportunity for individuals such as Dwight Eisenhower in 1952, John Kennedy in 1960, and George McGovern in 1972 to prove their popularity with the voters. Eisenhower, Kennedy, and McGovern, who were not the choice of the party leaders, might not have been nominated had it not been for the primaries. It can also be argued that the primaries provide an opportunity to test the two qualities most needed in a presidential candidate —the ability to appeal successfully to the great bulk of American voters, and the ability to gain the support of group leaders, who themselves wield considerable political power. In the words of George Romney, a presidential contender in 1968, "The primary process is expensive and grueling, but nevertheless, it helps to eliminate those who aren't thoroughly qualified and indicates those who are."

Allocation of delegates. Both parties have followed the general rule of allocating delegates to the national convention according to the representation each state has in Congress. Republicans and Democrats use different formulas, and minor rule changes through the years have allowed differing numbers of delegates. In the 1976 Democratic presidential convention there were 3,008 voting delegates, and in the Republican conventions of 1956–1976, the number of delegates ranged from 1,308 to 2,259.

Convention procedure. The conventions of the two major parties follow remarkably similar procedures, considering that they have developed independently and are not regulated by legal provisions. Both parties have made some changes because of television. For instance, nominating speeches have been shortened, and the principal addresses and other events are scheduled so that they can be viewed by the maximum television audience. Convention coverage by the networks provides the political parties with several days of free television time, which would cost millions of dollars to purchase.

Next to the nomination of the President and Vice-President, the most important function of the convention is the drafting of the party platform. Occasionally a dispute will erupt on the floor of the convention over some provision, but commonly platforms are adopted with little opposition. Although the platforms often look similar, a careful reading will reveal important differences. Party platforms serve the purpose of uniting the party as well as helping to elect the President, so they must necessarily avoid some issues and be vague and ambiguous on others.

Presidential nominations generally may be classified in three categories. First, if a President is seeking a second term, he is generally nominated by acclamation. Second, in conventions at which a President is not seeking renomination, the strongest candidate is often nominated on the first ballot because he has obtained sufficient delegate support prior to the convention. In the last half century, two-thirds or more of the nominees of both parties have been nominated on the first ballot. Third, in the remaining cases, two or more ballots have been required for a nomination.

The greater tendency to nominate candidates on the first ballot in recent years is due in part to the combined influence of television, public-opinion surveys, and the presidential primaries. Television converts presidential contenders into public personalities whose vote-getting appeal may be measured in opinion surveys and the primary contests.

Vice-presidential nominations. By tradition, the presidential nominee is permitted to choose his running mate. Vice-presidential candidates are usually selected primarily "to balance the ticket," from the standpoint of both factions within the party and geography. More recently, owing to the death in office of Presidents Roosevelt and Kennedy and the illnesses of other Presidents, the qualification for the presidency in the selection of vice-presidential candidates has been given greater attention. Yet in 1968 Nixon chose Spiro Agnew as his running mate primarily to win southern support, and in 1972 McGovern chose Sargent Shriver largely because of his Catholic religion and his close connection with the Kennedy family.

Presidential campaigns and elections

Presidential campaigns are the most elaborate, spectacular, and expensive feature of American politics, and they differ sharply from election campaigns anywhere else. In no other country do so many people expend so much effort over such a vast expanse of territory and over so long a time soliciting the votes of such a large electorate. In most Western democracies, the chief executive is a member of the legislature. Like all other national legislators, he is elected by the voters of one constituency rather than by the entire electorate of the country. In countries where a president is elected by the general electorate, as in France, campaigns are much shorter, the distances to be traveled are less, the electorate is smaller, and the communications media play a much smaller role than in the United States. As the first presidential primary in the United States is held in March, American presidential candidates must usually plan for an active campaign of at least nine months, and various presidential aspirants have campaigned for a year or more prior to the first presidential primary. Four of the contenders for the 1976 Democratic nomination had established their formal campaign committees and announced their candidacies for the presidency by February, 1975, nearly two years before the election. By comparison, Italian campaigns are restricted by law to six weeks, and British campaigns are customarily limited to three weeks, as are French presidential campaigns.

Winning the nomination. One of the popular myths regarding the American presidency is that the office customarily seeks the man; in reality few presidents have been elected who have not actively sought the office. Most presidential candidates must conduct two campaigns—the first to obtain the nomination and the second to win the election. Each of the campaigns requires careful and detailed planning, a personal campaign organization, and ample funds. Often presidential aspirants lay the groundwork for their presidential campaigns several years prior to actually seeking the nomination and election.

One of the first steps in the campaign for the nomination is the "build-up," through which the aspirant hopes to gain sufficient national prominence and stature to be considered "presidential timber." If the aspirant is a United States senator or a governor of a populous state, the publicity ordinarily received in such an office helps him gain national prominence. In addition, prospective candidates solicit invitations to appear on television programs and to address national conventions of powerful interest groups as well as political rallies or fund-raising dinners. Many prospective candidates travel abroad, hoping to gain a reputation for being well informed regarding foreign affairs. By noting the individuals engaging in activities of these types in the year or two prior to the conventions, one can compile a fairly accurate list of those persons who hope to be nominated as presidential candidates.

Campaign strategy. Presidential campaigns are seldom conducted with the view to appealing equally to all voters. Instead, the electorate is usually considered as comprised of groups of voters, and greater efforts are made to influence some groups than others. Customarily, much of the campaign output is directed toward specific geographic and group targets. The aim of each candidate is to win the election in enough states to receive 270 or more electoral votes. As the candidate who carries a state receives its entire electoral vote, candidates concentrate their efforts on the large doubtful states and spend relatively little time in the less populous states and those considered "safe" for one or the other nominee. Presidential candidates usually spend at least half of their time campaigning in the seven largest states—California, Illinois, Michigan, New York, Ohio, Pennsylvania, and Texas.

In addition to geographic targets, campaigns are usually waged with the view of attracting the votes of specific socioeconomic groups. Programs are developed that appeal to voters as businessmen, laborers, farmers, physicians, and members of ethnic minorities. In employing group appeals, candidates run the risk of alienating some groups by appealing for the support of others.

Among the target groups are the members of the candidate's party. Research on voting behavior has verified what practical politicians have long believed: Individual voting decisions are generally based on the voters' perceptions of three factors—the parties, the issues, and the candidates. Campaigns are usually designed to win votes on the basis of each of these variables. From the standpoint of party affiliation, voters are viewed as strong partisans, weak partisans, independents, and members of the opposite party, and each group is considered as a specific target. Issues are formulated with a view toward activating strong partisans, to strengthening the party ties of weak partisans, and to converting independents and members of the opposite party.

Campaign organizations. A bewildering number of organizations participate in presidential campaigns. In most elections these organizations may be grouped into four categories. First, there are the official party organizations, which are active between campaigns and whose staffs are greatly expanded in the months prior to the election. Second, often a candidate for the presidency or other major office establishes a personal organization that will work directly with him. Many times these organizations are formed to help the candidate win the nomination and will then be integrated with the national committee staff. Third, various *ad hoc* groups are established, and subsidiary party organizations are activated. Each party creates temporary organizations, such as Independents for Nixon–Agnew and Citizens for McGovern–Shriver, to attract the active support of individuals who might not want to work with the regular party organizations. Uniquely American are the organizations of registered voters of one party for the candidate of the opposite party—such as "Democrats for Nixon" and "Republicans for McGovern." Fourth, special-interest groups have political action committees that participate in election campaigns. Well-known examples of such groups include the AFL–CIO Committee on Political Education and the American Medical Association Political Action Committee.

In most presidential campaigns, the candidate, after winning the nomination, selects a new national committee chairman whose principal responsibility is to conduct the general election campaign. In seeking reelection, Nixon established in 1971 an organization called the Committee to Reelect the President (commonly called by the acronym CREEP) and gave it primary responsibility for running his campaign. Thus the Republican national chairman and national committee were relegated to minor roles in the election. CREEP was originally organized by Attorney General John N. Mitchell and H. R. Haldeman, Nixon's chief of staff at the White House. In February, 1971, Mitchell resigned as Attorney General to devote full time as head of CREEP. Several members of the White House staff were subsequently transferred to CREEP, including G. Gordon Liddy, who planned the break-in of the Democratic National Committee headquarters at the Watergate complex. Shortly after this break-in, Mitchell resigned and was succeeded by Clark MacGregor, a former White House staff member. Nixon also created a separate fund-raising committee, the Finance Committee to Reelect the President, and appointed as its head Maurice H. Stans, who until then had been his Secretary of Commerce.

Professional campaign management and opinion surveys. With the increased use of television and the decline in the old-style political machine, there has developed a new type of firm dedicated to political public relations and campaign management. For a handsome fee, such firms will take the responsibility for virtually every aspect of a campaign. They will plan the general strategy, raise funds, recruit campaign workers, write speeches, prepare campaign literature, handle press conferences, make arrangements for the candidate's public appearances, and prepare advertising copy and film used in the press and on television. Many candidates for major office do not engage a professional campaign management firm, but may employ a variety of persons or firms with specialized knowledge—including a pollster, an advertising agency, a film-maker, a speech writer, a direct-mail organization, and possibly an accounting firm. Another example of the new professionalism in campaigns is the extensive use of public-opinion surveys. Most candidates for major offices carefully analyze the opinion polls appearing in the press and employ private polling organizations to conduct more specialized surveys. The results are often used in planning campaign strategy, in deciding what questions to discuss, and in determining how to handle specific problems.

Electoral college. Although the people vote for the President on the first Tuesday after the first Monday in November, the formal election of the President does not occur until over a month later, when the presidential electors, who were originally selected by their respective state political party organizations, meet in their states and go through the formality of casting their ballots for the President and Vice-President. Virtually every aspect of the Electoral College system has long been criticized. The "winner-take-all" system, by which the entire electoral vote of a state customarily goes to the candidate receiving a plurality of the state's popular vote, permits a candidate who was outpolled by his opponent to be elected President. Three times—in 1824, 1876, and 1888—the person elected President received fewer popular votes than another candidate. If the candidates of neither party receive a majority of the electoral votes, the President is elected by the House of Representatives (with each state casting one collective vote regardless of size) and the Vice-President is elected by the Senate. This system makes possible the election of candidates with fewer electoral (as well as popular) votes than an opponent, and the election of a President from one party and a Vice-President from the opposite party. Moreover, as the electors in less than one-third of the states are legally obligated to vote for the candidate of their party, a few electors have cast their ballots for other persons. For instance, in 1968, a Republican elector in North Carolina voted for George Wallace instead of Richard Nixon, the popular winner in that state.

Four proposals have long been discussed for changing the method for electing the President; three would abolish the office of elector but would retain the electoral votes. Under one plan, a state's electoral vote would automatically be awarded to the candidate who polled a plurality of the popular votes. A second proposal, the "proportional system," would allocate the electoral vote in every state according to each candidate's percentage of the popular vote. Under a third proposal, the "district plan," each candidate would receive an electoral vote for each congressional district he carried; in addition, two electoral votes in each state would go to the candidate winning a plurality of the state's popular votes. With any of these proposals, the possibility remains that the person elected President could have fewer popular votes than another candidate.

The most widely favored proposal would abolish the Electoral College altogether and elect the President by a direct, nationwide popular vote. This has been endorsed by the American Bar Association, and according to public-opinion surveys it has had the support of approximately eight out of 10 Americans. Under the plan suggested by the American Bar Association, if no candidate received at least 40 percent of the popular vote, there would be a runoff election between the two leading candidates.

Presidential elections classified. After the parades, the rallies, the informal speeches to small crowds, the television addresses to millions of viewers —after the campaigns have ended and the electorate has voted, what do the results mean? Presidential elections have often been interpreted as great collective decisions, and various systems have been devised for classifying the individual elections. The following classification based on the partisan affiliations of the electorate suggested by Professor Angus Campbell and his associates is possibly the most useful:[2]

1. *Maintaining elections.* In maintaining elections, the prevailing pattern of partisan identification has continued, and the party holding office has been returned to power. During the past century, most elections have been of this type, Recent examples include the elections of 1936, 1940, 1948, and 1964.
2. *Deviating elections.* In deviating elections, due to some event, set of circumstances, or candidate, the second largest party replaces the party which, during that era, has the support of the majority of the voters. These elections deviate from the normal pattern in that the basic division of partisan support remains unchanged, but the majority party is defeated. Examples are 1912 and 1916, when Wilson won during the period of Republican hegemony, and 1952, 1956, 1968, and 1972, when Eisenhower and Nixon were victorious even though the majority of the electorate retained its affiliation with the Democratic party.

[2]Angus Campbell, Philip E. Converse, Warren E. Miller, and Donald E. Stokes, The American Voter, New York: Wiley, 1960, pp. 531-538.

3. *Reinstating elections.* In reinstating elections, the dominant party is returned to office after being out of power. The elections of 1920 and 1960 are examples.
4. *Realigning elections.* In realigning elections are included those rare instances when a significant number of voters make a lasting change in their partisan identification. Since the formation of the present two parties, this type of election has occurred only twice—in 1860 and in 1932—and both were associated with major crises—the Civil War and the Great Depression.

CONGRESSIONAL CAMPAIGNS AND ELECTIONS

Every two years, campaigns are waged for all of the 435 seats in the House of Representatives and for one-third of the seats in the Senate. Many of these campaigns are miniatures of presidential campaigns. The candidate establishes a personal campaign organization, coordinates his efforts with those of other candidates and organizations, solicits support from influential interest groups, prepares campaign literature, purchases radio and television time and space in the press, and addresses organized groups and political rallies. Some candidates—in particular, those seeking to represent heavily populated states in the Senate—employ private polling organizations and public-relations personnel to assist them in their campaigns.

For a number of senatorial aspirants and more than half of the candidates for the House of Representatives, the direct primary is the crucial test. Those candidates residing in a "safe" district or state are virtually assured election once they have their party's nomination. For example, in 1970 and 1972, of the congressional incumbents seeking reelection, 96 percent were successful.[3] Moreover, after holding office for a term or two, their renomination becomes less difficult; in an election year, seldom are more than eight to 12 representatives defeated for renomination, and only rarely does a senator fail in his efforts to be renominated.

Most congressional candidates seeking nomination through the direct primaries tend to base their campaigns largely on their personal qualifications and to discuss few political issues. Unlike their counterparts in Great Britain, Scandinavia, and other democracies, those wishing to be nominated to the national legislature in the United States are not required to receive the endorsement of the national party organization or to support the party program. Any individual with the legal qualifications may enter a direct

---

[3]In 1974, largely owing to Watergate disclosures, the largest number of new lawmakers since 1948 was elected to Congress. In the 94th Congress, convening in January, 1975, there were 92 new members of the House of Representatives, of whom 75 were Democrats, and 11 freshman senators, of whom eight were Democrats.

primary, and if he wins, he becomes the candidate of the party. After winning the nomination, if he has sufficient popular support, he may be elected even though opposed by the leadership of the party.

The general election campaigns of candidates seeking seats in Congress in presidential election years tend to differ from those of off-year elections. In presidential election years, if the party's candidate for chief executive is likely to win, most congressional candidates gear their campaigns to his and attempt to ride into office on his "coattails." However, if the presidential candidate is unpopular, some congressional candidates ignore the national ticket, and others publicly disassociate themselves from it, as several Republicans did in 1964 and several Democrats did in 1972. In midterm congressional elections, a different situation prevails; without the influence of the presidential election, candidates tend to conduct individual campaigns often based on local issues or personalities. In recent presidential elections, only in 1956, when President Eisenhower was elected to a second term, and in 1968 and 1972 has the President's party failed to gain control of Congress.

POLITICAL FINANCE

Although more information is available regarding campaign contributions and expenditures in recent elections than for any previous period, political finance remains the "dark continent" of American politics. The numerous electoral contests, the many official and unofficial organizations involved in political campaigns, and the inadequacy of financial reports filed by candidates and political organizations render the task of compiling an accurate tabulation of political spending extremely difficult.

What campaigns cost

The costs of election campaigns are constantly mounting, owing principally to the growth of the electorate, the rise in the general price structure, and the increase in the use of television in campaigns. According to the most reliable estimates, campaign expenditures for candidates at all levels of government during presidential election years increased from $140 million in 1952 to $200 million in 1964, $300 million in 1968, and $400 million in 1972.[4]

Campaign costs for high political offices have also risen enormously.

---

[4]In addition, candidates and campaign organizations are given hours of volunteer labor and the use of automobiles, airplanes, office space, and other items of value without charge. Alexander Heard, *The Costs of Democracy,* Chapel Hill: University of North Carolina Press, 1960, pp. 7–8; Herbert E. Alexander, *Financing the 1968 Election,* Lexington, Mass.: Heath, 1971; and Robert A. Diamond (ed.), *Dollar Politics,* Washington, D.C.: Congressional Quarterly, 1974, vol. 2.

POLITICAL FINANCE **265**

"He's sworn to refuse any contribution over one hundred dollars, but nobody's offered him that much yet."
The New Yorker, October 14, 1974, p. 41.

Candidates for mayor of New York City and Los Angeles have spent more than $3 million on an election. In gubernatorial campaigns, Nelson Rockefeller in New York reported spending $5 million, and Ronald Reagan in California $3.8 million. The cost of senatorial campaigns has ranged from only a few thousand dollars in thinly populated states to as much as $5 million. The cost of election to a contested seat in the House of Representatives typically has been from $50,000 to $75,000, and in some elections candidates have spent as much as $200,000. As will be explained, ceilings were set by Congress for future elections to Congress and the presidency. Starting in 1976, the amount a senatorial candidate can spend depends on the size of the state. The maximum will range from $120,000 in Alaska to approximately $1.3 million in California.[5] Considerably more was spent

---

[5]*Congressional Quarterly Weekly Report*, 32 (October 12, 1974), p. 2867.

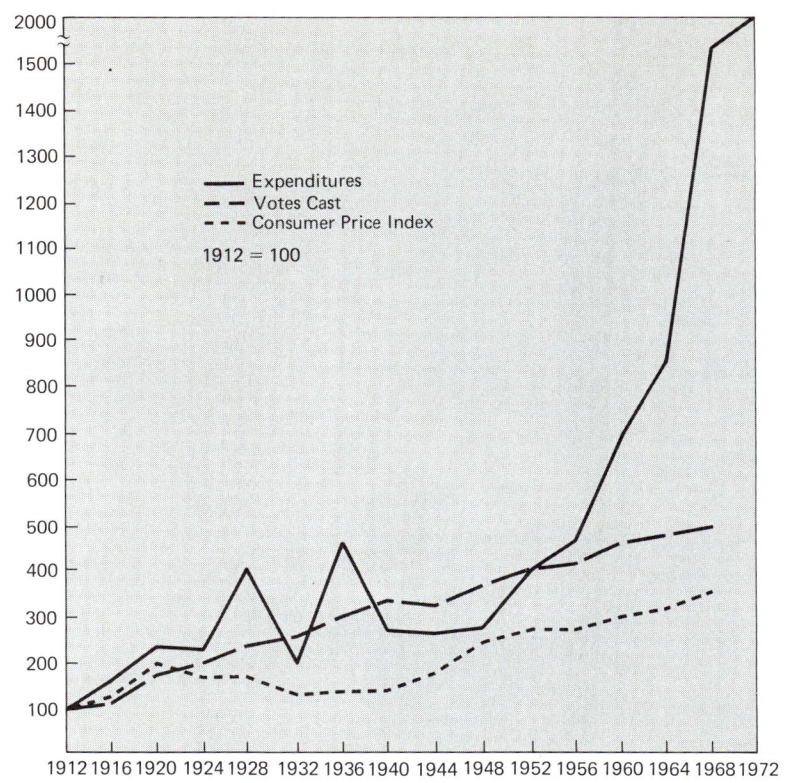

Figure 11-1 *Campaign spending (indexes of direct campaign expenditure by national-level committees, number of votes cast, and consumer prices)*
SOURCE: Robert A. Diamond, Dollar Politics, Washington, D.C. Congressional Quarterly, Inc., 1972, p. 3.

electing the President in 1968 and 1972 than in any previous election. The prenomination expenditures, the costs of the national conventions, and the amounts spent by other groups in the presidential races totaled about $100 million in 1968 and were approximately one-third higher in 1972. (See Figure 11-1.)

Regulation of campaign finance

1972 presidential campaign finance. For more than three decades political observers advocated a general overhauling of legislation regulating political finance. Finally Congress enacted the Federal Elections Campaign Act in 1971. The major provisions of the act limited the amount that could be spent in a campaign by the candidate and his family, placed ceilings on expenditures for media advertising in campaigns, and changed the provisions regarding the disclosure of campaign contributions and expenditures.

This latter provision, requiring reports to be filed with the General Accounting Office instead of, as formerly, with the Clerk of the House of Representatives and the Secretary of the Senate, proved to be of particular significance from the standpoint of illuminating the area of political finance.

Under the previous legislation, the Corrupt Practices Act of 1925, some candidates had failed to file reports and those filed often were incomplete; but owing primarily to the lack of an enforcing agency, during the half century the provisions were in effect no candidate for Congress was prosecuted under the law. Congress specified that the new law should take effect on April 7, 1972, and that the disclosure provisions of the previous legislation should expire on March 10, 1972. Thus there appeared to be a one-month hiatus during which contributions would not have to be reported.

The financial reports filed under the 1971 law enabled investigating committees and scholars to gain a more accurate picture than previously of presidential campaign finance. Because of the date that the law became effective, fund-raising for the Nixon-McGovern contest was divided into two periods: prior to April 7, 1972, and afterward. McGovern reported raising $1.2 million in the months prior to that date. In his report for that period McGovern listed the names of 42,040 contributors, of whom 86 persons gave $1,000 or more and no one over $25,000. Nixon's fund-raisers told donors that if they would contribute between March 10 and April 7, they would remain anonymous, and the fund-raisers refused to release the donors' names or the amount collected until they were required to do so by a court order on a suit filed by Common Cause. Reports of Nixon's fund-raising of March 10–April 7, 1972, showed a collection of $19.9 million, with more than 100 persons contributing over $40,000 each. Of these, 14 gave $250,000 or more; one person, insurance company executive W. Clement Stone, gave $2 million; and Richard Mellon Scaife, an heir to the Mellon family oil and banking fortune, gave nearly $1 million. Reports filed of campaign contributions and expenditures during the second period—April 7 through December 31, 1972—showed the two presidential candidates collecting and spending similar amounts. The Nixon–Agnew campaign reported receiving $43 million and spending $49 million; and the McGovern-Shriver campaign collected $48 million and spent $45 million. These reports and others obtained by the General Accounting Office indicate that the total Nixon campaign raised more than $62 million and the total McGovern campaign approximately $50 million.[6] When the amounts other candidates spent seeking the Democratic nomination are added to these sums, the total exceeds by as much as one-third that of any other presidential campaign.

Campaign finance abuses. In addition to providing more information on election finance in 1972 than in any previous election, the new disclosure

---

[6]Diamond, *op. cit.*, p. 64.

requirements and the Watergate investigations brought to light several illegal or highly questionable practices. Undoubtedly both parties had been guilty of some of these abuses in prior elections, but not to the extent that they were employed in the 1972 Nixon campaign. The following are noteworthy examples:

First, large sums were collected in cash in an apparent effort to conceal the source of the funds, and often how the money was spent. Numerous accounts of cash donations were reported. Billionaire Howard R. Hughes contributed $100,000 in cash to Nixon's close friend Charles "Bebe" Rebozo, who apparently never delivered it to the campaign committee. In another instance, an official of an oil firm told of delivering $100,000 in cash to Maurice H. Stans, chairman of the Finance Committee to Reelect the President, who "dumped it in the desk drawer and said 'thank you.' "[7] According to reports, Stans had as much as $250,000 in cash at times. Another $1 million in cash passed through the hands of Hugh Sloan, the committee treasurer; H. R. Haldeman at times had as much as $350,000 in cash, and Herbert W. Kalmbach, Nixon's personal attorney, $250,000.[8]

Second, although donations by corporations to federal campaigns had been illegal since 1907, Nixon fund-raisers obtained sizable amounts from corporations for his 1972 campaign. By the end of 1974 legal charges had been brought against 14 corporations, 13 of which pleaded guilty for contributing to the Nixon campaign. These corporations together contributed approximately $775,000 to Nixon, most of it in cash. Some of the corporations also made donations to Democratic candidates. For instance, a vice-president of Gulf Oil pleaded guilty to making an illegal contribution of $100,000 to Nixon, $10,000 to Senator Henry M. Jackson, and $15,000 to Representative Wilbur D. Mills, both of the latter declared Democratic presidential candidates. The Gulf Oil executive explained his reaction to the solicitation for a donation from Attorney General John N. Mitchell and Commerce Secretary Maurice H. Stans: "I considered it considerable pressure when two cabinet officers . . . were asking me for funds—that is, just a little bit different than somebody collecting for the Boy Scouts."[9]

Third, much of the cash collected was through "laundered" funds; that is, money which was transmitted through third parties in order to conceal its source. For example, Minnesota Mining and Manufacturing Company (3M), which used corporate funds for contributions to the presidential cam-

---

[7] Ibid., p. 11.

[8] Theodore H. White, *The Making of the President, 1972,* New York: Atheneum, 1973, p. 279.

[9] Diamond, *op. cit.* Gulf Oil was later charged by the Securities and Exchange Commission with making approximately $5.4 million in illegal campaign contributions from 1960 through 1974 from a secret fund maintained in the Bahamas. *Los Angeles Times,* March 12, 1975.

paigns of Nixon, Democratic Senator Hubert Humphrey, and Democratic Congressman Wilbur Mills, arranged for a Swiss consultant to submit false billings to the company. After the consultant was paid, he returned the money in cash to 3M officials, who gave the money to agents of the candidates.

Fourth, some contributions were made with the implied, if not explicit, understanding that the donors would receive something specific in return, either appointment to an office or favorable treatment regarding a particular issue or problem. The charge was made that the Nixon administration was brokering ambassadorships, and according to the Senate committee investigating Watergate, contributions of $1.8 million were made by persons holding or seeking ambassadorships. For instance, Mrs. Ruth L. Farkas, wife of the owner of a department-store chain, was appointed ambassador to Luxembourg after she and her husband contributed $300,000 to Nixon's campaign; of that amount, $200,000 was given after the election. Herbert W. Kalmbach, a leading fund-raiser, pleaded guilty to a charge of promising an ambassadorship in return for a $100,000 contribution; and a condition of the guilty plea was that he be granted immunity from prosecution regarding other "contributions from persons seeking ambassadorial posts."

Various examples can be cited of persons making contributions who wanted favorable treatment in specific cases. Critics have questioned whether such contributions should not be classified as bribes. A contribution of $200,000 in cash by Robert L. Vesco, who was at the time under investigation for stock fraud, led to the indictment but not conviction of two former Cabinet officers, Mitchell and Stans, for obtaining the contributions with the understanding that they would intercede in behalf of Vesco. Contributions totaling at least $2 million were promised by milk cooperatives following a decision by Nixon to increase milk price support subsidies. A third highly publicized example was the pledge by the International Telephone and Telegraph Corporation (ITT) of $400,000 toward financing the Republican National Convention at a time when ITT was involved in an antitrust suit, which was later settled in favor of ITT.

Fifth, some funds collected for Nixon's campaign were used for illegal or questionable purposes. The break-ins of the Democratic National Committee Headquarters at the Watergate complex in Washington, D.C., and of the Los Angeles office of the psychiatrist of Daniel Ellsberg, who had given the Pentagon Papers to the press, were financed by money donated for Nixon's election campaign. G. Gordon Liddy received $199,000 in cash before the break-ins, and afterward Watergate defendants received an amount estimated to exceed $400,000.[10] In addition to paying the burglars, campaign funds were used for their legal fees and for the legal fees of others involved in Nixon's campaign. The General Accounting Office reported that by June,

[10] Ibid., p. 10.

1974, more than $1.4 million was paid from campaign funds for legal fees of nearly 30 persons formerly involved in Nixon's campaign. These included Maurice Stans, John Mitchell, and Nixon's brother, Edward Nixon.[11]

Another example of illegal or questionable use of campaign contributions was the creation of a "dirty tricks department" to cause dissension among the various Democratic presidential aspirants, to conduct political espionage, and in other ways to disrupt Democratic primary campaigns. Donald R. Segretti, who headed a group employed for this purpose, and two of his associates were later sentenced to prison terms for their activities. A variety of "dirty tricks" were used, including paying individuals to infiltrate the committees of Democratic candidates for the purpose of disrupting their campaigns,[12] advocating highly unpopular causes in letters that appeared to be on an opposition candidate's stationery and over his name, and distributing other misleading literature purported to have originated with a Democratic presidential candidate.

The federal campaign election act of 1974

Watergate served as an impetus for the enactment of the 1974 Federal Campaign Election Act, which provided long-needed major changes regarding the financing of political campaigns. Public reaction to the campaign finance illegalities brought to light by Watergate virtually forced Congress to correct financing abuses, some of which had been prevalent in both Republican and Democratic contests. Because the 1974 legislation was so comprehensive, a survey of the regulations affecting federal elections involves primarily the provisions of this statute.

Limitations on contributions and expenditures. Formerly any person could contribute up to $5,000 to any one political candidate or committee, and there was no limit on the total amount a person could contribute to various candidates and committees. Because the federal gift tax applied to contributions of over $3,000, some people, in order to avoid the tax, made numerous contributions of that amount to several committees of candidates. A noteworthy example occurred in 1972 when Richard Mellon Scaife, in giving $990,000 to Nixon's campaign, wrote 330 separate $3,000 checks, each to a different committee.

Under the present law, persons other than family members may not give more than $1,000 to any candidate for a primary, general, or runoff election; and a person's total political contributions may not exceed $25,000 during a year. Political committees and other organizations may not con-

---

[11] *International Herald Tribune,* June 12, 1974.
[12] White, *op. cit.,* p. 276.

tribute more than $5,000 to an individual candidate for any election; however, there is no limit on the aggregate amount committees or organizations may contribute to candidates or political party committees. Cash contributions over $100 and foreign contributions are prohibited.[13] The 1974 law also retains the provision of the 1971 act which established $50,000 as the maximum amount a candidate or his family may contribute to his own campaign if he is running for the presidency or vice-presidency; $35,000 if he is seeking election to the United States Senate; and $25,000 if he is a candidate for the House of Representatives.

The following limits are established on campaign expenditures: $2 million for the presidential nominating convention; $10 million for any candidate seeking his party's nomination in presidential primaries; $20 million for each presidential candidate in the general election; $100,000 for senatorial candidates in primaries or eight cents per eligible voter, whichever is higher; $150,000 for senatorial nominees in the general election or 12 cents per voter, whichever is greater; and $70,000 for candidates for the House of Representatives for the primary and $70,000 for the general election. Every candidate for the above offices may spend for fund-raising 20 percent in addition to the allowed amounts; hence the actual limit on candidates for the House of Representatives in a primary or a general election is $84,000 if the full 20 percent is used for soliciting funds.[14]

Publicity of income and expenditures. The principle of public disclosure of the sources of funds is well established. Since 1910 the national government has required candidates for Congress and political committees under federal jurisdiction to file financial statements at given intervals. This principle was reasserted in the Campaign Election Act of 1974. Of particular importance in the new statute is the provision that each candidate must establish *one campaign committee through which all donations and expenditures must be reported,* and specific banks are to be designated as depositories of funds. Each candidate thus becomes personally responsible for funds collected and spent in his campaign. All candidates for federal offices and committees supporting them must file reports of all contributions and expenditures over $100 with the Federal Election Commission. The underlying assumption of this legislation is that by publicizing the names of the donors and the pur-

---

[13] The 1974 act also provides that no elected or appointed official shall receive more than $1,000 for any speech or article, and shall not receive a total of more than $15,000 in any year for speeches or articles. This provision was adopted to prevent an organization from making excessive political contributions under the guise of payment for speeches or articles.

[14] The 1974 statute removed the ceilings set in 1971 on campaign spending in the mass media.

poses for which funds are spent, the candidates will be more circumspect regarding the solicitation and use of funds, and the voters will be able to make more intelligent decisions regarding candidates. The 1974 election campaign reforms finally adopted two key principles that had successfully worked in Britain for nearly a century: first, an effective limitation on the amount of money that can be spent by a candidate in his campaign; and, second, the requirement that campaign funds have to be channeled through the candidate's agent, and through him alone.

Public financing of presidential elections. Theodore Roosevelt and various other political leaders and scholars since his day have advocated governmental financial contributions to political campaigns. Finally in 1974 Congress provided public financing for presidential but not for congressional campaigns. This section of the Federal Campaign Election Act is undoubtedly one of the most significant provisions of the law. No longer will presidential aspirants have to turn to wealthy persons and organized interest groups for the money necessary to run for the office of Chief Executive.

The 1974 act provides for a $2 million public subsidy for each major party for its conventions, funds for candidates entering presidential primaries, and public funding for the general election campaign. A candidate of a major party entering presidential primaries seeking his party's nomination may qualify for as much as $4.5 million on a matching basis; in order to obtain public financing each candidate must have raised more than $5,000 in sums not to exceed $250 from any individual in at least 20 states.

Nominees of the two major political parties for the presidency automatically qualify for full public financing ($20 million) for their *presidential election* campaigns. Minor party and independent candidates are eligible for a proportion of full financing based on current or past votes received. If a presidential candidate decides to accept public financing, no private donations are permitted.

Federal election commission. One of the weaknesses of previous legislation regulating political finance was the lack of an agency specifically charged with the enforcement of the regulations. The 1974 act provides for the establishment of an eight-member bipartisan Federal Election Commission. The President, President *pro tempore* of the Senate, and the Speaker of the House of Representatives each select one Democrat and one Republican, whose names are submitted for approval by a majority of the members of both Houses of Congress. The Secretary of the Senate and the Clerk of the House of Representatives, serving as *ex-officio*, nonvoting members of the commission, complete the membership of the commission. Obviously much of the effectiveness of the new campaign finance legislation will depend on the membership of the commission and the specific rules and regulations it establishes within the framework of the statute.

How the money is spent. The specific campaign expenditures vary, of course, according to the office sought, the candidate, his campaign strategy, and the availability of funds. In presidential campaigns, however, the amount paid for publicity dwarfs all other types of expenses. The largest single publicity expenditure is for television. In every presidential election since 1952—the first election in which television was used extensively—the cost of television and radio time in campaigns at all levels rose sharply from that of preceding years until 1972, when it declined slightly from the 1968 high of approximately $50 million. Another major expenditure in recent years has been for public-opinion polls. It has been estimated that in 1972 political candidates and committees at all levels of government paid at least $5 million for public-opinion surveys.

Sources of campaign funds

A vast amount of money obviously must be obtained to pay the legitimate costs of the thousands of political campaigns conducted in the United States. What are the sources of these funds? Although the 1974 Federal Campaign Election Act will have a substantial effect on campaign finance, especially through the provisions for public financing of presidential elections and limiting the amounts any person may contribute, most political funds in the future will probably come, as in recent years, from four sources.

First, there are contributions by the candidates, their relatives, and wealthy friends. In the past, if a candidate has the personal and family resources of Nelson D. Rockefeller or John F. Kennedy, he and his family may have contributed a large proportion of his campaign expenses. It is estimated that Nelson Rockefeller and members of his family have spent $25 million of their personal funds on his political career.[15] As previously noted, the 1974 act established limitations in federal elections on contributions by the candidate and his family.

Second, both parties have solicited and received numerous large and small gifts from private individuals. Public-opinion surveys show that in a given election year 10 to 12 percent of the electorate contribute to national, state, or local elections. Candidates for major offices have relied more on large gifts than on small ones. However, starting with Goldwater's 1964 presidential campaign, both parties have made greater efforts to obtain donations from rank-and-file voters through direct mail and radio and television solicitations. One may expect this trend to continue under the 1974 act. In 1972, McGovern received contributions from approximately 750,000 persons. These donations ranged from only a few dollars to the $724,000

---

[15] *Congressional Quarterly Weekly Report*, 32 (August 24, 1974), p. 2272.

contributed by Stewart Mott, a General Motors heir. To provide incentive for sizable contributions, the Democrats, after John Kennedy entered the White House, created the President's Club, consisting of persons who contribute $1,000 or more annually. The Republicans, with Richard Nixon as President, rewarded their $1,000 donors by giving them membership in a group known as The RN Associates.

Third, a major source of party funds has been derived from fund-raising activities, including $1 rallies, $5,000 dinners, and telethons. Over $40 million was collected from such events in both 1968 and 1972. On one night alone at dinners held simultaneously in 19 cities throughout the country, at which Richard Nixon was presented via closed-circuit television, $5 million was contributed to Republican party campaign coffers. In 1973 the Democrats raised over $5 million in an eight-hour telethon, featuring television and motion picture personalities.

Fourth, as is true in most Western democracies, political-interest groups both directly and indirectly make contributions to political parties and candidates. Previously government contractors, corporations, and labor unions were prohibited from making contributions to federal election campaigns. However, such organizations have used various means to bypass the spirit, if not the letter, of the law. One of the techniques employed by major corporations or several businesses in the same field of activity was to establish an organization to collect and distribute campaign funds.[16] These organizations operated under such names as the Effective Government Association and the Bankers' Political Action Committee. Labor unions and other groups have used similar methods of assisting candidates and party committees. As noted previously, the AFL–CIO has created a subsidiary organization, the Committee on Political Education, and the American Medical Association established its Political Action Committee, which collects and spends funds to aid political parties and candidates. The 1974 Federal Campaign Election Finance Act sanctions such practices by providing that unions, government contractors, and corporations may maintain separate, segregated political funds.

Additional political finance reforms

The 1974 Federal Campaign Election Act includes a number of long-advocated reforms. Yet there is widespread agreement that additional changes are needed.

---

[16]Another method used by some business organizations has been to give bonuses to their executives with the understanding that the money will be transmitted to a political party or candidate. For example, in 1972 officials of the leading government contractors gave $2,555,740 to Republicans and $319,983 to Democrats. *Congressional Quarterly Weekly Report,* 32 (October 5, 1974), p. 2671.

First, public financing should be extended to congressional as well as presidential elections. Some countries provide for complete or partial public funding of such elections. For instance, in West Germany the government provides the legislative candidates of each party approximately 78 cents for each vote received by the party's candidate in that district in the previous election. Such a system in the United States would greatly reduce the influence of interest groups in Congress.

Second, no person should be permitted to contribute to the campaign of a candidate for whom he is not qualified to vote. Such a step would prohibit parents of children under 18 years of age from making contributions in the names of the children. But, more importantly, it would prevent a person in Texas, for instance, from contributing to candidates in, say, South Dakota or Maryland.

Third, because of the various advantages incumbents have in seeking reelection, ceilings on campaign expenditures of nonincumbents should be higher than those placed on officeholders. Fourth, a highly questionable provision of the 1974 act permits candidates to use surplus campaign funds for other purposes. Such funds should be given to the party's national or state committee. Finally, proposals have been suggested for providing other than direct financial assistance to political candidates and committees. They include recommendations that political parties be granted a limited amount of free radio and television time, as they are in most European countries, Japan, Canada, and Australia; and that candidates be permitted to mail some literature free through a restricted use of the franking privilege, as candidates may in Japan.

12
Political-Interest Groups

12

Organized group action has long been a principal means for attempting to gain political and economic goals in America. One of the classic statements regarding political-interest groups was written by James Madison in 1788 when he observed in No. 10 of *The Federalist* that

> *a landed interest, a manufacturing interest, a mercantile interest, a moneyed interest, with many lesser interests, grow up of necessity in civilized nations, and divide them into different classes, actuated by different sentiments and views. The regulation of these various and interfering interests forms the principal task of modern legislation.*

Although organized interests have been active for many years in politics, in recent decades the number of such groups has vastly multiplied and their influence has greatly expanded. Today interest groups are active in virtually every area of political decision-making.

Various terms or phrases have been employed to describe the private organizations or groups that attempt to influence government. In the past, the most commonly used term was *pressure groups*, but the tendency in recent years is to refer to these organizations as *interest groups*. By definition, a political-interest group is any private group of people who seek to influence some phase of public policy. Hence legislative bodies or political parties are not political-interest groups, even though they influence public policies.

Only in democratic systems, where freedom of association and free speech and press are guaranteed, can political-interest groups, as we know them, organize and promote their interests. In democratic philosophy, no single individual or group has a monopoly on understanding and developing policies. By contrast, authoritarian and totalitarian doctrine holds that only one interest may be promoted—the interest of the state—and that the ruling party has the right and duty to determine and enforce that single interest.

Hence a basic difference exists between interest groups in nondemocratic and democratic regimes. The purpose of organized groups in the former is to transmit government policies to the group and its members. The purpose of interest groups in a democracy is to translate group interests into government policy. In totalitarian states, the government and the official party attempt to encompass or control all phases of group interests. Those in power determine what groups may organize, and either provide their leadership or rigidly supervise their activities. Other voluntary associations are prohibited, and all media of communication are strictly controlled to ensure support for the official policies and to prevent dissent. In short, in a nondemocratic system, competitive political-interest groups are not permitted.

FUNCTIONS OF POLITICAL-INTEREST GROUPS

In the United States and other Western democracies, political-interest groups perform several functions. First, they help to crystallize and aggregate opinions and stimulate discussion of political issues. Numerous amorphous ideas may be suggested as solutions to problems in any area of public concern. Many interest groups study and debate the various ideas and then develop and advocate concrete proposals, and thus stimulate discussion of political issues.

Second, organized interest groups provide a type of group representation. Because of the great diversity and complexity of many electoral districts, it is impossible for elected representatives to know the problems and opinions of all their constituents. Moreover, the primary interests of many individuals today are related more to occupational, fraternal, or ideological associations than to the specific problems of the geographic electoral district in which they live. Thus political-interest groups provide a channel of communication between their members and public officials. Many legislative and administrative officials readily admit that organized interests are a valuable source of much specialized and detailed information. The communication process, however, is not a one-way street, for often lobbyists or leaders of interest groups obtain information from the government agencies and transmit it to their members.

Third, political-interest groups help check on the activities of other interest groups and public officials. If an interest group makes extreme or unreasonable demands, it may be opposed by other groups. Interest groups also scrutinize the activities of public officials and help ensure that they perform their tasks in a responsible fashion.

GROUP TACTICS AND TECHNIQUES

Interest groups are pragmatic organizations. Aware of the crucial decision-making points in the political process, they generally follow the principle of taking whatever action will produce the maximum results for their members with the minimum expenditure of time and energy. The manner in which political-interest groups function in the United States is influenced basically by the political environment: the separation of powers, the federal form of government, the electoral system, technological developments, and the social and economic composition of the population.

Because of their different political and economic cultures, methods used by organized interest groups in Great Britain, France, or Switzerland might be different from those used by similar groups in the United States. Indeed, within the United States some political-interest groups tend to be more successful in some state capitals than in others. Moreover, actions that might be effective for one group might not succeed with another. The tactics and techniques employed would depend on such factors as the goals of the group, the status of the group, the cohesion of its members, its financial resources, the prestige position of the organization, the quality of its leadership, the size and geographic dispersion of its members, and its relations with the political parties and other interest groups.

Where, then, does the organized interest group attempt to exert influence? Depending on the goals and characteristics of the particular group, it may attempt to influence its own members, other organized interest groups, the public at large, legislators, executive and administrative personnel, and the courts—in short, the places where political decisions are made. The fact that there are so many places in the American political system where decisions are made contributes to the influence of organized interest groups.

Influencing the membership and other groups

Scholars have noted for many years that in most large organizations an active minority often controls the actions and policies of the group. This tendency is referred to as the "iron law of oligarchy." In many large interest groups, the leaders, officers, and paid staff form a small elite who run the organization and who, from the viewpoint of the initiation and adoption of policies, in effect become the organization.

The officers and staffs of many organizations often devote much time attempting to win a following and influence group members. Efforts are made to increase the cohesion of the group and to retain and enlarge the membership. In group publications, in national and state conventions, and in local meetings, these elites often attempt to get the members to accept and support the policies prepared by them and to engage in political activity that will promote the aims of the leaders of the organization.

The efforts of political-interest groups to influence public officials have tended to cause political observers to overlook the extent to which groups seek the cooperation of other organized groups. Pressure groups attempt to obtain the assistance of their allies and potential allies, the endorsement of groups not directly interested in their political programs, and the neutralization of opposing forces. Such cooperation may be accomplished by merely activating others, by "log-rolling"—agreeing to support each other's political goals—or by making compromises on proposed programs. A congressional committee investigating lobbying activities once commented on the "growing joint effort in lobbying" and added that "the general theme of combination rather than conflict grows bolder and more insistent every year."

Interest groups and the public

The idea that an organization with ample funds can sell any program to the general public has largely been disproved. Nevertheless, one of the noteworthy features of pressure-group activity has been the efforts to gain support for programs by using the mass media. Public-relations campaigns are directed primarily to the special publics likely to become concerned with a particular proposal and to other individuals referred to as "opinion leaders," who may influence many who might otherwise be uninterested in the issue.

Today many organizations employ public-relations counsels to advise them and to direct public-relations and propaganda campaigns. The use of public-relations experts is a distinguishing characteristic of modern propaganda. The rise of the public-relations counsel has occurred concomitantly with the growth of pressure groups and the extraordinary development of the communications media, particularly television.

Political-interest groups employ propaganda for both short-range and long-range goals; in either case, they attempt to make their programs appear synonymous with the "general welfare." The short-range goals of a public-relations campaign may be to give the impression that there is such widespread support for a proposal that the campaign itself will provide the momentum necessary to secure the acceptance of the policy, or the purpose of the campaign may be to stimulate a sufficient number of persons to urge public officials to adopt the desired program.

The long-range or strategic aim of propaganda campaigns tends to be ideological, usually urging the public to accept a particular philosophy of government. In brief, the purpose of such campaigns is to condition the attitudes of the people so that they will respond almost automatically with favor toward programs desired by the group and will automatically reject programs that the group opposes. The National Association of Manufacturers (NAM) has developed a strategic concept of propaganda that it refers to as its "bank account theory." In one of its publications, the Association explains that the theory requires making "regular and frequent deposits in the Bank of Public Good-Will" in order that "valid checks can be drawn on this account" on the proper occasions.

Some corporations employ institutional advertising, which does not promote a particular product but attempts either to expound a general philosophy such as "free enterprise" or to associate the organization in the minds of the people with some highly esteemed value or program. Business groups enjoy an advantage over other groups in this area, because the cost of such advertising may be deducted for tax purposes as an operating expense.

A number of the larger interest groups disseminate press releases, clip sheets, and prepared editorials to the press. The effectiveness of this type of propaganda is largely due to the fact that when it appears verbatim in newspapers or magazines, it gives the impression of straight reporting or editorializing by the staff of the periodical.

In their efforts to influence public attitudes, political-interest groups have not overlooked the educational system. Some groups, including the NAM, have prepared and distributed books, booklets, posters, film strips, and other "teaching aids" to the schools. The NAM once announced that it distributed "at least two million booklets" free to the schools every year.

In the late 1960s the mass demonstration came into widespread use to influence public attitudes toward a general problem. These were used extensively by civil-rights and antiwar groups, and undoubtedly scored considerable success in influencing public opinion and government leaders.

Interest groups and political parties

Although political-interest groups and political parties are similar, they can be readily distinguished. The major parties have as their fundamental purpose gaining control of the personnel and politics of the government; however, they tend to concentrate on the nomination and election of public officials rather than on the choice of policies. Political-interest groups are also interested in the personnel and policies of government, but they are primarily interested in public policies and the selection of public officials is only of secondary concern. Political-interest groups do not wish—and are not prepared—to take over and operate the entire government, which is the basic aim of a major political party. Political-interest groups do not periodically submit their program to the voters in an election; if they participate in the electoral process, it is customarily by supporting party candidates whose views are similar to theirs. Group leaders, realizing that much of their success in achieving their political goals may depend on the support they receive from one or both political parties, usually take one of two approaches toward political parties. Many groups—especially the smaller organized interest groups—avoid too close an identification with either party but attempt to secure the support of both parties. Other groups have tended to align themselves with one party, but still attempt to work with the other party.

Political-interest groups use a variety of methods to influence political parties. Several organizations urge their members to work actively in a party and, if possible, to be elected to a position in the party organization. Most of the larger interest groups appear before the resolutions committees of the parties to urge the adoption of their programs as planks in the parties' platforms. Often they attempt to obtain the endorsement of both parties and thus remove their proposals from the arena of partisan controversy. Although interest groups do not in their own name nominate candidates for public office, they often work for the nomination and election of certain candidates.

Pressures on legislators

In the past, organized groups in the United States concentrated most of their efforts on promoting and opposing legislative proposals. Although in recent years interest-group activities have expanded in other areas, the most obvious actions of pressure associations are still those in which they attempt to influence legislative decisions.

The principal organized interests maintain permanent staffs of professional lobbyists, press agents, research personnel, and secretaries in Washington, and have staffs in state capitals during legislative sessions. Organizations that have only an incidental interest in legislative proposals do not usually have a full-time lobby staff, but may employ a lobbyist to represent them on occasions when legislative issues of interest arise.

Los Angeles Times, January 18, 1975. Copyright, Chicago Sun-Times.

Lobbying consists basically of communicating with the legislators, and political-interest groups use every opportunity to inform legislators of their wishes. Although most major public policies are initiated by the President and his assistants or by congressional committees, available information indicates that political-interest groups originate a large proportion of the other measures introduced in Congress, as well as the great majority of bills in the state legislatures. If a measure sponsored by one group is opposed by another, the role of the legislators may resemble the role of officials refereeing a contest between two competing teams. Unfortunately, in such instances the interests of the public may be overlooked.

Committee hearings on bills provide the opportunity for interest groups to present information and arguments and also to show how strongly the members of the group favor or oppose a given proposal. Officers of organizations, their lobbyists, or lay members testify before committees, and occasionally delegations are organized to attend committee hearings. At crucial times—such as when a committee is considering a bill or when the measure is being debated by one of the houses of the legislature—political-interest groups may have their members write, telegraph, or telephone their legislators. Campaign contributions to congressmen may play an important role in the outcome of a bill. For instance, one congressman remarked that if lobbyists did not make campaign contributions, "the power of the lobbyists would be practically nil."[1]

Influencing the executive branch

As compared to interest groups in the United States, interest groups in Great Britain, with its parliamentary form of government and centralized parties, have directed more attention to the Cabinet and less to individual legislators. However, in recent years in the United States, too, political-interest groups have increased their efforts to influence the executive branch of the government. Aware of the expanded role of the chief executive as the chief legislator, pressure groups have importuned the President and governors to incorporate or omit particular proposals from their legislative programs and to increase or decrease specific budgetary requests. After the legislature enacts a controversial bill, it is not uncommon for political-interest groups to inundate the President with letters, telegrams, and personal calls urging him to veto or sign the measure. Individual Presidents,

---

[1] "Lobbies: Putting Pressure on Government," *Los Angeles Times*, March 17, 1972. Shortly before the 1974 election a congressman seeking reelection explained: "Certainly, the donors want influence. They want to be able to come in at any time and have you listen. . . . Of course, you'll take a longer look at their problems, and if it doesn't violate your principles, you'll try to lean their way, especially on an issue that doesn't involve a lot of other people." "Short Memory? Special Interests Spend Record Sums," *Wall Street Journal,* October 16, 1974.

because of their own backgrounds and sources of political support, have tended to be more amenable to the wishes of some groups than others.

As groups are aware that administrators may vigorously execute or virtually nullify a statute, it is understandable that organizations often seek the appointment of their members or of persons friendly to their group to administrative positions of concern to them. Pressure groups with friends in high administrative posts sometimes find that they have advantages not available to others in securing subsidies, contracts, permits, licenses, favorable adjustments of tax problems and antitrust suits, and other favors and privileges.

Pressure groups may also seek to influence administrative actions by working through legislators. Groups may urge the legislature to amend the statutes under which an agency functions, and they may urge increases or decreases in an agency's budget in order to expand or curtail its operations. It is not correct to assume that a hostile relationship always exists between political-interest groups and administrative agencies. On the contrary, it is not unusual to find political-interest groups, governmental organizations, and legislators working together for their mutual benefit—but especially for the benefit of the interest group.

Interest groups and the courts

Although political-interest groups devote less effort toward influencing policy through the courts than through the legislative or executive branches, a number of organizations, acknowledging the importance of the judiciary in the political process, have turned their attention to the courts. Many groups realize that they may be affected by judicial decisions that result from the power of judicial review, the interpretation of the Constitution, statutes, or treaties, by injunctions and other court orders, or by decisions in civil or criminal cases affecting personal and property rights. Hence, whether judges are elected or appointed, various organizations scrutinize the records of prospective judges and oppose those they believe are biased against their group. For example, in 1969 and 1970, bipartisan coalitions of civil-rights organizations, labor, and other groups were successful in getting the Senate to oppose two Supreme Court nominations made by President Nixon.

Various groups have sought to advance their interests by testing the constitutionality or interpretation of legislation or the actions of public officials. A noteworthy example is the National Association for the Advancement of Colored People, which has for years employed litigation as a principal means for upholding Negro rights. In winning court cases, such as *Brown* v. *Board of Education of Topeka* (1954), in which school segregation was outlawed, the NAACP won political victories fully as important as any gained in the halls of Congress. Some organizations intervene in suits as *amici curiae,* or "friends of the court," a device that permits them to file briefs in a case in which they are not a party and in this way to support other groups involved in litigation. For some interest groups, attempting to influence government is virtually an endless process; if the legislature enacts and the chief executive signs a measure considered undesirable, pressure organizations may seek to have it nullified, or at least amended, by judicial action.

THE VARIETY OF INTEREST GROUPS

Although political-interest groups have been studied and analyzed for many years, we still have only an approximate idea of how many groups seek to press their claims on government. Even less is known regarding the cost of interest-group activities. The Federal Regulation of Lobbying Act requires the registration of lobbyists and the filing of reports of group expenditures; however, various groups that attempt to influence legislation have never registered, and many groups that do register do not file complete reports. The aggregate of group legislative expenditures in the states probably exceeds the national figures. In California alone, more than 400 lobbying groups have reported expenditures in excess of $3 million during a single legislative session, and this amount includes only those costs related to the employment of registered lobbyists.

It is customary to classify interest groups according to their membership or primary interests, such as business, labor, farm, professional, religious, and ethnic. The following discussion begins with the economic-interest groups, which have the largest membership and which undoubtedly are the most influential in American politics.

Business groups

In all modern democracies, business groups have organized and have been active in the determination of public policy. Although business is represented in the political arena by a variety of organizations, three types are most prevalent. First, there are the "peak" associations, each of which includes as members a number of other organizations. Second, there are many trade associations that attempt to influence government, usually on the national or state levels. Third, some individual business corporations and firms are active in politics at all levels of government.

The National Association of Manufacturers, organized in 1895, in recent years has had a membership of between 14,000 and 18,000 individuals, firms, and corporations engaged in manufacturing. The organization tends to reflect the more conservative business viewpoint of the larger manufacturing firms. For instance, its members comprise only about 8 percent of the manufacturing firms in the nation, but they account for approximately 75 percent of the nation's industrial production.

The United States Chamber of Commerce, formed in 1912 after President Taft suggested that such an organization would help the government to "keep in closer touch with commercial affairs," is a federation composed of approximately 2,500 local and state branches, 1,000 trade and professional associations, and 45,000 corporation and individual members, and is found in every sizable community in the nation. Having a more diversified membership and interests than the NAM, the Chamber tends to take less specific stands on public issues and adopts policies that, in its words, "are general in application to business and industry." Like the NAM, the Chamber has opposed most legislative measures providing for social reforms and for benefits for organized labor. On some measure on which most elements of business are in general accord, the Chamber of Commerce, acting through its local chapters, can inundate Congress with literally thousands of letters, telegrams, and telephone calls. In the words of an official of the Chamber, "Our prime effort is at the grass roots. . . . We urge our members to write their representatives about bills. . . . We feel that personal letters and telegrams have more impact than petitions or resolutions."[2]

A third association for businessmen which has attracted considerable attention has been the Committee for Economic Development, which was formed by a number of the more liberal business leaders during World War II. This organization has not attempted to represent any particular business interest and has limited its activities largely to conducting research and issuing reports on a number of public questions. These reports have been carefully reasoned and informative and have undoubtedly helped to shape some public policies.

Of the business groups registering under the Federal Regulation of Lobbying Act, a large proportion are trade associations, multipurpose groups composed of competing firms, producing similar goods or rendering similar services. According to the Department of Commerce, there are some 14,000 trade associations, of which 1,700 are organized nationally. Although trade associations have been formed for a variety of reasons, most of them serve as channels of communications between the government and their industries. They have provided the primary means by which many business groups lobby public officials and obtain information from the government.

The term *political-interest group* also includes individual business concerns—primarily corporations—when they act politically, as many do. Throughout most of the nineteenth century and well into the twentieth, the main actors in the politics of interest were the owners, managers, and lobbyists of individual business concerns. During the past two decades there has been a growing tendency for major corporations to act on their own rather than to work through a trade association. Most major corpora-

---

[2]*Los Angeles Times,* February 25, 1973.

tions, including such firms as the Bank of America, Kaiser Steel Corporation, Shell Oil Company, Western Union, and numerous others, have registered as employing lobbyists.

Agricultural groups

One of the major population movements in the United States in recent decades has been the farm-to-city migration. In 1949 30.5 million Americans lived on farms, but by 1975 the number had decreased to about 10 million. Although the number of farmers has declined sharply, agricultural groups continue to exert much influence in areas of direct interest to farmers. The three major farm organizations in the United States are the Patrons of Husbandry (the Grange), organized in 1867; the National Farmers' Union, founded in 1902; and the American Farm Bureau Federation (the Farm Bureau), established in 1919.

The Farm Bureau, the largest and most influential of the farm organizations, has in recent years supported Republican policies more often than those of the Democratic party. Both the Farm Bureau and the Grange are conservative organizations whose statements on public policies often parallel those of organized business. Unlike the other two major farm organizations, the Farmers' Union has supported most of the policies of Democratic administrations and has been willing to work with labor unions. Among the benefits gained by these farm organizations are a complex of price supports and subsidies for farmers.

In addition to these major agricultural associations, there are hundreds of other farm organizations—producer associations, cooperatives, marketing groups, and others—actively involved in the political representation of agricultural interests. Many of these organizations are formed along farm commodity lines: the American Livestock Association, the National Apple Institute, the National Pork Producers Association, and the National Wool Growers Federation.

In 1974 two former top officials of the nation's largest dairy cooperative were sentenced to prison and fined for making illegal campaign contributions. The cooperative itself received the maximum fine for the illegal contributions, which included over $600,000 to the 1972 Nixon election campaign. According to congressional testimony, the money was part of $2 million pledged to Nixon in 1971 by the cooperative if he would raise milk price supports. In 1971, shortly after the pledge was made, milk price supports were increased.

Labor organizations

In the federal structure of organized labor, the basic building blocks are the 75,000 to 80,000 local unions. These local unions, which might be compared with our local units of government, are organized into approximately 130 national craft or industrial unions. These are the constituent units of the AFL–CIO, just as the 50 states are the constituent units of our federal government. In some respects the national unions, which usually have authority over such matters as calling strikes and establishing wage policies and work rules, are more powerful than the AFL–CIO itself. Some of the national unions are titans in their own right. The Steel Workers, Carpenters, and Machinists unions have memberships in excess of 750,000 each. By comparison, a number of other national unions are quite small; 40 percent of the national unions in the AFL–CIO have fewer than 25,000 members.

In 1973 about 12.3 million Americans belonged to unions affiliated with the AFL–CIO. Since the end of World War II, largely because of the relative decline of the number of the more easily organized blue-collar workers and the greater proportionate increase of white-collar workers, the rate of growth of the AFL–CIO has steadily declined in proportion to the total labor force, and some unions have lost in terms of total members. In addition to the unions affiliated with the AFL–CIO, there are some 50 national unions that are independent of that organization. These include the railroad brotherhood; the United Mine Workers, which was an early pillar of the CIO; the Teamsters, which has flourished despite its ouster from the AFL–CIO in 1957; and the United Automobile Workers (UAW). In 1968, shortly after withdrawing from the AFL–CIO, the UAW joined with the Teamsters to form the Alliance for Labor Action. Total membership of Americans in unions represents only about one-quarter of nonagricultural workers.

The political arm of the AFL–CIO is the Committee on Political Education (COPE) which engages in a variety of political activities, including, in the words of one COPE official, "screening candidates, ironing out differences to avoid conflict, allocating finances, and funneling in campaign workers." Whereas organized business derives its political power from its wealth and the status of its members, organized labor is influential because of the size of its membership. Although organized labor makes campaign contributions, its principal strength in the last analysis lies in its millions of voters.

The professions

Strictly speaking, the "professions" are those callings that regulate themselves on at least a semiofficial basis, and for which the principal condition of entry is the completion of a prescribed course of higher education. Because the licensing of professions falls within the jurisdiction of the states, professional associations generally are more concerned with state governments than with the national government. However, as the latter has expanded its activities, professional associations have found more reason to direct their attention to the national level. Of the various professional associations, the educational, medical, and legal groups are the largest and probably the most influential.

The educational lobby. Among the organizations seeking support and recognition for education, the National Education Association (NEA) and its various state affiliates, with over one million members, is the largest. Critics of NEA have insisted that the organization has not been sufficiently aggressive in seeking support for education. As the educators throughout the nation have witnessed a relative decline in their incomes in comparison with other professional groups and with certain unionized workers, some teachers have urged membership in teacher unions, including the American Federation of Teachers.

The medical lobby. The American Medical Association (AMA), organized nationally in 1901 by local medical associations and including in its present membership approximately 75 percent of all licensed physicians in the country, has been described by a well-known journalist as "the most powerful lobby in Washington."[3] The AMA Political Action Committee reported making donations of over $1.7 million in the 1974 midterm election campaign, with contributions going to 248 candidates for the House of Representatives and 22 Senate candidates.[4] During the past three decades the AMA has had a consistent record of opposing legislation that would provide government participation in meeting the mounting costs of medical care. Labeling such measures "socialized medicine," the AMA has attempted to organize its members in campaigns to defeat such proposals. In recent years, however, perhaps due to their increased income from Medicare and Medicaid payments, doctors' resistance to government assistance in health-care costs appears to be declining.

As noted above, approximately one-fourth of all doctors are not members of the AMA, and others are members only because membership in their local medical societies necessitates membership in the state and national associations. Furthermore, many younger doctors appear to be rejecting the self-protective stance of the AMA and accepting a broader concern and responsibility for the health care of all persons.

The legal lobby. In a society where "the rule of law" has deep institutional roots, it was inevitable that members of the legal profession should play a prominent part in government. By contrast with the AMA, the American Bar Association (ABA)—the major professional group for lawyers—has engaged in few highly controversial political issues. The historic role of the lawyer in American politics has been to represent interests other than his own. Hence his primary identification has been with his clients rather than

---

[3] TRB, "AMA Maintains Opposition to Health Bills," *Los Angeles Times*, March 24, 1971.

[4] Richard Diamond, (ed.), *Dollar Politics*, Washington, D.C.: Congressional Quarterly, 1974, Vol. II, p. 56.

with his professional associates. The ABA has ordinarily confined its activities to such professionally relevant problems as legal aid, defendants' rights, administrative procedures, and judicial personnel and jurisdiction. In 1971, however, the American Trial Lawyers Association, an affiliate of the ABA, was generally credited with the defeat of legislation by Congress and a number of states for "no-fault" automobile insurance. Since 1945 the ABA has assisted the Senate Judiciary Committee and the Department of Justice by reviewing the qualifications of prospective federal judges. With more than half of Congress numbered among its members, the ABA exercises considerable influence on such matters. Also, the most successful and highest paid of the Washington lobbyists are lawyers, many of whom have formerly served in Congress or in high administrative positions.

Other interest groups

Shared attitudes rather than property, occupation, or income constitute the group "interest." Therefore, the range of political-interest groups is virtually as wide and diverse as society itself. For instance, a highly effective interest group is the National Rifle Association. With a membership of over a million, it has been successful in preventing the enactment of a national gun-control law, although according to opinion surveys, such legislation is desired by a majority of Americans.[5] Many groups have shared attitudes due to common experiences, religious affiliations, or ethnic backgrounds. Examples of such organizations include the American Legion, the National Council of Churches, the National Catholic Welfare Conference, the National Jewish Welfare Board, and the National Association for the Advancement of Colored People.

A number of foreign governments and firms employ American professional lobbyists and seek to influence governmental decisions in the United States by using much the same tactics as the American interest groups. In recent years some 400 such "foreign agents" have been registered with the State Department. The countries that employ such agents apparently believe that American lobbyists will secure more favorable decisions in such areas as foreign aid, trade, and tariff adjustments than would their own representatives. For instance, it was reported that the Agriculture Committee of the House of Representatives gave preferential treatment to the sugar quotas of countries employing well-known American lobbyists.

Some scholars have suggested that a distinction be made between the groups that are organized to advance the personal interest of their members and those that advocate other causes. It has been proposed that the latter category be called "promotional" or "opinion" or "ideological" groups.

---

[5]*Wall Street Journal,* May 24, 1972.

While there is the obvious problem of classifying groups that advocate other causes as well as programs for their own personal benefit, the concept of the promotional or opinion group is useful. The variety of such shared attitude groups may be seen by noting such examples as the American Civil Liberties Union, the American Association for the United Nations, and the National Council for the Prevention of War. More recently, as a result of the women's liberation movement, several feminist organizations —the largest of which is the National Organization of Women (NOW)— have been formed.

The proliferation of interest groups has produced a reaction among individuals who are concerned that government may favor the special interests to the disadvantage of the general citizenry. As a result, ciizens have organized groups to defend the general interest. Examples of such "anti-special-interest groups" are the League of Women Voters; the National Committee for an Effective Congress; Ralph Nader's Public Citizen Incorporated; Common Cause; and the Sierra Club. Ralph Nader wrote:

> A way must be found for the individual citizen to provide an impact on government agencies and corporate boardrooms. . . . Bureaucrats cannot easily overcome the pressure brought by the hundreds of special-interest lobbyists in Washington and state capitals. A primary goal of our work is to build countervailing forces on behalf of citizens. . . .

Common Cause, organized by John W. Gardner, former Secretary of Health, Education, and Welfare, with the stated purpose "to uphold the public interest against all comers, particularly the special interests that dominate our lives today," has attracted over 300,000 dues-paying members. The influence of these public-interest groups may be indicated in the comment of a California state senator: "When the Sierra Club speaks, I listen."

The radical right and the radical left

In a democracy characterized by a highly heterogeneous population, it is not surprising to find radical groups on the right and the left whose views deviate sharply from those of the great majority of the population. These groups comprise a particular type of political-interest group in the United States. While some such groups have formed minor parties, others have not; and regardless of their names and forms of organization, they resemble typical political-interest groups more than they do major political parties. Such groups also exist in Europe and elsewhere, and in some multiparty systems they have formed political parties. These groups in the United States illustrate the problem of distinguishing precisely between political-interest groups and political parties.

In speaking of radical groups of either the right or the left, a distinction must be drawn between radicalism in the sense of extreme programs on

"*It seems a tragic waste when you consider what Ralph Nader's intelligence and drive might have accomplished in some legitimate walk of life.*"
Drawing by Reilly; © 1971 The New Yorker Magazine, Inc.

the one hand and radicalism in the sense of commitment to revolution and violence on the other. For example, on the radical right, a group that seeks to abolish the income tax and the social-security system is radical in the sense that it proposes what seem to nearly all Americans fundamental changes. This kind of radicalism is to be distinguished from that of groups opposing the democratic process itself. Similarly, on the left, any one of the socialist parties in the United States may be called radical because its program of public ownership of the means of production is totally opposed to the existing private-ownership system. Yet, when speaking of the U.S. Communist party and other revolutionary groups as radical, we refer to their official commitment to revolution as the means of bringing about their objectives.

Both radical-left and radical-right groups appear to proliferate during times of severe social and political tension and change. The post–World War II period, characterized by revolutionary technological innovations, major social transformations, and continual international crises, spawned an unprecedented number of radical-right groups, including the Reverend Billy James Hargis' "Christian Crusade," the Minutemen, and the John Birch Society. The Vietnam era brought forth many new radical-left groups, such as Students for a Democratic Society, the Progressive Labor party (a pro-Chinese Communist group), and the Weatherman, a group of terrorists.

As long as interest groups use constitutional means, they should be encouraged, for a complete and vigorous expression of the maximum number of viewpoints is a source of strength in a democratic society. However, some of the groups on both the radical left and the radical right do not believe in the democratic process and have resorted to slander, intimidation, and violence in pursuing their goals. The Constitution attempts to reconcile two values, each of which places limitations on the other: first, the right to speak, organize, protest, and demonstrate; and second, the need to maintain public order and to protect the rights of others.

PRESSURE GROUPS AND DEMOCRACY: THE DILEMMA OF REGULATION

The recent growth of political-interest groups has been partly due to governmental policies and processes, which one perceptive scholar has labeled "interest-group liberalism." According to him, the "operative principles" of interest-group liberalism are: "Destroy privilege by universalizing it. Reduce conflict by yielding to it. Redistribute power by the maxim of each according to his claim. Reserve an official place for every major structure of power."[6] More than at any time previously in American history, the principal key to success in politics is organized group activity.

What problems arise from interest-group activity? First, there is little doubt that some groups exert more influence and obtain more benefits than could be justified by the size of their membership or by their contributions to society. It is also well known that members of the upper and middle classes are more likely than the disadvantaged to be active in interest groups. Moreover, among those groups that are organized, some have more resources and influence than others, and as a consequence receive favored treatment from the government. As one student of interest groups has noted: "The fact that not all groups are organized and not all interests are represented has serious consequences. At the extreme they involve the virtual exclusion of some elements of the population from effective voice in affairs that deeply concern them."[7] Second, it is sometimes difficult to know who is represented by an organized group. An organization may have a name

---

[6]Theodore J. Lowi, *The End of Liberalism*, New York: Norton, 1969, pp. 292–293.
[7]Grant McConnell, *Private Power and American Democracy*, New York: Knopf, 1966, p. 7.

that indicates that it represents hundreds of individuals, when it actually is a "front" group for others who do not want their identity known. Third, some groups may employ methods and tactics—such as bribery, intimidation, or making campaign contributions with the implied if not explicit expectation of future favors—which, if used on a wide scale, would tend to undermine the political system.

Political-interest groups thus constitute a dilemma for democratic government. In order for a free society to flourish, individuals must be permitted to organize and take joint political action, and the First Amendment of the Constitution, which provides for freedom of speech and press and the right to assemble and to petition government, guarantees this right; yet, if unrestrained, interest groups might subvert the political system.

As a partial effort to solve the dilemma involving political-interest groups, laws have been enacted to require certain interest groups and their lobbyists to register with the government. The Federal Regulation of Lobbying Act, passed in 1946, provided that paid lobbyists and organizations that solicit, collect, and spend money for the "principal purpose" of influencing federal legislation must register with the Clerk of the House of Representatives and the Secretary of the Senate, and they must file quarterly reports listing all persons who have contributed $500 or more to the group and all persons to whom payments of $10 or more have been made. Lobbying-registration laws, some based on the federal statute, have been passed by most states.[8] The theory behind this legislation is that by disclosing information regarding those who are attempting to influence public policies, governmental decisions might be made more on the merits of the issues rather than on the amount of influence applied.

Largely because of defects in the phraseology of the law and because there is no agency specifically charged with its enforcement, many groups that lobby do not register; and others that do register do not file complete reports of their expenditures. Hence the legislation has had relatively little impact on the activities of pressure groups. The influence of pressure groups in general would no doubt be reduced if the Federal Regulation of Lobbying Act were amended to require the submission of additional information concerning lobbyists and organized interest groups. Proposals to strengthen the act have been introduced in virtually every session of Congress, but to this date none has been enacted.

The principal safeguards concerning pressure-group activity are not to be found in statutory regulations but in the total functioning of the political system. The political parties, elected officials, administrative personnel, the

---

[8] In addition to lobbying-registration laws, there are other federal statutes that require particular types of interest groups to register with the Securities and Exchange Commission or the Secretary of Commerce; and certain lobbyists or agents of foreign powers are required to register with the Department of State.

mass media of communication, and other pressure groups all serve as checks against any specialized interest or combination of interests—a "power elite" —gaining sufficient power to dominate the political or economic life of the nation. However, these checks have not prevented a variety of groups from gaining at times economic and political advantages which some consider to be adverse to the public interest.

13 Congress

13

LEGISLATURES IN THE POLITICAL PROCESS

The institutions discussed thus far, primarily interest groups and parties, have been concerned principally with the articulation and aggregation of interests—that is, they are concerned with the development of policy positions designed to promote the welfare of given groups within society. But to maintain the viability of a democratic system, conflicting interests must be reconciled, passions mollified, and demands converted into policy, and *legislatures* are a vital instrument in this conversion process.

Legislatures coexist with executives in a variety of patterns and relationships largely determined by constitutions and party systems. In most regimes throughout the world, the executive branch dominates the legislature through its use of extraordinary powers granted by the constitution or through its control of the party system. In the twentieth century, even in thoroughly democratic systems, the executive branch has enlarged its prerogatives and authority, but the extent of executive domination differs sharply from place to place. With a strong two-party system, the Cabinet in England has established its firm control of the government, although this control depends on satisfying "back benchers" that their wishes are being met satisfactorily, and this is not always an easy job. In France, beginning with the regime of De Gaulle, an independently elected president with broad powers to govern has put the French parliament into political eclipse. The United States Congress remains unique in its independence and in its capacity to influence the course of public policy by means of its criticism, its development of policy options, and, occasionally, its policy leadership.

Legislative-executive struggle in the United States

In one student's perceptive phrase, the Constitution of 1787 "is supposed to have created a government of 'separated powers.' It did nothing of the sort. Rather, it created a government of separated institutions *sharing* powers."[1] It is in this context that one must view the remarkable contests between Congress and Presidents Johnson and Nixon over Vietnam policy and between Congress and Presidents Nixon and Ford over a wide range

[1] Richard Neustadt, *Presidential Power,* New York: Wiley, 1960, p. 42.

of domestic and foreign policy issues. In each case Congress has endeavored to assert policy authority after a long period of relative acquiescence to the President.

There has been something of a cyclical pattern in the history of legislative-executive relations, depending to some extent on the President himself, his concept of the role that he should play in the constitutional system, and the circumstances under which he served. George Washington established the prototype of forthright presidential leadership, relying heavily on great personal prestige. Jefferson dominated Congress more subtly through his control of his party. Subsequently presidential leadership declined, notwithstanding the brilliance of Andrew Jackson and later of Lincoln during the Civil War. The Whigs and the Radical Republicans so dominated the government that Woodrow Wilson could write in 1885 that Congress was "the central and predominant power of the system," and that the U.S. government was "government by the Standing Committees of Congress."[2]

The transformation of the United States into an important world power in the twentieth century gave the executive branch an initiative in policy-making that far transcended diplomacy, reaching into the farthest recesses of domestic politics as well. The increasing reliance of the American people on the national government to mediate group conflict and to provide protection against the potential consequences of a complex economic system indicated a need for strong executive leadership. Congress continued to play an active role in an expanded realm of public policy, but was less well equipped to provide leadership, partly because of its own disintegrative nature, but perhaps more significantly because of the increasing expertise required in formulating solutions to problems of a highly technical character and of the contingent nature of most policy-making and execution. Although the broad outlines of policy can be enacted by Congress, the executive appeared to need great discretion in deciding what to do in the context of specific circumstances that Congress could only dimly foresee.

Nearly all modern presidents—both Roosevelts, Wilson, Truman, Kennedy, Johnson, and Nixon—have striven to provide a rallying point for the country and an agenda for Congress. But Congress has had a powerful influence in putting forward its own items for the legislative agenda and countering those acts of presidential authority and policy which it deemed unwise.

The office of the member of Congress

Formal eligibility requirements do not seriously constrain access to membership in the houses of Congress. Few are prepared to seek such offices

---

[2]Woodrow Wilson, *Congressional Government*, New York: Meridian Books, 1956, p. 23.

before reaching the minimum ages of 25 for a member of the House or 30 for the Senate. Members of Congress must be residents of the states they represent, and by tradition, House members must reside in the districts they represent.

The local-residence requirements for elected representatives ensure that members of Congress share the same experiences, values, and concerns of many of their constituents, thus making it unnecessary that they be pressured into taking certain courses of action. The congressman's deep identification with the majority of the constituents in his district is especially important with regard to his attitudes toward policy matters and his responsiveness to party discipline. The local party organization has often granted his nomination, or at least permitted it, and the representative may therefore be responsive to local party as well as community forces. The party differs from place to place, however, and therefore each representative may respond differently. A Democratic congressman from Chicago must be an "organization man" to survive, whereas a Republican congressman from the suburbs may act quite independently of the party. In either case, the congressman may defy the national party, secure in the protection afforded him by the local political structure.

The close identification of legislator with district distinguishes members of Congress from legislators in other countries. In Britain and France, for example, there is no local residence requirement, and candidates can be designated by the national parties to seek election in districts where they do not live. In systems of proportional representation, frequently encountered on the European continent, individuals represent primarily parties and not geographical areas.

The length of legislators' terms of office does have some effect on how they spend their time and how they perceive their jobs. The two-year terms for members of the House keep many members who have been elected by narrow margins constantly running for reelection, and this diverts them from their principal task of considering public policy. The longer term of the senator, combined with the larger size and greater heterogeneity of his constituency, may lead a senator to be a statesman for five years and a politician for one, hoping to curry favor with the electorate by more constituent-minded behavior as the election approaches.

President Johnson proposed in 1966 that the constitutional terms of office for members of the House be extended to four years with the terms to run concurrently with that of the President. The proposal was not seriously considered by Congress for a number of reasons—the most important being that most members of the House disliked increasing presidential influence by having to run only when he ran.[3]

---

[3] See Charles O. Jones, *Every Second Year: Congressional Behavior and the Two-Year Term*, Washington, D.C.: Brookings Institution, 1967.

The perquisites of office

Congressmen receive annual salaries in excess of $45,000, making them the best paid legislators in the world. The average member in addition receives fringe benefits that raise his salary effectively to $55,000. The average member of the House employs more than 10 persons on his personal staff at a cost of nearly $150,000 and with top salaries over $30,000. Senators maintain staffs ranging from 20 to nearly 100, at an annual cost ranging from $217,000 to $365,000; the size depends on the population of his state, committee staff members he may use, and sometimes on whether he is willing to spend his own money.

Members of Congress receive other perquisites including allowances for stationery, telephones, telegrams, travel, office rent in their home districts or states, the privilege of sending free mail exclusive of campaign literature to their constituents, free gymnasium, free medical service while at work, and subsidized services at the Capitol.

The perquisites of office for a congressman may seem more than ample. But seldom has the income of a congressman been sufficient to allow him to maintain his family adequately. He must maintain two residences, contribute to numerous worthy causes, and travel. Today, his is a full-time job, and the compensation should reflect his full-time duties.

The position of legislator has a widely varying character throughout the democratic world. In England, a member of the House of Commons is paid an annual salary of about $12,600. He has limited allowances for mail, telephone service, and secretarial assistance. The British have a fear of the "professional politician," and compensation is therefore deliberately kept at a low level. In France, a member of Parliament is paid a substantial salary, equal to that of the average highest civil-service class, although he spends only 5½ months in session.

HOW REPRESENTATIVE IS CONGRESS?

Method of representation

The Great Compromise of the Constitutional Convention basically provided equal representation for each state in one chamber and representation based on the proportion of the total population in the other chamber. New states, most recently Alaska and Hawaii, entered the Union on a completely equal basis, each receiving two senators and a proportional number of representatives. The result is that Alaska, having a population in 1970 of 304,000, has equal representation in the Senate with California, which had a population in 1970 of 20.1 million.

Reapportionment for the House of Representatives, unlike reapportionment and redistricting for state legislatures, is automatic and based on mathematical formula and reflects the decennial shifts of population. Thus

California, having 30 representatives in the 1950s, gained eight in the 1960s and five more in the 1970s for the largest delegation—43—in the nation. Other states, having had their proportion of the national population diminished, lost seats in Congress.

The politics of districting

State legislatures historically have had the responsibility for creating congressional districts. Some state legislatures have persistently ignored standards of compactness, contiguity, and equality of numbers, creating districts that were often political monstrosities. The glaring inequalities made the votes of some individuals far more important than those of others. For example, after the 1960 Census, the congressional district including Dallas, Texas, had a population of 951,527, and the 12th District in Michigan had a population of 177,431, making the vote in the 12th district worth 5.4 times more than that in Dallas.

The practical result was that the membership of the House of Representatives tended strongly to overrepresent the rural areas of the United States. These rural districts, being relatively homogeneous in population, tended to be "safe" districts in which one party tended to dominate from election to election. Representatives from these overrepresented districts thus could build up seniority in the House and increase their influence year by year. The heavily urban districts in the larger cities of the country were adequately represented simply because they began to lose population to the suburbs. It was in the latter category that the severest discrimination took place. These were the districts where party competition tended to be most intense, where either party might win a given election. Already disadvantaged by the malapportionment, the suburban districts also suffered because their representatives were less likely to develop long years of seniority.

Neither Congress nor state legislatures were willing to correct the situation until the Supreme Court in 1964 finally entered this political thicket and declared in the case of *Wesberry* v. *Sanders* that the provision of the U.S. Constitution that representatives should be chosen "by the people of the several states" meant that every citizen's vote should be of equal value. Under the watchful eyes of federal district courts, legislatures throughout the country drew up districting plans to achieve substantial equality. As cases came before the Supreme Court, it continued to insist on congressional districts as mathematically equal as possible, rejecting, for example, a total variance of the largest district to the smallest district in Missouri of 5.97 percent, and approving a variance of 0.159 percent in Texas. The Court appeared to reject such traditional justification of variations as geographical compactness, existing political boundaries, and population trends unless specifically justified.

Unfortunately, the emphasis on mathematical equality has left legislatures with golden opportunities for gerrymandering congressional districts. Using computers to calculate where boundaries should be drawn to maximize voter strength of the dominant party, legislatures have created congressional districts that divide communities on the one hand and on the other hand bring together widely separated areas in the same districts. The only type of gerrymandering specifically outlawed by the Supreme Court is that which is done for racial reasons—that is, to reduce the effective voting power of minority groups.

Impact of apportionment on the system of representation

In recent decades the Senate has been the more "liberal" of the two houses of Congress; that is, it has been more disposed to authorize and expand federal welfare programs and to impose controls over the economy. Senators represent entire states and therefore find within their constituencies a large assortment of conflicting interests, among which the senator must seek to strike a balance. In most states, urban interests, led by highly vocal groups that have the power of bloc voting, may be extremely influential. Organized labor and blacks in recent years have held this power and occasionally have used it effectively. The Senate is also a source of assistance to the relatively sparsely populated western states, whose equal representation in the Senate gives them disproportionate strength to bargain for favors for local mining, livestock, and agricultural interests.

The House has been the more conservative of the two chambers but in the future House districts will probably include more heterogeneous populations, and therefore be less dominated by single groups. There is some evidence, however, that the situation will benefit the Republican party, which tends to have the advantage in suburban districts. Outside the South, suburban Republicans tend to vote with their rural brethren, thus fragmenting the so-called urban vote. Thus the House may remain as relatively conservative as ever.

Many nations avoid the problems of apportionment and districting by adopting systems of proportional representation. Such systems do not require the establishment of districts, because the candidates usually run at large on party lists within a given electoral subdivision such as a province. The seats for each party are distributed roughly on the basis of the proportion of the total vote that each party received in that subdivision.

The recruitment process and membership in Congress

Despite the fact that nearly anyone is eligible for membership in Congress, only comparatively few have a serious chance of becoming candidates because the recruitment process in each district and state has its own bias.

In some areas, the dominant political machine controls nominations, and the likelihood of successfully challenging the machine is very small. In other areas, an interest group may be powerful in the nomination and electoral process. In still another, nominations may be free-for-all contests where sheer chance may play a greater role.

Three characteristics seem to be preferred by most voters in their candidates for Congress: (1) that they have previous political experience, (2) that they be lawyers, and (3) that they be incumbents. In 1975, 53 percent of the members of Congress were lawyers, 82 percent had had previous government service, either elective or appointive, and 89 percent were incumbents. In addition, such candidates have some natural advantages. Lawyers develop the political skills of debate and compromise and have a freedom to participate not permitted to salaried employees. Those with political experience, especially incumbents, have the advantage of being known to the public and the opportunity of using public office to gain higher public office.

For those seeking extreme change in society, Congress is not likely to be sympathetic. Men who have succeeded in the existing political system are older—the average age in 1975 was over 50—and are not likely to seek its radical transformation. Increasingly, membership in Congress is becoming a career, and this tends to isolate congressmen from the volatile forces in American life.

In terms of other broad population groups, Congress is both in some ways reasonably representative and in other ways very unrepresentative. Its numbers tend to reflect well the broad religious groupings in the United States—Catholics, Protestants, and Jews. Women are vastly underrepresented, having an all-time record of 19 in the 1975 session. Similarly, there were only 16 blacks in Congress in 1975.

Just how these background and constituency characteristics influence the way that legislators see their roles in Congress is not entirely clear, although one assumes they have some effect. A student of the Senate has classified senators in terms of their respect for the "folkways" of the Senate —the rules governing apprenticeship and respect for the rules of the institution—and has related their behavior to their backgrounds.[4] The two groups that he found to be most respectful of Senate traditions were the *patricians* and the *professionals*. The patricians are well-born, politicians by tradition, and seasoned veterans of politics when entering the Senate; the professionals rise from modest circumstances through political offices to the Senate. Together, these two classes form the ruling core of the Senate. *Amateurs,* on the other hand, "made it" in other walks of life, came to the Senate late in life, and found rules and traditions unwarranted impedi-

---

[4]Donald Matthews, *U.S. Senators and Their World,* New York: Vintage Books, 1960.

ments in seeking their goals. *Agitators,* elected by accident, are mavericks and are disdainful of all rules not to their liking.

A student of the House classified congressmen with respect to their orientation toward their districts and orientation toward the House as an institution.[5] Those coming from hotly contested, marginal districts tended to see themselves as delegates of their districts and spokesmen for their interests. Those from safer districts tended to emphasize the work of the House and service as trustees for national interests.

THE LAWMAKING FUNCTION

Representative assemblies did not begin as *legislatures* but as assemblies or *parliaments* consisting of representatives of the several privileged orders of medieval societies. They were places of discussion and consent, but not of lawmaking in the more direct and positive sense. The English Parliament today is still primarily a chamber for debate and discussion, especially with reference to the propositions laid before it by the Cabinet.

The American tradition diverged markedly from this pattern. In their contests with the royal governors, the colonial legislatures early asserted their supremacy over the executive and made their assertion effective in practice. This colonial experience established a strong tradition of legislative initiative, which has been an important element in the history of legislative-executive relations in this country. Article I of the Constitution begins by stating, "All legislative powers herein granted shall be vested in a Congress of the United States," and enumerates an extensive list of matters on which Congress is empowered to act. The Constitution subsequently involves the President in the lawmaking function through his obligation to send to Congress annually a message on the State of the Union and through his power to veto bills approved by Congress. Thus, from the very beginning, the Constitution provided the President *opportunity* for influence, but not the *substance* of influence itself. The substance would come when the circumstances required it.

In contrast with the conditions prevailing in the nineteenth century, both necessity and opportunity enhanced the role of the President in the twentieth century. Rather than reconciling diverse geographical interests, the political system took on a *national* focus. As the only elected national leader, the President was a natural agent in the formulation of national policy dealing with the economy. As the principal constitutional agent in foreign policy, he became the nation's leader in an area increasingly of concern to the public.

The function of Congress under these changed circumstances is debat-

---

[5]Roger H. Davidson, *The Role of the Congressman,* New York: Pegasus, 1969.

able with respect to both fact and value. While no one can gainsay the increased presidential role in policy-making, there can be little doubt that Congress remains a major alternative policy-initiator in the political system. In recent years, Congress has been the principal initiator of measures for the protection of the environment and expanded national health programs, and has challenged the President on crucial issues such as foreign trade and defense policies, and on domestic issues such as taxation and spending.

Consensus-building and legitimation

Although the President and his administration may claim to represent a numerical majority, there are innumerable individuals and groups whose more limited interests must be considered in the process of policy-making. It is generally agreed that Congress can usefully perform the function of conciliating the wide variety of individuals and groups that have a stake in federal policy. The final package—the result of intense bargaining—tends to reduce tensions among the conflicting groups in our society, and distribute the burdens and rewards in such a manner that no one group feels itself to be permanently disadvantaged. The problem is to ensure that all groups do get access to this process when a matter concerns their vital interests. Unfortunately, not all groups do have adequate access; the well-organized interest groups of business and labor unions are able to express their views very effectively, whereas the unorganized consumer groups and some ethnic minorities, often failing even to perceive their stake in a given policy, generally make little impact on Congress.

Congress performs its legitimation function when it represents the national community by approving policy and thus saying the policy is legal, right, and deserving of respect. The importance of the legitimation function may perhaps be best understood when Congress has failed to legitimize policy. Congressional attacks on Vietnam policy had much to do with undermining public support of that policy. Similarly, congressional opposition to the supersonic transport eventually created public opposition that resulted in the shelving of that project.

Providing funds

An integral part of the lawmaking function of Congress is its authority to determine the levels of spending of the national government. This it does through a series of annual appropriations bills that are handled by the appropriations committees of the two houses.

The President and his aides have tremendous influence, both in law and in practice. The President has the responsibility to deliver to Congress his estimates of the funds required to operate the government during the next year. The President and his principal advisers are aware of congressional attitudes on programs and spending levels, and in many respects they anticipate congressional reaction in putting together their spending packages. Nevertheless, the President determines the *basis* for discussion of expenditures in Congress.

The appropriations committees employ large staffs to examine the budget, but there are serious practical problems in attempting to understand and criticize a document running thousands of pages in length, and involving more than $350 billion, within a period of six months. Congress, therefore, resorts to various devices to simplify its task: increasing or decreasing amounts by percentages, accepting last year's budget and examining only requests for new funds, or giving an agency a "fair share" of the funds available.[6] The result is that Congress occasionally increases some amounts, but it usually cuts the budget, particularly in the case of relatively unpopular programs such as foreign aid. The overall budget seldom differs very much from what the President requests.

In 1974 Congress took a major step toward strengthening its role in overall budget policy through the creation of budget committees in both houses. These committees are designed to force Congress to examine the total impact of its appropriations on the economy and to reduce expenditures or increase taxes in accordance with agreed-upon spending levels. An ambitious reform, these committees may make Congress both a strong and responsible partner with the President in fiscal policy.

THE REPRESENTATIVE FUNCTION

Perhaps the most readily agreed-upon function attributed to members of legislatures is that of "representing" the interests of the people who elected them. But the concept of representation is a complicated one, involving both the attitudes and expectations of those who represent and those who are represented.

Relationships to the electorate

In electing a legislator, the voters may consider him to be a *delegate*, sent to Congress to undertake the accomplishment of certain objectives that are of great local interest. The available evidence, however, indicates that the electorate is not well informed regarding the candidate or the positions he has taken on the issues. In a study of the voters in several constituencies where a Republican candidate sought a congressional seat held by a Democrat, less than one voter in five knew something about both candidates, and more than half knew nothing about either. The usual comments about the

---

[6]See Aaron Wildavsky, *The Politics of the Budgetary Process*, Boston: Little, Brown, 1964.

candidates were such vague evaluations as "He's a good man," or "He understands our problems." Their formulations are in terms of general aims of government and how far government should go in achieving certain goals. Furthermore, three out of five voters appear to believe that a congressman should vote on the basis of his own judgment. In a sense, he is considered a *trustee* for their interests.

Even when the legislator makes a positive effort to know what his constituents desire, it is not always feasible to discover it. National opinion polls may have little relevance to his district. Only people who have some ax to grind may volunteer their views. There may be large numbers of people directly or indirectly affected by a given legislative issue who may not have perceived their involvement and who may therefore have failed to register their opinions. The representative will read his mail attentively, visit with various opinion leaders in his district, read his district's newspapers avidly, and still be unable to discern clearly the nature of constituent opinion.

Much depends on the congressman's perception of his role with regard to the constituency. Should he think of the interest of his district or of the nation? Most congressmen act both ways, depending on the issue, and they are often very sophisticated about how these roles can be played. On civil-rights issues, for example, congressmen are inclined to follow the dominant opinions of their constituency. It is hard to conceive, for example, of a representative from Harlem not voting for civil-rights legislation, and it is equally hard to conceive of a "black belt" congressman from Mississippi voting for it. On foreign-policy issues, they feel free to act more independently; on social-welfare issues, they are somewhere in between.

Determinants of congressional voting

The most important thing members of Congress do is vote, and the most reliable predictor of congressional voting behavior is party affiliation. Both in and out of Congress, the legislator identifies himself with his partisan colleagues, receives the benefit of their political and personal support, and fears the withdrawal of that support if he fails to "play ball." All of these factors propel him in the direction of the central tendency of his party. American parties are not highly disciplined either outside or inside the legislature, so they cannot compel acceptance of the party position. The fact that Senator Clifford Case (Republican, New Jersey) finds his voting record corresponding to the voting record of a middle-of-the-road Democrat, and that Senator John Stennis (Democrat, Mississippi) finds his voting record corresponding to the voting record of a middle-of-the-road Republican, indicates the divergence that is tolerated in the two parties.

In the period from 1968 to 1974, Democrats and Republicans tended by a margin of nearly three to one to vote with their partisan colleagues on issues on which a majority of one party opposed a majority of the other. In only one out of four cases did they vote in opposition to a majority of their own party.

Voting studies of congressmen suggest that much depends on the nature of the constituencies. In highly competitive districts—where either party stands a good chance of having its candidate elected—there is a tendency for the representative to take moderate positions on the issues. He "hedges his bets" by avoiding extremes, since his constituency tends to consist of highly diverse groupings of individuals with widely differing values and interests. On the other hand, the congressman from the "safe" district usually tends to represent a relatively homogeneous constituency and tends to vote its dominant interests, partly because its interests are more easily known. Similarly, representatives of districts that are "typical" of their party, that is, having similar social and economic groups within them, tend to vote with their party more than those whose districts are more typical of those of the opposition party.

How congressmen promote constituent interests

Not only must a congressman or senator decide how to vote, he must also find ways of using his position to advance the interests of his constituents. One approach is to find a strategic position in the legislature, especially a favorable committee assignment, where he may be influential. A congressman from a rural district may try to obtain a place on the agriculture committee; a representative from an urban, working-class district may look for a place on the education and labor committees. He may try to locate a spot for himself on some of the more prestigious committees having broad legislative authority, such as the Ways and Means Committee in the House of Representatives or the appropriations committee in either house.

By careful preparation, by "doing his homework," by winning reelection several times, he may become recognized as a leader on given types of legislation affecting his district and thus be able to promote its interests markedly. The large number of military bases in Georgia is not attributable solely to its favorable climate and topography, but rather to the fact that for many years the armed services committees of both Senate and House were chaired by Georgians.

Much of the representative's time is spent in responding to specific requests for assistance from individuals, public officials, and interest groups back home. These range from requests from students for help in writing term papers to requests from cities or interest groups for aid in negotiating with an administrative agency.

The voters base their requests on the correct assumption that the congressman speaks with a louder voice than does the individual citizen who seeks some favor or redress from an administrative agency. Thus when a citizen complains that he has not received his social-security check, the congressman can ascertain the reason for the delay in relatively short order. And if discretionary authority is necessary to determine whether the citizen is entitled to those checks, he has a "friend in court" to plead his case. These types of cases are handled routinely by staffs that have developed considerable skill in processing them.

Less routine are statewide or districtwide matters that involve decisions that can affect the welfare of thousands of people. Thus a decision of the Department of Defense to close military establishments in various parts of the country threatens the income and livelihood of many citizens. The congressman is called upon to demonstrate to Defense Department officials the importance of the specific base to the country's defense effort. Seldom would the congressman threaten reprisals for failure to receive favorable consideration for the plight of the people in his district, but the executive official may be aware of the weapons available to the congressman if he does not have a sympathetic hearing.

Members of Congress undertake most services with alacrity and conviction, because they recognize that they are performing services for individuals and groups who may have legitimate grievances with administrative agencies and because the performance of these chores creates goodwill at home and identifies them as someone who "can get something done in Washington." Presumably, this pays off at election time. On the other hand, they also recognize that such demands on their time and attention mean that they cannot dedicate sufficient time to informing themselves about the nation's problems.

THE OVERSIGHT FUNCTION

Closely related to Congress's legislative and representative functions is the function of checking on and exercising control over the administrative agencies that carry out its will as expressed in legislation or resolution. Each congressional committee has the responsibility to exercise "oversight," or to maintain close surveillance over the activities of agencies subject to its legislative jurisdiction. Having granted discretionary authority, congressional committees hold administrators accountable for following their intentions through hearings, committee reports, debate, and private conversations.

For the most part, these inquiries are conducted quietly, the purpose being to achieve significant improvements in administrative methods and to obtain additional information that provides the basis for remedial legislation when required. The performance by administrative officials, especially before appropriations subcommittees, establishes a kind of rough "rating" on the agency and its chief personnel.

In England and in many continental European countries, the scrutiny of administrative behavior occurs principally through question periods in Parliament or the practice of *interpellation.* In each case, the Cabinet minister appears before the entire chamber for questioning on matters relating to the conduct of business in his department. Under interpellation a debate may ensue, even to the point of taking votes on the chamber's support of the policy in question. Although interpellation has been repeatedly recommended by various observers for adoption in the United States, it has never found favor.

The informing function

Congress has an obligation to keep the country informed regarding the pressing issues of society. Critics, however, point to the uninspiring debates in the chambers of Congress and to the inadequate manner in which they are reported in the press and on radio and television.

The critics, however, tend to overlook the occasional effectiveness of Congress in floor debate and the continuous performance of Congress in its committees. Extended debate has often led to significant changes in public policy, and these debates have been widely reported in the press. Similarly, extended congressional hearings have provided a wealth of ammunition for both sides in the public debate over both foreign and domestic policy. Perhaps the most dramatic example was the televised hearings conducted by the Senate Foreign Relations Commission on the Vietnam war during the late 1960's. Those opposed to the war were able to obtain a forum for their views almost equal to that of the President, and certainly equal to that of the Secretary of State.

Formal parliamentary debates in England and in most Commonwealth countries are given wide publicity and therefore help to stimulate the debate itself. In Australia, for example, debates in the national legislature are broadcast. The serious press in England reports the parliamentary debates in considerable detail and provides the focus of political discussion in that country. The reason for the difference may be that the Prime Minister and Cabinet sit in Parliament and thus force debate, and that the attention of the British citizen is not distracted by state politics.

Congressional studies and investigations

Less spectacular than hearings oriented toward specific policy proposals are inquiries conducted by congressional committees for the purpose of gathering information that may be used in dealing with policy issues later. Thus the House Committee on Science and Astronautics conducts an annual seminar on some social problem to which science might address itself and invites leading political, scientific, and academic figures to testify and to discuss these matters. The Joint Economic Committee, since it has no legislative authority, has no other purpose than to conduct studies and make policy recommendations.

As an instrument of "informing," Congress has yet to find a method as effective as the congressional investigation, perhaps because of the tendency of investigating committees to search for "good guys" and "bad guys" in any affair under scrutiny. These investigations at times take on the characteristics of trials, and they excite all the interest that normally attaches to a trial when an individual's life, liberty, or property may be at stake.

The most spectacular congressional investigation of recent decades was the Senate investigation of the Watergate burglary and the subsequent efforts to cover it up by President Nixon and his chief aides. Its hearings were televised daily and the cast of characters included virtually every high official of the White House, several Cabinet members, and Republican party officials. These hearings were full of drama and showed that a congressional investigation can be carried on with dignity and respect for law.

It is generally conceded that Congress has, and should have, the power to investigate in order to inform itself and the nation regarding problems possibly requiring legislative action. The reservations held by many concern the extent of congressional authority when it threatens, through exposure for the sake of exposure, the rights guaranteed to the individual by the First, Fourth, and Fifth Amendments to the Constitution.

Decisions of the Supreme Court and actions by the House of Represensatives have rectified some of the worst abuses of the past. The purpose of the investigations must be demonstrably relevant to a legislative purpose of Congress, witnesses are allowed to have counsel, and under certain circumstances testimony may be taken in executive session.

In England, the Royal Commissions of Inquiry, appointed by the Crown and consisting of experts or prominent public men, study problems and make reports. Their procedures are dignified and sober and in sharp contrast with the conditions often prevailing in congressional investigations. Recent presidential commissions to investigate civil disorders, violence, pornography, and drugs suggest one major alternative to congressional investigations.

Advise and consent

Congressional control of administration is strengthened in another way: through the powers granted to the Senate to advise on, and consent to, treaties and appointments of officers of the government. In each case, the power of the Senate generally lies not in any open, formal exercise of this power, but in the threat of its use unless the administration consults on matters that are likely to be controversial.

Treaties. With regard to treaties—which require the approval of two-thirds of the senators present—much of what might formerly have been handled by treaty is now dealt with by means of executive agreements and through legislative actions implementing foreign economic policy. These actions require authorization by a regular legislative bill and appropriations through the normal funding procedures. Furthermore, the President is frequently given blanket authorization to take certain actions in foreign policy. One example of this is the Vietnam resolution of 1964, which authorized him to "take all necessary measures to repel any armed attack against the forces of the United States and to prevent further aggression." Treaties are still important instruments of policy-making, however. One notable recent treaty, the Nuclear Nonproliferation Treaty, banned the transfer by nuclear powers of nuclear weapons and devices to countries not having nuclear capability.

Since Woodrow Wilson failed to consult with senators on the Treaty of Versailles and thereby doomed the League of Nations, presidents have been careful to keep senators informed regarding negotiations and have even included them in the process of formulating international agreements. The presence of senators at the San Francisco conference to create the United Nations and their continued presence on UN delegations is a testament to this experience.

Appointments. Appointments require the approval of a simple majority of the senators, and those who are nominated usually have advance senatorial approval. If a serious fight develops between the Senate and the President over a nomination, either someone has seriously miscalculated the attitude of the Senate or the President is willing to risk a defeat. Presidents are seldom defeated, but the occasional instances confirm the reality of senatorial power.

But few nominations raise such political ire. Senators recognize it as a prerogative of the President to select his own team of officials, even while pressing upon him the credentials of some other individual. Most presidents are not averse to acceding to senatorial recommendations, because they recognize them as coin of the political realm that can be called upon when they need credit. Over certain categories of federal offices, however, such as district court judges, marshals, district attorneys, and in some instances heads of federal field offices, senators of the President's party do claim some control. If they are not accorded deference they may ask their Senate colleagues to join them in rejecting the presidential candidates according to the custom of "senatorial courtesy." This custom dictates that senators will decline to approve a candidate who is "personally obnoxious" to a senator from the candidate's state. In doing so, the senators protect their colleague against the possibility of contrary factional elements developing within his own state.

Judicial functions

In the past decade Congress has revived judicial powers that had appeared to be dead letters in the constitutional charter. The power of impeachment, while occasionally discussed abstractly, had not been used against a President since the trial of Andrew Johnson in 1868 and against a judge since 1936. Until the impeachment proceedings against President Nixon, there had been only 12 impeachments in American history. Of these, 11 went to trial, with seven acquitted and four convicted.

The Constitution provides that a President, Vice-President, and all civil officers may be removed from office on impeachment for and conviction of "treason, bribery, or other high crimes and misdemeanors." The House of Representatives draws up and approves articles of impeachment by a majority vote and the Senate tries the accused, with a two-thirds vote required for conviction. While treason and bribery have reasonably precise meanings, "other high crimes and misdemeanors" are less well defined. As stated by President Ford, when as House Republican leader in 1970 he pressed for impeachment of Justice William O. Douglas,

> *an impeachable offense may be whatever a majority of the House of Representatives considers it to be at a given moment in history; conviction results from whatever offense or offenses two-thirds of the other body considers to be sufficiently serious to require removal of the accused from office.*

In the case of the effort to impeach President Nixon in 1974, however, it appears that the members of the House Judiciary Committee took a much more restrained view. The articles of impeachment charged that Nixon

1. Engaged in a course of conduct or plan designed to "delay, impede and obstruct the investigation" of unlawful entry at Democratic National Headquarters; and to "cover up, conceal, and protect those responsible" and "to conceal the existence and scope of other unlawful covert activities."
2. Abused his powers with respect to Internal Revenue Service records, unlawful surveillance of citizens, and misuse of federal investigative agencies.
3. Failed to produce records in response to congressional subpoenas.

The committee approved these articles in preparation for a final House vote. Further revelations of the President's complicity in the Watergate cover-up led to his immediate resignation, precluding further action by the House or Senate on the articles of impeachment.

The two houses of Congress also have the responsibility for judging the qualifications of their own members, i.e., to decide whether to exclude or expel a member. Only 13 times in American history have the two bodies taken such action, with the last instance occurring in 1967 when the House of Representatives excluded Adam Clayton Powell. He was, however, re-elected, and the Supreme Court decided that the House had unconstitutionally excluded him. In 18 instances the House and Senate have expelled members; in virtually all cases expulsion was for support of rebellion in the Civil War, and none has been expelled since that time.

CONGRESSIONAL ORGANIZATION: FORMAL AND INFORMAL

Congress is a problem-solving place, and it is therefore necessary to develop rules and customs to keep inevitable conflict within reasonable bounds. The ritualistic character of congressional procedure may be explained in part by the fact that each member has equal standing in the chamber. He is elected by his own constituency and owes his presence to the voters, not to his colleagues in Congress. Having independent political support, he therefore expects the same deference from his colleagues that he is prepared to give to them. This deference manifests itself in innumerable ways: in respect for the rights of the others in debate, in accommodation in scheduling consideration of bills, and in defense of a colleague under attack by a common opponent, such as the executive.

Because serving in Congress tends to be a permanent career for many of its members, there is deep concern for the maintenance of the institution itself and the traditions it embodies. One tradition emphasizes hard legislative work and attention to the business of each chamber; failure to follow this tradition imposes large burdens on the rest of the legislature. Another tradition is respect for seniority and its reverse: patient service during a quiet apprenticeship. Since most members seldom have opportunities to realize higher ambitions, longevity becomes a basis for advancement and respect.

These rules are enforced subtly and effectively by the congressional "establishment,"[7] which usually controls committee assignments, perquisites such as space, and opportunities for travel and for conducting investigations. Legislators who enter Congress with strong ideological commitments or a sense of personal mission to remake society often find the system oppressive and deserving of radical change. Moreover, the "outsider," the maverick, the individualist may equally well reflect his own constituency and may make proportionate contributions to the legislative product through agitation and dissent. The contributions of men such as Congressman Wilbur Mills of Arkansas and Senator George McGovern of South Dakota are different, but who is to say which is more valuable? It should be noted also that membership in the "establishment" is neither an automatic disqualifica-

---

[7] See William S. White, *Citadel*, New York: Harper & Row, 1956; and Joseph S. Clark, *The Senate Establishment*, New York: Harper & Row, 1964.

tion nor an advantage in moving upward. Both John F. Kennedy, who was not a member, and Lyndon Johnson, who was, became Presidents.

Differential access to congressional power

The formal organization of Congress, its internal distribution of power, and its procedures provide unequal access to congressional power. Some groups, regions, and administrative agencies have preferential opportunities for influence.

To illustrate, the agriculture committees of both the Senate and House have jurisdiction over legislation dealing with all phases of agriculture and forestry. The membership of these committees consists almost exclusively of representatives of the food- and fiber-producing areas of the United States, chiefly from the Midwest and the South. Since Congress does its real legislative work at the committee level, the crucial decisions on agricultural legislation are made by those who have a direct interest and stake in these matters. Agricultural policy, however, concerns not only the producers of farm products, but also the consumers, processors, distributors, and taxpayers, who are not represented at the committee stage and thus are seriously disadvantaged. If they find agricultural legislation not to their liking, they must make an effort to block it on the floor of the chamber, where the weight of tradition and of parliamentary procedure is very much against them.

Differential access is further demonstrated by the fact that the South has traditionally returned its elected representatives term after term, resulting in a disproportionate number of southerners occupying committee chairmanships when the Democrats control Congress. From these vantage points, southern interests have been advanced or protected whenever the Democrats are in power. The power of Senator James Eastland of Mississippi in obstructing or slowing down consideration of civil-rights legislation from his position as chairman of the Senate Judiciary Committee is a dramatic example of a relatively common phenomenon.

The role of party

The fundamental principle in the organization of the Congress is party, with the Democrats and Republicans uniformly lining up with their partisan colleagues in contesting for control. The party that gains a majority in the House of Representatives, for example, can rest assured that it will control the leadership positions in the House. Through control of these positions, the party has the means to manage effectively the machinery of the two houses for whatever purposes the majority party agrees upon. But there is the rub—getting agreement.

American political parties are characterized by their lack of internal discipline and their inability to bring together the many diverse factions that are within them. Thus the majority party, although in nominal control of the machinery of the two houses, seldom can exhibit sufficient unity to agree on every program and to implement it. Fortunately or unfortunately, the minority party normally manifests similar unseemly divisions in its ranks and thereby presents the perfect setting for "coalition politics": Factions in each of the parties coalesce to form roadblocks to action until a bargain is struck among the contending interests. Unless one party has extraordinary majorities, as was the case during the 1975 session of Congress, the leadership must bargain with potential supporters, using whatever enticements or threats seem suitable, in order to build its majority. This results in "back-scratching," a practice that is much condemned but widely used, in which members of the legislature trade votes on issues that are of vital interest to some but of lesser consequence to others.

The most enduring example of this factionalism is the southern wing of the Democratic party. Not only on issues of race but also on questions such as government spending, federal-state relations, and foreign trade the southern Democrats have often found themselves in opposition to their northern colleagues. Because of the strategic positions that the southerners occupy in committee chairmanships, their influence over policy decisions far exceeds their numerical strength.

Nevertheless, given the organization of Congress and the ties between the legislator and his party in the constituency, the opinion of a majority within a party is still the single most influential force in Congress. The congressman was elected in a partisan campaign, usually with formal party support, which normally involves some financial assistance; he probably identifies with his party because of some ideological affinity; when he arrives in Congress, he is immediately introduced to members of his own party, and he continues to associate with them; he is physically separated from the opposition on the floor of the chamber; and he is often subjected to partisan appeals by those with whom he works. If the White House is occupied by a President of his party, he may find himself the object of considerable persuasion if not outright arm-twisting by the chief executive and his emissaries.

All of this means that the party has an important, but not always decisive, role in Congress. Other "reference groups" are significant to the congressman: large national interests with which he may identify, or local groups in his own constituency. When the pull of the other groups is powerful, he may ignore the dominant opinion in his party and vote with the opposition, absent himself, or vote to eviscerate the bill.

Such laxity in party discipline is almost unheard of elsewhere, except in France. Failure to support the party position even once on a major issue might be sufficient grounds for expulsion from the party in many European countries. In part, this is explained by the importance of ensuring parliamentary support for the government. If the government in Britain, for example, loses a vote in Parliament, there is almost automatically a call for a new election. Members of the majority are under heavy pressure to avoid such an occurrence.

Whatever the merits of such systems, they are inconceivable in the American context. The continental nature of our republic, the traditional alliances of region and party, the complex array of interest groups, and the lack of interdependence between the chief executive and the Congress all militate against such a disciplined party system. Modest efforts to reform the system along more ideological or programmatic lines may prove successful, but it is more likely that increased party cohesion, if it comes to pass, will reflect more profound changes in the economic and social structure of the United States.[8]

THE AGENTS OF LEADERSHIP

Power in Congress is decentralized and therefore leadership is shared. Moreover, leadership is of a special kind, emphasizing arts of compromise, avoidance of open dictation, and subtle inducements and penalties. Leadership roles are shared among the elected leaders, the committee or seniority leaders, and the informal leaders who lead by the personal qualities they exhibit.

The elected leaders

Elected leaders of the two houses of Congress owe their positions to the selections made by the caucuses of the two parties in each house. Thus the House caucuses choose candidates for the speakership, majority leader, whips, and leadership of such party organs as policy and campaign committees. In strict party-line voting, the candidates of the majority party take the formal leadership positions with the minority party candidates taking on roles as minority leaders. Similarly, the parties choose their majority and minority leadership in the Senate.

Historically, the Speaker of the House has been on occasion a virtual dictator of the House. In the present era, however, the Speaker derives his influence from the prestige of his office, his personal influence resulting

---

[8] But there are limits to violation of party support, as two Democratic congressmen discovered in 1965. Both were from the South and both had openly supported the candidacy of Senator Barry Goldwater for the presidency. The Democratic caucus voted to strip them of their seniority rights on their committees. One resigned and was immediately reelected as a Republican. In 1969, House Democrats stripped Congressman John Rarick (Democrat, La.) of his seniority for supporting George Wallace in the 1968 presidential campaign.

from many years of experience in the House, and effective use of certain formal powers such as his power to recognize members to speak and make motions, to interpret and apply the rules, and to refer bills to committees. Even with regard to these rules, his discretion is severely circumscribed by precedent. He is a very influential man, however, especially on committee assignments and scheduling of legislation. He is deferred to by both members and people outside the House who want the House to act favorably in their cause.

The leadership in the Senate is similarly dependent on a combination of formal and informal power. The Senate majority leader must bargain with the chairmen of the standing committees, who have powerful claims to the loyalty of the members because of the rules of specialization. As with the Speaker, the influence of the majority leader varies with the character of the officeholder. Senator Mike Mansfield, the successor to Lyndon Johnson, prefers to lead by quiet and patient consultation rather than by maneuver and personality, as did his predecessor.

Other instruments of leadership in the two houses consist of the majority leader of the House, the assistant majority leaders, and the whips. They lead by controlling the lines of communication in the chambers and through the development of the legislative program. They are in constant contact with the Speaker (in the House) and with the committee chairmen, ascertaining their intentions, counseling urgency or delay, as they attempt to establish the working schedule for the chamber. They work closely with the President and his agents in attempting to implement the President's program, when the Congress and the presidency are controlled by the same party.

Minority leaders perform essentially the same functions for their membership, although they have no formal responsibility for planning the program of the Senate or House. They are vital cogs in the machinery of the two houses, because so much of the business of the two houses is carried on by unanimous consent. Particularly in the Senate, where there is no limitation on debate, either on motions to take up bills or on the bills themselves, acceptable arrangements with the minority must be made. The mutual respect that the leaders of both parties develop for each other over the years ensures that the legislative process will function with a minimum of acrimony and foot-dragging.

The committee system of Congress

The fact that Congress is a legislative body and not merely a debating society requires that it organize itself to deliberate over proposals. The nature of lawmaking is too exacting and complex to permit consideration of more than the major features of the legislation during debate on the floor of the chambers. The tedious struggle over the purposes, the means, and the language of legislation must be left to smaller bodies—the committees and subcommittees of Congress—where members can develop expertise and therefore be in a position to make informed judgments on legislative proposals. Of the 10,000 or more bills introduced each year, only a small fraction receive serious committee consideration.

When legislative proposals are reported to the entire body of the Senate or the House of Representatives, there is a presumption that relevant alternatives have been studied, technical problems have been eliminated, and significant issues have been carefully examined. The entire membership is then prepared to make its decision on the desirability of that specific proposal, but is seldom prepared to rewrite the legislation on the floor of the chamber.

It is clear that there are mutual sets of expectations on the part of the committee members, the total membership of each house, and the clientele groups that have a stake in committee actions. The Appropriations Committee of the House, for example, is expected to finance the government economically; to oversee the expenditures by executive agencies; to follow consensus-building procedures that ensure that all sides have been heard and all conflicts ironed out; to avoid legislating as distinct from appropriating; and to keep the House informed.[9] In return, the Appropriations Committee expects, and usually receives, deference to its judgment and relative autonomy in the way it carries out its business.

The House Education and Labor Committee, because of the controversial nature of the legislation coming before it, has been a constant battleground organized along relatively strict party lines and with interest-group lobbyists playing major roles. Incapable of solving the hot political issues within the committee, the committee members more frequently than not bring their fights out on the floor of the House, with pitched battles ensuing. Failure to resolve issues internally means that the Education and Labor Committee seldom inspires confidence in House members, and all of its proposals are carefully scrutinized on the floor.

Committees of Congress are not of equal importance. Some committees year after year handle legislation of crucial importance while others have extremely limited jurisdictions or are "housekeeping" in nature. In both houses, the committees dealing chiefly with financing the government and public expenditures—the Senate Finance Committee and House Ways and Means Committee and the two committees on appropriations—rank highest in significance and in status among congressmen. The Senate Foreign Relations Committee, the House Rules Committees, and the Armed Services and Judiciary Committees also rank very high. At the other end are the committees dealing with administration of the legislative bodies, the District of Columbia, and veterans' affairs.

[9]Richard F. Fenno, Jr., *Congressmen in Committees*, Boston: Little, Brown, 1973.

Membership on the committees is allocated to the two parties in accordance, roughly, with the proportion of membership of each party in the entire chamber. Thus the overwhelming Democratic majorities in 1975 were reflected in 2–1 majorities in each committee. The committees on committees within each party attempt to meet both the demands of balanced representation on the committees and the wishes of the individual member to serve on committees that rank high in the hierarchy of committees or that affect his district. Control over these appointments, usually well within the orbit of party leadership influence, provides the party leaders with great bargaining power over new members who are hoping for congressional careers.

Committee staff. Among the most important aides to congressmen are the professional staffs of the committees, which are gradually growing in number and professionalism. A 1975 decision by the Democratic caucus permitted each committee to employ 42 persons, with 26 asigned to the majority party and 16 to the minority. On some committees, however, the staff members are so thoroughly professional that they all serve members of the committee irrespective of party. Where staff members achieve such competence and where they are used effectively by the members of the committee, they are an invaluable resource in providing Congress with alternative approaches to policy.

Chairmanships and the seniority rule. One of the most controversial features of congressional organization and procedure is the rule of seniority. This rule provides that the chairmanship of the committee automatically goes to that member of the majority party who has served the longest continuous period *on the committee*. The status of each member is rigidly determined by the length of his continuous service, and one can hope to achieve chairmanship only by outlasting the other members of his party and by the providence of his party winning a majority in that chamber.

The chairmanship confers both prestige and power over the members of the committee and the fate of legislation that is referred to it. It affords the chairman the opportunity to be an autocrat or a democrat, according to his own personal inclinations. Specifically, the chairman appoints chairmen and members of subcommittees, and thereby determines the extent to which individual members of the committee can make their imprint felt on legislation and their names known to the public. He chairs committee meetings and can affect the fate of bills by his rulings on procedure. Moreover, his long experience gives him status to which the other members usually defer. Outside the committee, the chairman often carries the main responsibility during floor debate and in conference committee.

The seniority rule favors those who have the highest likelihood of returning to Congress after each election, that is, those who come from safe districts. Thus when the Democrats control Congress, the chairmanships have tended to go to congressmen and senators from the southern states. When the Republicans are in control, the chairmanships have tended to fall into the hands of members from the strongholds of rural Republicanism in the Midwest. In both cases, it is argued, the committees are dominated by men, often extremely old, who are least responsive to the trends of contemporary political life. The liberal members of both parties therefore must struggle mightily to overcome a decided disadvantage in promoting legislation to their liking.

With the convening of the 1975 session of Congress and under the influence of a sweeping Democratic victory that brought 92 new members into the House, the seniority system suffered its most telling defeat in over 50 years. The Democratic caucus took the authority to name committee members from the Democratic membership of the Ways and Means Committee and gave it to a newly created Steering and Policy Committee. This committee tends to reflect House leadership and broad membership more effectively. The result was action by the caucus to strip four chairmen—all southerners—of their positions and to replace them with high-ranking but not always second-ranking members of the committees. The reasons for removing the particular chairmen varied: advanced age and inability to lead; arbitrary and unresponsive behavior; major policy differences; irrational behavior. The Democratic caucus claimed the right to name even subcommittee chairmen of the Appropriations Committee. In the Senate, the Democrats adopted a rule that allows a secret ballot on committee chairmen whenever one-fifth of the members of the caucus request it.

Two lessons seem clear. Committee chairmen are no longer secure in their positions if they fail to provide leadership that responds to the wishes of the members of the committees themselves, for most of the dissatisfaction was expressed by those committee members. Secondly, the seniority rule was only modified, not rejected. In most cases, second-ranking members were chosen to replace the chairmen. Long uninterrupted service on committees would still appear necessary for committee leadership.

Defense of the seniority rule stresses the need for experienced men with long acquaintance with the problems of the agencies with which they have to deal, with the rules of the Congress, and with the substantive issues that arise. Furthermore, it is argued that the automatic rule avoids divisive struggles over committee leadership that many other methods would invite. Finally, it is contended that the generalized description of chairmen as dictators and mossbacks misses the mark by far. Many of the chairmen are extremely permissive, and many of the chairmen from the South, far from being conservative and out of step, are progressives, such as Senator John Sparkman of Alabama (chairman of the Senate Foreign Relations Committee), or at least reasonable party men, such as Congressman George Mahon of Texas (chairman of the House Appropriations Committee).

The committee system of the British Parliament stands in sharp contrast to that of Congress. Committees in Parliament are not specialized, but deal with all types of legislation. Members are appointed each session, but the membership may change as the issue changes. Cabinet ministers carefully guide the committees in their deliberations. Parliamentary committees help the Cabinet, but do not pretend to rival it. The American political system, by contrast, aims at dispersing power as much as possible, making unified leadership difficult and at times impossible.

THE LEGISLATIVE PROCESS

Legislative success depends not only on the intrinsic merits of proposals but also on good strategy, adequate resources, and to some extent good fortune. Dedication to the end sought is important, but equally important are flexibility and willingness to compromise.

The origin of legislation is complex. In a technical sense, congressmen are authors of bills and can rely on the technical and research services of legislative counsels, committee staffs, and the Congressional Research Service of the Library of Congress in preparing bills. But the content of legislation is usually the result of a long process of negotiation that may include administrative officials, private interest groups, university professors, and state and local units of government. The bill introduced may be a compromise between what interested groups want and what they think they can get out of Congress.

Illustrative of this process is the history of legislation dealing with health and medical services. President Truman in 1949 made the first determined but unsuccessful bid for passage of a prepaid medical-insurance program for all persons. A movement begun in 1957 to incorporate medical care for the aged within the social-security system resulted in 1960 in an act providing for grants to the states to help pay for medical care for the "medically indigent" and in 1965 in Medicare, a program based on the social security program. With medical and hospital costs soaring, the movement for a federally sponsored medical program for all citizens is generating considerable support. In this political process, important roles are played by presidents, administrators in the Department of Health, Education, and Welfare, individual congressmen, committees and their staffs, and private organizations such as the American Medical Association and the American Hospital Association.

The rules of Congress

The rules of Congress naturally impose some constraints on strategy. The Constitution requires all revenue bills to originate in the House of Representatives, and by tradition all appropriations bills also originate in the House. This makes the House the principal battleground for these measures,

HOW A BILL BECOMES A LAW

Legislation Usually Begins as Similar Proposals in Both Houses

Introduction

HR-1 Education Problem → Introduced in House

S-2 Education Problem → Introduced in Senate

Committee Action

Referred to Committee—Committee Holds Hearings and Recommends Passage (House)

Referred to Committee—Committee Holds Hearings and Recommends Passage (Senate)

Floor Action

House Debates and Passes

Senate Debates and Passes

All Bills Must Go Through Both Houses Before They Reach the President

House and Senate Committee Members Confer—Reach Compromise

House and Senate Approve Compromise

Enactment into Law

President Signs Bill into Law

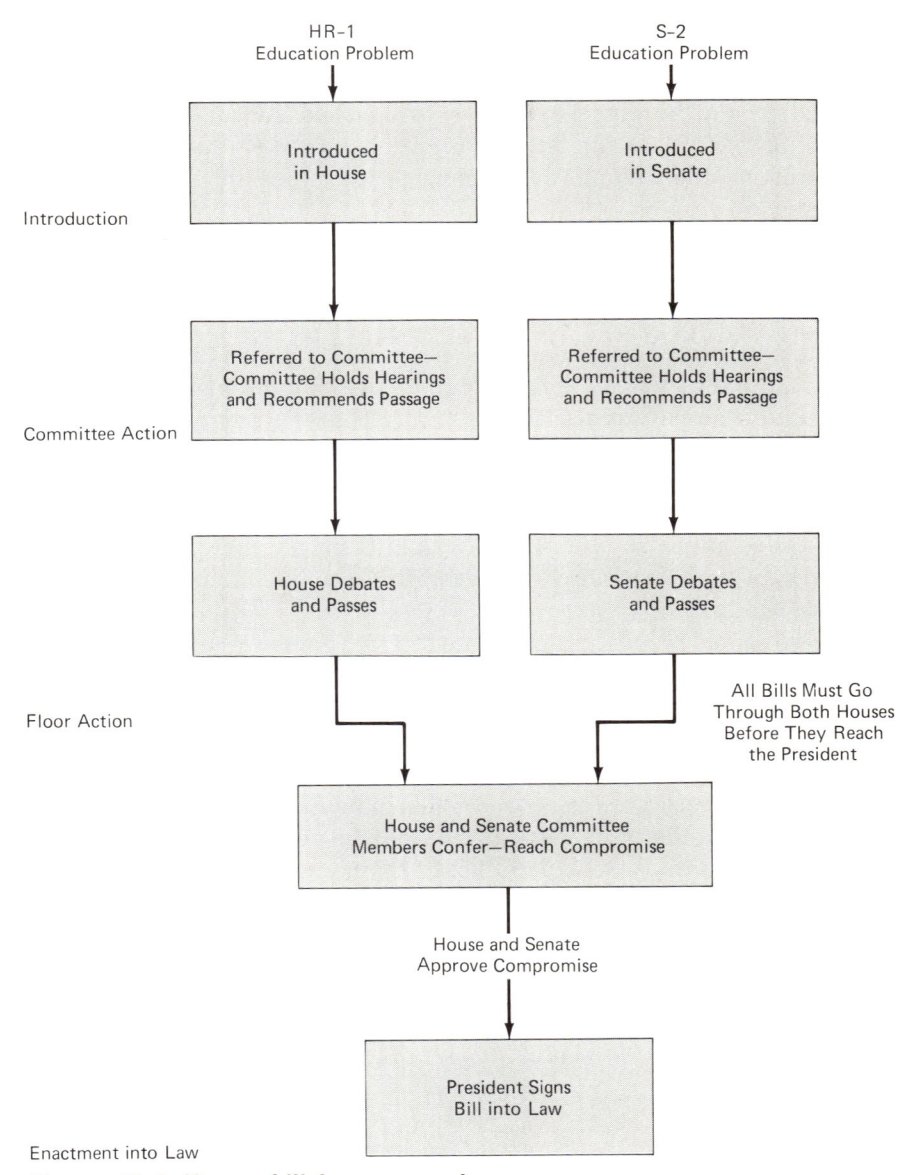

Figure 13–1 *How a bill becomes a law*

with the Senate serving as a kind of appeal body. The rules largely dictate which committees will consider certain bills, although some discretion is left in the hands of the presiding officers. Occasionally this discretion may prove important, as in the passage of the 1964 Civil Rights Act. The legislation was written to emphasize the power of Congress to regulate interstate commerce and thus provided justification for referring the act to both the Interstate and Foreign Commerce Committee and the Judiciary Committee of the Senate. Since the latter committee was likely to bury such legislation, reference to the Commerce Committee made possible hearings and a favorable committee report.

Committee deliberations

Committee proceedings normally are undertaken at two levels: public hearings and staff investigations. Hearings provide opportunities for the administration, interest groups, members of Congress, subject-matter experts, and sometimes even crackpots to express themselves on legislation. For the members of the committee, hearings are useful in establishing a record and in exploring possible areas of compromise among contending parties. For the parties appearing before the committees, the hearings probably provide them with their best single opportunity to publicize their views and thereby create support.

Owing to recent reforms, nearly all committee hearings are public. Executive sessions for purposes of achieving agreement on a bill's final form were usually held behind closed doors, but increasingly these are open to the public also. At this stage, the bargaining becomes even more intense. There may be further consultation with executive officials, with representatives of interest groups, and with academicians; these parties, however, participate at the sufferance of the committee. The procedure normally is relatively informal, with modifications made through the give-and-take of discussion and compromise. On controversial legislation, however, all of the devices of parliamentary law may be employed to promote or impede a bill. Any bill leaving a committee usually strongly reflects the chairman's viewpoint.

The result of committee deliberations may be a completely new or "clean" bill. The original proposal may have been transformed through the addition of wholly new provisions or the deletion of major parts of the original proposal.

The House Rules Committee

In the House of Representatives, the Rules Committee is responsible for determining when and under what conditions major legislation will be considered.[10] The committee is empowered to specify the length of time a bill may be considered, motions that may be made, and whether amendments may be proposed.

With the majority party firmly in control, the committee usually works with the majority leadership in scheduling legislation. But it has also shown a propensity for ignoring the will of the majority, principally by delaying or even refusing to grant "rules" permitting the legislation to be considered on the floor of the House. When a coalition of southern Democrats and Republicans used this power excessively during the 1950s and early 1960s, the House to some degree restricted the committee's use of this power by altering its membership and forcing regular procedures on it. The result has been that few bills are now held up arbitrarily in that committee.

Nearly everyone agrees the Rules Committee performs a useful function, however, in preventing embarrassing legislation from reaching the floor. For example, House members would find it difficult to vote against excessive veterans' benefit legislation, and the Rules Committee prevents them from having to do so. Its restrictions of amendments, usually imposed on tax legislation, also prevent the worst cases of logrolling. Moreover, a really determined majority can outmaneuver the Rules Committee by means of a discharge petition. This route is followed as often as one time per session; the threat of its use made possible the passage of the Civil Rights Acts of 1960 and 1964.

Consideration on the floor of the House of Representatives

The House considers legislation in the Committee of the Whole, where 100 members constitute a quorum, and where the debate is controlled by a floor manager of the bill—a member and often the chairman of the committee—and a representative of the minority. Speeches are concise explanations of the bill, criticisms of it, or enthusiastic outbursts of oratory. Debate is better attended in the House, at least in part because votes so closely follow upon debate, but it is doubtful that many minds are changed as a result of the oratory.

Until 1970, decisions rendered in the Committee of the Whole were by voice, teller, or division voting, and in no case were individual votes recorded. Since 1970, however, when individual votes are taken by tellers they are recorded, and this has narrowed the opportunity for members of the House to scuttle a bill in this committee beyond the eyes of colleagues, press, and constituents. Most students of Congress consider this a major change in the direction of responsible government.

[10]Bills reported by the committees are placed on one of several "calendars," or schedules, that govern the order in which legislation is considered on the floor of the House.

Decisions made in the Committee of the Whole are generally subject to review by the entire House. At the final stages of considering controversial legislation, the House usually votes once to recommit the bill to committee and then again on final passage. Approval requires a majority of those present and voting.

THE SENATE

As a second legislative chamber, the Senate is unique because of its equal standing with the House. Second chambers elsewhere often have only the power of delay, and in some countries there is no second chamber at all. Most federal systems have second chambers to represent the territorial units of the federal union.

Because of its smaller size and different traditions, the Senate operates much more informally. Some commentators refer to it as a "club." Decisions on most matters—bringing bills to the floor, scheduling and imposing limits on debate—are made by unanimous consent. By a process of consultation and negotiation, the various factions in the Senate reach agreement on procedure. The majority leader is the crucial figure in bringing about such consensus.

The "style" of the Senate is noticeably different from that of the House, largely because it operates on the basis of unanimous consent. Senators consider themselves the "upper house" and therefore patronize the House members, to the chagrin of the latter. Constantly sought out for their views on all manner of public issues, the senators are much more likely to consider themselves fountains of wisdom on a diverse range of topics. Some of them are considered presidential "timber" and therefore have a national audience to address. Instead of serving on one or two committees, senators may serve on as many as five important committees, and they must equip themselves to deal with widely diverse topics.

Its responsibility for giving advice and consent on treaties signed by the President has given to the Senate an important role in the field of foreign affairs. The major debates on foreign policy usually occur in the Senate, and these are given wide coverage by the communications media. The Senate Foreign Relations Committee has been recognized as the chief congressional instrument for consultation with the President on foreign policy and for guidance of the Congress with regard to foreign policy. As foreign policy has required financial support, the House has acquired more influence than it used to have. But in the public discussion of foreign-policy issues, the Senate still retains its primacy.

The filibuster

The Senate's informal method of operation makes it vulnerable to the most famous feature of Senate procedure—the filibuster or extended debate. By sustaining its traditional opposition to curtailing debate until every individual has had an opportunity to speak, the Senate thereby permits an individual or determined minority to stall the Senate and prevent it from acting on the legislation under consideration. The intent is clearly to prevent action when a minority recognizes that it will be defeated. The filibuster is a last-ditch technique, and is relatively seldom used. In recent decades, the filibuster has been used principally by southern senators to prevent the passage of civil-rights legislation. In the 1970s, however, liberals talked to death the supersonic transport and filibustered on diverse subjects such as extension of the military draft, loans to Lockheed Aircraft, and funding of the Vietnam War.

Effective filibusters are conducted by a band of senators who are determined to hold the floor until the majority despair of breaking their will and either make major concessions or move to consider other legislation. Filibusters are especially effective toward the end of the session of Congress, when little time remains to complete the business on hand.

The cloture rule. The cloture rule permits a two-thirds majority of those present and voting to limit debate. Once this rule is adopted, each senator is allowed only one hour to speak on all amendments and on final passage of the bill. Cloture has been adopted infrequently—only 21 times—since its adoption by the Senate in 1917. This record testifies both to the infrequent need for formal limitations on debate and to the inefficacy of the cloture rule for closing off debate. A determined minority opposed to some policy, plus those who revere the principle of unlimited debate, can usually combine to defeat a cloture motion. Cloture was invoked, however, in considering the Communications Satellite Act (1962), the Civil Rights Act (1964), the Voting Rights Act (1965), and open housing (1968).

Efforts to reform the cloture rule were moderately successful in 1975. The required proportion of senators to close debate on substantive issues was reduced from two-thirds to three-fifths, but leaving the two-thirds requirement for changes on the rules themselves. Even with the adoption of such a change, the filibuster will be only marginally less effective as a minority weapon.

The filibuster has its share of critics and supporters. The critics (principally the liberal elements in both parties) argue that it prevents majorities from acting and makes a mockery of the legislative process in that it prevents decision on the *merits* of legislation and denies the capacity of argument to persuade. The defenders of the filibuster (principally the conservatives in both parties) urge its retention as a means of protecting minority rights against the tyranny of numbers, either to prevent action or to force some acceptable compromise. An intransigent minority can prevent the majority from acting irresponsibly under the influence of momentary passion or crisis; the filibuster provides senators an opportunity to inform the nation of important issues. The Senate is the only legislative body in the world in which a minority is able to impose its will on the majority by means of the filibuster.

The conference committee

Important legislation seldom passes the two houses of Congress in identical form. If the differences are minor, the originating house may agree to the amendments proposed by the second chamber, thus obviating any further reconciliation of differences. Generally, however, it is necessary to reconcile such differences through the appointment of conference committees, which consist of the committee chairmen, the ranking minority leaders, and other seniority leaders on the committees in each house.

The conferees are expected to defend the position assumed by each chamber, but the overriding consideration is resolution of the conflict in a manner that will prove acceptable to the members of both houses. They are under considerable time pressure, especially as the session draws to an end and the members are anxious to clear the legislative decks. Their reports are usually accepted with little or no debate. Beginning in 1975, it may be expected that conference committees will be open unless specifically closed by committee vote, thus subjecting the committee members to pressures they were previously able to avoid in considerable measure. The result, however, will continue to be compromises between positions taken in each house and an occasional deadlock when neither house will retreat.

The President decides

Once majorities of the houses have agreed on the legislation in identical form, the bill is sent to the President for his signature. At this point the Office of Management and Budget (OMB), acting for the President, circulates the bill among the departments and agencies concerned with the subject matter, and asks for their comments and views. If there is serious objection from the departments, OMB, or his own staff, the President may decide to veto the bill. In so doing, he must consider the extent of support the bill received in the two houses, because they may override his veto by a two-thirds majority of those present and voting. The President may normally expect that a number of legislators of his party will change their initial votes in deference to his role as the party leader. If he fears defeat, there are other options open to him. He may refuse to sign a bill passed less than ten days from the end of the session, thus killing the bill by a "pocket" veto; or he may sign the bill and at the same time ask for revisions. Each of these actions softens the edge of the veto and reduces the sharpness of the conflict between the two branches.

The few times each session that the President exercises this prerogative attests to the care with which Congress acts to avoid the veto. The infrequency of its use indicates also the desire of Congress to legislate rather than to create issues.

Reform of Congress is dependent on what members and the general public expect of congressional performance. If they subscribe to what has been called the "literary" interpretation of the Constitution, they may well prefer a Congress whose members are localistic in their orientation, ready to do battle with a President who claims to represent the nation as a whole. They may prefer weak parties so that congressmen can vote local interests even at the expense of some notion of party responsibility. Indeed, they may urge further strengthening of Congress by providing it with more professional staffs of its own and making it less dependent on the executive branch.

Others subscribe to the "executive dominance" and "party government" approaches to legislative evaluation. They emphasize the need for party responsibility to the electorate in terms of clear-cut programs and effective action to implement programs while in office. If these approaches were followed, Congress would become less a policy partner and more a place for airing divergent opinions with respect to programs initiated by the executive branch.

The different conceptions clearly reflect the enduring problem of reconciling majority rule with minority rights and ensuring effective action on public issues. The "literary theory" emphasizes minority rights and reconciliation of them through a process of bargaining. The executive dominance or party theory emphasizes majority rule and presumably more responsible government. It seems clear that the present system is heavily weighted toward the "literary theory," except under conditions of very heavy congressional majorities. Change will occur only as rather fundamental changes are made in the character of American society—its stratification, its sense of geographical attachments, and its fundamental institutional arrangements, such as the federal system and the separation of powers.

14 The Presidency

14

Modern democracies may be broadly classified into two types: parliamentary and presidential. Under the parliamentary system, executive powers are divided between the titular chief of state, the political executive, and the cabinet. The chief of state may be a hereditary monarch as in Britain, Belgium, and Japan, or he may be a president elected for a fixed term of office as in West Germany, Ireland, and Italy. In either instance, he exercises very little political power; other than performing ceremonial functions, his primary responsibility is to designate the political executive, who may be called prime minister, premier, or chancellor. The political executive holds office because he is the leader of the majority party or is able to organize a coalition cabinet that has the support of a majority in parliament.

The presidency is one of America's principal political innovations. The presidential system which originated in the Constitutional Convention in Philadelphia in 1787 was unlike any governmental organization then in existence. The experience of the Founding Fathers with the British monarch George III led them to realize the danger inherent in an executive unrestrained by law and institutional checks. Yet they recognized the weakness of government under the Articles of Confederation, where there had been a legislature but no separate executive. From the writings of political theorists, Locke and Montesquieu in particular, as well as from experience with colonial and state governments, most of the delegates came to favor a government based on the principle of separation of powers.

ASPECTS OF THE PRESIDENCY

Qualifications and perquisites

The Constitution provides that the President must be at least 35 years of age, a resident of the United States for at least 14 years, and a "natural born citizen." Apparently included among "natural born citizens" are persons born abroad of American parents. Although Theodore Roosevelt succeeded to the office at age 42, John Kennedy at age 43 was the youngest elected President, and he followed Dwight Eisenhower, who, at age 70 when he left the White House, was the oldest person to hold that office.

The precedent of a President holding office for only two terms was established by George Washington and was not broken until Franklin

Roosevelt's election to a third term in 1940 and a fourth in 1944. The Twenty-Second Amendment, which went into effect in 1951, limits the President to two elections and no more than ten years in office.

Today the American President receives far more in salary and perquisites than the chief executive of any other Western democracy. Congress has provided the President with an annual salary of $200,000 plus a $50,000 tax-free expense account. By comparison, the Prime Minister of Great Britain receives an annual income in salary and allowances totaling about $75,000, and the Prime Minister of Canada approximately $55,000. In addition, the President has funds for various expenses including travel, entertainment, and staff salaries; he is also provided a mansion, vacation retreats, fleets of limousines, airplanes, helicopters, and a yacht with funds for their maintenance, as well as Secret Service protection for himself and his family.[1] When a President retires from office, he is given a liberal allowance for his transition to private life, a $63,000 annual pension, office space for himself and his staff, $96,000 a year for staff salaries and other office allowances, and protection by the Secret Service. If a President or former President dies before his wife, she receives an annual pension of $20,000. Former President Nixon, by resigning, assured himself of these retirement benefits, none of which would have been his had he been impeached and convicted.

Presidential succession

In a country with a parliamentary government, if the prime minister dies or is unable to continue in office, there is little danger of the country's remaining without a chief executive for long, because the parliament may select a new prime minister at any time. The election of the President for a fixed period of time led the Founding Fathers to provide for a reserve or stand-by President—the Vice-President. The Constitution provides that "in case of the removal of the President from office, or of his death, resignation, or inability to discharge the powers and duties of said office, the same shall devolve on the Vice-President."

The Twenty-Fifth Amendment to the Constitution, ratified in 1967, provides that whenever the office of Vice-President becomes vacant, the President shall nominate a Vice-President, who takes office after a vote of confirmation by Congress. If the President believes he is unable to perform the duties of office, he so informs Congress in writing, and the Vice-President serves as acting President until the President is ready to resume his duties. Should the President become disabled and unable to communicate this fact, the Vice-President with a majority of the Cabinet, notifies Congress. The

---

[1]In 1973 President Nixon had five Boeing jetliners, 16 helicopters, and 11 Lockheed Jetstars. TRB, "Americans Get What They Want: His Royal Majesty, the President," *Los Angeles Times,* November 27, 1973.

Vice-President then serves as acting President until the President has recovered. In case of a disagreement regarding the President's disability or recovery, Congress has the power to decide whether the President or the Vice-President should carry out the duties of the office.

At the time of its adoption the general assumption was that the Twenty-Fifth Amendment would be used primarily to fill vacancies created by the death of a President or Vice-President. However, on October 10, 1973, Vice-President Spiro T. Agnew resigned, pleading "no contest" to charges of failing to pay income taxes on funds accepted as bribes from construction contractors while he was serving as governor of Maryland and as Vice-President.[2] President Nixon then nominated as Vice-President Gerald R. Ford, the minority leader in the House of Representatives, and Congress confirmed him on December 6, 1973. On August 9, 1974, Richard Nixon became the first President to resign, after having been told by Republican congressional leaders that he had no other alternative to impeachment and conviction by Congress. Immediately after Nixon's resignation, Ford was sworn in as the 38th President of the United States. Ford then nominated and Congress approved on December 29, 1974, Nelson A. Rockefeller as Vice President. This sequence of events resulted in having a President and Vice-President neither of whom had been elected by a nationwide vote.

Growth of the presidency

The twentieth century has witnessed the continual expansion of the office of chief executive in Western democracies, with most of the growth of executive power occurring since the 1930s. In the United States, starting with the administration of Franklin Roosevelt, the role of the federal government in the lives of the American people has greatly increased, there has been an aggrandizement of executive power vis-à-vis Congress, and the nation's involvement in world affairs has grown tremendously. As it was once asserted that the sun never set on the British Empire, it could now be said that the sun never sets on American military forces. Thus, because of the expansion of the federal government and America's changed position in world affairs, as well as the organization of our governmental system, the responsibilities and burdens of the American President are undoubtedly greater than those of any other single official.

Article II of the Constitution, which states that the "Executive Power shall be vested in a President of the United States," is one of the most indefinite in the Constitution. This lack of rigidity in the Constitution has made it possible for the presidency to expand or contract to meet conditions of changing times. The powers and influence of the American chief executive, like those of the British Cabinet system, result more from custom,

---

[2] Agnew was sentenced to three years' probation and was fined $10,000.

practice, and the impact of personality than from the prescriptions set forth in a written document.

THE ROLES OF THE PRESIDENT

Calvin Coolidge said that "the presidency does not yield to definition," and Woodrow Wilson asserted that it was "one thing at one time, another at another." In an attempt to understand this complex office, the presidency today might be analyzed as seven offices in one. The President is at once the chief of state, national leader, leader of his party, chief legislator, chief administrator, chief diplomat, and commander-in-chief. All presidential duties cannot be neatly classified into one and only one of the seven categories; in fact, most major presidential decisions and actions may relate to responsibilities in several areas. Furthermore, the President's success in one role—for instance, as chief legislator or as national leader—may strengthen his position in another, such as chief administrator or commander-in-chief. At the same time, functions performed by the President as party leader may conflict with his efforts as chief diplomat or chief legislator.

The obvious conflict occurs between the role of the President as chief of state and his other roles, all of which involve political leadership and decision-making. As chief of state, the President has great prestige, for in this role he is the symbol of the country. But in performing his various other responsibilities, he must make decisions that will lead to opposition and criticism. This combination of functions creates confusion and psychological tensions not experienced in parliamentary countries, where citizens may criticize the prime minister and at the same time show respect for the monarch as the chief of state. A British writer has observed:

> Whenever there has been a national crisis, . . . I have found myself worried by the interventions and appearances of the President. Who, I always want to know, is speaking? The Head of the State? The Commander in Chief? The head of a temporary administration? The temporary head of a political party? It is never quite clear. . . . All right: 'Hail to the Chief!' But, what chief, I ask, and chief of what?"[3]

When making decisions the President seldom thinks of himself in a fragmented role as chief administrator, or chief of state, or commander-in-chief; instead, he thinks of himself as *the President*. Nevertheless, this method of classification provides a convenient way to study the office of the President.

---

[3]Henry Fairlie, "Thoughts on the Presidency," *Public Interest*, no. 9 (Fall, 1967), p. 29.

The President as chief of state

As chief of state, the President performs many of the functions of monarchs in such countries as Great Britain, Holland, Sweden, and Japan. The fact that these democracies retain their monarchs is evidence that in those countries the royal family is believed to fill a useful role. The President—like hereditary monarchs—serves as the symbol of the unity, continuity, and purpose of the country. These leaders help to personalize what might otherwise appear as a distant and impersonal government. Just as in countries where the royal family adds interest, glamour, and pageantry to the lives of the people, in the United States, following the activities of the "first family" of the nation provides interest and some vicarious pleasure to many Americans. This tendency of Americans to view a middle-class American family—the Johnsons, the Nixons, the Fords—as celebrities, if not royalty, is partly due to the press. The personal lives of the President, his wife, and their children become, in effect, public lives, as the newspapers almost daily report on their social activities, habits, the way they dress, and the things they do. Possibly both the President and the nation would benefit if the President and his family were permitted more privacy.

Ceremonial head of the nation. As the ceremonial and symbolic head of the nation, the president engages in a variety of activities. He greets and entertains visiting dignitaries from other countries. He receives delegations of businessmen, labor leaders, and representatives of many other groups. He addresses such groups as the United States Chamber of Commerce, AFL–CIO, and the American Legion. While he may delegate some of these responsibilities to the Vice-President, Cabinet members, or leaders of Congress, he personally performs most of these activities, because in their performance he is adding to his own stature, prestige, and influence. He thereby enhances all of his roles and powers, for he is seen as the representative of the entire nation, the symbol of the country.

Chief magistrate. The Founding Fathers obviously intended that the President should be the nation's chief magistrate. This role is indicated by his judicial powers. Although it created a judicial branch of government separate from the executive, the Constitution authorized the President to appoint judges and "to grant reprieves and pardons for offenses against the United States except in cases of impeachment." With this power, the President can temporarily postpone punishment, reduce a sentence, issue a pardon with certain restrictions, or grant a complete release from penalty. Annually the President, acting on the advice of the Attorney General, rules on thousands of requests for reprieves and pardons, and neither Congress nor the courts can overrule his decisions. No doubt the most celebrated and controversial presidential pardon was President Ford's pardon on September 8, 1974, of former President Nixon "for all offenses against the United States which he . . . has committed or may have committed."[4]

The President as national leader

The President has the responsibility of providing leadership for the nation in the same sense that the British Prime Minister and the West German Chancellor provide political leadership for their countries. Because the role of national leader involves the President in political or policy-making issues, it is essentially different from the ceremonial and symbolic role of chief of state. As the only official other than the Vice President to be chosen by the entire electorate, he must be the spokesman and representative of all the people, although, in fact, most Presidents have tended to promote the interests of some groups more than others.

An articulate President can do much to unify the country if he can express the aspirations of the great majority of the people. There are times when the President must be spokesman for the majority interest against pressure groups seeking special advantages. There are other times when he is obligated to defend the interests of minority groups, as in the case of civil rights and liberties. Most definitely, the responsibility of the President is not merely to represent or reflect majority attitudes. Indeed, when the President believes the majority is unconcerned, uninformed, or wrong, it is his duty to attempt to change their attitudes. He cannot impose his opinions on the people, but as national leader he has the responsibility to educate and inform the public on any matter of national concern.

Many believe that the President should stand as the conscience of the people. As Franklin Roosevelt once remarked, "The presidency . . . is preeminently a place of moral leadership." Some Presidents have failed to understand that the moral and ethical standards associated with them tend to influence the behavior of many others, and that a "credibility gap," associated with Johnson's administration, and Nixon's Watergate scandals produced a feeling of cynicism and disillusionment toward the entire political system.

Presidential leadership in economic policy. The President has always been expected to be the spokesman and guardian of the national interest. Traditionally he has responded wtih federal aid in times of natural disaster anywhere in the nation. As the federal government has assumed greater

---

[4]For the text of President Ford's statement pardoning former President Nixon, see *Congressional Quarterly Weekly Report,* 37 (September 14, 1974), p. 2455.

responsibility for social and economic problems, the role of the President as guardian of the national interest has taken on new meaning.

The President, as the chief administrator of the economy, is now expected to initiate fiscal and monetary policies to stimulate economic growth, maintain a stable economy, prevent depressions before they occur, and eradicate poverty. Both Nixon and Ford, faced simultaneously with the problems of inflation and recession, found their responsibilities in the field of economic policy among their most perplexing and difficult tasks.

Leading public opinion. The success of the President as a national leader depends in large measure on his efforts and ability at guiding and directing public opinion. The more dynamic and influential twentieth-century Presidents have all understood, as did Lincoln, the importance of public opinion. In Lincoln's words: "Public sentiment is everything. With public sentiment nothing can fail; without it, nothing can succeed."

Television has greatly enhanced the opportunity of the President to fulfill his role as national leader. Prior to radio and television, relatively few persons ever heard the voice of the President. Today the President—his personality, mannerisms, and voice inflections—is more familiar to millions of Americans than their congressmen or their mayors. With a studio in the White House, television is always at the President's disposal, and recent Presidents have utilized it frequently to make announcements of major policies or appointments.

THE PRESIDENTIAL PRESS CONFERENCE. The presidential press conference is a uniquely American institution. In no other country does the chief executive meet the press so often or under similar conditions. Although the press conference has been compared with the question hour in the House of Commons and the interpellation in the French Parliament, it is not actually comparable, because the latter two are means by which not the press but members of the legislature may question ministers.

The growth of the presidential press conference has paralleled the establishment of the modern presidency. Woodrow Wilson is usually credited with initiating presidential press conferences to which all accredited White House reporters were invited. Franklin Roosevelt, who held more press conferences than any other President, established the press conference as a precedent that has been followed by all of his successors. Under the postwar Presidents, the presidential press conferences became more institutionalized and the formal press conference came to resemble semipublic mass meetings, with as many as 450 reporters attending. Kennedy was the first President to allow a number of his press conferences to be directly televised. Johnson, Nixon, and Ford continued the practice of having formal televised sessions. Nixon held fewer press conferences than any of his immediate predecessors,[5] preferring instead television addresses and rare televised interviews. Ford, who upon taking office announced that he planned to meet with the press frequently, averaged slightly more than one conference a month during his first year in office.

The present-day televised press conferences with many of the several hundred reporters present competing to ask questions in the relatively short period of 30 minutes is undoubtedly not as useful in informing the public as were the nontelevised, smaller conferences held by such Presidents as Franklin Roosevelt and Harry Truman. Today's press conferences may give the appearance of a staged television performance and have often been used by the President primarily to promote specific policies with the television audience. Smaller conferences limited to 40 to 50 representatives of the wire services, broadcasting networks, and major papers and magazines that have full-time reporters assigned to the White House would permit the President to explain his programs in greater depth and the reporters to ask more significant and probing questions.

QUALITIES OF OPINION LEADERSHIP. Presidents have varied considerably in their efforts and talents for mobilizing public sentiment. Although opinion leadership obviously requires the ability to communicate with the people, it does not demand that the President be a gifted speaker. Of recent Presidents, Truman, Eisenhower, and Ford were not accomplished orators, but they had the capacity to communicate effectively with the public. More important than oratory is the moral quality of a President's leadership, the extent to which his statements and actions generate confidence, and his capacity to perceive and to personify the temper of the times. The President's capacity for national leadership is evidenced by his ability to strike the proper balance between communicating sufficiently and overexposure, in his timing in presenting information and arguments, and in the sense of urgency he attaches to a particular problem. By the priority he places on current problems and by bringing them to the attention of the nation, the President is able—more than any other person—to determine the key political issues of the day.

The President as party leader

The remaining five principal roles of the President can be grouped into two broad categories—domestic and international. In the first category are his tasks as leader of his party, chief legislator, and chief administrator.

[5] Franklin Roosevelt, in a little over three terms, held 1,000 press conferences; Truman held over 300, and Eisenhower 200. John Kennedy averaged two a month, or 66 in all, and Lyndon Johnson held 158 in five years. Nixon held 28 press conferences in his first four years in office.

Even individuals with little prior experience in partisan politics—such as college president Woodrow Wilson and generals Zachary Taylor and Dwight Eisenhower—have been elected as party men. Regardless of the President's previous positions and experience, upon his nomination he becomes the leader of his party and he continues in that capacity as long as he is in the White House. As Clinton Rossiter has said, the President is the "Chief Republican" or the "Chief Democrat," and he must "put his hand firmly to the plow of politics." The President's statements become the most authoritative pronouncements on party policies. He is expected to carry out the party platform, which often he has helped to draft, and while in office he usually develops his own program, which then becomes the party program. As noted in Chapter 11, the national party organization is closely identified with the President. The national chairman, although formally elected by the national committee, is selected first by the President and serves as his agent. Because American national parties tend to be loose alliances of state and local party organizations and are not highly unified or disciplined, as they are in Great Britain, the President has relatively little control over his party.

The President and his party cooperate out of mutual need. The President must have the support of the party to be elected and to secure the adoption of his legislative program. Conversely, the success of the party and its candidates throughout the 50 states is dependent on the popularity and program of the President. As party leader, the President is expected to help raise campaign funds, to select most of his appointees from his party, to attend and address party meetings and rallies, and to assist in the election of at least some partisan candidates.

The President's varied responsibilities as political and party leader require him to assume a dual personality. Most Presidents have been active in partisan politics prior to their election. After election, each one is expected to lead his party and to work for its success. On the other hand, it is assumed that the President will adopt a nonpartisan role in many matters and be the political leader and spokesman for all the people. In short, the President is expected to be both a partisan and nonpartisan political leader. Most Presidents have attempted to solve this apparent dilemma by performing many of their responsibilities in a nonpartisan fashion and at the same time performing those tasks expected of the leader of the party.

The President as chief legislator

The President's legislative responsibilities cast him in a role somewhat comparable to that of a prime minister. Although following the Watergate investigations many political observers urged Congress to assume a stronger role in its relations with the executive branch, there remains widespread agreement that the President must provide leadership for Congress. The reason is simply that in the formation of public policy there is no official or group within Congress capable of providing continuous leadership. As Senate Majority Leader Mike Mansfield explained: "We want him [President Ford] to exercise the leadership he is exercising, but we would appreciate closer cooperation. . . . It is easier for one man to take the lead than it is for five hundred and thirty-five members of the House and Senate." The President is the only person who has the responsibility and the facilities to develop a comprehensive nationwide program, and whose position enables him to organize sufficient support from the public and the legislators to secure its adoption.

A variety of circumstances makes it difficult for Presidents to exercise effective legislative leadership, in particular in promoting domestic programs. The principle of separation of powers complicates the President's leadership problems. The executive and legislature are coordinate branches of government, each receiving its authority from the Constitution and jealously guarding its prestige and independent status. Usually, many members of Congress are older than the President, have been in public office longer, believe they know more about political problems, and are reluctant to accept his guidance. As the members of Congress and the President are elected by different constituencies, they view political issues from different perspectives; many members of Congress take a local, more provincial view of issues, whereas the President in reaching decisions should consider the broader national and even international aspects and ramifications. In addition, the Constitution provides the President few means for inducing Congress to follow his lead. Unlike the British Prime Minister, he cannot dissolve the legislature and call a new election, nor can he require the members of his party in the legislature to vote for his proposals.

There has been a remarkable variation in the success of the several

Santa Barbara News–Press, April 18, 1973. Copyright, Washington Star Syndicate, Inc.

Presidents in providing legislative leadership. This variation has been due not only to their differing personalities and abilities and their conception of the President's legislative responsibilities, but also to the times during which they occupied the White House. Some Presidents, in particular Woodrow Wilson and Lyndon Johnson, established impressive legislative records only to find later that national and international events had greatly diminished their influence with Congress. Other Presidents have served when the times and the general public did not seem to require aggressive executive leadership.

Constitutional powers. The Constitution, which made few provisions for presidential direction in the formation of legislative policy, grants the President two relatively important legislative powers—the message and the veto powers—and one that is comparatively unimportant—the authority to call special sessions.

LEGISLATIVE MESSAGES AND RECOMMENDATIONS. The Constitution enjoins the President to "give to the Congress information of the State of the Union, and recommend to their consideration such measures as he shall judge necessary and expedient." During the nineteenth century, Presidents tended to interpret this provision literally and limited themselves merely to calling the attention of Congress to current problems. Starting with Theodore Roosevelt, most Presidents have interpreted the message power as authorization to develop a legislative program and to work for its enactment.

In the weeks prior to the opening of a congressional session, the President and his assistants sift through the recommendations submitted by the executive agencies and presidential advisers and prepare the President's legislative program. These proposals will be outlined by the President in the "State of the Union" message, which is usually followed by the budget message and by several other messages recommending particular policies that are often accompanied by drafts of bills.

THE VETO POWER. The President participates directly in the legislative process through his power to approve or veto legislation. Most Presidents prior to the Civil War took the view that they should veto only those bills they believed to be unconstitutional; consequently, they vetoed relatively few bills. More recent chief executives have used the veto as an instrument to exert legislative leadership and have vetoed bills they believed to be not in the national interest.

Because of the difficulty of obtaining the two-thirds vote needed to enact a bill over a presidential veto, a President may be able to forestall the adoption of particular bills by simply announcing that he will veto them if they are enacted. Thus, at times, congressmen have changed the content of legislative measures to meet presidential approval.

CONTROL OF LEGISLATIVE SESSIONS. A third, and less consequential, constitutional provision authorizes the President to call special sessions of Congress and to adjourn the two houses "in case of disagreement between them with respect to time of adjournment." As the two houses of Congress have never disagreed regarding adjournment, the latter authority has never been exercised. Moreover, since the adoption of the Twentieth Amendment, providing for Congress to convene each year in January, Congress has usually been in session for eight or more months each year, and there has been little reason for calling special sessions.

Extraconstitutional powers. Because the Constitution makes so few provisions for presidential leadership in the formation of legislative policy, the President's success as a national legislator is dependent on his knowledge of extraconstitutional institutions and methods and his skill in utilizing them.

PUBLIC OPINION AND LEGISLATIVE LEADERSHIP. One of the President's principal sources of strength in working with Congress is his ability to influence public opinion. The President can focus attention on his legislative program through press conferences, in news releases, and in other public statements and addresses. Recent Presidents have often used television to appeal directly to the public for support for legislative measures. The President, by calling particular issues to public notice, is often able to increase the "attentive" public and bring the pressure of their opinions to bear on members of Congress.

THE PRESIDENT'S PARTY LEADERSHIP IN CONGRESS. Although American legislators, unlike their British counterparts, refuse to bind themselves to support their party's legislative proposals, American government is nevertheless party government. No President has achieved an enviable legislative record whose party did not control both houses of Congress and who did not energetically assert his role as party leader. Hence the likelihood of securing the enactment of a legislative program is greatest if the President's party has sizable majorities in each house and if a number of the legislators believe they owe their election to the President. Woodrow Wilson, Franklin Roosevelt, and Lyndon Johnson all enjoyed this advantage, and all established substantial legislative records.

The President has relatively little influence over the selection of his party's leaders in the House and Senate, but he must secure their cooperation if his proposals are to be adopted. Before the opening of a legislative session, the President usually discusses his proposed program with congressional party leaders and throughout legislative sessions he customarily meets weekly with congressional leaders to discuss the progress of bills and the tactics to be employed.

PARTICIPATION IN THE LEGISLATIVE PROCESS. Recent Presidents and their assistants have participated directly or indirectly in virtually every phase of the bill-passing process. It is now accepted practice for executive officials to draft the bills that comprise the President's legislative program. All recent Presidents have placed a high priority on cooperating with Congress, but the formalization of executive-legislative relations into a full-time staff activity developed during the administrations of Eisenhower, Kennedy, and Johnson. Previously, liaison between the Executive and Congress had been more informal and often on an *ad hoc* basis. In addition to White House staff members, other congressional-relations officers are spread throughout the departments and agencies.[6] In the State Department, the official charged with congressional relations customarily has held the rank of assistant secretary.

PERSONAL PERSUASION. While key administration bills are under consideration by Congress, the President's congressional liaison officers spend much time on Capitol Hill supplying information regarding bills, helping arrange for influential persons to testify at committee hearings, and attempting to persuade reluctant congressmen to vote as the administration wishes. Votes may be obtained on a *quid pro quo* basis. One of Johnson's White House staff members once explained: "Sometimes you have to offer a dam here, or a defense project there, to get a bill through. This is a tough game, and sometimes we do make deals."

The President himself may grant numerous minor favors that will add to the prestige and status of congressmen of both parties and increase their indebtedness to him. Such efforts at personal persuasion are usually reserved for occasions when an informal poll of the House or Senate shows that a presidential measure may fail by a few votes to be enacted.

In his relations with Congress, the President has occasion to recall that politics is both "the art of the possible" and "a struggle for power." As members of Congress have political power in their own right, the President's power to persuade often becomes the power to negotiate, and not uncommonly he is required to compromise—to accept half a loaf or nothing at all.

The President as chief administrator

As the framers of the Constitution conceived the office, the President's primary role would be that of chief administrator. In accordance with the tripartite division of power, the President as head of the executive branch

---

[6]President Ford adopted the practice of meeting daily with the head of his congressional relations staff and four other top advisers when Congress was in session. "New Life for White House Liaison with Congress," *Congressional Quarterly Weekly Report*, 33 (February 1, 1975), p. 226.

is enjoined by the Constitution to "take care that the laws be faithfully executed."

The President's role as chief administrator has been vastly expanded by congressional delegation of broad discretionary powers to administrators. This is largely a twentieth-century development. In our early history, much legislation was self-executing—Congress passed laws and left the enforcement to individuals who brought action in court against offenders. As society has grown more complex and the activities of government have multiplied, Congress has created numerous administrative agencies to enforce public policies. Congress has delegated to the President and other executive officers the responsibility of determining when these conditions exist, and for filling in the details of the law through the issuance of executive directives—orders, rules, and regulations. These executive directives, known as "delegated legislation," have the force of law and are published in the *Federal Register*.

Although the President as chief administrator has the responsibility for directing and coordinating some 1,800 governmental agencies, several reasons make it difficult for him to exercise effective control. As the principal manager of the world's largest conglomerate, the President is faced with all the problems of central management that characterize other conglomerates. In addition, his managerial powers are more circumscribed than are the powers of managers of corporate conglomerates. Moreover, because of his various other responsibilities, the President is able to devote very little time to supervising the myriad departments and offices.

The President shares with Congress control over the federal agencies. Congress creates the agencies, defines their functions, appropriates funds for their operations, and often specifies their procedures and organization. Thus, as was explained previously, the Constitution provides for a system of *shared powers* rather than a clear-cut separation of powers. Furthermore, several administrative units—including the Interstate Commerce Commission, Federal Reserve Board, and others—have an independent or semi-independent status; and some agencies, such as the Army Corps of Engineers, because of their particular relationship with members of Congress, are relatively free from presidential direction. Finally, other factors—such as the demands of political-interest groups or bureaucratic inertia and tradition—may lead an executive agency to ignore the wishes of a President.

Means of administrative control. The principal means by which the President may exercise control over the administrative establishments are the executive budget, his power to reorganize, and his appointment and removal powers.

BUDGETARY CONTROL. As will be explained, the President has an effective instrument for administrative control through the Office of Management and

Budget in the preparation of the federal budget, and, after its approval by Congress, in its supervision of the execution of the budget.

ADMINISTRATIVE REORGANIZATION. Since the late 1930s, Presidents have had greater power than formerly over the executive branch through their authority to reorganize the administrative agencies. Although Congress creates the agencies and prescribes their activities, it has been recognized that the President as the chief administrator should have the authority to transfer and regroup administrative units. When a reorganization of an agency or agencies is desired, the President may submit the proposed reorganization to the House of Representatives and the Senate, and if within 60 days neither of the houses rejects the plan, it goes into effect.

APPOINTMENT POWERS. After a new President takes office, he may appoint as many as 1,000 to 1,500 persons to top-level and middle-level executive positions.[7] By comparison, when one party replaces another in Great Britain, the only changes in personnel are ministers and their immediate parliamentary assistants, a total of some 70 individuals. Historically, one reason for the large turnover in the executive branch in the United States was the demand of political parties for patronage, but patronage pressures have greatly declined, and today the need of the President to staff his administration with loyal supporters is a more important reason. As the President, unlike the British Prime Minister, is not guaranteed control of the legislature or the united backing of his political party, he must establish a personal organization that will enable him to exercise the necessary leadership. In short, Presidents, lacking institutional controls and the support of a unified party, find that their best assurance of securing cooperation and assistance is by appointing the optimum number of loyal top-level and middle-level executives.

The types of individuals selected for executive positions are influenced by the President's background and personality as well as by his party; with a change of Presidents, the character of the administration is usually sharply altered. After Eisenhower took office, there were more businessmen in high governmental positions than at any time during the preceding 20 years. Under Kennedy, Washington was said to resemble "an extension division of Harvard." Presidents have also expressed a geographic bias in their appointments, perhaps a natural phenomenon, since most of their acquaintances

---

[7]When Richard Nixon became President in 1969, he found that he could make approximately 6,500 patronage appointments and that as many as 1,500 of these could be considered policy-making positions. The largest number of patronage positions are in the State Department (1,012), the Interior Department (816), and the Department of Agriculture (716). For a listing of these positions, see U.S. House of Representatives, Committee on Post Office and Civil Service, "Policy and Supporting Positions," 90th Congress, 2d Session, 1968.

come from the area in which they themselves have lived. For example, Johnson surrounded himself with many Texans in positions of close personal confidence, and Nixon installed in high positions more Californians than any previous President. Change in personnel from one administration to the next helps to provide a dynamic quality to the government, a periodic infusion of new ideas, and a fresh look at domestic and world problems.

The Constitution provides for the President to make two types of appointments. First, it states that the President "shall nominate, and by and with the advice and consent of the Senate, shall appoint ambassadors, other public ministers and consuls, judges of the Supreme Court and all other officers of the United States, whose appointments" are not otherwise provided by law. Second, Congress may authorize the President, or department heads, to appoint, without Senate confirmation, "inferior officers," and Congress may determine which officials are to be so classified.

Of the officials requiring confirmation, the Senate generally permits the President virtually complete freedom in choosing persons who will fill key positions—such as the department secretaries and the personnel of the Executive Office of the President. The Senate also usually approves with little debate the President's nominations for other administrative positions, diplomatic posts abroad, and justices of the Supreme Court, although, as noted earlier, the Senate in 1968 and 1970 refused to confirm Supreme Court appointments.

"Senatorial courtesy" applies to most other positions requiring Senate confirmation. According to custom, the President, prior to sending such nominations to the Senate, consults the senators of his party from those states in which the appointments are to be made. Included among positions affected by senatorial courtesy are district court judges and federal marshals. If the President fails to consult with a senator of his party on such an appointment, the senator may declare the appointment "personally obnoxious" and request that confirmation be refused, and the Senate usually complies. In practice, senatorial courtesy places with the senators of the President's party the power to fill most federal positions in their states.

REMOVAL POWERS. The Supreme Court ruled in 1926 (*Myers v. U.S.*) that the President could remove any appointive official who performs executive functions and that Congress may not limit that power. In later decisions the Supreme Court announced that members of the independent regulatory agencies, such as the Interstate Commerce Commission and the Federal Communications Commission, who perform quasi-legislative or quasi-judicial as well as executive duties, could be removed only for such causes as neglect of duty, inefficiency, or malfeasance in office (*Humphrey's Executor v. U.S.*, 1935, and *Wiener v. U.S.*, 1958). Civil-service employees can be removed from office only in accordance with civil-service rules.

In all large organizations—major corporations as well as governments—

the principal executive power is the power of persuasion and not the power of command. The President's success as an administrative leader depends largely on his ability to persuade those directly under him to support his policies, and he will find that giving an order will not necessarily assure that it is carried out. Harry Truman commented shortly before Dwight Eisenhower succeeded him in office: "He'll sit here, and he'll say, 'Do this! Do that!' *And nothing will happen. Poor Ike*—it won't be a bit like the Army."[8]

The President as chief diplomat

Most Presidents have been more successful in obtaining support from Congress and the American people for policies related to international affairs than for their domestic programs. This higher degree of success can be attributed to at least three factors. First, Americans in general tend to be less well informed and interested in international policies than in domestic issues. Second, there are fewer political interest groups concerned with external than with internal policies. Third, Presidents have often used the argument of national security in their efforts to obtain support for programs related to foreign affairs, and few persons have the facts necessary to counter such arguments.

The Founding Fathers were aware that responsibility for conducting foreign relations must necessarily rest with the chief executive. The Constitution authorizes the President to appoint and to receive "ambassadors and other public ministers," and "to make treaties." These powers, however, are shared with Congress, especially with the Senate and the Senate Foreign Relations Committee. Appointments to diplomatic positions must be approved by the Senate, and treaties require a two-thirds vote in the Senate. In addition, Congress, of course, has established the State Department and other agencies involved in foreign affairs and must appropriate funds for salaries and for expenditures related to the implementation of foreign policies and programs.

Conducting foreign relations. Until the beginning of this century, American interest in foreign problems was sporadic, and the nation's influence in international affairs was slight. The entry of the United States into World War I and the leadership of Woodrow Wilson at the peace conference projected the nation fully onto the world scene, but disillusionment with postwar developments caused many Americans to favor withdrawing behind the apparent security of the Atlantic and Pacific oceans. The subsequent rise of Nazi Germany and World War II illustrated dramatically that the United States could never again isolate itself from world politics. At the

---

[8]Quoted in Richard E. Neustadt, *Presidential Power,* New York: Wiley, 1960, p. 26.

conclusion of World War II, the United States became increasingly involved in leadership throughout the world.

Constitutionally, the President is the single official channel of communication between the United States and foreign powers. Any doubt regarding this point was answered when the Supreme Court ruled that the President has "exclusive power . . . as the sole organ of the Federal Government in the field of international relations" (*U.S. v. Curtiss-Wright Export Corporation*, 1936). Neither members of Congress nor private citizens may legally negotiate with foreign governments. Conducting foreign relations requires unified action, occasionally a considerable degree of secrecy, and often swift decisions. Congress obviously is not constituted to function in this manner. The Secretary of State, ambassadors, and other Foreign Service personnel are representatives of the President and not of Congress.

The President's preeminence in foreign affairs today stems in part from the staff, information, and facilities at his command. From American embassies, consulates, intelligence agencies, other governmental agencies, and even private citizens, an overwhelming mass of information is collected regarding foreign developments. The State Department, White House staff, National Security Council, Central Intelligence Agency, and other government units assist the President in making decisions by sifting and analyzing these data.

From the days of George Washington, the Secretary of State has been the ranking Cabinet officer and the President's chief adviser and agent in foreign affairs. However, the role of the Secretary of State has varied from one administration to another. For instance, Dwight Eisenhower permitted John Foster Dulles broad discretionary powers in conducting foreign relations, but Woodrow Wilson (who sometimes typed his own diplomatic messages) was virtually his own Secretary of State. Henry Kissinger, as Nixon's personal assistant, had more influence over foreign policy than did Secretary of State William Rogers. However, when Kissinger was Secretary of State under both Nixon and Ford, his influence in foreign policy matters due to his vast range of knowledge and experience was undoubtedly as great as that of any previous Secretary of State.

One of the prerogatives of a sovereign nation is the right to recognize or to refuse to recognize foreign governments. The President's authority to receive ambassadors carries with it this power. By recognizing a new regime, the President may add to its prestige and domestic support. Conversely, by refusing recognition, the President may hope to encourage opposition to a new government and lead to its demise. Recognition has also been withheld because of dislike for certain policies and practices of the government. The United States withheld recognition from the Soviet Union for 16 years after the Bolshevik Revolution, and refused to recognize Communist China for over two decades. In such instances, the President must decide whether more is to be gained by attempting to stigmatize the government by refusing recognition or by granting recognition and establishing means of communicating with the government and its people.

Treaties and executive agreements. As the United States has become increasingly involved in international politics, the government has entered numerous agreements with foreign countries. These are of two general types —treaties and executive agreements. The process of negotiating treaties is solely within the purview of the President. However, Wilson's experience in failing to secure the necessary two-thirds Senate approval for the Versailles Treaty and the League of Nations has led his successors to appoint influential senators to delegations negotiating treaties and to keep other senators informed of proposed treaties.

Executive agreements, although not mentioned in the Constitution, have long been used by Presidents for reaching formal understandings with foreign governments. During this century, the United States has negotiated far more executive agreements than treaties with other countries, largely because the latter require approval by a two-thirds vote in the Senate, whereas executive agreements require no more than a simple majority in each house, and some require no congressional approval. Often executive agreements are based on authority previously delegated to the President by Congress. Examples include the reciprocal trade agreements that date to the 1930s and the numerous postwar foreign-aid arrangements between the United States and other countries.

The President as commander-in-chief

The President is designated by the Constitution as the supreme commander of the armed forces. The Founding Fathers, expecting that Washington would be elected President, intended for him to have the authority to take personal command of the troops. However, as one scholar has written, "The Napoleonic concept of the warrior-statesman has not taken root in the United States."[9] Although a number of Presidents—including Washington, Jackson, Grant, and Eisenhower—had had extensive military service, they, unlike Charles de Gaulle of France and political leaders of various other countries, chose not to wear military uniforms while serving as chief executive. In the United States, the President serves as the living embodiment of the American belief in the supremacy of civil over military authority.

Although the primary purpose of the military forces is to protect the security of the nation against external enemies, the President may utilize the regular armed forces and the National Guard for suppressing riots and internal disorders. As commander-in-chief, the President is responsible for

---

[9]Joseph E. Kallenbach, *The American Chief Executive,* New York: Harper & Row, 1966, p. 527.

commissioning the officers, deciding on promotions, selecting the officers for the top command and staff positions, and determining the relative strength and particular missions of each branch of the armed services. Naturally, the President delegates most of these tasks to his subordinates in the Department of Defense and to the top-ranking military officers.

The President shares power over the military with Congress. The Constitution authorizes Congress "to raise and support armies" and "to provide and maintain a navy." All appropriations for the military must be provided by the legislature. Congress, not the President, is authorized by the Constitution to declare war, but in actuality the President tends to take the initiative in such declarations, and Congress tends to go along with him. Of the five congressionally declared wars, only one—the War of 1812—may be said to have been initiated by Congress. In the other four—the war with Mexico, the Spanish-American War, and the two World Wars—Congress acted after the President had recommended that war be declared; in fact, events prior to those declarations or actions by the Presidents left Congress little alternative. In addition, Congress has at times given the President virtually a free hand to conduct military operations without a formal declaration of war. In the 1950s, Congress adopted a resolution permitting President Eisenhower to determine whether an attack by Communist China on the Formosa Straits would justify a military response. President Johnson, in maintaining more than half a million troops in Vietnam, relied in part on the Gulf of Tonkin Resolution (1964), which authorized the President "to take all necessary measures to repel an armed attack against the forces of the United States and to prevent further aggression," and President Nixon bombed Cambodia for four years and sent American troops into that country and Laos without prior consultation with Congress.

The widespread aversion to the undeclared war in Southeast Asia resulted in the repeal of the Tonkin Gulf Resolution in 1971. Two years later Congress passed, over President Nixon's veto, the War Powers Act, which has two key provisions: First, if the President sends troops into foreign combat, he must notify Congress within 48 hours and must cease military action in 60 days unless Congress approves his action. Second, Congress, by a joint resolution that is not subject to presidential veto, may require the President to remove the troops within less than 60 days.

Wartime powers. During times of major wars, when the very survival of the nation has appeared to be at stake, the President's powers based on his role as commander-in-chief have expanded so greatly that this role overshadowed all others. Under war conditions, all aspects of life must be geared to the war effort; thus Presidents, especially during the Civil War, World War I, and World War II, have felt compelled to take whatever actions they considered essential for winning the war.

During World War II, Franklin Roosevelt assumed broader powers than any previous President. On his order, 100,000 American citizens and aliens of Japanese descent were evacuated from the West Coast; more than 60 strike-bound or strike-threatened industries and plants were seized and operated; and a wide array of emergency boards and offices were created to control virtually every phase of economic life, from the allocation of raw materials needed for war production to the establishment of price control on consumer goods.

Most wartime Presidents have participated as commanders-in-chief in planning overall military strategy. Before the nuclear age, the autonomy of field commanders was respected military doctrine, and it was commonly accepted that the President should not determine the tactics of individual battles. Now, because of the gravity and complexity of the times, the President is often intimately involved with details of military tactics. There is widespread agreement that military decisions that may have far-reaching political implications should not be left to the generals.

THE PRESIDENT'S ASSISTANTS

An important factor in determining the success of a President is his ability to recruit intelligent and knowledgeable assistants and to make the most effective use of their capabilities. To a large extent the tone or quality of an administration may be determined by as few as 200 to 300 of the most influential officials. Of these, the most important to the success of a President are the members of the Executive Office of the President and the Cabinet. Hence attention will be directed here primarily to them. The President must rely on these officials for advice, information, and the performance of many tasks.

The Executive Office of the President

For a century and a half, the American Presidents performed their duties with very little personal assistance. For instance, at the time of World War I, President Wilson had only one presidential secretary and approximately 45 clerks, stenographers, and messengers. Herbert Hoover added two presidential secretaries, but the organization of the President's office was largely unchanged until Franklin Roosevelt's administration. The Executive Office of the President, created by Roosevelt in 1939, has never been a single organization as the name implies, but a title covering a group of individuals and agencies that assist the President in the performance of duties that are strictly the President's responsibility.

Other than the White House staff and the Office of Management and Budget (formerly the Bureau of the Budget), all units of the Executive Office of the President have been created since World War II. The specific units have changed as some are terminated or transferred to a department and others are created. The establishment of these newer agencies reflects the increased involvement of the President in national defense, economic policy, and urban problems. During Nixon's administration the staffs expanded until over 2,500 people (not including the personnel of the Central Intelligence Agency) were employed in the agencies and offices—more than 50 times the number of people that assisted Wilson.[10] Thus in a few decades the presidency has been transformed from virtually a one-man operation to a highly staffed institution. Today the chief executive of no other country has a comparable staff.

The White House office. Of the several units of the Executive Office, the White House staff exercises the strongest influence on presidential policy and leadership. The character, size, and functioning of the staff vary according to the needs of the particular President and his method of working. President Eisenhower, no doubt owing to his army background, organized the personnel in a manner somewhat similar to a military general staff. When Kennedy took office, he dropped the chief-of-staff approach and worked more directly with key members of the White House office. Nixon sharply increased the number of personnel, adopted the chief-of-staff approach, and appointed H. R. Haldeman, his long-time associate, as the chief of staff.[11] When Ford became President, he announced that instead of adopting the chief-of-staff approach, he would have several top aides of equal rank and would be readily accessible to all of them.

The range of the tasks of White House staff members is as broad as the President's responsibilities. Some may be given a variety of general assignments, whereas others perform specialized functions. Aides are commonly assigned to oversee the major areas of presidential responsibility—public opinion, international relations, national security, and relations with Congress and administrative agencies. The President has a personal secretary; one White House staff member usually serves as appointments secretary, determining who may see the President; and another is usually assigned the tasks of recommending persons to be appointed to governmental positions. Staff members write speeches, investigate or make studies of special problems, and coordinate programs. There is always a press secretary, who has several assistants. White House staff members are typically a diversified group and will include attorneys, journalists, university professors, businessmen, and former assistants to members of Congress. A few key members of the White House staff have Cabinet status, and they have their offices near the President in the west wing of the White House.

The presidency has been greatly strengthened by the White House staff,

---

[10]U.S. Senate, Committee on Government Operations, *Organization of Federal Executive Departments and Agencies,* 93d Congress, 1st Session, 1973.

[11]At the time Nixon resigned, the White House staff consisted of approximately 540 persons, ranging from messengers and typists to the top-ranking members with titles of Counselor to the President and Assistant to the President.

but the President himself may be limited by his staff in that it is often they who decide what issues are brought to his attention and whom he shall see. The staff in turn may be limited by lack of knowledge and a sense of what is important. In their zeal to protect the President and guard his time, the White House staff may form a barrier between the President and other policy-making officials; as a result, the President is sometimes too isolated. Nixon's staff was sometimes referred to by journalists as the "Berlin Wall," or the "Palace Guard."

The President, protected by his staff, guarded by the Secret Service, and insulated from the people, may come to lose his perspective and have an exaggerated sense of his own importance. As Mme. de Gaulle is reported to have once said to her husband, "Charles, you are not yet France," so American Presidents may need to be reminded that they are not yet the United States. A former White House assistant has suggested that

> *the real question every president must ask himself is what he can do to resist the temptations of a process compounded of idolatry and lofty patriotic respect for a national symbol. . . . The atmosphere of the White House is calculated to instill in any man a sense of destiny.*[12]

Even with a large and able staff, the President still has the responsibility for decision-making. One former White House assistant observed, "The real strain comes from the agonizing decisions and unanswerable questions that simply cannot be delegated or divided."[13] John Kennedy similarly remarked, "The President bears the burden of the responsibility. . . . The advisers move on to new advice."

The Office of Management and Budget. The Office of Management and Budget (OMB) provides the President with a powerful instrument for administrative control and coordination as well as a means for exerting legislative leadership. The OMB is, except for the White House staff, the most influential unit of the Executive Office of the President. The director heads a permanent staff of able, experienced, and professionally trained individuals.

The chief function of OMB is to prepare the national budget which the President will present to Congress. Preparing the budget is not just a mechanical ordering of income and outgo, but an arrangement of national priorities. All federal agencies are required to submit to OMB detailed estimates of their proposed expenditures for the forthcoming fiscal year. The OMB staff holds budget hearings, and revises the proposed expendi-

---

[12] George E. Reedy, *The Twilight of the Presidency,* New York: World, 1970, pp. 14–15.

[13] Theodore C. Sorensen, "But You Get to Walk to Work," *New York Times Magazine,* March 19, 1967, p. 171.

tures so that the plans of the various agencies conform with the President's general program. In establishing his budgetary policies, the President makes important priority decisions.

The OMB is also the President's chief legislative clearinghouse. All legislative proposals originating with executive agencies, before being sent to Congress, must be submitted to the Legislative Reference Office of OMB to determine if they are in conformity with the President's general program and policies. No agency can request congressional appropriations directly, but must make requests through OMB.

The Council of Economic Advisers. The Council of Economic Advisers (CEA) consists of three professional economists who are appointed by the President with the consent of the Senate. In recent administrations, the chairman of the CEA has been an important adviser to the President. The CEA, with its staff of economists and statisticians, undertakes a continuing analysis of national economic trends and developments, appraises the economic programs and policies of the government, and advises the President regarding policies that will encourage economic growth and stability. The CEA prepares for the President an annual report on the national economy which the President transmits to Congress.

The National Security Council. The National Security Council (NSC) is charged with the responsibility for advising the President "with respect to the integration of domestic, foreign, and military policies relating to national security." The NSC is composed of the President, who serves as the chairman; the Vice-President; the Secretary of State; and the Secretary of Defense. The Assistant to the President for National Security Affairs serves as executive director of the NSC. The President frequently invites other persons to attend meetings, including the U.S. Ambassador to the United Nations, the Chairman of the Joint Chiefs of Staff, the Director of the Central Intelligence Agency, and members of the White House staff.

The principal purposes of the NSC are to bring together the top officials who have responsibilities for national security and foreign policies, and to provide them with information that will permit a thorough analysis of all aspects of such policies. Information and analysis of relevant factors are provided by the staff of the NSC; governmental units represented on the NSC; and the Central Intelligence Agency, which operates under the direction of the NSC. The NSC thus serves as a planning and coordinating agency.

The Domestic Council. The membership of the Domestic Council includes the President, Vice-President, all members of the Cabinet except the Secretary of State and Secretary of Defense, and members of the White House staff who have responsibility in the domestic area. In creating the Council,

President Nixon stated he planned to rely on it in formulating solutions to domestic problems, just as he would rely on the National Security Council in developing foreign policy. Hence its principal purpose is to develop and coordinate domestic policies, in particular in such areas as housing, health, education, and civil rights. The Council usually functions through a series of *ad hoc* interdepartmental committees, each assigned a specific project or task.

Other Units of the Executive Office. In addition to the five offices just discussed, there are 10 other specialized offices in the Executive Office. The purpose and activities of these units are largely described by their titles. These include the Office of Economic Opportunity, (the "war-against-poverty" agency), the Council on Environmental Quality, and the other units of the Executive Office of the President that are shown in Figure 14–1.

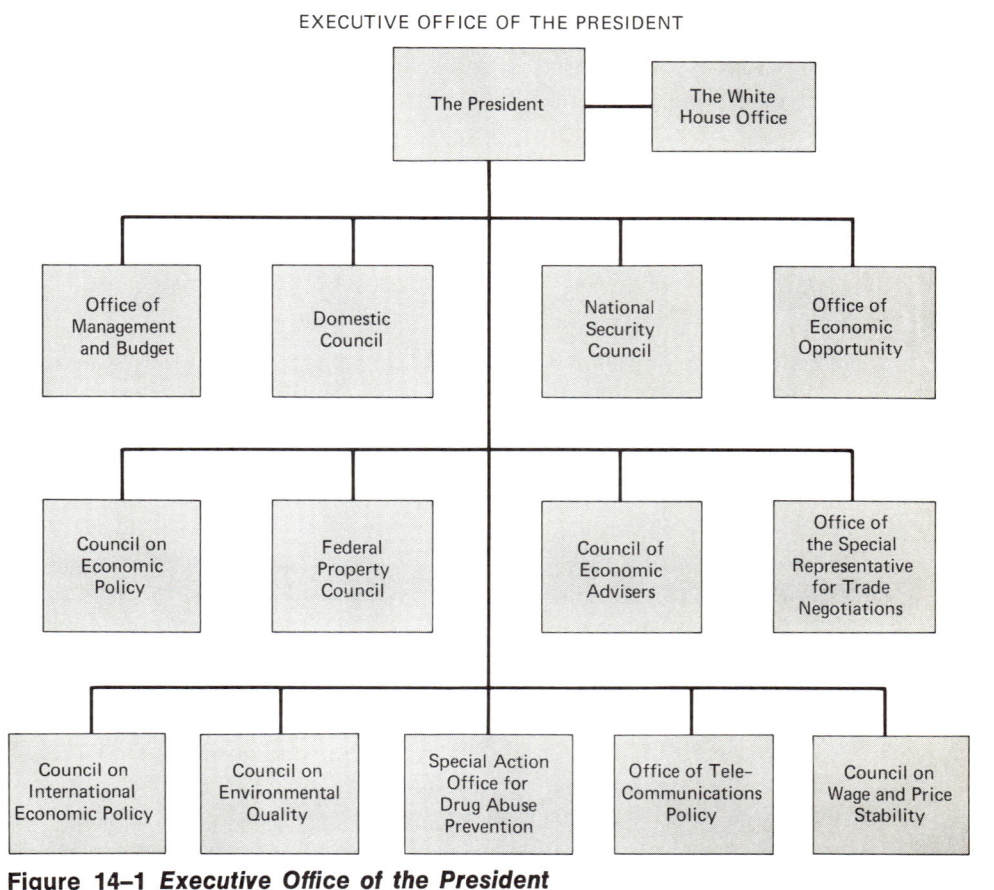

EXECUTIVE OFFICE OF THE PRESIDENT

```
                                The President ─── The White House Office
                                     │
     ┌──────────────┬────────────────┼────────────────┬──────────────┐
  Office of       Domestic         National        Office of
  Management      Council          Security        Economic
  and Budget                       Council         Opportunity
     │               │                │                │
  Council on      Federal         Council of       Office of
  Economic        Property        Economic         the Special
  Policy          Council         Advisers         Representative
                                                   for Trade
                                                   Negotiations
                                     │
     ┌──────────────┬────────────────┼────────────────┬──────────────┐
  Council on     Council on      Special Action   Office of Tele-  Council on
  International  Environmental   Office for       Communications   Wage and Price
  Economic Policy Quality        Drug Abuse       Policy           Stability
                                 Prevention
```

Figure 14–1 *Executive Office of the President*
SOURCE: *United States Government Manual* 1974–1975. Washington, D.C.: U.S. Government Printing Office, 1974.

The Cabinet

Many Americans apparently believe that the American Cabinet should perform the same functions as the British. A comparison of the American and British Cabinets, however, illustrates a fact of political life—governmental institutions with the same name may in reality be quite different. Although the American Cabinet derived its name from the British institution, the two bodies are dissimilar. The British Cabinet is composed of elected leaders of the majority party in Parliament, each member sharing with the Prime Minister responsibility for developing and defending governmental policies and for running the government. None of the U.S. Cabinet members is elected, and the President alone is politically and constitutionally responsible for developing public policies and administering the government. Whereas British policies are collective decisions of the entire Cabinet, the President may ignore the Cabinet; and if he does consult it, he can say, as did Lincoln, "Seven nays, one aye, the ayes have it."

The Cabinet was instituted by Washington, who called meetings of his department heads to discuss governmental problems. It was not until 1907 that the Cabinet was referred to in a federal statute, and it was not mentioned in the Constitution prior to the Twenty-Fifth Amendment. There are now 11 executive departments: State; Treasury; Defense; Justice; Interior; Agriculture; Commerce; Labor; Health, Education, and Welfare; Housing and Urban Development; and Transportation. The Post Office Department, which was formerly of Cabinet status, has been changed to a government corporation.

Selection of Cabinet members. In choosing his Cabinet, a President must consider many factors. The Cabinet traditionally has been chosen almost entirely from the President's party, but occasionally opposition-party members have been chosen, in particular when a President wanted to remove the operation of a department from the arena of partisan conflict. During World War II, President Roosevelt appointed two well-known Republicans; and President John F. Kennedy, after his extremely narrow victory, selected Republicans as secretaries of the Defense and Treasury Departments, both of which are often focal points of political controversy.

A President, also for practical political reasons, may attempt to select his department heads so that each major geographic area will be represented. Various other political considerations help to determine certain Cabinet appointments. President Ford chose as Secretary of Transportation William T. Coleman, the second black to serve in the Cabinet; and he appointed as Secretary of Housing and Urban Development Mrs. Carla Hills, the third woman to serve in such a position. Almost invariably a President will appoint one or more of his department heads in order to repay political debts, to give representation to different factions in the party, or to utilize a person's political knowledge and presumed ability to work with Congress.

Executive experience, specialized knowledge of the work of a particular department, and acceptability to the clientele of a department have all been important factors in determining the choice of Cabinet members. In an apparent effort to reestablish confidence in the Justice Department which was diminished by the involvement of former Attorney General John Mitchell in the Watergate scandals, President Ford appointed as Attorney General Edward H. Levi, who at the time of his appointment was President of the University of Chicago and had formerly served as the dean of its law school. As heads of certain departments—including Agriculture, Commerce, and Labor—Presidents customarily appoint persons who have knowledge of those areas and who are acceptable to leading organized groups interested in the work of the department. For similar reasons, the Secretary of the Interior usually is a westerner and is acquainted with conservation problems, which are the primary concern of that department. In addition to selecting department heads because of political considerations and their qualifications for particular positions, Presidents have customarily made some selections for personal reasons; Kennedy's choice of his brother Robert as Attorney General, and Nixon's appointment of his friend and law partner John Mitchell to the same post are notable examples.

The role of the Cabinet. Not only is the American Cabinet different from those of other countries, but through the years its own role has changed. The Cabinet members are commonly considered to have two principal functions: Individually they serve as the administrative heads of the departments, and collectively they serve, presumably, as advisers to the President. In reality, the Cabinet's role has been determined by the President's conception of it, his personality, and the growth and organization of the government.

Changes in the organization and operation of the executive branch have had a greater impact on the role of the Cabinet than is generally understood. As all executive agencies were originally grouped within the departments, formerly the President in Cabinet meetings could obtain the views of the head of every agency, and he might give directives that could be transmitted to each unit in the executive branch. Toward the end of the nineteenth century, Congress began establishing agencies outside the departments, and today some of these—such as the Veterans Administration and the National Aeronautics and Space Administration—have more personnel than certain executive departments. Thus no longer do the heads of all executive agencies, or even the largest ones, have Cabinet status.

Franklin Roosevelt began the practice, followed by his successors, of inviting persons other than Cabinet members to attend Cabinet meetings. Among those attending Cabinet meetings from time to time are the Ambassador to the United Nations, heads of various other executive agencies, and members of the White House staff. This increase in the number attending Cabinet meetings has diminished the potential usefulness of the Cabinet as an advisory body. A larger group reduces the effectiveness of discussion, multiplies the possibility that confidential information may be leaked to the press, and decreases whatever collegial relationship might develop from meetings of a smaller, more well-defined group.

An important governmental change that has reduced the influence of the Cabinet was the establishment of the Executive Office of the President. Within the White House office, the President has a number of assistants who can advise him; and units of the Executive Office that cut across departmental lines, such as the National Security Council and the Domestic Council, offer advice on specialized problems.

In the past, the Cabinet served for certain Presidents both as a political council and as an agency for coordinating administrative activities; in recent years it has performed neither function. The primary responsibility of Cabinet members now is to serve as administrative heads of their departments. The decline in the frequency of Cabinet meetings is an indication of the diminished role of the Cabinet. Whereas some earlier Presidents held regularly scheduled Cabinet meetings twice a week, President Nixon often allowed more than a month to elapse between meetings. Early in his administration, President Ford announced his intention of restoring the prestige and influence of the Cabinet and making himself readily available to its members. No doubt meetings of the Cabinet will continue to serve as a sounding board for certain presidential ideas and proposals, as a means of communicating information to top officials, and as a method of establishing an *esprit de corps* within the administration, but it is unlikely that the Cabinet will again serve as an important political council where collective decisions are made on major policies.

The Vice-President as presidential assistant

The office of Vice-President is a paradox. It is the second highest office in the nation and has been filled by many able individuals, yet Vice-Presidents have wielded little influence or power. The responsibilities and influence of the Vice-President have increased in recent decades, but even now congressional leaders, Cabinet officers, and White House staff members have greater influence on public policy than he does.

The vice-presidency provides an illustration of a deviation from the separation-of-powers theory. Although the Vice-President is an executive official, he is also President of the Senate. His formal powers in that capacity are minimal: He votes only in case of a tie, and he has the customary powers of a presiding officer. Vice-Presidents such as Alben Barkley, Richard Nixon, Lyndon Johnson, and Hubert Humphrey, who have previously served in the Senate, may have some influence and may help promote the President's program through their personal friendships and knowledge of the Senate. But even these individuals have found they had less influence in the Senate as Vice-President than they previously had as senator. Because the Vice-President's role of presiding officer may be temporarily filled by a senator, his attendance is not required throughout every session, and he consequently has time for other tasks.

In the past, Vice-Presidents were virtually ignored by the Presidents and other top officials. For instance, during the half year that Wilson's illness rendered him unable to meet with his Cabinet, Vice-President Thomas Marshall was neither included in Cabinet meetings nor otherwise informed regarding governmental decisions. The first President to invite the Vice-President to Cabinet meetings was Franklin Roosevelt; but when Roosevelt died, Harry Truman had little information regarding the current activities of the government.

Eisenhower, more than other Presidents, encouraged his Vice-President to engage in a variety of activities. As Vice-President, Richard Nixon traveled abroad, addressed various organized groups, campaigned for political candidates, and presided over meetings of the Cabinet and National Security Council when Eisenhower could not attend. Under subsequent Presidents the Vice-Presidents have engaged in fewer but similar activities. After Rockefeller's confirmation, President Ford stated that he planned to make the new Vice-President an active member of his administration, and appointed him as the active head of the Domestic Council.

That the office of Vice-President has gained status and importance is apparent. No Vice-President from Van Buren (1836) until Nixon (1960) had been nominated for the presidency without first having succeeded to that office on the death of the President. Yet in 1968 both presidential nominees were former Vice-Presidents. Moreover, of the past nine Presidents, five had previously served as Vice President.

Why does the Vice-President play such a minor role in the determination of public policy? Why does the President, so obviously overburdened, make such limited use of the Vice-President? First, political power tends to be positional—it is commonly associated with an office or position, and the office of Vice-President provides the incumbent with relatively little power. Second, the Vice-President may have competed against the President for the presidential nomination—as had Johnson against Kennedy in 1960. Thus the President may be reluctant to give him assignments that would possibly enhance the Vice-President's political stature at the expense of his own.

Probably of more importance is the need for the President to have assistants who are directly accountable to him, who are amenable to his wishes, whose best interests are identical with his own, and who may be dismissed at any time. The fact that the Vice-President may have a considerable political following and is elected for a four-year term excludes him from that category. Each President is aware that friction may develop between him and the Vice-President and that the latter may not give his complete support to the President's program. The role of any particular

Vice-President is determined by the President. Vice-President Humphrey once commented: "A Vice-President will be and is what the President wants him to be," and Vice-President Rockefeller similarly remarked: "The role of a Vice-President totally depends on the President."

THE IMPLICATIONS OF WATERGATE

The abuse of executive power

On August 9, 1974, only one year and a half after the beginning of his second term, Richard Nixon resigned as President of the United States. The initial act that led eventually to his resignation occurred over two years earlier, when on June 17, 1972, seven men employed by the Committee to Reelect the President (CREEP) were arrested after breaking into the headquarters of the Democratic National Committee in the Watergate building complex in Washington, D.C. The name Watergate soon became the code word or symbol used to designate the illegal acts and misdeeds performed by members of the Nixon administration and employees of CREEP.

Following the trial and conviction of the Watergate burglars and the two who had planned and directed the break-in—G. Gordon Liddy and E. Howard Hunt, both former CIA agents and both of whom had also been employed by the White House—the Senate, by a unanimous vote, created the Select Committee on Presidential Campaign Activities (commonly called the Senate Watergate Committee or the Ervin Committee, after its chairman, Senator Sam J. Ervin of North Carolina). Investigations by this committee, the Justice Department, special Watergate prosecutors, and the press led to the filing of criminal charges against more than 40 persons associated with the Nixon administration or CREEP. Included were four former Nixon Cabinet officers: Attorneys General John Mitchell and Richard Kleindienst, Secretary of Commerce Maurice Stans, and Secretary of the Treasury John Connally; the lieutenant governor of California; the two top-ranking White House staff aides, H. R. Haldeman and John Ehrlichman, and nearly a dozen others; and employees of CREEP.

Among the information revealed by the Senate Watergate Committee was the fact that Nixon had secretly begun in 1971 taping all conversations, including telephone calls, made in the President's office. Nixon first refused to relinquish the tapes of these conversations to the investigating committees and the special prosecutor's office, using the arguments of separation of powers, executive privilege, and the need for confidentiality of presidential conversations. Later he made available transcripts of some of the tapes; and finally, after a unanimous decision by the Supreme Court in 1974 requiring that the tapes be released, he agreed to make available whatever Watergate-related tapes were wanted.

In the spring of 1974, aided by information produced by other investigations, the House Judiciary Committee began inquiries regarding the alleged involvement of President Nixon in the Watergate cover-up, the misuse of federal agencies for personal or partisan reasons, the secret bombing of Cambodia, and other matters that might lead to a recommendation for the impeachment of the President. After concluding its investigation, the committee held televised hearings, and by bipartisan votes approved three articles of impeachment for submission to the full House of Representatives for its consideration. (See Appendix 3 for the three impeachment articles.)

During the months following the Watergate break-in, Nixon had steadfastly insisted that he was unaware of the involvement of White House or CREEP personnel in illegal activities, including the cover-up of the involvement of higher government or CREEP officials. A few days after the House Judiciary Committee voted to recommend impeachment, Nixon released a transcript of a taped conversation between himself and Haldeman on June 23, 1972—six days after the Watergate break-in—which clearly showed Nixon's knowledge and participation by that early date in Watergate cover-up activities. After this release, all Judiciary Committee members who had previously voted against recommending impeachment stated that if they had had this information, they would have joined with the majority in voting for at least one of the impeachment articles. Soon afterward, Nixon, informed by the Republican leadership in the House and Senate that his impeachment and conviction appeared to be inevitable, announced his resignation.

Volumes have been produced regarding the unlawful acts and misdeeds leading to Nixon's resignation as President.[14] Watergate-related campaign finance illegalities are discussed in Chapter 11, and other aspects of Watergate are presented elsewhere in this book. Hence the account here of unlawful activities and the abuse of executive power will focus primarily on the principal charges considered by the House Judiciary Committee in recommending impeachment.

The first article of impeachment charged President Nixon with the obstruction of justice by using his office to cover up and protect those involved in the Watergate break-in, withholding evidence, making false and misleading statements, interfering with government investigations, counseling witnesses to commit perjury, and approving the payment of money to obtain the silence of witnesses or to influence their testimony. The second article accused the President of "repeatedly" violating the constitutional

---

[14]For the most complete accounts, see U.S. Senate, Select Committee on Presidential Campaign Activities, *Presidential Campaign Activities of 1972,* Books 1–8, 93d Congress, 1st Session, 1973; U.S. House of Representatives, Committee on the Judiciary, *Impeachment of Richard M. Nixon, President of the United States,* 93d Congress, 2d Session, 1974; *Watergate: Chronology of a Crisis,* vols. 1–2, Washington, D.C.: *Congressional Quarterly,* 1974; Carl Bernstein and Bob Woodward, *All the President's Men,* New York: Warner, 1975.

rights of American citizens by misusing the Internal Revenue Service, the FBI, the Secret Service, and the CIA, and by authorizing "a secret investigative unit" within the White House which engaged in covert and illegal activities. The third article charged Nixon with failing to provide the Judiciary Committee with evidence subpoenaed during its impeachment inquiry.

Among American political scientists and historians there is virtually unanimous agreement that Nixon's presidency has the dubious distinction of being the most corrupt in American history, surpassing even the Grant and Harding administrations. Moreover, the underlying motivation of the Nixon administration misdeeds tends to be different from that for the corruption in previous administrations. Previously, corrupt acts associated with a presidency were usually committed by one or a few persons seeking financial gain. In Watergate, most of the illegal acts were committed for the primary purpose of gaining or retaining political power.

Explanations for Watergate. In the months since Watergate has become a household word, various explanations or interpretations have been suggested regarding the underlying factors that contributed to the illegal acts and abuse of executive power. First, the Nixon administration was an aberration traceable principally to the personality, character, and experience of the President and his top assistants.[15] A few earlier Presidents apparently have engaged in some Watergate-type activities—for instance, rewarding campaign contributors with ambassadorships and attempting to use the FBI or the Internal Revenue Service for partisan purposes—but the cumulative total abuses of power and unlawful acts of the Nixon years are without precedent. According to a second interpretation, Watergate and the distressed condition of the presidency were the results of the American socio-economic system and the pressures to which it and the presidency had been subjected during preceding decades.

A third interpretation is that Watergate resulted largely from what has come to be called the "imperial presidency." The term "imperial presidency"[16] as now used refers to two related developments. First is the tendency of recent Presidents and their top assistants to expand their concept of the President's prerogatives and powers to near-imperial dimensions. A second aspect of the imperial presidency syndrome is the growth of presidential perquisites: the limousines, airplanes, helicopters, White House aides acting as courtiers, and the deference—usually reserved in other countries for royalty—now given the President and his family.

A fourth interpretation of the underlying causes of Watergate holds

---

[15]James David Barber, *The Presidential Character: Predicting Performance in the White House,* Englewood Cliffs, N.J.: Prentice-Hall, 1972.

[16]The term is used by Arthur Schlesinger, Jr., as the title for a book, *The Imperial Presidency,* Boston: Houghton Mifflin, 1973.

that the corruption and misdeeds occurred because of the institutional setting of the presidency and the failure of the system of checks and balances. It is apparent that the system of separation of powers has not worked entirely as envisaged by the Founding Fathers. Earlier in this chapter the increase in executive power was noted. President Nixon sought in various ways to expand further the authority of the presidency. He instituted changes intended to centralize in the White House powers formerly held by department heads. Through the assertion of executive privilege, the impoundment of funds appropriated by Congress, and the unauthorized committing of troops to foreign combat, he extended the President's authority in relation to Congress. Yet in the end the separation of powers did work. The Senate Select Committee on Presidential Campaign Activities unearthed many of the Watergate illegalities; the Supreme Court ruled against Nixon's expanded concept of "executive privilege" by requiring him to produce the Watergate tapes; and the House Judiciary Committee's articles of impeachment led to Nixon's resignation.

A post-Watergate presidency

Since the establishment of the American presidency a fundamental question has been how to provide the nation's Chief Executive with the power needed to exercise strong, effective leadership and at the same time hold him responsible for his actions. Events of the Johnson and Nixon administrations—especially the Vietnam war and Watergate—have focused particular attention on this issue.

Starting during the latter part of the nineteenth century, several plans have been proposed to institute changes that might provide stronger and more responsible executive leadership. Some have suggested establishing a cabinet form of government somewhat similar to that in Britain, Canada, and Australia, arguing that by thus uniting the executive and legislative branches, the executive would have the power necessary to provide forceful leadership and at the same time the legislature could more effectively hold the executive accountable for its actions. Others have urged that efforts be made to achieve more energetic and responsible governmental action through stronger and more centralized political parties. Neither proposal seems likely to be implemented in the near future.

Today there is widespread agreement that the American people have come to expect too much from the President, and that it is time to de-emphasize the office of the presidency and the myth of an omnipotent President sitting in his White House office making decisions that can solve the problems not only of the United States, but of much of the world. Moreover, there is also a general consensus among students of politics that the system of checks and balances should be strengthened. Actions taken by Congress and the courts will help prevent another Watergate. Congress, through such actions as the adoption of the War Powers Act and the Federal Election Campaign Act, the creation of the House and Senate Budget Committees, the modification of the seniority system in selecting chairmen of standing committees, the request that President Ford appear before a committee to explain his pardon of Nixon, and investigations of the misuse of the FBI and CIA, seems to be reasserting its role as a co-equal branch of the federal government. The federal courts, through rulings on impoundment of funds and executive privilege, have placed restrictions on powers claimed by President Nixon. In addition, the press, by exercising its investigatory and adversary roles, may be expected to serve as a check on questionable executive actions.

The principal potential danger in presidential government lies in the power that one man—the President—has to make decisions in the international sphere. In the domestic area the President can take no important action without the continued support and approval of Congress, which must provide the funds and personnel necessary for any government program. Although Congress can limit the President's actions in domestic affairs, it does not serve as an adequate check in international relations, even with the enactment of the War Powers Act. The President can be restrained only by his advisers, most of whom he has appointed. Rash or irrational presidential decisions could possibly lead to a war that might be avoided by a more restrained or intelligent chief executive. The problem is not due to new presidential power; the President, acting on his authority as commander-in-chief, has always been able to commit the nation to policies that might result in armed conflict. It is the possibility of modern nuclear warfare which inserts a new element of danger.

More than three decades ago, Edward S. Corwin pointed out that one of the hazards of the presidential system is that "there is no governmental body which can be relied upon to give the President independent advice and which he is nevertheless bound to consult."[17] A characteristic of the British cabinet system that has recommended it to some American political scientists is the collegial nature of major political decisions. Congress created the National Security Council as an advisory body to the President on military and foreign policy. But the President is not required to act on the advice of the Council; moreover, a strong President may so dominate the Council, whose members are selected by him, that they may be reluctant to assert opposing views. Major presidential decisions on national security and foreign policy are, of course, customarily made only after the President has consulted with various political leaders and experts. The President can find many people who will support him in what he wants to do; what he needs are men who will not hesitate to oppose him when they feel he is wrong.

[17] Edward S. Corwin, *The President: Office and Powers*, 2d ed., New York: New York University Press, 1941, p. 316.

15
Running the National Government

15

In 1974, after an airliner crashed in Virginia killing 92 persons, the Federal Aviation Administration adopted a rule requiring airlines to equip jet airplanes with ground proximity warning systems—a proposal that had been urged upon the FAA since 1969. The Administrator of the Environmental Protection Agency in 1974 issued regulations requiring the states to classify all lands for the purpose of determining the extent to which new industrial, utility, or residential activity would reduce air quality.

Both of these examples illustrate how governmental activity impinges on the individual citizen: in some cases to improve his lot in life, in others to worsen it; in some cases to increase his freedom of action, in others to decrease it. It is the administrative branch of government, the bureaucracy, that implements programs and makes policy meaningful to the citizenry. In terms of the number of employees involved, the amounts of money spent, the individual contacts with citizens, and the significance of decisions made by public employees, the administrative agencies that implement general policy constitute the heart of government.[1]

DIMENSIONS OF THE BUREAUCRACY: SIZE AND VARIETY OF ITS ACTIVITIES

To appreciate what federal administration means in terms of management and coordination, one must have some conception of its dimensions and scope of activities. The United States government today employs about 2.8 million civilian employees, or 3 percent of the total civilian labor force in the United States. By far the largest proportion of those employees work outside of Washington, D.C.; only about 10 percent are employed in the nation's capital. Federal employment may be placed in perspective by noting that public employment at the state level is over three million, and it is well over eight million at the local level.

The variety of activities and programs of the federal government ranges from operating the Alaska Railroad to managing medical research on major diseases to transporting and delivering mail. There is no citizen whose life is not touched in some way by some activity of the federal government,

---

[1]Throughout this discussion, the term *bureaucracy* is used in a nonprejorative sense; that is, as a neutral term referring to the federal public service.

whether it be in the payment of taxes, the observance of federal safety regulations, participation in federally sponsored school lunch programs, or in using interstate highways.

Such varied activities require the services of every skill known to man. The nuclear physicist may be employed in discovering new radioactive isotopes that may be useful in medical practice or research; the engineer may be working on the design of water-delivery systems as a part of a hydroelectric power and water project; the economist may be involved in assessing the impact of American foreign-aid programs on the developing economies of new nations.

THE RISE OF THE ADMINISTRATIVE STATE

The growth in the size of the national bureaucracy, the variety of its programs, and the frequency of its impact on the individual's life have been subjects of much lamentation. For some critics, the growth of the bureaucracy is visible evidence of the moral degradation of the American people or an insidious plot to destroy freedom and to regiment the public under controls exercised by power-hungry individuals who think they know what is good for everyone else.

Although these assertions may have a trace of truth, they fail to credit the transformation of the character of American society under the impact of the industrial revolution as the chief element in the changed and changing role of government. The automobile provides the best illustration. Motorists have bought increasingly powerful cars and have demanded increasingly greater mobility. In response, government, acting through the Bureau of Public Roads and state highways agencies, has constructed an extraordinarily extensive network of highways throughout the country. Air pollution—60 percent of the total estimated to be from car exhausts—became a serious problem, leading to the creation of the Environmental Protection Agency and its air-pollution regulations. Traffic safety became a serious problem, leading to the creation of the National Highway Traffic Safety Administration. The demand for foreign and domestic oil reflected the needs of an automotive society, and resulted in a complex system of laws to regulate the petroleum industry at both the national and state levels. Such an example could be multiplied a hundredfold.

In newly developing areas throughout the world, the bureaucracies are carrying a far heavier burden of modernization. In the absence of private capital, the state has become the primary instrument for economic betterment, and the civil servant has become the administrator of the national wealth. Since, in these areas, the civil service often constitutes the single largest concentration of educated and experienced personnel, it has a far greater influence over the direction and speed of development than does the civil service in the United States. Moreover, in the newly developing areas, civil servants play an important *political* role in inculcating a sense of national identity among people who previously were loyal only to their local community or tribe.

THE SPIRIT OF THE BUREAUCRACY

"Pure" bureaucracy has been characterized by (1) specialization of roles, (2) selection on the basis of achievement, (3) advancement on the basis of established rules, (4) full-time salaried employees who are committed to the bureaucracy as a career, and (5) decision-making according to rules within a hierarchical set of relationships. To a certain extent, every bureaucratic system in the world satisfies these criteria. But the startling differences among the administrative patterns of various societies testify to the powerful impact of culture, because administrative relationships are not only formal relationships among people within the bureaucracy but are patterns of interaction among administrators, the public, and the other institutions of government.

Illustrative of one administrative pattern is the French bureaucracy. The French administrative structure developed from the royal household, but was adapted to the purposes of the modern nation-state with the overthrow of the monarchical system. The civil service was already powerful and relatively professional; only its master had changed. The top-ranking bureaucrats were often drawn from a narrow social class that had access to higher education. Because of political instability, the bureaucracy provided the necessary continuity in government and often made crucial political decisions that others were not prepared to make. The bureaucracy was fortified, moreover, by guarantees of security, adequate pay, and official rank, all of which contributed to high social status. Much of this remains applicable to France today.

The American administrative system may be distinguished for its *representative* rather than its *class* character. Far from being a social, economic, or political elite, its personnel is recruited nationwide and from all classes of the population. There are no formal and few informal barriers to internal advancement. Entry is permitted at all levels, making the infusion of new blood both a possibility and a practical reality.

American bureaucrats are distinctive in their high degree of professionalization among federal executives. A much higher percentage in the federal service has had advanced professional training and has worked in professional capacities than is characteristic of other groups, such as business executives. Moreover, in comparison with business executives, governmental executives have a broader occupational experience and mobility and have moved in and out of public life relatively freely.

Although representation is normally thought to be the exclusive prerogative of the elected representative, the American political system creates an expectation that the bureaucrat will also respond to the public's conception of the general interest. The administrator therefore faces serious political issues, not by simply looking for direction from the Congress or the President, but by grappling with them himself and with other participants in the administrative process.

This suggests that all of the lines of influence in the American bureaucracy are not hierarchical according to the vertical lines normally found on organization charts. The bureaucrat is subject not only to immediate legal superiors in the government agencies but to the host of other individuals and groups that have a stake in the outcome of an administrative decision, because each recognizes the bureaucrat's authority to make binding decisions affecting his welfare. The contests that take place in administrative settings may indeed appear to be almost as political as those that occur in Congress, where bargaining is the normal method of problem-solving.

BUREAUCRACY AND POLICY-MAKING

The complexity of the issues in modern society have required the bureaucracy to become a full partner in virtually every phase of the policy-making process. The development of new programs in the federal government requires integration of what exists, what is proposed, and the avoidance of measures that are obviously impractical or have failed in the past. It requires an awareness of all of the technical and procedural ramifications involved in inaugurating a new program and an appreciation of the substantive values of existing programs and adeptness in improving the programs. The bureaucracy has collective experience and knowledge that must be consulted in any major effort to change policy. For example, when and if a national health program is adopted in the United States, it will almost certainly benefit from, and perhaps be based upon, past experience and extensive studies conducted within the Department of Health, Education, and Welfare. It should be noted, however, that a bureaucratic agency, if it wishes, can use that same collective experience to obstruct innovation and perpetuate programs that no longer have significant social value.

Moreover, the constitutional-legal description of the role of bureaucracy fails to recognize that the bureaucracy is a human institution, peopled by individuals with commitments to, and dependence on, their activities within their agencies. These commitments, coupled with personal ambitions, social affiliations, and professional pride, tend to develop within agency personnel strong policy drives that in time become traditions and even dogma. The Federal Bureau of Investigation, for example, has developed an *esprit* as well as a reputation that only the most intrepid critics challenge.

Policy promotion

The bureaucracy, although formally neutral, actively promotes by various methods the policy programs in which it believes. Public-information officers provide reams of information about government programs to interested parties, and operating personnel in the field discuss their activities before luncheon clubs and professional groups. Agencies develop close relationships with interested groups that can be relied on to cooperate in promoting programs of mutual concern. Experienced bureaucrats work with sympathetic congressmen, lobbyists, newspapermen, and other executive officials to create a favorable climate for their propositions.

The bureaucracy is subject to political control, however, through the President and Congress, and it must respond when the political winds change, as painful as such response is for people who have committed themselves to existing programs. In some instances, the response may be lethargic, but this then requires more dynamic and forceful political leadership and perhaps the removal of those unwilling to follow new paths. The fact that there was almost no complaint about bureaucratic sabotage during the Eisenhower-Kennedy and Johnson-Nixon transitions testifies to the ability of the bureaucracy to serve different masters.

Policy implementation

The nature of public policy also requires the delegation of broad discretion to the administrators in the application of general laws and guidelines to specific cases. Congressional legislation increasingly has the character of general statements of purposes to be achieved, of classes of individuals who are eligible or subject to the statute, and of conditions under which the provisions of the statute should be applied. Congress cannot foresee every contingency that might arise under a statute, so the burden falls on the bureaucracy. For example, the Food and Drug Administration is required to approve all new drugs for both safety and effectiveness. Safety and effectiveness are not terms with self-evident meanings when it is considered that several thousand prescription drugs and 100,000 to 500,000 nonprescription drugs are sold over drug counters each year to millions of people with innumerable ailments, each having its peculiar symptoms and remedies. The FDA is therefore charged with the extraordinarily complex and expensive task of ascertaining these qualities in drugs, and incidentally leaving itself open to criticism and possible court action by pharmaceutical manufacturers or consumer groups who may disagree with an FDA judgment.

POLITICAL LEADERSHIP AND CONTROL

In the constitutional sense, the President has authority over, and is responsible for, the activity of every member of the executive establishment. When he knows what he wants, when his principal aides and executives are in agreement, and when he exercises the full authority of his office, undoubtedly he can have his way. Unfortunately, he is but a single man, and even though his reach is much extended by his personal aides, the Office of Management and Budget, and the National Security Council, he cannot commit himself to more than a fraction of the public business. He must rely on the judgment and loyalty of his administrative subordinates, and this is often risky business, because Cabinet and sub-Cabinet officers often have their own clienteles and may be responsive to influences other than the President's.

Congress is a worthy competitor with the President for control of the bureaucracy. Administrators make decisions that materially affect the constituents of members of Congress, and this creates considerable incentive for intervention. Moreover, Congress and its committees are intensely jealous of their prerogatives as lawmakers, and they use a variety of techniques to ensure their influence. Committee members maintain close relationships with bureau chiefs, and these are often more enduring than the relationships between political executives and bureau personnel. Congress may pass legislation in defiance of presidential wishes; it may cut or increase a bureau's budget; it may set personnel ceilings on an agency or alter its organization. It may investigate the agency or authorize the General Accounting Office to do so.

The success of some administrative agencies and their allies on the committees on Capitol Hill in avoiding presidential or political-executive control has led one commentator to describe these relationships as "subgovernments." The committees and agencies are usually closely associated with interest groups that are intensely involved in the policies followed by the agencies. A classical illustration of such close association among an interest group, congressional committees, and an executive agency is in the broad area of veterans' benefits.

ORGANIZATION OF THE EXECUTIVE BRANCH

The formal structure of the executive branch follows no single pattern (see Figure 15–1), nor can it be based on a single principle of organization. Rather, its design must be based on the purpose or objective for which a public agency is created. For example, it may be appropriate to centralize research activities dealing with a given problem in a single agency if a major attack is to be made on that problem. In other cases, research may be appropriately divided among agencies if that research is vital for the accomplishment of those agencies' missions. Congress had to balance conflicting public needs in 1974 when it made fundamental changes in the structure of the atomic energy program. For nearly 30 years all activity at the federal level dealing with atomic energy was under the direction of the Atomic Energy Commission, but in 1974 Congress separated research and regulation by creating the Energy Research and Development Administration and a

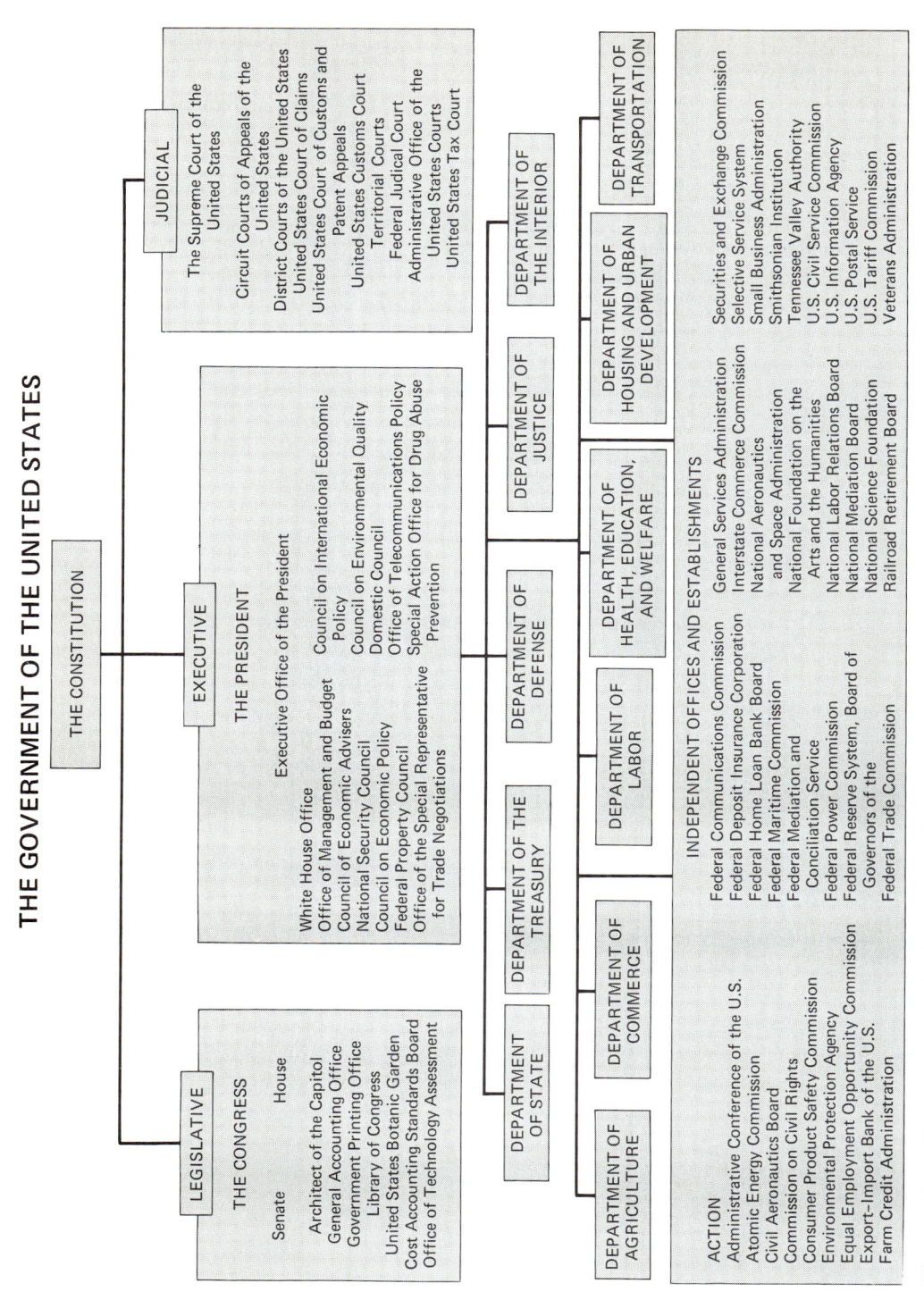

THE GOVERNMENT OF THE UNITED STATES

THE CONSTITUTION

LEGISLATIVE

THE CONGRESS

Senate   House

Architect of the Capitol
General Accounting Office
Government Printing Office
Library of Congress
United States Botanic Garden
Cost Accounting Standards Board
Office of Technology Assessment

EXECUTIVE

THE PRESIDENT

Executive Office of the President

White House Office
Office of Management and Budget
Council of Economic Advisers
National Security Council
Council on Economic Policy
Federal Property Council
Office of the Special Representative for Trade Negotiations
Council on International Economic Policy
Council on Environmental Quality
Domestic Council
Office of Telecommunications Policy
Special Action Office for Drug Abuse Prevention

JUDICIAL

The Supreme Court of the United States
Circuit Courts of Appeals of the United States
District Courts of the United States
United States Court of Claims
United States Court of Customs and Patent Appeals
Territorial Courts
United States Customs Court
Federal Judicial Court
Administrative Office of the United States Courts
United States Tax Court

DEPARTMENT OF STATE
DEPARTMENT OF THE TREASURY
DEPARTMENT OF DEFENSE
DEPARTMENT OF JUSTICE
DEPARTMENT OF THE INTERIOR
DEPARTMENT OF AGRICULTURE
DEPARTMENT OF COMMERCE
DEPARTMENT OF LABOR
DEPARTMENT OF HEALTH, EDUCATION, AND WELFARE
DEPARTMENT OF HOUSING AND URBAN DEVELOPMENT
DEPARTMENT OF TRANSPORTATION

INDEPENDENT OFFICES AND ESTABLISHMENTS

ACTION
Administrative Conference of the U.S.
Atomic Energy Commission
Civil Aeronautics Board
Commission on Civil Rights
Consumer Product Safety Commission
Environmental Protection Agency
Equal Employment Opportunity Commission
Export-Import Bank of the U.S.
Farm Credit Administration
Federal Communications Commission
Federal Deposit Insurance Corporation
Federal Home Loan Bank Board
Federal Maritime Commission
Federal Mediation and Conciliation Service
Federal Power Commission
Federal Reserve System, Board of Governors of the
Federal Trade Commission
General Services Administration
Interstate Commerce Commission
National Aeronautics and Space Administration
National Foundation on the Arts and the Humanities
National Labor Relations Board
National Mediation Board
National Science Foundation
Railroad Retirement Board
Securities and Exchange Commission
Selective Service System
Small Business Administration
Smithsonian Institution
Tennessee Valley Authority
U.S. Civil Service Commission
U.S. Information Agency
U.S. Postal Service
U.S. Tariff Commission
Veterans Administration

Figure 15-1 The government of the United States
SOURCE: *United States Government Manual 1974–1975*, Washington, D.C.: U. S. Government Printing Office, 1974.

new Nuclear Regulatory Commission. The purpose in doing so was to stimulate energy research but also to ensure that public and environmental safety was not endangered by the overenthusiasm of scientists and administrators who did research on nuclear energy.

Departments

The principal form of organization is the *department*, headed by a secretary who is appointed by the President, is confirmed by the Senate, and sits in the President's Cabinet. By far the largest number of federal employees are found in these departments.

Although the general departmental structure has many similarities, it is misleading to classify together such incongruous organizations as the Department of Defense, with its three constituent military services and its one million civilian employees (and 2.2 million uniformed servicemen), and the Department of Labor, with its 13,000 employees. Both the size of these two organizations and their traditions and missions make them extremely different. Every Secretary of Defense has testified to the difficulty in exercising control and coordinating the efforts of the military departments, owing to the strong loyalties and professional commitments to the individual services that were developed during their separate existence and as a result of the tensions that exist between civilian and military leaders.

Independent agencies

A second major type of government unit is the independent agency, which is headed by a single administrator who does not carry Cabinet rank. These agencies are usually more specialized than the major departments; a typical agency is the Veterans Administration.

The justification for the creation of agencies of this type is far more political than administrative. Proponents of independent agencies often argue that there is something unique about their programs that necessitates separate organizational existence. In some instances, this may have the ring of reality, as in the case of the National Aeronautics and Space Administration, which embarked on obviously novel efforts in space exploration. But this position is hardly tenable with regard to the Veterans Administration, which engages in programs closely related to and sometimes identical with programs conducted in, for instance, the Department of Health, Education, and Welfare.

The real justifications for independence are found in the desire of interested parties—members of Congress, interest groups, or both—to ensure responsiveness to their wishes, and the desire of Presidents to launch new programs unfettered by the traditional orientations and ways of doing things in old-line departments. Thus the Environmental Protection Agency was made independent of old-line departments concerned with the environment because its role was to challenge actions of possible detriment to the environment, whether by federal agencies or private parties.

Independent regulatory commissions

A third organizational form is the independent regulatory commission, which, as its name implies, is an organization headed by a plural body and concerned principally with regulating some essentially private economic activity. Examples of these commissions are the Interstate Commerce Commission, which is concerned primarily with regulating the railroad and trucking industries, and the Federal Power Commission, which regulates the electric-power and natural-gas industries.

Congress created these commissions because it felt that neither the courts nor Congress would be able to master the complex technical subject matter and handle cases expeditiously. Because the commissions were given broad authority to establish standards and rules, and because they decided cases among parties, they were considered quasi-legislative and quasi-judicial bodies. They were protected from political influence in that their members were given long and staggered terms, were bipartisan, and were not subject to removal by the President.

Since these commissions deal with corporations having virtual monopolistic power over such vital public industries as telephone service and the transmission of energy, it is naive to believe that they are independent of politics. The President has some influence through his appointments to the commissions, but the economic interests and committees of Congress are often far more influential, because they can deny the commissions the resources they need to do an effective job of regulation. As a result, persistent accommodation of regulated industries by at least some of the independent regulatory commissions (such as the Interstate Commerce Commission) has often had the result that the regulated become the regulators.

Corporations

Government corporations are organized to operate more or less as business enterprises, freed from the normal budgetary and financial controls imposed on regular administrative agencies. Examples of such corporations are the Tennessee Valley Authority, which generates enormous quantities of hydroelectric power and manages a variety of resource-oriented activities in the Tennessee Valley, and the Federal Deposit Insurance Corporation, which insures depositors of funds in member banks against loss. The independence of these enterprises is demonstrated by the fact that they are not dependent on annual appropriations and are free to reinvest their funds as they deem wise. The advantages are flexibility and ability to adapt to novel situations quickly. Despite its businesslike character, the corporate form does not necessarily lead to increased efficiency or better service, as demonstrated by the U.S. Postal Service and its continuing problems after becoming a federal corporation.

These corporations are not totally without external controls, however. The President appoints and may remove their heads, and they must follow federal personnel and accounting practices. They are not completely self-financing and must occasionally seek congressional appropriations. Having responsibilities that overlap with other agencies, they inevitably must seek support elsewhere to do their jobs.

Internal organization and processes

In the typical department, the secretary is accompanied by an under secretary, a number of assistant secretaries, and other aides who are appointed either by the President or the secretary and are responsible to the secretary. It is this corps of political leaders that changes when a new administration takes office and directs the efforts of the bureaucracy toward the goals of the new President and his party.

It is not easy to guide or redirect the bureaucracy. To do so requires sophisticated knowledge of the substantive work of the department and persistence in overcoming the lethargy, if not outright opposition, of bureau personnel; it also demands a clear perception of the goals to be achieved, which hardly can be gleaned from reading partisan platforms. Many political executives arrive poorly equipped and do not remain in the job long enough to see the job through.

The internal structure of departments is typically based on operating bureaus, sometimes headed by political appointees and sometimes not. These bureaus are the operating agencies of the departments, and often their existence far antedates that of the departments themselves. Often having strong congressional and clientele support, they have a momentum behind their programs that makes difficult any assertion of control by political officials at nominally higher echelons. Thus the Forest Service operates autonomously in the Department of Agriculture.

The central offices of these bureaus are in Washington, and it is there that general policy decisions are finally made. The headquarters staff usually includes specialists in budgeting, programming, personnel, and information, as well as experts in the various technical fields that constitute the work of the bureau. The large majority of the personnel of these operating units are found in field offices throughout the United States and the world. Civil servants function in widely diverse circumstances and are subjected to pressures to modify accepted practice from local interests as well as from their own recognition of the difficulties of applying general policy to given situations. The result is strained relations between the central and field offices and accusations of overcentralization and bureaucratic red tape from persons who rely on the bureau's service.

Equal treatment and decentralization

Both equal treatment and decentralization are cherished values in American society, but they sometimes conflict. Thus, for example, the Federal Housing Administration determines what factors of income will be considered, and to what extent, in guaranteeing a loan made on a house. It would be manifestly unfair for the FHA to apply certain guidelines in one area and others in another. Moreover, guidelines are necessary to deal promptly with routine cases; the more difficult cases may be referred to the central office. But real estate prices fluctuate from region to region, as do incomes. Moreover, incomes are often related to racial and social characteristics, so there is a built-in inequality in the FHA's guidelines. Frequent inspections and audits can assure adherence to standards.

Many of the problems attacked by federal programs involve the activities of several federal, state, and local agencies, and thus the problems of centralized control and administrative responsiveness are compounded. As a partial remedy, 10 regional councils have been created to bring together the major federal departments engaged in domestic social welfare and planning. They are designed to reconcile policy conflicts and facilitate state and local requests for grants, but they have only partially overcome the compartmental character of federal organization.

Planning and budgeting

The diversity, size, and cost of federal programs have led to serious concern for improved planning, budgeting, and evaluation. Greater attention is being paid to definition of goals, exploration of alternative means, and explicit statements of costs and benefits. By the utilization of computers and techniques such as systems analysis and operations research, it is hoped that greater efficiency will be achieved in the expenditure of public money for both military and civilian purposes. The most noteworthy effort in this direction has been the Planning, Programming, and Budgeting system, made the official practice during the Johnson administration.

Available evidence suggests that the results have been mixed. Greater attention has been paid to objectives and evaluation of the extent to which those objectives have been achieved. Alternatives have been explored more comprehensively and their consequences assessed before embarking on programs. On the other hand, there has been a recognition that the information demands for true systems analysis are excessive, that objectives frequently remain unclear, that experience may still be a better teacher than analysis, and that ultimately decisions must be made on the basis of values and not of mathematical equations that have the appearance of certainty.

ADMINISTRATIVE MEASURES AND PROCEDURES

For the public, the major questions in judging an administration are whether it has acted fairly, expeditiously, and in accordance with procedures that are understandable and predictable. Organization and control are important only insofar as they contribute to the realization of these goals and increase public confidence in the bureaucracy's capacity to achieve them. In general terms, administrative actions either regulate public behavior or provide services, and for each purpose there are distinctive procedures.

Regulatory and enforcement measures

The most direct and uncompromising form of administrative action is enforcing the law. Even in the field of criminal law, which is generally a preserve of the states, a significant number of federal statutes are enforced by federal agents. The Lindbergh Act, an antikidnaping statute, and narcotics statutes are enforced by federal agents through police-type activities. Federal narcotics agents, for example, are empowered to seize illegally possessed narcotics and to take into custody those who have them in their possession.

An extremely powerful weapon in the hands of the bureaucracy is the power to issue a license—in other words, to grant a privilege to engage in a form of activity that is otherwise proscribed by law. Thus no one may engage in the commercial transmission of messages by radio without a license from the Federal Communications Commission. Nor may an airline fly a plane or a pilot navigate that plane without obtaining licenses for that purpose. To obtain the privilege to engage in those activities, it is necessary to satisfy the licensing authority that one has complied with the statutory requirements imposed by Congress and with the regulations made pursuant to those statutes.

Another form of administrative activity concerns issuing orders to individuals or groups to desist from a given practice or to comply with a decision rendered by the agency. The Federal Trade Commission, for instance, may issue "cease and desist" orders to companies that make false or misleading claims in their advertising.

Less sweeping and general, but no less direct and binding are other actions taken to secure compliance with the requirements of law. Typical would be the situation of the individual taxpayer, who is required to file an income-tax return each year. Failure to report or to pay the amount justified by one's income, or intentional or unintentional errors in the return, will result in personal contacts with Internal Revenue Service agents who will

"Licensing is going to lead to government confiscation of automobiles, mark my words!"
Conrad in *The Los Angeles Times*. Reprinted by permission of The Register and Tribune Syndicate.

attempt to bring about a resolution of discrepancies. Failure to pay promptly may result in fines, and evidence of deliberate fraud may bring a criminal indictment for tax evasion.

In fact, much of the contact between the public and officials is of this character. Rather than highly formalized proceedings, there are negotiations in which each side explains and justifies his actions, almost always with reference to a given statute or regulation. Thus complaints about discriminatory practices in housing may be registered with the Secretary of Housing and Urban Development, who is authorized by the 1968 fair-housing legislation to eliminate discriminatory practices by "informal methods of conference, conciliation, and persuasion," all of which are to take place in private. Only when a pattern of resistance to the statute exists does the Attorney General take enforcement action.

Providing government services

The federal government is engaged in providing an almost infinite variety of services to its citizens—medical services, educational programs, social security, recreational benefits. In addition, it aids its citizens indirectly by subsidizing airlines and merchant ships and through research carried out by federal employees and federal contractors. In some instances, the government may even actively promote its services, as it did in advertising benefits under Medicare.

Direct government services are granted through individual application and a sometimes lengthy process of verifying qualifications. A veteran may apply to the Veterans Administration for admission to a VA hospital for treatment of an ailment that he claims was incurred during military service. Once his case has been decided favorably, the veteran is thereafter eligible for treatment under whatever regulations apply.

In many instances, the applying entity is not an individual but a city, university, or corporation. A city may seek funds for improving local transportation or housing under the Model Cities program of the Department of Housing and Urban Development. A university may seek federal funds for undertaking research or to support a new graduate program. A corporation may apply for a loan from the Small Business Administration or from the Department of Commerce under its program of aid to depressed areas. In many of these instances, a demonstration of the applicant's willingness and ability to share some of the financial burden may be an important factor in deciding whether federal funds should be granted.

Except in cases of deliberate fraud, the only sanction against failure to abide by the standards established by the agency is withdrawal of funds. But this may be a powerful weapon when the recipients have depended on the service or the funds and have planned their programs on the basis of this assistance. The Office of Education, for example, has the authority to withhold funds from school districts that fail to desegregate their facilities.

THE PUBLIC SERVICE

The administration of public programs in the United States requires public servants who have demonstrated qualifications to perform the tasks assigned to them, who can be responsive to change when society dictates a different direction for policy, and who can equitably apply laws and regulations to all persons. It is difficult to find these qualities in a single individual, but they may be found in the public service as a whole.

The quality of demonstrated qualifications is found in the merit principle, applicable today to the recruitment and selection of 90 percent of the people employed by the federal government. It applies to jobs ranging from nuclear physicists to clerk typists. While a significant number of positions are not subjected to strict examination conditions, less than 1 percent of all appointments are on a patronage basis.

The principle of responsiveness is considered in the appointment of political executives—Cabinet and sub-Cabinet officers and their aides, White House staff, agency heads, and some bureau chiefs. The President and his party, when anxious to turn the country in a particular direction, look to these officials, who are overwhelmingly chosen on a partisan basis, to provide the policy leverage. They presumably will serve the man who appointed them.

The third principle, equity, is strongly emphasized in the public service, despite the occasional scandal or misreading of the law. The legal requirement of equal treatment is reinforced by a sense of professionalism, by the legal constraints imposed on public servants, and by an awareness of the procedural requirements for ensuring that all interested parties have adequate opportunity to express their views. Indeed, there are those who find the bureaucracy an important bulwark of the constitutional system, because of its representative character and its passion for proper procedure.

To be sure, the application of these principles creates tensions. Civil servants who are pledged to objectivity and neutrality run the risk of simply trying to maintain the status quo. Political executives, in their passion for change, may be less patient with procedure and less cognizant of conflicting points of view. In the clash of the two principles one hopes for balance and stability moderated by changes having adequate political support.

Political executives

The job of the political executive is a difficult one, facing inward toward the bureaucracy and at the same time facing outward toward a sometimes hostile environment. He must learn to operate at the proper level, not substituting his judgment for the technical information provided by the bureaucracy, yet using bureaucratic expertise in the accomplishment of administration objectives. In the latter respect, the political executive is immersed in outside relationships: formulating and defending a budget and a legislative program to White house staffers, the Office of Management and Budget, and members of Congress. In addition, he must seek support from the powerful interest groups that carefully watch administrative actions.

Political executives for the most part are not neophytes to politics or the public service, and they are therefore acquainted with the strains and stresses of public life. Over the past several decades, approximately three-fourths of all political executives have had previous political experience.

The effectiveness of political executives depends also on their length of service, because considerable experience is required to reorient an agency that has developed its own momentum over a number of years. The reshaping of agency policy is an incremental process, a slow and cumulative chipping away and adding on in small pieces, and this requires persistence, ingenuity, and the building of political and administrative support. High turnover among political executives has been a serious problem.

The Civil Service: recruitment, selection, and classification

The distinctive feature of the civil service is its recruitment and selection on the basis of merit. The concept of merit suggests that the choice of candidates for office depends on demonstrated competence measured by objective examination techniques. Ties of family, party affiliation, education at the "right" schools—all of which may be considered relevant in nonmerit systems—are disregarded in favor of measured capacity for administrative tasks.

A fundamental issue, however, is whether one should measure basic intelligence, which presumably indicates general capacity to deal with complex problems, or specific skills and knowledge that equip a person to perform the tasks of the immediate position for which he is being recruited. In general, the American practice has been directed toward the choice of the best person for the position to be filled, with less concern for general ability to assume the duties of that office and perhaps higher positions in the administrative hierarchy. In large part, this preference is an expression of the American egalitarian spirit, which emphasizes equal opportunity for all people for public employment. In contrast, British civil-service examinations, especially for the higher civil service, tend to be geared to the classical and humanistic traditions of the major British universities. Examinations for the American Foreign Service resemble those used in the British system, which partly explains the "Ivy League" flavor of the Foreign Service.

All the positions in the federal public service have been classified according to the duties to be performed, their placement in the hierarchy, and the responsibilities they carry. Such classification facilitates personnel actions such as recruitment, transfers, equitable salary administration, training, and promotions. While this method of classification sometimes appears to be arbitrary and designed to prevent the most effective and flexible use of personnel, it is difficult to conceive of personnel management in the federal service without it. Federal employees have been grouped into approximately 10,000 different classes.

A contrasting system used in the military service, to some extent in the Foreign Service and the Public Health Service, and widely used in foreign countries, follows the "rank" concept. Under this system, individuals receive pay and perquisites according to their rank, but their actual duties depend entirely on how the agency feels they may be most effectively utilized. Entrance is usually only at the bottom and advancement is based entirely on satisfactory performance within the service. In non-"rank" systems, a new employee may begin at any level.

The federal government attempts to recruit qualified personnel in a highly competitive labor market, one in which the more immediately attractive incentives are normally found in private enterprise. Pay scales for administrative and technical personnel are often higher in private industry, and personnel policies of corporations sometimes are less hemmed in by rules and regulations that are imposed by Congress on public employees. The "image" of the public service often is a negative one, especially among the better educated and higher occupational classes, who tend to regard government service as involving excessive paper work and clerical duties. Many public servants, however, particularly on higher policy-making levels, find exciting careers in the public service.

To meet competition from the private sector, Congress has improved the conditions of public service. Facing a severe shortage of trained scientists and technical personnel, Congress established in 1958 several "supergrades." The pay for the entire civil service increased significantly, especially for those at the higher administrative levels. In 1962 Congress for the first time adopted federal pay scales comparable to those in private enterprise. For many years this principle had been followed with regard to blue-collar employees and lower clerical grades. Recent civil-service pay boosts, while not achieving precise comparability with private industry, particularly at the very top, where private salaries vary widely, have moved strongly in that direction.

In comparing the financial benefits of government employees with those of employees in private business, it should be remembered that the annual wage or salary is not the only ingredient. Federal employees (like most employees in state and local government) enjoy security of employment, pension rights, and other fringe benefits that are not, or only partly, available to employees in the private sector of the economy.

In addition to improved pay, recent years have witnessed other forms of incentives for public-service employment. Career-development programs have been inaugurated, providing for in-service training as well as for more extensive educational programs at the university level. Special examinations have been devised to select especially qualified college graduates for intensive career-development programs that will lead to accelerated movement into the higher echelons of the federal service.

The problems of neutrality, loyalty, and ethnic employment

While the bureaucrat performs a political function of the very highest order because of his skills and experience, he is under obligation to perform his duties in a nondiscriminatory way for all citizens and avoid political partisanship in any form. He can hardly be neutral in pursuing government policy, but he must be neutral with respect to the political parties.

Restrictions on political activities. The excesses of the spoils system of the past led to the adoption of measures to guarantee the position of the employee against the most severe forms of partisan intrusions in the administrative process. Perhaps the most stringent limitation is found in the restriction on political activities by civil servants. Although civil servants may vote and discuss politics privately, they may not actively promote the interests of a political party, participate in campaigns, run for office, serve on party committees, or solicit funds. They are protected against unwarranted partisan pressures by prohibitions against party campaign solicitations, which traditionally constituted assessments on politically appointed officeholders. Such restrictions may be necessary to ensure public confidence in the impartiality of federal civil servants, yet the fact that they are civil servants does not necessarily diminish their interest in politics. There has been some sentiment for revising these restrictions on political participation, particularly in allowing public servants to run for local office.

Loyalty. In 1947 the Truman administration established a loyalty program for all civil servants. In 1956 the Supreme Court ruled, however, that the security program for federal employees applied only to "sensitive jobs," such as in national defense, secret scientific research, or intelligence. In Britain the loyalty program has applied only to sensitive positions from its inception in 1947.

Necessary as these actions were and are, they raise important questions of citizen rights as well as of desirable policy. The very definition of loyalty is subject to varied interpretations, because opinions and general attitudes rather than specific overt acts are often questioned. For this reason, procedural safeguards are all the more important. An individual accused of being a security risk must receive a written statement of charges, be given an opportunity to answer, and be given a hearing; and his case must be reviewed by the agency head.

Employment of minorities. The federal government considers itself a "model" employer and as such has tried to provide equal opportunities for all citizens, regardless of ethnic background. In 1973, 16.3 percent of all federal classified employees were members of minority groups—about the percentage of minority groups in the total population. However, minority members were concentrated in the lower grades 1 through 4, where they held 28.3 percent of jobs in these grades. In the top grades 12 through 18, minority members held 14.3 percent of jobs—a vast improvement over 1967, when only 3.3 percent of jobs in grades 12 through 18 were held by minority members. In 1973, women held 34 percent of all federal white-collar jobs—about the percentage of women in the total labor force. However, women held 46.6 percent of jobs in the lowest grades 1 through 6, as compared with 4.5 percent of the top grades 13 through 18. Thus it appears that, whereas racial minorities have attained much higher proportions of better paying and more responsible positions, women still have a long way to go before attaining substantial equality.

A RESPONSIBLE BUREAUCRACY IN THE DEMOCRATIC SYSTEM

Large-scale public enterprise has resulted in the creation of bureaucratic structures of immense size and power, capable of administering gigantic undertakings such as the worldwide security programs of the Department of Defense. Millions of citizens depend on the administration of programs that are vital to their health, education, mobility, employment, and general welfare.

Given this power, how is the bureaucracy to be made responsible, and to whom? The question is not easily answered either for the polity or for the bureaucrat, because responsibility implies many things.

1. He is responsible to the law prescribing goals, methods, and procedures.
2. He is responsible to higher authority, ultimately to the President.
3. He is often responsible to a set of professional ethics, whether of engineering, law, or accountancy.
4. He is responsible to the clients of his organization who depend on his services.
5. He is responsible to the public interest, however vague and elusive the concept may be.

Given the multiple focuses of responsibility, it is understandable that a bureaucrat may be a cautious man and that he may take refuge in procedures. He knows that audacious behavior is likely to arouse opposition among one influential group or another and make life difficult. His protection is in playing the game by the rules purportedly designed to guarantee fairness to everyone. The bureaucrat also knows that the conflicting demands on him force him to defend the public interest in terms of his own integrity and sense of fairness. The external controls that exist—Congress and the courts—help to reinforce this personal sense of responsibility in establishing limits of irresponsible behavior. The bureaucrat has great power that is tempered by an awareness of conflicting values and the necessity of achieving a reconciliation of these values through patient encouragement of consensus rather than through authoritative fiat. Most of all, he must ensure equitable treatment for all who depend on him.

16
The American Political Economy

16

AMERICAN ATTITUDES TOWARD GOVERNMENT INTERVENTION IN THE ECONOMY

The dominance of empiricism

The empirical and pragmatic outlook of Americans reflects the experience of the frontier, where survival and prosperity depended on the ability to adapt to new and rapidly changing conditions rather than on the capacity to spin out intellectual arguments to their logical conclusion. In economics, as in politics, pragmatism has prevailed from the very beginning of the American experience. While the ideas of Adam Smith and laissez-faire were considerably in vogue in the late colonial and early independence periods, they did not have the dominance in America that they enjoyed in England.

The federal union, created by the Founding Fathers, was based on one free market, with one uniform currency, one national policy in foreign trade, one system of postal communication and highways, and one national policy of taxing and spending for the common defense and the "common welfare." The framers clearly realized that there could be no powerful and prosperous nation without national economic policies, and therefore, in Article I, the economic powers of Congress are more specifically enumerated than any other category. Although, collectively, these powers do not form any complete and clear-cut system or "ism," they at least reflect the view of the Founding Fathers that government is not an inactive bystander in the economic process.

THE CONSTITUTION AND ECONOMIC POLICIES

Flexibility of constitutional language

The Constitution has been invoked to justify low and high taxes, laissez-faire and government intervention in economic affairs, and the priority of economic rights over human rights and vice versa. As has been true so often, in the long run the Supreme Court also followed election results in this area. In the era of laissez-faire, or from about 1880 to the 1930s, the Supreme Court struck down many economic reforms, particularly of the states, such as minimum wages for women, limitations on hours of employment, and price controls. Since the middle 1930s, the Court has recognized that the majority of the people need and desire government action in economic matters, and it has consistently refused on constitutional grounds to interfere with such policies, state or federal.

The language of the Constitution is flexible enough to allow both a narrower—laissez-faire—interpretation and a broader interpretation, such as was used, for example, in an earlier period by the Supreme Court under Chief Justice Marshall and more recently under Chief Justice Warren. The powers of Congress to "lay and collect taxes" (Article I, Section 8), to "provide for the common defense and general welfare of the United States," and to regulate interstate commerce can be used for governmental economic policies that go beyond anything that has been done so far.

Private property and eminent domain

Under the Fifth and Fourteenth amendments, private property may be taken by the federal or state governments, provided due process is observed, the property so taken is for public use, and just compensation is paid. The key phrase is "public use." The courts at one time interpreted public use in a very narrow sense—that is, the private property taken had to be used by a governmental authority or by the general public. More recently, courts have taken a much broader approach. A city may, for example, condemn slum dwellings and build public-housing projects on that land for "persons of low income." In the first test case, decided by New York State's highest court in 1936 (*New York City Housing Authority* v. *Muller*), the main issue was the meaning of "public use." The property owners argued that public-housing projects for "persons of low income" was "class legislation" not meeting the constitutional standard of public use, because only low-income persons were eligible for the project and they alone would use it. By contrast, the court took a broader view and interpreted "public use" to mean "benefit to the public," stating that "the essential purpose of the legislation is not to benefit that class or any class; it is to protect and safeguard the entire public from the menace of the slums."[1]

"Business affected with a public interest"

The pragmatic nature of American governmental economic policies can perhaps best be seen in the concept of "business affected with a public interest." In 1877 the Supreme Court had to decide whether an Illinois statute fixing maximum rates charged by grain elevators was constitutional. In upholding the statute (*Munn* v. *Illinois*, 1877), the Court laid down the prin-

---

[1] For a fuller discussion, see William Ebenstein, *The Law of Public Housing*, Madison: University of Wisconsin Press, 1940.

ciple that government regulation, including price control, is constitutional in the case of businesses "affected with a public interest." Looking back to the (precapitalist) common law, the Court found that when private property is "affected with a public interest, it ceases to be *juris privati* only." The Court then stated:

> When, therefore, one devotes his property to a use in which the public has an interest, he, in effect, grants to the public an interest in that use, and must submit to be controlled by the public for the common good, to the extent of the interest he has thus created.

The courts have never drawn up a list of businesses affected with a public interest and therefore subject to governmental regulation. Insurance companies, tobacco warehouses, milk producers and marketers, coal producers, and many other types of businesses have been held to be subject to price regulation—in some cases minimum prices and in other cases maximum prices. The Supreme Court has pointed out that "public interest" is not a mystical quality that inheres in some types of business but not in others. Public interest means no more, the Court held in *Nebbia v. New York* (1934), "than that an industry, for adequate reason, is subject to control for the public good."

No specific economic theory enshrined in the Constitution

The absence of a clearly defined economic theory about the nature and limits of governmental policies in economic affairs has been most clearly stated by Justice Holmes. In 1905 the Supreme Court (in *Lochner v. New York*) struck down a New York statute limiting the hours of work in bakeries to 10 hours per day and to 60 hours per week, such limitation being held by the Court's majority to be a deprivation of liberty without due process. This majority decision—a high point of dogmatic laissez-faire argumentation in the Court's history—was sharply attacked by Justice Holmes in one of his most famous dissenting opinions: "The Fourteenth Amendment does not enact Mr. Herbert Spencer's *Social Statics*." Holmes went on to say that *"a constitution is not intended to embody a particular economic theory, whether of paternalism and the organic relation of the citizen to the state or of laissez-faire."*

One of the most frequently used arguments in favor of laissez-faire and against any government action in economic matters is that "one thing leads to another," and that, once government intervenes in economic life, the "road to serfdom" (the title of F. A. Hayek's famous book) is inevitable.[2] In less analytical terms, this logic is often expressed in the phrase *creeping*

---

[2]F. A. Hayek, *The Road to Serfdom,* Chicago: University of Chicago Press, 1944.

socialism. In 1911 the Supreme Court upheld the constitutionality of an Oklahoma statute that subjected state banks to assessments for a Depositor's Guaranty Fund (*Noble State Bank* v. *Haskell*). In challenging the constitutionality of the statute, the appealing bank argued along the customary lines of "one thing leading to another." Speaking this time for the majority of the Court, Justice Holmes rebutted such argumentation as follows: "It is asked whether the State could require all corporations or all grocers to help to guarantee each other's solvency, and where we are going to draw the line? But the last is a futile question, and we will answer the others when they arise."

CURBING CONCENTRATION OF ECONOMIC POWER

The rise of trusts

The era after the Civil War was characterized not only by rapid industrialization and the appearance of big business organizations, but also by various monopolistic devices that enabled a single corporation to control an entire industry. The most effective of these devices was the *trust*. Through a trust agreement, stock of competing corporations was handed over to a board of trustees in return for "trust certificates." The trustees were then in a position to fix prices and exclude competition in an entire industry. Later, the term *trust* came to mean any big corporation that had large power in its industry. Particularly in political parlance, "trust-busting" and "anti–big business" became virtually identical. This terminological ambiguity reflected from the beginning the suspicion that mere bigness is, or may be, a threat to the free market, although no specific acts of restraint of trade are committed by the big corporation.

The first major trust was formed in 1882 by John D. Rockefeller from about 40 oil companies, and his Standard Oil Company controlled 90 to 95 percent of the petroleum industry in the United States. Trust agreements in other industries followed swiftly; around the turn of the century, 26 corporations controlled 80 percent or more of the output in their fields.

The Sherman Antitrust Act

Since the states were powerless to curb these monopolistic giants (and in many states there was not even a desire to curb them), pressure for federal action against monopolies became more and more intensive because trusts were national in scope and impact. Bipartisan support for the defense of the free market against restraint of trade through monopolies resulted in the Sherman Act of 1890, the first major antitrust legislation in the United States (and in any Western country).

The Sherman Act has two important provisions. First, it declares illegal "every contract, combination in the form of trust or otherwise, or conspiracy, in restraint of trade or commerce among the several states or with foreign nations." The second main provision declares any person guilty of a misdemeanor who "shall monopolize, or attempt to monopolize, or combine or conspire with any other person or persons, to monopolize any part of the trade or commerce among the several states, or with foreign nations."

The restriction on interstate and foreign trade has been interpreted broadly by the courts. Thus restraints of trade within a single city or state are held illegal if they significantly impinge on interstate commerce. As to foreign trade, agreements between American corporations and foreign corporations reducing competition in United States exports or imports are illegal. Even agreements among foreign corporations are held illegal if they aim at price-fixing or other anticompetitive or monopolistic practices in the United States.

Breakup of monopolies. In the first phase of its operation, the most notable successes in breaking up monopolies were scored against Standard Oil of New Jersey and the American Tobacco Company, both cases decided by the Supreme Court in 1911. Like Standard Oil of New Jersey, American Tobacco had bought up its competitors, and finally controlled 95 percent of the cigarette industry. Both monopolies were ordered to dissolve.

The third major antimonopoly case involved the steel industry, and was directed against the United States Steel Corporation (*U.S. v. U.S. Steel Corp.* [1920]). U.S. Steel was formed in 1901 out of nine large previous corporations, and by 1908 accounted for slightly over half of all steel production. Suit against it was brought in 1912, and finally decided by the Supreme Court in 1920. The Court did not order its dissolution, because it found that competition still existed, and that U.S. Steel had discontinued its famous "price-fixing dinners" and other "predatory" and anticompetitive practices.

Criminal prosecutions under the Sherman Act. Under the Sherman Act, the Department of Justice can bring both civil and criminal suits against persons or corporations charged with violations under its provisions. In criminal actions, the penalty for each violation may be a fine of up to $100,000 for an individual or of up to $1 million for an offending corporation, and the prison term for offending individuals may run up to three years. Criminal proceedings are instituted in flagrant cases of deliberate violation of the law, and within that category, jail sentences are given in particularly extreme cases.

A new approach in the fight against monopoly: the factor of size

A breakthrough in antitrust policy occurred in the aluminum industry (*U.S. v. Aluminum Company of America*), decided by the federal Court of Appeals as the court of last resort in 1945. At the time of bringing the lawsuit against Alcoa, the company controlled over 90 percent of primary aluminum production in the United States. Until the Alcoa case, the government always felt it had to prove "predatory practices" and "unworthy motives" of a company before it could be held an illegal monopoly: "The law does not make mere size an offense" (*U.S. v. U.S. Steel Corporation* [1920]). In the Alcoa case, the Court of Appeals expressed the new doctrine that mere monopolistic size was enough to constitute a monopoly, even if no specific "predatory practices" could be charged, because the very possession of monopolistic power meant that Alcoa would sell at a price fixed by itself, with no interference from nonexisting competitors. Alcoa was ordered to dispose of its Canadian interests, but was otherwise left intact. Instead of breaking it up, the government turned over wartime production facilities to Alcoa's emerging rival companies, Reynolds Metals and Kaiser Aluminum, to create more balanced competition.

Expanding governmental protection of the free market: the Clayton Act

Although the Sherman Act was a big step forward in the protection of the free market, it suffered from two basic defects. First, it was couched in such general language that the courts had almost complete discretion to determine the meaning of such general terms as *restraint of trade* and *monopolize*. The second main defect was, at least until the Alcoa case in 1945, that the Sherman Act dealt with accomplished facts: It was punitive rather than preventive.

The desire for specific anticompetitive prohibitions and for preventive action found its legislative expression in the Clayton Act and the Federal Trade Commission Act of 1914. The Clayton Act outlawed price discrimination, such as selling below cost to drive competitors in specific areas out of business, or granting large buyers price concessions that go beyond the cost-saving resulting from large sales to one buyer; interlocking directorships, or serving on the board of directors of two or more competing companies; and acquisitions of share capital of competing corporations.

All these practices are illegal when the "effect may be to substantially lessen competition or tend to create a monopoly." Here lies perhaps the biggest difference between the Clayton Act and the Sherman Act. Whereas the Sherman Act seeks to remedy past offenses, the Clayton Act looks to the probable future: All the government has to prove is that anticompetitive acts *may* result in less competition, or that they *tend* to create a monopoly.

The Federal Trade Commision. The Federal Trade Commission (FTC) was entrusted with the administration and enforcement of the provisions of the Clayton Act, sharing these activities with the Department of Justice. In setting up the FTC, the act of 1914 also provided that "unfair methods of competition in commerce and unfair or deceptive acts or practices in commerce" are illegal. The outlawing of unfair and deceptive methods goes even beyond the prohibitions of the Sherman and Clayton Acts, because the aim of the FTC is to protect the buyer and consumer against unfair and deceptive practices rather than to prevent monopolies. The Truth-in-Packaging Act of 1966 and the Truth-in-Lending Act of 1968 are two major legislative measures designed to protect the consumer and borrower against misrepresentation in advertising, packaging, and consumer-credit terms. Unfair practices include false or misleading advertisements, false endorsements, commercial bribery or spying, deceptive pricing, and "payola." In advertising, for example, calling one's product perfect, marvelous, wonderful, and stunning is allowed, but suggesting that "calories don't count" in a dietary regime is not permissible.

Curbing the urge to merge

Section 7 of the Clayton Act forbade acquisition of share capital of one company by another if both were in a competitive position. If one company buys up another competing company, such mergers are called *horizontal*. But under the Clayton Act, two other types were permissible until 1950: *vertical* mergers (or "integration") between a supplier and a customer, as for example between a manufacturer of steel ingots and an iron-ore mining company, or between a shoe manufacturer and a retail chain outlet; and *conglomerate* mergers, or the merging of two corporations in different lines of business. This loophole was closed by Congress in 1950, when it forbade such acquisitions and mergers if substantial reduction of competition would be the probable effect "in any line of commerce in any section of the country."

Particularly attacked by the federal government are conglomerate mergers, where the acquiring company has such vast financial resources that future competition in the acquired company's business might thereby be weakened. For example, in 1967 the Supreme Court ordered Proctor & Gamble to divest itself of Clorox Company, which it had acquired in 1957. The main argument of the Court was that Proctor & Gamble, the nation's largest advertiser, had financial and promotional resources that would tend to create monopolistic conditions in the liquid bleach market in which Clorox was a leader.

GOVERNMENT AND LABOR

Areas exempt from antimonopoly policies

Public utilities such as gas and electric companies, communications such as telephone and radio and television broadcasting, and transportation companies such as railroads are exempt from the provisions of antimonopoly

"Either we buy a new desk or we stop adding to the conglomerate."
Drawing by Mahood; © 1971 Saturday Review, Inc.

laws to the extent that their activities are regulated by state and federal regulatory commissions—the Interstate Commerce Commission, the Federal Power Commission, and the Federal Communications Commission.

Agriculture is another area in which combination is not only tolerated but often governmentally encouraged and sponsored in various allocation and marketing programs through which farmers are assured minimum prices for some of their products. The Clayton Act specifically exempted farmers' mutual-help organizations from its antimonopoly provisions.

The rationale behind the encouragement of labor unions

The most important exemption from the general principle against combination is with respect to labor. Here, the purpose of public policy is to make possible the democratic method of bargaining between employers and workers. However, in a corporate economy the individual worker does not possess bargaining power in dealing with his employer. His employer (or prospective employer) is not as eager a buyer of his individual labor power as he is an eager seller of his services. An employer of 10,000 workers who lets one man go loses $1/100$ percent of his work force, and at worst, if he cannot find an immediate replacement, he has to get along without this small fraction of his labor force. A worker who loses his job, or does not get one, has to forgo 100 percent of his wage. Only if workers combine in a union can they match the bargaining power of the employer. This is particularly true when the employer himself does not act alone, but acts with other employers in a particular line of business locally or nationally in determining wage rates or other working conditions.

The National Labor Relations Act: the Magna Carta of labor

The National Labor Relations Act of 1935 (often referred to as the Wagner Act, named after its chief author, Senator Robert Wagner of New York) finally brought organized labor what it wanted. The two most important provisions of the act were (1) employees were given the right to organize unions and take part in their activities, without restraint or coercion by employers in the exercise of their rights; (2) employees were given the right to bargain collectively with the employers through their elected representatives, and the employer could not refuse to bargain. Employers were also forbidden to set up "company unions" (that is, unions controlled by the employers), to discriminate against union members, or to dismiss or otherwise penalize a worker for having exercised his rights under the act.

The philosophy of the National Labor Relations Act was based on the democratic principle that social conflicts should be settled through peaceful negotiation rather than through violence. The act does not compel unions and managements to agree; they are merely compelled to bargain their disputes collectively. If they do not agree, strikes (by employees) and lockouts (by employers) are still legal.

For enforcement, the act also set up the National Labor Relations Board (NLRB), an independent regulatory body made up of five members, appointed by the President, with the consent of the Senate, for five-year terms. One of its main functions is to determine, in case of disagreement, the legitimate representative union of workers, and to hold supervised elections to make that determination in instances where several unions claim to represent the majority of the employees. In addition, the NLRB has the authority to investigate charges of unfair labor practices, and to issue "cease-and-desist" orders in the light of its findings.

The Taft-Hartley Act

As a result of the National Labor Relations Act and the pro-labor attitude of the New Deal administration under Franklin D. Roosevelt, union membership jumped from 3.6 million in 1935 to over 10 million in 1941. Yet, as time went on, the feeling grew in Congress that the pendulum had swung too far in the direction of labor, and that a new balance between labor and management should be established. This led to the Labor-Management Relations Act of 1947, commonly referred to as the Taft-Hartley Act. The two basic principles of the Wagner Act—the right of labor to organize unions and to bargain collectively—were preserved, but important restrictions on labor were added. Some of the most important innovations of the Taft-Hartley Act are:

1. A cooling-off period of 80 days, initiated by the President in cases of threatening or actual strike situations, if he finds that stoppage of work would imperil national health or safety.

2. Prohibition of the *closed shop,* under which an employer can hire only persons who are union members. The *union shop* was allowed to continue: Under the union-shop arrangement, new employees must join the union, provided a majority of the workers has voted in favor of a union shop, and provided union shops are not forbidden by state right-to-work laws.

3. Prohibition of unfair labor practices by unions. Whereas the Wagner Act focused on unfair labor practices by employers, the Taft-Hartley Act made numerous labor practices by unions illegal. Such prohibitions include the following: the refusal to bargain collectively; coercion of, or discrimination against, employees for exercising their rights; and featherbedding—that is, forcing employers to pay for work not done or not intended to be done—and the contributing of union funds in federal elections.

The Landrum-Griffin Act

A decade after Taft-Hartley, Congress passed another major reform as the result of congressional investigations of abuses in labor-management relations. The chief objective of the Labor-Management Reporting and Disclosure Act of 1959, commonly referred to as the Landrum-Griffin Act after its House sponsors, was to protect union members against improper union practices.

First, the reform gave union members a "bill of rights," guaranteeing them

1. The secret vote in union elections
2. "Reasonable rules and regulations" for participation in union meetings
3. Full and fair hearings in disciplinary proceedings of unions
4. The right to appear before a governmental body without union coercion or interference
5. The right to sue unions in a federal court for infringing any of the "bill of rights."

The second main objective of the Landrum-Griffin Act was to strengthen the character of leadership positions in unions as positions of trust and responsibility. The misappropriation or embezzlement of union funds became a federal crime, and union officials handling union money have to be bonded.

Finally, the act had three provisions aimed directly at a hoodlum element that had penetrated a few unions.

1. It prohibited picketing for the purpose of extortion.
2. It prohibited management to pay, or for union officers to receive, bribes for "sweetheart contracts," that is, labor contracts between

union leaders and management that are favorable to management and that corrupt union leaders arrange in return for cash.
3. It prohibited persons convicted of serious felonies from holding union offices for at least five years.

PUBLIC POLICIES FOR ECONOMIC GROWTH AND STABILITY

The Employment Act of 1946

The principal legal commitment of national policy to maintain economic stability and encourage economic growth is expressed in the Employment Act of 1946. Little known to the general public, it is one of the most important acts of Congress in this century.

The act declares that it is the "continuing policy and responsibility of the Federal Government" to create and maintain "conditions under which there will be afforded useful employment opportunities, including self-employment, for those able, willing, and seeking work, and to promote maximum employment, production, and purchasing power." The act provides further that the President transmit annually to Congress by January 20 an economic report, presenting an analysis of the state of the economy during the preceding year, the prospects and needs for the coming year, and programs and legislative proposals for the maximum utilization of manpower and resources.

The Joint Economic Committee and the Council of Economic Advisers.

The act also established two committees: first, the Joint Economic Committee, composed of eight members of the Senate and eight members of the House of Representatives. Its main function is to serve as a guide to congressional committees dealing with legislation relating to the economic report, and to submit to Congress annually by March 1 its own findings and recommendations with respect to presidential proposals in the report. The second committee established by the Employment Act of 1946 is the Council of Economic Advisers in the Executive Office of the President. The council consists of three members, appointed by the President with the consent of the Senate. The main function of the council is to assist the President in the preparation of the annual economic report, and to "develop and recommend to the President national economic policies" aiming at full employment of manpower and resources.

The problem of inflation

Just as the military are often said to prepare for the last war, economists and policy-makers are prone to get ready for the last major economic dislocation. The Employment Act of 1946, with its priorities of maximum employment, production, and purchasing power, was passed against the background of the Great Depression of the 1930s, when unemployment was the major economic evil. Yet since the middle 1960s a new economic calamity has ravaged the advanced industrial nations, including the United States: *inflation*. In the 1950s and the first half of the 1960s, the annual rate of inflation, as measured by the consumer price index, averaged between 2 and 3 percent. From the late 1960s, the rate dramatically increased, reaching 8.8 percent in 1973 and 12.2 percent in 1974—the first "double-digit" inflation in the United States in several decades.

The Employment Act of 1946 did not even mention inflation, and some economists have therefore suggested that the act be amended so as to include a reasonable stability of prices as a top priority of governmental economic policy. Such a commitment on the part of government would be particularly important, since the new type of calamitous double-digit inflation has been accompanied by steeply rising rates of unemployment. Whereas in the past rising unemployment generally had a deflationary effect on prices, causing them to drop or to rise only moderately, the new type of inflation has been accompanied by rising unemployment, resulting in "stagflation," or stagnating economic activity plus inflationary price rises at the same time.

Runaway inflation also poses a direct threat to the stability and possibly even to the survival of democratic institutions. In the early 1920s, Germany passed through a period of wild inflation, in which a loaf of bread finally cost several million marks, and such feverish social disorder was one of the major causes of the early rise of Nazism. In Latin America, runaway inflation in recent decades has been one of the persistent factors in the decline of democratic institutions in such nations as Argentina, Brazil, and Chile. In recent years Italy has suffered from the highest rate of inflation among the major industrial nations of Europe, and such inflation has been accompanied by a weakening of democratic institutions. By contrast, West Germany has experienced the comparatively mildest inflation in Western Europe, and her political stability has consequently remained at a high level. If democratic governments are unable to cope with inflation, masses of people are easily persuaded or cajoled into accepting authoritarian governments that impose economic discipline and stability—by force, if necessary.

The use of fiscal and monetary policies

Basic economic policies of most governments today are guided by a twofold concept: to use fiscal and monetary policies as instruments of economic stability and of growth. The purpose of both "tools" of economic policy is to match at all times, as much as is feasible, total spending (aggregate demand) with productive capacity in the economy.

The use of fiscal policies. If total spending is below productive capacity, or threatens to fall below it, the government can employ either (or both) of the following fiscal policies: It can either increase government spending, thus driving up demand, or it can reduce taxes so that private individuals and businesses have more money to spend on consumer goods and to invest in productive facilities. This dual policy of both cutting taxes and increasing government expenditures has been followed since the middle 1960s.

President Kennedy favored a sizable cut in taxes, although the budget was in a state of deficit. After his assassination, Congress enacted the Revenue Act of 1964 and the Excise Tax Reduction Act of 1965. Despite the reduction in the rates of both income and excise taxes, federal revenue did not decline, but rose sharply in subsequent years, because the increased spending by private individuals and corporations stimulated business activity and reduced unemployment to such an extent that more tax revenue was generated than would have been possible under the previous higher tax and excise rates. In 1968 Congress enacted a 10 percent surcharge on personal and corporate income taxes to help pay for the rising costs of the Vietnam war and to correct the growing balance-of-payments deficit. The surtax came three years too late, was not high enough, and failed to stem the rising tide of inflation and the growing deficit of the balance of payments. In 1971 and 1975 Congress reverted again to tax cuts as a means of stimulating the sagging economy and reducing the rising unemployment. but neither measure was an unqualified success, for unemployment remained at high levels, exceeding 8 percent of the labor force in 1975. Fiscal policies have not always been as successful as their proponents would have wished; this is partly because such policies are not properly timed or not vigorous enough, and partly because economists disagree among themselves as to the proper timing and scope of such fiscal policies.

The use of monetary policies. Monetary policy is the second main instrument of the government in promoting economic stability and growth. Unlike fiscal policy, which is handled by the federal government, monetary policy is handled by the Federal Reserve System, a semi-independent body established in 1913. The system is made up of 12 regional Federal Reserve Banks, owned by the private member banks in the system. Nearly half of the 14,000 banks in the United States are members of the Federal Reserve System, but this half controls over 80 percent of bank assets and deposits. The system is directed by a Board of Governors in Washington, made up of seven members who are appointed by the President with the consent of the Senate. To make the board politically independent, its members are appointed for staggered 14-year terms, and members may not be reappointed for a second term. In addition to controlling the supply of money and credit available to banks and borrowers, the Board of Governors sets the interest rate at which it lends money to private banks, which in turn make loans to businesses and individuals. The interest rate is raised in inflationary or near-inflationary periods to decrease the demand for credit. Thus less money enters the spending stream in the economy, and there is therefore less pressure on existing resources. By contrast, when there is a slack in the economy—when manpower and resources are underemployed—a decrease in the interest rate, or "easy money," stimulates the demand for credit, and these additional funds enter the spending stream by increasing expansion of plants, inventories, and the production of consumer goods.

Limits of monetary policies. The great—and as yet not completely resolved—dilemma in using monetary tools in economic policy has both an economic and a political aspect. Economically, manipulating credit volume and interest rates seems to be even less predictable than fiscal policies. When the government increases expenditures or cuts taxes in time of underemployed workers or resources, money immediately enters the spending stream and stimulates production and investment. By contrast, even the policy of very low interest rates during the Great Depression in the 1930s did not have the desired effect in any decisive manner. If credit is easily available at low interest rates, potential borrowers may still abstain from borrowing if they feel pessimistic about the future of the economy. Similarly, if in a period of inflation credit is tightened and interest rates are raised, optimistic individuals or corporations may still borrow money to expand plant facilities, to buy consumer goods on credit, and to purchase stocks or gold in anticipation of future profits.

Monetary policy has also been used with limited effectiveness in defending the value of the dollar. The stability of the dollar was seriously threatened in the late 1960s and early 1970s, mainly because the United States suffered alarmingly large deficits in its balance of payments with the rest of the world. After repeated official assurances that the dollar would not be devalued, the dollar was devalued by almost 10 percent in 1971, and by another 10 percent in 1973. While the depreciation of the dollar stimulated American exports, particularly of basic agricultural and industrial commodities, increased exports also had the less pleasant side effects of shortages and increased prices for the American consumer. Moreover, the potentially beneficial effect of devaluation and increased earnings from exports was vitiated by the fact that the cost of imported oil alone rose from $7.5 billion in 1973 to about $25 billion in 1974.

Federal insurance of deposits and credits

Because the safety of credit affects both the stability and growth of the economy, the federal government is involved in various programs. The Federal Deposit Insurance Corporation (FDIC), established in 1933, at the depth of the Great Depression, insures deposits in banks up to $40,000 for each account. Nearly all of the country's 14,000 banks participate in this program. The Federal Savings and Loan Insurance Corporation insures deposits up to $40,000 per account in participating savings and loan associations (S&L's). Individual savings and time deposits in banks and S&L's exceed $300 billion, and the overwhelming majority of American families are protected by these federal insurance programs.

In addition to depositors in banks and S&L's, another large group that has received financial protection from the federal government is composed of the shareowners who leave their securities in the custory of their brokers. The number of shareowners increased from 6.4 million in 1952 to 31 million in 1974. After nearly a hundred brokerage firms went bankrupt in 1968–1970, Congress created the Securities Investor Protection Corporation (SIPC) in 1970. SIPC provides protection of up to $50,000 for shareowner-customers whose brokerage firms go bankrupt.

In the field of foreign trade, the federal government established in 1934 the Export-Import Bank to facilitate foreign trade through the granting or insuring of credit, particularly where private banks are unwilling or unable to assume the risks. Such risks may be political, as in trade credits granted to Communist governments or to politically unstable non-Communist countries, or where the credits are for projects with uncertain financial returns.

BUILT-IN STABILIZERS OF THE ECONOMY

In addition to *ad hoc* public policies and discretionary fiscal policy aiming at economic stability, governmental intervention and long-range policies have developed "built-in stabilizers" that tend to lessen the impact of sharp upswings or declines in economic activity.

Government spending

One built-in stabilizer is the size of government itself, currently employing (on the federal, state, and local levels) about 16 percent of the civilian labor force, as compared with 6 percent in 1929. As to government spending, federal, state, and local government expenditures amounted to about 10 percent of national income in 1929, but climbed to about 40 percent in the mid-seventies. Thus government employment and expenditures have proportionately risen three to four times since 1929.

Unlike families and business enterprises, which in the long run must spend less when they take in less, government (particularly on the federal level) can keep on spending more than it receives through the process of borrowing. In fact, since the 1930s, when the English economist John Maynard Keynes published his policy proposals for combating depressions, his key idea has been generally accepted: that government *should* increase its expenditures in times of shrinking economic activity to make up for the loss of demand on the part of family households and private businesses.

"Transfer payments"

An even more important "built-in" stabilizer in the economy derives from the phenomenal growth of "transfer payments" (payments resulting not from current production but from public and private pensions, social-security benefits, unemployment insurance, veterans' benefits, and the like). In 1929 transfer payments amounted to only 1.7 percent of total personal income, but in the 1970s the share of transfer payments in personal income was over 12 percent. Most of these payments, such as pensions or social-security benefits, remain stable in recessions. Some types of transfer payments even rise in recessions; for example, as unemployment increases, unemployment-assistance payments increase. As for the impact of inflation on personal incomes, social-security benefits in the 1970s have been better protected by congressional legislation than have wages; in fact, social-security benefits in the 1970s have risen faster—in terms of purchasing power—than have wages and salaries. Thus transfer payments play an increasingly important role in periods of either recession or inflation, and in periods that suffer from both.

EXECUTIVE POWER IN DEFENSE OF PRICE AND WAGE STABILITY

Until recently, both the government and the public accepted the economic proposition that the movement of wages and prices—except in a few regulated industries—was the product of market forces that should not be interfered with in normal times. Only in wartime was the whole economy considered to be "affected with a public interest" and therefore subject to federal regulation of prices, as happened in both world wars.

Holding the line in basic industries

This traditional pattern of governmental economic policy was changed in 1962. In that year the major steel companies announced a substantial increase in steel prices; President Kennedy reacted swiftly, attacked the announced price rises as inflationary and detrimental to the public interest, and insisted, by various veiled and not-so-veiled threats, that the steel companies rescind the increases. Within a few days the disagreement became more than a struggle between two principles—free price determination by business versus government control—or even between two impersonal forces—government versus the steel industry. It appeared to the public as a struggle between the President of the United States and the chairman of the board of U.S. Steel, who took the lead in defending the price increases. The steel industry backed down, particularly after it became clear that public opinion was on the side of the President.

In 1965, during the Johnson administration, price increases in aluminum and copper were rescinded after vigorous protests by leading administration spokesmen and threats by the federal government to unload aluminum and copper from its own stockpile of both materials and thus drive the prices back to what it considered noninflationary.

During the period of 1962–1965, the federal government also attempted to keep wage increases in line with the rising productivity of labor. According to calculations of the Council of Economic Advisers, issued by it in the form of "guideposts," such wage increases were, on the average, to be kept to 3.2 percent per year. However, the restraints on prices and wages became ineffective from 1966 on, since the substantial decline of unemployment and the growing inflation, both largely the result of the escalation of the Vietnam war, drove prices and wages sharply upward.

Economic controls in the 1970s

On coming into office in 1969, President Nixon persistently rejected the Kennedy-Johnson controls through guideposts and "jawboning," partly because these policies were too closely identified with his two Democratic predecessors in the presidency, and partly because he preferred letting the market find its own equilibrium to imposing government controls.

From early 1971, however, the combined pressures of inflation, unemployment, and the weakness of the dollar gradually convinced President Nixon that only the federal government had the power to mitigate the causes and symptoms of the developing economic crisis. In August, 1971, he finally decided to use those powers in view of the deepening economic problems both in the United States and abroad. The main features of the "new economic policy" included a freeze on prices, wages, rents, and dividends for 90 days; a temporary surcharge of 10 percent on imports; and tax cuts for individuals and corporations. The 90-day freeze on wages and prices was followed by Phase II of economic controls, which lasted from November, 1971, to January, 1973. On the whole, the controls worked. In 1969 and 1970, the last two years prior to economic controls, the consumer price index had risen by 6.1 percent and 5.5 percent respectively. In 1971 and 1972, the consumer price index rose by only 3.4 percent in each year.

In January, 1973, Phase II was replaced by Phase III, which lasted until June, 1973. Mandatory controls were replaced by self-administered guidelines, which did not work. Prices started to explode, particularly in the farm and food sectors of the economy. In June, 1973, President Nixon imposed a 60-day freeze on prices, but shortages occurred, since producers of industrial and agricultural goods knew that prices would soon rise again. After the 60-day freeze on prices expired in August, 1973, Phase IV of less than halfhearted controls was inaugurated, lasting until April, 1974, and ending in failure. The consumer price index rose by 8.8 percent in 1973, and in 1974 the rate of increase was 12.2 percent, one of the highest inflationary movements in American history. The failure of Phases III and IV was also partly due to international economic developments: In 1973 and 1974, food shortages in many parts of the world increased the demand for American farm products, thus driving prices upward at an unusually sharp rate.

In view of the comparative ineffectiveness of direct price and wage controls under the preceding three administrations, President Ford tried to achieve economic stability through tax, tariff, and fiscal policies, without entirely abandoning occasional interventions in the area of prices. Thus when U.S. Steel announced price increases of 4.7 percent in 1974, President Ford appealed to the company to show more restraint, as a result of which the increases by U.S. Steel were reduced to about 4 percent—a small victory for the government.

FEDERAL SUBSIDIES

The federal subsidy program is another direct federal economic policy aiming at stability in selected sectors, although it may also pursue other objectives, such as raising income (as in farming) or output (as in air or sea transportation). Between 1950 and 1970, the total amount spent on federal subsidy programs exceeded $130 billion, and the long-term trend per average year has been upward. In the 1970s federal subsidy programs have exceeded $10 billion per year.

Subsidies to transportation

Historically, the federal government has always been concerned with encouraging all forms of transportation. In the nineteenth century, for example, land grants to railroads amounted to 183 million acres, and the federal and state governments contributed close to $1 billion to the construction of railroads. The railroads prospered until the late 1940s, but from the 1950s on, intercity passenger traffic by rail became increasingly unprofitable because of the growing competition of buses, air lines, and private automobiles. Under the High Speed Ground Transportation Act of 1968, Congress authorized subsidies for the development of high-speed trains in highly congested areas, such as the Boston-Washington corridor. These trains, traveling at over 100 miles per hour, are modeled on French and Japanese trains and are intended to relieve pressure on overcrowded highways and airports.

Amtrak. In 1970 Congress established the National Rail Passenger Corporation (popularly known as Amtrak) for the purpose of operating intercity passenger traffic. Amtrak is a semipublic corporation, in which the majority of the board of directors is appointed by the President, so that the government can always maintain control. Amtrak has been consistently losing money, and by the mid-seventies governmental subsidies came to about $200 million a year. Going a step further toward the gradual nationalization of railroads, Congress in 1974 set up the Consolidated Rail Corporation (CRC) out of seven bankrupt railroads serving 17 states in the East and Midwest. The cost to the taxpayer will be over $2 billion.

Urban mass transportation. Since the 1960s, mass transportation in the cities has been a growing problem of national dimensions. Under the Urban Mass Transportation Act of 1964, Congress authorized the expenditure of $375 million by state and local agencies for the improvement of mass transportation services in large metropolitan areas. However, federal outlays quickly rose and reached over $1 billion in 1974, used primarily for capital expenditures. In the Mass Transit Act of 1974, Congress authorized, for the period of 1975–1980, almost $8 billion for capital grants and $4 billion for operating expenses or capital grants.

Air carriers. Air carriers have been another major recipient of federal subsidies. Annual subsidies to air carriers have amounted to about $75–100 million in recent years. Some of these funds go to small local-service carriers, and some go to international air lines, which have been greatly troubled financially by the skyrocketing fuel costs since 1973. In addition to direct subsidies to air carriers, the federal government spends annually over $300 million on the planning and development of airports.

Shipping. Direct aid to shipping dates back to 1789, when the first Congress passed legislation in favor of American vessels. Mail subsidies have been granted to maritime carriers since 1845. Under the Merchant Marine Act of 1936, the federal government subsidizes American shipping engaged in foreign commerce by paying the difference between the cost of building or operating American vessels and the corresponding lower costs abroad. The main rationale for these subsidies is the need for a merchant marine in national emergencies.

Subsidies through postal services

Annual postal budgetary deficits in the 1950s were around $500 million. In the 1960s and early 1970s, the deficits kept increasing, until they greatly exceeded $1 billion per year. First-class mail and airmail are the only two services that yield consistent profits. The biggest money losers are second-, third-, and fourth-class mail. The constantly increasing deficits combined with a decline in the quality of the postal service finally induced Congress to adopt a basic reform. On July 1, 1971, the Post Office Department became the U.S. Postal Service, an independent government corporation. The main feature of the reform was to eliminate congressional and political influence over appointments and postal rates.

GOVERNMENT AND THE ENERGY CRISIS

Cheap, abundant supplies of coal, petroleum, and natural gas have been among the major factors behind the growth of the American economy. The American people were suddenly jolted out of their complacent belief in cheap and unlimited energy supplies by the embargo on oil exports to the United States by the oil-exporting Arab states in October, 1973. Gas stations sold gasoline in limited quantities to each customer, were out of gasoline early in the day, and generally closed on Sundays. Long lines of eager buyers formed at gas-station pumps, tempers flared, and there were sporadic incidents of violence.

The energy problem painfully and dramatically came to the attention of the American public in 1973, but its roots lie in developments over many years. Most importantly, there has been a substantial shift from the most abundant source of energy—coal—to the scarce sources of energy—oil and gas. Nineteen-forty-six was the last year in which the United States exported more oil than it imported. In the 1950s and throughout most of the 1960s oil imports rose at an increasing but still not alarming rate. But from the late 1960s on, oil imports accelerated rapidly. In 1969 imported crude oil and refined products accounted for 22 percent of domestic consumption; but by 1973 the proportion rose to 36 percent. During that period, domestic production stagnated, so that imports had to supply the entire increase in oil consumption in the United States. Whereas in 1950 oil accounted for 37 percent of all energy consumed, in 1973 it accounted for 46 percent.

Natural gas also increased its share of energy consumption. In 1950 natural gas accounted for 18 percent of all energy, but by 1973 the proportion rose to 31 percent. Throughout most of the period, domestic production was able to keep pace with the growing demand, but from 1969 on, production slowed down and had to be supplemented by imports. The sharply rising demand for gas was due to two factors: First, the price of gas was kept at a low level by the Federal Power Commission; and second, gas became attractive as a clean fuel, as environmental limitations were increasingly imposed on the use of high-sulfur coal.

By contrast with oil and gas, the production of coal was about the same in 1973 as in 1950, but the proportion of coal in the total consumption of energy dropped from 37 percent in 1950 to only 18 percent in 1973. Strict federal health and safety regulations, high costs of transportation, and restrictions or prohibitions of the use of high-sulfur coal kept the production of coal at a stagnatingly low level, and induced many users to shift to oil or gas.

Project Independence

The shift in energy consumption from abundant coal resources to the scarce and diminishing resources of oil and gas inevitably led to the dependence of the United States on the major oil-exporting states. The quadrupling of oil prices from 1973 to 1974 raised the cost of imported oil from $7.5 billion in 1973 to $25 billion in 1974, adversely affecting the balance of payments of the United States and significantly contributing to its rate of inflation. The Arab oil embargo from October, 1973, to March, 1974, also showed that a high degree of dependence on imported oil made the United States vulnerable to blackmail in foreign policy, particularly in the crucial region of the Middle East.

On November 7, 1973, President Nixon launched Project Independence, to make the United States capable of meeting its energy needs by 1980, without depending on any foreign sources. Both targets quickly proved unrealistically optimistic. In his State of the Union address of January 15, 1975, President Ford adopted 1985 as the target date for independence in energy. He also made it clear that self-sufficiency was not meant to be absolute or complete, in the sense of total cessation of all imports of energy, particularly oil. The objective, the President said, was to "end vulnerability to economic disruption by foreign suppliers by 1985." Obviously, oil imports on a moderate scale from Canada greatly differ from huge oil imports from Saudi Arabia with respect to the likelihood of economic disruption or political blackmail.

Federal policies aiming at reasonable self-sufficiency in energy have two main components: first, restraint in energy consumption, and second, expansion of available energy supply.

Conservation of energy. In the program of conserving energy, the automobile is one of the prime areas of concern, since it accounts for 13 percent of total energy consumption. The design of lighter, gas-saving automobiles, supplemented perhaps by a slowing down of additional emission standards, might bring about an improvement of gas mileage by 40 percent within possibly five years, as was proposed by President Ford in 1975. Another approach to reducing energy consumption by the automobile is reflected in the federal programs of aiding mass transportation and in the continued retention of a nationwide speed limit of 55 miles per hour, enacted by Congress in 1973. Finally, conservation of energy will also be achieved through more efficient design of buildings and improved power and heating technologies in industrial plants and private homes.

Expansion of energy production. In addition to conservation of energy, the federal commitment to reasonable self-sufficiency by 1985 includes a substantial expansion of the production of energy. The exploitation of vast oil and gas deposits in Alaska was delayed for several years by litigation and unfavorable court decisions reflecting the concerns of environmentalist groups. But as the nation was shocked by the energy crisis in the fall of 1973, Congress quickly enacted legislation authorizing construction of the Alaska pipeline. By 1980 Alaska oil production is expected to run to over two million barrels per day—about 20 percent of domestic production in the early 1970s. Since 1973 the federal government has also stepped up its leasing program for the outer continental shelf in the Gulf of Mexico, the Gulf of Alaska, and the Atlantic Ocean.

Among available energy sources ready for substantial expansion, coal is the most important. The United States has almost half of the world's known coal reserves, and at current rates of production there is enough coal for a period of between 500 and 800 years. The Federal Energy Office estimated in 1974 that coal production could be tripled from 600 million tons a year in 1973 to 1.8 billion tons a year by 1985. The federal government owns about 40 percent of coal reserves, located mostly in several western states, and is thus in a position to contribute directly to increased production of coal through an accelerated program of leased coal lands. Both the mining and burning of coal create environmental problems, however, and new technologies will have to be developed to produce cleaner coal. Coal can also be converted into synthetic gas or petroleum, and the federal government has funded a pilot plant to explore the long-range technical and commercial feasibility of converting coal into gas and petroleum.

Another new promising energy source in which the federal government has taken an interest is the recovery of oil from shale. Shale deposits are abundant in Colorado, Wyoming, and Utah, and much of the land is owned by the federal government. The technology of recovering oil from shale is available, although still in an early stage of sophistication. The most critical difficulties stem from the fact that vast amounts of water are required for the recovery of the oil, and that huge amounts of waste would have to be disposed of if the environment is to be protected. In 1974 the federal government leased several substantial tracts of land with shale deposits to some major oil companies, and has provided some aid for research and development.

The federal government has also increased its financial support for two possible energy sources that at best will take about two decades for sizable results: solar and geothermal energy. Part of the appeal of these forms of energy lies in the fact that the heat in the earth and the sun are virtually limitless, and that both are clean and harmless to the environment. By contrast, the federally planned expansion of nuclear energy has been opposed by some scientists and others on the ground that nuclear accidents or sabotage might cause disastrous damage of unimaginable proportions.

Energy Research and Development Administration. Two difficulties will have to be overcome if the major aspects of Project Independence are to be realized: time and money. Up to the present, it has taken three to five years to open a coal mine, eight to 10 years to plan, design, and build a nuclear power plant, and several years to convert coal into synthetic gas or petroleum. In the case of geothermal power and solar energy, the lead time must be measured in decades rather than in years. Technological progress may be achieved by massive federal injections of funds for research and development. In December, 1974, Congress enacted a federal commitment of $20 billion for research and development in the nonnuclear energy field for a period of 10 years. Such programs will be coordinated by the newly created Energy Research and Development Administration (ERDA). Capital investments from the private sector for the achievement of self-sufficiency in energy are projected to run to at least $250 billion, and may end up requiring over $500 billion from the middle 1970s to the middle 1980s. Such outlays of private capital may be forthcoming only with further federal commitments, such as price guarantees for new products derived from high-risk investments. Considering that the atom bomb was developed at a cost of $2 billion, and that the Apollo space program cost $25 billion, the magnitude of Project Independence becomes readily apparent as the most ambitious national 10-year program in the history of the United States.

GOVERNMENT AND AGRICULTURE

Agriculture is the sector of the American economy in which the intervention of government is more clearly and strongly visible than in any other branch of the economy. Public policies in agriculture are not marginal as in some other areas, but provide the setting within which the American farmer can function and maintain his economic identity and existence. In no other Western nation is there the strong commitment of government to the maintenance of a healthy farm economy that has evolved in the United States.

The growth of farm productivity

The main asset of American farming is its tremendous capacity to produce an ever increasing amount of food and fibers with less and less land and human energy. In popular thinking, the technological revolution of the last century is identified with increased industrial productivity. In the United States, however, the increase of agricultural productivity in recent decades has outstripped the growth of the whole economy. Since 1950, for example, productivity in farming (or output per man-hour) has increased at twice the rate of the nonfarm economy. In 1950 one farm worker produced enough food, fiber, and other agricultural raw materials to supply himself and 9.7 others; in the 1970s, he supplied himself and more than 50 others. Between 1950 and the mid-1970s, farm output increased by over 60 percent, whereas the input of labor decreased by about 60 percent and the use of cropland by 6 percent. The number of farms declined from 5.6 million in

1950 to 2.8 million in the 1970s, and the portion of the national population living on farms went down from 15 percent in 1950 to 4.5 percent in the 1970s.

The high productive capacity of American agriculture is also important in the international perspective. With 1 percent of the world's agricultural labor force, the United States is the largest exporter of farm products, and accounts for over one-sixth of world agricultural exports. In the principal nontropical crops, the productivity of American farming is of crucial importance to the rest of the world: In 1973, for example, the United States accounted for 44 percent of world wheat exports, 76 percent of world corn exports, and 85 percent of world soybean exports. If many other countries depend on farm-product imports *from* the United States, the United States increasingly depends on farm-product exports *to* other countries for its balance of payments, particularly in view of the astronomical increases in the cost of imported oil. Agricultural exports tripled from $6 billion in 1969 to $18 billion in 1973, and the agricultural share of all exports rose from 16 percent in 1969 to 26 percent in 1973. In the process of sharply increasing its agricultural exports, particularly since 1972, the United States also depleted its reserves, leading to substantial increases of food prices in the domestic market. These high food prices, going up faster than the consumer price index for all commodities, contrasted unfavorably with the low food prices of the 1950s and 1960s, when American agriculture suffered from excess capacity and production, leading to government-financed storing of vast quantities of farm products that were eventually either sold commercially or given away by the government to poor countries.

Reasons behind government aid to farming

The rationale behind government aid to farming is based on several factors. First, there is the factor of social justice, according to which the farm sector of the economy should be entitled to share fairly in the general prosperity of the nation. Second, there is the economic consideration, according to which an ailing agriculture cannot but have harmful effects on the rest of the economy. A prosperous agriculture is an important market for many products and services that come from the nonfarm sectors of the economy. For example, farmers, less than 5 percent of the population, account for up to 20 percent of the market for steel, rubber, petroleum, and other basic products.

Finally, there is the problem of unregulated competition in farming, which only government can resolve. Farming is less able than industry to adjust production to demand. In a major industry such as steel or automobiles, a few leading companies can normally plan production in line with anticipated demand, and still make profits. By contrast, farm production is determined by a few million independent production units. Greater ignorance of market conditions, uncertainty of weather conditions, and excessive optimism of the individual farmer that he can beat the next fellow—all may result in unbridled competition with a disastrous imbalance between production of and demand for farm products.

The Great Depression provided a telling illustration of the problem. Between 1929 and 1933 farm output dropped by only 6 percent, but prices of farm products dropped by 63 percent. By contrast, during the same four years production of farm implements dropped by 80 percent, but prices declined by only 6 percent, because an industry dominated by a few large corporations could regulate production more effectively by cutting output to a level at which it was still profitable. Government, and government alone, could bring about a better balance between agricultural supply and demand, so that farm prices and incomes could be maintained at a fair level.

"Parity" prices

Although aid to farming dates back to the earliest days of the Republic, the current massive and detailed aid and regulation of agriculture started under President Franklin D. Roosevelt in the 1930s. The key economic concept in aid to farming is "parity" between prices of farm products and nonfarm products. The period 1909–1914 was chosen as the base period because the purchasing power of farm products during those five years was considered a fair and reasonable one by Congress in the 1930s. If a farmer could buy 10 of a nonfarm article for one bushel of wheat in 1909–1914, but can buy only eight of the same article with one bushel of wheat today, then parity has gone down by 20 percent. The purpose of the price-support policies of the federal government since the 1930s has been to make sure that the parity ratio does not drop below a certain level in predetermined "basic" commodities. In general, price-support policies have ranged from 60 to 90 percent of parity. The main commodities that benefit from price-support programs are the "basic" commodities such as cotton, wheat, corn, tobacco, rice, and peanuts, and some "nonbasic" commodities such as dairy products, soybeans, sugar beets, sorghum grain, oats, and barley.

Price-support programs

The main instrumentality of supporting prices is the Commodity Credit Corporation (CCC). The common procedure is for the individual farmer to obtain a loan from the CCC when his crop is ready for marketing. The loan is equivalent to the support price of the commodity. If the market price of the commodity goes above the support price, the farmer sells his crop in the open market, repays the loan, and keeps the difference between the support price and the higher market price. If at the time the loan becomes due the market price has not risen to the level of the support price, he forfeits his crop by not repaying the loan, and the CCC keeps the crop. In effect, therefore, the loan constitutes a guaranteed price for the farmer's crop, with the government bearing all the risks if prices drop.

The government also supports crop prices and farm incomes through direct payments to farmers. Under the Agriculture and Consumer Protection Act of 1973, the government sets "target" or guaranteed prices for cotton, wheat, and feed grains at predetermined levels. If the farmer sells at a market price that is lower than the target price, the government pays the farmer the difference between the lower market price and the higher target price. The farmer is thus guaranteed a fair price. Another innovation of the Agriculture and Consumer Protection Act of 1973 was the limiting of subsidy payments to $20,000 per farmer.

In times of chronic farm-product surpluses, the reduction of acreage has been used by the government to regulate and reduce farm output. Such programs have included acreage allotments, land diversion, and soil conservation. Removing land from production in a period of surpluses not only contributes to decreased production and therefore to greater price stability, but also expands available resources for recreation, conservation, and a better environment. As the era of surpluses has vanished since 1973, temporarily at least, acreage restrictions have been lifted, and the government has called on farmers to raise output to maximum capacity.

In its broadest sense, the price-support program has aimed at assuring the farm population a standard of living that is equivalent to that of the nonfarm population. This objective has been attained. In 1960 the average per capita farm income was about half of the average per capita income in the nonfarm sectors of the economy. By 1973 the gap was closed, and average per capita farm income was even slightly above that of average per capita nonfarm income.

THE MIXED ECONOMY

The historical encounter between socialism and capitalism in the context of democratic government has led to a growing *rapprochement* between the two ideologies. Capitalism has moved toward socialism with respect to economic regulation and the welfare state, because the democratic ethos is incompatible with personal insecurity, want, and suffering when the means are available to remedy such conditions. Socialism, on the other hand, has moved in the direction of capitalism with respect to the issue of private ownership of productive property, because the democratic political value of diffusion of power and of personal liberty is incompatible with total ownership and management of the economy by the state.

The evolving economy in non-Communist countries, whether governed by socialist or nonsocialist parties, is neither capitalist nor socialist, if capitalism means laissez-faire and if socialism means public ownership. No generally agreed-upon name has so far been found for this type of economy, because it has developed gradually and pragmatically rather than

"Never breathe this to another soul, Morton, but the only real money I've ever made was under socialistic, pinko, Democratic administrations."
Saturday Review, February 8, 1975, p. 27.

according to some preconceived ideology or master plan. Probably the most widely used term for economic systems operating within the framework of constitutional government is "mixed economy," indicating the mixture of predominantly private initiative and property on the one hand and of predominantly public responsibility for economic regulation and social welfare on the other.

17 The Welfare State

17

The growth of the welfare state is the result of long-term structural changes in American society and of specific political demands made by the people on government. In the United States, welfare-state policies have not been the products of a master plan or ideology, but of the slow and cumulative responses to practical situations. The Constitution states in the Preamble that one of the main purposes of forming this nation is to "promote the general welfare."

REASONS FOR THE GROWTH OF THE WELFARE STATE

Changing structure of the population

The first structural change is the rapid urbanization of American society. Whereas in 1910 less than half of the American people lived in urban areas, at present over 70 percent are urban residents. By the year 2000, four out of five Americans will live in urban areas. Within urban areas, there is growing concentration of population in metropolitan areas. Currently over one-third of the American people live in metropolitan areas of over 1 million population, and that proportion is growing, too, as more people move into the suburbs that cluster around large metropolitan centers.

The anonymity of urban life makes the needy person dependent on public assistance, because the community ties of small-town or rural life are gone. Moreover, the number of those needing public welfare in cities is growing faster than the population of the cities. As the middle- and high-income groups have left the "central cities" for the suburbs, their place has been taken by low-income groups, inevitably creating problems of governmental aid. In New York City, for example, close to 2 million whites, mostly from the middle class, have moved out of the city since 1950 and have been replaced by about the same number of nonwhites, mostly blacks with low incomes. Welfare rolls expanded in the 1950s and exploded in the 1960s: In 1960, welfare recipients numbered 328,000, and in 1975 the number had jumped to more than 1 million, or about 13 percent of the total population of the city. Several other large cities show similar percentages of welfare populations.

In the period 1950–1970, the percentage of blacks in a few typical large cities rose as follows: from 9.5 to 21.2 in New York, from 13.6 to 32.7 in

Chicago, from 16.2 to 43.7 in Detroit, and from 23.7 to 46.4 in Baltimore. Washington, D.C., Atlanta, and Newark now have majorities of blacks, and Baltimore, Detroit, St. Louis, and New Orleans will soon have black majorities. While the total populations of many of these large cities have been growing slowly, their welfare populations have risen at a very fast pace during the "black urbanization" of the 1960s. During the same period, several of the southern states lost part of their black population, since many blacks went North, attracted by the prospect of better-paying jobs and higher welfare benefits in the North and West.

The age composition of the nation's population has also changed. The number of old (65 and over) and the number of young (18 and under) have grown at a faster rate than the population as a whole. Since the incidence of poverty is higher among the very young and the very old than among other age groups, the result is increased welfare needs for children and the old. This structural change in the age composition of the population is aggravated by growing urbanization, because an urban economy makes little provision for the chores and part-time jobs that are available in a farm economy to the very young and the very old.

The political factor: the welfare state as a response to popular demands

The third major reason for the growth of the welfare state is political. Where constitutional government has been firmly established, as in North America, northwestern Europe, Australia, and New Zealand, the use of the vote, of free labor unions, and of a free press proved powerful weapons in the arsenal of social reform. Democracy can work—at least with respect to social and economic issues—only if the more affluent classes are willing to share their wealth with the less affluent ones.

The democratic process itself inevitably leads to social change and reform, because for many it is the main instrument through which they can hope to improve their lot significantly. The demand for publicly provided educational opportunity is not the product of "statist" thinking, but the logical consequence of an advanced economy that demands constantly rising educational standards from its work force. Similarly, economic performance in an advanced industrial society also requires high standards of health.

If private industry itself were able and willing to provide such educational and health needs, there would be no reason for government to take over these responsibilities. In the preindustrial society, the owners of large estates assumed such responsibilities as a matter of course. But in the modern industrial society, as Tocqueville clearly saw in his *Democracy in America*, the employer no longer feels the same sense of responsibility—and the vacuum is inevitably filled by government.

The welfare state and the voter

Because the number of voters who need, or will need, *some* form of public aid is vastly greater than that of the well-off who can go it alone, it comes as no surprise that welfare expansion is "good politics." This fact is evident particularly in a two-party system: Both parties show a natural tendency to promise more and more social welfare, and no party has a monopoly in promoting welfare policies. In Britain, the Conservative party has ruled most of the time in the last four decades, because it has avoided the impression that it is the party of the rich and opposed to welfare-state measures. And it has been able to avoid such an impression not by any clever publicity or gimmickry, but by the simple device of actually promoting social change and welfare. By contrast, the Republican party in the United States has shown occasional deep cleavages within its ranks on the issue of the welfare state. Candidate Goldwater's statement early in the presidential campaign in 1964 that he would prefer private, voluntary social insurance to the existing compulsory public system contributed to his defeat.

By contrast, Richard Nixon, both during his election campaign in 1968 and during his administration, showed that he was sensitive to the major issue of welfare. In 1969 he proposed what no Democratic president had ever dared to advocate: a family-assistance plan that came close to a guaranteed annual income. The federal budget for 1971 was the first in 20 years in which more money was spent on human resources (education, health, income security, and veterans' benefits) than on defense. This ratio of expenditures improved in subsequent budgets: In the budget for 1975, expenditures for human resources were earmarked at 50 percent of total expenditures, as compared with 29 percent for defense. (See Figure 17–1.) By contrast, in the 1963 budget of President Kennedy—before any major involvement in Vietnam—29 percent of the budget was spent on human resources, and 47 percent on defense.

This is not to suggest that politicians view welfare politics solely from the vote-getting angle. Many political leaders in both parties favor such policies because they sincerely believe in human welfare, but they are not displeased that what seems the right thing to do also pays off politically. As in so many other instances, actions need not fail in order to establish their virtuous character.

Welfare policies as insurance premiums

Welfare policies can also be viewed as insurance premiums that the better-off pay in the interests of social and political stability. It is perhaps no coincidence that states with the most advanced welfare policies also enjoy the highest degree of political stability—the Scandinavian countries, Britain,

CHANGING PRIORITIES IN THE FEDERAL BUDGET

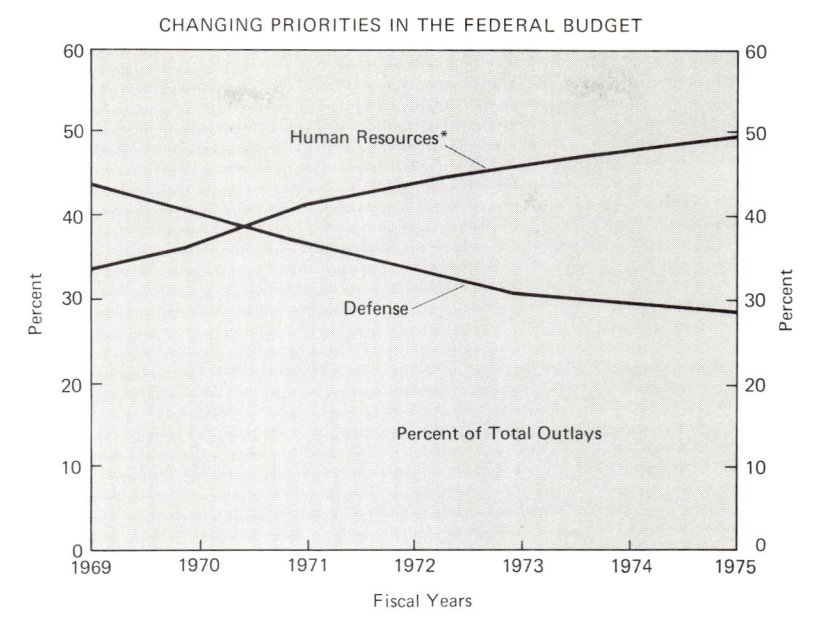

*Education and Manpower, Health, Income Security, and Veterans Benefits

Figure 17–1 *Federal expenditures on defense and human resources*
SOURCE: The United States Budget in Brief: Fiscal Year 1975. *Executive Office of the President, Office of Management and Budget,* 1974.

Holland, Switzerland, Australia, New Zealand, and Canada, to mention but a few. Political stability cannot be ensured solely by political instruments—constitutions, free elections, a free press, and the right to vote—but must have a solid foundation of social and economic equity and justice. If people are to feel that they have a stake in their community, the best way of ensuring that feeling is to give them the stake rather than to substitute exhortation and indoctrination for it.

SOCIAL SECURITY AND WELFARE

Social security is the provision to a working person and his family of a guaranteed income in the case of retirement, unemployment, disability, or death. In nearly all other advanced industrial societies, social security also protects the population against the economic hazards of illness—but this protection is not yet available in the United States, or only to a limited extent since 1965. Until the Great Depression of the 1930s, the generally accepted attitude in the United States was that each individual was responsible for planning ahead for emergencies resulting from loss of income.

The shattering experience of the Great Depression—one out of four in the labor force was out of work—broke down a key principle of traditional individualism, according to which a person could always find a job if he looked hard enough for one. More and more people realized that the American economy had become a *national* economy, that unemployment was a national problem, and that therefore only the national government could provide the resources and administrative machinery of a system of economic security. This was accomplished in the Social Security Act of 1935, the most important in this area until that time, and still the greatest single act of Congress relating to social security.

Highly innovative in the perspective of American government, the Social Security Act of 1935 was less innovative in the perspective of comparative government. Germany had established an old-age pension and disability system in 1889, followed by Britain, France, and Sweden early in this century. By the time the Social Security Act was passed in 1935, more than 50 nations had adopted systems that often were more comprehensive than the American social-security system.

Old-age, survivors, and disability insurance

Although, as we shall soon see, social security provides for several other contingencies, to most people it is almost synonymous with old-age, survivors, and disability insurance (OASDI). Social security is generally identified with these three types of protection because they are its most important part, affecting more people than any other form of social security.

OASDI covers citizens and noncitizens, and applies to nearly all forms of employment and self-employment. Federal and railroad employees are covered by separate retirement systems. Coverage of state and local government employees cannot be compulsory, because under our federal system the national government cannot tax state governments and their subdivisions. However, the states may voluntarily join the social-security system, and more than three-fifths have done so. Similarly, there is no compulsory OASDI for nonprofit organizations of an educational, religious, charitable, or scientific character, because such entities are tax-exempt. However, such organizations may join the social-security system by waiving their tax exemption for this specific purpose. In fact, nearly all nonprofit organizations of this type have joined. Teachers and administrative employees in private schools and colleges are probably the largest single group benefiting from social security in this category. Well over 90 percent of all gainfully employed (including self-employed) persons are now covered by social security.

Many economists argue that OASDI in its present form is not based on the insurance principle in any case. The main distinction between OASDI and private insurance is that OASDI does not accumulate reserves equal to outstanding liabilities, as in done by private insurers. Essentially, OASDI is a pay-as-you-go system, with benefits paid out of current tax receipts. The current level of OASDI trust funds would be enough to pay benefits for less than one year if no tax payments were received by the funds. Basically, OASDI is a system that taxes the working population to support payments to beneficiaries under the various OASDI programs. The working population has the moral commitment of Congress that they, in their turn, will likewise receive benefits from the working population when they become eligible.

The contributory element is the main feature that OASDI shares with private insurance. However, in private insurance, contributions are paid voluntarily, whereas in OASDI such contributions are taxes levied on a compulsory basis. Also, in private insurance the relation between payments and benefits is clearly defined in actuarial terms, whereas in OASDI the relation between a person's tax contribution to OASDI and his benefits is tenuous, since payments and benefits are revised by Congress every few years.

OASDI is financed by social-security taxes paid by employees, employers, and self-employed persons. The maximum annual earnings on which social-security taxes are paid were $14,100 in 1975, and the payroll tax rate was 5.85 percent each for employer and employee. Maximum taxable earnings, tax rates, and benefits have consistently gone up in the past and are scheduled to go up in the future. First, as the ratio of wage earners to retirees declines because of lower birth rates, fewer workers will have to pay higher payroll taxes for the benefits of more retired workers. Second, Congress has been aware of the factor of inflation, and has continuously adjusted retirement benefits on an *ad hoc* basis every few years. Beginning in 1975, OASDI benefits have been tied to the rising consumer price index, so that benefits will henceforth rise automatically in line with the rate of inflation.

A person who retired at 65 in 1975 needed only six years of "work credit" to be covered by social security. Monthly retirement, disability, or survivor benefits range between $125 and $450, depending on the amount of the employee's contribution and the number of persons in the family entitled to benefits. Social-security benefits differ from fixed private pensions in two important respects: First, social security makes additional payments to retirees' dependent wives, widows, and children. *Need* after retirement or disability is thus recognized. Second, the element of *equity* is also taken into account: Social-security retirees in the lowest income bracket receive benefits amounting to about 60 percent of final pay; in the case of middle-income retirees the percentage drops to 45; and in the case of higher-income brackets (at or above the maximum taxable base) the percentage is only about 33. The system as a whole is thus biased in favor of low-wage earners and those with dependents—another indication that social security is not a pure insurance system.

Private pensions

Social-security benefits increased about twice as fast as wages and the cost of living in the years 1969–1974, but unless a retiree can supplement such benefits with some personal savings or a private pension, his overall income will be low. Responding to the needs of elderly persons for higher retirement incomes, private pension plans have grown faster than government pensions. The number of employees covered by private plans rose from 4 million in 1940 to over 30 million in 1975. During that period, assets of private pension funds jumped from $2.4 billion to over $160 billion, and now considerably exceed the assets of governmental (federal, state, and local) pension funds.

Employee Benefit Security Act. Until 1974 the main disadvantage of private pension plans was that a worker could lose his pension rights if he changed jobs, or if his company or pension fund went broke. The Employee Benefit Security Act of 1974 removed both threats to private pensions for workers. Under the act, workers who change jobs retain part or all of the accumulated pension rights, depending on the length of their employment. The act also set up a Pension Benefit Guaranty Corporation to insure workers' pension rights against loss in case of insufficient assets in private pension funds. This insurance program is financed by premiums paid by employers and administered by the Department of Labor. Some other nations—Britain, Holland, Switzerland—have been moving in the same direction of protecting workers' pension rights in private plans, and Finland has the distinction of being the only Western nation in which private pension plans are mandatory.

Unemployment insurance

Unlike OASDI, which is directly administered by the federal government, unemployment insurance is a joint federal-state effort. The federal government sets minimum standards of law and administration, but the state determines who is to be covered, how large the unemployment insurance tax is, how large benefits are to be, and for how long. The program is financed by the unemployment insurance tax of 3.2 percent on the first $4,200 paid to each employee. The tax is paid entirely by the employer. The federal government retains 0.5 percent of the 3.2 percent payroll tax. It uses these funds to help states defray the costs of administering the unemployment insurance programs, and it also makes loans and grants to the states as the need arises, particularly in periods of high unemployment. In some states the taxable wage base is higher than $4,200, going up to $10,000 in Alaska. There is also flexibility in determining the tax liability of the individual employer. The employer who has laid off few workers pays a lower unemployment insurance tax rate than the employer with a high layoff record, thus giving employers a financial incentive to maintain high employment.

Current maximum weekly unemployment benefits for individuals range between $50 and $120, but many states pay allowances for dependents, in which case the maximum weekly benefits go up to between $75 and $150. The general goal in setting benefit rates is to provide the unemployed worker with an income that is about half his customary weekly wage, up to a maximum amount determined by law. Benefits are typically paid for a period of 26 weeks, but in times of high unemployment the benefit period is extended by an additional 13 to 26 weeks. However, the actual average period during which an unemployed person receives benefits is only about 13 weeks in a typical year. Many workers in highly unionized industries receive additional unemployment benefits from their employers under union contracts.

Public assistance

In addition to maintaining insurance programs against the economic hazards of old age, death, disability, and unemployment, the federal government is operating public-assistance programs for various categories of needy persons outside of the social-security system. Whereas insurance programs are financed by contributions of employers and employees, assistance programs are funded out of general tax revenues.

Supplementary security income. This program aids the needy aged, blind, and disabled. Until the end of 1973, this type of assistance was rendered through three joint federal-state programs, administered by the states with federal grants paying more than half of the cost. On January 1, 1974, the three separate programs were integrated into one and taken over by the federal government, which now administers it through the Social Security Administration and also bears the entire cost. The federalization of assistance to the needy aged, blind, and disabled provides financial relief to the state and local agencies formerly involved in it, and also provides, for the first time, a uniform national minimum income for three classes of especially disadvantaged individuals. In most states, the federally established SSI (Supplementary Security Income) grants are higher than they had been before 1974, when the states administered the assistance programs for the needy aged, blind, and disabled. However, states that had provided higher assistance levels than the new SSI grants must supplement the federal grants up to the previous state level, so that no SSI grantee would receive less under the new system than under the old. Also, eligibility requirements for SSI have been relaxed so that more persons now receive aid than before. Prior to 1974, about 3.2 million persons received assistance under state

Copyright © 1965 Jules Feiffer. Courtesy Publishers-Hall Syndicate.

programs for the needy aged, blind, and disabled; under SSI, the number of aid recipients in these three categories has climbed to about 5 million.

Food stamps

Set up in 1964, the food-stamp program is administered by the Department of Agriculture through state and local welfare offices. The entire cost of the program is borne by the federal government. The original purpose of the program was to improve the diet of low-income families and to help farmers dispose of surplus food. However, since 1972 food surpluses have vanished, so that the single purpose of the program now is to help low-income individuals and families obtain food at no cost or at less cost than market prices.

Eligible persons or families can buy food stamps at banks, welfare offices, or post offices. The price of the stamps is always lower than the redemption value at the supermarket. The cost of the stamps is determined by net income and family size. Thus in early 1975 a family of four with a monthly income of less than $30 could obtain food stamps worth $150 per month and pay nothing for the stamps. The same family of four had to pay $126 to buy $150 worth of food if its monthly income was $500. If its net monthly income was $510 and above, the family was not eligible for food stamps. These income figures refer to *net* income. To arrive at the net income figure, food stamp recipients may deduct from gross income state and federal income taxes, social-security taxes, union dues, medical expenses in excess of $10 per month, child-care expenses in connection with employment, and various other allowable expenses.

The food-stamp program has shown phenomenal growth over the years. In 1965, 425,000 persons received food-stamp aid at a cost of $33 million to the federal government. In 1975, over 19 million persons were aided, at an annual federal expenditure of about $5 billion. Whereas in the past most food-stamp recipients were on welfare and received multiple benefits under various welfare programs, the majority of food-stamp recipients in 1975 were in the labor force, either earning low net incomes or temporarily out of work.

In addition to the food-stamp program, the federal government operates various other food programs, such as the provision at low or no cost of breakfasts, lunches, and milk in elementary and secondary schools. The most important is the school-lunch program, which currently benefits 26 million schoolchildren, or one-half of all schoolchildren. The total cost of such child nutrition programs was about $2 billion in 1975.

Aid to families with dependent children (AFDC)

Since the 1960s, the decade of the "welfare explosion," the greatest increase of welfare recipients has been in the aid to families with dependent children

(AFDC) program. In 1960 there were about 3 million AFDC recipients, and the cost of the program was about $1 billion. By 1973 the number of AFDC recipients had almost quadrupled to about 11 million, and the cost had risen sevenfold to over $7 billion.

One of the most baffling aspects of AFDC is the fact that it has continued to expand rapidly even during periods of prosperity and sharply declining unemployment. Between 1961 and 1969, for example, the rate of unemployment dropped from 6.7 percent of all workers to 3.5 percent—a record low in peacetime—yet the number of AFDC recipients more than doubled during those years. It became obvious that the previously unchallenged view of a direct correlation between worsening economic conditions and rising numbers of welfare recipients simply did not hold true. More complex social changes—particularly changing attitudes toward work and the progressive disintegration of the family—seemed to be responsible.

AFDC was originally conceived as a program for widows and orphans or for families who needed temporary help because of special hardships. In the 1930s, when AFDC started, about 75 percent of benefit recipients were children of fathers who had died or who were totally disabled; currently less than 20 percent of children in AFDC are in this category. The remaining 80 percent of the AFDC children have living and able-bodied fathers, but their fathers have deserted their families or were never married to the mothers of the children. Starting out as a program to help fatherless and husbandless families, AFDC has ended up creating such families, by "establishing incentives for families to split up or never to form."[1] In the most comprehensive study of welfare ever done by Congress, the Joint Economic Committee found, on the basis of data collected from 100 local areas that "the financial incentives for family breakup averaged $3,000 a year in July 1972,"[2] and that a single woman about to have her first (illegitimate) child would receive in various welfare benefits over $1,100 more per year than she could obtain as a needy individual.[3]

The unwed pregnant mother has, in many cases, no material incentive to marry the man who made her pregnant, since AFDC will provide financial support for her and her child. By the same token, the unwed father loses the economic incentive to marry the mother, since he knows that AFDC and other welfare programs will provide the material aid for the unwed mother and child if he does not marry the mother. During the period of 1961–1969, the number of illegitimate children on AFDC rolls more than doubled, whereas the number of illegitimate children in the general population rose by

---

[1] Joint Economic Committee of Congress, Subcommittee on Fiscal Policy, *Income Security for Americans: Recommendations of the Public Welfare Study*, Washington, D.C.: U.S. Government Printing Office, 1974, p. 48.
[2] *Ibid.*, p. 78.
[3] *Ibid.*, p. 80.

only one-third. During the same period, the proportion of illegitimate children receiving AFDC benefits rose from 37 percent to 65 percent; that is, two out of three illegitimate children are currently receiving AFDC benefits. About one-third of all children in AFDC were born out of wedlock, and this proportion is more than three times higher than in the general population.

In addition to the "perverse anti-family incentive" in AFDC plus other welfare benefits, the Joint Economic Committee noted the "perverse anti-work incentive" in such programs. In 1974, a welfare family of four received, in tax- and expense-free AFDC benefits and food stamps alone, an annual income that, translated into taxable earnings, was $600 higher than the median earnings of full-time women workers. However, AFDC families receive more than AFDC payments and food stamps: Nearly all such families also receive free medical care and free school lunches for their children, and some AFDC families also benefit from public housing and other assistance programs. The combination of such benefits can, in the words of the Joint Economic Committee, "provide total maintenance income larger than many welfare mothers could hope to earn."[4]

While there has been almost general agreement that AFDC has been a failure despite its high cost, there is much less agreement on what should replace it and particularly on whether a new welfare system should contain the principle of a guaranteed annual income. In public-opinion polls, about two-thirds of those questioned are opposed to the principle of a guaranteed annual income (GAI). Working-class opposition to GAI is particularly strong. Explaining to an inquiring political scientist that support for GAI would be political suicide, a congressman stated: "My supporters are primarily working-class people; they oppose the notion of something for nothing. They tell me they bust their butts over their jobs, and they're not about to have somebody living off the fruits of their energies."[5] To many working-class and middle-class people, GAI is objectionable not only because of its costs, but because it runs counter to the basic American values of dignity and achievement through work.

HEALTH AND MEDICARE

Government involvement in health services

Public responsibility for minimum health standards affecting the safety of the community is one of the oldest functions of government, going back to colonial times, and beyond that to Elizabethan England. The Public Health Service of the United States, founded in 1789, originally provided for all

[4]*Ibid.*, p. 99.
[5]Quoted in Aaron Wildavsky, *The Revolt Against the Masses: And Other Essays on Politics and Public Policy,* New York: Basic Books, 1971, p. 75.

"Frankly, I feel we can learn much from China. For example, restoring dignity to the concept of menial labor."
Drawing by Lorenz; © 1971 The New Yorker Magazine, Inc.

medical and hospital needs of merchant seamen in federal hospitals. Currently the Public Health Service provides such services not only for about 120,000 merchant seamen, but also for 340,000 Indians and other groups, totaling about 800,000. In addition, the federal government provides, in federally operated hospitals, for the health needs of 22 million war veterans and for 3 million members of the armed forces (active and retired), plus 4 million of their dependents. Thus more than 30 million persons receive health and hospital services directly from the federal government in federal hospitals staffed by federally appointed physicians. In addition, under Medicare the federal government provides for the cost of health care for about 22 million persons aged 65 and over; about 24 million persons are covered under federally subsidized state programs for the medically indigent, regardless of age (Medicaid). The number of persons under all these programs amounts to at least 80 million, or about 40 percent of the population.

In recent years; federal expenditures on health have risen enormously in dollar amounts and as proportions of the federal budget. In the federal budget for 1965, $1.7 billion, or 1.4 percent of the budget, was devoted to health. In the federal budget for 1975, $26.3 billion, or 8.6 percent of the budget, was earmarked for health. Currently, well over $100 billion are spent annually on health care; government on all levels (federal, state, and local) pays for about 40 percent of the nation's total health bill.

Medicare: toward a national health insurance program? One of the main arguments against a government health-insurance program, even if limited to those over 65 years of age, has been the tremendous growth of private health insurance. The proportion of Americans who are protected by some form of private health insurance rose from 9 percent in 1940 to 80 percent in 1965. Yet the benefits provided by such insurance covered only 25 percent of the cost of illness in 1965, and the old and the poor often could not afford to buy private health insurance, or, if they were over 65, found it difficult to obtain insurance because of the higher risk involved.

In 1965 Congress finally made the historic decision to provide health insurance for all persons over 65 by passing the Health Insurance for the Aged Act, popularly known as Medicare. Under this program, 17 million persons covered by social security were automatically eligible to receive Medicare benefits starting July 1, 1966. An additional 2 million persons over 65, who were not covered by social security, were also declared eligible for Medicare.

There are two parts to Medicare: *hospital insurance* and *medical insurance*. Hospital insurance, covering automatically all persons 65 and over entitled to social-security benefits, pays for hospitalization, convalescence in a hospital or nursing home after an illness, and for home visits by nurses following hospitalization. Hospital insurance is financed by a portion of the social-security payroll tax. In 1975 medical insurance cost the subscriber $6.70 a month and paid for physicians' and surgeons' services, home health services, outpatient therapy and treatment, and various diagnostic tests. Medical insurance does not cover anyone automatically and requires voluntary enrollment by persons 65 and over.

State medical programs. The Medicare law of 1965 provides that the federal government may contribute varying grants to state Medicare programs ("Medicaid") for families with dependent children "whose income and resources are insufficient to meet the costs of necessary medical services." There is no age limit in this provision, and it is the state's responsibility to determine a maximum level of income below which families are eligible for Medicaid. Since the start of Medicaid in 1966, the cost has risen beyond the expectations of its original proponents. In fiscal 1975, the federal budget earmarked $6.5 billion for Medicaid, or 55 percent of the estimated total cost.

Medicare and Medicaid have stimulated the desire for a still broader and better coordinated national health insurance program which could put an end to the existing fragmentation of the health-care delivery system.

Congress has been considering, during the past several years, a number of national health plans, with varying mixes of elements of insurance and welfare. As in other countries, a complete national health-care delivery system will not come in one sweep, but will be instituted in stages.

THE EXPANDING FEDERAL EFFORT IN EDUCATION

The role of education in American development

Among the elements that contributed to rapid economic growth in the United States from its very inception, education deserves an important place. This does not mean that the purpose of education is economic growth, but there can be no rapid economic growth without education. No ill-educated nation has ever attained significant economic progress, and no highly educated nation has ever been extremely poor.

The first state university was established in 1785 by the state of Georgia, followed by North Carolina in 1789. Jefferson founded the University of Virginia in 1816, and from then on public colleges and state universities proliferated throughout the land. Before the Civil War, 182 colleges and universities existed in the United States—more than in any other country in the world. In 1862 the Morrill, or Land Grant, Act provided federal public lands to the states and territories for the purpose of creating and maintaining tax-supported colleges and universities. Many students of American history consider the state universities to be among the unique innovations of the United States, since the state universities reflected the first commitment of a modern nation to make higher education available to broad masses of people rather than to a small elite. Since 1900, the population of the United States has increased less than threefold, but the number of college students has risen by eightyfold. One-third of the world's college students and professors and one-quarter of all institutions of higher learning are currently in the United States.

The magnitude of the educational effort

About 30 percent of the American population is involved in education. Out of a population of more than 215 million, more than 60 million are enrolled in schools (from kindergarten to college), about 3 million are teaching, and about 250,000 serve as administrators in the nation's schools. Thus the educational effort is, in economic terms, the largest single "industry" in the United States, and one that has grown faster than the economy as a whole.

The growth of education is reflected in financial effort and cost. In 1950, private and public expenditures on education were 3.4 percent of gross national product. Currently the share of gross national product devoted to education is about 8 percent—one of the highest in the world. Government on all levels (federal, state, and local) pays for about 80 percent of the cost of education, the rest being borne by private sources. In 1975 total educational outlays exceeded $100 billion for the first time.

The increases in educational expenditures have raised educational levels substantially. Between 1955 and 1975, college enrollments rose from 2.7 million to about 8.5 million, or more than three times. In 1940, 34 percent of high school graduates went on to college; currently the percentage is about 60. Within the sector of higher education, the role of private institutions has declined, whereas the share of enrollments in public institutions has constantly increased, thus further increasing the financial responsibilities of government. In 1950, about half of the American college students were in public colleges and universities; currently over 70 percent attend public institutions.

Federal aid to education

Until 1965, federal involvement in education was generally specific or on an *ad hoc* basis. Traditionally, education has been thought of as the domain of state and local authorities, and federal involvement on a large and general scale was fought off on two grounds: First, the states' righters claimed that federal aid would mean federal control and uniformity. Second, there was the religious issue; if federal money were to benefit parochial (mostly Roman Catholic) schools, the objection was raised that the separation of state and church would thereby be violated. If federal aid would be withheld from Roman Catholic schools, members of that faith in Congress would oppose federal aid to schools on the grounds of anti-Catholic discrimination. The combination of (generally) southern states' righters and northern Roman Catholic leaders thus seemed to create an insurmountable obstacle.

Federal involvement in education was therefore confined to those areas in which there was either an identifiable federal interest or an element of pork-barrel politics. Educational grants to veterans after World War II clearly involved a federal responsibility to members of the armed forces. Federal aid to "federally impacted areas" (that is, areas suffering from additional educational burdens because of sizable defense installations or similar activities) was a mixture of both federal interest and local politics.

The Elementary and Secondary Education Act of 1965

Direct federal aid to elementary and secondary schools was legislated by Congress in 1965 in the Elementary and Secondary Education Act. Like the establishment of Social Security in 1935 and Medicare in 1965, this is one of the great legislative breakthroughs in the history of social welfare in the United States. Federal aid to elementary and secondary schools was made possible in 1965 because of two factors: first, the realization that, owing to the growing interdependence of states and communities, quality differentials were a national concern. During the 1964–1965 school year, expenditures per pupil in public elementary and secondary schools ranged from $273 in Mississippi to $790 in New York. Because of the great mobility of the population, poor levels of education in one state affect all other states. Second, aid to education was justified as a main line of attack on poverty, which President Johnson had stressed in his 1964 campaign and in his subsequent legislative proposals to Congress.

Most of the funds are designed to strengthen education in aid-receiving school districts, including the building of school facilities and the hiring of teachers for new programs. The act emphasizes services that improve education rather than routine services. Typical services financed under the act include preschool or afterschool programs, guidance counseling, educational radio and television, speech therapy, remedial education, mobile services, library resources, and equipment and facilities.

Funds under the act can go only to public schools, but the special programs they set up and the special equipment they purchase are also available to children from parochial schools if such schools have the prescribed number of children from low-income families. Because parochial schools cannot directly receive any federal funds, the state-church issue was thus avoided. The intent of the law is to help educationally deprived children, not to aid religion.

With respect to the issue of potential federal control over elementary and secondary education, the act specifically prohibits any federal officer

> to exercise any direction, supervision, or control over the curriculum, program of instruction, administration, or personnel of any educational institution or school system, or over the selection of library resources, textbooks, or other printed or published instructional material by any educational institution or school system.

Federal aid to elementary and secondary education currently amounts to about $4 billion per year; so far, these large grants have provoked not the fear of government control, but the demands for increasingly more federal money for elementary and secondary schools.

The Higher Education Act of 1965

The single most important provision of the Higher Education Act of 1965 is the allocation of substantial funds for direct federal undergraduate scholarships for needy students. These "Basic Educational Grants," as they later were called, have expanded in scope in the last few years. In fiscal 1973 the federal budget allotted $122 million for such grants; in the budget for 1975 the amount climbed more than tenfold to $1.3 billion. In subsequent amendments of the Higher Education Act of 1965, the federal government has developed several other assistance programs for college students. Currently about half a million needy students benefit from the "work-study" program in colleges, with the federal government contributing over 80 percent of the cost. There is also a fast-growing program of government-guaranteed student loans; the loans are obtained from private lenders, mostly banks, but the federal government guarantees repayment and additionally defrays part of the interest. Undergraduates may borrow up to $2,500 a year, to a maximum of $7,500. Graduate students may borrow up to a maximum of $10,000. Currently about one million such loans are arranged annually; at the end of 1974, the total amount of loans outstanding was over $5 billion.

Among the other federal aid programs in higher education, two deserve special mention. Veterans attending college are entitled to various benefits paying for subsistence, tuition, and other educational expenses. Such educational assistance may run up to 36 months. The cost of this program in the 1970s has ranged between $2 and $3 billion annually. The second special program is in the health area. In 1971 Congress passed the comprehensive Health Manpower Training Act and the Nurse Training Act, authorizing the expenditure of $3 billion for 1972–1974 for the training of an increased number of physicians, dentists, nurses, and other health professionals. The acts provide funds for student grants and loans as well as for the construction of medical and related professional schools. The budget for 1975 allocated about $800 million for health manpower training. Finally, the federal government is also the principal source of funds for biomedical research. Currently annual federal expenditures are over $2 billion, or about four-fifths of the entire cost of biomedical research in the United States.

HOUSING AND URBAN RENEWAL

Just as the creation of a Cabinet-level Department of Health, Education, and Welfare in 1953 was a belated recognition of social welfare as a national responsibility, the creation of the Cabinet-rank Department of Housing and Urban Development (HUD) in 1965 finally took official cognizance of the fact that the urbanization of American society had created problems that were beyond the capacity of state and local governments to solve.

Federal activities in housing and urban renewal are centered in several major areas. Insurance is the oldest. During the Great Depression, the federal government entered the home-financing business on a small scale in 1932. Two years later, the Federal Housing Administration (FHA) was established to encourage the flow of private mortgage funds through federal insurance. Currently FHA-insured loans amount to $10–12 billion annually. The Veterans Administration (VA) insures loans to veterans of World War II, Korea, and Vietnam, the amount of such loans running to $5–8 billion annually. In both FHA- and VA-insured mortgages the maximum amount is (since 1974) $45,000 for a single-family dwelling (before 1974, the maximum insured mortgage was $33,000). The maximum for insured home-improvement loans is $10,000 ($5,000 before 1974). The federal government also lends money directly through the Farmers Home Administration to assist rural housing. Low-income farmers receiving such loans pay an interest rate that is considerably lower than what the government itself has to pay.

Slum clearance and public housing. Since the middle 1930s, the federal government has helped local housing authorities to clear slums and build public housing for low-income families and the elderly. The local housing authorities own and manage these housing projects, but the federal government grants or insures loans to public housing authorities, and also makes annual subsidies to cover the difference between operating costs and rents received. By 1973, over 1 million public housing units for about 4 million people had been built under this program.

However, since the late 1960s, there has been a growing disenchantment with large (and often high-rise) public-housing projects. As more and more fatherless welfare families with numerous children and teenagers moved into such large projects, they became high-crime areas with serious problems of drugs and vandalism, so that in some cases projects became gradually uninhabitable and had to be bulldozed: "Ironically, a public effort to build decent housing for the poor has produced housing whose reputation is worse than that of the slums."[6]

In recent years the federal government has therefore explored new directions in providing housing for low- and moderate-income families. Under two major housing acts passed by Congress in 1968 and 1974, the federal government helps such families to buy one-or two-family houses, new or old. The government insures the mortgage and subsidizes a portion of the monthly payments of the buyer. The size of the subsidy is geared to the buyer's income. In another new program set up by the Housing Acts of 1968 and 1974, the government grants low- and moderate-income families rental assistance in existing, rehabilitated, or new housing. Under this program, the landlord rents an apartment to a qualified family at less than the going rate, and the federal government pays the landlord the difference between what the subsidized family pays and what other tenants pay. Under both the assisted home-ownership and rental programs, the government avoids going directly into the business of constructing and managing public housing and instead gives the subsidized family the choice of finding suitable housing on its own.

Since 1950, housing in the United States has greatly improved in quantity and quality. The number of housing units has risen much faster than the number of households, and the proportion of substandard housing units has declined dramatically since 1950. In 1950, 34 percent of housing units

[6]E. D. Huttman, "The Pathology of Public Housing," *City,* 5 (Fall, 1971), p. 32.

HOUSING AND URBAN RENEWAL 433

THE IMPROVEMENT IN HOUSING CONDITIONS, 1950-1970

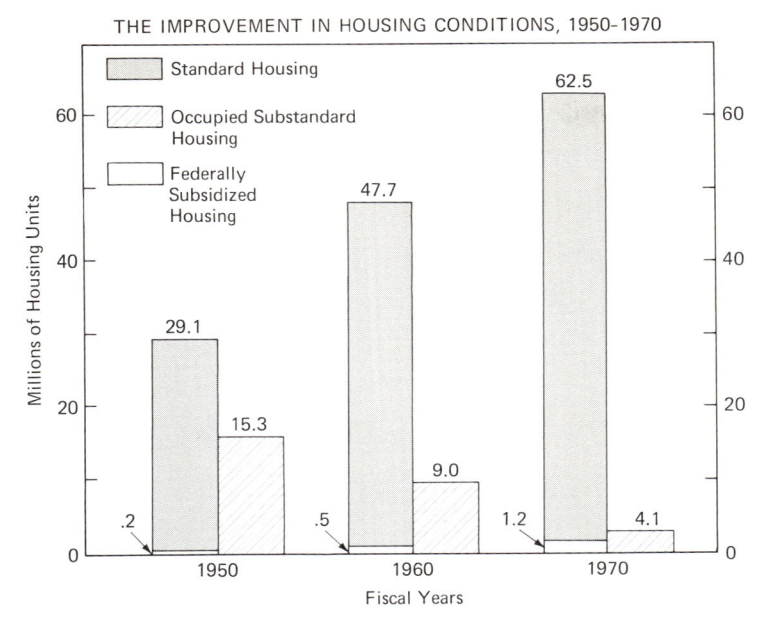

Figure 17–2 *The improvement in housing conditions, 1950–1970*
SOURCE: The United States Budget in Brief; Fiscal Year 1975. *Executive Office of the President. Office of Management and Budget, 1974.*

were substandard, dropping to 16 percent in 1960, and declining still further to 6 percent in 1970. (See Figure 17–2.) Some of this progress has undoubtedly been due to federal policies—both specific housing policies and more general monetary and fiscal measures that indirectly benefit home construction and ownership.

Urban renewal and community development. The federal government's activity in housing has inevitably led to its involvement in urban renewal and community development, for cities are more than conglomerations of physical structures. Urban decay, particularly in the inner cities, has been reflected in unsafe streets, rising crime and drug abuse, and diminishing business and employment opportunities. The federal government has steadily increased expenditures in this area. Between 1965 and 1975, the annual federal budget allocation for community development rose from $0.5 billion to $2.9 billion, or almost sixfold. In 1974 Congress authorized a three-year, $8.6 billion program for community development in the cities. Time will tell whether even the infusion of massive federal funds into urban renewal and community development will stem the outflow of middle-class families from the inner cities into the suburbs, which has sapped the economic and civic vitality of the cities. The issue of whether the cities can regain their one-time social, economic, and cultural role may well become one of the main issues shaping American government and politics in the next 30 years.

18 American Foreign Policy

18

FROM COLONY TO WORLD POWER

Never before in history has a nation been catapulted so rapidly as the United States from colonial insignificance to world power. From a population of about 3 million at the time of independence, the United States now numbers over 200 million and is the fourth most populous nation in the world, exceeded only by China, India, and the Soviet Union. Beginning its economic career as a simple farm community with little impact on the international economy, it is now the most advanced industrial society in the world. Militarily weak at the outset, the United States has become one of the strongest military forces on earth.

Inward-looking in its early years, seeking to go it alone by opening up the vast stretches of an empty continent, deliberately shunning entangling foreign commitments, the United States now finds itself with responsibilities and entanglements throughout the world. The first major step in projecting American power beyond the U.S. borders was the Monroe Doctrine (1823), in which the United States made clear its determination to keep European imperialistic and expansionist states out of the Americas. Later in the nineteenth century, American foreign policy became deeply involved in East Asia, particularly in China, Japan, and the Philippines. After defeating Japan in World War II and giving independence to the Philippines in 1945, the United States found itself more deeply involved in East Asia than ever before, with Communist China its main problem. By historical tradition averse to entanglements in Europe, the United States was called on to restore the European balance of power in World Wars I and II, and through NATO, set up in 1949, it has assumed long-range responsibilities in Europe. Other multilateral and bilateral defense treaties of the 1940s and 1950s with Latin American, Asian, and Pacific nations committed the United States to the defense of nearly 50 countries. No other nation in history has ever taken on burdens of this magnitude, and after the Vietnam experience it is doubtful whether the United States has the will or capacity to ensure the integrity and existence of so many states on five continents.

Expenditures on national defense have substantially declined as percentages of the federal budget and of gross national product in recent years. In 1960, before the Vietnam war, defense expenditures accounted for 49.8 percent of the federal budget and for 9.3 percent of GNP. In 1975, defense expenditures dropped to 29 percent of the federal budget and to below 6 percent of GNP. (See Figure 18–1.) The size of the armed forces, too, was trimmed from 2.5 million in 1960 to 2.1 million in 1975.

The weakening of the defense effort can also be seen in the fact that the proportion of expenditures on weapons has declined by comparison with expenditures on personnel. In 1968, at the peak of the American involvement in Vietnam, defense personnel (military and civilian) accounted for 42 percent of the defense budget, but by 1975 the percentage had risen to 55. This trend has been accentuated by the ending of compulsory military service in 1973 and the adoption of a volunteer army. In the short period of 1968–1975, the average annual pay for military personnel doubled, from $5,500 to $11,000.

In spite of the decline of defense expenditures as a share of the federal budget and GNP, many Americans feel that too much money is spent on defense. According to a Gallup poll in 1974, 44 percent of the interviewees thought that too much was being spent on defense, 32 percent thought defense expenditures were about right, and only 12 percent held the view that too little was being spent (12 percent had no opinion). By contrast, when a similar poll was taken in 1960, before the Vietnam war, only 18 percent of interviewees felt that too much was being spent for defense.[1]

Domestic and foreign affairs

The paramount importance of foreign relations goes beyond statistically provable facts and figures. It has become increasingly difficult to keep "domestic" issues separate from "foreign" issues. Tariff and immigration laws are a case in point, for they affect both spheres, although to different degrees. From the American viewpoint, an increase in tariffs on coffee or bananas may affect only a fraction of 1 percent of the American economy, but the nations affected by such tariff changes may depend for 60 to 70 percent of their foreign currency earnings on exports to the United States.

Even without initiating any specific policy, the United States—solely because it is what it is—profoundly affects the rest of the world. The whole non-Communist world, for example, keenly watches the performance of the American economy at all times. If the American economy is buoyant and expanding, the outlook for shared prosperity in many other nations looks bright. If American economic activity is sluggish, tremors immediately seize many another nation. The same holds true of noneconomic issues. Most Americans regard racial problems as a strictly domestic affair, but to hundreds of millions throughout the world—whites as well as nonwhites—racial equality is the crucial test of the role of the United States in the world community, because the vast majority of the human race is not white.

[1] *The New York Times,* October 10, 1974.

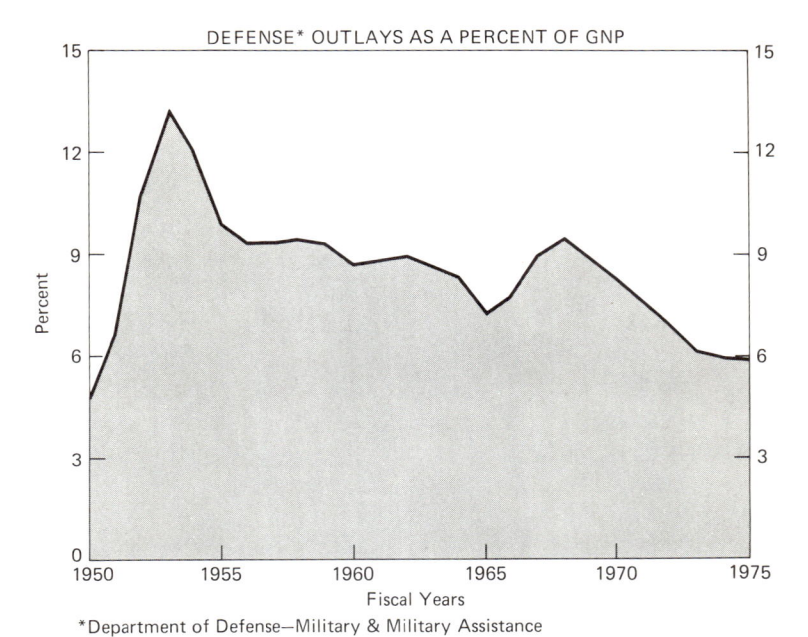

Figure 18-1 Defense outlays as a percent of GNP
SOURCE: The United States Budget in Brief: Fiscal Year 1975. *Executive Office of the President, Office of Management and Budget,* 1974.

That the American people have not fully adjusted to the importance of foreign affairs can be seen in the selection of this century's presidential candidates. In the earlier days of the Republic, six Secretaries of State became President: Jefferson, Madison, Monroe, John Quincy Adams, Van Buren, and Buchanan. But, although experience in foreign affairs for the presidential office has become infinitely more important in this century than in the last, no Secretary of State in this century has become President. Perhaps as the nation has become more "democratic" in the sense of being more responsive to demands by specific major groups (workers, farmers, racial minorities), it has put a premium on the ability to recognize and meet such demands rather than on experience in foreign policy. Lyndon Johnson amply demonstrated his ability to build a national consensus out of conflicting group demands in domestic affairs, but he failed to forge the same consensus in foreign affairs, particularly on Vietnam. In his 1968 and 1972 presidential campaigns, Richard Nixon successfully stressed his deep knowledge of international affairs and his personal relations with many world leaders. Yet, as John F. Kennedy had done in 1960, Nixon chose Vice-Presidents (Agnew in 1968 and Ford in 1973) who had had no experience in international politics.

DEMOCRACY AND FOREIGN POLICY

Inherent tensions between democracy and foreign policy

Alexis de Tocqueville, although viewing the American experiment in democracy with friendly sympathy, had grave doubts whether democracy and foreign affairs were compatible:

> *Foreign politics demand scarcely any of those qualities which a democracy possesses; and they require, on the contrary, the perfect use of almost all those faculties in which it is deficient. Democracy is favorable to the increase of the internal resources of the State; it tends to diffuse a moderate independence, it promotes the growth of public spirit, and fortifies the respect for law in all classes of society; and these are advantages which only exercise an indirect influence over the relations which one people bears to another. But a democracy is unable to regulate the details of an important undertaking, to persevere in design, and to work out its execution in the presence of serious obstacles. It cannot combine its measures with secrecy, and will not await their consequence with patience.*[2]

Whether Tocqueville is basically right or not, there is little doubt that some of his criticisms are amply borne out by historical experience. Many a democracy has dearly paid for hoping that critical international situations will fade out of existence by ignoring them.

In World War I the United States entered the conflict in 1917 and then proceeded to build up its military strength. However, by the time World War II broke out in 1939, the United States had again disarmed and was shaken out of its lethargy only after the fall of France in 1940, when the invasion and conquest of Britain by Nazi Germany seemed imminent. Immediately after World War II was over, the nation disarmed at the fastest possible rate in a fitful attempt to return to "normalcy," just as it had done after World War I. The Communist takeover of Czechoslovakia in 1948 and the attempted Communist conquest of Korea in 1950 rudely awakened the American people from the unrealistic illusion of trying to meet its international responsibilities without being militarily prepared. In the age of atomic weapons, the United States—for the first time in its history—can no longer buy time by relying on its *potential* military power, but must have at all times a variety of forces-in-being capable of acting without delay. If West Berlin were captured in a few hours or if Western Europe were overrun in a few days or weeks by conventional armed forces, the United States—were it to rely solely on nuclear weapons—would be faced with

---

[2] Alexis de Tocqueville, *Democracy in America*, London: Longmans, 1835, vol 1, pp. 236–237.

the grim choice of abandoning those areas or courting global destruction with nuclear arms. Few believe that the second option would be chosen; if the nuclear deterrent is to be credible, it must be supported by an array of conventional forces.

The difficulty of reconciling democracy and foreign affairs also appears when a democratic nation becomes too involved in international politics. First, excessive involvement in foreign affairs shifts the balance between the executive and legislative powers in the direction of the executive, since the conduct of foreign policy is by its very nature a function of the executive, as is also recognized by the Constitution. Such tilting of the balance not only may lead to a strong executive, but may result in the abuse of executive power under the cloak of "national security," as was shown by the Nixon administration, which heavily stressed foreign policy over domestic concerns. Second, the key objective of democratic government is welfare, whereas foreign policy ultimately hinges on power. Power politics require —and cultivate—attitudes and goals that are different from, and antagonistic to, welfare politics. Finally, overcommitments in international politics are extremely costly, and therefore necessitate a restructuring of social priorities, since no country possesses unlimited resources allowing it to produce abundant guns and abundant butter.

In seeking to resolve conflicts with other nations, a democratic society thus permanently oscillates between two major dangers: If it tries to isolate itself from foreign involvements and is unprepared in its defenses, it may suffer defeat or lose its existence. On the other extreme, if a democratic

"Can't you ever have enough over-kill capacity?"
Wall Street Journal, July 27, 1971.

nation becomes too involved in foreign commitments, it may lose its democratic political system.

Weakness of the rule of law and of a sense of community

Another inherent tension—or even incompatibility—between democracy and foreign affairs lies in the different qualities required for their successful operation. Two of the fundamental features of democracy—the rule of law and the consciousness of community—exist but in a rudimentary form among sovereign nations. In a democracy, the rule of law means not only that there is a legal answer to every problem and conflict, but also that the rule of law is mindful of legitimate interests and is enforced by an impartial authority. If the law is unjust, the pressure of the community will eventually bring about its substitution by a just rule. By contrast, in the society of nations, binding international law is still in its infancy, struggling for recognition and respect, and lacking an essential feature of national law—a machinery of impartial adjudication and enforcement. Thus every nation, particularly if it happens to be a great power, is judge and policeman in its own cases.

Collective defense agreements as a substitute for the rule of law

It is argued by some historians that Germany and Austria-Hungary might not have precipitated World War I in 1914 had they known in advance that Britain (and, later, the United States) would fight on the side of France and Russia. Similarly, in the 1930s, Nazi Germany and Japan assumed (or at least hoped) that the United States would not enter the conflict, and this uncertainty was, again, a contributing factor in shaping their war plans. The takeover of eastern Europe by Soviet armed forces after World War II indicated that Soviet imperialism followed a clear pattern of expansion, yet the United States still did not react with a basically new foreign policy. Only after Czechoslovakia was communized in 1948 did the conviction grow in the United States that American policies of waiting and seeing would lead to eventual major conflict, as they had done in 1914 and 1939. Seeking to learn a lesson from the errors of the past, the United States therefore joined with other like-minded nations in setting up the North Atlantic Treaty Organization (NATO) in 1949. Its most important provision is in Article 5, in which members of NATO "agree that an armed attack against one or more of them in Europe or North America shall be considered an attack against them all." Like all alliances in history, NATO has had its ups and downs, but its main purpose—the deterrence of Soviet aggression against any NATO member—has been achieved. Its main failure showed up during and after the Arab oil embargo in 1973, when each member of NATO sought to make its own arrangements with the Arab oil-exporting states, thus preventing a united front on the oil issue with its grave implications for the defense of the West.

The Korean conflict. Whereas mutual defense pacts do not provide absolute or complete security against aggression, the absence of advance commitments may encourage aggression. Korea is a case in point. The invasion of South Korea by North Korea in 1950 occurred after the United States had failed specifically to include South Korea in the American "defense perimeter," where aggression would be resisted by American armed force. Interpreting this omission as American lack of commitment, North Korea, backed by Russia and China, felt encouraged to attack South Korea. This calculation proved wrong, because President Truman, after securing U.N. approval, dispatched air and naval forces to Korea. After three years of heavy fighting, the invasion was stopped, and the Republic of Korea was saved from military conquest. In 1953 the United States and the Republic of Korea signed a mutual-defense pact. Since then there have been hundreds of border incidents between North Korea and the Republic of Korea, but North Korea has abstained from another major invasion attempt, and one reason for this may be the fear that any such attack would result in military response by the United States. The United States has similar defense pacts with Taiwan (Republic of China) and Japan.

Vietnam. The case for American involvement in Vietnam was much less clear than it had been in Korea. In Korea, the attempt to conquer South Korea was carried out by the invasion of South Korea by regular North Korean armies. There was a stable government in South Korea, and North Korea completely failed to produce Communist guerrillas or other tools of civil war.

By contrast, South Vietnam had not had a stable government since the French were ejected in 1954. Communist guerrillas, the Vietcong, spread throughout the country, and set up their rule in many villages and towns. Increasingly the guerrillas were augmented by regular North Vietnamese troops. Thus the issue arose of whether the conflict was primarily an internal civil war or whether it was largely carried on by outside forces, the armies of North Vietnam, supplied with (mostly) Soviet and (some) Chinese weapons. On the first supposition, it was argued by many that the United States had no legal or moral right to intervene in the internal conflict of another nation. On the second supposition, American intervention could be more properly justified, since its purpose would then be to aid an independent state against armed aggression from the outside.

A second major issue was that of national interest. When Lyndon Johnson became President in 1963, there were 16,000 American "advisers" in Vietnam. When he left office five years later, there were almost 550,000 American troops in South Vietnam. Opposition to the escalation of American involvement, leading to the longest war in American history, was largely based on the growing popular conviction that no vital national interest was at stake in Vietnam that was worth the sacrifice of more and more men and of higher and higher expenditures.

The growing disenchantment with the war was also deepened by the changing international environment in the 1960s. The conflict started in a "bipolar" world, in which the Communist countries, led by the Soviet Union, and the non-Communist countries, led by the United States, faced each other in terms of both ideology and power. As the war progressed, this bipolar international structure was replaced by one that was more complex. Rivalry between China and Russia replaced the former unity of the Communist bloc; in the non-Communist world, the United States ceased to be the undisputed leader, as western Europe and Japan became major economic powers, and many Americans felt that the United States could not—and should not—carry the defense burdens of non-Communist countries almost singlehandedly. Recognizing these changes in the world situation and American reactions to them, the Nixon administration gradually wound down American involvement through "Vietnamization," or the turning over of major fighting responsibilities to South Vietnamese forces. After four years of gradual withdrawals of American troops, the war was officially ended on January 27, 1973, when a treaty was signed in Paris by the United States, North Vietnam, South Vietnam, and the Vietcong. The cost of American involvement in Vietnam was high: 56,000 dead (of whom 46,000 were killed in combat), over 300,000 wounded, and about $140 billion in expenditures. Yet these sacrifices failed to achieve the objective of safeguarding the independence of South Vietnam. In the spring of 1975, two years after the total withdrawal of United States combat forces from Vietnam following the Paris treaty, North Vietnam and the Vietcong succeeded in gaining control of all South Vietnam.

Changing attitudes toward America's role in the world

The basic weakness of bilateral or multilateral defense agreements as a substitute for the rule of law lies in the fact that each nation still has to determine under what conditions it will consider itself bound by such agreements in a specific case. For example, since the *rapprochement* between China and the United States in the early 1970s it is questionable whether the United States would go to war with China over Taiwan, although there is a mutual defense pact between Taiwan and the United States.

The era of widespread American commitments throughout the world, which began in 1940, seemed to draw to a close by the late 1960s and early 1970s. In a public-opinion poll in 1964, 55 percent of the respondents felt that the United States should concentrate more on domestic than on international concerns; 32 percent put international concerns above domestic ones (13 percent had no opinion). In 1974, 77 percent favored domestic over international concerns; only 14 percent took the opposite view (9 percent had no opinion).[3]

More detailed public-opinion polls on changing attitudes toward internationalism and isolationism in the years 1964–1974 clearly show an erosion of internationalist sentiment and a corresponding increase of isolationist or middle-of-the-road positions. As Table 18–1 shows, the two most striking changes in attitudes in 1964–1974 were the drop of the completely internationalist category from 30 percent in 1964 to 11 percent in 1974 and the rise of the completely isolationist group from 3 percent in 1964 to 7 percent in 1974. The combined group of internationalists (complete and predominant) dropped from 65 percent in 1964 to 41 percent in 1974, whereas the total of isolationists (complete and predominant) rose from 8 percent in 1964 to 21 percent in 1974. Interestingly enough, the percentage of the mixed or middle-of-the-road group also increased, from 27 percent in 1964 to 38 percent in 1974. Even in 1974 the total of internationalists (41 percent) was still about twice as large as the total of isolationists (21 percent), but this was a sharp drop from 1964, when the total of internationalists (65 percent) was eight times as large as the total of isolationalists (8 percent). Thus, whereas the data in Table 18–1 do not indicate a complete turnabout of public opinion from internationalism to isolationism, they do suggest a continuous process of turning inward, of caution, of withdrawal from overextended international commitments.

The Vietnam war probably accelerated this process of introversion but did not generate it. In the view of some historians of American foreign policy, the American public was bound to adopt a changed stance in the

Table 18–1 *Internationalist/isolationist trends, 1964–1974*

	1964	1968	1972	1974
Completely internationalist	30%	25%	18%	11%
Predominantly internationalist	35	34	38	30
TOTAL INTERNATIONALISTS	65	59	56	41
MIXED	27	32	35	38
TOTAL ISOLATIONISTS	8	9	9	21
Predominantly isolationist	5	6	5	14
Completely isolationist	3	3	4	7

Source: William Watts and Lloyd A. Free, *State of the Nation 1974*, Washington, D.C.: Potomac Associates, 1974, p. 219 (distributed by Basic Books, New York).

[3] Donald R. Lesh (ed.), *A Nation Observed: Perspectives on America's World Role*, Washington, D.C.: Potomac Associates, 1974, p. 144 (distributed by Basic Books, New York).

late 1960s, since they view the whole history of American foreign policy as alternating roughly every 25 to 30 years between cycles of introversion and extroversion. Frank L. Klingberg has suggested the sequence of cycles shown in Table 18–2. Writing in 1952, Klingberg predicted that the then dominant mood of strong extroversion would not last forever, but would continue only until well into the 1960s. His prediction has come true, and if the underlying concept of cyclical alternations of American foreign policy is valid, the current mood of weariness of international commitments will not last forever either, but is likely to be replaced by a new phase of extroversion in about two decades.

THE EMPHASIS ON POWER AND NATIONAL INTEREST

In the 1920s and 1930s, the Western democracies—both students and practitioners of foreign policy—disregarded power as a key element in world politics and hoped that peace could be maintained solely through international treaties outlawing war and through appeals to morality. This neglect of the role of power by the democracies encouraged the fascist states to prepare for war and led the Soviet Union to believe that the Western democracies were decadent and on the way out as major forces in world affairs.

After World War II, the pendulum of opinion and criticism swung to the other extreme, and power, or national interest, became the sole yardstick by which some students and diplomats judged foreign policy. According to this view, foreign policy should pursue only the national interest and avoid the tempting chimeras of "legalistic" and "moralistic" ideas. In analyzing American diplomacy between 1900 and 1950, George F. Kennan, the most distinguished American representative of the "national-interest" school of thought, comes to the following conclusion: "I see the most serious fault of our past policy formulation to lie in something that I might call the legalistic-moralistic approach to international problems."[4]

The national-interest school deserves credit for reminding us that there

Table 18–2 *Introvert and extrovert phases*

Introvert Dates	Extrovert Dates
1776–1798	1798–1824
1824–1844	1844–1871
1871–1891	1891–1919
1919–1940	1940–

Source: Frank L. Klingberg, "The Historical Alternation of Moods in American Foreign Policy," World Politics, 4 (January, 1952), p. 250. Reprinted by permission of Princeton University Press.

[4] George F. Kennan, *American Diplomacy: 1900–1950*, Chicago: University of Chicago Press, 1951, p. 95.

can be no realistic foreign policy without a recognition of the factors of power and national interest. The emphasis on national interest as a key element in the making of foreign policy is a useful antidote to the unctuous hypocrisy that often obscures the pursuit of very material interests.

Difficulty of defining the national interest

Foreign policy, however, is not easily explainable in terms of national interest. In the first place, there is the difficulty of defining the national interest. Disagreements over issues of American foreign policy are not in the main between "idealists" seeking to uphold legal or ethical standards in international life and "realists" coldly pursuing the national interest, but among those who agree that the national interest should guide American foreign policy but who differ over what the national interest is in a particular case.

After the United States defeated Mexico in 1846 and took over half of its territory, some Americans urged that all of Mexico plus a few Central American republics ought to be annexed. Those who opposed such a policy did so, among other reasons, on the ground that such excessive imperialist aggrandizement of the United States would not be in the American interest, because it might permanently poison U.S.–Latin American relations. A century later, when Mexico nationalized the oil industry and expropriated several American oil companies in 1938, some Americans urged tough action against Mexico in order to protect the national interest. President Roosevelt, in resisting such a policy, also thought of the national interest: He was sure that war would soon descend upon the world, and that a friendly Mexico (which in World War I almost sided with America's enemies) and a friendly Latin America would be vital in the coming world conflict. His policy was confirmed by subsequent events. When the United States was drawn into World War II, all Latin American republics (with the exception of fascist-dominated Argentina) quickly declared war on the Rome-Berlin-Tokyo Axis, and Mexico, in particular, made an important contribution to the American war effort. In the Vietnam war, too, the major disagreement was not between idealists and realists, but between those who thought that United States interests in Southeast Asia required intervention in Vietnam and those who asserted that such involvement would hurt American interests at home and abroad.

Civilian supremacy over the military. If democratic nations insist on civilian supremacy over the military, they do so because they believe that "war is too important to be left to the generals," as the French statesman Georges Clemenceau put it. In the view of democrats, the civilian mind is more likely to pursue national objectives in the light of long-term considerations and overall political factors, whereas the military mentality may be more inclined to concentrate on immediate and tangible results that can be obtained by the use of armed force. The temptation for "final" military solutions is by no means without appeal in democracies too.

In the Korean conflict, for example, General Douglas MacArthur publicly criticized the American policy of confining the war to Korea, and was eager to carry the war to the Chinese "sanctuary," thus ending the Chinese threat "once and for all." President Truman asserted the constitutional tradition of civilian supremacy by firing the general for his impetuous criticisms and stuck to his concept of confining the war to the Korean theater of operations because of the larger political issues involved. At the time, a substantial segment of American public opinion sided with General MacArthur, but in the end, President Truman's judgment was accepted as having served the American national interest more effectively by avoiding a possible world war.

The constitutional principle of civilians rather than the military determining the national interest offers little protection against the danger of civilian officials adopting a military viewpoint. The fateful decision of solving the problem of Vietnam through massive military escalation in 1965 was President Johnson's, and it was only in 1968 that he realized the issue could not be settled by military means, as viewed in the perspective of either Saigon or Washington. Postmortemizing on the American experience in Vietnam, Bernard Brodie, one of the leading scholars in the field of strategy and military affairs, wrote: "Our failures there [in Vietnam] have been at least 95 percent due to our incomprehension and inability to cope with the political dimensions of the problem, not forgetting that part which is internal to the United States."[5]

The national interest and foreign policy. The difficulty of defining the national interest and its relation to the conduct of foreign policy by a democratic government was highlighted more recently by the debate over the activities of the Central Intelligence Agency in Chile in 1970–1973. In 1974 it was revealed that the CIA had spent $8 million in 1970–1973 in Chile to help opponents of Marxist President Salvador Allende resist the growing trend toward one-party rule. Most of the money had gone to anti-Allende newspapers, politicians, and striking workers and shopkeepers. The CIA was particularly alarmed by the increasing introduction into Chile of Soviet and Cuban personnel and weapons, suggesting the possibility or probability of a Communist preemptive takeover of total power by the minority government of President Allende.

This prospect was frustrated by the forcible overthrow of the Allende government by the Chilean military in September, 1973, but revelations of

[5]Bernard Brodie, "Why Were We So (Strategically) Wrong?" *Foreign Policy*, no. 5 (Winter, 1971–1972), p. 157.

CIA covert activities in Chile prior to the overthrow raised numerous issues of American foreign policy, although there was no evidence that the CIA was involved in the preparation of the military coup. When asked about the CIA activities in Chile, President Ford stated in his press conference of September 16, 1974, that "our government, like other governments, does take certain actions in the intelligence field to help implement foreign policy and protect national security." Concerning the aid given secretly to anti-Allende newspapers and political parties, President Ford said, "I think this is in the best interest of the people of Chile and certainly in our best interest."

President Ford's position did not resolve the problem of whether a democratic government has the right to intervene in the internal affairs of other nations in pursuit of its national interest. Moreover, by claiming that the CIA activities in Chile were also in the best interests of Chile, President Ford implied that the United States government has the right to define the national interest of *other* nations—a novel doctrine that may generate new dimensions of tension and conflict, since other governments may take the position that they are better judges of their national interests than the government of the United States. Very likely, the government of the United States, too, would not be too eager for other nations to determine its national interest.

"Are other countries allowed to do things for reasons of overriding national security?"
Drawing by Stevenson; © 1971 The New Yorker Magazine, Inc.

DEMOCRATIC CONTROL OF FOREIGN POLICY

From Jefferson on, democratic leaders have held that democracy requires not only a public that cares about public affairs but also an informed public. In domestic affairs, information is backed up by personal experience. The average voter thus feels he can judge public issues on the basis of interest, personal involvement, and information. Also, special-interest groups perform an important function in this process, because in trying to promote a cause, they disseminate information, slanted and one-sided as it may be. Although interest groups influence foreign policy, as on the issue of trading with Communist countries, they are not as large or as influential as the special-interest groups that are concerned with domestic issues.

Low level of interest and information in foreign affairs

By contrast, the citizen of a democratic country has neither the intensity of interest nor the level of information about foreign affairs that he brings to bear on domestic issues. The more general an issue of foreign policy is, the more it affects the nation as a whole, as over the issue of high tariffs versus free trade in general, but it seems to affect the citizen less as an individual. Where any foreign-policy issue directly affects a particular group—as when workers become jobless because of tariff cuts on a specific product—those affected express their intense interest as loudly as they can. But where an issue of foreign policy goes beyond the interests of a special group, public opinion tends to accept the decisions made by the President or the Secretary of State.

Periodically the public can become deeply interested or aroused when the conduct of foreign policy generates either drama or crisis. Thus a visit of the President to Peking or a 10-day trip of the Secretary of State to the Middle East, shuttling back and forth between a dozen countries on a nonstop peace mission, are dramatic enough to arouse momentarily the interest of even the most lethargic, since such events immediately fill the newspaper pages and the television screens. Public opinion also becomes interested and aroused when foreign policy leads to a crisis or the threat of war. For years energy experts had warned the public that the United States was running out of domestic oil and becoming too dependent on Middle East, mostly Arab, oil exporters. Yet the public became concerned about the subject of energy only after the Arab oil embargo in the fall and winter of 1973–1974, when gas shortages resulted in long queues at gas station, considerable frustration, and sporadic violence.

Public interest in foreign policy becomes most intense in case of threat of war or actual war, because war affects every family through military service, economic controls, and many other dislocations of personal life. Such public interest becomes even deeper if the war goes badly, as it did in Vietnam, or if the outcome is inconclusive, as it seemed to many at the end of the Korean war.

The growing role of science and technology

The problem of the low level of interest and information in foreign affairs has been intensified by profound scientific and technological changes in recent decades. As science and technology have increasingly come to determine the complicated weapons and weapons systems on which the United States must rely in the last resort, the layman—and even most congressmen, high executive officials, and newspaper commentators are in this category—feels more bewildered than ever. As foreign policy has become more and more determined by scientific and technological developments, strategy, too, has become increasingly removed from the range of interest or understanding of the average citizen. When he therefore encounters terms such as "megatons," "spasm warfare," "MIRV" (Multiple Independently Targeted Reentry Vehicle), "MRV" (Multiple Reentry Vehicle), "payload," and "throw weight," he may throw up his hands in despair and feel that all this is beyond his grasp and ought to be decided by experts.

Foreign affairs have thus become the domain of "small" publics, made up largely of scientists, professional strategists, government policy-makers, and highly influential small private groups such as the Council on Foreign Relations. Although hard thinking in these groups is a continuing process, few pronouncements on foreign policy by these experts ever reach the television screen or the daily papers. It could perhaps be argued that the very smallness and expertise of these "small publics" in the field of foreign policy may help to eliminate demagoguery and keep thought on a high level. But even if such were the case, the problem of democratic control of foreign policy—as of any policy—would thereby not be solved, because under democratic control the people through their elected representatives are supposed to control the experts, high-minded as they may be, and not vice versa. Sometimes even experts disagree among themselves, as happened during the Vietnam war and as periodically occurs whenever experts compare the overall military power of the United States with that of the Soviet Union. Such disagreements among experts accentuate the difficulties of the average citizen in trying to judge foreign-policy issues knowledgeably and intelligently.

The citizen, and even Congress, can turn away from foreign affairs, but the government cannot. Ultimately policy decisions on the highest level are made by a small group of political, administrative, and military leaders. This innermost circle of decision-makers includes the President, who has supreme responsibility and authority in foreign policy, the Secretaries of State and Defense, the Chairman of the Joint Chiefs of Staff, and the Director of the Central Intelligence Agency.

The changing role of Congress

In its power to appropriate money, Congress still tries to maintain some control over foreign policy. This is particularly noticeable in areas that do not require highly specialized information and in which the issues involved can be easily grasped. This happens annually, for example, in congressional discussions of foreign aid. All the traditional formal and informal practices (such as logrolling) come into play: In the classical congressional approach to foreign aid, those who oppose aid to Greece yield on this issue if Turkey gets its cut, and partisans of massive aid to India make concessions on aid to Pakistan. But in the crucial decisions affecting national security and survival and involving the expenditure of billions of dollars, Congress, too, has generally relied on the testimony of experts, although it has—particularly in the last few years—sought to assert its independence by slashing specific defense expenditures or by stretching the development and production of costly new weapons systems over a longer period. In critical situations, such as developed under Truman in Korea, under Kennedy in Cuba, and under Johnson and Nixon in Southeast Asia, Congress felt that it had to give the President almost complete discretion, even if his actions involved the deployment of armed forces abroad.

More recently, however, Congress has balked against exclusive presidential control of military and foreign affairs. Despite the commitment of over half a million men and the expenditure of more than $100 billion on the Vietnam war, the United States failed to achieve a military solution to the conflict. This failure greatly weakened the confidence of many Americans in the military establishment, and the corrosion of confidence was also reflected in Congress. From the late 1960s on, Congress has scrutinized more closely the size of the military establishment and has increasingly examined charges of waste in military procurement.

The National Commitments Resolution. Since military commitments are closely related to foreign-policy objectives, Congress has also challenged the presidential predominance in this field, and has sought to restore a constitutional balance between the President and Congress in decisions that may lead to armed conflict. In 1969 the Senate passed the National Commitments Resolution, designed to strengthen the role of Congress. The resolution defined a national commitment as the use of armed forces on foreign territory or the promise to assist a foreign country with armed forces, and expressed the sense of the Senate that such national commitments be made only by means of a treaty, statute, or concurrent resolution of both houses of Congress. Although the Senate National Commitments Resolution did not have binding legal force on the President, it conveyed the message that he ought to consult with Congress more actively in matters involving the use of armed forces abroad. After President Nixon staged the armed incursion into Cambodia in 1970 without prior consultation with Congress, Congress passed amendments to appropriation bills forbidding him to use funds for introducing armed forces into Laos, Thailand, and Cambodia.

The War Powers Act. The efforts of Congress to reassert itself in foreign policy and national security culminated in the War Powers Act of 1973, unsuccessfully vetoed by President Nixon. Under the act, the President may commit U.S. forces without a prior declaration of war or specific statutory authorization only in case of attack or imminent attack upon the United States or its armed forces. The President must report such commitment of armed forces to Congress within 48 hours, and obtain congressional authorization within another 60 days or terminate his military action. The 60-day period may be extended by 30 days if such extension is required for the safe withdrawal of American forces.

The role of Congress in the decision-making process. The purpose of the National Commitments Resolution of 1969 and of the War Powers Act of 1973 was not to enable Congress to conduct foreign policy or military operations, but to ensure for itself a significant role in the decision-making process in these vital areas. The conflict between Congress and the President over control of foreign policy goes back to the days of George Washington, and changes in the balance between presidential and congressional powers do not occur abruptly. It remains to be seen whether the self-assertive recent posture of Congress primarily reflects a temporary mood of "No more Vietnams" (and perhaps also of "No more Watergates") or whether it foreshadows a long-term shift of power in the direction of more congressional sharing of authority in formulating foreign policy.

Veto limits of public opinion

Public opinion still serves an important function in setting some veto limit to foreign-policy proposals. In 1937 President Roosevelt made his famous "quarantine speech," in which he urged the American people to join with the other Western democracies in quarantining the fascist aggressor states (Germany, Italy, and Japan). But Congress and the public were not ready for this policy, and for over half a year the President refrained from discussing major issues of foreign policy. In 1951 President Truman found that public opinion—particularly organized Protestant groups—would not stand for his proposal to send a regular and permanent ambassador to the Vatican. From 1966 on, President Johnson became keenly aware of the declining popular support of his conduct of the Vietnam war. After this support dropped to about 40 percent in 1967 and early 1968, the President sought peace talks with the other side and announced the cessation of

American bombing of North Vietnam north of the 20th parallel, two important steps to extricate the United States from the conflict. In wars, in particular, public opinion can have a strong veto power on foreign policy, since the successful conduct of a war—unlike the passing of a bill in Congress—requires more than a mere 51 percent of popular support.[6]

Bipartisanship in foreign policy

The inherent tension between democracy and foreign policy can also be seen in the concept and practice of bipartisanship. After President Woodrow Wilson's debacle in the Senate over the issue of American membership in the League of Nations, later presidents have made it a point to consult in advance with congressional leaders of both parties on important foreign-policy matters. The aim has been to build a foreign policy that could be accepted by both parties.

President Kennedy appointed several Republicans to high foreign-policy and national-security positions, including Henry Cabot Lodge as ambassador to the United Nations and Robert S. McNamara as Secretary of Defense. President Johnson retained Kennedy's Republican appointees. As in the case of Eisenhower, Johnson encountered his major foreign-policy troubles —as over the intervention in the Dominican Republic in 1965 and the Vietnam war—among elements in his own party, led by Senators Eugene McCarthy and J. William Fulbright. Partly because his major emphasis in the campaign had been on foreign affairs, President Nixon returned to the Eisenhower approach of appointing Republicans to top foreign-policy and defense positions, including the Cabinet members in these two areas.

If bipartisanship in foreign policy merely means that vital issues of American security be considered by everybody, regardless of party, in a rational and objective manner, and that foreign-policy issues not be exploited for partisan purposes, there is no special problem of democratic government here, because the same attitude should ideally prevail in domestic politics, too. However, the problem arises when bipartisanship in foreign policy leads to an excessive emphasis on "closing the ranks," "standing shoulder to shoulder," and unity for the sake of unity. Bipartisanship may then become a threat to the functioning of traditional democratic processes.

China is a case in point. After the Communists won the civil war in 1949, nonrecognition of Communist China by the United States became a bipartisan dogma. For years, persons who questioned the wisdom of nonrecognition often did not dare to raise the issue in public lest they be

---

[6]See John E. Mueller, "Trends in Popular Support for the Wars in Korea and Vietnam," *American Political Science Review,* 65 (June, 1971), pp. 358–375, with interesting comparative references to American attitudes toward World Wars I and II.

thought "soft on communism." The spell of hostility between the United States and China was broken only after President Nixon's visit to Peking in 1972 opened new channels of communication and dialogue between the two countries. Perhaps only a President of impeccable anti-Communist credentials and background as well as conservative leanings could have brought about this change of American attitudes almost overnight, and if there was an American public figure who could not be charged with being soft on communism it was Richard M. Nixon. But behind President Nixon's China coup there lurked the danger of a new bipartisan dogma—that the new China policy be accepted by all without cool and careful scrutiny.

THE LONG-RANGE CHALLENGES TO AMERICAN FOREIGN POLICY

Gradually, the realization has dawned on American policy-makers that the protracted war on hunger and poverty throughout the world is likely to last even longer than the cold war with communism, because communism is only the froth on the surface of much bigger problems, such as overpopulation, racial conflicts, and economic want.

The widening gap between rich and poor countries

In 1970, per capita gross national product was $2,701 in the developed countries and only $208 in the developing countries of the world.[7] This represents a ratio of 13 to 1. Within the developed countries, per capita GNP was highest in North America, or $4,670, and in the poorest region of the world, South Asia (including India and Pakistan), per capita GNP was $103; the ratio between the richest and the poorest regions is thus about 45 to 1.

What is most alarming about this gap between developed and developing countries is that it is persistently widening rather than narrowing. Gross national product has grown at almost the same rate in developing as in developed countries in the last two decades. However, per capita income has grown much more slowly in developing countries, since population growth is much more rapid there than in the developed nations.

The effects of the currently widening gaps between developed and less developed (or "aspiring") nations are projected for the year 2000 in Figure 18–2. Taking an example from the non-Communist world, the differential between the per capita GNP in the United States and India was $3,420 in 1966, but is projected to be $9,890 for the year 2000. The chart also shows that the population in the United States is assumed to rise by about one-half in the years 1966–2000, whereas that of India is projected to double during

[7]U.S. Bureau of the Census, *Statistical Abstract of the United States, 1974*, p. 825.

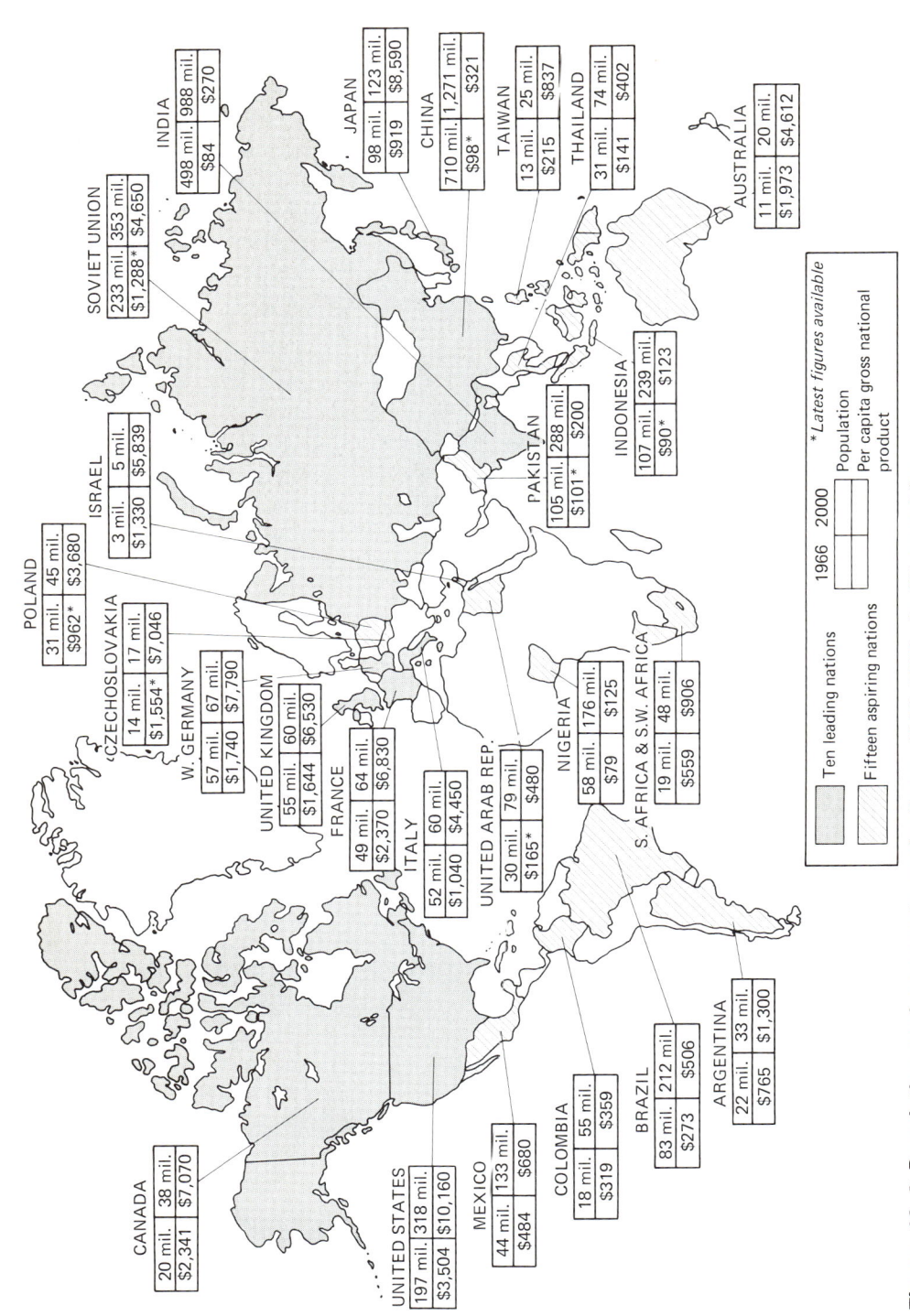

Figure 18–2 Population and economic projections, 1966–2000, in 25 countries
SOURCE: The New York Times, January 6, 1969. © 1969 by The New York Times Company. Reprinted by permission.

the same period. However, the widening differential between developed and developing nations also applies to the Communist world. The per capita GNP differential between the Soviet Union and China was $1,190 in 1966, but is projected to rise to $4,329 by the end of this century. These trends and projections clearly show that the significant line that divides humanity is not political or ideological, as the expression "East-West" suggests, but that it is economic, roughly corresponding to a "North-South" division, since most of the less developed nations are in the southern portion of the earth.

American economic aid to developing countries has amounted to about $80 billion in the period 1946–1973. In recent years, annual American assistance to developing nations has been about $3 billion, but the share of GNP used for this purpose declined from 0.56 percent in 1962 to 0.29 percent in 1972. The same has been true of developed countries as a group: In 1962, their aid to developing countries was 0.52 percent of their GNP, dropping to 0.34 percent in 1972.[8]

The oil crisis. Since 1973, the quadrupling of oil prices in one year by the Organization of Petroleum Exporting Countries (OPEC) has revolutionized the entire structure of the world economy. The developed countries have suffered from enormous balance-of-payment deficits, double-digit inflation, and high unemployment—unfavorable conditions for generous aid to developing countries. The oil-importing developing countries have been hit even harder, since they have no reserve strength to cope with the disaster of the new oil prices.

By contrast, the developing countries in OPEC (above all, Saudi Arabia, Iran, Libya, and Kuwait) have emerged as new financial giants. Since most OPEC countries are unable to spend the vast funds flowing into their national treasuries on internal development, they are expected to accumulate between $300 and $500 billion by 1980. So far, OPEC countries have invested the huge surpluses from their oil monopoly primarily in safe capital markets, such as New York, London, and Zurich, while giving to the developing oil-importing countries only paltry amounts of aid—mostly in the form of credits rather than grants.

Thus the oil-importing developing countries find themselves in a distressing situation: The traditional providers of economic assistance—countries like the United States, Britain, Japan, and France—are in deep economic trouble themselves, unable to provide massive aid even if they wanted to, whereas the new oil-rich countries are accumulating annually tens of billions of dollars but are unwilling to aid substantially the oil-importing developing nations. If the United States, comparatively less

---

[8] James W. Howe and the Staff of the Overseas Development Council, *The U.S. and the Developing World*, New York: Praeger, 1974, p. 196.

dependent on oil imports than the other major industrial nations, will recover from inflation and recession and increase its independence in energy, it will face what may perhaps be the greatest challenge in its history: how to share its restored economic and political strength with the developed and developing nations so deeply wounded by the energy crisis.

The paradox of power and influence

Before the United States attained the status of a superpower after World War II, its influence in the world was much greater than its "raw power." During the nineteenth century, for example, the United States got along without information agencies in foreign countries to explain and justify American policies. The tens of millions of immigrants who came here from all over the world did not need any official American propaganda to explain the United States to them. During the eighteenth and nineteenth centuries, liberals everywhere looked upon the United States as the "conscience of democracy," the haven of the lowly and oppressed from all four corners of the globe.

Paradoxically, as American power reached its zenith after World War II, it lost much of its previous influence, for it ceased to be regarded as the conscience of democracy. For the first time in American history, the necessity arose to explain the United States and its foreign policies to other nations. If the contemporary struggle in the world will be decided in the minds of men rather than on the battlefields, the performance of American ideas and institutions at home will be closely watched by the rest of the world.

In 1776 the worldwide impact of the American call for freedom, of defiance of privilege and authority, was enhanced by America's economic and political weakness. Having attained material power unprecedented in history, can the United States survive in a dangerous world, live up to its original ideals, and strengthen and expand freedom and welfare throughout the world? Or will it follow other great powers in history that went down failing to see that power can endure only if it is justified not by those who possess it, but by those who do not?

Appendix 1
The Declaration of Independence

Appendix 1
The Declaration of Independence

When in the course of human events, it becomes necessary for one people to dissolve the political bands which have connected them with another, and to assume among the Powers of the earth, the separate and equal station to which the Laws of Nature and of Nature's God entitle them, a decent respect to the opinions of mankind requires that they should declare the causes which impel them to the separation.

We hold these truths to be self-evident, that all men are created equal, that they are endowed by their Creator with certain unalienable Rights, that among these are Life, Liberty and the pursuit of Happiness.—That to secure these rights, Governments are instituted among Men, deriving their just powers from the consent of the governed, That whenever any Form of Government becomes destructive of these ends, it is the Right of the People to alter or to abolish it, and to institute new Government, laying its foundation on such principles and organizing its powers in such form, as to them shall seem most likely to effect their Safety and Happiness. Prudence, indeed, will dictate that Governments long established should not be changed for light and transient causes; and accordingly all experience hath shown, that mankind are more disposed to suffer, while evils are sufferable, than to right themselves by abolishing the forms to which they are accustomed. But when a long train of abuses and usurpations, pursuing invariably the same Object, evinces a design to reduce them under absolute Despotism, it is their right, it is their duty, to throw off such Government, and to provide new Guards for their future security.—Such has been the patient sufferance of these Colonies; and such is now the necessary which constrains them to alter their former Systems of Government. The history of the present King of Great Britain is a history of repeated injuries and usurpations, all having in direct object the establishment of an absolute Tyranny over these States. To prove this, let Facts be submitted to a candid world.

He has refused his Assent to Laws, the most wholesome and necessary for the public good.

He has forbidden his Governors to pass Laws of immediate and pressing importance, unless suspended in their operation till his Assent should be obtained; when so suspended, he has utterly neglected to attend to them.

He has refused to pass other Laws for the accommodation of large districts of people, unless those people would relinquish the right of Representation in the Legislature, a right inestimable to them and formidable to tyrants only.

He has called together legislative bodies at places unusual, uncomfortable, and distant from the depository of their Public Records, for the sole purpose of fatiguing them into compliance with his measures.

He has dissolved Representative Houses repeatedly, for opposing with manly firmness his invasions on the rights of the people.

He has refused for a long time, after such dissolutions, to cause others to be elected; whereby the Legislative Powers, incapable of Annihilation, have returned to the People at large for their exercise; the State remaining in the mean time exposed to all the dangers of invasion from without, and convulsions within.

He has endeavoured to prevent the population of these States; for that purpose obstructing the Laws of Naturalization of Foreigners; refusing to pass others to encourage their migration hither, and raising the conditions of new Appropriations of Lands.

He has obstructed the Administration of Justice, by refusing his Assent to Laws for establishing Judiciary Powers.

He has made Judges dependent on his Will alone, for the tenure of their offices, and the amount and payment of their salaries.

He has erected a multitude of New Offices, and sent hither swarms of Officers to harass our People, and eat out their substance.

He has kept among us, in times of peace, Standing Armies without the Consent of our legislature.

He has affected to render the Military independent of and superior to the Civil Power.

He has combined with others to subject us to a jurisdiction foreign to our constitution, and unacknowledged by our laws giving his Assent to their acts of pretended legislation:

For quartering large bodies of armed troops among us:

For protecting them, by a mock Trial, from Punishment for any Murders which they should commit on the Inhabitants of these States:

For cutting off our Trade with all parts of the world:

For imposing taxes on us without our Consent:

For depriving us in many cases, of the benefits of Trial by Jury:

For transporting us beyond Seas to be tried for pretended offences:

For abolishing the free System of English Laws in a neighboring Province, establishing therein an Arbitrary government, and enlarging its Boundaries so as to render it at once an example and fit instrument for introducing the same absolute rule into these Colonies:

For taking away our Charters, abolishing our most valuable Laws, and altering fundamentally the Forms of our Governments:

For suspending our own Legislature, and declaring themselves invested with Power to legislate for us in all cases whatsoever.

He has abdicated Government here, by declaring us out of his Protection and waging War against us.

He has plundered our seas, ravaged our Coasts, burnt our towns, and destroyed the lives of our people.

He is at this time transporting large armies of foreign mercenaries to compleat the works of death, desolation and tyranny, already begun with circumstances of Cruelty & perfidy scarcely paralleled in the most barbarous ages, and totally unworthy the Head of a civilized nation.

He has constrained our fellow Citizens taken Captive on the high Seas to bear Arms against their Country, to become the executioners of their friends and Brethren, or to fall themselves by their Hands.

He has excited domestic insurrections amongst us, and has endeavoured to bring on the inhabitants of our frontiers, the merciless Indian Savages, whose known rule of warfare, is an undistinguished destruction of all ages, sexes and conditions.

In every stage of these Oppressions We have Petitioned for Redress in the most humble terms: Our repeated Petitions have been answered only by repeated injury. A Prince, whose character is thus marked by every act which may define a Tyrant, is unfit to be the ruler of a free People.

Nor have We been wanting in attention to our British brethren. We have warned them from time to time of attempts by their legislature to extend an unwarrantable jurisdiction over us. We have reminded them of the circumstances of our emigration and settlement here. We have appealed to their native justice and magnanimity, and we have conjured them by the ties of our common kindred to disavow these usurptions, which would inevitably interrupt our connections and correspondence. They too have been deaf to the voice of justice and of consanguinity. We must, therefore, acquiesce in the necessity, which denounces our Separation, and hold them, as we hold the rest of mankind, Enemies in War, in Peace, Friends.

We, therefore, the Representatives of the United States of America, in General Congress, Assembled, appealing to the Supreme Judge of the world for the rectitude of our intensions, do, in the Name, and by the Authority of the good People of these Colonies, solemnly publish and declare, That these United Colonies are, and of Right ought to be Free and Independent States; that they are Absolved from all allegiance to the British Crown, and that all political connection between them and the State of Great Britain, is and ought to be totally dissolved; and that as Free and Independent States, they have full Power to levy War, conclude Peace, contract Alliances, establish Commerce, and to do all other Acts and Things which Independent States may of right do. And for the support of this Declaration, with a firm reliance on the Protection of Divine Providence, we mutually pledge to each other our Lives, our Fortunes and our sacred Honor.

Appendix 2
The Constitution of the United States

Appendix 2
The Constitution of the United States

[Preamble]

We the people of the United States, in Order to form a more perfect Union, establish Justice, insure domestic Tranquility, provide for the common defence, promote the general Walfare, and secure the Blessings of Liberty to ourselves and our Posterity, do ordain and establish this Constitution for the United States of America.

ARTICLE 1
Section 1
[Legislative Powers]

All legislative Powers herein granted shall be vested in a Congress of the United States, which shall consist of a Senate and a House of Representatives.

Section 2
[House of Representatives, How Constituted, Power of Impeachment]

The House of Representatives shall be composed of Members chosen every second Year by the People of the several States, and the Electors in each State shall have [the] Qualifications requisite for Electors of the most numerous Branch of the State Legislature.

No Person shall be a Representative who shall not have attained to the Age of twenty five Years, and been seven Years a Citizen of the United States, and who shall not when elected, be an Inhabitant of that State in which he shall be chosen.

Representatives and direct Taxes shall be apportioned among the several States which may be included within this Union, according to their respective Numbers, which shall be determined by adding to the whole Number of free Persons, including those bound to Service for a Term of Years, and excluding Indians not taxed, three fifths of all other Persons. The actual Enumeration shall be made within three Years after the first Meeting of the Congress of the United States, and within every subsequent Term of ten Years, in such Manner as they shall by Law direct. The Number of Representatives shall not exceed one for every thirty Thousand, but each State shall have at Least one Representative; and until such enumeration shall be made, the State of New Hampshire shall be entitled to chuse three, Massachusetts eight, Rhode-Island and Providence Plantations one, Connecticut five, New York six, New Jersey four, Pennsylvania eight, Delaware one, Maryland six, Virginia ten, North Carolina five, South Carolina five, and Georgia three.

When vacancies happen in the Representation from any State, the Executive Authority thereof shall issue Writs of Election to fill such Vacancies.

The House of Representatives shall chuse their Speaker and other officers; and shall have the sole Power of Impeachment.

Section 3
[*The Senate, How Constituted, Impeachment Trials*]

The Senate of the United States shall be composed of Two Senators from each State, chosen by the Legislature thereof, for six Years; and each Senator shall have one Vote.

Immediately after they shall be assembled in Consequence of the first Election, they shall be divided as equally as may be into three Classes. The Seats of the Senators of the first Class shall be vacated at the Expiration of the second Year, of the second Class at the Expiration of the fourth Year, and of the third Class at the Expiration of the sixth Year, so that one third may be chosen every second Year; and if Vacancies happen by Resignation, or otherwise, during the Recess of the Legislature of any State, the Executive thereof may make temporary Appointments until the next Meeting of the Legislature, which shall then fill such Vacancies.

No Person shall be a Senator who shall not have attained to the Age of thirty Years, and been nine Years a Citizen of the United States, and who shall not, when elected, be an Inhabitant of that State for which he shall be chosen.

The Vice-President of the United States shall be President of the Senate, but shall have no Vote, unless they be equally divided.

The Senate shall chuse their other Officers, and also a President pro tempore, in the Absence of the Vice-President, or when he shall exercise the Office of President of the United States.

The Senate shall have the sole power to try all Impeachments. When sitting for that Purpose, they shall be on Oath or Affirmation. When the President of the United States [is tried] the Chief Justice shall preside: And no Person shall be convicted without the Concurrence of two thirds of the Members present.

Judgment in Cases of Impeachment shall not extend further than to removal from Office, and disqualification to hold and enjoy any Office of honor, Trust or Profit under the United States: but the Party convicted shall nevertheless be liable and subject to Indictment, Trial, Judgment and Punishment, according to Law.

Section 4
[Election of Senators and Representatives]

The Times, Places and Manner of holding Elections for Senators and Representatives, shall be prescribed in each State by the Legislature thereof; but the Congress may at any time by Law make or alter such Regulations, except as to the Places of chusing Senators.

The Congress shall assemble at least once in every Year, and such Meeting shall be on the first Monday in December, unless they shall by Law appoint a different Day.

Section 5
[Quorum, Journals, Meetings, Adjournments]

Each House shall be the Judge of the Elections, Returns and Qualifications of its own Members, and a Majority of each shall constitute a Quorum to do Business; but a smaller Number may adjourn from day to day, and may be authorized to compel the Attendance of absent members, in such Manner, and under such Penalties as each House may provide.

Each House may determine the Rules of its Proceedings, punish its Members for disorderly Behaviour, and, with the Concurrence of two thirds, expel a Member.

Each House shall keep a Journal of its Proceedings, and from time to time publish the same, excepting such Parts as may in their Judgment require Secrecy; and the Yeas and Nays of the Members of either House on any question shall, at the Desire of one fifth of those Present, be entered on the Journal.

Neither House, during the Session of Congress, shall, without the Consent of the other, adjourn for more than three days, nor to any other Place than that in which the two Houses shall be sitting.

Section 6
[Compensation, Privileges, Disabilities]

The Senators and Representatives shall receive a Compensation for their Services, to be ascertained by Law, and paid out of the Treasury of the United States. They shall in all Cases, except Treason, Felony and Breach of the Peace, be privileged from Arrest during their Attendance at the Session of their respective Houses, and in going to and returning from the same; and for any Speech or Debate in either House, they shall not be questioned in any other Place.

No Senator or Representative shall, during the Time for which he was elected, be appointed to any civil Office under the Authority of the United

States, which shall have been created, or the Emoluments whereof shall have been encreased during such time; and no Person holding any Office under the United States, shall be a Member of either House during his Continuance in Office.

Section 7
[Procedure in Passing Bills and Resolutions]

All Bills for raising Revenue shall originate in the House of Representatives; but the Senate may propose or concur with Amendments as on other Bills.

Every Bill which shall have passed the House of Representatives and the Senate, shall, before it becomes a Law, be presented to the President of the United States; if he approve he shall sign it, but if not he shall return it, with his Objections to that House in which it shall have originated, who shall enter the Objections at large on their Journal, and proceed to reconsider it. If after such Reconsideration two thirds of that House shall agree to pass the Bill, it shall be sent, together with the Objections, to the other House, by which it shall likewise be reconsidered, and if approved by two thirds of that House, it shall become a Law. But in all such Cases the Votes of both Houses shall be determined by Yeas and Nays, and the Names of the Persons voting for and against the Bill shall be entered on the Journal of each House respectively. If any Bill shall not be returned by the President within ten Days (Sundays excepted) after it shall have been presented to him, the Same shall be a Law, in like Manner as if he had signed it, unless the Congress by their Adjournment prevent its Return, in which Case it shall not be a Law.

Every Order, Resolution, or Vote to which the Concurrence of the Senate and House of Representatives may be necessary (except on a question of Adjournment) shall be presented to the President of the United States; and before the Same shall take Effect, shall be approved by him, or being disapproved by him, shall be repassed by two thirds of the Senate and House of Representatives, according to the Rules and Limitations prescribed in the Case of a Bill.

Section 8
[Powers of Congress]

The Congress shall have the Power To lay and collect Taxes, Duties, Imposts and Excises, to pay the Debts and provide for the common Defence and general Welfare of the United States; but all Duties, Imposts and Excises shall be uniform throughout the United States.

To borrow Money on the credit of the United States;

To regulate Commerce with foreign Nations and among the several States, and with the Indian Tribes;

To establish an uniform Rule of Naturalization, and uniform Laws on the subject of Bankruptcies throughout the United States;

To Coin Money, regulate the Value thereof, and of foreign Coin, and fix the Standard of Weights and Measures;

To provide for the Punishment of counterfeiting the Securities and current Coin of the United States;

To establish Post Offices and post Roads;

To promote the Progress of Science and useful Arts, by securing for limited Times to Authors and Inventors the exclusive Right to their respective Writings and Discoveries;

To constitute Tribunals inferior to the supreme Court;

To define and punish Piracies and Felonies committed on the high Seas, and Offences against the Law of Nations;

To declare War, grant Letters of Marque and Reprisal, and make Rules concerning Captures on Land and Water;

To raise and support Armies, but no Appropriation of Money to that Use shall be for a longer Term than two Years;

To provide and maintain a Navy;

To make Rules for Government and Regulation of the land and naval Forces;

To provide for calling forth the Militia to execute the Laws of the Union, suppress Insurrections and repel Invasions;

To provide for organizing, arming, and disciplining, the Militia, and for governing such Part of them as may be employed in the Service of the United States, reserving to the States respectively, the Appointment of the Officers, and the Authority of training the Militia according to the discipline prescribed by Congress;

To exercise exclusive Legislation in all Cases whatsoever, over such District (not exceeding ten Miles square) as may, by Cession of particular States, and the Acceptance of Congress, become the Seat of the Government of the United States, and to exercise like Authority over all Places purchased by the Consent of the Legislature of the State in which the Same shall be, for the Erection of Forts, Magazines, Arsenals, dock-Yards, and other needful Buildings;—And

To make all Laws which shall be necessary and proper for carrying into Execution the foregoing Powers, and all other Powers vested by this Constitution in the Government of the United States, or in any Department or Officer thereof.

Section 9

[Limitation upon Powers of Congress]

The Migration or Importation of such Persons as any of the States now existing shall think proper to admit, shall not be prohibited by the Congress prior to the Year one thousand eight hundred and eight, but a Tax or duty may be imposed on such Importation, not exceeding ten dollars for each Person.

The Privilege of the Writ of Habeas Corpus shall not be suspended, unless when in Cases of Rebellion or Invasion the public Safety may require it.

No Bill of Attainder or ex post facto Law shall be passed.

No Capitation, or other direct, Tax shall be laid, unless in Proportion to the Census or Enumeration herein before directed to be taken.

No Tax or Duty shall be laid on Articles, exported from any State.

No Preference shall be given by any Regulation of Commerce or Revenue to the Ports of one State over those of another; nor shall Vessels bound to, or from, one State, be obliged to enter, clear, or pay Duties in another.

No Money shall be drawn from the Treasury, but in Consequence of Appropriations made by Law; and a regular Statement and Account of the Receipts and Expenditures of all public Money shall be published from time to time.

No title of Nobility shall be granted by the United States: And no Person holding any Office of Profit or Trust under them, shall, without the Consent of the Congress, accept of any present, Emolument, Office, or Title, of any kind whatever, from any King, Prince, or foreign State.

Section 10
[Restrictions upon Powers of States]

No State shall enter into any Treaty, Alliance, or Confederation; grant Letters of Marque and Reprisal; coin Money; emit Bills of Credit; make any Thing but gold and silver Coin a Tender in Payment of Debts; pass any Bill of Attainder, ex post facto Law, or Law impairing the Obligation of Contracts, or grant any Title of Nobility.

No State shall, without the Consent of the Congress, lay any Imposts or Duties on Imports or Exports, except what may be absolutely necessary for executing its inspection Laws: and the net Produce of all Duties and Imposts, laid by any State on Imports or Exports, shall be for the Use of the Treasury of the United States; and all such Laws shall be subject to the Revision and Controul of [the] Congress.

No State shall, without the Consent of Congress, lay any Duty of Tonnage, keep Troops, or Ships of War in time of Peace, enter into any Agreement or Compact with another State, or with a foreign Power, or engage in War, unless actually invaded, or in such imminent Danger as will not admit of any delay.

ARTICLE 2
Section 1
[Executive Power, Election, Qualification of the President]

The executive Power shall be vested in a President of the United States of America. He shall hold his Office during the Term of four Years, and, together with the Vice-President, chosen for the same Term, be elected as follows.

Each State shall appoint, in such Manner as the Legislature thereof may direct, a Number of Electors, equal to the whole Number of Senators and Representatives to which the State may be entitled in the Congress; but no Senator or Representative, or Person holding an Office of Trust or Profit under the United States, shall be appointed an Elector.

The Electors shall meet in their respective States, and vote by Ballot for two Persons of whom one at least shall not be an Inhabitant of the same State with themselves. And they shall make a List of all the Persons voted for, and of the Number of Votes for each; which List they shall sign and certify, and transmit sealed to the Seat of the Government of the United States, directed to the President of the Senate. The President of the Senate shall, in the Presence of the Senate and House of Representatives, open all the Certificates, and the Votes shall then be counted. The Person having the greatest Number of Votes shall be the President, if such Number be a Majority of the whole Number of Electors appointed; and if there be more than one who have such Majority, and have an equal Number of Votes, then the House of Representatives shall immediately chuse by Ballot one of them for President; and if no Person have a Majority, then from the five highest in the List the said House shall in like Manner chuse the President. But in chusing the President, the Votes shall be taken by States, the Representation from each State having one Vote; A quorum for this purpose shall consist of a Member or Members from two thirds of the States, and a Majority of all the States shall be necessary to a Choice. In every Case, after the choice of the President, the Person having the greatest Number of Votes of the Electors shall be the Vice-President. But if there should remain two or more who have equal Votes, the Senate shall chuse from them by Ballot the Vice-President.

The Congress may determine the Time of chusing the Electors, and the Day on which they shall give their Votes; which Day shall be the same throughout the United States.

No person except a natural born Citizen, or a Citizen of the United States, at the time of the Adoption of this Constitution, shall be eligible to the Office of President; neither shall any Person be eligible to that Office who shall not have attained to the Age of thirty five Years, and been fourteen Years a Resident within the United States.

In Case of the Removal of the President from Office, or of his Death, Resignation, or Inability to discharge the Powers and Duties of the said Office, the Same shall devolve on the Vice-President, and the Congress may by Law provide for the Case of Removal, Death, Resignation or Inability, both of the President and Vice-President, declaring what Officer shall then act as President, and such Officer shall act accordingly, until the Disability be removed, or a President shall be elected.

The President shall, at stated Times, receive for his Services, a Compensation, which shall neither be encreased nor diminished during the Period for which he shall have been elected, and he shall not receive within that Period any other Emolument from the United States, or any of them.

Before he entered on the Execution of his Office, he shall take the following Oath or Affirmation:—"I do solemnly swear (or affirm) that I will faithfully execute the Office of the President of the United States, and will to the best of my Ability, preserve, protect and defend the Constitution of the United States."

Section 2
[Powers of the President]

The President shall be Commander in Chief of the Army and Navy of the United States, and the Militia of the several States, when called into the actual Service of the United States; he may require the Opinion, in writing, of the principal Officer in each of the executive Departments, upon any subject relating to the Duties of their respective Offices, and he shall have Power to grant Reprieves and Pardons for Offences against the United States, except in Cases of Impeachment.

He shall have Power, by and with the Advice and Consent of the Senate, to make Treaties, provided two thirds of the Senators present concur; and he shall nominate, and by and with the Advice and Consent of the Senate, shall appoint Ambassadors, other public Ministers and Consuls, Judges of the supreme Court, and all other Officers of the United States, whose Appointments are not herein otherwise provided for, and which shall be established by Law: but the Congress may by Law vest the Appointment of such inferior Officers, as they think proper in the President alone, in the Courts of Law, or in the Heads of Departments.

The President shall have Power to fill up all Vacancies that may happen during the Recess of the Senate, by granting Commissions which shall expire at the End of their next Session.

Section 3
[Powers and Duties of the President]

He shall from time to time give to the Congress Information of the State of the Union, and recommend to their Consideration such Measures as he shall judge necessary and expedient; he may, on extraordinary Occasions, convene both Houses, or either of them, and in Case of Disagreement between them, with Respect to the Time of Adjournment, he may adjourn them to such Time as he shall think proper; he shall receive Ambassadors and other public Ministers; he shall take Care that the Laws be faithfully executed, and shall commission all the Officers of the United States.

Section 4
[Impeachment]

The President, Vice-President and all civil Officers of the United States, shall be removed from Office on Impeachment for, and Conviction of, Treason, Bribery, or other high Crimes and Misdemeanors.

ARTICLE 3
Section 1
[Judicial Power, Tenure of Office]

The judicial Power of the United States, shall be vested in one supreme Court, and in such inferior Courts as the Congress may from time to time ordain and establish. The judges, both of the supreme and inferior Courts, shall hold their Offices during good Behavior, and shall, at stated Times, receive for their Services, a Compensation, which shall not be diminished during their Continuance in Office.

Section 2
[Jurisdiction]

The judicial Power shall extend to all Cases, in Law and Equity, arising under this Constitution, the Laws of the United States, and Treaties made, or which shall be made, under their Authority;—to all Cases affecting Ambassadors, other public Ministers and Consuls;—to all Cases of admiralty and maritime Jurisdiction;—to Controversies to which the United States shall be a Party;—to Controversies between two or more States;—between a State and Citizens of another State;— between Citizens of different States; —between Citizens of the same State claiming Lands under Grants of different States, and between a State, or the Citizens thereof, and foreign States, Citizens or Subjects.

In all Cases affecting Ambassadors, other public Ministers and Consuls, and those in which a State shall be Party, the supreme Court shall have original Jurisdiction. In all the other Cases before mentioned, the supreme Court shall have appellate Jurisdiction, both as to Law and Fact, with such Exceptions, and under such Regulations as the Congress shall make.

The Trial of all Crimes, except in Cases of Impeachment, shall be by Jury; and such Trial shall be held in the State where the said Crimes shall have been committed; but when not committed within any State, the Trial shall be at such Place or Places as the Congress may by Law have directed.

Section 3
[Treason, Proof and Punishment]

Treason against the United States, shall consist only in levying War against them, or in adhering to their Enemies; giving them Aid and Comfort. No

Person shall be convicted of Treason unless on the Testimony of two Witnesses to the same overt Act, or on Confession in open Court.

The Congress shall have Power to declare the Punishment of Treason, but no Attainder of Treason shall work Corruption of Blood, or Forfeiture except during the Life of the Person attainted.

ARTICLE 4
Section 1
[Faith and Credit Among States]

Full Faith and Credit shall be given in each State to the public Acts, Records, and judicial Proceedings of every other State. And the Congress may by general Laws prescribe the Manner in which such Acts, Records and Proceedings shall be proved, and the Effect thereof.

Section 2
[Privileges and Immunities, Fugitives]

The citizens of each State shall be entitled to all Privileges and Immunities of Citizens in the several States.

A Person charged in any State with Treason, Felony, or other Crime, who shall flee from Justice, and be found in another State, shall on Demand of the executive Authority of the State from which he fled, be delivered up, to be removed to the State having Jurisdiction of the Crime.

No person held to Service or Labour in one State, under the Laws thereof, escaping into another, shall, in Consequence of any Law or Regulation therein, be discharged from such Service or Labour, but shall be delivered up on Claim of the Party to whom such Service or Labour may be due.

Section 3
[Admission of New States]

New States may be admitted by the Congress into this Union; but no new State shall be formed or erected within the Jurisdiction of any other State; nor any State be formed by the Junction of two or more States, or Parts of States, without the Consent of the Legislatures of the States concerned as well as of the Congress.

The Congress shall have Power to dispose of and make all needful Rules and Regulations respecting the Territory or other Property belonging to the United States; and nothing in this Constitution shall be so construed as to Prejudice any Claims of the United States, or of any particular State.

Section 4
[Guarantee of Republican Government]

The United States shall guarantee to every State in this Union a Republican Form of Government, and shall protect each of them against Invasion; and on Application of the Legislature, or of the Executive (when the Legislature cannot be convened) against domestic Violence.

ARTICLE 5
[Amendment of the Constitution]

The Congress, whenever two thirds of both Houses shall deem it necessary, shall propose Amendments to this Constitution, or, on the Application of the Legislatures of two thirds of the several States, shall call a Convention for proposing Amendments, which, in either Case, shall be valid to all Intents and Purposes, as Part of this Constitution, when ratified by the Legislatures of three fourths of the several States, or by Conventions in three fourths thereof, as the one or the other Mode of Ratification may be proposed by the Congress; Provided that no Amendment which may be made prior to the Year One thousand eight hundred and eight shall in any Manner affect the first and fourth Clauses in the Ninth Section of the first Article, and that no State, without its Consent, shall be deprived of its equal Suffrage in the Senate.

ARTICLE 6
[Debts, Supremacy, Oath]

All Debts contracted and Engagements entered into, before the Adoption of this Constitution, shall be as valid against the United States under this Constitution, as under the Confederation.

This Constitution, and the Laws of the United States which shall be made in Pursuance thereof; and all Treaties made, or which shall be made, under the Authority of the United States, shall be the supreme Law of the Land; and the Judges in every State be bound thereby, any Thing in the Constitution or Laws of any State to the Contrary notwithstanding.

The Senators and Representatives before mentioned, and the Members of the several State Legislatures, and all executive and judicial Officers, both of the United States and of the several States, shall be gound by Oath or Affirmation, to support this Constitution; but no religious Test shall ever be required as a Qualification to any Office or public Trust under the United States.

ARTICLE 7
[Ratification and Establishment]

The Ratification of the Conventions of nine States, shall be sufficient for the Establishment of this Constitution between the States so ratifying the Same. done in Convention by the Unanimous Consent of the States present the Seventeenth Day of September in the Year of our Lord one thousand seven hundred and Eighty seven and of the Indpendence of the United States of America the Twelfth In witness whereof We have hereunto subscribed our Names.

Go. Washington
Presidt and deputy from Virginia

New Hampshire	John Langdon Nicholas Gilman
Massachusetts	Nathaniel Gorham Rufus King
Connecticut	Wm Saml Johnson Roger Sherman
New York	Alexander Hamilton
New Jersey	Will: Livingston David Brearley Wm Paterson Jona: Dayton
Pennsylvania	B. Franklin Thomas Mifflin Robt Morris Geo. Clymer Thos. FitzSimons Jared Ingersoll James Wilson Gouv Morris
Delaware	Geo. Read Gunning Bedford jun John Dickinson Richard Bassett Jaco: Broom

Maryland	James McHenry Dan of St Thos. Jenifer Danl Carroll
Virginia	John Blair— James Madison Jr.
North Carolina	Wm Blount Richd Dobbs Spaight. Hu Williamson
South Carolina	J. Rutledge Charles Cotesworth Pinckney Charles Pinckney Pierce Butler
Georgia	William Few Abr Baldwin

AMENDMENTS TO THE CONSTITUTION

[The first ten amendments were proposed by Congress on September 25, 1789; ratified and adoption certified on December 15, 1791.]

Amendment I
[Freedom of Religion, of Speech, of the Press, and Right of Petition]

Congress shall make no law respecting an establishment of religion, or prohibiting the free exercise thereof; or abridging the freedom of speech, or of the press; or the right of the people peaceably to assemble, and to petition the Government for a redress of grievances.

Amendment II
[Right to Keep and Bear Arms]

A well regulated Militia being necessary to the security of a free State, the right of the people to keep and bear Arms, shall not be infringed.

Amendment III
[Quartering of Soldiers]

No Soldier shall, in time of peace be quartered in any house, without the consent of the Owner, nor in time of war, but in a manner to be prescribed by law.

Amendment IV
[Security from Unwarrantable Search and Seizure]

The right of the people to be secure in their persons, houses, papers, and effects, against unreasonable searches and seizures, shall not be violated, and no Warrants shall issue, but upon probable cause, supported by Oath or affirmation, and particularly describing the place to be searched, and the persons or things to be seized.

Amendment V
[Rights of Accused in Criminal Proceedings]

No person shall be held to answer for a capital, or otherwise infamous crime, unless on a presentment or indictment of a Grand Jury, except in cases arising in the land or naval forces, or in the Militia, when in actual service in time of War or public danger; nor shall any person be subjected for the same offense to be twice put in jeopardy of life or limb; nor shall be compelled in any criminal case to be a witness against himself, nor be deprived of life, liberty, or property, without due process of law; nor shall private property be taken for public use, without just compensation.

Amendment VI
[Right to Speedy Trial, Witnesses, etc.]

In all criminal prosecutions, the accused shall enjoy the right to a speedy and public trial, by an impartial jury of the State and district wherein the crime shall have been committed, which district shall have been previously ascertained by law, and to be informed of the nature and cause of the accusation; to be confronted with the witnesses against him; to have compulsory process for obtaining witnesses in his favor, and to have the Assistance of Counsel for his defence.

Amendment VII
[Trial by Jury in Civil Cases]

In Suits at common law, where the value in controversy shall exceed twenty dollars, the right of trial by jury shall be preserved, and no fact tried by a jury, shall be otherwise reexamined in any Court of the United States, than according to the rules of the common law.

Amendment VIII
[Bails, Fines, Punishments]

Excessive bail shall not be required, nor excessive fines imposed, nor cruel and unusual punishments inflicted.

Amendment IX
[Reservation of Rights of the People]

The enumeration in the Constitution, of certain rights, shall not be construed to deny or disparage others retained by the people.

Amendment X
[Powers Reserved to States or People]

The powers not delegated to the United States by the Constitution, nor prohibited by it to the States, are reserved to the States respectively, or to the people.

Amendment XI

[Proposed by Congress on March 4, 1794; declared ratified on January 8, 1798.]

[Restriction of Judicial Power]

The Judicial power of the United States shall not be construed to extend to any suit in law or equity, commenced or prosecuted against one of the United States by Citizens of another State, or by Citizens or Subjects of any Foreign State.

Amendment XII

[Proposed by Congress on December 9, 1803; declared ratified on September 25, 1804.]

[Election of President and Vice-President]

The Electors shall meet in their respective state, and vote by ballot for President and Vice-President, one of whom, at least, shall not be an inhabitant of the same state with themselves; they shall name in their ballots the person voted for as President, and in distinct ballots the person voted for as Vice-President and they shall make distinct lists of all persons voted for as President, and of all persons voted for as Vice-President, and of the number of votes for each, which lists they shall sign and certify, and transmit sealed to the seat of the government of the United States, directed to the President of the Senate;—The President of the Senate shall, in the presence of the Senate and House of Representatives, open all the certificates and the votes shall then be counted;—The person having the greatest number of votes for President, shall be the President, if such number be a majority of the whole number of Electors appointed; and if no person have such majority, then from the persons having the highest numbers not exceeding three on the list of those voted for as President, the House of Representatives shall choose immediately, by ballot, the President. But in choosing the President, the votes shall be taken by states, the representation from each state having one vote; a quorum for this purpose shall consist of a member or members from two-thirds of the states, and a majority of all the states shall be necessary to a choice. And if the House of Representatives shall not choose a President whenever the right of choice shall devolve upon them, before the fourth day of March next following, then the Vice-President shall act as President, as in the case of the death or other constitutional disability of the President.—The person having the greatest number of votes as Vice-President, shall be the Vice-President, if such number be a majority of the whole number of Electors appointed, and if no person have a majority, then from the two highest numbers on the list, the Senate shall choose the Vice-President; a quorum for the purpose shall consist of two-thirds of the whole number of Senators, and a majority of the whole number shall be necessary to a choice. But no person constitutionally ineligible to the office of President shall be eligible to that of Vice-President of the United States.

Amendment XIII

[Proposed by Congress on January 31, 1865, declared ratified on December 18, 1865.]

Section 1
[*Abolition of Slavery*]

Neither slavery nor involuntary servitude, except as a punishment for a crime whereof the party shall have been duly convicted, shall exist within the United States, or any place subject to their jurisdiction.

Section 2
[*Power to Enforce This Article*]

Congress shall have power to enforce this article by appropriate legislation.

Amendment XIV

[Proposed by Congress on June 16, 1866; declared ratified on July 28, 1868.]

Section 1
[*Citizenship Rights Not to Be Abridged by States*]

All persons born or naturalized in the United States, and subject to the jurisdiction thereof, are citizens of the United States and of the State wherein they reside. No State shall make or enforce any law which shall abridge the privileges or immunities of citizens of the United States; nor shall any State deprive any person of life, liberty, or property, without due process of law; nor deny to any person within its jurisdiction the equal protection of the laws.

Section 2
[Apportionment of Representatives in Congress]

Representatives shall be apportioned among the several States according to their respective numbers, counting the whole number of persons in each State, excluding Indians not taxed. But when the right to vote at any election for the choice of electors for President and Vice-President of the United States, Representatives in Congress, the Executive and Judicial officers of a State, or the members of the Legislature thereof, is denied to any of the male inhabitants of such State, being twenty-one years of age, and citizens of the United States, or in any way abridged, except for participation in rebellion, or other crime, the basis of representation therein shall be reduced in the proportion which the number of such male citizens shall bear to the whole number of male citizens twenty-one years of age in such State.

Section 3
[Persons Disqualified from Holding Office]

No person shall be a Senator or Representative in Congress, or elector of President and Vice-President, or hold any office, civil or military, under the United States, or under any State, who, having previously taken an oath, as a member of Congress, or as an officer of the United States, or as a member of any State legislature, or as an executive or judicial officer of any State, to support the Constitution of the United States, shall have engaged in insurrection or rebellion against the same, or given aid or comfort to the enemies thereof. But Congress may by a vote of two-thirds of each House, remove such disability.

Section 4
[What Public Debts Are Valid]

The validity of the public debt of the United States, authorized by law, including debts incurred for payment of pensions and bounties for services in suppressing insurrection or rebellion, shall not be questioned. But neither the United States nor any State shall assume or pay any debt or obligation incurred in aid of insurrection or rebellion against the United States, or any claim for the loss or emancipation of any slave; but all such debts, obligations and claims shall be held illegal and void.

Section 5
[Power to Enforce This Article]

The Congress shall have power to enforce, by appropriate legislation, the provisions of this article.

Amendment XV

[Proposed by Congress on February 26, 1869; declared ratified on March 30, 1870.]

Section 1
[Negro Suffrage]

The right of citizens of the United States to vote shall not be denied or abridged by the United States or by any State on account of race, color, or previous condition of servitude.

Section 2
[Power to Enforce This Article]

The Congress shall have power to enforce this article by appropriate legislation.

Amendment XVI

[Proposed by Congress on July 12, 1909; declared ratified on February 25, 1913.]

[Authorizing Income Taxes]

The Congress shall have power to lay and collect taxes on incomes, from whatever source derived, without apportionment among the several States, and without regard to any census or enumeration.

Amendment XVII

[Proposed by Congress on May 13, 1912; declared ratified on May 31, 1913.]

[Popular Election of Senators]

The Senate of the United States shall be composed of two Senators from each State, elected by the people thereof, for six years; and each Senator shall have one vote. The electors in each State shall have the qualifications requisite for electors of the most numerous branch of the State legislatures.

When vacancies happen in the representation of any State in the Senate, the executive authority of such State shall issue writs of election to fill such vacancies: *Provided,* That the legislature of any State may empower the executive thereof to make temporary appointments until the people fill the vacancies by election as the legislature may direct.

This amendment shall not be so construed as to affect the election or term of any Senator chosen before it becomes valid as part of the Constitution.

Amendment XVIII

[Proposed by Congress on December 18, 1917; declared ratified on January 16, 1919.]

Section 1
[National Liquor Prohibition]

After one year from the ratification of this article the manufacture, sale, or transportation of intoxicating liquors within, the importation thereof into, or the exportation thereof from the United States and all territory subject to the jurisdiction thereof for beverage purposes is hereby prohibited.

Section 2
[Power to Enforce This Article]

The Congress and the several States shall have concurrent power to enforce this article by appropriate legislation.

Section 3
[Ratification Within Seven Years]

This article shall be inoperative unless it shall have been ratified as an amendment to the Constitution by the legislatures of the several States, as provided in the Constitution, within seven years from the date of the submission hereof to the States by the Congress.

Amendment XIX

[Proposed by Congress on June 4, 1919; declared ratified on August 26, 1920.]

[Woman Suffrage]

The right of citizens of the United States to vote shall not be denied or abridged by the United States or by any State on account of sex.

Congress shall have power to enforce this article by appropriate legislation.

Amendment XX

[Proposed by Congress on March 2, 1932; declared ratified on February 6, 1933.]

Section 1
[Terms of Office]

The terms of the President and Vice-President shall end at noon on the 20th day of January, and the terms of Senators and Representatives at noon on the 3rd day of January, of the years in which such terms would have ended if this article had not been ratified; and the terms of their successors shall then begin.

Section 2
[Time of Convening Congress]

The Congress shall assemble at least once in every year, and such meeting shall begin at noon on the 3rd day of January, unless they shall by law appoint a different day.

Section 3
[Death of President Elect]

If, at the time fixed for the beginning of the term of the President, the President elect shall have died, the Vice-President elect shall become President. If a President shall not have been chosen before the time fixed for the beginning of his term, or if the President elect shall have failed to qualify, then the Vice-President elect shall act as President until a President shall have qualified; and the Congress may by law provide for the case wherein neither a President elect nor a Vice-President elect shall have qualified, declaring who shall then act as President, or the manner in which one who is to act shall be selected, and such person shall act accordingly until a President or Vice-President shall have qualified.

Section 4
[Election of the President]

The Congress may by law provide for the case of the death of any of the persons from whom the House of Representatives may choose a President whenever the right of choice shall have devolved upon them, and for the case of the death of any of the persons from whom the Senate may choose a Vice-President whenever the right of choice shall have devolved upon them.

Section 5

Sections 1 and 2 shall take effect on the 15th day of October following the ratification of this article.

Section 6

This article shall be inoperative unless it shall have been ratified as an amendment to the Constitution by the legislatures of three-fourths of the several States within seven years from the date of its submission.

Amendment XXI

[Proposed by Congress on February 20, 1933; declared ratified on December 5, 1933.]

Section 1
[National Liquor Prohibition Repealed]

The eighteenth article of amendment to the Constitution of the United States is hereby repealed.

Section 2
[Transportation of Liquor into "Dry" States]

The transportation or importation into any States, Territory, or possession of the United States for delivery or use therein of intoxicating liquors, in violation of the laws thereof, is hereby prohibited.

Section 3

This article shall be inoperative unless it shall have been ratified as an amendment to the Constitution by conventions in the several States, as provided in the Constitution, within seven years from the date of the submission hereof to the States by the Congress.

Amendment XXII

[Proposed by Congress on March 21, 1947; declared ratified on February 26, 1951.]

Section 1
[*Tenure of President Limited*]

No person shall be elected to the office of the President more than twice, and no person who has held the office of President, or acted as President, for more than two years of a term to which some other person was elected President shall be elected to the office of the President more than once. But this Article shall not apply to any person holding the office of President when this Article was proposed by the Congress, and shall not prevent any person who may be holding the office of President, or acting as President, during the term within which this Article becomes operative from holding the office of President, or acting as President during the remainder of such term.

Section 2

This Article shall be inoperative unless it shall have been ratified as an amendment to the Constitution by the legislatures of three-fourths of the several States within seven years from the date of its submission to the States by the Congress.

Amendment XXIII

[Proposed by Congress on June 17, 1960; declared ratified on May 29, 1961.]

Section 1
[*District of Columbia Suffrage in Presidential Elections*]

The District constituting the seat of Government of the United States shall appoint in such manner as the Congress may direct:

A number of electors of President and Vice-President equal to the whole number of Senators and Representatives in Congress to which the District would be entitled if it were a State, but in no event more than the least populous State; they shall be in addition to those appointed by the States, but they shall be considered, for the purposes of the election of President and Vice-President, to be electors appointed by a State; and they shall meet in the District and perform such duties as provided by the twelfth article of amendment.

Section 2

The Congress shall have power to enforce this article by appropriate legislation.

Amendment XXIV

[Proposed by Congress on August 27, 1962; declared ratified on January 23, 1964.]

Section 1
[Bars Poll Tax in Federal Elections]

The right of citizens of the United States to vote in any primary or other election for President or Vice-President, for electors for President or Vice-President, or for Senator or Representative in Congress, shall not be denied or abridged by the United States or any State by reason of failure to pay any poll tax or other tax.

Section 2

The Congress shall have power to enforce this article by appropriate legislation.

Amendment XXV

[Proposed by Congress on July 6, 1965; declared ratified on February 10, 1967.]

Section 1
[Succession of Vice-President to Presidency]

In case of the removal of the President from office or of his death or resignation, the Vice-President shall become President.

Section 2
[Vacancy in Office of Vice-President]

Whenever there is a vacancy in the office of the Vice-President, the President shall nominate a Vice-President who shall take office upon confirmation by a majority vote of both Houses of Congress.

Section 3
[Vice-President as Acting President]

Whenever the President transmits to the President pro tempore of the Senate and the Speaker of the House of Representatives his written declaration that he is unable to discharge the powers and duties of his office, and until he transmits to them a written declaration to the contrary, such powers and duties shall be discharged by the Vice-President as Acting President.

Section 4
[Vice-President as Acting President]

Whenever the Vice-President and a majority of either the principal officers of the executive departments or of such other body as Congress may by law provide, transmit to the President pro tempore of the Senate and the Speaker of the House of Representatives their written declaration that the President is unable to discharge the powers and duties of his office, the Vice-President shall immediately assume the powers and duties of the office as Acting President.

Thereafter, when the President transmits to the President pro tempore of the Senate and the Speaker of the House of Representatives his written declaration that no inability exists, he shall resume the powers and duties of his office unless the Vice-President and a majority of either the principal officers of the executive department or of such other body as Congress may by law provide, transmit within four days to the President pro tempore of the Senate and the Speaker of the House of Representatives their written declaration that the President is unable to discharge the powers and duties of his office. Thereupon Congress shall decide the issue, assembling within forty-eight hours for that purpose if not in session. If the Congress, within twenty-one days after receipt of the latter written declaration, or, if Congress is not in session, within twenty-one days after Congress is required to assemble, determines by two-thirds vote of both Houses that the President is unable to discharge the powers and duties of his office, the Vice-President shall continue to discharge the same as Acting President; otherwise, the President shall resume the powers and duties of his office.

Amendment XXVI

[Proposed by Congress on March 23, 1971; declared ratified on June 30, 1971.]

Section 1
[Enfranchises citizens eighteen years of age or older]

The right of citizens of the United States, who are eighteen years of age or older, to vote shall not be denied or abridged by the United States or any state on account of age.

Section 2

The Congress shall have the power to enforce this article by appropriate legislation.

Appendix 3
Articles of Impeachment Against Richard M. Nixon, President of the United States

Appendix 3

Articles of Impeachment Against Richard M. Nixon, President of the United States

The Committee on the Judiciary, to whom was referred the consideration of recommendations concerning the exercise of the constitutional power to impeach Richard M. Nixon, President of the United States, having considered the same, reports thereon pursuant to H. Res. 803 as follows and recommends that the House exercise its constitutional power to impeach Richard M. Nixon, President of the United States, and that articles of impeachment be exhibited to the Senate as follows:

RESOLUTION

Impeaching Richard M. Nixon, President of the United States, of high crimes and misdemeanors.

Resolved, That Richard M. Nixon, President of the United States, is impeached for high crimes and misdemeanors, and that the following articles of impeachment be exhibited to the Senate:

Articles of impeachment exhibited by the House of Representatives of the United States of America in the name of itself and of all of the people of the United States of America, against Richard M. Nixon, President of the United States of America, in maintenance and support of its impeachment against him for high crimes and misdemeanors.

Article I

In his conduct of the office of President of the United States, Richard M. Nixon, in violation of his constitutional oath faithfully to execute the office of President of the United States and, to the best of his ability, preserve, protect, and defend the Constitution of the United States, and in violation of his constitutional duty to take care that the laws be faithfully executed, has prevented, obstructed, and impeded the administration of justice, in that:

On June 17, 1972, and prior thereto, agents of the Committee for the Re-election of the President committed unlawful entry of the headquarters of the Democratic National Committee in Washington, District of Columbia, for the purpose of securing political intelligence. Subsequent thereto, Richard M. Nixon, using the powers of his high office, engaged personally and through his subordinates and agents, in a course of conduct or plan designed to delay, impede, and obstruct the investigation of such unlawful entry; to cover up, conceal and protect those responsible; and to conceal the existence and scope of other unlawful covert activities.

The means used to implement this course of conduct or plan included one or more of the following:

(1) making or causing to be made false or misleading statements to lawfully authorized investigative officers and employees of the United States;

(2) withholding relevant and material evidence or information from lawfully authorized investigative officers and employees of the United States;

(3) approving, condoning, acquiescing in, and counseling witnesses with respect to the giving of false or misleading statements to lawfully authorized investigative officers and employees of the United States and false or misleading testimony in duly instituted judicial and congressional proceedings;

(4) interfering or endeavoring to interfere with the conduct of investigations by the Department of Justice of the United States, the Federal Bureau of Investigation, the Office of Watergate Special Prosecution Force, and Congressional Committees;

(5) approving, condoning, and acquiescing in, the surreptitious payment of substantial sums of money for the purpose of obtaining the silence or influencing the testimony of witnesses, potential witnesses or individuals who participated in such unlawful entry and other illegal activities;

(6) endeavoring to misuse the Central Intelligence Agency, an agency of the United States;

(7) disseminating information received from officers of the Department of Justice of the United States to subjects of investigations conducted by lawfully authorized investigative officers and employees of the United States, for the purpose of aiding and assisting such subjects in their attempts to avoid criminal liability;

(8) making false or misleading public statements for the purpose of deceiving the people of the United States into believing that a thorough and complete investigation had been conducted with respect to allegations of misconduct on the part of personnel of the executive branch of the United States and personnel of the Committee for the Re-election of the President, and that there was no involvement of such personnel in such misconduct; or

(9) endeavoring to cause prospective defendants, and individuals duly tried and convicted, to expect favored treatment and consideration in return for their silence or false testimony, or rewarding individuals for their silence or false testimony.

In all of this, Richard M. Nixon has acted in a manner contrary to his trust as President and subversive of constitutional government, to the great prejudice of the cause of law and justice and to the manifest injury of the people of the United States.

Wherefore Richard M. Nixon, by such conduct, warrants impeachment and trial, and removal from office.

Article II

Using the powers of the office of the President of the United States, Richard M. Nixon, in violation of his constitutional oath faithfully to execute the office of President of the United States and, to the best of his ability, preserve, protect, and defend the Constitution of the United States, and in disregard of his constitutional duty to take care that the laws be faithfully executed, has repeatedly engaged in conduct violating the constitutional rights of citizens, impairing the due and proper administration of justice and the conduct of lawful inquiries, or contravening the laws governing agencies of the executive branch and the purposes of these agencies.

This conduct has included one or more of the following:

(1) He has, acting personally and through his subordinates and agents, endeavored to obtain from the Internal Revenue Service, in violation of the constitutional rights of citizens, confidential information contained in income tax returns for purposes not authorized by law, and to cause, in violation of the constitutional rights of citizens, income tax audits or other income tax investigations to be initiated or conducted in a discriminatory manner.

(2) He misused the Federal Bureau of Investigation, the Secret Service, and other executive personnel, in violation or disregard of the constitutional rights of citizens, by directing or authorizing such agencies or personnel to conduct or continue electronic surveillance or other investigations for purposes unrelated to national security, the enforcement of laws, or any other lawful function of his office; he did direct, authorize, or permit the use of information obtained thereby for purposes unrelated to national security, the enforcement of laws, or any other lawful function of his office; and he did direct the concealment of certain records made by the Federal Bureau of Investigation of electronic surveillance.

(3) He has, acting personally and through his subordinates and agents, in violation or disregard of the constitutional rights of citizens, authorized and permitted to be maintained a secret investigative unit within the office of the President, financed in part with money derived from campaign contributions, which unlawfully utilized the resources of the Central Intelligence Agency, engaged in covert and unlawful activities,

and attempted to prejudice the constitutional right of an accused to a fair trial.

(4) He has failed to take care that the laws were faithfully executed by failing to act when he knew or had reason to know that his close subordinates endeavored to impede and frustrate lawful inquiries by duly constituted executive, judicial, and legislative entities concerning the unlawful entry into the headquarters of the Democratic National Committee, and the cover-up thereof, and concerning other unlawful activities, including those relating to the confirmation of Richard Kleindienst as Attorney General of the United States, the electronic surveillance of private citizens, the break-in into the offices of Dr. Lewis Fielding, and the campaign financing practices of the Committee to Re-elect the President.

(5) In disregard of the rule of law, he knowingly misused the executive power by interfering with agencies of the executive branch, including the Federal Bureau of Investigation, the Criminal Division, and the Office of Watergate Special Prosecution Force, of the Department of Justice, and the Central Intelligence Agency, in violation of his duty to take care that the laws be faithfully executed.

In all of this, Richard M. Nixon has acted in a manner contrary to his trust as President and subversive of constitutional government, to the great prejudice of the cause of law and justice and to the manifest injury of the people of the United States.

Wherefore Richard M. Nixon, by such conduct, warrants impeachment and trial, and removal from office.

Article III

In his conduct of the office of President of the United States, Richard M. Nixon, contrary to his oath faithfully to execute the office of President of the United States and, to the best of his ability, preserve, protect, and defend the Constitution of the United States, and in violation of his constitutional duty to take care that the laws be faithfully executed, has failed without lawful cause or excuse to produce papers and things as directed by duly authorized subpoenas issued by the Committee on the Judiciary of the House of Representatives on April 11, 1974, May 15, 1974, May 30, 1974, and June 24, 1974, and willfully disobeyed such subpoenas. The subpoenaed papers and things were deemed necessary by the Committee in order to resolve by direct evidence fundamental, factual questions relating to Presidential direction, knowledge, or approval of actions demonstrated by other evidence to be substantial grounds for impeachment of the President. In refusing to produce these papers and things, Richard M. Nixon, substituting his judgment as to what materials were necessary for the inquiry, interposed the powers of the Presidency against the lawful subpoenas of the House of Representatives, thereby assuming to himself functions and judgments necessary to the exercise of the sole power of impeachment vested by the Constitution in the House of Representatives.

In all of this, Richard M. Nixon has acted in a manner contrary to his trust as President and subversive of constitutional government, to the great prejudice of the cause of law and justice, and to the manifest injury of the people of the United States.

Wherefore Richard M. Nixon, by such conduct, warrants impeachment and trial, and removal from office.

Bibliography

Chapter 1
CONCEPTS OF DEMOCRACY

Adorno, T. W., et al. *The Authoritarian Personality.* New York: Harper & Row, 1950.
Aron, Raymond. *Democracy and Totalitarianism.* New York: Praeger, 1969.
Dahl, Robert A., and Edward R. Tufte. *Size and Democracy.* Stanford: Stanford University Press, 1973.
De Grazia, Alfred. *Eight Bads—Eight Goods: The American Contradictions.* Garden City, N.Y.: Anchor Press/Doubleday, Anchor Books, 1975.
Dobzhansky, Theodosius. *Genetic Diversity and Human Equality.* New York: Basic Books, 1973.
Ebenstein, William. *Today's Isms: Communism, Fascism, Capitalism, Socialism,* 7th ed. Englewood Cliffs, N.J.: Prentice-Hall, 1973.
Kristol, Irving. *On the Democratic Idea in America.* New York: Harper & Row, Harper Torchbooks, 1973.
Lipset, Seymour Martin. *Political Man.* Garden City, N.Y.: Doubleday, 1960.
Macpherson, C. B. *Democratic Theory: Essays in Retrieval.* New York: Oxford University Press, 1973.
Orwell, George. *1984.* New York: New American Library, Signet Books, 1950.
Padover, Saul K. *The Meaning of Democracy.* New York: Praeger, 1963.
Pickles, Dorothy. *Democracy.* New York: Basic Books, 1970.
Schattschneider, E. E. *The Semisovereign People: A Realist's View of Democracy in America.* New York: Holt, Rinehart & Winston, 1960.
Sniderman, Paul M. *Personality and Democratic Politics.* Berkeley: University of California Press, 1974.

Chapter 2
CONFLICT RESOLUTION IN THE POLITICAL PROCESS

Coser, Lewis. *The Function of Social Conflict.* New York: Free Press Paperbacks, 1964.
Deutsch, Morton. *The Resolution of Conflict: Constructive and Destructive.* New Haven: Yale University Press, 1973.
Edinger, Lewis J. (ed.). *Political Leadership in Industrialized Societies.* New York: Wiley, 1967.
Ellul, Jacques. *The Technological Society.* New York: Random House, Vintage Books, 1964.

Friedrich, Carl J. *The Pathology of Politics: Violence, Betrayal, Corruption, Secrecy, and Propaganda.* New York: Harper & Row, 1972.
Hirsch, Herbert, and David C. Perry. *Violence as Politics.* New York: Harper & Row, 1973.
Janowitz, Morris. *Political Conflict: Essays in Political Sociology.* Chicago: Quadrangle Books, 1970.
Lamb, Robert and Robert Gilmour. *Political Alienation.* New York: St. Martin, 1975.
Nelson, William R. (ed.). *The Politics of Science.* New York: Oxford University Press, 1968.
Rose, Arnold M. *The Power Structure: Political Process in America Society.* New York: Oxford University Press, 1967.
U.S. Department of Health, Education, and Welfare. *Records, Computers, and the Rights of Citizens: Report of the Secretary's Advisory Committee on Automated Personal Data Systems.* Washington, D.C.: U.S. Government Printing Office, 1973.

Chapter 3
CONSTITUTIONAL GOVERNMENT

Chase, Harold W., and Craig R. Ducat (eds.). *Edward S. Corwin's The Constitution and What It Means Today,* 13th ed. Princeton, N.J.: Princeton University Press, 1973.
Kelly, Alfred H., and Winfred A. Harbison. *The American Constitution: Its Origins and Development,* 4th ed. New York: Norton, 1970.
Levy, Leonard W. (ed.). *Essays on the Making of the Constitution.* New York: Oxford University Press, 1969.
——— (ed.). *Judgments: Essays on American Constitutional History.* Chicago: Quadrangle Books, 1972.
McLaughlin, Andrew C. *The Confederation and the Constitution, 1783–1789.* New York: Collier, 1962.
Mitchell, Broadus, and Louise Pearson Mitchell. *A Biography of the Constitution of the United States,* 2d ed. New York: Oxford University Press, 1975.
Murphy, Paul L. *The Constitution in Crisis Times, 1918–1969.* New York: Harper & Row, 1972.
Pritchett, C. Herman. *The American Constitution,* 2d ed. New York: McGraw-Hill, 1968, chaps. 3, 4.
Swindler, William F. *Court and Constitution in the Twentieth Century: The New Legality, 1932–1968.* Indianapolis: Bobbs-Merrill, 1970.
Van Doren, Carl. *The Great Rehearsal: The Story of the Making and Ratifying of the Constitution of the United States.* New York: Viking, 1948.

Chapter 4
FEDERALISM

Duchacek, Ivo D. *Comparative Federalism: The Territorial Dimension of Politics.* New York: Holt, Rinehart & Winston, 1970.

Elazar, Daniel J. *American Federalism: A View from the States.* New York: Crowell, 1966.
Goldwin, Robert A. (ed.). *A Nation of Cities.* Chicago: Rand McNally, 1968.
——— (ed.). *A Nation of States: Essays on the American Federal System.* Chicago: Rand McNally, 1963.
Grodzins, Morton. *The American System: A New View of Government in the United States.* Chicago: Rand McNally, 1966.
Leach, Richard H. *American Federalism.* New York: Norton, 1970.
Oates, Wallace E. *Fiscal Federalism.* New York: Harcourt Brace Jovanovich, 1972.
Reagan, Michael D. *The New Federalism.* New York: Oxford University Press, 1972.
Wheare, Kenneth C. *Federal Government,* 4th ed. New York: Oxford University Press, 1964.
Wildavsky, Aaron. *American Federalism in Perspective.* Boston: Little, Brown, 1967.

Chapter 5
THE COURTS AND JUDICIAL REVIEW

Abraham, Henry J. *The Judicial Process,* 3d ed. New York: Oxford University Press, 1975.
Becker, Theodore L., and Malcolm M. Feeley (eds.). *The Impact of Supreme Court Decisions,* 2d ed. New York: Oxford University Press, 1973.
Bickel, Alexander M. *The Least Dangerous Branch.* Indianapolis: Bobbs-Merrill, 1962.
Chase, Harold W. *Federal Judges: The Appointing Process.* Minneapolis: University of Minnesota Press, 1972.
Eisenstein, James. *Politics and the Legal Process.* New York: Harper & Row, 1973.
Goulden, Joseph C. *The Benchwarmers: The Private World of the Powerful Federal Judges.* New York: Weybright & Talley, 1974.
Jacob, Herbert. *Justice in America,* 2d ed. Boston: Little, Brown, 1972.
Kurland, Philip B. *Politics, the Constitution, and the Warren Court.* Chicago: University of Chicago Press, 1970.
Murphy, Walter F., and C. Herman Pritchett. *Courts, Judges, and Politics,* 2d ed. New York: Random House, 1974.
Pritchett, C. Herman. *The American Constitution,* 2d ed. New York: McGraw-Hill, 1968, chaps. 7–9.
———. *The Roosevelt Court: A Study in Judicial Politics and Values, 1937–1947.* Chicago: Quadrangle Books, 1969.
Schubert, Glendon. *Judicial Decision Making: The Political Role of the Courts,* rev. ed. Glenview, Ill.: Scott, Foresman, 1974.
Simon, James F. *In His Own Image: The Supreme Court in Richard Nixon's America.* New York: David McKay, 1973.
Steamer, Robert J. *The Supreme Court in Crisis.* Amherst: University of Massachusetts Press, 1971.
Swindler, William F. *Court and Constitution in the Twentieth Century: A Modern Interpretation.* Indianapolis: Bobbs-Merrill, 1974.

Chapter 6
CRIMINAL PUNISHMENT AND THE CONSTITUTION

Bedau, Hugo Adam. *The Death Penalty in America.* Garden City, N.Y.: Doubleday, Anchor Books, 1967.

Casper, Jonathan D. *American Criminal Justice: The Defendant's Perspective.* Englewood Cliffs, N.J.: Prentice-Hall, 1972.

Frankel, Marvin E. *Criminal Sentences: Law Without Order.* New York: Hill & Wang, 1973.

Graham, Fred P. *The Self-Inflicted Wound.* New York: Macmillan, 1970.

Kalven, Harry, Jr., and Hans Zeisel. *The American Jury.* Boston: Little, Brown, 1966.

Karlen, Delmar. *Anglo-American Criminal Justice.* New York: Oxford University Press, 1967.

Lefcourt, Robert (ed.). *Law Against the People.* New York: Random House, 1971.

Levy, Leonard W. *Against the Law: The Nixon Court and Criminal Justice.* New York: Harper & Row, 1974.

Lewis, Anthony. *Gideon's Trumpet.* New York: Random House, 1964.

Meltsner, Michael. *Cruel and Unusual: The Supreme Court and Capital Punishment.* New York: Random House, 1973.

Nagel, Stuart (ed.). *The Rights of the Accused.* Beverly Hills, Cal.: Sage, 1972.

Pritchett, C. Herman. *The American Constitution,* 2d ed. New York: McGraw-Hill, chap. 30.

Wilson, James Q. *Varieties of Police Behavior.* Cambridge: Harvard University Press, 1968.

Chapter 7
LIBERTY

Abraham, Henry J. *Freedom and the Court.* New York: Oxford University Press, 1972.

Berns, Walter. *Freedom, Virtue, and the First Amendment.* Baton Rouge: Louisiana State University Press, 1957.

Chafee, Zechariah, Jr. *Free Speech in the United States.* Cambridge, Mass.: Harvard University Press, 1941; Atheneum, 1969.

Clor, Harry. *Obscenity and Public Morality.* Chicago: University of Chicago Press, 1969.

—— (ed.). *Censorship and Freedom of Expression.* Chicago: Rand McNally, 1971.

Dorsen, Norman (ed.). *The Rights of Americans.* New York: Pantheon, 1971.

Emerson, Thomas I. *The System of Freedom of Expression.* New York: Random House, 1970.

Kalven, Harry, Jr. *The Negro and the First Amendment.* Chicago: University of Chicago Press, 1966.

Meiklejohn, Alexander. *Political Freedom.* New York: Harper & Row, 1960.

Miller, Arthur R. *The Assault on Privacy.* Ann Arbor: University of Michigan Press, 1971.

Morgan, Richard E. *The Supreme Court and Religion.* New York: Free Press, 1972.

Murphy, Paul L. *The Meaning of Freedom of Speech: First Amendment Freedoms from Wilson to FDR.* Westport, Conn.: Greenwood, 1972.
Pritchett, C. Herman. *The American Constitution,* 2d ed. New York: McGraw-Hill, 1968, pt. 6.
The Report of the Commission on Obscenity and Pornography. New York: Bantam, 1970.
Shapiro, Martin. *Freedom of Speech: The Supreme Court and Judicial Review.* Englewood Cliffs, N.J.: Prentice-Hall, 1966.
Westin, Alan F. *Privacy and Freedom.* New York: Atheneum, 1967.

Chapter 8
EQUALITY

Bardolph, Richard (ed.). *The Civil Rights Record.* New York: Crowell, 1970.
Bickel, Alexander M. *The Supreme Court and the Idea of Progress.* New York: Harper & Row, 1970.
Dorsen, Norman. *Discrimination and Civil Rights.* Little, Brown, 1969.
Goldwin, Robert A. (ed.). *One Hundred Years of Emancipation.* Chicago: Rand McNally, 1964.
Hamilton, Charles V. *The Bench and the Ballot: Southern Federal Judges and Black Voters.* New York: Oxford University Press, 1973.
Harris, Robert J. *The Quest for Equality.* Baton Rouge: Louisiana State University Press, 1960.
Peltason, Jack W. *Fifty-eight Lonely Men: Southern Federal Judges and School Desegregation.* New York: Harcourt Brace Jovanovich, 1961.
Polsby, Nelson W. (ed.). *Reapportionment in the 1970s.* Berkeley: University of California Press, 1971.
Pritchett, C. Herman. *The American Constitution,* 2d ed. New York: McGraw-Hill, 1968, pt. 7.
Storing, Herbert J. (ed.). *What Country Have I?: Political Writings by Black Americans.* New York: St. Martin, 1970.
Ten Broek, Jacobus. *Equal Under Law.* New York: Collier, 1965.
Voce, Clement E. *Caucasians Only.* Berkeley: University of California Press, 1959.

Chapter 9
PUBLIC OPINION AND POLITICAL PARTICIPATION

Almond, Gabriel, and Sidney Verba. *The Civic Culture: Political Attitudes and Democracy in Five Nations.* Princeton, N.J.: Princeton University Press, 1963.
Bartley, Numan V., and Hugh D. Graham. *Southern Politics and the Second Reconstruction.* Baltimore: Johns Hopkins University Press, 1975.
Campbell, Angus, et al. *The American Voter.* New York: Wiley, 1960.
———. *Elections and the Political Order.* New York: Wiley, 1967.
Cobb, Roger W., and Charles D. Elder. *Participation in American Politics.* Baltimore: Johns Hopkins University Press, 1975.
Dawson, Richard E., and Kenneth Prewitt. *Political Socialization.* Boston: Little, Brown, 1969.

Easton, David, and Jack Dennis. *Children in the Political System: Origins of Political Legitimacy.* New York: McGraw-Hill, 1969.
Flanigan, William H. *Political Behavior of the American Electorate,* 2d ed. Boston: Allyn & Bacon, 1972.
Key, V. O., Jr. *Public Opinion and American Democracy.* New York: Knopf, 1961.
———. *The Responsible Electorate.* Cambridge: Harvard University Press, 1966.
Lazarsfeld, Paul F., et al. *The People's Choice: How the Voter Makes Up His Mind,* 3d ed. New York: Columbia University Press, 1968.
Monroe, Alan D. *Public Opinion in America.* New York: Dodd, Mead, 1975.
Scammon, Richard, and Ben J. Wattenberg. *The Real Majority: An Examination of the American Electorate.* New York: Coward, McCann & Geoghegan, 1970.
Verba, Sidney, and Norman H. Nie. *Participation in America: Political Democracy and Social Equality.* New York: Harper & Row, 1972.

Chapter 10
THE PARTY SYSTEM

Chapter 11
THE ELECTORAL PROCESS

Barber, James D. (ed.). *Choosing the President.* Englewood Cliffs, N.J.: Prentice-Hall, 1974.
Bone, Hugh A. *American Politics and the Party System,* 4th ed. New York: McGraw-Hill, 1971.
Broder, David S. *The Party's Over.* New York: Harper & Row, 1971.
Burnham, Walter Dean. *Critical Elections: The Mainsprings of American Politics.* New York: Norton, 1970.
Davis, James W. *Presidential Primaries: Road to the White House.* New York: Crowell, 1967.
Diamond, Robert A. (ed.). *Dollar Politics,* 2d ed. Washington, D.C.: Congressional Quarterly, 1974.
Dunn, Delmer D. *Financing Presidential Campaigns.* Washington, D.C.: Brookings, 1972.
Duverger, Maurice. *Political Parties: Their Organization and Activity in the Modern State.* New York: Wiley, 1956.
Epstein, Leon D. *Political Parties in Western Democracies.* New York: Praeger, 1967.
Heidenheimer, Arnold J. (ed.). *Comparative Political Finance.* Lexington, Mass.: Heath, 1970.
Key, V. O.., Jr. *Politics, Parties, and Pressure Groups,* 5th ed. New York: Crowell, 1964.
Ladd, Everett Carll, Jr. *American Political Parties: Social Change and Political Response.* New York: Norton, 1970.
Matthews, Donald R. *Perspectives on Presidential Selection.* Washington, D.C.: Brookings, 1973.
Mazmanian, Daniel A. *Third Parties in Presidential Elections.* Washington, D.C.: Brookings, 1974.
Patterson, Ernest. *Black City Politics.* New York: Dodd, Mead, 1974.

Polsby, Nelson W., and Aaron B. Wildavsky. *Presidential Elections: Strategies of American Electoral Politics,* 3d ed. New York: Scribner, 1971.
Pomper, Gerald M. *Elections in America.* New York: Dodd, Mead, 1968.
Sayre, Wallace, and Judith H. Parris. *Voting for the President: The Electoral College and the American Political System.* Washington, D.C.: Brookings, 1970.
Sorauf, Frank, Jr. *Political Parties in America,* 2d ed. Boston: Little, Brown, 1972.
Sundquist, James L. *Dynamics of the Party System.* Washington, D.C.: Brookings, 1973.
White, Theodore H. *The Making of the President, 1972.* New York: Atheneum, 1973.

Chapter 12
POLITICAL-INTEREST GROUPS

Bachrach, Peter (ed.). *Political Elites in a Democracy.* New York: Atherton, 1971.
Blaisdell, Donald C. (ed.). "Unofficial Government: Pressure Groups and Lobbies," *Annals of the American Academy of Political and Social Science,* vol. 319, September, 1958.
Diamond, Robert A. (ed.). *The Washington Lobby,* 2d ed. Washington, D.C.: Congressional Quarterly, 1974.
Gerberding, William P., and Duane E. Smith. *The Radical Left: The Abuse of Discontent.* Boston: Houghton Mifflin, 1970.
Lipset, Seymour Martin, and Earl Raab. *The Politics of Unreason: Right-Wing Extremism in America, 1790–1970.* New York: Harper & Row, 1970.
Lowi, Theodore J. *The End of Liberalism.* New York: Norton, 1969.
McConnell, Grant. *Private Power and American Democracy.* New York: Knopf, 1966.
Malecki, Edward S., and M. R. Mahood. *Group Politics: A New Emphasis.* New York: Scribner, 1972.
Milbrath, Lester W. *The Washington Lobbyists.* Chicago: Rand McNally, 1963.
Olson, Mancur, Jr. *The Logic of Collective Action.* Cambridge: Harvard University Press, 1965.
Truman, David. *The Governmental Process.* New York: Knopf, 1951.
Zeigler, Harmon, and G. Wayne Peak. *Interest Groups in American Society,* 2d ed. Englewood Cliffs, N.J.: Prentice-Hall, 1972.

Chapter 13
CONGRESS

Clausen, Aage R. *How Congressmen Decide: A Policy Focus.* New York: St. Martin, 1973.
Cleaveland, Frederic N., et al. *Congress and Urban Problems.* Washington, D.C.: Brookings, 1969.
Cummings, Milton C., Jr. *Congressmen and the Electorate.* New York: Free Press, 1966.

Davidson, Roger H. *The Role of the Congressman*. Indianapolis: Bobbs-Merrill, Pegasus, 1969.
Fenno, Richard F., Jr. *The Power of the Purse: Appropriations Politics in Congress*. Boston: Little, Brown, 1966.
———. *Congressmen in Committees*. Boston: Little, Brown, 1973.
Froman, Lewis A., Jr. *The Congressional Process: Strategies, Rules, and Procedures*. Boston: Little, Brown, 1967.
Hinckley, Barbara. *Stability and Change in Congress*. New York: Harper & Row, 1971.
Mayhew, David, *Party Loyalty Among Congressmen*. Cambridge: Harvard University Press, 1966.
Polsby, Nelson W. *Congressional Behavior*. New York: Random House, 1971.
Ripley, Randall B. *Power in the Senate*. New York: St. Martin, 1969.
Saloma, John S., III. *Congress and the New Politics*. Boston: Little, Brown, 1969.
Truman, David B. *The Congress and America's Future*, 2d ed. Englewood Cliffs, N.J.: Prentice-Hall, 1973.

Chapter 14
THE PRESIDENCY

Bailey, Thomas A. *Presidential Greatness*. New York: Appleton-Century-Crofts, 1966.
Bernstein, Carl, and Bob Woodward. *All the President's Men*. New York: Simon & Schuster, 1974.
Cornwell, Elmer E., Jr. *Presidential Leadership of Public Opinion*. Bloomington: Indiana University Press, 1965.
Cross, Mercer (ed.). *The Complete Watergate*. Washington, D.C.: Congressional Quarterly, 1975.
Hargrove, Erwin D. *Presidential Leadership: Personality and Political Style*. New York: Macmillan, 1966.
Johnson, Richard T. *Managing the White House*. New York: Harper & Row, 1974.
Koenig, Louis W. *The Chief Executive*, 3d ed. New York: Harcourt Brace Jovanovich, 1975.
Mosher, Frederick C., and Others. *Watergate: Implications for Responsible Government*. New York: Basic Books, 1974.
Neustadt, Richard E. *Presidential Power*. New York: Wiley, 1960.
Rather, Dan, and Gary Paul Gates. *The Palace Guard*. New York: Harper & Row, 1974.
Reedy, George E. *The Twilight of the Presidency*. New York: World, 1970.
Schlesinger, Arthur, Jr. *The Imperial Presidency*. Boston: Houghton Mifflin, 1973.
Sorenson, Theodore C. *Decision Making in the White House: The Olive Branch or the Arrows*. New York: Columbia University Press, 1963.
Tugwell, Rexford G., and Thomas E. Cronin (eds.). *The Presidency Reappraised*. New York: Praeger, 1974.
U.S. House of Representatives, Committee on the Judiciary. *Impeachment of Richard M. Nixon*. 93d Congress, 2d Session. Washington, D.C.: U.S. Government Printing Office, 1974.

Chapter 15
RUNNING THE NATIONAL GOVERNMENT

Downs, Anthony. *Inside Bureaucracy.* Boston: Little, Brown, 1967.

Dye, Thomas R. *Understanding Public Policy,* 2d ed. Englewood Cliffs, N.J.: Prentice-Hall, 1975.

Henry, Nicholas. *Public Administration and Public Affairs.* Englewood Cliffs, N.J.: Prentice-Hall, 1975.

Kaufman, Herbert. *Administrative Feedback: Monitoring Subordinates' Behavior.* Washington, D.C.: Brookings, 1973.

Lindblom, Charles. *The Intelligence of Democracy: Decision-Making Through Mutual Adjustment.* New York: Free Press, 1965.

Macmahon, Arthur W. *Administering Federalism in a Democracy.* New York: Oxford University Press, 1972.

Pressman, Jeffrey L., and Aaron Wildavsky. *Implementation: How Great Expectations in Washington Are Dashed in Oakland; Or, Why It's Amazing That Federal Programs Work at All, This Being a Saga of the Economic Development Administration as Told by Two Sympathetic Observers Who Seek to Build Morals on a Foundation of Ruined Hopes.* Berkeley: University of California Press, 1973.

Seidman, Harold. *Politics, Position, and Power.* New York: Oxford University Press, 1975.

Sharkansky, Ira. *Public Administration: Policy-Making in Government Agencies,* 3d ed. Chicago: Rand McNally, 1975.

Waldo, Dwight. *Public Administration in a Time of Turbulence.* Scranton, Pa.: Chandler, 1971.

Wildavsky, Aaron. *The Politics of the Budgetary Process,* 2d ed. Boston: Little, Brown, 1974.

Chapter 16
THE AMERICAN POLITICAL ECONOMY

Bell, Daniel, and Irving Kristol (eds.). *Capitalism Today.* New York: Basic Books, 1971.

Committee for Economic Development. *A New U.S. Farm Policy for Changing World Food Needs.* New York: Committee for Economic Development, 1974.

Freeman, S. David. *Energy: The New Era.* New York: Walker (for the Twentieth Century Fund), 1974.

Fuchs, Victor R. *The Service Economy.* New York: National Bureau of Economic Research, Columbia University Press, 1968.

Ginzberg, Eli, et al. *The Pluralistic Economy.* New York: McGraw-Hill, 1965.

Haberler, Gottfried. *Economic Growth and Stability: An Analysis of Economic Change and Policies.* Los Angeles: Nash, 1974.

Joint Economic Committee, Congress of the United States. *Federal Subsidy Programs.* Washington, D.C.: U.S. Government Printing Office, 1974.

Kahn, Alfred E. *The Economics of Regulation: Principles and Institutions,* 2 vols. New York: Wiley, 1970–1971.

Liebhafsky, H. H. *American Government and Business.* New York: Wiley, 1971.

Phillips, Almarin (ed.). *Competition and Regulation.* Washington, D.C.: Brookings, 1974.
Schumpeter, Joseph A. *Capitalism, Socialism, and Democracy.* New York: Harper & Row, Harper Torchbooks, 1962.
Tobin, James. *The New Economics One Decade Older.* Princeton, N.J.: Princeton University Press, 1974.

Chapter 17
THE WELFARE STATE

Alford, Robert R. *Health Care Politics: Ideological and Interest Barriers to Reform.* Chicago: University of Chicago Press, 1974.
Banfield, Edward C. *The Unheavenly City Revisited.* Boston: Little, Brown, 1974.
Brown, J. Douglas. *An American Philosophy of Social Security.* Princeton, N.J.: Princeton University Press, 1972.
Cornuelle, Richard C. *Reclaiming the American Dream.* New York: Random House, 1965.
Ginzberg, Eli, and Robert M. Solow (eds.). *The Great Society: Lessons for the Future.* New York: Basic Books, 1974.
Joint Economic Committee, Congress of the United States. *Income Security for Americans: Recommendations of the Public Welfare Study.* Washington, D.C.: U.S. Government Printing Office, 1974.
Miller, Herman P. *Rich Man, Poor Man.* New York: Crowell, 1971.
Mosteller, Frederick, and Daniel P. Moynihan (eds.). *On Equality of Educational Opportunity.* New York: Random House, 1972.
Rivlin, Alice M. *Social Policy: Alternate Strategies for the Federal Government.* Washington, D.C.: Brookings (General Series Reprint 288), 1974.
Stein, Bruno, and S. M. Miller (eds.). *Incentives and Planning in Social Policy: Studies in Health, Education, and Welfare.* Chicago: Aldine, 1973.
Wilensky, Harold L. *The Welfare State and Equality: Structural and Ideological Roots of Public Expenditures.* Berkeley: University of California Press, 1974.

Chapter 18
AMERICAN FOREIGN POLICY

Bloomfield, Lincoln P. *In Search of American Foreign Policy: The Humane Use of Power.* New York: Oxford University Press, 1974.
Cochran, Charles L. (ed.). *Civil-Military Relations: Changing Concepts in the Seventies.* New York: Free Press, 1974.
Cohen, Bernard C. *The Public's Impact on Foreign Policy.* Boston: Little, Brown, 1973.
Crabb, Cecil V., Jr. *American Foreign Policy in the Nuclear Age,* 3d ed. New York: Harper & Row, 1972.
Howe, James W., et al. *The U.S. and the Developing World: Agenda for Action.* New York: Praeger, 1974.
King, Alexander. *Science and Policy.* New York: Oxford University Press, 1974.

Kissinger, Henry A. *American Foreign Policy,* expanded ed. New York: Norton, 1973.

Lesh, Donald R. (ed.). *A Nation Observed: Perspectives on America's World Role.* Washington, D.C.: Potomac Associates, 1974 (distributed by Basic Books, New York).

Spanier, John, and Eric M. Uslaner. *How American Foreign Policy Is Made.* New York: Praeger, 1974.

White, John. *The Politics of Foreign Aid.* New York: St. Martin, 1974.

Wilcox, Francis O. *Congress, the Executive, and Foreign Policy.* New York: Harper & Row, 1972.

Yager, Joseph A., et al. *Energy and U.S. Foreign Policy.* Cambridge, Mass.: Ballinger, 1975.

Index

ABA. *See* American Bar Association
A Book v. Attorney General of Massachusetts, 152
Abortion laws, 171
Abrams v. United States, 164
Act of Settlement (1701), 55
ACLU. *See* American Civil Liberties Union
Adams, John, 112
Adderly v. Florida, 159–160
AFDC. *See* Aid to Families with Dependent Children
AFL-CIO, 288
Africa, 26
Aggression, 39–40
Agnew, Spiro T., 200, 226, 333
Agriculture
  committees on, 315
    government and, 408–411
    parity prices and, 410
    price-support programs and, 410–411
    productivity and, 408–409
Agriculture and Consumer Protection Act of 1973, 411
Aid to the Blind, 94
Aid to Families with Dependent Children, 423–425
Air carriers, 404
Alaska pipeline, 407
Alcoa, 391
Alexander v. Holmes County Board of Education, 182
Alien and Sedition Act, 81, 163
Alien Enemies Act, 81
Allende, Salvador, 446–447
AMA. *See* American Medical Association
Amalrik, Andrei, 59
American Bar Association, 289–290
American Civil Liberties Union, 144
American Farm Bureau Federation. *See* Farm Bureau
American Foreign Service, 381
American Independent party, 246
American Institute of Public Opinion, 195
American Medical Association, 289
American Revolution, 48–49
American Tobacco Company, 390
Amtrak, 403–404
Anarchism, 8–9

Anti-Riot Act, 157
Appeal, 99
Appellate courts, 102
Appellate jurisdiction, 99
Apportionment, 302
Appropriations Committee, 319
Aristotle, 2
Articles of Confederation, 60–61, 68
Assassinations, 48
Association, freedom of, 162–163
Austria, 215
Authoritarian government, 23–26
Autobiography (Jefferson), 13
Autocracy, 7

Bail, 132
Bail bondsmen, 132
Bail Reform Act of 1966, 132
Baker v. Carr, 118, 119
Barron v. Baltimore, 73, 125
Basic Educational Grant, 430
Beauharnais v. Illinois, 150
Belle Terre v. Boraas, 184
Benton v. Maryland, 135
Bett v. Brady, 134
Bill of Rights (1689), 55
Bill of Rights, 61, 68, 73, 76, 145–146
Black, Hugo, 38, 106, 117, 125, 168
Blackmun, Harry A., 106
Blacks, 15
  educational equality and, 178–182
  equality of opportunity and, 175–176
  equal voting rights for, 176–177
  population changes and, 414–415
  prison reform and, 135
  voting and officeholding increase by, 214–215
Block grants, 92
Board of Education v. Allen, 170
Boddie v. Connecticut, 186
Brandeburg v. Ohio, 164
Brandeis, Louis D., 105, 170
Branzburg v. Hayes, 149
Brazil, 25
Brennan, William J., Jr., 73
Brezhnev, Leonid, 26
Bricker Amendment, 71
Brodie, Bernard, 446

503

Brown v. Board of Education, 103, 117–118, 119, 176, 179
Brown v. Louisiana, 159
Bryce, James, 190
Buchanan v. Warley, 183
Bukovsky, Vladimir, 59
Bureaucracy, 366–370
  policy-making and, 369–370
  political leadership and control in, 370–371
Bureau of the Budget. *See* Office of Management and Budget
Bureau of Public Roads, 367
Burger, Warren, 105, 127, 142, 170
Burger Court, 127
Burke, Edmund, 23, 242
Business affected with public interest, 387–388
Business men, 4–5
Busing, 182

CAA. *See* Community-action agency
Cabinet, the, 356–357
Calhoun, John C., 82
California, 88
Calley, William, 140
Cameron v. Johnson, 159
Campaign
  organizations in, 260
  presidential, 258–263
  strategy in, 259–260
Campaign committees, 232
Campaign Election Act of 1974. *See* Federal Campaign Election Act
Campaign finance
  abuses and, 268–270
  cost of, 264–266
  reforms and, 274–275
  regulation of, 266–267
  sources of, 273–274
Canada, 215
Candidate orientation, 213
Candidates, 255
CAP. *See* Community-action programs
Capitalism, 28–29, 411
Capital punishment, 119, 137
Cardozo, Benjamin, 125, 127
Carswell, G. Harrold, 106
Case, Clifford, 307
CCC. *See* Commodity Credit Corporation
CEA. *See* Council of Economic Advisers
Censorship, 147
Center for Political Studies of the University of Michigan, 195–196
Central Intelligence Agency, 446–447
Chafee, Zecharaiah, Jr., 138
Chaplinsky v. New Hampshire, 156

Checks and balances. *See* Separation of powers
Chicago Seven, the, 157
Chief Justice, 111
Chile, 446–447
Chimel v. California, 126
China, 25, 26, 452–453
Circuit court. *See* District court
Civil disobedience, 161–162
Civil Rights Act of 1866, 183–184
Civil Rights Act of 1875, 177
Civil Rights Act of 1964, 178, 181, 185, 324
Civil Rights Cases decision, 177
Civil Service, 381–383
Clayton Act, 391, 392, 393
Clear and present danger doctrine, 163–164
Closed shop, 395
Cloture rule, 327–328
Cohen v. California, 156
Coleman, William T., 356
Collective needs, 2
Committee for Economic Development, 286
Committee on Political Education, 288
Committee for Public Education v. Nyquist, 170
Committee to Reelect the President, 260, 360, 361
Commodity Credit Corporation, 410–411
Common Cause, 291
Communes, 8–9
Communication
  free flow of, 36–39
  taboo issues and, 40–41
Communism, 27, 40. *See also* Marxism-Communism
Communist party
  in England, 166
  in United States, 164–165
Community-action agency, 91
Community-action program, 91
Community development, 433
Concurrent jurisdiction, 101
Concurring opinions, 110–111
Confederation, 78
Conference committee, 328
Confessions, 129–131
Conflict
  cooperation and, 3
  socialization of, 240–241
Conflict resolution
  government and opposition in, 36
  leadership, and role of, 31–32
  power, transfer of, and, 32
  processes of, 31–36
Conglomerate mergers, 392
Congress, U.S.
  advise and consent role of, 311
  appointments and, 312

committee system of, 318–322, 324
conference committees of, 328
constituent interests of, 308–309
Constitution, interpretation of, and, 72
constitutional powers delegated to, 63–64
differential access to, 315
electorate, relationship to, of, 306–307
foreign policy role of, 450, 451
information function of, 310
investigations by, 310–311
judicial functions and, 313–314
leadership role of, 317–322
legislative process and, 322–326
as legislature, 304–306
membership requirements of, 298–300, 302–304
office of the member of, 298–300
organization of, 314–317
oversight function of, 309–314
party role of, 315–317
representation in, 300–304
rules of, 322–323
salaries in, 300
Senate as chamber of, 326–329
seniority rule in, 320–322
separation of powers principle and, 65, 66–67
treaties and, 312
voting in, 307–308
Connally, John, 360
Conscientious objection, 167–168
Consensus, 31. *See also* Conflict resolution
Consolidated Rail Corporation, 404
Constitutional Convention, 61, 70, 98
Constitutional Council (France), 121
Constitutional government, 55–56
Constitutional interpretation, 71–74
Constitution of the United States, 11, 461–485
  amending process of, 69–71
  amendments to, 68–69
    1st, 9, 67, 73, 146, 166
    4th, 126, 128
    5th, 129, 132, 165
    6th, 133
    8th, 132
    10th, 64
    11th, 68
    12th, 69
    13th, 68
    14th, 60, 67, 68, 115, 125, 176
    15th, 60, 68, 176, 251
    16th, 68, 117
    17th, 11
    18th, 69
    19th, 11, 69, 251
    20th, 69
    21st, 69, 332–333
    22nd, 60, 69, 71, 232
    23rd, 69
    24th, 55, 69, 177
    25th, 69, 332–333
    26th, 55, 68, 71, 252
    27th, 69, 185
  Articles of
    I, Section 8, 63
    III, 97
    V, 69
    VI, 64, 101
  checks and balances in, 66–67
  comparison of, with English and Soviet constitutions, 59–60
  domestic violence and, 83
  economic policies and, 386–389
  equal footing doctrine and, 84–85
  extradition and, 87–88
  federal-state relations and, 82–88
  Federalism principle in, 63–64
  full faith and credit provision in 86–88
  history of, 60–61
  interstate privileges and immunities and, 86–88
  interstate relations and, 85
  limited government principle and, 62–68
  and new states, admission of, 83–85
  popular sovereignty principle in, 61–63
  presidential power in, 341–342
  Republican form of government and, 83
  separation of powers principle and, 65–68
  states and commerce in, 85
  world significance of, 74–76
Constitutions, foreign
  of England, 55–58
  of France, 74, 75
  of Germany, 75
  of Latin America, 75
  of Soviet Union, 58–59
  unwritten, 55, 56–58
Continental Congress, 60
Convention, national, 231
Convictions, review of, 135–137
Cooper v. Aaron, 81, 103, 181
COPE. *See* Committee on Political Education
Corrupt Practices Act of 1925, 267
Corwin, Edward S., 364
Council of Economic Advisers, 354, 396
Council on Environmental Quality, 355
County courts, 102
Courts. *See* Federal court system; State courts; Supreme Court
Courts-martial, 139–140
Court system, crisis in, 140–141
Cox v. Louisiana, 157, 158, 159
Cox v. New Hampshire, 158

506 INDEX

CRC. *See* Consolidated Rail Corporation
CREEP. *See* Committee to Reelect the President
Crime
   political, 52–53
   and the social order, 50–51
Crime Control Act of 1968, 127, 128
Crime Control and Safe Streets Act of 1968, 118
Criminal punishment, 125
Criminal suspect, rights of, 126–128
   coerced confessions and, 129–131
   electronic eavesdropping and, 128–129
   self-incrimination and, 129–131
   wiretapping and, 128–129
Cromwell, Oliver, 57
Cruel and unusual punishment, 137–138

Data banks, 47
Dean, John W., 36
Declaration of Independence, 12, 61–62, 144, 458–460
Delegated legislation, 344
Democracy, 7
   American political commitment to, 12–16
   anarchism and, 8–9
   communes and, 8–9
   concepts of, 7–23
   developing countries and, 27–29
   feudalism's contribution to, 10
   foreign policy and, 438–444, 448–453
   free speech, role of, in, 41–43
   government and opposition in, 35–36
   historical overview of, 9–10
   leadership role in, 31–32
   majority and minority in, 33–35
   Marxist-communist concept of, 26–27
   modern Western concept of, 10–12
   moral integrity in, 22–23
   operational concept of, 16–20
   political order of, 20–23
   as system of power, 7–9
   taboo issues in, 40–41
   voluntary associations and, 9
Democracy in America (Tocqueville), 44
Democratic party, 12, 219–220, 224–225, 227–230
   composition of, 207–212
   racial composition of, 210–211
   religious groups and, 210–211
Democratic-Republican party, 12
Demonstrate, freedom to, 157–161
Demonstrations
   breach of the peace and, 159–161
   constitutional status of, 158–159
Dennis v. United States, 164
Department of Defense (U.S.), 47
Desegregation, 180–182

De Tocqueville, Alexis, 44, 438
Devaluation of the dollar, 399
Developing countries
   American foreign policy and, 453–456
   capitalism and, 28–29
   democracy in, 27–29
   single-party dominance in, 28–29
Direct democracy, 16
Direct election of senators, 11
Direct primary, 254
Dirksen, Everett, 118
Dirty-tricks department, 270
Dissenting opinions, 110–111
District courts, 102
Districting, 301–302
Diversity of citizenship cases, 101
Dixiecrats, 246
Doe v. Bolton, 171
Domestic Council, 354–355
Domestic violence, 83
Dossier society, 47
Double jeopardy, 134–135
Douglas, William O., 142, 171
Draft-card burning, 161
Dred Scott case, 73–74, 116
Due process of law, 115
Dulles, John Foster, 348

Eagleton, Thomas, 232
Eastland, James O., 315
Easton, David, 189
Economic Opportunity Act of 1964, 91
The Economist (London), 16
Economy, U.S.
   fiscal policies and, 397, 398
   government spending and, 400
   inflation and, 396–397
   mixed economy and, 411–412
   monetary policies and, 397, 398–399
   Nixon's "New Economic Policy" and, 402–403
   price and wage stability and, 401–403
   transfer payments and, 401
Education
   desegregation and, 180–82
   federal aid to, 429
   role of, in America, 428–429
   role of political participation in, 208–209
   segregation in, 178–180
Educational equality, 178–183
Edwards v. South Carolina, 157, 160
Ehrlichman, John, 52, 360
Eighteen-year-old vote, 71
Eisenhower, Dwight David, 71, 83, 116, 175, 179, 180, 210–211, 225, 331, 338, 345, 348, 350, 352, 359
Elections, campaign, 258–263
Electoral college, 11, 221, 261–262

Electorate, 251–252
Electronic eavesdropping, 128–129
Elementary and Secondary Education Act of 1965, 169, 429–430
Elitism, 4–5, 6
Ellsberg, Daniel, 148
Emigration, 25–26
Eminent domain, 387
Employee Benefit Security Act, 420
Employment Act of 1946, 396
Energy crisis, 405–408
Energy Research and Development Administration, 497–508
Engel v. Vitale, 169
Engels, Friedrich, 27
Environmental Protection Agency, 367
Equal footing doctrine, 84–85
Equality, 13–14
Equality of opportunity, 173–176
Equal Pay Act, 184
Equal protection of the laws, 60, 115, 173, 185–187
Equitable abstention, doctrine of, 103
ERDA. *See* Energy Research and Development Administration
Ervin, Sam, 165, 360
Ervin Committee. *See* Senate Watergate Committee
Escobedo v. Illinois, 118, 130
Establishment clause, 168
Everson v. Board of Education, 168
Excise Tax Reduction Act of 1965, 398
Exclusionary rule, 126, 127
Executive agreements, 349
Executive branch. *See also* Presidency; President
  budgeting and, 376–377
  departments of, 313
  government corporations and, 374–375
  independent agencies and, 373–374
  independent regulatory commissions and, 374
  internal organization and processes of, 375–376
  organization of, 371–377
  planning, 376–377
Executive Office of the President, 351–355
Executive power, abuse of, 360–362
Export-Import Bank, 400
Extradition, 87–89

Family, the, and political process, 205–206
Farm Bureau, 287
Farmers Home Administration, 432
FCC. *See* Federal Communications Commission
FDA. *See* Food and Drug Administration

FDIC. *See* Federal Deposit Insurance Corporation
Federal Bureau of Investigation, 47
Federal Campaign Election Act of 1974, 270–275
Federal centralization, 93–95
Federal Communications Commission, 198
Federal court system
  appointment of judges for lower courts in, 104
  federal courts in, 98–101
  appointment of Supreme Court justices in, 104–107
  jurisdiction of, 100–101
  relations between states and, 102–103
  Supreme Court in, 99–100
Federal Deposit Insurance Corporation, 374, 399–400
Federal Elections Campaign Act of 1971, 266–67
Federal Elections Commission, 272
Federal grants-in-aid, 89–92
  block grants as, 92
  effects of, 90–91
  objections to, 91–92
Federalism, 63–64, 79–82
The Federalist (Madison/Hamilton/Jay), 61
  No. 78 of, 97
Federalist party, 222
Federal judges, 66
Federal Housing Administration, 376
Federal questions, 100
Federal Regulation of Lobbying Act, 285, 294
Federal Reserve System, 398–399
Federal Savings and Loan Corporation, 400
Federal subsidies, 403–405
Federal system, 78, 80–81, 82
Federal Trade Commission, 377, 391–392
Feiner v. New York, 157
Feudalism, 10
FHA. *See* Federal Housing Administration
Fielding, Dr. Lewis, 52
Filibuster, 326–327
Finance of campaigns. *See* Campaigns, finance
Fiscal policies, 397, 398
Flannigan, William H., 209–210
Flast v. Cohen, 169–170
Food and Drug Administration, 370
Food stamps, 423
Ford, Gerald, 226, 313, 333, 338, 352, 356, 358, 359, 406, 447
Foreign policy
  bipartisanship in, 452–453
  Congress, U.S., role of, 450, 451
  democracy and, 438–444
  democratic control of, 448–453

Foreign policy . . . (Continued)
  national interest and, 444–447
  President and, 347–349
Fortas, Abe, 105
Fowler v. North Carolina, 137
France, 59, 368–369
Frankfurt Constitution of 1849, 75
Frankfurter, Felix, 74, 117, 119, 142
Freedom, individual, 163–166
Freedom of expression, 146–147
  restraint on, methods of, 147–148
  as safety valve, 40
Freedom of Information Act, 37
Freedom of the Coffeehouse, 25
French Revolution, 12
Friedrich, Carl J., 76
Frontiero v. Richardson, 186
Fulbright, J. William, 452
Full Employment Act of 1946, 175
Full faith and credit, 86–87
Furman v. Georgia, 137

GAI. *See* Guaranteed Annual Income
Gallup, Dr. George, 195
Gardner, John W., 291
Genocide, 26
Germany, 75
Gibbons v. Ogden, 115
Gideon v. Wainwright, 100, 134
Gillette v. United States, 168
Ginsberg v. New York, 153
Ginzburg v. United States, 152
Gitlow v. New York, 146, 164
Glorious Revolution, 10, 12
GNP. *See* Gross National Product
Goldwater, Barry, 273, 416
Gooding v. Wilson, 156
Government. *See also* Constitutional government
  agriculture and, 408–11
  by discussion and consent, 36–55
  collective needs and, 2
  in education, role of, 428–431
  energy crisis and, 405–408
  health service and, 425–428
  in housing and urban renewal, role of, 431–433
  as institutionalized political power, 7
  labor and, 392–396
  lawlessness in, 52–55
  and opposition, 35–36
  organizing and conducting, 238
  and rising expectations, 44–46
Government services, 378–379
Grandfather clause, 176
Grand jury, indictment by, 132
Grange, the, 287
Grant, U. S., 117

Grants. *See* Block grants; Federal grants-in-aid
Grasso, Ella, 215
Great Britain, 217
  Official Secrets Act of, 38–39
  opposition, role of, in, 36
  party system in, 243
  policy of, on totalitarian parties and political violence, 166
  racial discrimination in, 184
Great Depression, the, 410, 417–418
Greek city-states, 9–10
Green v. School Board of New Kent County, 181
Green v. United States, 134, 135
Greenstein, Fred, 205
Griffin v. Illinois, 186
Griffin v. School Board of Prince Edward County, 181
Griswold v. Connecticut, 171
Gross national product
  defense spending and, 435–436
  worldwide comparison, 453–455
Grovey v. Townsend, 176
Guaranteed Annual Income, 425
Guideposts, 402
Guinn v. United States, 176
Gulf of Tonkin Resolution, 350
Gun control laws, 51

Habeas corpus, writ of, 67, 138
Hague v. C.I.O., 159
Haldeman, H. R., 268, 352, 360
Hamilton, Alexander, 61, 67, 97, 221
Hand, Learned, 68
Harlan, John, 106, 119, 156
Harper v. Virginia State Board of Education, 177
Harrington, Michael, 37
Harris, Louis, 196
Harris Survey, 196
Haynsworth, Clement F., 105–106
Health Insurance for the Aged Act. *See* Medicare
Health Manpower Training Act, 431
Health services, 425–428
Heart of Atlanta Motel v. United States, 178
Higher Education Act of 1965, 430–431
High Speed Ground Transportation Act of 1968, 403
Hills, Carla, 356
Hoffman, Julius, 157
Holmes, Oliver Wendell, 105, 115, 119, 173, 388–389
Hoover, Herbert, 351
House Committee on Un-American Activities, 165

House Judiciary Committee, 361
House of Commons, 10–11
House of Lords, 10–11, 57
House of Representatives, 11
    Appropriations Committee of, 319, 321
    Education and Labor Committee of, 319
    leadership, 318
    legislation in, consideration of, 325–326
    Rules Committee of, 319, 324–325
    Steering and Policy Committee of, 321
    Ways and Means Committee of, 319
Housing, equal access to, 183–184
Housing and Urban Development, Department of, 431
Housing and urban renewal, 431–433
HUD. See Housing and Urban Development, Department of
Hughes, Charles Evans, 105, 107, 111, 116
Hughes, Howard R., 268
Humphrey, Hubert H., 225–226, 360
Humphrey's Executor v. *U.S.*, 346
Hunt, E. Howard, 360
Hurtado v. *California*, 132

Illinois v. *Allen*, 141
Impeachment, 313–314
    Nixon, Richard M., and, 361–362, 486–491
Imperialist capitalism, 28
Imperial presidency, 362
Income and political participation, 208–209
Income tax, federal, 70, 71
Independent regulatory commissions, 374
Independents, 235–236
Independent short-term parties, 246–247
Indian Supreme Court, 121
Indirect democracy, 17
Inflation, 396–399
In forma pauperis, 99–100
Information
    free flow of, 36–39
    and taboo issues, 40–41
Initiative, 195
In re Gault, 139
Internal Revenue Service, 47
Internal Security Act of 1950, 164
Internationalism, 443–444
Interposition, 81–82
Interstate compacts, 85
Interstate privileges and immunities, 86–88
Interstate relations, 85
Investigations, legislative, 165
Isolationism, 443–444
Italian Constitutional Court, 121
Italy, 217

Jackson, Andrew, 12, 82, 120
Jacksonian democracy, 222
Jacobellis v. *Ohio*, 152

James, William, 39–40
Jay, John, 61
Jefferson, Thomas, 11, 12, 13, 22, 32, 81, 112, 113, 221, 222
Jeffersonian Republicans, 222
Jenkins v. *Georgia*, 153
Jim Crow rules, 177–178
Johnson, Lyndon, 36, 105, 120, 169, 181, 225, 299, 346, 350, 451, 452
Joint Economic Committee, 396, 425
Jones v. *Alfred H. Mayer Co.*, 183–184
Judges
    selection of, 103–109
    state, 102, 107–108
    tenure of, 108–109
Judicial review
    of congressional and presidential acts, 112–114
    congressional statutes, and interpretation of, 116
    controversy over, 116–119
    democracy and, 119–120
    and *Marbury* v. *Madison*, 112–114
    in other countries, 120–121
    power of, 111–121
    state legislation, and constitutionality of, 114–116
Judiciary Act of 1789, 64, 98, 113
Jury trials, 133
Justice
    English criminal, 141–142
    for juveniles, 139
    military, 139–140
Justice-of-the-peace system, 101–102
Juveniles, justice and, 139

Kahn v. *Shevin*, 186
Kalmbach, Herbert W., 268, 269
Kastigar v. *United States*, 129
Katz v. *United States*, 128
Kennan, George F., 444
Kennedy, John F., 83, 120, 181, 210, 225, 331, 337, 345, 352, 356, 401, 452
Kennedy, Robert F., 48, 51, 357
Kentucky Resolution, 81, 82
Kentucky v. *Dennison*, 88
Key, V. O., Jr., 19–20, 190
Keyes, Sir Roger, 669
King, Dr. Martin Luther, Jr., 48, 51, 161–162
Kissinger, Henry, 348
Kleindienst, Richard, 360
Klingberg, Frank L., 444
Korean conflict, 441
Krushchev, Nikita, 26
Kunz v. *New York*, 155

Labor-Management Relations Act of 1947. See Taft-Hartley Act

Labor-Management Reporting and Disclosure Act of 1959. *See* Landrum-Griffin Act
Labor-management violence, 49–50
Labor unions, 393
Land Grant Act, 89, 428
Landrum-Griffin Act, 395–396
Latin America, 75
The Law of the Soviet State (Vishinsky), 58
Leadership
 in congress, 317–322
 in democracy, 31–32
Legal Services Corporation, 91
Legal Tender Cases, 117
Legislative process, 322–326, 339–343
Lemon v. *Kurtzman,* 170
Lenin, V. I., 27
Levi, Edward, 357
Libel, 150–152
Liberty League, 144
Licensing, 377
Liddy, G. Gordon, 360
Limited government, 12–13, 67–68
Lincoln, Abraham, 82, 138, 174, 224
Literacy tests, 177
Lobbying, 283, 285, 294
Lochner v. *New York,* 388
Locke, John, 61
Long range doctrinal parties, 245–246
Lord Bolingbroke, 74
Louisiana, 88
Loyalty, 383

MacArthur, Douglas, 446
McCarthy, Eugene, 452
McCarthy, Joseph, 165
McCulloch v. *Maryland,* 74
McGovern, George, 226, 231, 256, 273–274
Madison, James, 22, 61, 78, 112, 277
Magna Carta, 12, 55
Majority rule principle, 33–35
Malloy v. *Hogan,* 129
Managed news, 200
Mansfield, Mike, 318, 340
Manual Enterprises v. *Day,* 152
Mapp v. *Ohio,* 118, 127
Marbury v. *Madison,* 103, 112–114
Marshall, John, 73, 74, 111, 112
Marshall, Thomas, 359
Marx, Karl, 26–27
Marxism-Communism, 26–27
Massachusetts Bill of Rights, 62
Mass media
 government control of, patterns of, 198
 impact on public opinion of, 197–202
 performance of the, 198–202
Mayflower Compact of 1620, 62

Medicaid, 427–428
Medicare, 427
Meek v. *Pittenger,* 170
Mergers, 392
Mexico, 217, 249, 445
Milbrath, Lester, 202–203
Military, 4–5, 435–437
Military justice, 139–140
Miller v. *California,* 153
Milliken v. *Bradley,* 182
Minority groups, 15–16, 383
Minority protection principle, 33–35
Miranda v. *Arizona,* 118, 130–131
Missouri plan, 108
Mitchell, John N., 260, 357, 360
Monetary policies, 397, 398–399
Monopolies, 390, 392–393. *See also* Trusts
Monroe Doctrine, 435
Morrill Act. *See* Land Grant Act
Multiparty system, 247–248
Municipal courts, 102
Munn v. *Illinois,* 387–388
Myers v. *U.S.,* 346

NAACP. *See* National Association for the Advancement of Colored People
NAACP v. *Alabama,* 163
NAACP v. *Button,* 163
Nader, Ralph, 291
National Advisory Commission on Civil Disorders, 186
National Association for the Advancement of Colored People, 162–163
National Association of Manufacturers, 280, 285
National chairman, 232
National Commission on the Causes and Prevention of Violence, 48
National Commitments Resolution, 450–451
National convention, 255–256
National defense, U.S., 435–436
National Defense Education Act of 1958, 91
National Education Association, 289
National health insurance program, 427
National Highway Traffic Safety Administration, 367
National interest, 444–447
National Labor Relations Act of 1935, 15, 394
National Labor Relations Board, 394
National Organization of Women, 291
National Rail Passenger Corporations. *See* Amtrak
National Rifle Association, 290
National Security Council, 354
NATO. *See* North Atlantic Treaty Organization
Nazi Germany, 25

NEA. *See* National Education Association
Newberry v. *United States,* 176
New Deal, 117–119, 175
Newspapers, 199–202
New York Times v. *Sullivan,* 150–151
New York Times v. *United States,* 148
Nixon, Richard M., 36, 93, 94, 105, 106, 118, 181, 200, 225, 256, 267, 333, 337–338, 346, 350, 352, 355, 358, 359, 360, 361, 362, 363, 402, 416, 450, 451, 453
    impeachment proceedings and, 313–314, 486–491
NLRB. *See* National Labor Relations Board
Noble State Bank v. *Haskell,* 389
"No knock" law, 127
Nominations, 252–258, 258–259
Nonvoting, 215–217
North Atlantic Treaty Organizations, 435, 440
NOW. *See* National Organization of Women
NSC. *See* National Security Council
Nullification, 82
Nurse Training Act, 431

OASDI. *See* Old-age, survivors, and disability insurance
Obscenity, 152–154
Office of Economic Opportunity, 91, 355
Office of Management and Budget, 328, 353–354
Official Secrets Act, 38–39
Oil crisis, 455–456
Old-age assistance, 94
Old-age survivors, and disability insurance, 418–419
Oligarchy, 7
Olmstead v. *United States,* 128
OMB. *See* Office of Management and Budget
One man, one vote, 118
OPEC. *See* Organization of Petroleum Exporting Countries
Open-occupancy law, 183
Opinion leaders, 191–192
Opposition (government), 35–36
Organization of Petroleum Exporting Countries, 455
Organized labor, 15
Original jurisdiction, 99

Pacific States Telephone & Telegraph Co. v. *Oregon,* 83
Packer, Herbert, 123, 124
Palko v. *Connecticut,* 125, 135
Parity prices, 410
Parker, John J., 105
Parliament (England), 57–58

Parliament Acts of 1911 and 1949, 55–56
Parochial schools, 169–70
Party organization
    local, 234
    national, 231–232
    state, 232–234
Pension Benefit Guaranty Corporation, 420
Pentagon Papers, 37–39, 52, 148
Petition of Right (1628), 55
Picketing, 158
Plea bargaining, 140
Plessy v. *Ferguson,* 178, 179
Plumbers, 52
Pluralism, 3–4, 6
Pocket veto, 328
Poland, 25
Political candidates, 213–214
Political crime, 52–53
Political executives, 380
Political interest groups
    agricultural, 287
    business groups and, 285–287
    the courts and, 284–285
    education and, 289
    functions of, 278
    labor organizations and, 287–288
    legal, 289–290
    medical, 289
    political parties and, 281
    public and, 280–281
    regulation and, 293–295
    tactics and techniques of, 278–285
Political leadership, 4–5
Political participation, 202–217
    age, as influencing, 211–212
    income and education in, role of, 208–209
    occupation in, role of, 207–208
    race in, role of, 210–211
    regional and residential influences in, 209–210
    religion in, role of, 210–211
    socioeconomic class in, role of, 206
    trends in, 214–217
Political parties
    affiliation with, 212–213
    changing attitudes toward, 235–237
    characteristics of, 241–248
    Congress and, 315–317
    development of, 219–221
    functions of, 237–241
    minor parties as, 245–247
    multiparty system and, 247–248
    one-party system and, 222–227, 248–249
    party organization and, 230–234
    President's role in, 338–339
    public interest groups and, 281
    two-party system and, 241–248

Political power, 6–7
Political trials, 141
Politics, defined, 189
Polls, 195–197
Poll tax, 55, 177
Popular sovereignty, 61–63
Populist party, 246
Port of New York Authority, 85
Post office, 148–149
Postal services, 404–405
Powell, Adam Clayton, 314
Powell, Lewis F., Jr., 107
Powell v. *Alabama,* 133–134
Power, 3–7
  elitist conception of, 4–5
  pluralist conception of, 3–4
  political, 6–7
  transfer of, 32
Presidency
  growth of, 333–334
  post-Watergate, 363–364
  qualifications for and perquisites of, 331–332
  succession in, 332–333
President
  administrative control by, means of, 344–345
  assistants to, 351–360
  as chief administrator, 343–347
  as chief legislator, 339–343
  as chief of state, 335–336
  as commander-in-chief, 349–351
  Constitution, interpretation by, 72
  constitutional powers of, 341–342
  economic policy leadership and, 336–337
  executive agreements and, 349
  extraconstitutional powers of, 342–343
  foreign affairs role of, 347–349
  legislative role of, 328–329
  as national leader, 336–338
  nomination of, 255–258
  as party leader, 338–339
  public opinion and, 337–338, 342
  roles of, 334–351
  separation of powers principle and, 65, 66–67
  Supreme Court and, 120
  treaties and, 349
  wartime powers of, 350–351
Presidential elections, 272
Presidential primaries, 256–257
Press, censorship of, 148–150
  fair trials and, 149–150
  freedom of, 148–154
Press conference, presidential, 337–338
Pressure groups. *See* Political interest groups
Preventive detention, 142

Price, Don K., 46
Price and wage stability, **401–404**
Primaries, 256–257
Prior restraint, 147
Privacy, right to, 170–171
Private pensions, 420
Private property, 387
Progressive party, 246
Project Independence, 406
Public accommodations, equal **access to,** 177–178
Public assistance, 421–423
Public Health Service, 425–426
Public housing, 432–433
Public interest, 388
Public opinion
  assessing, 193–197
  defined, 189–190
  function of, 192–193
  mass media impact on, 197–202
  President and, 337–338
  surveys of, 195–197
  veto limits of, 451–452
Public service, 379–380
Punishment, 135–137
  cruel and unusual, 137–138

Quickie divorces, 87

Racial discrimination, 176
  in Britain, 184
  housing and, 183–184
  in education, 178–180
  public accomodations and, 177–178
Racial segregation, 117–118
Racial violence, 49
Radical left groups, 291–293
Radical right groups, 291–293
Reagan, Ronald, 265
Rebozo, Charles, 268
Recall, 195
Reed v. *Reed,* 185–186
Reference group, 212
Referendum, 195
Rehnquist, William H., 107
Reitman v. *Mulkey,* 183
Released-time program, 169
Religion
  aid to parochial schools and, 169–170
  establishment clause and, 168–170
  freedom of, 166–168
  political participation, and role in, 210–211
Representation of the People Act, 56
Representative government, 17
Republic, 11, 78
Republican form of government, 83

Republican party, 12, 224–225, 225–226, 227–230
　composition of, 207–212
　formation of, 221
Restrictive covenant, 183
Revenue Act of 1964, 398
Revenue sharing, 92–93
Right to counsel, 133–134
Robinson v. *California*, 137
Rockefeller, John D., 389
Rockfeller, Nelson, 226, 265, 273, 333, 360
Rodino, Peter, 165
Roe v. *Wade*, 171
Rogers, William, 348
Roman rule of law, 10
Romney, George, 257
Roosevelt, Franklin D., 60, 71, 109, 117, 225–226, 337, 350–351, 357, 359, 451
Roosevelt, Theodore, 104, 225, 331
Roper, Elmo, 195
Roper Survey, 195
Rossiter, Clinton, 339
Roth v. *United States*, 152
Royal Commissions of Inquiry, 311
Rules Committee, 324–325
Russian Constitution of 1820, 75

Sakharov, Andrei, 59
San Antonio School District v. *Rodriguez*, 183
Sartori, Giovanni, 56, 247
Scaife, Richard Mellon, 267, 270
Scales v. *United States*, 164
Schenck v. *United States*, 163–164
Schmitz, John G., 247
School District v. *Schemp*, 73, 169
Searches and seizures, 126–127
Secession, 82
Secessionist parties, 246
Secular-regulation rule, 167
Securities Investor Protection Corporation, 400
Segregation, 81–82, 178–180
Select Committee on Presidential Campaign Activities. *See* Senate Watergate Committee
Self-evident truths, 13
Self-incrimination, 129–131
Senate, 326–329
　cloture rule, 327–328
　filibuster in, 326–327
　leadership in, 318
Senate Finance Committee, 319
Senate Foreign Relations Committee, 319, 326
Senate Select Committee on Watergate. *See* Senate Watergate Committee
Senate Watergate Committee, 52, 165, 360

Senatorial courtesy, 346
Separate but equal doctrine, 178–179
Separation of powers, 65–68
Settlement Act of 1701, 97
Single-party dominance, 28–29
SIPC. *See* Securities Investor Protection Corporation
Sit-in, 178
Shapiro v. *Thompson*, 86
Sheppard, Dr. Samuel, 149
Sheppard v. *Maxwell*, 149
Sherbert v. *Verner*, 167
Sherman, Roger, 78
Sherman Antitrust Act, 389–390
Shipping, 404
Shriver, R. Sargent, 232
Slavery, 13
Sloan, Hugh, 268
Smith Act, 118
Smith v. *Allwright*, 177
Smith v. *Goguen*, 161
Socialism, 411
Social security, 417–425
Social Security Act of 1935, 94, 418
Solid South, 224
Soviet Union, 25, 26, 58–59
Spain, 25
Speaker of the House, 317–318
Speech, freedom of, 36–37, 41–43, 55–57, 161
Speedy trial, 140
Splinter parties, 246
Split-ticket voting, 35
Spock, Dr. Benjamin, 157, 247
SSI. *See* Supplementary security income
Stagflation, 397
Stalin, Joseph, 26
Standard Oil Company, 389
Stanley v. *Georgia*, 153
Stans, Maurice H., 268, 360
State courts, 101–102, 102–103, 107–108
State medical programs, 427–428
States
　admission of new, 83–85
　and commerce, 85
　federal centralization and, 93–95
　federal grants-in-aid, and role in, 89–92
　future of, 95
　revenue sharing, 92–93
　weaknesses of, 88–93
States' rights, 225, 246
State universities, 428
Steel industry, 401
Steering and Policy Committee, 321
Stennis, John, 307
Stone, Justice, 119
Stone, W. Clement, 267
Stotland v. *Pennsylvania*, 159

Street v. New York, 161
Submerged Lands Act of 1953, 85
Subsequent punishment, 147
Sunday Closing cases, 167
Supplementary security income, 421–423
Supremacy clause, 64, 101
Supreme Court, 66, 71, 97, 99–100
    Chief Justice's role on, 111
    concurring and dissenting opinions of, 110–111
    and constitutional interpretation, 72–74
    and judicial review, 111–121
    justices for, appointment of, 104–107
    operation of, 109–110
    the New Deal and, 117–119
Supreme Court of Japan, 121
Swann v. Charlotte-Mecklenburg Board of Education, 182
Swiss constitution of 1848, 75
Switch-voting, 237
Symbolic speech, 161

Taboo issues, 40–41
Taft, William Howard, 105, 225
Taft-Hartley Act, 394–395
Talmadge, Herman, 52
Taney, Roger B., 73–74, 138
Television, 199, 337–338
Tennessee Valley Authority, 374
Terminiello v. Chicago, 156
Terry v. Ohio, 126
Texas v. White, 82
Thornhill v. Alabama, 158
Ticket-splitting, 236–237
Tinker v. Des Moines School District, 161
Totalitarian government, 23–26
Transactional immunity, 129
Transfer payments, 401
Transportation, 403
Treaties
    Congress's role in making, 312
    President's role in making, 344
Trial courts, 102
Truman, Harry, 114, 338, 343, 446, 451
Trust certificates, 389
Trusts, 389
Truth-in-Lending Act of 1968, 392
Truth-in-Packaging Act of 1966, 392
Two-party system, 241–248

Ulmann v. United States, 74, 129
Unemployment Insurance, 420–421
Union shop, 395
Unitary government, 79–80
United States Chamber of Commerce, 286
United States Steel Corporation, 390
United States v. Butler, 119
United States v. Calandra, 127

United States v. Classic, 177
United States v. Nixon, 114
United States v. O'Brien, 161
United States v. Seeger, 167–168
U.S. v. Aluminum Company of America, 390–391
U.S. v. U.S. Steel Corporation, 390, 391
Universal suffrage, 251
Unwritten constitution, 55–58
Urban mass transportation, 404
Urban renewal, 433
Use immunity, 129

VA. *See* Veterans Administration
Vesco, Robert L., 269
Veterans Administration, 431
Veto, 328–329, 341
Vice-presidency, 258, 332–333, 358–360
Vietnam, 441–442, 446
Violence
    in American democracy, 47–55
    crime rate and, 50–51
    labor-movement and, 49–50
    in the 1960s, 48
    and political crime, 52–53
    racial, 49
Virginia Resolution, 81
Vishinsky, Andrei, 58
Voluntary associations, 9
Voting
    eighteen-year-olds and, 71
    versus nonvoting, 215–217
Voting rights, 176–177, 251–252
Voting Rights Act, 11, 60, 94, 177

Wagner Act. *See* National Labor Relations Act
Walker v. Birmingham, 155
Wallace, David, 205
Wallace, George, 48, 246
War Powers Act, 350, 364, 451
Warren, Earl, 105
Warren Court, 117, 118, 125
Washington, George, 22, 221, 451
Watergate, 32, 360–364
Watergate complex, 269–270
Watkins v. United States, 118, 165
Weber, Max, 189
Weeks v. United States, 126
Welfare state, 414–417
Welfare system, 94
    social security and, 417–425
Welsh v. United States, 168
Wesberry v. Sanders, 301
West German Federal Constitutional Court, 121
West Germany, 215, 217
White-collar workers, 46

INDEX **515**

White House office, 352–353
Whitman, Walt, 12
Whitney v. California, 164
Wiener v. U.S., 346
Williams v. Illinois, 186
Williams v. Mississippi, 176
Williams v. North Carolina, 87
Will the Soviet Union Survive Until 1984? (Almarik), 59
Wilson, James Q., 45
Wilson, Woodrow, 12, 225, 298, 312, 337, 348
Winthrop, John, 11
Wiretapping, 128–129

Wisconsin v. Yoder, 167
Witherspoon v. Illinois, 137
Wolf v. Colorado, 127
Women's liberation movement, 184–187, 215
Work-study program, 431
World War I, 438
World War II, 438
Writ of *certiorari,* 99
Wyman v. James, 127

Yates v. United States, 118
Yugoslavia, 25

Zorach v. Clauson, 169

JK261 47904773
.A66 1976

AMERICAN DEMOCRACY
IN WORLD PERSPECTIVE

MONTGOMERY COLLEGE LIBRARIES
JK 261.A66 1976
germ, circ
American demo

0 0000 00160283 8

76 77 78 79   9 8 7 6 5 4 3